HERE FOR CANADA

ALSO BY STEPHEN J. HARPER

Flags of Canada

Right Here, Right Now

A Great Game

HERE FOR CANADA

MEMOIRS OF THE 22ND PRIME MINISTER

STEPHEN J. HARPER

SIGNAL
McCLELLAND & STEWART

Hardcover edition published 2026

The authorized representative in the EU for product safety and compliance is Penguin Random House Ireland, Morrison Chambers, 32 Nassau Street, Dublin D02 YH68, Ireland, https://eu-contact.penguin.ie

Library and Archives Canada Cataloguing in Publication
Title: Here for Canada : memoirs of the 22nd prime minister / Stephen J. Harper.
Names: Harper, Stephen, 1959- author
Description: Includes bibliographical references.
Identifiers: Canadiana (print) 20260155535 | Canadiana (ebook) 20260155780 | ISBN 9780771004049 (hardcover) | ISBN 9780771052071 (hardcover ; signed edition) | ISBN 9780771004056 (EPUB)
Subjects: LCSH: Harper, Stephen, 1959- | LCSH: Prime ministers—Canada—Biography. | LCSH: Canada—Politics and government—21st century. | LCSH: Canada—Foreign relations—1945- | CSH: Canada—Foreign relations—21st century. | CSH: Canada—Politics and government—2006-2015. | LCGFT: Autobiographies.
Classification: LCC FC651.H37 A3 2026 | DDC 971.07/3092—dc23

All photographs credited to Jason Ransom, Deb Ransom, Jill Propp, and Jill Thompson, Official Photographers to the Prime Minister 2006–2015, are Property of the Crown.

Cover design by Andrew Roberts
Cover art: Jason Ransom / Library and Archives Canada / Stephen J. Harper fonds / R16093-17581-6
Typeset in Garamond 3 LT Pro by Erin Cooper

Printed in Canada

Signal, an imprint of McClelland & Stewart
Penguin Random House Canada
320 Front Street West, Suite 1400
Toronto, Ontario, M5V 3B6, Canada
penguinrandomhouse.ca

1 2 3 4 5 30 29 28 27 26

Penguin Random House Canada

To those many thousands of Canadians who gave their time, their money, their prayers, and even part of their working lives to support me.

CONTENTS

PART ONE: 1959–2006

PART TWO: 2006–2008

PART THREE: 2008–2011

PART FOUR: 2011–2015

PART ONE

1959–2006

1

BEGINNINGS

HERITAGE AND FAMILY

I AM A SEVENTH-GENERATION CANADIAN. My family history in Canada extends back before the American Revolution. My paternal great-great-great-great-grandfather, Christopher, came to Nova Scotia in 1774 from Yorkshire, England. From an extensive family history my father worked on in the 1970s, we know that the Harpers had migrated between southern Scotland and northern England in the preceding generations. Still, it is safe to say that Christopher Harper was English, given his declaration as Methodist upon arrival.

Those were troubled times in the Maritimes, as sentiment became bitterly divided between loyalist (pro-British) and revolutionary (pro-American) sympathizers. Christopher Harper found himself quickly drawn in as those arguments turned bloody. They culminated in the November 1776 Eddy Rebellion and the Battle of Fort Cumberland. A band of revolutionaries led by Jonathan Eddy surprised the poorly maintained and defended fort, not far from where Harper had settled. A loyalist militia leader, he and his family* sought refuge in the fort, watching helplessly as their pioneer home was burned to the ground. In the weeks that followed, the defenders successfully

* Christopher Harper and his wife Elizabeth (née Leppington) Harper had ten children, two of whom had died in infancy.

drove off the rebels and won the engagement. Rebel homes were then razed in retaliation.

From that point of the War of 1812, Christopher Harper was a polarizing figure in a polarized society. He successfully ran for the legislature of Nova Scotia in 1785, but he was ultimately excluded from that body when his political opponents discovered that his home was actually a mile inside New Brunswick. The new province had been partitioned from Nova Scotia the previous year. Electoral boundaries then, as now, can make or break political careers. As near as I can tell, no Harper would run for public office for the next two hundred years!

Part of Christopher Harper's lineage stayed in New Brunswick, through to my father, Joseph Harris Harper. He was born in Moncton, the son of a teacher, and, like the Harpers before him, raised solidly middle class.

On my mother's side, I am a sixth-generation Canadian. William Johnston, my great-great-great-grandfather, came from Lincolnshire, England in 1849. People were evidently more mobile at the time than is now appreciated because, while the Johnston name is Scottish and generally Presbyterian, Lincolnshire is nowhere near Scotland and William was listed as Anglican when he came to Canada. He settled in Grey County—one of the last opened parts of southern Ontario—beginning a long tradition of farming. It was still the predominant family occupation when my mother, Margaret Frances Johnston, was born in the town of Durham. Somewhere along the line, my mother's forebears returned to their Scottish faith, as she was raised Presbyterian.

So, my background is mainly English-Scottish, although my father discovered traces of Irish, Welsh, Dutch, and German as well. As far as we can tell, despite the diverse ethnic streams that crossed the Harper paths over the years, my entire religious heritage is Protestant.

As is true of many older Canadian families, the Harpers spread out over the generations. Some moved elsewhere in Canada, but just as many emigrated, especially to the United States, where distantly related Harpers are said to have achieved prominence.

It is often difficult to identify specific influences in family trees, but I have always found genealogical research fascinating. We are, consciously or otherwise, imbued with the memories, the stories, and the beliefs of those who have gone before. For me, it is important to be grounded in the flow of time and space, and that has become more so as I have gotten older.

My mother and father found their separate ways to Toronto, via very different routes.

My mother came from a struggling farm family. My grandparents, Rupert and Catherine (née Herd) Johnston, married in 1928 and took out their mortgage just before the Great Depression and then war engulfed the world. They raised six children in what were truly tough times. Back then, once kids were of an age to support themselves, they were expected to do so, as did my mother. At just sixteen, she moved to Toronto, initially finding work as a maid. Later she went to secretarial college and worked in that occupation at various businesses, pretty much up to the time of my birth.

My dad was raised in Moncton. After high school he trained as a chartered accountant. His life was upended in 1950 when his father, Harris Chapman Harper, disappeared. There was a massive manhunt at the time, and the story became the source of voluminous speculation and numerous rumours that continued for decades.

Some thirty-five years later (and completely coincidentally), I came to know one of the lead detectives on the case, who had long since retired from active policing. He told me that the unsolved disappearance of my grandfather had always haunted him. Harris Harper was a prominent citizen—a school principal, a militia leader, a volunteer in local activities—who was widely recognizable, yet there were no sightings or even the thinnest of leads to go on. The former officer said he and his colleagues could never even arrive at a theory of what might have happened that day. A mystery it will remain, but one that could not help but impact my father, although I did not fully appreciate how until many years later.

There is no doubt, however, that it led my father to seek a change in life. Not long after becoming a chartered accountant, he headed off to Toronto, where he met my mom at the local United church. They had their first date on February 6, 1952, a hard day in history to forget because that is the day King George VI died and Queen Elizabeth II ascended to the throne. My parents were attending a concert, and the scheduled program was replaced by more fitting mournful music.

Married in 1954, my parents were a typical post-war, middle-class couple. Dad was the primary breadwinner, while Mom eventually became a full-time mother. In the days when both employers and employees wanted long-term commitments, my dad signed on with Imperial Oil in 1955 and worked there for the next thirty-one years. Surprisingly, this chartered accountant spent most of his career not in accounting, but in the company's nascent computer department in the early years of the "information technology revolution." In fact, in 1957, he was one of a team of eleven people that set up the first commercial mainframe and computer department in Canada.

In 1961, my father was seconded by Imperial Oil to the Glassco Commission. Officially the Royal Commission on Government Organization, it was established under Prime Minister John Diefenbaker to examine how the civil service could be reorganized to incorporate contemporary private-sector management techniques. It ultimately issued a five-volume report recommending, among other things, that departments be managed on a decentralized basis, that senior management rotate between departments, and that the Treasury Board be restructured. The six months my dad worked on that project exposed him to the inner workings of Ottawa and left strong impressions about how the public service functioned. His reflections would prove to be of benefit to me many years later.

I was born on April 30, 1959, and my two brothers followed in due course. Grant was born in 1961, while my dad was working on the Glassco Commission, and Robert was born in 1964. They both went on to become chartered accountants like our father—who would have loved for me to have taken a similar path. Alas, it would not be so. A line I have used often is that I did not have the charisma to be an accountant!

GROWING UP IN LEASIDE AND RICHVIEW

MY MIDDLE-CLASS FAMILY LIVED IN what was then the most middle-class of communities: Leaside, Ontario. Designed by the owners of the Canadian Northern Railway and opened in 1913, Leaside was the first planned suburb in Canada and, when I was a boy, an independent municipality. It was comfortable and affordable for a young family starting out—very different from today. I tell people that, as prime minister, I earned far more in relative terms than my dad earned at that point in his life. Yet, as prime minister, I could never have remotely afforded to buy the house that I grew up in.

Despite its proximity to downtown Toronto, Leaside was a safe neighbourhood, and tightly knit. It had lots of green space and the full range of sports and recreational activities. It was close to bustling industrial and commercial areas, where young Leasiders would often stay to work after growing up in the community and marrying high-school sweethearts. In other words, Leaside had all the advantages of both big city and small town, which is why I have often said that I grew up "in a small town in Toronto." It was just a great place to be a kid.

I had a wide variety of interests over the years. I was an avid collector, focusing at different times on stamps, coins, hockey cards, and much else. My intellectual interests were broad and eclectic: I devoured history, geography, astronomy, science, and even heraldry, which I admit is something your average young Canadian has never given much thought to!

I also was attracted to music from an early age. There was certainly an aptitude for it within my broader family. My uncle George (my dad's brother) was a very talented multi-instrumentalist, who put himself through college, in part, by performing in a band. My grandmother, Faye (née Coy) Richardson (her name through remarriage to my grandfather Beecher some years after her husband Harris Harper disappeared), played piano quite well. My parents were not musical, but my father had a keen appreciation of music. His particular love was Duke Ellington, and he probably had the largest collection in the world of the Duke's recordings.

I was eight when I told my parents I wanted to play the piano. They must have been skeptical because, while they promptly enrolled me in lessons, they did not buy an instrument right away. So I initially learned by first hearing a tune, then fingering the notes on a cardboard keyboard, and later playing it for my teacher. Once assured of my commitment, my parents shelled out for a piano. I persevered all the way up to completing my grade 9 Royal Conservatory exam, which I think technically qualified me to be an introductory teacher. But honestly, I barely scraped through because at that level proficiency requires far more practice than I was willing to put in. Besides that, any dream of a musical career was also hampered by the fact that, when nervous, my hands would become shaky—obviously fatal for a pianist. (That tic had an interesting consequence. Because shaky hands were my only visible sign of nervousness, I learned to speak publicly without notes early on, memorizing my speeches and occasionally ad libbing. It was something that would certainly prove useful down the road.)

Another interest I had at an early age was the French language. This was very much supported by my parents, especially my dad, with his New Brunswick background. My first exposure to French was in 1968, just after I finished grade 3. It was at a time when Pierre Trudeau's bilingualism policies were popular and expanding. To make up for a shortage of French teachers, the local school boards put on special summer courses to try to rapidly train up new instructors. They put out a call for students to attend these classes as guinea pigs for the training, and my parents enrolled me in one of the programs. It involved me travelling a few kilometres away to a completely different neighbourhood (Deer Park). It was a real adventure because it meant I was riding the transit by myself and finding my way around town, exploring Toronto. Looking back now—an unattended nine-year-old riding around on public transit in a large city—it sounds crazy, but it tells you how much safer things were then. Or at least perceived to be safer.

I learned only the most elementary French that summer—I was, after all, quite young. By the time I graduated from high school, I could read and write it quite well, but in a conversation, I could barely speak a word or understand anything said to me, much like how I learned Latin. I did take an immersion course at the University of Victoria in the summer of 1978, but I really only became fluent in French years later, through using it with increasing frequency during my political career.

Like most boys, I was also interested in sports. But, in truth, I was never an athlete. I just lacked the natural abilities. It did not help that, when I was growing up, I was plagued by serious asthma and allergies. I was in the hospital at least once a year until I was ten. The doctors thought I would be a chronic case, but I largely grew out of these maladies in my teens—much too late to excel in sports. That is not to say I didn't try; I actually became a cross-country runner in high school. I did it, in part, to put my asthma behind me. I was terrible, always finishing near the bottom, but I still jogged my four or five miles every day and did my best to compete.

And then there was hockey—especially hockey. It took a big chunk of my childhood. The Maple Leafs' last Stanley Cup championship and Canada's victory over the Soviets in the first Summit Series will forever be hard-wired in my brain. Over the years people have wondered how my interest in the sport led me all the way to authoring a book on its history. The fact is that taking an academic approach to the sport was my way of making up for my utter lack of ability as a player. I became a reader, an intellectual child, and transferred my interests in sports into their study, especially into the history.

I have also been asked when and how my aspirations for leadership developed. That is a hard question to answer because I was not a naturally sociable child. Most of my early pursuits were solitary, and I was slow to make real friends. However, at a young age I became involved in scouting—cub scouts in particular. In my local troop at Northlea United Church, I became the "senior sixer," which was the youth leader of the whole pack. However, I did not continue with scouting after grade 7.

My memories of childhood are overwhelmingly positive. I am not referring just to the long days of pickup sports, especially road hockey, with my brothers and our friends, and the many hours of family board games. We had great family vacations as well. We seldom went to the typical getaway spots, preferring road trips and visits to relatives. Many weekends were spent at our Johnston grandparents' family farm near Durham, and we had a few memorable visits to my Richardson grandparents in Moncton. One special highlight was a long drive in a camper across Western Canada in 1970.

My brothers and I were very close growing up, in all the meanings of that term. There were lots of shared experiences and great moments, interspersed with frequent squabbling and fighting. But having brothers is still one of the best things in my life. And we have remained close. They were supportive of my political career at every stage, and extraordinarily tolerant of all the attention and oxygen I have taken over the decades.

When I look back now, especially on my childhood, this is what I see: I was raised in a very stable, very loving family. My father had both a big influence and a keen interest in his boys' hobbies,* and my mother dedicated her life to raising our family. Of course, at the time, I really did not fully appreciate this. What I saw was mainly the peculiarities and the warts because no family is perfect. But that start in life was a big part of any success I had later, and nothing can really replace that.

Just as I was becoming a teenager, we moved out to central Etobicoke, the west end (at that time) of the city. The Richview area was a very different kind of community than the one from where I had come, a much more upper-middle-class neighbourhood. Although property values in Leaside are much higher today, the opposite was the case in 1971.

My schooling was what you would expect it to be in that era: public. I had gone to Northlea Elementary School when we lived in Leaside, and I would attend John G. Althouse Middle School and Richview Collegiate Institute in Etobicoke. I was a decent student, but not particularly studious through elementary and middle school. I did, however, excel in math, where I was naturally gifted, but overall, I usually did just enough to pass without really trying.

That changed in grade 10. I got very serious about my studies and decided that I wanted to excel in academics. I do not remember exactly why.

---

* One of the many examples of that was my dad's encouragement of my interest in heraldry and vexillology (the study of flags). After many years of painstaking research, he and Frank Dunbar of the Royal Ontario Museum authored *Old Colours Never Die*, the complete history of military flags in Canada.

Perhaps it was because I got my glasses that summer and could actually see the blackboard! Whatever the reason, it seemed to work.

In grade 13—yes, there was a grade 13 then—I appeared on *Reach for the Top*, a popular televised high school quiz show. Richview Collegiate had not participated in years, but one of the other students spearheaded getting us on and I made the team. I did reasonably well in our first episode, which became the team's only appearance: we got defeated by a wide margin. The embarrassment of this loss was mitigated somewhat by the fact that the team who beat us went on to be the national champion!

In recalling some scattered memories from childhood, I would say my political consciousness emerged gradually. I was too young, for example, to remember the Kennedy assassination, although I have vague recollections of people talking about it. But I do remember the flag debate in 1964–1965. In fact, I naively surveyed family, friends, and neighbours about their preferred choice and recall well the intensity of the views expressed.[†] I also remember when we took the old Canadian Red Ensign down and put the new maple leaf flag up at my school, and peace gradually returned to the neighbourhood![‡] I also remember very clearly Winston Churchill's death and funeral in 1965, as well as the assassinations of 1968 (Martin Luther King Jr. and Robert F. Kennedy).

My recollection of political events became more comprehensive around the age of ten. At that point, my parents insisted that I read the front section of the newspaper—the *Toronto Star*—and be able to discuss current affairs in an informed and intelligent (and sometimes animated) manner at

---

† My parents were among those who believed we needed a new, distinctively Canadian flag. They preferred the one proposed by Prime Minister Lester Pearson, which had blue bars instead of red bars and a three-maple-leaf symbol in the centre, rather than just a single maple leaf.

‡ This period led to my interest in flags. In 2025, I authored *Flags of Canada,* a consequence of my excessive free time at home during the early stages of the Covid-19 pandemic. The book recounts, among other things, the flag debate of 1964–1965.

the dinner table. I credit those dinnertime discussions with the beginning of my interest in politics, the first emergence of my own views, and the early acquisition of debating skills.

My parents were not terribly partisan. They would have been what political strategists call "Liberal-Conservative switchers," and there was no pressure on me or my brothers to adopt one political view or another. My father's family were mostly Conservative; a grand uncle named Ewart Atkinson served for ten years in the New Brunswick legislature. My mom's family were traditionally more Liberal. In fact, my grandmother Johnston supported the Progressives when she was young, around the time women got the right to vote. Her member of Parliament was Agnes Macphail, the first woman elected to the House of Commons, who went on to join the Co-operative Commonwealth Federation (CCF).

My parents may not have been partisans, but they were very serious about politics. They were informed on the issues of the day, tried to meet the candidates, and voted in elections at every level without fail. But I am not exaggerating when I say that they did not want their young son to be a politician. In fact, I distinctly remember my mother saying, "I don't care what profession you choose, but I hope you won't be a politician or a minister." Being as serious about church attendance as she was about voting, I am not sure why she felt that way. My father, of course, wanted me to be a chartered accountant, but he never pressured me on it.

My budding interest in politics developed further in high school. By that time, I had developed a few opinions, which were conventionally left-of-centre, although I was briefly further left when, in grade 10, I was "elected" for the New Democratic Party (NDP) in a mock election in which each of our seven history classes constituted a designated riding in various parts of the country. I was drafted as the NDP candidate—I do not remember the riding, but it was somewhere in Ontario—and I won it fairly handily.

A couple of years later, my high school friend Paul Watson—an eventual Pulitzer Prize–winning photojournalist—set up a Liberal youth club in Etobicoke Centre and convinced a few of us to join. He had political ambitions and wanted to go to the Liberal convention. I became secretary of the club and came very close to meeting Pierre Trudeau. He was going to be visiting the area and had agreed to meet the club, but for reasons I cannot remember, I had to be out of town that day. Thus, it never happened. (The closest I came would be passing Mr. Trudeau on a Montreal street many years later, a few months before his death.)

I have never denied that at one time I held left-of-centre views. But lest anyone accuse me of jumping back and forth politically, I say this: the evolution of my political philosophy was the result of reflection, education, and experience.

I got a great deal out of high school. I was fortunate to have had many good teachers, and I learned a lot. I was also very busy, developing a personal discipline that would serve me well in life. I was a straight-A+ student; I was taking my grade 9 Royal Conservatory piano exam; I was running on the cross-country team; and I long had my own paper route, where I learned some basic business and entrepreneurial skills.

Despite having so much going on—probably too much—I was increasingly unhappy in those years. Yes, I was, after all, a teenager. But it was more than that. I had not developed any passions. As university approached, I became ever more uncertain about what I wanted to study and why, let alone what I wanted to do in life. In truth, I just did not want to live like I was living—not having much fun—and four years of university sounded like more of that. My musings on this subject led to increasing tension with my parents.

I finally enrolled at University of Toronto in a commerce program, with some abstract notions of going into law. But those were simply vague ambitions at the time. I felt like I was doing what was expected of me rather than pursuing any real personal goals. After a few weeks, it was clear that my heart was not in it. So I left school. Believing this would make life at home unpleasant, I decided to leave Toronto as well. The late-1970s oil boom was underway, so I moved out to Alberta, where I figured it would be easy to get a job. I was doing what many young people were doing at the time: trying to figure out who I was and what I wanted to do.

There were those at the time who did not understand what I was doing and, even now, people for whom my actions back then make no sense. Yet

I have never once doubted that I made the right decision. There came a point when I realized that I was only going to be happy if I could make my own life choices. And that is what I did.

CHANGE IS IN THE (ALBERTA) AIR

I APPLIED FOR WORK at a few places in my new hometown of Edmonton. The first job offer came, ironically, from my father's former employer, Imperial Oil, a company that often preferred to hire relatives of employees. My initial job was as a file clerk, followed by stints in the mailroom and accounts receivable. But it was when I was hired into the computer department (where, incidentally, my father no longer worked) that opportunities began to open up for me.

I became a computer operator and then what was known as an "applications programmer." In those days there was such a shortage of programmers in Alberta that it was possible to become one with no computer science education. All you had to do was train yourself. So, I learned several programming languages. I was employed like that for about two years, and I used the skills to help put myself through university later on.

By twenty-two, I found myself making very good money with as much job security as the private sector had to offer. But I never viewed it as a career. It was interesting, but it was not something I wanted to do for life. Besides, I could see the rapid changes that were coming to information technology. Without going into detail, the future direction of the field would require me to become far more of a technical specialist, and that was not the part of the job that interested me.

I was already leaning toward a return to school when developments at work dovetailed with my plans. Imperial Oil intended to move its entire computer department, including its IBM mainframe computer system, to Calgary in 1981, where I had chosen to go to university. At the time, this was a very bold undertaking. Few major corporations had ever attempted such a move, and those tries had mostly been disastrous.

With the understanding that I would go to school after the relocation, I was assigned to a small team that would spend six months travelling back and forth between Edmonton and Calgary, making all the plans for a "seamless transition." That meant we had to take the system down one Friday night and have it operating Monday morning without anyone noticing. There was no "cloud" back then. This required backing up all software and data on tapes and disks, dismantling the hardware, moving it down Highway 2, and then re-assembling it all in a brand-new facility. It involved multiple backup plans and built-in redundancies. And we did it: we moved the entire computer department without a hitch—the first time that had ever been accomplished.

It was a great way to end my full-time employment with Imperial, although I would return for the next three summers. I learned a lot during my time with Esso. I witnessed the workings of a large and complex organization, including its management, accountability, and cost structures. And, of course, being part of project management teams, particularly around the big computer relocation, was just one of the diverse career experiences I would accumulate along the way.

By the time I moved to Calgary in the summer of 1981, I had been in the province for almost three years. I had enjoyed living in Edmonton, and I would grow to like Calgary even more. I was increasingly seeing Alberta as my home province. I guess it was inevitable that my "liberal-ish" worldview would change in the Alberta air.

I love Alberta and the vibrancy of its society. It has a dynamism and an entrepreneurial culture that resembles the best of the United States. But it does not have that kind of anarchic, sometimes-violent side of American society. It is still an orderly, very polite, Canadian place. As well, old money and old connections matter far less than in Toronto or Montreal, so it truly is a land of opportunity. Alberta is just a great place to live, and working in its thriving energy sector, I could see up close how important business really is to the creation of wealth and the well-being of society. Of course, holding a job, incurring bills, and paying taxes really does alter one's view of the world.

My perspective was already beginning to change when the Trudeau Government embarked on the National Energy Program (NEP). I watched as

Alberta's unemployment rate went up by about 10 per cent in six months. All this happened simply because those in power in Ottawa, who had no idea what they were doing, decided they would re-engineer a major industry. Witnessing such unbridled and arrogant government overreach made a lasting impression on me. It began to solidify my views about what role government should and should not be playing in the economy. And those views led me toward a conservative philosophy, at least on economic matters.

It was not long after that—I was attending the University of Calgary by then—that I started dating a girl, Cynthia Williams, who was a strong Progressive Conservative and who wanted to get involved in party politics. It was 1982 and the party was in the midst of a leadership race. Joe Clark, of whom I was never a supporter, had resigned the leadership after getting an approval vote of only 66 per cent at the party's convention. I became a party member, and I supported Brian Mulroney. After Mr. Mulroney won the leadership in 1983, I joined my local riding association in Calgary West. Not long after that, I met my member of Parliament, Jim Hawkes, and that is when my serious and ongoing involvement in politics really began.

Jim Hawkes was a smart, hard-working, and approachable member of Parliament. I first met him at one of the monthly townhall meetings he held in his riding. I took an instant liking to his cerebral approach to issues—Jim was a rare Ph.D. in the House of Commons—and joined his riding executive during the next year. When Hawkes was challenged for his nomination (having been on the wrong side of the leadership race), I began to work for him in earnest and set up a youth club in his riding. One of the new executive members was John Weissenberger, an ex-Montrealer who would be at my side politically for the next three decades. I then became the Calgary West PC youth chairman during the 1984 election campaign.

My growing involvement in politics coincided with my progress at U of C. Unlike my first go-round in Toronto, this time I had taken a very different approach to my education. I did not enrol in one particular program. Instead, I decided to take courses in a range of subjects that interested me to see where that might lead. For a year and a half, I was in what was called

General Studies. By the middle of my second year, however, I had settled on economics as my major. I liked its unique combination of big-picture thinking and rigorous mathematics. I still think it is the ideal intellectual preparation for a wide range of occupations.

As I entered my final year, I admit that I had not done much thinking about what I would do next. Imperial Oil was always a possibility, although I had no interest in returning to programming. I suppose, even then, my real interest was in public policy. Then, one day, when I was sitting with a small group of my senior riding association colleagues talking with Jim Hawkes, he said, "Why don't you come work for me? I'm going to have an opening in my Ottawa office in the fall." Without much hesitation, I said: "Well, yeah, that sounds interesting. I'll do that."

I did not suspect it at the time, but that quick decision set the professional direction of my life. I still marvel at how life can surprisingly put one on a particular path. And working for Jim Hawkes was a great introduction to politics in Ottawa—one that served me in good stead for many years to come.

Jim and I were never really on the same page philosophically. He was a fairly Red Tory, although he had an eclectic mixture of views. But he was a very good boss; he was serious, and he was decent, even though, I would tell people, he did not really need me. Jim worked tirelessly, and he briefed himself thoroughly on anything he needed to know. He showed me the ropes and gave me lots of interesting experiences. A particularly vivid, and useful, one was speaking on his behalf to a very hostile union audience.

One thing I learned from him was how to make the most of one's position. Jim was a smart guy who knew the political lay of the land. He knew he would never be in Cabinet. That is often just the way the numbers work, especially when you are a Conservative from Alberta. Cabinet at that time already had powerful Albertans—Don Mazankowski, Joe Clark, and Harvie Andre. Even if you were in Parliament twenty more years, you were not going to be in Cabinet in a PC government.

Understanding that reality, Jim developed a strategy. He found smart young people, employed them for a while, taught them the system, and then helped them find jobs in ministers' offices. Through that network of staffers, he got insight and more "indirect" influence over what was going on in the government. That was (and largely still is) the way things worked for political staffers in Ottawa. One would usually start as a legislative assistant to a backbencher, maybe even as an intern, and then, after a year or two, look for opportunities in ministers' offices. Cabinet ministers are always on the lookout for talent and experience.

In Jim's mind, the time was soon coming for me to make such a move. One night over dinner, he asked me whether I was ready. My answer must have disappointed him. Although I had expressed some misgivings before, this time I was categorical about my disillusionment with the government. I had become a philosophical conservative in the preceding years, but now I found myself working for a government that simply was not that. I was also troubled by the separatist elements we had in the Quebec wing of the party. Most important to me, I had come to Ottawa to be part of eliminating Pierre Trudeau's enormous deficit, which I considered essential for Canada's long-term growth. I told Jim it was not personal; I just saw no prospect that the PC Government was ever going to balance the budget. That, of course, turned out to be true, although Jim was kind enough not to remind me that he had expressed his own doubts on that when I had first agreed to come to Ottawa.

The Mulroney Government did do some good things, and it was, without a doubt, superior to the government it had replaced. Yet one of the problems, I had concluded, was the ideological heterodoxy of the PC caucus. The Mulroney PCs had won a massive majority in 1984, but they had done so more on a "throw the bums out" coalition than on any detailed plan for governing. The caucus reflected that, with a dizzyingly wide range of political views. A few people were well to the right of your typical Blue Tory; a lot were redder than Red. I will never forget my first meeting with a group of legislative assistants to Alberta MPs. For the most part, they were actually in favour of the National Energy Program! And the Quebec caucus had its own unholy diversity, ranging from the closet separatists I mentioned to genuine, hard-core federalists—something that would haunt the PC Government when it later embarked on constitutional reform.

Frankly, the whole thing was not my cup of tea. I told Jim I was instead going back to university to take my master's. I was also leaning into a possible life in academia, though that was hardly set in stone.

Jim had no hard feelings and even signed a reference letter to the U of C's economics department. That summer, I left Ottawa for a brief stint in the constituency office and then headed to grad school. As far as I was concerned, partisan politics had been an interesting experience, but that was the end of it for me.

2

—

"THE WEST WANTS IN!" AND BUILDING REFORM

AN EVOLVING POLITICAL PHILOSOPHY

THE YEAR 1986 and my return to Calgary from Ottawa was a time of transition in my life. I was back at the University of Calgary, now in the master's program in the economics department. It was a comfortable place. In university I had quickly figured out how to balance my studies and other elements of my life much more successfully than I had in high school. I now knew how to work just hard enough to do very well. And I was pursuing studies that deeply interested me.

The topics and research areas I focused on in my course work were not typical in economics at that time. The areas of concentration were mostly centred on econometrics and statistical methodologies. Of course, I did study those things, but I directed my attention more to economic history and the responses to that history in the development of economic theory over time. I then leaned on that knowledge when doing policy analysis and evaluation. I was particularly drawn to macroeconomics, especially fiscal policy, which I ultimately did my thesis in. It was not the usual route, but I enjoyed it, as well as life in general, and initially thought I would pursue a Ph.D.

Contrary to the PC Government for which I had worked, the conservative bent of my political thinking had been hardened by my time in Ottawa. It was now being reinforced in my scholastic studies and other intellectual readings. What is called public choice theory played a key role in the development of my thought. Applied to economics, its essence is that government policy must be understood in its institutional framework. Political actors can no more be assumed to be all-benevolent and all-knowing than can participants in the markets. The vested interests of government itself can never be ignored, and so real-world market options should be measured against real-world government policy, not theoretical ideals.*

I also ventured beyond my studies, reading broadly in classical liberal economics and conservative political theory. Together, my studies and readings helped me understand that conservatism is not an abstract ideology the way other isms are. It is wisdom derived from both an understanding of human nature and the lessons of human experience. The end result was that I became much more philosophically grounded in my thinking, greatly deepening the shift in worldview that had started a few years earlier.

FINDING FAITH

PROFOUND CHANGES WERE HAPPENING elsewhere in my life as well. In particular, my religious outlook began to alter. Despite growing up in a church-going household, I had never been attracted to religion. On the contrary, from at least late childhood I considered myself an atheist, and I refused to be confirmed when I was a teenager.†

Over the next few years, my deepening conservative convictions convinced me of the reality and importance of values that transcend time and place.

---

* As an example, my thesis was on the application of "political business cycle" theory to federal fiscal policy in Canada. The theory is that macroeconomic policy is not designed to smooth business cycles, as conventional economic theory suggests, but instead to exploit electoral cycles for the benefit of incumbent governments. My statistical study, covering the period from 1953 to 1988, found elements of both motives.

† I suppose I was a type of atheist that I have discovered is very common—one who does not believe in God but is quite angry with Him!

One obvious source of those, anywhere, is religion. In the process of reading what Malcolm Muggeridge, C.S. Lewis, and others had written, I undertook a similar spiritual journey. This was not just a change of perspective but also a learning experience, because I came to realize how surprisingly shallow was my understanding of Jesus and the Christian faith.

In time, there came the point when I believed in Christ and the Christian message of hope and salvation. I became an adherent through the Christian and Missionary Alliance and one of its local Calgary ministers, Brent Trask. I had met Brent during the 1988 election campaign, and he has become my personal pastor over these many years.

I am often asked why I do not talk more openly about my faith. Besides it not being politically very advisable to do so today, I think proselytizing is usually ineffective and often best avoided. Over the years, the people in my life who drew me to faith, albeit very slowly, were those whose lives and characters I wanted to emulate. I discovered only later that such men were Christians. I am not confident that I am the kind of example that would lead others to the Christian faith. And I am certain that I would not convert anyone by overtly trying to do so.

Still, my faith is very real to me. I have felt the presence of God often since my conversion, in good times as well as bad. Knowing Christ has relieved me of much of the emotional turmoil I once had in my soul. It has also made me far more appreciative of all that I have. And understanding that there is a world beyond the material—a world that is beyond us—is something I find of great comfort.

PRESTON MANNING AND THE REFORM PARTY

THIS WAS ALSO a time when my political philosophy began to find an outlet. After all, people who do economic research often get into public policy. This was true of me.

I became involved with a group of professors and students who often talked about what was happening in Ottawa and why. My experiences in the nation's capital were of interest to them. One day in May 1987, Bob Mansell, head of the graduate program in the economics department and my interim thesis supervisor, said to me, "I've met this guy, Preston Manning. He's the son of a former premier.* You might have heard of him. He's trying to put something together politically. He's having this Western Assembly in Vancouver to discuss political reform. I can't go—would you go for us?"

By then I was thoroughly disillusioned with the direction of the PC Government. I had already let my membership lapse for numerous reasons—and then came the Bristol Aerospace incident in late 1986. The Mulroney Government took a contract rightfully awarded under the official process to Bristol Aerospace in Winnipeg and gave it to a Montreal company. Despite their vehement denials—I certainly was not convinced—it was clear that this was purely an act of regional politics. This blatant political favouritism began to shake the confidence of even long-time western PCs.

I decided to take Mansell up on his offer. Preston Manning did a terrific job that day. I got to meet him afterwards and found him intellectually engaging, very smart, but also down to earth. I did not expect this. Here was someone who was part of Alberta political "royalty" but also just an ordinary guy. I found him highly intriguing, and my interest was piqued.

I met other interesting people as well. At a social event during the assembly, I wound up sitting beside a woman named Diane Ablonczy. I had heard of her before because she had been an independent candidate for "Provincial Rights"—a group that existed briefly after Social Credit broke up—in Calgary-Mountain View in the 1982 provincial election. As we talked, she confided that she was likely to become the first chairman of the new party they were starting (she called herself "chairman"). She asked me what I thought about this political enterprise. I told her I really liked Preston Manning and found him thoughtful and compelling as a potential political

* Preston Manning is the son of Ernest Manning, Alberta's eighth premier, who served between 1943 and 1968—longer than any other Alberta premier and the second-longest-serving provincial premier in Canadian history.

leader. Then she asked me whether I would be interested in taking on a role in the new political party he was planning.

I said I was interested in helping Manning, but I did not think it would draw that heavily on my time "because," I said, "this isn't going to go anywhere. Preston's clearly smart and we can do some stuff, but if his ideas get any traction, the PCs will move to occupy that space."

My frank response apparently did not put her off. Following the convention, Mansell and Preston Manning asked me to draft one of the papers for what would become the Reform Party of Canada's founding convention in Winnipeg in October 1987. With the input of my friends and academic colleagues, I created a document that examined how the West had been treated in Confederation in economic, political, and constitutional terms, and what could be done about it. It leaned heavily on the confident economic conservatism of the era that was flourishing outside Canada, and it combined that with the key themes Manning had been espousing.

When I presented it in Winnipeg—it was in a keynote speech—it was a big hit. I cannot say it was my best work, but it was one of the better papers presented. After the convention, Manning, newly elected first leader of the Reform Party of Canada, asked me to serve as the party's first policy chief. I accepted, even though it was becoming apparent that helping out would take a bit more time than I had originally expected. It was still part-time, unpaid work, other than a few expenses. I certainly did not anticipate it was going to become a full-time gig anytime soon. Little did I know.

My tenure as Reform's policy chief also introduced me to populism. It has become commonplace these days for people to equate populism with demagoguery and other negative traits, but in Western Canada and the western United States, where the term originates, it had a more respectable and distinctive meaning.

In the late nineteenth century, populist movements sprang from early-stage agrarian societies. They sought to represent the interests of the mass of the local people, who were largely farmers or labourers, as opposed to the interests of economic elites—railways, banks, grain companies, and the like—which, although highly influential in regional politics, were quite small in number and often represented organizations headquartered hundreds or even thousands of miles away. Such movements could be of the left, the right, or the centre, but what united them was the belief that the bulk of the population shared common interests and values. Because of this philosophy, they often decried party politics, at least in its traditional forms.

Alberta has a unique history of populism. For most of its first three-quarters of a century as a province, its politics tended to be dominated by a single, broad-based political party, extensively organized at the grassroots level. Most relevant was the history of Social Credit. A truly desperate populace had given a landslide victory to William Aberhart, an evangelical preacher, in the Depression election of 1935, on what was then, even for the times, a radical populist agenda. When Aberhart died in 1943, his young lieutenant, Ernest Manning, converted that populism into what was, policy-wise, a largely mainstream conservative movement. But it was one that right to the very end kept its roots among ordinary working-class, farming-class, middle-class people.

It is now commonplace to remember Social Credit for some peculiarities of its era. However, I think it is indisputable that the mix of populist and conservative policies inspired a period of development that was spectacular and left the province in very good political, social, and economic shape—that it still benefits from to this day. More than once I have argued that the advent of Manning in Alberta in 1943 and the turn to Tommy Douglas's CCF in Saskatchewan in 1944 would define a half century of growth in the former and of decay in the latter. It is an underappreciated story in Canadian history.

I would also contend that virtually all parties in democracies use fundamentally populist appeals in one way or another, that is, they often argue that they represent "the people" broadly while their opponents are the expressions of "special interests." Of course, that is often superficial and cynical. I like to joke that the real difference between democracy and populism these days is whether one likes an election result. If one does, it is democratic; if one does not, then it is populist.

At that point I did not have trouble in squaring populist and conservative ideas. As elites of all kinds were becoming more liberal, the idea of conservatism as a populist force was taking hold. Certainly, in economics, new thinkers were challenging the established, left-liberal Keynesian policy consensus from the right. This was not all rhetorical positioning. For example, although both Ronald Reagan and Margaret Thatcher were seen as close to the interests of business, they were in fact strongly opposed by the traditional economic elites within their respective parties, at least in their early days.

More importantly, I became convinced that a populist ethos was inescapable for the Reform Party. The party had no significant corporate support and few large donors. There were no full-time professional staff. And Reform was ineligible for the tax credits and subsidies received by the other political parties. We were raising most of our money from small donations by passing KFC buckets at numerous grassroots meetings. In that environment, it was essential for the party leadership to very quickly figure out how to be "populist" in the sense of responding to the actual concerns of our members and followers. Addressing the priorities and perspectives of regular voters, in language they understand, was one of the key lessons I learned during this period and from working with Preston Manning.

I was one of the few people who could write speeches for the leader because I was able to write in his voice. For a time, you could say, I was doing Preston Manning's "veeshion" just as well as Preston Manning, which was necessary, because he had me leading the policy process in those early years. I was responsible for preparing first drafts of policies, which were then vetted by a broad-based group of policy experts and enthusiasts gathered from across the West. The proposals that emerged were ultimately debated and affirmed or rejected at a Reform Party convention. The platform, I hasten to say, was not all mine by any means. But I had a ringside seat and was able to see how populism and policy could work together.

A fundamental lesson I learned from this process was that good policy is the result of healthy debate and lively give-and-take. Senior leadership will undoubtedly have their ideas about the direction of policy. And good, principled people will have the philosophies and theories that they want to base policy on. But as a political practitioner, one's political ideas cannot just be your own; they have to be other people's ideas as well. Politics is not an exercise in solipsism. Sometimes you are pushing people in a direction; other times they are pushing you in a direction. The point is to unite people around a program. That was the real success I observed during that period: within a brand new party, creating a good degree of consensus around its major policy ideas.

FIRST POLITICAL CANDIDACY (1988)

WE WERE GETTING CLOSE to the 1988 federal election. To this point, I was basically a policy guy. But political necessity was about to intrude. The Reform Party was founded in October 1987 with the intention of running eighty-eight candidates in Western Canada in the upcoming federal election. As we would say, "the West wants in!" But six months later the party had only two nominated candidates. That was when Preston approached me with a non-policy request. "We've got to get some candidates," he said. "Will you be next? Would you consider running against Jim Hawkes in Calgary West?"

I was initially caught off guard, but Preston's explanation was straightforward. He was running against Joe Clark in Yellowhead. The two had known each other since university days, and the announcement had attracted attention. "If you do the same thing in Calgary West, it will have the same effect. It will put us on the political map, and we need that."

I decided to do it, the decision made easier by the fact that I did not think I had any chance of winning. Jim was not really surprised I was going to run. He knew where I had been moving politically for the previous couple of years. And we both knew I was not going to win.

That might seem like an odd understanding to have with a political opponent, but we both knew the score. Whatever dissatisfaction there was in the West with the Mulroney PCs, they had just inked a major free trade agreement with the United States. With the Liberal-dominated Senate refusing to pass the deal in advance of the election, we knew it was going to polarize the electorate—the Reform Party supported the agreement, by the way—and dominate the election. The bulk of wavering conservatives were going to return to the PC fold. In such an election, Reform would have little chance, and I would have none in Calgary West.

I think that is one way in which I am different from a lot of other people in politics. In my experience, most people need the assurance that they can win to find the motivation to be energized. I am comfortable advancing a political cause or argument if I think it is true and the right thing to do regardless. But, of course, it was always important to convey the possibility of victory to my supporters.

I proceeded with getting the Reform nomination in Calgary West, only the third in the party's history and, given the circumstances, uncontested. My acceptance speech included some thoughts on the PCs new "star" Quebec Cabinet minister, one Lucien Bouchard. Reviewing what Bouchard had said about Quebec, the Meech Lake Accord, and his constitutional views, as well as what I had seen in the Quebec PC caucus, I predicted that he would someday lead a separatist party in the House of Commons.

As it turned out, my assessment of my electoral chances was correct. The pleasant surprise to me—and to more neutral analysts—was how well I had done. Despite being largely ignored by the mainstream media—except for deliberate inaccuracies, as when the *Calgary Herald* renamed us the Western Reform Party, "WRP"—we had made a mark with the electorate. In Calgary West, I had received nearly ten thousand votes, constituting about 17 per cent of the total, and a clear, if distant, second place.

We had run a good, well-focused local campaign in Calgary West and worked hard to get our message out. I even got my deposit back.* And this was not the only riding where that happened. Despite failing to win a seat, Reform's success in the popular vote was truly unique; a new party had not had this kind of breakthrough in Alberta in fifty years. Clearly, something was going on.

---

* In those days, Elections Canada (and often other provincial and municipal electoral administrators) required a monetary deposit from candidates to ensure that they were serious about running. If the candidate received 15 per cent of the vote in the election, the deposit would be fully refunded. Beginning in 2000, both the deposit and the refunding were progressively liberalized. In 2017, such deposits were ruled unconstitutional by the courts.

Until then, I was still, at least in my own mind, a policy guy. I had not planned to be a politician and had almost zero interest in becoming one. Even in my student days, I had never been one to run for office, and I did not consider myself all that suited for it. But I had done it, and had learned that it was not so bad. I cannot say that I loved campaigning, but I discovered that I was reasonably good at it, and that I could occasionally even get a little enjoyment out of entering the fray.

However, the real benefit was that Reform started to get attention. Manning had been right; my candidacy did generate some local press and, post-election, requests for media interviews with the party's "chief policy officer" became more frequent. Those included French-language interviews. As the only one around Preston Manning who spoke any French—mine was still very basic conversation-level at that point—I filled the hole. Fortunately, the expectations were not high, but I would dread ever watching those early interviews today!

Although we had attracted many former Progressive Conservative voters, actual PC Party activists were few and far between at the time of the 1988 election. I was an exception, and so were a few people around me in Calgary West. One of my colleagues from the University of Calgary economics master's program, Ken Warenko, was my campaign manager. But he was a novice, as were most of the organizers and workers. Those with experience were usually older people who had cut their teeth a generation or more earlier with Social Credit. Reform was, in other words, a rudimentary political machine, and it was largely dependent on Ted Byfield's *Western Report* media network to circulate its messages. That would soon start to change.

A "PARLIAMENTARY PARTY" TAKES SHAPE

THE REFORM PARTY WOULD not stay out of Parliament for long. In the northeastern Alberta riding of Beaver River, winning PC candidate John Dahmer was very sick and died before he could be sworn in. For the by-election, to be held on March 13, the PCs fought about who they should run: Dahmer's widow or another candidate. They chose the latter, which was a serious political error. Reform, on the other hand, had a brilliant candidate, a hold-over from the general election.

Her name was Deborah Grey. She was a schoolteacher with no previous background in politics. She was not overly philosophical, certainly not a policy person, but she understood the Reform agenda and was an outstanding, natural communicator. She excelled in debates, and she easily absorbed what she needed to know. She was also great with people, and they responded to her. As the campaign progressed, Preston told me, "She's going to win this by-election." I was skeptical, but he insisted: "There's no free-trade debate anymore. We're onside with people on the issues; we're going to win the by-election." And we did.

Reform had its first seat in Parliament—a highly strategic beachhead. Preston then asked me if I would go with Deborah to Ottawa to be her legislative assistant. It was not the easiest decision for me; I was supposed to be working on my thesis. But the timing was not terrible. I had finished my course work, and with the election intervening, my thesis was not yet underway. I was also considerably invested in this enterprise by now, and taking the job would start to pay the bills. Not to mention, I was now in on the ground floor of something that was getting interesting.

The fact was that the future of the party hinged on Deborah Grey being successful in Ottawa. We were sending a young woman to Parliament Hill who had no political background or experience; she would be alone, politically and socially. And there was little doubt that she was going to face a hostile environment. I decided I would take Preston up on his offer. I would go for a year or so. Besides, when would I get another chance to do something like this again?

This time in Ottawa, things were different. Deborah was a great boss, but Jim Hawkes had been a veteran parliamentarian who knew the system inside out. With Jim, I was just out of university, a kid with everything to learn. With Deborah, although she was the MP, I was the one with some Parliament Hill experience. And to boot, as a party official, I was there, in part, to make sure that she remained closely linked with the head office.

In the end, Deb Grey was a very fast learner and did a great job for the party. I have to say that Preston Manning was very fortunate having her as Reform's first MP, because it was a tricky dynamic in a young political party. When you have a single MP or representative who is not the leader, it is quite likely to go one of two ways—both bad. They are alone and may not have the skills to succeed, in which case they fail. Or they are really good, and think, "Why am I not the leader?" And everybody else tells them they should be the leader, which starts to poison the relationship at the top.

Neither of those scenarios happened with Deborah. And she was about to get company. By 1989, Brian Mulroney's Meech Lake constitutional deal, designed to address Quebec's opposition to Pierre Trudeau's 1982 constitutional amendments, was in real trouble. Under pressure from Reform and others, Alberta Premier Don Getty called the province's first Senate election. Military hero and Reform candidate Stan Waters won. To prove Senate reform could happen under Meech—contrary to the critique offered by many Westerners—Getty persuaded Mulroney to appoint Waters to the Senate. Now Reform had a person in each chamber.

With that, I began running what we called our weekly "caucus meeting." We would get everyone together—our MP, our senator, and me, usually in Deb's office, with Preston on the phone—and make sure we knew what was on the parliamentary agenda and the positions we would take. We coordinated everything and ensured we had our policies straight. It was actually a lot of fun because it was starting to feel like a real party, and we were establishing valuable disciplines for the years ahead.

I learned things too. For instance, my earlier prediction to Diane Ablonczy about the PCs filling any Reform "space" did not happen. Instead, the PCs started moving in the opposite direction. Whatever Reform proposed—whether it was with the deficit, or the constitution, or immigration, or anything else—got vigorously attacked by the PCs. And it was not just the policies that were attacked but our supporters as well. According to the PCs, Reformers were off their rocker, kooks, radicals, racists, and bigots. But if you are going to call people those kinds of names, you had better not be asking for their votes later. As a result, our supporters, who had started out as disaffected PCs, were becoming entrenched in their loyalty to Reform.

For Deborah, though, those were tough times. She was a rookie who had won a by-election in an obscure riding. In Ottawa, this was initially viewed as a quaint, one-off thing. But as Reform's numbers continued to rise, PCs in ridings like hers in the West, especially in Alberta, began to recognize her, and the ideas she stood for, as a threat. They responded accordingly, some getting quite nasty.

Not everyone behaved that way; there were notable exceptions. For instance, our office had a good relationship with Jim Hawkes, who was by then the chief government whip. He and I often met on house business. (There were, of course, practical reasons for his openness; a single MP denying unanimous consent can complicate the Government's business in the House.)

Former prime minister John Turner was another exception. When Deborah gave her maiden speech in the House of Commons, Turner, then leader of the Opposition, left his parliamentary office, came down to a virtually empty chamber, listened to her carefully, and then congratulated her afterwards. Turner and his party often disagreed vehemently with the positions Deborah took, but in the range of treatment we got from parliamentarians, no one was ever as consistently gracious and thoughtful as he was. It is one reason I maintained a relationship with Mr. Turner until his passing in 2020.

REFORM GOES NATIONAL

REFORM WAS NOW SHOWING UP with greater frequency on the general public's radar. Obviously, Deborah Grey and Stan Waters attracted attention, particularly on local and western regional issues. But beyond that, Reform was now part, albeit in a small way, of debates around issues of national relevance: unemployment, the deficit, inflation, tax hikes, the GST, the Meech Lake Accord, and many others. The economy was especially top of mind for the public because Canada was slipping into recession.

As a party, we were attracting interest from people of more varied background (but especially disillusioned PCs) than ever before. We could sense that we were gaining momentum. By late 1990, I could see scenarios where we might win a bunch of seats (mine included) in a federal election campaign. However, I also saw one very significant obstacle.

The key to Reform's continued growth was to make it a national party. Even in the West, even among people who were focused on western grievances, there were just too many voters who would not cast a ballot for a purely regional party. They liked what we stood for, but, in their minds, if we were not running candidates in most ridings, we were never going to be in the game. In Reform's senior circles, I thus became an advocate for eastern expansion. I was not the only one, but I was probably the most vocal and aggressive about it. My intention was to advance the cause in two ways.

One was by putting together proposals around expansion that could get the support of Reform's leaders and riding associations at a party convention. Issues like entrenching equal representation by province on National Council and regional protections into policy adoption were key. As was an expanded set of policies, especially on constitutional matters, that assured party members we had no intention of "going soft" on the themes that had brought us into existence.

My other contribution was a careful tracking of interested eastern voters from Deborah Grey's office in Ottawa. Our MP's office was usually the key point of approach for eastern Canadians who had some interest in the party. I arranged for the party to send packages out, and I followed up more promising recruits with phone calls. I kept growing files on the various eastern constituencies, which, in some cases, started to construct nascent if unofficial riding associations.

There was one key wrinkle in the eventual expansion package we proposed at the April 1991 Reform Assembly in Saskatoon: while the party would become officially national, we would defer expansion into Quebec. The reasons were largely pragmatic. As the country's constitutional debates were heating up, Reform was unique in offering a constitutional reform agenda that was not Quebec-centric. It would be impossible to compete on that ground in Quebec, and attempting to do so would muddy our message elsewhere. Besides, with the emergence of Lucien Bouchard's Bloc Québécois, Quebec already had its own new, insurgent party. Any support

Reform would get in the interim would therefore come from more radical elements of the anglophone community, which would forever limit any future growth. Manning's unilingualism, which he then showed no interest in addressing, was also a practical consideration.

There was certainly resistance to eastern expansion, but as the assembly approached, that seemed to decline dramatically. Press coverage notwithstanding, it all but collapsed at the convention itself. It was another successful exercise in Reform's practice of grassroots democracy: bring people into the debate early, address their concerns, and build consensus around common objectives. Most of all, treat people as reasonable, and they are more likely to act that way.

The Saskatoon assembly was important for another, very special reason: it is where I first met, albeit briefly, the woman who would eventually become my wife. Laureen Teskey had come on her own as a delegate from her riding. Although she had done some paid work for the party, I did not know her at all. She came over and introduced herself at the convention. We had some mutual friends, and it was not long after that we had our first date and then started going out.

It quickly became apparent that my expansion thesis was correct. Once Reform went national, the party went from single digits in the polls to mid-double digits overnight, and the biggest growth was in the West, although quite significant in Ontario. We were now on the national radar to stay.

It helped that the PCs continued to have troubles. Their gradual decline from their early years in office, which had been temporarily reversed by the free trade agreement, had resumed. The philosophically unrooted nature of their electoral coalition, combined with the immense stresses around the constitutional agenda and the economy, were to blame. The latter was now in full-blown recession, and the unresolved deficit was haunting the government.

Through ongoing spending restraints and incremental tax increases, the PCs had done just enough to keep the deficit from getting worse, but they had not solved the problem. In other words, the file was all bad news with little to show for their efforts. Now that we were a serious national party, it was Reform's intention not just to benefit from disaffection but also to proactively exploit the government's failures on this and other matters.

Immediately after the Saskatoon assembly, Preston Manning moved to deepen Reform's organizational capacity and professionalism. These were times of real growth. As my future Conservative fund chair Irving Gerstein would later say, "Message creates momentum, which raises money." With expansion and attention quickly came new members and much more revenue. Reform added to its ranks a full-time executive director; professional administrators; and policy, strategy, and communications staff. It was no longer just Preston Manning sitting at a table with a kitchen cabinet. The Reform Party now had a half-dozen-plus smart, capable, experienced, eager senior people. There was Dr. Tom Flanagan, who had been hired from the University of Calgary as director of policy and research; Rick Anderson, who had come over from the Liberal Party, as an election planner and strategist; and lawyer Cliff Fryers as party chairman. His drive and organizational energy were critical to making the trains run on time.

However, as the Reform Party's appeal became broader, new and different challenges appeared on the scene. For one, we had to deal with undesirables who had the potential to hijack the movement. In some parts of Eastern Canada, our constituency associations were weak or non-existent. These became targets of some very radical groups whose deliberate strategy was to take over our riding associations to embarrass us. These were not people with merely "'politically incorrect' conservative views outside the liberal mainstream." They were actual fascists: ideologically race-oriented Holocaust deniers and defenders of far-right regimes. Even in small numbers, they were an existential threat.

At the party's bidding, I joined a small committee tasked with identifying these people and ensuring they were expelled from the membership. It was a nasty and delicate business because this had to be done without stifling legitimate debate. It was an ugly episode that taught me some valuable political skills: like how to identify these kinds of people and the methods they use.

THE CHARLOTTETOWN ACCORD AND THE 1993 ELECTION

DESPITE MY ROLES IN POLICY, in Ottawa, and in the expansion effort, my place in Reform had been diminishing even prior to the Saskatoon convention. In 1990, after returning to Calgary from my time with Deborah Grey, I became quite ill, being hospitalized and largely out of commission for some months. I had contracted viral pneumonia, brought on by a gradual and unrecognized return of asthma. It had been twenty years since I had had anything like this, and fortunately, I have had nothing like it since. After recovery, my first priority was completing my master's degree, something I accomplished in just a few months. However, it took me further out of the day-to-day at Reform headquarters.

After the convention, despite my pay going up in the newly professionalized party, my role continued to decline. In part, this was a natural consequence of the organization getting bigger. There were, however, more subtle shifts that would soon have consequences.

While things were evolving rapidly with Reform, national politics were not standing still. Most prominent was the constitutional file. The national drama that was the Meech Lake Accord process, which the Reform Party had strongly opposed, finally came to an unsuccessful end. Then the Mulroney Government tried to do it over again. It was a catastrophic mistake that ultimately led to the referendum on the Charlottetown Accord in October 1992.

Reform's response to the Charlottetown Accord came close to creating a serious schism within the party. Some of the party's new advisors believed Reform should support the agreement, and Preston appeared open to that point of view. I must admit that I still do not understand why. Thanks to the pressures Reform had created, the new Accord did address issues well beyond the Meech Lake deal, like Senate reform. But the specifics clearly ran against the grain of our overall constitutional agenda, which had been a big factor in our rise. As such, it had precious little support among our membership—something those of us opposed quickly provided hard data on. Besides, even if the deal was initially popular, it was hard to see how Reform being a fourth "Yes" vote could do anything other than relegate us to complete irrelevance.

Tom Flanagan and I developed the eventual compromise, which was the "kNOw more" position. In other words, the more the public learned about the accord, the more likely it would be to oppose it. That was because the accord was, in numerous areas, little more than a framework for further negotiations. The idea that it would resolve the constitutional and national-unity debates—a big part of the argument for it—was an illusion.

Our framing of Reform's position was clever. It was also true. And it accurately predicted how the debate unfolded. The Yes side, despite having the support of the three traditional parties and almost the entire Canadian institutional establishment, saw its support steadily erode and was defeated in virtually every part of the country.

On the other hand, Reform's position on the substance of the deal had been muddied in the process. Some of the HQ relationships had also become strained, including between Preston and myself. We had disagreed before, of course, but without rancour. Although we patched things up, the conflict had some lingering effects.

The defeat of the Charlottetown Accord should have been a great victory for Reform. However, the internal conflict (which had been leaked) and the loss of definition of our constitutional position kept us from taking full advantage. Preston tried to adjust to the new issue mix, particularly with the development of the "Zero in Three" plan of federal deficit reduction—the development of which I again played a central role in. Nevertheless, in the months following the Charlottetown referendum, Reform's support began to fall back. When the PCs got a new leader in the form of Kim Campbell, polling had us at barely 10 per cent.

During this period, election speculation was building: we were approaching the maximum limit of a five-year term. I had decided some time before to run again, and I had again secured the Calgary West nomination unopposed. Following the referendum, I took a leave of absence from the Reform national office to concentrate on trying to win the seat.

The election was finally called on September 8, 1993. Notwithstanding Reform's recently weakened position, this campaign was going to have much better odds for us than its predecessor. Our level of organization in Calgary West, which was good in 1988, was even better in 1993 under campaign manager John Weissenberger. The party as a whole was also far better organized, but the key difference was that people now knew about us. There was no more "Who are you and what are you talking about?" when door knocking. Whether or not they liked us, they knew who the Reform Party was, and they had heard of Preston Manning.

Yet there was still a long way to go. In fact, few pundits were predicting much of an improvement for Reform. We were still trailing the PCs, even in an urban Alberta riding like mine.

Things started to change the moment the election was called. I remember sitting in my basement suite in University Heights in Calgary, on the phone with Laureen—by now my fiancée—watching, almost in disbelief, Kim Campbell's initial gaffe-filled press conference. I said to Laureen, "You know, I might win this after all."

As it turned out, that press conference was the high point of the PC campaign. You could see this clearly in the electoral trenches, where I was now spending my every waking hour. In most campaigns, it is standard practice to get your signs up immediately. Our people now had the organizational capacity to get that done. In the early days of the election in Calgary West, you would see some Reform signs, more PC signs, and the odd Liberal or NDP sign. Then, halfway through the campaign, those PC signs started to come down.

This was an amazing development in and of itself. People who put up signs early tend to be hard-core supporters. So the PCs were clearly in big trouble. Then, within about a week, Reform signs began going up on lawns that had previously had PC signs. Core supporters of the PC Party were switching their vote to us, and right in the middle of the election, no less. A dramatic shift—in fact, a historic realignment—of the electorate was underway, and not just in Calgary. What we were seeing, in real time, was the disintegration of the PC Party nationally into three parts:

a rump Red Tory base of loyal PC supporters; those who shifted their allegiance to the Reform Party; and, in Quebec, those who defected en masse to the Bloc Québécois.*

The results of this fracturing could not have been more dramatic, as was demonstrated in my riding of Calgary West. In 1988, Jim Hawkes finished forty-two points ahead of me. In 1993, I finished thirty-seven points ahead of him. He was not even second. Although some of this swing happened well before the election—maybe a quarter of it—most of it occurred right in the middle of the campaign.

In my constituency, the critical shift occurred among right-of-centre voters. Most were attracted to what we stood for, but many still preferred a PC government to a Liberal government, and they doubted whether Reform could win the riding. However, as the polls kept shifting, a PC defeat started to look inevitable nationally, and it became clear we had a shot at winning locally. Once we began to pass the PCs in polling support, the rationale for sticking with them simply began to evaporate. It was like a snowball gaining size and momentum as it goes down a hill, and it simply rolled over the PCs.

In truth, I always had mixed emotions about winning that election. My parents had come out from Etobicoke to work on that campaign, as they had in 1988, and there were certainly shared moments of elation and pride when my victory was called on television. All I could think was, "Gee, I really won. I am actually a member of Parliament!" It seemed a bit surreal to me. I was also very excited about the dramatic results for the Reform Party. Fifty-two Reformers were heading to Ottawa to change the country.

---

* The 1993 election was held on October 25, and it was an unprecedented reordering of Canadian politics. Jean Chrétien's Liberal Party of Canada won 177 of 295 seats for a majority in the House of Commons. Lucien Bouchard's BQ won 54 seats, followed by Reform with 52. The New Democratic Party won 9 seats, followed by the Progressive Conservatives, who were nearly wiped out when their seat count plummeted from 154 to 2. One former PC was also elected as an Independent.

Yet I also harboured a pang of regret about defeating my friend and mentor Jim Hawkes. That had not been my objective: I had first become the candidate in Calgary West to advance the Reform cause when I knew I had no chance of winning. Now I had beaten him, and there was a part of me that felt uneasy about that. Since Jim and I stayed in touch over the years, at one point I broached the issue and told him I was sorry. He was beyond gracious about it, explaining that it would not have mattered who ran against him, he was never going to win. The party got wiped out in that election. He also reminded me that he was dealing with some health issues at the time, and if he had not been forced out of politics, he might not have survived.

From the day I was elected a member of Parliament, and through my tenure as prime minister, Jim was always a good source of advice. I know he took pride in having played a role in training a future prime minister of Canada. And although he was never a fan of Reform, once we formed the new Conservative Party of Canada, he became a strong partisan supporter as well. Jim passed away in 2019.

A REFORM MP IN OTTAWA (1993–1997)

WHEN FIFTY-ONE REFORM COLLEAGUES and I arrived in Ottawa in the fall of 1993, we were eager to take on the world. Obviously, Ottawa was a dramatically changed place in light of the results of the election. The PCs and NDP no longer had official party status. Our caucus was actually the third party. The Bloc had won fifty-four seats and were accorded the role of Official Opposition—a pretty dubious designation in our view, given it was a separatist party with no intention of offering the country an alternative government. But strange things can and do happen in Ottawa—especially when they are in the Liberals' interests—and we had to make the best of it. Of our fifty-two-member caucus, Deb Grey used to say, "We got the full deck and they [the Bloc] got the jokers." As an aside, Prime Minister Chrétien constantly referred to us as the "turd" party—a slip that, despite his thick French-Canadian accent, could not have been accidental.

Regardless, we were actually in Ottawa, in the House of Commons. Our caucus were all rookies, except for Deb Grey and Ray Speaker,* but we Reformers brought a lot of varied, outside-professional experience, judgment, and enthusiasm to our new roles. Even though I was the second-youngest member of caucus, I had as much Ottawa experience as anyone, which led to a number of very interesting assignments. For starters, I was appointed to the Board of Internal Economy (BOIE), which is effectively the management committee of the House of Commons. I served stints as Reform's constitutional critic, deputy whip, and a sometimes finance critic. I also chaired internal caucus committees on pay, perks, and pensions, as well as ethics. It was not all fun, but everything I did then brought useful experience and lessons learned for later.

I have always believed that the processes in large organizations really matter, but until then, I had never been in management. House of Commons management was a microcosm of the federal public service. Moreover, I was on the BOIE at a time when the Liberals had signed on to dramatic budget cuts. I worked on an internal committee of three: Alfonso Gagliano, chief government whip for the Liberal Party; Gilles Duceppe, chief whip in the Bloc Québécois; and myself. Our task was to turn the administration inside out to find financial savings. You could not think of three more different people, politically or personally. The work was intense and lengthy, but it was a great experience. We also worked well together. Despite Mr. Duceppe's very different view of the country and Mr. Gagliano's later political issues, these were very capable and, in my experience, straightforward individuals.

---

* Ray was a rookie in the House of Commons, but he had served for almost three decades in the Alberta Legislature.

REFORM AND THE 1995 QUEBEC REFERENDUM

WITHOUT A DOUBT, my most exciting experience during this time was as Reform's constitutional critic during the 1995 Quebec referendum campaign. Reform played little role in the actual referendum itself, as the party had only the tiniest presence in the province. But I had followed the Meech and Charlottetown Accords intensely—I was virtually part of the academic "constitutional industry" for a time—and as the only Reformer who used French regularly, I got a front-row seat for the drama that ensued.

One small but useful contribution I made was spearheading the formation of the *"ADQ pour le Non."* The Action démocratique du Québec (ADQ) was a small, centre-right nationalist party that had been formed by former Quebec Liberal youth leader Mario Dumont to oppose the Charlottetown Accord. Dumont was supporting the "Yes" side in the sovereignty vote, but the party's supporters were very divided on the question. With the help of a couple of federal Reformers within the ADQ, I pulled together about twenty former ADQ candidates who opposed separation. We launched a little campaign within that party to promote the "No" side. Did it move a lot of votes? I do not know, but ADQ voters were the swing voters and the No side only won by 1 per cent. So, it could not have hurt!

By far Reform's most substantive contribution to the referendum was our publication of two papers that laid out for all Canadians, especially Quebecers, the possible implications of the referendum vote, whether No or Yes. Although I led a small team, including future MP Scott Reid, that did most of the drafting, this was Preston Manning's initiative. He was highly attuned to the stakes involved in this referendum—I would argue even more so than Prime Minister Chrétien, especially during the early days.

This was an example of Preston Manning's special gift. He had a knack for figuring out what people really had on their minds, especially things that traditional politicians wanted to avoid, and then giving those things a voice. The political establishment and all the talking heads would condemn his proposals, but they invariably intrigued a big portion of the public.

In this case, Preston was the only one with a bullhorn, because there was virtually no substantive discussion around the referendum, not on the No side anyway, and certainly none that involved Canadians outside Quebec. In retrospect, it is shocking how unprepared the federal government was for the campaign and, in contrast, how close a very well-prepared Quebec premier, Jacques Parizeau, came to winning the vote.

The first paper we called "Plan A." It explored how our party believed, in the case of a No vote, we could reform Confederation and make Quebecers feel more comfortable within it. These were reasonable and attractive propositions that sought common ground between alienated Westerners and discontented Quebecers. A lot of the ideas revolved around decentralization, and though viewed as controversial in some quarters, they were thoughtful nonetheless.

The second paper, "Plan B," was far more contentious and just as necessary. Virtually nobody had done any serious thinking out loud about what a successful Yes vote might bring and, in particular, how to defend the interests of loyal Canadians, both outside and inside Quebec. On the separatist side, it was clear that they expected that they could just declare independence—on their own terms, no less—and all would be roses.

The fact was that nobody on the federalist side seemed to be taking that possibility seriously. One wonders, in hindsight, how did the country ever go along with this? Well, for the longest time, nobody really believed the sovereigntists could win. After all, in the 1980 referendum, with Pierre Trudeau leading the No side, they were defeated handily. And as the 1995 campaign started, they were well behind. But things started to change, and very quickly. There is little doubt that a sense of complacency existed in the federal Liberal Government. They simply believed that calling this second referendum would be the death knell of the Parti Québécois.

Reformers had a very different perspective. What if the separatists did win? What then? Who would speak for Canada? With this in mind, we put out the Plan B paper, which outlined the issues involved in the tough, cold-blooded negotiations that Canadians would have to undertake with Quebec. As unpleasant as these topics were, such a discussion was needed for the sake of the rest of Canada. The reaction of the political establishment was negative and shrill, but in short order, these were the issues that people were talking about.

Both papers made a significant contribution to the debate.* After all, the Liberal Government put out precisely nothing on either option A or B. The benefit for me was the invitation to numerous debates and interviews, inside and outside Quebec, in both French and English, during the campaign.

Most memorable was referendum night, October 30, 1995, in Montreal. I had gone there to be a panelist on CBC Television's national coverage of the result. I did not intend to stay in the city. By that point, it was clear that the vote could go either way. With tensions ratcheting up rapidly, we considered widespread violence a real possibility. I had planned a safe exit route back to Ottawa as soon as I was off the air.

Before heading to the studio, I ended up having a surprise dinner in the Peel Pub with Mordecai Richler. A passionate Canadian, Richler was well known for his contempt for the separatists. In truth, my views of the sovereignty movement have always been more nuanced. As a Canadian nationalist—which I am—I have never supported their cause, but I understand it, and I understand why some Québécois do. I also understand its dark side. In fact, on the air that night, I stated that "ethnic nationalism" was one element of the Quebec separatist movement. That got a sharp rebuke from other panelists, who later had to reverse themselves after Parizeau made his infamous "money and the ethnic vote" concession speech.

We can debate how much influence Reform's papers had during the referendum, but there is no doubt that both, especially the Plan B initiative, had a big impact in its aftermath. When the Yes side failed by just 1.16 per cent (officially 54,288 votes) in a 93.52 per cent turnout, the terms of the

---

* The two papers were consolidation into a Reform Party publication entitled "20:20—20 Proposals for a new confederation—20 Realities about secession—A Vision for the Future of Canada."

debate changed forever. In short order, few disputed that the consequences of separation had to be laid out.

I pushed the matter further by tabling my own private member's bill (PMB) in the Commons. It would have created a federal framework for any future Quebec referendum. My PMB was very clear on how any future federal government should handle the referendum, how it should recognize or not recognize the question, and how it should deal or not deal with the result. I know for a fact that it attracted attention in the highest echelons in Ottawa in both political and bureaucratic circles.

It is generally acknowledged that my PMB was a precursor to the Clarity Act introduced by Stéphane Dion in 2000. The eventual Liberal legislation was a somewhat watered-down version. But it did not matter. The debate had shifted. This was now recognized universally as a critical issue. During the 1995 referendum, a lot of Quebecers had voted Yes, believing they would not really separate, but seeing this as a way of creating leverage, getting attention, and maybe even forcing Ottawa to make changes. The Plan B paper, my PMB, and the eventual Clarity Act put paid to that notion. The consequences of a vote to separate would be very different than the picture the sovereigntists had painted.

In fact, the whole post-referendum period played out far differently than virtually anyone thought it would at the time. With the big increase in support for sovereignty and an emotional surge propelling the popular Lucien Bouchard to the premiership of Quebec, expectations were high for an imminent and final federalist–separatist showdown. But the opposite happened. Almost as soon as the 1995 contest was over—or at least within six months of it—the air started to go out of the whole debate. Mario Dumont, a great reader of public opinion—the closest thing to Preston Manning in Quebec—stated that there should be no more referendums for at least ten years. In Quebec City, Bouchard became mired in Quebec's fiscal problems.

The sovereignty issue began to recede, slowly at first, but with increasing momentum. This is not to say the issue has vanished. It clearly has not. But

I have no doubt that the Plan B discussion, by creating a more realistic and more challenging view of what separation would actually look like, set us down a different path.

REFORM AND THE LIBERAL BALANCED BUDGET

I CONSIDER REFORM'S BIGGEST impact during that Parliament to be preparing the ground for the balancing of the federal budget, which began with our "Zero-in-Three Plan," a central plank in our 1993 election campaign. It was based on the conviction that Canada's finances were in dreadful shape, a significant drag on economic growth, and a crisis-risk for the country. Led once again by Preston Manning, we proposed a major, detailed, three-year cost-cutting exercise to balance the books. All our political competitors, including the PCs, attacked the plan as being completely outrageous.

Indeed, Jean Chrétien dismissed the paper's core assumption, saying explicitly in the campaign that the deficit was not a priority and was not going to be his focus going forward. And that is how he acted for about a year and a half. Then, in 1995, Mexico had a peso crisis and Canada was, by some accounts, hours away from a crisis of our own. Apparently, the folks running Canada's finances discovered that borrowing a lot of money is a good idea until people develop some hesitation about continuing to lend. Suddenly, the Liberals woke up and understood that crippling deficits matter, and if you do not have a credible financial story to tell markets, you are in big trouble.

In fairness, once the Liberals resolved to tackle the deficit, they did so with gusto. They effectively ended up doing "zero in two"—eliminating the deficit in two years. The spending reductions they made were in fact far deeper than Reform had proposed. Those included steep cuts to transfers to the provinces for healthcare and other social programs, which had been only a small part of our proposals. Of course, by then, two years lost through inaction had made the problem that much worse. Still, they did it, and they deserve credit for doing what needed to be done. But I would argue that Reform's leadership and presence played a big part in their change of direction.*

In contrast, remember that, when the Mulroney Government had tried to tackle the deficit, the parliamentary environment had been entirely unhelpful. No matter what the PCs tried to do, even the smallest and most reasonable things, they were pilloried by the Opposition, including by the Liberal Party that had created the mess in the first place. Yet suddenly the Liberal Party was able to eliminate the deficit quickly and successfully, almost overnight. Why was that? Because they knew they had support from Reform for the general direction of balancing the budget and that, thanks to Reform, Canadians had increasingly become aware of the need for dramatic action. So, yes, that was an achievement for the Liberal Party, and Canada as a whole ultimately benefitted from it. But there is no reason to believe it would have happened, short of a financial crisis, unless there had been that caucus of fifty-two Reform MPs committed to fiscal sanity and discipline.

LEAVING OTTAWA AND THE REFORM CAUCUS

BY LATE 1996, we were approaching election time, and I had a made a critical decision. I had decided to leave Parliament. It was the right thing for me, and for the party. For a number of reasons. I had had a lot of interesting roles, to be sure. I had had my share of successes, as well as some failures. But a major factor were the periodic clashes I continued to have with Preston Manning, which made for an increasingly uneasy relationship. I have to bear significant responsibility for that. There were some genuine, principled areas of disagreement between us, but I also acknowledge that much of the fallout reflected my immaturity at the time.

---

* By the way, this was not the first time Reform had inspired dramatic fiscal change. In 1992, Alberta premier Ralph Klein, fearing the emergence of a provincial Reform Party, among other reasons, had done it as well.

Being a member of Parliament had been a privilege and an honour, but I really did not like Reform's chances going forward. By 1995, I had become convinced that Reform had to clearly define itself as a conservative political party (albeit a grassroots one) and to fully displace the PCs on the right if we were to continue to grow. With a sense of urgency, I placed an article in the *Globe and Mail* to that effect.*

I will not speak for Preston, but he had a different view and a different strategy at that point for the way he thought we should go forward, which emphasized Reform's populism. By the end of 1996, I had become convinced of two things: that his approach was going to fail, and that the party might not outlast Preston Manning's leadership. That said, I did not get into politics to fight Preston Manning. That would not have been useful for anybody. I had run for office because of Preston Manning, and I had been there to help Preston Manning. So given how I now felt, it made sense for me to do other things, not fight the direction in which he was trying to take the party.

In late 1996, I quietly announced that I would not be a candidate in the next federal election. I ultimately resigned my parliamentary seat on January 14, 1997, before the expected spring election.

CHANGING THE POLITICAL STATUS QUO

I THINK IT IS appropriate to reflect upon the influence Reformers had upon the Ottawa we came to change. Granted, we were a bit naive about the scope of the change we thought we could drive. Yet the impact of the Reform Party has been dramatically minimized by most observers.

I have already talked about how Reform shifted the debate on both the constitutional/national unity and economic/fiscal agendas. These changes

---

* "Where does the Reform Party go from here?" the *Globe and Mail,* March 21, 1995.

were transformational in nature, and they lasted for a generation.† It also ought to be noted that Reform added an element of decorum to Parliament by ending the tradition of desk thumping in the House of Commons. People forget that, but it was much needed.

Reform also had considerable influence on the machinery of political parties. The party brought in national membership lists. Previously, riding associations could be so-called rotten boroughs—the personal fiefdom of a member of Parliament. We made the parties more open. Leadership campaigns turned into broad-based membership votes instead of elite, delegated conventions. The governing bodies of political parties were also restructured along more democratic lines.

None of this would have been accomplished without Preston Manning, whose many achievements should not be overlooked. He is the only person since Confederation to start a political party and build it into a national entity virtually from scratch. Granted, he had some background in Social Credit, and there was a residual base there. But that party had ceased to exist for more than a generation.

The fact is that without Preston Manning and the Reform Party, the modern Conservative Party of Canada would never have been formed, and I would never have become prime minister. There is no way I could have ever taken Reform from a populist movement outside Parliament to national party status; I did not have the skills. Nor, frankly, did anyone else. Although Preston did not succeed in his ultimate ambition, he had a profound impact upon Canadian politics and upon my life. Both Canada and I are better for it.

---

† But just a generation, unfortunately. With *Trudeau-fils*, we landed back in the *Trudeau-père* environment of deep national divisions and out-of-control deficit spending after 2015.

3

THE ROAD TO LEADER OF THE OPPOSITION

NATIONAL CITIZENS COALITION

FROM MY DAYS as the policy chief of the Reform Party, I had maintained connections with conservative-leaning organizations in Canada—not that there were a lot of them! One was the National Citizens Coalition (NCC). Although it has since receded in prominence, the NCC was, from its founding in 1967 through the 1980s, the only broad-based conservative political action group in the country.

The NCC's agenda was summarized by its slogan "more freedom through less government." Limited government has been, of course, a central tenet of modern conservatism in all Western societies, especially as it pertains to economic matters. This was where the NCC was always most focused, although it weighed in from time to time on national defence and foreign affairs and on constitutional and unity debates. On the other hand, it explicitly avoided issues of a "social" or moral nature. It was an agenda close to my own, and I had been a supporter for several years.

I had come to know both NCC chairman Colin T. Brown, son of the organization's founder, and long-time president David Somerville. In the latter part of 1996, David made it clear he was ready to move on. I was the ideal candidate to fill the eventual vacancy, and the timing was perfect given my planned departure from Parliament. Shortly after I announced my intention to leave, we reached an agreement on a transition plan. I would join the NCC in early January, serve as its vice president for the balance of the year, and succeed David when he departed at the end of 1997. Most of the NCC's two-dozen-plus staff were located at the head office in Toronto, but David had relocated to Calgary, my adopted hometown.

In the 1990s, other conservative activist groups started to appear, and the NCC's relative position had begun to shrink. Yet it still had a considerable budget of about two-and-a-half million dollars a year. That was all raised through private donations without tax support—the NCC was structured as a not-for-profit business not a charity—and there were very few sizable donors. I certainly saw this new job as a chance to use some of my political skills on issues I was passionate about.

That said, the key attraction to me of the NCC position was not political at all. It was an opportunity to run an organization for a few years and broaden my employability after that. I had spent time in a large corporation and in government, and in both I had absorbed important management techniques. But I had no such direct experience myself. In terms of future jobs in the business world, I had no interest in returning to computer programming, where my skills were by then anachronistic, and my economics education did not have a strong business bent. So this was first and foremost the chance to operate a business, to learn management skills, and to meet a payroll.

The National Citizens Coalition did not intervene in party politics per se, but we certainly were very active on the political issues of the day. We published our views through in-house newsletters and periodicals. We bought advertising to spread our messages through other media. We litigated and spent a fair amount of time and money on court cases. And we did fundraising, essential to building any kind of political organization—and another skill that would come in handy for me personally down the road.

The litigation activities of the NCC, which are done mainly by constitutional foundations now, became a growing focus during my time as president. We defended free speech against arbitrary restrictions on independent (non-political party) election spending. We fought for marketing freedom for grain farmers. We sued the B.C. government of Glen Clark when it won its re-election on a blatantly fraudulent budget. All these actions were supported by publicity campaigns, as were battles against government waste, the "gold-plated" MP pension plan, fiscal irresponsibility, and similar causes.

Another initiative that briefly gathered significant attention was the Alberta Agenda of 2001—the "firewall letter" written by me and five other prominent Alberta conservatives.* It urged the provincial government to strengthen the province against intrusions by the federal government by fully exercising its own constitutional jurisdictions. The initiative was sparked by the 2000 federal election campaign, when the federal Liberal Party had demonized Alberta as a campaign tactic.

Needless to say, Albertans were infuriated by what had transpired, regardless of how they felt about the election's outcome. Our argument was that if Alberta was frustrated by its treatment in Confederation, why not fully use its powers the way Quebec does? Indeed, a lot of Alberta's authority, including powers over policing, pensions, and taxation, for example, have actually been lent to Ottawa to exercise on its behalf.

Although it made many headlines at the time—including demagogic accusations of "separatism"—the initiative had zero political impact back then. Despite its strong financial position, the Ralph Klein Government did not want to touch the issue and made that clear. Interestingly, now, over two decades later, the Alberta Agenda is back on the province's radar and part of the political discussion.

Although I remained a Reform (and later Alliance) supporter during these years, my official "non-partisanship" at the NCC allowed me to periodically weigh in on national issues independent of the parties' positions. My consistent focus was on the political situation that had led to my 1995 *Globe and Mail* article and my exit from Parliament—the prospect of perpetual

---

* They included Andy Crooks, chair of the Canadian Taxpayers Federation, and Ken Boessenkool, a former Stockwell Day policy advisor whom I had worked with as a Reform MP and who later had roles in my office and on my various campaigns. There were also three University of Calgary political science professors—Ted Morton, Rainer Knopff, and Tom Flanagan. Morton was later an Alberta provincial cabinet minister.

Liberal government despite its modest levels of support. Yes, the Liberal Party had a significant and robust electoral coalition behind it. But its persistence in office—particularly its majority status in the Commons—was in large part due to a divided opposition. The opposition vote was increasingly shared by four medium-sized parties: the Reform Party, the PC Party, the NDP, and the Bloc Québécois. Each had enough support to win a substantial block of seats, but none had any possibility of forming a government.

I was focused on explaining how this situation arose and how it could be overcome. Obviously, my interest was in the ways conservatives could overcome it. That began by recognizing that right-of-centre voters, while substantial in number, were divided among the different political parties. They could be found in the Reform Party, for sure, but they were also still very much present among the ranks of the PC Party. Conservatives could also be found within the Bloc Québécois, a nationalist/sovereigntist party whose voters ranged from the very left to the very right. There was also a conservative-leaning constituency within the Liberal Party, attracted by Jean Chrétien's and Paul Martin's deficit-busting, (modest) government downsizing, and even tax-cutting agenda in the early 2000s.

My thesis, articulated largely in my writings at the time, was based on the nature of conservatism. It is not an ism like, say, socialism, communism, libertarianism, or fascism, in that it has never provided a blueprint for society or a detailed policy agenda. It is about broad principles based on human experience, human nature, and a cautious approach to political change. As such, the cultural context of conservatism matters a lot.

The challenge, therefore, for conservatives in Canada, is the culturally complex nature of the country. I argued that in Canada we have three broad political cultures—on both the left and the right, incidentally, but certainly on the right. In the anglophone part of Eastern Canada, there is what I would call the Tory tradition—a very institutional-based kind of conservatism. In Western Canada, conservatism flows out of the right side of the populist tradition, which is a values-based, grassroots, freedom-oriented version. And in Quebec and among French-Canadians generally, conservatism is rooted in a nationalism that emphasizes, across the spectrum, a collective identity and its survival. I laid out the view that the key to building a long-term conservative coalition was to combine these three cultures in a single political party.

This analysis was not typical among those who advocated "unite the right," that is, the growing call for a merger or accommodation between the Reform Party and the PC Party. Typically, they would emphasize the need to bring together economic conservatives and social conservatives. In my view, such a division, while real, was largely irrelevant in terms of the partisan politics of the day. The Reform Party was unambiguously both more economically conservative and more socially conservative than the PC Party. In short, the division was much deeper than those labels, based, as I contended it was, on recurring patterns in Canadian history.

My historical argument went as follows: the person—really the only person—who had successfully brought Canada's conservative traditions together was our longest-serving prime minister, Sir John A. Macdonald.* It is true that Western conservatism was not a big factor at the time, but Macdonald nevertheless cemented together a broad conservative coalition over an incredible period of time and national evolution. An ongoing conservative majority has not been secured since his passing in 1891.

Conservative governments have since tended to come about during challenging times, not as an exercise in conscious coalition-building but through a disparate "throw the bums out" coalition opposing long-standing Liberal governments. As such, those governments had been prone to fragmentation when they were defeated, leading to more long periods in opposition. Robert Borden's unusual and very different electorates in 1911 and 1917

---

* William Lyon Mackenzie King is usually credited as being Canada's longest-tenured PM. That is certainly true since Confederation, having served roughly twenty-one-and-a-half years to Macdonald's nineteen. However, Macdonald was also the joint first minister of the pre-Confederation United Province of Canada (the "Canadas") for an additional nine years. In fact, besides being the pre-eminent Father of Confederation, he was our dominant political figure for almost four decades.

fell apart under Arthur Meighen with the rise of the Progressives and the total loss of Quebec. R.B. Bennett's Depression Government dissolved with a split (H.H. Stevens' Reconstruction Party) and the emergence of conservative populism (Social Credit). John Diefenbaker's defeat in 1962–1963 also witnessed the reappearance of Social Credit, this time in both the West and Quebec. Of course, the most vivid and complete explosion had taken place at the end of the Mulroney-Campbell Government in 1993.

THE 1997 ELECTION AND ITS CONSEQUENCES

MUCH OF THE MUSINGS from me and others about the state of conservative politics had been conditioned by the results of the 1997 federal election. For Reform, there was some good news. The party had become the Official Opposition with an improvement of eight seats and slightly more popular vote. But the disappointments were larger. The PC party had returned to official status with twenty seats scattered from Newfoundland to Manitoba, and it had won almost the same number of votes as Reform, which had lost its only Ontario seat. In short (and as I suspected), Reform had utterly failed to consolidate the right-of-centre vote, and its growth potential was now severely limited.

Yet the PCs, who were still the fifth-place party, had to know that their prospects for further success were just as constrained. That is no doubt part of the reason why their leader, Jean Charest, was persuaded to leave in March 1998 and take the helm of the Quebec Liberal Party for the upcoming battle against Lucien Bouchard's Parti Québécois. His departure meant that the PCs needed a new leader, and a campaign was announced. At that point, I began to receive approaches from some PCs to run for the leadership. To me, this came totally out of left field (so to speak).

I suppose I should not have been so surprised. My NCC role had made me a commentator on Canadian politics from a conservative, admittedly Reform-sympathetic, but otherwise non-partisan perspective. I was also travelling frequently, spending a lot of time working out of our Toronto head office, but also meeting our supporters and conservative partner organizations in different parts of the country. I had a background in the PC Party and my "unite the right" views were well known in those circles. My declarations during my time as an MP had been generally consistent with the views of Blue Tories, and I had avoided Reform's harder-edged social stands. I spoke passable French. It was also true that the federal PCs' potential leadership ranks were pretty thin.

I used the attention to give a couple of speeches about the need to create a broad conservative movement. I also made some connections in the PC Party that would prove valuable some five years down the road.

Yet this was not part of a "master plan" to lay the groundwork to become prime minister. I wish I could say I had such a clear objective. True, I had not completely ruled out returning to politics someday, but neither was I certain I ever would. And, frankly, the events that would ultimately propel me back into the federal arena happened entirely outside my control.

In fact, my decision not to contest the PC leadership was relatively quick and unequivocal. First, I had just committed to a new job, and it would have been inappropriate for me to leave so soon. Second, there were family considerations: Laureen and I had married just after the 1993 election, and my son Ben had been born toward the end of my tenure as an MP. We were paying down a mortgage and had hopes of growing our little family. That happened the following year with the arrival of our daughter Rachel.

There was also the naked political reality that there was no way I could have won that leadership race. Most of the "real" conservatives were in the Reform Party at that point and would not be joining to vote for me in a leadership race. The PC Party had gravitated to a virtual left-of-centre-ish philosophy, and with former prime minister Joe Clark entering the race, the victor was preordained. I was also under no illusion that some of the people approaching me to run had ulterior motives. They wanted a former Reform MP in the race to show "Reformers returning to fold," knowing full well that I would not win, and hoping to split the Reform Party in the process.

Still, it was clear that the "unite the right" concept was in the air, and Preston Manning quickly saw which way the political winds were blowing.

As Joe Clark was heading to a PC leadership coronation on a no-deal-ever-with-Reform platform, Preston came out in favour of a broader coalition to end the vote-splitting that was keeping the Liberals in power. Going even further, at the Reform Assembly in London in May 1998, he declared that the party had gone as far as it could and that he would stay on only if he could lead a new, broader party.

Thus the United Alternative movement was born. Preston never used the term "unite the right," but his objective was clear, and he pursued a systematic outreach strategy in putting the new party together. Precious few federal PCs were tempted, but key provincial players in Ontario and the West got on board. After all, the federal split, if it persisted, could eventually become a threat to their own electoral fortunes. And Manning was frank and sincere about the issue that mattered most: leadership. While he would contest the leadership of the new party—the eventual Canadian Reform Conservative Alliance—it would be a wide-open affair. It was set for July 8, 2000, and turned out to be wide open indeed.

Given my advocacy of a united conservative movement in Canada, it would have been natural for people to think that I might have been interested in the leadership of this new entity. But the answer was absolutely not. I had been enjoying my job and learning a lot as president of the NCC. At this point I had no desire to return to party politics, choosing instead to be a father and enjoy the early years with my family. I still consider those years some of the best of my life. On a personal level, I was not tempted in the least.

But there was also a political calculus. I was not involved in the formation of the Canadian Alliance. And I would never have considered running against Preston Manning. I still retained some misgivings about having run and ultimately defeated Jim Hawkes. Politics being what it is, there was no way, if I ran in the Canadian Alliance leadership race, that it would be interpreted as anything but Preston and me having a showdown, which I did not want to be part of. Preston had led the initiative to create the Canadian Alliance and, once again, deserved enormous credit for taking that project as far as he had. He had every right to seek the leadership without getting a challenge from the likes of me.

Yet neither did I support Preston. I considered his leadership bid doomed. The argument that Reform had gone as far as it could, but that a new party could go further with the same leader, was not going to hold up to serious scrutiny. Preston's conversion to a conservative coalition-building strategy in place of his earlier "populist" one, while welcome, was frankly too late. I made my choice during the Canadian Alliance leadership campaign to support Tom Long, whom I knew from his lengthy and successful background as an Ontario political activist. I liked the fact that he was focused on a clear economic agenda, which had always been the most solid ground for conservatives over time.

Ultimately, Stockwell Day won. He was perfectly positioned to get both PC and Reform votes. He had a good reputation as a provincial PC Cabinet minister in Alberta. Yet he was clearly on the "right" side of the party and in no way identified with the federal PCs. He also spoke passable French, unlike his opponents. I did not know Stock at all, and I did not support him, but I had no reason to oppose him either. If Preston had won, I would have been fine with that. But from early in the race, we at the NCC knew that Stock was going to win.* I was just as happy with that outcome.

THE 2000 ELECTION AND ITS FALLOUT

THE NEW CANADIAN ALLIANCE would be quickly tested at the polls. Partly out of political opportunism, partly because he was goaded into it, Jean Chrétien called an election on October 22, 2000. The new party was not ready, and it showed during the campaign and in the results. When the ballots were tabulated on November 27, even though the Alliance's votes had increased significantly over Reform's, the party had only gained

---

* The NCC had tens of thousands of contacts, and we ran an in-house tele-fundraising program. Because of that, we always had large-scale, real-time data on what conservative supporters were thinking.

six seats. Worse yet, Joe Clark's PCs, though reduced to twelve seats, had retained official party status. This was a massive disappointment to a lot of the people involved.

I was disappointed too, especially, as I have said, with the way the Liberals had gratuitously demonized Alberta during the campaign. All the same, I thought that, under the circumstances, the Alliance's results were not all that bad. Yes, Stockwell Day had made mistakes, but who hasn't? I certainly thought he had the right to continue to lead the party.

There were others who clearly did not agree. Within months of the election, a rebellion began brewing in the party, the likes of which we had not seen in Canadian politics in a long time, if ever. Growing numbers of MPs and other senior Canadian Alliance people—almost all supporters of Manning in the leadership race—launched attacks on Stockwell's leadership. This was not some behind-closed-doors, in-caucus criticism; it was a full-bore public assault. Stockwell Day's team responded with an all-guns-blazing counterattack of their own.

The result was a full-scale civil war. It is hard for people who were not around then to imagine what the reporting was like at that time. It was unbelievable. Every night, Canadians had a front-row seat to a party literally tearing itself to pieces. Screaming matches and vicious personal attacks in front of cameras and microphones became a regular occurrence.

Then matters got even worse. Some thirteen Canadian Alliance MPs split off to form their own (now third) "conservative" group in Parliament. Calling themselves the Democratic Representative Caucus (DRC), they included the key people in Reform under Preston Manning. But it did not stop there. In short order, they teamed up with Joe Clark to form a PC-DRC coalition in the House of Commons.

From the point of view of this outsider, it was a catastrophe. Conservatives were further fragmenting, and Joe Clark was the one with the wind in his sails. This was the summer of 2001. There were growing expectations that deficit-slaying, tax-cutting Paul Martin would become the leader of the Liberal Party. So if Clark emerged from the rubble of what remained of the conservative parties, the governing Liberals would have a leader more "right-of-centre" than we did. That could have very well meant the end of conservatism as an independent force in federal politics.

I had tried to warn Stock's people early on that this kind of thing could happen. I had long had the view that if Preston ever ceased to be leader, there was a real risk that self-destructive forces could be released within the party. However, I never imagined the magnitude and ferocity they would have, and the direction they would take. In any case, by July 2001, the situation was beyond saving. Stockwell Day was forced to resign by caucus and to call a leadership race.

MY BIG DECISION

EVEN BEFORE THE RACE started, calls began trickling in from Alliance members of Parliament I knew asking if I would consider running for the leadership. Initially, I was not just surprised but taken aback, because I did not support the overthrow of Stockwell Day, and I did not wish to be associated with the attempt to do so. But the people who were calling were not from the DRC. Indeed, they were not even publicly aligned with Stock's critics. And they largely shared my views that the assault on the leadership was very damaging to the party. Still, they had concluded that, whether it was right or wrong, Stock's days were numbered. They also confided in me that, for all but a handful of loyalists, the caucus had lost confidence in him and that he would have few MPs supporting him in the inevitable leadership race.

Once Stock stepped down, the trickle turned into a torrent as both former colleagues and new MPs, as well as National Councillors and other senior party members, inquired about my interest in seeking the top job. By now, I had been out of the cut and thrust of partisan politics for some time, so the apparent strength of interest in my candidacy did catch me off guard. But it should not have. From both my Reform days and my NCC presidency, I still had a high profile within the Alliance voting universe. Moreover, being completely uninvolved in the civil war and on neither side of the Manning–Day fight were advantages over any other potential leadership candidate.

There were, however, very real reasons for me to be cautious about this. The fact that an outsider could be an instant leadership frontrunner was a telling comment on just how deep the problems were in the Canadian Alliance. There was also the not insignificant matter of my existing professional obligations. The unwritten understanding was that I would serve as NCC president for at least five years. I had been in that role for three and a half, and I had just started thinking about what I would do next. Until then, I had not ruled out staying on, but I had been contemplating other options in the business world rather than a return to politics.

The NCC obstacle quickly proved to be no obstacle at all. About that time, I was in the Toronto office—I always spent at least a week a month there—for our regular board meeting. Before we got started, somebody joked about me running for the Alliance leadership. I initially brushed it off, but it quickly became apparent that there was a unanimous opinion by the board that I should consider the possibility. Their view was that the situation was dire, and if I did not run, it was unclear who could lead the conservative movement. As much as the NCC was their baby, without a viable national conservative party, its mission would be hopeless.

My conversations with senior Alliance people soon became much more serious as I began to genuinely weigh the possibility of running. The support was clear, and the barriers were few. For one thing, Laureen and I had just paid off the mortgage on our home. We had always lived way below our means, taken on relatively short (fifteen-year) home payment obligations, and made prepayments whenever possible. We had a comfortable amount of savings, and Laureen operated a graphic design and computer consulting business out of our house. Even with a long campaign, which the Alliance race was shaping up to be, we would face no financial pressures.

One day in late July, I came home and told Laureen that I was inclined to jump into the race. She was a bit surprised because she knew that, through all the previous leadership races and speculations, I had never seemed interested. Why this time? "Well," I said, "if I run, I'm going to have the overwhelming majority of the caucus behind me, and lots of senior support beyond that as well. I'll also have strong support from the NCC membership, which is a big part of the Alliance's activist and donor base. I have no doubt I will win if I run. And once I win, no matter how bad shape the party appears to be in, I will be the leader of the Opposition." And then I said what was really driving me. "I know the campaign will be hard, but I'm basically having the position of leader of the Opposition handed to me. If I don't take this opportunity, I'll spend the rest of my life wondering if I should've tried."

Laureen was certainly not opposed to the idea—after all, like me, she was a true believer in the cause—but she did think the state of the party was quite concerning. This was the commitment I made to her: "I don't know how far I can take it. But the day it's clear we're not going further, we're not going forward, then we'll both leave Ottawa and never look back." And with that, Laureen agreed.

On August 1, 2001, I travelled to Prince Albert, Saskatchewan, to speak at a party event. It was the first time I had done such an event since 1996. The local MP was Brian Fitzpatrick, whom I did not know. He had briefly been a member of the DRC but had agreed to come back into the Alliance caucus once Stock stepped down, in the hope that I would seek the leadership. In Prince Albert, I publicly declared my intention of exploring a leadership bid (there being a fair amount of work to actually get such a thing organized from scratch). There was some note of that in the media, although the focus of coverage remained on the ongoing infighting.

In September, I took a leave of absence from the NCC presidency, with the full blessing of the organization. In fact, in the early days of my campaign, most of my donations came from NCC contributors. Still, that was not the most important asset I had gained in my time there.

In retrospect, the NCC was a critical chapter in my professional life. Indeed, I think my tenure at NCC was probably the single most important experience I had in preparing me for the Prime Minister's Office. It is one thing to have political experience on the hustings, in the House of Commons, and in the media. Those are prerequisite skills. It is also very useful to have academic knowledge of an area like economics and to have worked in the various environments I had been exposed to. But being in charge of an organization, with all the issues, personalities, challenges, and responsibilities stopping at your desk, was invaluable. I cannot imagine being prime minister without having some kind of leadership experience like that.

CANADIAN ALLIANCE LEADERSHIP CAMPAIGN, 2001–2002

I WAS IN THE RACE. My campaign strategy took shape early. It would be unusual but fit the circumstances. I would not attack Stockwell Day. In fact, I even fired a couple of campaign people early on for attacking him. I had no gripe with Stockwell Day, and I knew that he could not win the leadership, for much the same reasons as Preston Manning could not win in the previous race. Attacking him would be counterproductive.

Nor did I attack the Manning supporters. Early on, I did attack the DRC MPs for aligning with Joe Clark. Clark certainly has some admirable qualities as a public figure, but for many in my generation, he had long been viewed as anything but a real conservative. That he now stood to pick up the pieces if the Canadian Alliance experiment failed was something we saw as a betrayal of everything we had wanted to change in federal politics. I instinctively found aligning with him inexcusable.

I made a point of seeking the sage political advice of Ray Speaker. I had first met Ray, whom I call "the last of the Alberta Socreds," when the Reform Party was first established. Over the years, particularly during our shared time in Parliament, we had become close (and have remained so). Ray counselled that the DRC people were a tiny minority, out of step with most Manning supporters who had stayed in the Canadian Alliance (Preston's own views on this development were never known). For those supporters, I was the closest thing to Preston Manning. Whatever the complexity of the relationship, Preston and I had long been joined at the hip in their minds. Besides, what the party really needed was unity, Ray said, and me attacking any bit of it undermined my message and appeal.

Ray's advice made sense and was confirmed by some "demon-dial" polling we did of the party membership. I had the overwhelming support of those who had supported Manning in the last leadership race. I also had a significant minority of those who had supported Day. Just as importantly, the Stock people were not at all hostile to my candidacy. I also had close to three-quarters of the caucus supporting me, from different previous leadership camps. They were led by Scott Reid and James Rajotte, but a large number were putting in significant effort on my behalf. In short, I was (as I had surmised) well ahead.

There was another group that I had to pay some attention to. They had not joined the DRC, but they believed that the Canadian Alliance's highest priority had to be to "unite the right." I tried to appeal to this group by emphasizing my long-standing support for a broad conservative movement and by committing to pursue unity when it was feasible to do so. But I also emphasized that this could never happen with Joe Clark, who was deeply opposed to any such union and, indeed, to conservatism itself. I meant what I said, but there were members who saw this as, in fact, opposition to conservative unity and sought candidates who would pursue "unity at all costs" (my phrase, not theirs).

One such group were former Reformers close to the DRC, and they settled on Diane Ablonczy as their leadership candidate. Another group were former PCs who had come over to the Alliance, and they drafted Dr. Grant Hill as theirs. Both groups wanted the next leader to commit to pursuing a deal with Joe Clark. However, the prospects of both candidates were dead in the water when the "unity" folks could not even unite around a single nominee! Consequently, although both were good candidates, they were never serious contenders.

In the end, I ran a campaign that did not focus on my leadership opponents. Instead, I put myself forward as the alternative to someone not in the race: Joe Clark. Who did the supporters of the Canadian Alliance members trust to lead Canada's conservatives—me or Joe Clark? It was not just a line; that was the real choice before them.

There was one other issue, however, that I had to handle during the campaign, and which was critical to both our unity and our prospects with the wider public: abortion. I made it very clear to everyone that, while I would respect a range of opinions on the issue, as leader of the party, abortion was off the table. I had my reasons for that decision, including the fact that it had never been a burning issue for me personally.

There was more to it, though. I had been in Ottawa in 1989, as Deborah Grey's legislative assistant and Reform's chief policy officer, following a Supreme Court decision that struck down Canada's abortion law. The Mulroney Conservatives attempted to bring in a new law to address what was then a legal vacuum. Getting a consensus, even among PCs, was no easy task. But in the end, they cobbled together a compromise position that would carry the support of the clear majority of their caucus. They then put the issue to an open debate and free vote in the House of Commons. It was a far from perfect law, but they had attempted to do what they felt was right and responsible.

I had a front-row seat to the debate that unfolded. Pro-life groups launched a bitter attack on the proposed legislation. Their position was that if they could not have a perfect abortion law, they wanted no law at all. And they threatened Deborah Grey and everybody else: "If you vote for anything other than the full outlawing of abortion, we will campaign against you." I had long conversations with these folks and told them that, if they succeeded in defeating this bill, the country would likely have no abortion law whatsoever. In their zeal, that is what they preferred. "Better we have no law than support a law that allows some abortion." That is what they got.

Ultimately, everyone hated the Mulroney Government for the outcome. Pro-life advocates had rejected the Government's compromising stance on the issue. Pro-choice hard-liners were angry that the PCs had tried to restrict abortion. Everyone else—most Canadians who are conflicted on the issue—resented having gone through arguments with their co-workers, friends, and families, only to see nothing resolved.

I may be a philosophical conservative, and even accused by some of being an ideologue, but the lesson I took from this was to never become wholly impractical as a politician. I will not align myself with people who pride themselves on defeat as a strategy. Hence my determination not to ever take my party into that kind of a quagmire. The social conservative element of the party understood this for the most part. Despite the ongoing opposition of pro-life organizations throughout my nearly fourteen years as party leader, I got a fair portion of their supporters during that campaign and virtually all of it later.

As for the race itself, it was one thing to be confident of victory, but another thing to put together and execute a winning campaign. Not to mention the nearly nine months I spent campaigning. It was a long, tough slog, because the real campaign was not about winning votes but about rebuilding the party. This became readily apparent in the first few months: I was often unable to find anyone from the executive of a riding to organize a meeting. Outside of MPs' constituencies, Canadian Alliance associations were, for the most part, just shells.

Assembling a team to run the campaign was not easy. We initially brought on a professional group. But money was tight, it did not work, and we eventually let them go. It was a difficult process in the early days, to say the least. I was often driving myself, riding to riding, campaign materials in the trunk. One day, in Estevan, Saskatchewan, in the fall of 2001, I stopped at a run-down roadhouse restaurant to have some lunch before a meeting. In a dimly lit room, a few locals were playing slot machines, and believe me, they had not been winning. I could relate. (In the background, the Eagles' song "Hotel California" started playing. I thought to myself, Maybe I'm actually in the Hotel California—and I can never leave!)

A poll had the Canadian Alliance at just 6 per cent. As MP Jim Abbott—a long-time friend and early supporter—said to me, "Are you sure you want to do this? That's almost the margin of error. We could be at zero!" And I will not lie, things looked so bad that I did consider throwing in the towel at one point.

Around December, though, the situation began to improve slowly but steadily. Mark Kihn, whom Laureen and I had known for years, came over from the NCC to start our direct-mail fundraising, and serious money started to come in. We were able to make a few hires. One was Carolyn Stewart-Olsen, a former Reform communications officer. Another early recruit was Ray Novak, who had worked briefly with me before on an NCC-sponsored research project, and who, of course, has worked with me in many different roles to this day. Tom Flanagan chaired the campaign, with John Weissenberger as the day-to-day manager.

Still, our campaign continued to be low-key. To some degree, this was a deliberate strategy on my part. I saw no merit in greatly exposing myself to the media, while Stock kept himself in the news. We knew that dynamic did not hurt me at all, given my lead and his negatives. We also knew that our campaign, like the party, remained weak, and we did not want too much scrutiny.

In the last couple of weeks, media attention finally shifted to the race. It was as if reporters suddenly woke up and realized that whatever the state of the Canadian Alliance, whoever won this was indeed going to be leader of the Opposition. Fortunately, the party apparatus had arranged a professional-looking leadership announcement in Calgary. March 20, 2002, was the date.

I knew I would win, and we were quite confident that it would be on the first ballot. And it was, with a solid 55 per cent support. After a lengthy campaign that had been largely in the shadows, the tight, crowded environment in the Calgary Telus Convention Centre was exhilarating. I remember Laureen and my parents being very excited, although a bit uneasy with the crush of bodies on the floor that almost engulfed them! Ben was six, and Rachel was three. Although they barely understood what was happening, they were two little kids clearly swept up in the atmosphere and having the time of their lives.

OPPOSITION LEADER (2002–2003)

THERE WERE POSITIVE SIGNS in the wake of the leadership race. The Canadian Alliance had inched up in the polls to the low double digits. A couple of months later, the party staged a convention, and it was also well organized, demonstrating that the constituency associations were coming back to life. Our finances were also in relatively decent shape, and we were starting to collect funds for future campaigns. In the end, it looked like I had actually won something.

Not that downtime or rest followed. I may have been the prospective Leader of Her Majesty's Loyal Opposition, but I was not yet in Parliament. I had to win a seat. The opportunity presented itself when a by-election was called for May 13, 2002, in Calgary Southwest, the riding Preston had vacated the previous year. There was no doubt I would win the race. As is the tradition, the governing Liberals did not put up a candidate. Neither did the PCs. Their nominee, Jim Prentice, whom I did not know at that point, phoned to let me know, indicating his hope that I would be open to conservative unity when the opportunity presented itself.

Despite the inevitable results, we still had to run a campaign, and that exercise exposed some of the great challenges that remained within the Canadian Alliance. What I found was a riding association hopelessly split between hard-core supporters of Preston Manning and hard-core supporters of Stockwell Day. They had largely supported me in the leadership race, but they remained at each other's throats. In the worst cases, they were suing each other. It may sound like I am making this up, but we had to ensure the two camps stayed separated when we put door-knocking teams together, lest all hell break loose. I even had to bring in an outside campaign manager in Glen Herring from Oakville, Ontario. Calgary Southwest was a deeply divided organization deeply in debt—and I knew there were plenty more ridings like it.* But we plowed through, and after winning the by-election, I promptly headed to Ottawa. With still no rest for the weary.

I faced a couple of key tasks when I arrived in the nation's capital. I had to start building an office and a team, and I needed to reach out to my caucus. My first stop was to see John Reynolds, the party's interim leader, who had stood in when Stockwell stepped down. John deserves great credit for

---

* It took well over a year before the Calgary Southwest Canadian Alliance Association was finally brought together in one, coherent, supportive team. That was accomplished under the presidency of Gwen Podborski. Gwen later served as my Calgary Southwest campaign manager in 2008.

managing our fractured party during that time. He effectively rallied the troops and gave people confidence. As interim leader, he had also been very careful not to do anything that would step on the incoming new leader's prerogatives. A long-time conservative operative, Jim MacEachern, had stepped in temporarily to ensure that basic functions of the Office of the Leader of the Opposition (OLO) were being competently executed. Still, the staff was small, as those who had departed to work on Stock's campaign had not been replaced. Although I had a competent team around me from the leadership race, it was also small. There was a long way to go to put together a full OLO, let alone prepare for a federal election.

On the other hand, my early engagement with the Canadian Alliance caucus was quite encouraging. They united behind me very quickly, in large part because I had most of them on my team, but also because Stockwell Day gave me his full support right out of the gate. That support continued for the next eight years, and Stock became a trusted lieutenant for the remainder of my leadership. Equally fast, we were able to end the caucus leaking that plagued us during the Alliance's civil war. The key, I found, was to restrict caucus meetings almost exclusively to MPs. In my experience, the way to keep things in confidence is to make sure only those in the circle of confidence are in the room.

My next task was to try to reconcile with the DRC. We had had a good start during the campaign, during which six of the thirteen had already returned to the Alliance—most to support my candidacy. Then, shortly after I became leader, I got a call from Chuck Strahl, the official leader of the DRC. Chuck and I had never been close when we were MPs together, but I welcomed his outreach. He said that most of the remaining DRC members wanted to return, and he gave me an interesting backstory.

According to Chuck, Joe Clark had become convinced that Stockwell Day would win the Canadian Alliance leadership race. He had effectively been fooled by my low-key strategy. Thus, in the closing stages of the campaign, Clark had given the DRC an option—join the PCs or you are out. There would be no United Alternative–type merger, not even the pretense of one. As Chuck said, whatever people might think of what they had done, they were genuinely trying to unite the right. What Joe had now laid on the table was not what they had signed up for. "So," Chuck said, "we would like to come back if people will have us."

While this was a positive development, I expressed some caution to Chuck. For one thing, I would have to build support to move this through caucus. I met Chuck and four other DRC members to assure them I was serious, and I began to socialize the idea with my key caucus supporters. But the other matter, I told Chuck, was Joe Clark. He had also called me after the leadership race to propose that we meet to discuss "unity." I suggested we both keep this CA-DRC reconciliation under wraps until we figured out what Joe was up to. Chuck agreed.

The meeting with Joe Clark was "plus ones," and Ray Speaker came with me. Ray, besides being my most trusted and experienced political advisor, knew all the players, including Joe Clark, whom he had watched for years. In the meeting, Joe put forward a very elaborate proposal: a series of committees and processes that would discuss unity items and possible common ground. But it was soon clear that he was making no commitment to the idea of actual unity.

Now, I may be many things, but I am not a fool. Chuck Strahl had already given me insights into Joe's true feelings and objectives: he was hoping that our party would continue wallowing in this eternal debate, questioning its purpose, and failing to ready itself for an election. So I had come to the meeting with my own proposal—one that would catch Joe completely off guard.

The idea had been suggested to me by David Prest. David was a key person in the whip's office. He had worked for Jim Hawkes, and I had taken Jim's advice in getting him hired by Reform after the election in 1993. The essence of the idea was this: I proposed that our model for unity be Joe Clark's own, that is, I proposed that the PC-DRC arrangement be converted into a CA-PC arrangement. Of course, I knew that both my caucus and the DRC would be prepared to support such a thing. As I said to Joe: "You already put together this coalition between the PCs and the DRC that you said was a model for bringing the parties together. Why don't we just change that into a CA-PC coalition? Exactly the same principles."

Joe rejected this proposal—immediately, categorically, and angrily. I was glad Ray was there, because his "fatherly" presence kept me from losing my cool. The discussion rapidly broke down. In the subsequent press conferences, it became clear that Clark was rejecting his own model. His motives became evident to all. By the next week, the DRC had parted ways with PCs. Within a few weeks Joe Clark had resigned his leadership. I would not have to compete with him for "conservative leadership" in the House of Commons.

With all these preliminaries out of the way, we got down to business. The performance of the Canadian Alliance in Parliament was dramatically improved. We were united. We were increasingly competent. The OLO had been built back up, after Tom Flanagan took over for a time as my chief of staff, eventually settling on long-time Reform/Alliance staffer Phil Murphy for the role longer term. We were also on point, especially around the growing number of "corruption" scandals involving the Liberal Government.

However, there was one problem—me. My own performance was very spotty, very hit and miss (with more misses than hits). Part of the reason was that I was utterly exhausted. Between the leadership campaign, my by-election campaign, and setting things up in Parliament, I had been working non-stop for almost a year, often with little help, and with only the rarest of breaks. I was physically and emotionally drained.

During my first year in Opposition, I became conscious of a deeper problem: I was not psychologically prepared to be leader. The fact is, I had really not aspired to leadership for most of my life, and although others clearly saw it in me, I did not mentally prepare myself. I was always saying to myself, "What should the leader do?" not "What would I do if I were a leader?" Because the truth is, I had not thought deeply about being the leader.

To deal with my weak performance, I did a few things, including getting some executive coaching. That process led me to answer the question "What is your ideal job?" I confessed that it was something like what I had once had when I was with Preston Manning—being the guy close to the leader, working to make sure the parts came together, and translating ideas into actual operations. In government, that probably meant being deputy prime minister. And that was a problem.

Intellectually, I knew where I wanted to go. But in terms of the psychology, the emotional stamina, the mental toughness, the formative vision and energy it takes to build, sustain, and truly lead a team of people and a movement—this was all new for me. On some of those scores, I was simply inadequate. So I did some soul searching, understood where I was not measuring up, and faced the need to improve. When you are the leader, it is not always sufficient to have others compensate for your weakness; sometimes you must simply get stronger in those areas yourself. You must grow as a person.

There was, however, a challenge beyond my own performance. We had to, once again, build a compelling and relevant political agenda. Our movement had become a victim of the (underappreciated) success of Reform and Preston Manning. A lot of the issues we championed when we arrived in Ottawa were now largely irrelevant. The things that had motivated me to get involved in federal politics in the 1980s—Canada's fiscal woes and statist economic policy, Quebec separation and the constitutional battles—were now either resolved or off the table. On policy, we were increasingly running on fumes.

To this point, the Chrétien Liberals, for all their deficiencies, had done a good job of covering their key vulnerabilities. Ironically, it was their ongoing comfort in office that became their key liability. But even that would, at first, be a problem for us.

I had only been leader for three weeks and was still trying to find my feet when the Liberals, then unassailable in the polls, began to have a unity crisis of their own. Tension had been gradually building between Jean Chrétien and Paul Martin on the certainty and timing of the former's eventual departure. On June 2, 2002, that tension became a crisis with Martin either having resigned or been fired as finance minister. (We never really knew which it was. I think they will each tell you a different story.)

Day after day, the Liberal fight was all over the news, but the media played it very differently than the Alliance civil war. The Liberals were in government, but now, we were told, with Paul Martin, they were also their own "opposition party." So with four parties still splitting the actual opposition and far from power, the Liberals were then dominating both sides of the federal political scene.

A FORK IN THE ROAD

THE CALGARY SOUTHWEST BY-ELECTION had been accompanied by some others, with several more such electoral tests over the next year. To the extent we were gauging our performance, it was usually as fellow also-rans against the PCs. Sometimes we were ahead of them; sometimes they were ahead of us. But few of these were in even remotely winnable ridings.

That would change with the Perth–Middlesex by-election scheduled for May 21, 2003. It would be a legitimate measure of our electoral prospects. The Liberals had won the riding in 2000, as they typically did in rural Ontario, on a CA-PC split vote. We had been a good third, at 23 per cent, but that performance was deceptive. It had been bolstered by our candidate—a former Liberal but hard-line pro-life MP—which had given us a strong core vote but little room to grow.

That turned out to be the least of our limitations. Early in the contest, I made my first visit to the riding. It was instantly apparent that we were in terrible shape. We had a decent candidate in Marian Meinen, but we also had all the same weaknesses I had seen in Calgary Southwest. Nominally the members were all behind me, but the Stock people and the Manning people used all their energy hating each other. But this was not Calgary Southwest; both groups were small, and we simply could not afford to be divided. My assessment, without any hard data, was that we were running in low single-digit support and headed to a very bad fourth place.

That was confirmed in some polling that we immediately commissioned, although the situation was actually worse, if that were possible. We discovered a deep problem with the Canadian Alliance brand. It was not the common refrain from liberal media that we were toxic, but rather that the Canadian Alliance had no brand at all. For those who were Reformers, the Alliance brand was just a watered down, feckless version of Reform. For those PCs who had joined the Alliance, it was a stillborn merger attempt. And for the general public—at least for our accessible voters—it meant nothing. In fact, they identified the PC Party with various "conservative" policy positions, even where our positions were much more clearly so. In other words, their name had a brand, whether accurate or not; ours had none.

I moved quickly to fix the problems on the ground. I recruited a talented organizer named Doug Finley to take over the campaign. Doug hailed from Scotland and had spent many years as a senior business executive. He had some political experience as a one-time Liberal organizer, and he had been around the Reform/Alliance for a few years. Doug had nearly been hired when I first filled the position of director of political operations a year earlier, but he had lost a split decision among the interviewers.

Doug immediately moved down to the riding and proved to be a tough, practical, no-nonsense political operator. He replaced anyone who wanted to fight with people who wanted to work. With only three weeks or so to go, he identified our core vote and got it out to the polls. We finished at 17 per cent—a barely respectable third—but probably triple where we had been headed before. It secured Doug's appointment as the new director of political operations. The PCs squeaked out a victory with Gary Schellenberger as their candidate, who was a well-known and well-regarded local politician.

As the dust settled, I privately gave Laureen my evaluation of what it all meant. With our current political assets, the Canadian Alliance brand, and the ongoing vote-split, our chances in the next election were severely limited. With Paul Martin as Liberal leader—his victory in the Liberal civil war was becoming a certainty—and his "centre-right" economic brand, we would be fighting to hold our base. We would survive. We could probably win most of our existing ridings. But we would not grow. The PCs were facing a similar situation, but with an even smaller and more fragile base.

The upshot, I told Laureen, is that I would have to get a merger with the PCs if this were to go anywhere. The opportunity would come when the PCs finally picked a new leader, which was scheduled for May 31. At that point, I would do whatever was necessary, including sacrificing my own leadership, to make a merger happen.

The date was not far off, and on that evening, I was at Stornoway in the third-floor family room with Ben and Rachel watching the Stanley Cup playoffs. I had been following the PC vote earlier, and when I flipped over to the hockey game, it was apparent that Peter MacKay was far enough ahead that he would win on a subsequent ballot.

Then Laureen appeared upstairs. "You have to come and see this." I followed Laureen down to the second floor and there, on the television, were Peter MacKay and David Orchard—an even stronger opponent of the merger than Joe Clark—embracing on the convention floor and vowing "to build this party together."

"I guess that kills any possibility of a merger," said Laureen. I looked at her, paused a moment, and I said, "No. You're wrong. The merger just happened."

4

—

THE PATH TO CONSERVATIVE MERGER AND POWER

LAYING THE GROUNDWORK FOR THE MERGER

I WAS OPTIMISTIC ABOUT a merger because the PCs had, in effect, already decided on that path. But the particular merger that they had chosen—a merger with the forces of David Orchard—was not feasible.

To this day, I really do not know what to make of David Orchard. Although he clearly identified with the PC Party, Orchard had a very strange notion of conservatism. He embraced every conceivable left-wing cause, but what really animated him and his followers was their opposition to free trade, based on a virulent anti-Americanism. If this was conservatism at all, it was the conservatism of the War of 1812, as epitomized by the 1911 election slogan "no truck nor trade with the Yankees!"

The problem for Orchard was that free trade had become the central feature of the modern PC Party. The Mulroney Government's Canada-United States Free Trade Agreement (CUSFTA) and subsequent North American Free Trade Agreement (NAFTA) were its defining achievements. Whether party supporters had gravitated to the Reform/Alliance or the Bloc Québécois or were the reddest of Red Tories, backing free trade was the one thing they all had agreed on.

It is worth remembering the fight for free trade—the critical issue of the 1988 election campaign. Its opponents had argued the deal would impoverish the Canadian economy and end the country's sovereignty. They had lost the election, but more importantly, their arguments had been utterly discredited by subsequent events. That is why the Liberal Party and even the NDP had become reconciled to CUSFTA and NAFTA. The idea that it would be abandoned by the remnants of the PC Party was absurd.

However, David Orchard's followers—I called them the "Orchardistas"—were united and determined. Having now been fully embraced by the PC Party, they were about to become a force within it. With the party's weakness in many parts of the country, PC constituency organizations were very vulnerable to takeover. Indeed, my sources confirmed that that process began almost as soon as the PC leadership race ended. The next stage would be a civil war over the party's most fundamental beliefs.

As I told Laureen that night, "The PCs will quickly discover that they must get out of this merger with the Orchardistas. It is untenable. If we make a good offer, and we play our cards right, the alternative of a merger with us will look infinitely better." They now needed us, and they would soon realize it. After all, besides greater philosophical coherence, the Canadian Alliance was a real party, not a fringe movement.

I did not think the PCs would survive on their current path. But we also needed them. The Canadian Alliance needed the PCs to capture the "conservative" brand, broaden our base, and have a decent shot at fighting Paul Martin. The days when we could simply displace the PCs, as I believe Reform could have done in the mid-1990s, were long gone.

In short order, we launched our "unity campaign." In the days and weeks to come, I and some of my most trusted colleagues put out feelers to key people in the PC Party. Our aim was to lay out the scenarios as we saw them and show our genuine desire for unity.

There were many conduits through which we sought dialogue. However, a big stumbling block was reaching out to the leader himself. I had only met Peter MacKay a couple of times before on the briefest of occasions. His agreement with Orchard at the convention made an immediate conversation seemingly impossible.

That soon changed when Belinda Stronach, daughter of industry mogul Frank Stronach and then-president of Magna International, showed up at my Stornoway door. My intelligence was that she was very close to Peter MacKay and wanted to facilitate a discussion. I was also aware that the Stronachs had been key behind-the-scenes players in the United Alternative process. Why exactly, I had not surmised, but it did not matter to me at that point.

Over the next few weeks, Belinda assisted in getting Peter MacKay and me together for our first sit-down to explore whether a merger was actually possible. MacKay expressed openness, and although he was circumspect, it was apparent to me that he realized how dangerous the Orchardista presence in their party was becoming.

In due course, we agreed to strike a committee of six highly trusted and experienced people, three from each side, to discuss the merger issue. The thinking was that the process would work better without the two ultimate leadership aspirants in the room. The choices were very good ones.

Peter named Don Mazankowski—former deputy prime minister under Brian Mulroney; Bill Davis—the once and long-time premier of Ontario; and Loyola Hearn—a former provincial Cabinet minister in Newfoundland who was now an influential MP in the PC caucus. I called once again upon Ray Speaker, who had served as a provincial minister for both the Socreds and PCs. I also employed our lone senator, Gerry St. Germain. Gerry had been PC Party president during the Mulroney era before being named to the Upper Chamber. I also asked Scott Reid. Scott and I had collaborated on policy in the Reform Party as far back as my pre-MP days, and he had been one of my earliest and strongest leadership supporters. Tom Jarmyn, an attorney and National Councillor from Nova Scotia, provided me with valuable legal advice, and the indispensable Ray Novak also assisted.

Although this high-profile group met and started discussions quickly, things soon began to drag. My PC contacts told me that Joe Clark and his people were making progress difficult internally, and a senior member confided, "We could use a bit of a shove!" That we soon provided.

In late September, I held a national press conference to lay out our offers to the PC Party. They included our preferred options, particularly on the leadership process, but were otherwise broad in nature. Most were quite acceptable to the PCs, and I indicated a willingness to negotiate on those that were not. That did the trick. While there were loud protestations that

I was being heavy-handed and putting undue pressure on the PCs, the six-member committee began to engage on specifics.

There was one substantial benefit to the drawn-out discussions with the PCs. The process allowed Peter MacKay and me to connect on a professional and personal level. We began to discuss the bigger picture, find instances where we could co-operate legislatively, and just generally get to know each other. As the committee battled over party principles and constitutional structures, he and I concentrated on building a better chemistry. It turned out we were not really that far apart. He identified with the "blue" (versus "red") side of the PC Party. I came more from the conservative (versus populist) side of the Reform/Alliance. In any case, I came to really like Peter, and we developed a strong relationship.

There is no shortage of utterly false narratives that circulate in media. They call them "perceptions"; I call them "facts that aren't true." One of those media perceptions was that Peter and I did not get along. According to this narrative, we remained political rivals, authors of a cynical bargain who nursed a simmering conflict. That could not have been more wrong.

It is true that Peter and I are different people, with different styles, and sometimes different views. But he was a trusted colleague during all those years in opposition and government. Through his father, long-time PC Cabinet minister Elmer MacKay, Peter was born into politics, and he was educated as a lawyer. He had strong views on some subjects, but I think his character in the political arena was most shaped by his athletic background, especially as a rugby player. He is the ultimate team player, always trustworthy to his colleagues and tough as nails to his opponents. He has weathered the ups and downs of political life with extraordinary resilience. The merger would not have happened without him. And his role was also critical to the many successes in the years that followed.

Peter and I became friends, and we spent some personal time together while I was in office. For me, that was unusual. Except for pre-existing relationships, I kept almost all my associations as prime minister on a strictly business level. I tell people that Peter even became a kind of a surrogate father-figure to Ben when I was opposition leader and prime minister, travelling around the country. It was a natural role for him, given his long association with Big Brothers and Big Sisters of Canada, and something I hugely appreciated. Peter and I have continued to have a close relationship to this day.

HAMMERING OUT THE DETAILS

MEANWHILE, THE ACTUAL MERGER discussions began to make substantial progress. The PCs came to see that we were genuinely serious. We also discovered surprisingly wide areas of agreement on political principles and policy.

One was the basic structuring of the new party. There were a couple of reasons for the consensus. For one, legislative changes over the years had opened the parties' Funds (the fundraising and business arms) to greater transparency. Also, the PCs, reacting (belatedly) to the threat from Reform, had overhauled their constitution and governance in the previous decade to strengthen their connections to the grassroots of the party. This common ground led, for example, to our early agreement on having a membership vote, rather than a delegated convention, for choosing the next leader.

But the agreements with the PCs on structure were not just on things we shared, but also on things we felt needed to be changed. For instance, in both the Progressive Conservatives and Canadian Alliance, our Funds had effectively become fused with our National Councils (which generally regulate constituency affairs and nomination processes). This meant that the people spending the money were not the people raising it, nor were they the people responsible for financing election campaigns. In both our parties this was leading to a lot of—to be polite—suboptimal expenditures. We agreed early on that restoring the independence of the Funds was critical, particularly as the new entity would inherit the PC Party's significant debt.

We also agreed early on to a revamping of the National Councils. In both parties, there were around three dozen members, making them costly and frequently dysfunctional. The interim council of the new party would be just a dozen members, six nominated by each existing council, and the permanent body would not exceed twenty members. We also agreed that, while representation on the council would not be equal by province, it would be heavily weighted to the smaller jurisdictions. The PCs had also developed a wider body consisting of party presidents and/or candidates-of-record from each of some three hundred ridings. That was clearly unworkable and had to go.

The name of the new party was also less contentious than might be expected, but it was an area where the passions of some ran high. Near the beginning, I had suggested something along the lines of the Reform Progressive Conservative Alliance Party of Canada—in other words, just throw in the kitchen sink. The eventual choice, the Conservative Party of Canada, came from PC Senator David Tkachuk. "Keep it clean and simple," he said. I liked it, but I also knew that it was much closer to the Progressive Conservative Party of Canada than to the Canadian Reform Conservative Alliance. It was going to be a problem for some on our side. (On their side was a contingent opposed to any name change, but they also tended to be those who were fundamentally opposed to merger.)

The most divisive issue came down to—and this should not surprise anyone—how to choose the leader? And particularly, how to choose the first leader? We had agreed that, under the new constitution, any interim leader would not be eligible for election—a wise provision that precludes the most obvious manipulation of a leadership race. Neither Peter nor I would be the interim leader.

As I said, the PCs were willing to go to a membership vote, but they wanted to adopt the formula used in some of their provinces, which granted every riding an equal one hundred points. The Alliance, being of purer grassroots pedigree, wanted to retain our one-member-one-vote system. We had a long back-and-forth about this. Compromises were offered and rejected on both sides. We seemed to be at loggerheads.

I was not naive about the outcomes these choices entailed. If we got one-member-one-vote, it was tantamount to the PCs agreeing to crown me as leader. The CA had a much larger and more unified membership than they did. On the other hand, an equal-votes-per-riding formula, given conservative weakness in many constituencies (even after merger), meant the real risk of electing a leader without broad membership support and, especially, without broad support in the areas we could win in a general election. That "equal riding" formula also took away any reward for a riding with a large membership and any penalty for one with a small membership. It could open the door to the rotten borough constituency associations that Reform had worked so hard to change.

One resolution was discussed only among my senior leadership team. I raised the possibility that I not be a leadership candidate in exchange for the PCs accepting the one-member-one-vote system. My people rejected it out of hand. I was told bluntly that, as the CA's best—and maybe only—leadership contender, they would not agree to the merger without assurance that I would run. So my offer was off the table.

I mention all this detail to convey some of the lessons I learned along the way about negotiating. Focus early on elaborating common objectives and developing chemistry. Build momentum around the easiest things on which to get consensus. Have bottom lines, but look for flexible ways of achieving them. Especially understand that nothing is settled until everything is settled. The toughest decisions come at the end, can only be made by the person at the top, and will only be resolved just before negotiations break down. That is where we were now at.

It was around that time that I had a conversation with Gwyn Morgan, then-CEO of Encana Corporation. Gwyn is a conservative, but he is much more a citizen than a partisan. He did, however, believe that the country's governance was suffering because of the lack of a competitive alternative to the Liberal government. He had become a confidant. He asked me in some detail where things stood on the negotiations. Without commenting greatly on the particulars, he said to me, "The question you ultimately have to ask yourself in a negotiation is: 'Is the price of the compromises worse than the benefit you would get from reaching a deal?' Always keep that measure in mind, and don't lose the forest for the trees."

With that perspective, there soon came a point when I realized the deal was not going to get significantly better than the one then on the table. And that deal was much better than no deal. I also knew that, with some grumbling, my party would follow my lead on any compromises that remained. With that, I conceded on all remaining points, including the leadership selection process.

Peter MacKay and I rounded out the talks in a short meeting at Stornoway. Laureen and my father-in-law, Dennis Teskey, who happened to be in town on a visit, were present. The only people in the room were our respective lawyers, the late Paul Lepsoe and Tom Jarmyn, who we needed to advise us on such matters.* Shockingly, all the power necessary to make such a decision under the relevant statutes, regardless of party constitutions, rested with the two of us as leaders. Shortly thereafter, on October 15, 2003, Peter and I announced in the National Press Theatre that we had a comprehensive agreement to create the new Conservative Party of Canada.

THE MERGER CAMPAIGN

GETTING AGREEMENT in the tight circles of negotiators was obviously very different than getting party-wide endorsement, which the merger would ultimately require. For me, this was no big deal. I had done what I said I would do—get a unity agreement between the CA and PCs when the opportunity presented itself. More than that, at every step in the process, I had kept the Alliance caucus and National Council† informed on the negotiations, on my bargaining positions, and on the likely outcomes. When the

* It should be noted that there were two other lawyers, both senior party officials, who played significant roles in drafting the agreement-in-principle and new party constitution – the late John MacDonell for the PCs and Mike Donison for us.

† National Council, which had taken shape before I became leader, was very problematic for a time. By now, however, it was under the presidency of Don Plett, a longtime Manitoba PC who had joined the Alliance, and it had become a well-functioning and co-operative body. Don would go on to eventually become Conservative leader in the Senate. He was succeeded as president by John Walsh, who performed exceptionally for my remaining years.

time came, there were no big surprises, and the endorsement from each body was virtually unanimous.

The unity behind me and behind the merger agreement in the Canadian Alliance was not shared by Peter MacKay on the PC side. He had been the leader for just a few months. The leadership factions had not settled in behind him, and there was widely divergent opinion on the party's future. His National Council was chaotically divided. Peter therefore decided—quite courageously, I might add—to approve the agreement in his capacity as leader without putting it to them. He would take the deal directly to the membership and let them speak.

However, the PC caucus, which was also split, could not be avoided. There were some, led by Joe Clark, who had been opposed to the negotiations even happening. Clearly, Peter needed some help, so I came up with an idea. At the Stornoway meeting, I said, "Why don't we do this. You know my views on Joe Clark. But he is the most senior political person in both caucuses. He's a former prime minister. Let's offer him the interim leadership. He's certainly capable of doing the job. It will allow him to retire on a high note. And maybe it will help the process."

Peter agreed, and to this day, I still think that was the best option. He took the agreement and our offer to Joe. Before Peter could finish going through the agreement, Joe denounced it, and him, and stormed out of the room, to publicly oppose the deal almost immediately. Peter never had the chance to make the offer to him.

So that was that. But Peter and I still had to find an interim leader. After a brief discussion, our second choice was John Lynch-Staunton, the Opposition leader in the Senate. John was thoughtful, laconic, and very well regarded, and he had also been an influential behind-the-scenes voice in encouraging the merger process. He had the confidence of the vast majority of PC senators, as well as Senator St. Germain. He had also never said or done anything to upset people of Reform/Alliance background. So John Lynch-Staunton it was, for party leader at large and in the Senate. In the Commons, we chose Grant Hill. Grant was always highly respected by his colleagues and had particularly good relations with the PC element in the Canadian Alliance. He did a first-rate job as opposition leader in the House.

The next step was to get the two caucuses together. This was a shining success. Of course, all Canadian Alliance members joined the new Conservative Party of Canada (CPC) caucus. But so did all but four PC senators and four PC MPs. We stood twenty-six strong in the Senate and seventy-two in the Commons. And collegiality developed, believe it or not, right off the bat.

In light of the many long-time rivalries and grievances between (and within) the two sides, this might have come as a surprise. But it was a situation not unlike what I inherited in the Alliance. It worked because things had been so ugly for so long that everybody recognized the situation had become existential. No one could survive any further political bloodshed. People wanted to move on. Contrary to periodic media reports about tensions between PCs and Reform/Alliance members, those labels simply became irrelevant in very short order. Our parliamentarians had crossed the Rubicon and were focused on the future.

Despite the great progress in bringing the teams together in Ottawa, there was still the issue of party membership buy-in. Both parties had committed to taking this agreement to a referendum of their supporters. Again, on the Alliance side, I did not see endorsement as a particularly tough goal.

Folks on the PC side were more divided, and all of us campaigned hard to get the support we needed. Prominent members of the PCs and Canadian Alliance made a point of campaigning together to set an example. Of course, we believed that there was a significant majority of PCs who favoured merger. Those ranks swelled during the campaign, as many of the federal PCs who had been sitting on the sidelines, especially those more on the right, came back to cast a ballot.

In the end, either because we had swayed opinions or because we had overestimated the opposition, the idea of union was even less controversial among the membership than it was among the party elites. On our side, it was 96 per cent in favour. But, even on the PC side, over 90 per cent came out for the agreement. Mr. Clark campaigned against it, but he lost the vote even in his own constituency.

There were PCs who walked away, but they were the exception. The vast majority of members of both "legacy parties" were not just behind the new CPC, they were enthusiastic. For the first time in a long time, we had a promising future. What had started with good chemistry between Peter and me had translated into a broader consensus and a new eagerness to confront the Liberals instead of each other.

CPC LEADERSHIP RACE

THERE WAS STILL the "small matter" of choosing a leader for the new party. My decision to contest the leadership was, as I said, part and parcel of the merger process itself. It was no secret that I would do so.

We had used the merger campaign to prepare for my eventual leadership bid. In particular, we had identified key PCs who would support my campaign, as we believed it important to show cross-legacy-party appeal. Member of Parliament Greg Thompson from New Brunswick and Saskatchewan senator David Tkachuk were important early supporters. I also received unexpected backing from a few PC councillors and senior staff members. My active speaking tour during the merger referendum had also allowed me to make new connections.

We had done some polling, too. The results, as I recall them, had been surprising. It was no shock that I was the overwhelming leadership choice of Alliance party members (and, of course, among the Alliance caucus and senior personnel). The surprise was how fragmented the opinion of PC Party members was. Joe Clark was still high in their estimation, but he had zero crossover appeal. I polled as well as any potential candidate from outside the federal PC Party. Even with the equal-votes-per-riding voting system, my chances were very good.

Of course, Peter MacKay also had significant support among PCs and had some crossover potential. We had presumed he would be a viable leadership candidate, notwithstanding the controversies within the PC ranks over the preceding months. But some unexpected developments ultimately blocked his path. The first problem, as I recall, occurred early during the merger campaign. Peter injured himself playing rugby and was forced to go on crutches for a period. It quite literally hobbled his ability to use the referendum to build a leadership campaign.

Soon, however, Peter faced a bigger problem. It became apparent that Belinda Stronach was planning her own leadership bid. That did more than just weaken Peter's potential. Belinda jumped into the race with big piles of family dollars, hiring all the PC (and a few CA) operatives at rates well above what they would normally charge. There was simply not enough talent left for anyone else from the PC side to launch a serious campaign.

Only Tony Clement, a former Ontario PC minister, managed to get anything off the ground. However, with Stronach absorbing so many resources, his campaign had limited funds and organizational support. He was a credible candidate, but he could not get beyond his core group (that is, those PCs who had earlier joined the Canadian Alliance) .

The field was set, and the rules were in place. I had made my own assessment of Belinda over the course of the merger process, but I wanted to see how she would appear on a public platform. Laureen and I tuned into her launch press conference in the small working office at the Stornoway residence. We came to our verdict quickly. Laureen said simply, "It's over. You're going to win."

While I felt the same way, we would take nothing for granted. This was especially true given the points system we were fighting under, knowing there were as many as one-third of the country's ridings (particularly in Quebec and Atlantic Canada) where the Alliance organization had been very weak. But I had a team, led by Tom Flanagan and Doug Finley, both inside and outside caucus, that was loyal and dedicated and could fight an effective campaign with a fraction of the dollars Belinda was spending. And, of course, I went to as many parts of the country as I could get to.

The conclusion of the campaign was anticlimactic. On March 20, 2003 (coincidentally exactly two years after the conclusion of my first leadership race), I got decent support in the east and ever-larger majorities as the vote went west. I won 56 per cent of the total points, and almost 70 per cent of the raw vote. Belinda Stronach's campaign had increasingly concentrated on racking up support in weaker ridings. As a result, her 35 per cent of points masked the fact that she only had some 22 per cent of the popular vote.

I remain very proud of this accomplishment. I had received a higher vote in the merged party than I did in the Alliance itself when I ran for leader. The support of Stockwell Day and other erstwhile Canadian Alliance adversaries had allowed my campaign to carry some 90 per cent of our former membership. But we had also won at least 40 per cent of former Progressive Conservatives.

This kind of big victory is critical in leadership races. Provided one is a "good winner," it is what puts "divided party" narratives behind you. It also gives you a margin of error. As leader, especially a new leader (as I still was), it allows you to survive the mistakes you inevitably make. Having your membership, and especially your caucus, invested in your leadership inclines them to rally around you to validate their choice, even when times are tough.

In the end, I also concluded that I had been wise to accept the equal-votes-per-riding leadership system. The one-member-one-vote system removes the necessity of organizing a leadership campaign at the constituency level. That is what had happened in 2001–2002. My leadership organization had, with rare exceptions, never been organized below the "regional" level, that is, never below groupings of ridings at the sub-provincial level. Thus, when we were later faced with fighting by-elections, I frequently found that the Alliance had no effective constituency organization. That, of course, is the level at which elections are actually fought. While the PC system was (and still is) far from perfect, its advantages had become evident.

ELECTION 2004

ALMOST AS SOON AS the leadership campaign ended, the prospect of a general election appeared. The Liberals would want to catch us unprepared, as they had in 2000 with Stockwell Day and the Canadian Alliance. They had excuses to do so—a government approaching the fourth year of its mandate and a new prime minister wanting his own.

I was not looking forward to the challenge. I knew we would not be fully ready—that was inevitable under the circumstances—and I was coming off a very rough three years. In fact, it was the toughest period of my professional life by far. I think that, in our system, being leader of the Opposition is tougher than being prime minister. As opposition leader, I had significant profile and even greater expectations, but unlike the prime minister, almost no way of fulfilling them. I had few rewards or punishments that could be marshalled. You are in constant persuasion mode, with little power to back it up. Of course, there was also no government plane to quicken travel and avoid making connections. For those years, road trips were frequent, long, and hard, with a small staff travelling with me.*

On top of those realities, I also had an unusual series of tests as opposition leader. For starters, I had had to contest and win two leadership campaigns. As far as I can tell, that makes me the only person in our parliamentary history to have to win two leadership races before fighting his first general election. And I had run a merger campaign. And I had my own by-election campaign, having to rebuild a riding association from scratch. And I had fought numerous other by-election campaigns. I had not stopped campaigning for three years, all the while trying to build an opposition leader's office and campaign machine where almost nothing had existed before. To say it had been exhausting is an understatement.

However, the Liberals did have challenges of their own. These began with a damning report from the auditor general on a major sponsorship program. Eventually dubbed the "sponsorship scandal," the allegation, coming from a highly credible source, was that the Liberals had used public funds for blatantly partisan purposes—funds that now could not be fully accounted for. That story had broken early in 2004, its coverage overwhelming Martin's intended agenda.

---

* Those trips, as often on the road as in air, usually included combinations of Ray Novak, Carolyn Stewart-Olsen, Dimitri Soudas, Dennis Gagnon, and Colin McSweeney. We developed some camaraderie, but it was still tough work.

How should Martin have responded? It is difficult say. But his decision to call a Royal Commission of inquiry, ultimately headed up by Justice John Gomery, kept the issue in the news. It was also highly divisive within the Liberal Party. Martin's landslide win in the leadership race had temporarily masked the scars of his usurpation of Jean Chrétien's mantle. The commission was seen by many Liberals as a renewed assault on Chrétien and his legacy.

The party's difficulties at this point should not be overstated, however. In comparison, we still had a huge mountain to climb. Our party was brand new, had never fought an election, and, when Governor General Adrienne Clarkson dropped the writ on May 23, I had been leader for all of nine weeks. Our election preparations had been minimal.

Nevertheless, we came out with guns blazing. Obviously, the sponsorship scandal was a great target, and we hit the Liberals hard on that. The polls narrowed dramatically. But, in the process, we also made some miscalculations.

Reform-like, we had a number of policy promises to rush out. But we erred in loading these announcements into the front of the campaign. By mid-campaign we had basically run out of script, not to mention our lack of a campaign-long advertising strategy. When you do not have a script, it is pretty easy to go off-script, and that also happened. Ever more frequent mistakes were made by me and others on the campaign trail.

We were also increasingly kept off-balance by Liberal attacks. As a long-time political activist, both inside and outside Parliament, I had made no shortage of statements on issues, many of them admittedly controversial. Since through most of those years I had never dreamed of being prime minister, I had probably said some things I would not have said, or would have said differently, if that is what I had been thinking. Ironically, though, even the most controversial of those statements did not have much impact. The Liberals instead focused on what I had *not* said, in particular on an issue I had rarely spoken about: abortion.

According to the Liberals, my utter lack of focus on abortion in my public career was evidence of a "hidden agenda" on the issue. The fact that I had told pro-life activists in two leadership campaigns that I would not open the issue and did not want their support was apparently even greater proof of my intention of keeping the agenda hidden. The media dutifully amplified the message by asking me about the issue virtually every day. This was the Liberal campaign machine at its effective best and cynical worst.

By voting day on June 28, we knew our chances of winning were slim. And there was a brutal reality behind it. Our lack of preparation showed, and indicated to the Canadian people that we were not ready to form a government. I could not disagree; we were not ready.

In the end, however, we held the Liberal Government to a minority. They had won 135 seats, and we had taken 99,* easily confirming our status as Official Opposition. That was not bad, considering Paul Martin had been expected, only weeks before, to win the largest majority in Canadian history. With the Bloc Québécois at 54 seats, the NDP with 19, and former Conservative MP Chuck Cadman elected as an Independent, Martin would face some very challenging arithmetic in the House.

I was not surprised on election night. I had not expected to win, but I had thought we would do somewhat better. I could have done better. Employing my ability to separate my intellectual read of the situation from my emotions, I was also concerned. I was worried that the Liberal attacks had taken their toll on my "electability" longer term.

Before people started asking whether I should stay on as leader, I asked myself that question. To answer it, I began with an even more fundamental question: "Does the party want me to stay on as a leader?" I was in politics to fight for conservatives, not to fight with conservatives. If the party did not want me, so be it. I could leave then with conservatism at the national level in far better shape than I had found it.

I made a point of having a few conversations with people I respected—not all of them hard-core Harper loyalists, by the way—asking them if I should stay. To my surprise they unanimously and insistently urged me to do so. One

---

* That included my riding of Calgary Southwest, where the campaign manager was Rob Griffith. A longtime volunteer, Rob was again campaign manager in 2006 and remained a key volunteer until 2015.

of those people—I wish I could remember who—helped me put things in perspective. He said, "Leader,"—they called me that then— "if at the beginning of the campaign in March, Paul Martin had said to you, 'I'll give you ninety-nine seats and take a minority government if you'll agree to call off the election,' would you have taken that deal?" And I said, "Oh, God, yeah. I mean, at that point we were way behind and barely ready." To which he responded, "Well, exactly. Most people in the party think we did okay. They're not unrealistic."

Wise words, but I needed a more convincing argument. I asked for polling to be done to learn the views of the party membership and wider public. The polls revealed that, generally, the CPC membership had a positive view of my performance. The big majority who had voted for me as leader wanted me to continue as leader. And contrary to much media commentary, the public—at least that part of the public open to voting Conservative—had not closed its mind to me being prime minister in the future. We were still in the game.

THE MINORITY PARLIAMENT AND THE MONTREAL CONVENTION

WHEN PARLIAMENT RETURNED on October 5, it was clear we had a complex and interesting situation in the House. The last minority government ended in 1980, so this was new ground for everyone involved. To Prime Minister Martin's credit—and unlike Prime Minister Chrétien—he consulted his opposition leaders regularly, trying to feel us out. The difficulty, though, was that it was never clear where he was going. Some of that might have been Liberal caginess, but certainly not all. It is not easy to work with a guy whose direction is not clear.

To be fair, though, working with Martin was not my primary strategic objective. We were in the opposition, and I focused on discovering the degree to which I could work with Gilles Duceppe and Jack Layton to increase our muscle in the House of Commons. Maybe, if I could find some common ground with the other opposition leaders, we could force the government to do some things differently.

The search for common ground included talking to the Bloc, although I should add that later stories about me trying to form a "coalition" with the Bloc are just nonsense. I had done a lot of polling back when I was NCC president on what I call the "macro mindset" of the Canadian public. I knew, far better than most, how toxic the Bloc was outside Quebec. It was also clear early on that the Liberals' media supporters would attack us anytime we sought to work with the Bloc, no matter what the issue. But the reality was that we did have common ground in opposition, particularly in making the Liberals pay politically for the sponsorship scandal.

Our first exercise in common cause was an amendment to the Liberals' Speech from the Throne. All three opposition parties had agreed to add some items to Parliament's agenda. The NDP signed on to that but, in short order, backed away and became the party propping up the government.

Given the parliamentary math—Liberals + NDP = 154, Conservatives + BQ + Cadman = 154, there was bound to be some political drama. I believed that the government should not fall on the Throne Speech—certainly not on the substance of our amendment—and I said so, but they threatened to call an election anyway. So it became an early test of wills. Could we get the government to make changes? Could they force us to acquiesce by threatening an election? In the end, Paul Martin came to me, the government blinked, and a revised version of our amendment passed. The world did not come to an end.

The real test, however, was the 2005 budget, tabled on February 23. It put us in a tough spot, because it was not our kind of budget. It proposed a lot of spending increases. What tax breaks it offered were not the ones we would have liked to see. Yet the fiscal position of the government was strong, and there was nothing in the document sufficiently offensive to trigger a new election.

I took the issue to our caucus. Not wishing to support the budget, but not wanting an election, we decided to abstain. I knew we would be roundly criticized, and we were. Abstention is one position on any political issue that never gets you much credit. No one likes it, and the media in particular hate you dodging controversy. That said, this ended up being an incredibly fortuitous decision, because it kept our options open as the budget measures proceeded through the parliamentary process. In the meantime, however, it made the party—especially me as leader—look weak.

No doubt this situation made us uneasy as we faced the first convention of the Conservative Party of Canada, set for Montreal on March 17–19. We were already looking forward to this event with a mixture of excitement and anxiety. After all, this would be the first time the whole new party came together. People from all regions and both political backgrounds would be there, in one place. The party machinery would all be new and tested for the first time. And, of course, there was to be a leadership review vote. There were so many unknowns. What was the dialogue going to be like? Would the delegates get along?

I need not have worried. Everybody was in a fantastic mood in Montreal. The deliberations were amiable, and the outcomes were common sense. Most importantly, people were happy. Here we were, the second-place party in a minority parliament, seemingly on the cusp of power. Less than two years before we—whether Canadian Alliance or Progressive Conservative—had been facing electoral disaster.

To my relief, the leadership review vote was not even close. By this point, my team was strong and deep. Tom Flanagan, Doug Finley, Ian Brodie, and many others had marshalled my support. This was obviously very satisfying to me personally and a strong affirmation of the work my team had been doing for the last three years. Unlike, say, in Stockwell Day's situation, there was also the "discipline of power" beginning to set in. In a minority parliament, a leadership fight would unquestionably cost the CPC the next election. Our people knew that, and they also knew that, if we held together, we had a shot at winning.

SAME-SEX MARRIAGE

THAT IS NOT TO SAY that everything was easy going coming out of the Montreal convention. We had a challenging issue before us—same-sex marriage.

While Paul Martin was pushing it forward, the debate in Parliament had been initiated under Jean Chrétien. Paul Martin was a practising Catholic and had been on the other side of the issue at one time. Although he had recently changed his view (ostensibly in light of court rulings), it was an uneasy situation for him. I have to believe that Chrétien, savvy political operator that he was, had not left this grenade (and some others) lying around for Mr. Martin by accident.

Public opinion on this issue had already shifted significantly over the past decade. In the 1990s, while the Liberals were putting "sexual orientation" in the Canadian Human Rights Act, they were still denying that same-sex marriage would ever be on the table. That debate had been badly mishandled by the Reform Party back then, creating internal division and external brand damage. I was determined to avoid a similar fate, although the reality was that same-sex marriage remained very unpopular among the vast majority of our supporters.

I was also opposed to same-sex marriage, but I established some ground rules for the debate. First, it would be a free vote in our caucus. Second, that would not mean anything goes. I made it clear that the positions expressed had to be respectful of the fact that other Conservatives held different opinions. I had been tested on this by one member who insisted on equating homosexuality with pedophilia, and I expelled the individual from caucus.

For my part, I argued against same-sex marriage but not against the legal recognition of same-sex unions as the equivalent of a marriage arrangement. If that is what consenting adults want, then I saw no reason why the state should not accommodate it. But I was leery about changing the definition of this millennia-old institution, and I worried that this might be the start of a broader anti-family and anti-freedom-of-religion campaign. Most of our caucus shared my opposition, although some were much more deeply opposed. A significant minority supported same-sex marriage.

Mr. Martin's Government ended up pushing same-sex marriage through, and public opinion continued to move rapidly in that direction afterward. Yet looking back on this issue with the benefit of hindsight, I see it as a situation where somebody wins the battle but loses the war. Paul Martin won the battle. I won the war.

My campaign against same-sex marriage had been vocal but measured. I did not attack people who were on the other side. Those who had voted against my position in our caucus had felt no antagonism, pressure, or sanction. And my position appealed to many voters who had been not just traditionally Liberal but hard-core Liberal. I think in particular of practising Catholics and some cultural communities.

While my position did not lose any significant mass of Conservatives, the Government's position increasingly alienated Liberals on the other side. The Liberal Party's position was, in fact, openly contemptuous of the other view. Egged on by their media allies, the Liberals made it clear that they thought of opponents of same-sex marriage as bigots and homophobes. In much the same way that the old PC Party drove some voter groups to Reform, the Liberals were now driving some of their electorate to us. The same moral applies: if you want people to vote for you, do not call them names.

We did not engineer this debate, and frankly, I did not particularly relish it. Nevertheless, it served the electoral strategy I had been developing as leader of the Opposition. I believed that our route to government did not lie in a traditional Red Tory strategy, that is, in watering down conservatism to attract affluent Liberals whose parents and grandparents were once Conservative. Instead, our path would be to show "aspirational" voters who were traditionally Liberal (or NDP, or Bloc for that matter), that their views were more in line with what Conservatives stood for. This was particularly true in many ethnic and religious communities that were philosophically conservative but traditionally Liberal. In the same-sex marriage debate, the Martin Liberals ended up doing my work for me.

It is worth reflecting on my stance on same-sex marriage then, and what I think about it now. Although I still do worry about the extremes on the left who want to (and periodically do) attack the family and religion, Canada did not go down that path after the legal recognition of same-sex marriage. (Of course, a subsequent decade of Conservative government may have played a part in that.) On the other hand, I believe that gay people have benefitted greatly from that recognition. Certainly, for gay people that I have known—and there was no small number of gay people who supported me, for a range of reasons—it has unambiguously been a good thing in their lives and their communities. Same-sex marriage has also benefitted Canadian society in general by sharing the benefits of this institution with gay people who, I believe, have become more centred on stable relationships, family life, and conservative values generally.

THE MAY 2005 PARLIAMENTARY CRISIS

ONE MATTER ULTIMATELY DOMINATED everything that happened in the 38th Parliament. The sponsorship scandal did not die with the election; it moved things to a whole other level. This was a result of the Gomery Commission that Paul Martin had appointed, which was then holding its hearings. It uncovered some explosive information that, despite a supposed blackout on reporting, found its way into the public domain. The extent of direct Liberal Party corruption became very apparent. This led to a huge public backlash across Canada, especially in Quebec.

For a government in a minority parliament, this was deadly stuff. The Martin Liberals sought to avoid opposition confidence votes on the sponsorship scandal, but they could not avoid confidence votes on budgetary legislation, which was still making its way through the Commons. Because we had abstained on the earlier votes, we were now in a position to vote no if we chose. Tactically speaking, it was not a large leap as we had been clear about our dislike of several budget measures. We were headed into our first real showdown on the survival of the Martin Government.

It provided high drama. In the end, Paul Martin survived by one vote. On May 19, 2005, with the support of the NDP and Chuck Cadman, the House voted 152–152 on Bill C-48, an amendment to the budget that added $4.6 billion in social spending and delayed corporate tax cuts. That left Speaker Peter Milliken to break the tie, and in line with parliamentary precedent, he voted to sustain the government.

Although we lost by that one vote, I was not disheartened. In fact, I was encouraged, although this view was not unanimous. There were some in the party who were very upset that we had forced this vote and had lost. But I believed that, once again, Martin had "lost the war."

Two things happened that saved the Martin Government for a time but hurt them longer term in the eyes of the electorate. The most important was a decision to secure NDP support by making substantive amendments to the budget. Done in a private hotel meeting between Paul Martin and Jack Layton, it was more than just unseemly: it transformed Paul Martin from the principled leader who slew the deficit to just another cynical Liberal who could not be trusted on economic and fiscal issues.

Trust is especially critical in a minority parliament. In our system, even when it does not have a majority, the Government has an absolute veto on the integrity of the fiscal framework. Too few people understand this. Spending measures require a royal recommendation—in other words, permission from the Government to proceed as legislation. It is true that the Government may not have the votes to pass its budget measures, but the opposition, even combined, cannot pass a different budget without the Government's acquiescence. Martin's willingness to give up that control hurt him badly with the business Liberals and other right-of-centre "fiscal conservative" voters he had long cultivated. It was a genuinely dangerous decision.

The second thing that damaged the Martin Government was its complicity in having Belinda Stronach cross the floor to become a Liberal Cabinet minister—minister responsible for democratic renewal, no less. To this point, Martin had benefitted from his talk about addressing the "democratic deficit." Yet here was a leader buying someone off with a Cabinet post to save his own skin. He was giving "democratic renewal" to the heiress of a corporation built on a dual-class shareholder structure that denied most of the company's owners a say in the business. It was not a good look.

I use the description of Martin's "complicity" in the Stronach affair deliberately because I also played a role. In the lead-up to the parliamentary confrontation, Belinda had been cagey in caucus about her support for the strategy. Outside the room, she planted the story in the media that she was not onside with the "Harper approach" and would be able to pick up the pieces if I failed to win the subsequent election.

I have never begrudged other caucus members having ambitions, including the ambition of being leader. You want people of ability around you, and you should assume that people of ability are also people of ambition. There is no point getting paranoid—and ultimately isolated—over that reality. But you must insist that ambition be pursued in ways that assist the common enterprise. This, by contrast, was an effort to advance ambition by undermining the team effort. Nor was it an isolated one. I was not going to tolerate it.

In the days immediately preceding Stronach's departure, I met her in my office to discuss this behaviour. I made it clear that, while there was no certainty I would succeed in my efforts and become prime minister, I would use my influence to ensure that she never became party leader in a subsequent leadership race. I understood the implications that the meeting might have, but I was not going to be sabotaged from within.

The upshot is that, when Belinda left, I was neither surprised nor dismayed, even though I knew it probably had cost us the vote. Again, I was playing a longer game. I was also clear about where that game was headed for her. As I told Laureen that day, "Belinda now knows the leadership of the Conservative Party is not in the cards. She'll find out in short order that leadership of the Liberal Party won't be in the cards either. Within two years, she'll be out of politics." That was ultimately what happened. Whatever help Stronach had been in the CPC merger, she was not committed, in my judgment, to the party's success. She was a problem, and frankly, one that precious few in caucus missed. Again, what Martin thought helped him actually hurt him and helped us instead.

While I never felt bad about the departure of Belinda Stronach, the opposite is true of Chuck Cadman. It is important for me to correct many untruths about my relationship with Chuck. First and foremost, I thought Chuck was a very good member of Parliament. He had also been a strong supporter of mine in both leadership races, and I liked him. Our parting of the ways came about for reasons that had nothing to do with my wishes or our relationship.

After the merger, while I was fighting the leadership race, Chuck got challenged for his nomination. We were prepared to do whatever we could to support him, and I told Chuck as much. But he was up against an ethnic candidate who had sold a lot of memberships, and Chuck became convinced that he could not win the nomination. In fact, I believe, in the end, he did not even attend the nomination meeting. So we lost Chuck. But then he ran as an Independent and won because he was a good MP. I still think that if he could win the riding, he could have won his nomination, but he saw things otherwise.

Having been elected as an Independent, Chuck decided that he would act as an Independent. As the Parliament progressed, he also became increasingly ill, and it was an open secret that he was suffering from terminal cancer. As the big confidence vote loomed, I talked to him. He was clear with me; he did not think the country wanted an election at that time, so he was going to vote against non-confidence. He also told me confidentially that he did not think our party was ready for an election.

I had accepted that, and I was confident Chuck was not going to change his mind. Nevertheless, I was pressed by Tom Flanagan and Doug Finley, who wanted to meet with Chuck to hear what his resistance was and whether his reasons could be addressed. You can imagine my shock when, some years later, it was alleged that Chuck had been offered a life insurance policy by the party in exchange for supporting the non-confidence vote.

To this day, I do not know where that story came from. We know that Chuck privately made this allegation before his passing. We also know conclusively, from our investigation, that Tom Flanagan and Doug Finley made no such offer. We could not find any evidence of any other party official meeting with Cadman on the date he said the offer was made. And frankly, it never made any sense: It is not easy, and it would be, at the very least, prohibitively expensive, to obtain a life insurance policy for a man with terminal cancer.

I found this all very sad because it put a cloud of ugly rumours around a great guy who was just doing what he thought was right. I was very pleased that later, his widow, Dona Cadman, ran and became a Conservative member of Parliament.

THE END OF THE BEGINNING

THE EVENTS OF MAY 2005 proved Chuck Cadman right on one critical matter: we were not ready to fight an election. In fact, as we continued our preparations to the day of the vote, it became apparent to me that we were not much more ready than we had been in 2004. It was a blunt reminder that, in a minority parliament, you must be prepared for an election at all times.

As a consequence, beginning in June, I began to make changes, starting right at the top. Doug Finley became the guy solely responsible for the national campaign, with the urgent task of nailing down a much better team and better-defined campaign plans. Ian Brodie, who had been performing very well as executive director of the party, became my chief of staff, with his own instructions to make further changes. With that, we started to kick into gear to get operationally ready for an eventual election.

I also developed my own plans for the defeat of the Liberal Government in the fall. The key—provided we were fully ready, of course—was to bring Jack Layton and the NDP on our side. The opportunity was obvious, as the sponsorship scandal and its drip of revelations continued unabated. What we did was simple. We had a line: "The NDP is supporting Liberal corruption." We repeated it in the House and on the hustings. Members were instructed to use it whenever possible in media, whether national, regional, or local.

I believed that the cumulative impact of this attack on the NDP would be severe. When a political attack is both true and important, it works. It was awkward enough for the NDP to be the party propping up the Government, regardless of what policy wins they might be achieving. Doing so for a party under constant corruption revelations would be unbearable.

Eventually, Jack himself privately admitted to me that the line was sticking. That was late fall, and he indicated that, if we could agree on the wording of a non-confidence vote, he would support it. The Bloc was already a done deal; the sponsorship scandal was causing support for Quebec sovereignty to rise after several years of decline. Thus, on November 28, 2005, by a vote of 171–133, we brought the Government down and headed for an election.

We were behind in the polls, but I felt good. Indeed, in the weeks leading up to the vote I felt confident, for the first time in my life, that I might actually become the prime minister of Canada. It was not just because of the sponsorship scandal. By then, Paul Martin's growing list of "priorities" and his lack of concrete accomplishments had undermined confidence in his leadership ability. The "Mr. Dithers" label was beginning to stick. That was on top of his loss of credibility on both democratic reform and economic management. The latter was astounding, given that the economy was in good shape.

My private confidence was completely contradicted in the media. That fall, there seemed a virtual press consensus that I would never be prime minister. Front-page stories featured polls purporting to show that I could never win an election. "Prominent Conservatives," whom I did not know and, for the most part, had never even heard of, echoed the propaganda there and elsewhere.

I considered such coverage more an annoyance than a problem. I had the caucus, party officials, and the grassroots fully behind me. We were also doing our own polling, which told a very different story. It did not say that I was going to win for sure, but it did show the continual erosion of public confidence in Paul Martin. People also widely believed that his Government had no direction—a common view even among those who continued to support him. Canadians were not necessarily ready to elect me as prime minister, but they were not closed to the idea, and they were open to not having Paul Martin as PM any longer. In strategic terms, we had an adequate "accessible voter pool" for an election.

As the campaign began, my team and I were optimistic. Public opinion was where we needed it to be. We were prepared operationally. We had a strategy. We had more detailed plans beyond that. The only rub was that expectations for our success were very low. But that would turn out to be our biggest asset.

5

GAINING POWER AND SETTING UP THE GOVERNMENT

ELECTION 2006

WITH THE FALL of Prime Minister Martin's Government and the election date set for January 23, 2006, we were ready. Our team was much stronger than it had been in 2004, and we had a comprehensive plan.

We would announce policies each day, very steadily. Unlike 2004, we were not going to release expansive policy proposals early. Our strategy this time around was the opposite: roll out micro, single-policy announcements daily to set the policy agenda of the campaign. As it turned out, this approach surprised opponents and pundits alike.

We decided to take a largely positive, proactive, constructive approach to the campaign. This surprised our opponents even more. After all, we had just defeated the Government on a non-confidence motion on the sponsorship scandal. This was after months when I had focused almost exclusively on that issue while providing little in the way of alternatives. Therefore, everybody assumed we would come out of the gate hitting them hard, negative and repeatedly on sponsorship and corruption. Of course, we did have a couple of days where we focused on that, and we looked to respond when new corruption revelations came out. But we largely changed course almost as soon as the campaign got underway. We would reserve the really big attacks for the back end, if needed, after the campaign's positive themes had been firmly established.

We also developed a strategy to insulate ourselves from what we knew would be inevitable, predictable, baseless Liberal attacks. We expected they would come after us as supporting two-tier healthcare, so we had prepared for that. Obviously, they were going to drag out abortion again. And the issue of same-sex marriage was still in play, as I had promised that a Conservative government would hold its own free vote on the issue.

On abortion, we had learned a key lesson from 2004: do not get drawn into constantly answering questions about it. Even a clear policy will be a liability if you are still answering questions every day. People get the impression that something must be on the table—why else do you keep talking about it? I was clear on day one: a Conservative government would not open the abortion issue, period. After that, the word "abortion" did not cross my lips.

I felt same-sex marriage had a similar risk. Public opinion in Canada then remained evenly split, if not even slightly opposed. But it was not what most people wanted to hear us talking about. Once again, on the first day I was proactive and crystal clear that we would have a free vote and that I would vote for the "traditional definition of marriage." It made headlines and a lot of our people questioned the wisdom of my hitting this issue head-on so early. My response was, "Exactly. That's why I got it over with on day one."

Our plan was clear. But it quickly became evident that the Liberals' strategy was not. In fact, to this day, the Liberal campaign plan remains a mystery to me.

Inexplicably, they apparently vacated the field in the first weeks of the election. Each day, we made an announcement, which dominated the news cycle. The Liberals, in contrast, made few statements. Even their attacks were muted. In fact, they did not seem to campaign very actively at all.

It was an odd campaign period, both for its length and for overlapping with the Christmas–New Year's period. Paul Martin began to appear prominently only just before Christmas. Then, like all the leaders, he was by necessity off the major airwaves through the holiday lull.

Maybe the Liberals just thought we would repeat what we did last election: blast out all our policies, scream about corruption, and then, us having shot our bolt, they would take over. Perhaps they bought into the earlier media narrative that there was no way we could possibly win. Whatever the reasons, in the meantime, we began to establish our brand with Canadians.

THE "FIVE PRIORITIES"

WE FOCUSED ATTENTION on five headline commitments. These were concrete, achievable, and covered important matters. Our campaign strategist, Patrick Muttart, had worked with me in helping pick these to ensure they addressed key concerns of the electorate. These five priorities also contrasted sharply with the Martin Government's increasingly diffuse and unfocused agenda.

The first and leading commitment was a federal Accountability Act in response to the Liberal scandals. This issue was top of mind for all Canadians. Our policy would be a positive response to the Government's problems. It would, of course, simultaneously reiterate the negative brand that had developed around the Liberal Party from the auditor general's findings of February 2004 to Justice Gomery's report of November 2005. We had brought the Government down on this issue, and we were determined to be seen as the party that would clean up the mess, not just decry it.

At this point, I believed we did not need to hit them all that much more. Instead, what we needed to do, through the Accountability Act, was show Canadians that we had practical measures to give the system greater integrity going forward.

The issue of accountability was the key for us, but following very closely behind was our second focus: cutting the GST. Obviously, any Conservative government worth its salt is going to talk about cutting taxes. This was a natural differentiator from the Liberals. They had been using recent budget surpluses for some tax cutting, but their focus had been on expanding government spending. Ours would be on the hard-working taxpayers rather than the tax-takers.

But why promise to cut the GST? Again, it was a lesson from 2004. The last time, we had proposed several tax reductions, but they had not established a tax-cutting brand for us. The cut to the GST—as we said, from "7 to 6 to 5 per cent"—could not be ignored. It was the single most visible tax paid by the most Canadians, by far. Some economists contended that the GST was the wrong tax to cut, that it was a comparatively "good tax." That is a perspective conservatives should reject; all taxes hurt the people who pay them.

Taxation is a necessary evil—necessary to fund (one hopes) essential government services despite their cost. Taking money out of people's pockets should always be a tough thing, and governments should never casually resort to taking more. Our philosophy of government, therefore, was not that there are good taxes and bad taxes; it was that there are higher taxes and lower taxes. Any time you can lower a tax, that is good; any time you must raise a tax, that is bad. That is how we saw the world, and we believed that Canadians would agree.

The third priority would become known as the Universal Child Care Benefit (UCCB). It continued the theme of delivering benefits directly to Canadians. In short, we promised a direct payment of $1,200 per year per child under six to all families to help support the cost of raising children. It would replace the Liberals' plan for a national daycare program.

It is worth putting this promise into perspective. We were running against a Liberal Party that had, for thirteen years, in election after election, promised to institute a national daycare program. Yet year after year, they never did it. Instead, preliminary funds—not an inconsiderable amount by the way—had gone to fund daycare advocates. Consequently, when they rolled that promise out again, all shiny and new, they simply hurt their credibility.

As conservatives, we had no interest in a national program, outside our area of jurisdiction, to expand government at the expense of citizen choice. We wanted to empower families to make their own choices. We believed then, and still do today, that the private sector can deliver these services more effectively than government. Laureen and I had used a range of child-care options ourselves, including part-time institutional care. We understood that what was philosophically sound for us as conservatives would appeal to many other Canadians as well.

As it turned out, not only were we right, but we had also underestimated the impact this policy would have on the election. All thanks to the ill-considered attacks the Liberal Party launched against it. First, they overestimated their own credibility on the subject. But then they got ideological, contending that giving money directly to parents would be wasting it. The infamous phrase was that parents would just "spend it on beer and popcorn."

From a tactical standpoint, we could not have asked for a better Liberal response. It was elitist, condescending, and reinforced the notion that the real purpose of a state-funded daycare program was to deprive parents of choice in the matter. It raised the profile of the issue and made our case for us. It was just another one of those things that broke our way.

Our "soft" social policy on childcare was balanced by our fourth focus, one more expected of a conservative party: a crackdown on crime. All good campaigns have a mixture of appeals to a party's base and to uncommitted voters. Criminal justice was certainly more targeted at Conservative voters. But not completely.

There had been a noticeable rise in "gun, gang, and drug" violence, especially in the big urban centres, in the years preceding the election. The Liberals' response—establishing a gun registry—had done nothing to reduce gun violence. How could it? Instead, we proposed several measures to deal with violent crime and violent offenders.

The difference between our two philosophies came to the fore in the early days of the campaign as a result of a gang-related shooting of an innocent woman, Jane Creba, in the heart of Toronto's business district on Boxing Day. The Liberals responded to the event with compassion, but they failed to understand both the outrage and the fear that such incidents produce. It was offside with the public mood. Criminal justice and "law and order" became an issue that, although initially targeted at our own people, quickly moved into the mainstream.

Our final big priority was the proposed "wait time guarantees" for key healthcare services. Frankly, it was designed to be a "shield" against the inevitable Liberal attacks that we favoured "American-style" healthcare. Personally, I always found this vulnerability peculiar. There had never been a major figure in the party—or its legacy parties—advocating the dismantlement of the public healthcare system. There was no Conservative provincial premier advancing the idea. On top of that, for a federal Conservative, respect for provincial jurisdiction was fundamental. Unlike the Liberals, we had no intention of telling the provinces how to run the healthcare system.

Nevertheless, there was no avoiding the healthcare issue in Canada—then or now. We concluded it was better to have something proactive to say on the matter than to play defence. Healthcare had been rising in the public consciousness, in a difficult way for the Liberals, ever since the big Chrétien-Martin budget cuts of the 1990s. Martin had taken the initiative to reverse this, stumbling—that is a whole other story—into a major healthcare deal with the provinces in 2004. That agreement had put significant amounts of federal money back into the system. We had supported that accord. Still, it was evident that the public had little sense of where the money was going, and news stories repeated the accusation that wait times were growing.

Hence our proposal to work with the provinces to develop wait-time standards around some core health services. Not surprisingly, there were provinces—many of which had Conservative governments—that were concerned we might be interfering in their healthcare systems. We assured them that this was the last thing on our minds. I made it very clear, in public but also in private, that this was not about trying to dictate to them or embarrass them. We were going to continue the elevated levels of transfer payments. We wanted to work with them to show Canadians the concrete benefits of the enhanced funding, but we had no desire to become co-managers of the system.

THE FIVE PRIORITIES IN QUEBEC

THERE WAS A TWIST to the five priorities in our Quebec campaign. The province's unique cultural and institutional realities must be factored into any election. For starters, the main campaign language is different. But that does not give one a free pass to say one thing in French and another in English. We were acutely aware of the lessons in that regard demonstrated by the breakup of Brian Mulroney's PC coalition. We needed a distinct Quebec approach, but it could not be at odds with our overall national campaign.

There were also some specific realities to be dealt with in 2006. One was that the sponsorship scandal had occurred almost entirely within Quebec. Quebecers were both angry and embarrassed by the image this was creating for their province. Worse, because the original program had been a federalist campaign against the separatist movement, the whole thing had now backfired. Support for sovereignty—in steady decline since 1995—had jumped considerably. We were very concerned about that as a party, and I was always careful to use lines like "ce n'est pas un scandale québécois; c'est un scandale libérale." It had the advantage of being understood and regularly applauded by audiences both inside and outside Quebec.

Needless to say, we were also concerned about our own electoral weakness in Quebec. The 2004 election results in the province had been dismal for us, and that hurt our image as a national party. This time around, we felt that circumstances really could allow us to offer a "federalist alternative," but we had to find some ways of differentiating ourselves. We did have a greater respect for provincial jurisdiction than our Liberal rivals, but we still had to avoid any suggestion to Conservatives outside Quebec that we were offering "special status."

One way that was done was in a different emphasis on the fifth priority. In Quebec, we stressed the underlying "déséquilibre fiscal" that was at the root of the challenges in the healthcare system. This "fiscal imbalance" was a big topic of discussion in the province, but it had little traction in the rest of Canada, at least not by that name.

This issue went back to the Chrétien-Martin budget cuts of 1995–1997. They had imposed enormous reductions in transfers to the provinces—the magnitude was around 25 per cent, in absolute terms. In subsequent years, the federal government had not only achieved balance but also, by the early 2000s, was accumulating huge surpluses—enough to throw around in new program spending, some debt repayment, and the odd tax cut. Meanwhile, the provinces had been left holding the bag on financing education and healthcare, for which pressures—especially for the latter—were constantly rising.

This was a reality that could not be ignored. In Quebec, we stressed resolving the fiscal imbalance as the fifth priority. It did not replace the wait time guarantees—call it 5(a) of our five priorities. In fact, it was much broader in nature and would prove to be a major undertaking.

We did go further in Quebec-specific commitments as well. The highlight was a speech I gave in Quebec City where I addressed some local issues and announced what we called our "fédéralisme d'ouverture." It was a phrase suggested by my French speechwriter, Paul Terrien, and one of our key Quebec candidates, Lawrence Cannon. Lawrence was a Quebec Liberal and one-time Robert Bourassa Cabinet minister. He is also a grandson of the famed Charles (Chubby) Power, a former minister in the government of Mackenzie King. His defection to the federal Conservatives was a significant coup for us.

The term does not translate particularly well. English Canadians would call it "open federalism." A better translation might be "federalism of openness." However you translate it, we believe that this is part of the genius of Canada's constitutional structure, as it allows for greater flexibility for specific needs within a federal system. There are those—many being federal Liberal elites—who decried this approach as somehow promoting the breakup of the country. But we saw it as exactly how the country is supposed to work. Sir John A. Macdonald, Sir George-Étienne Cartier, and their colleagues created a federation. They understood that provinces had specific powers and distinct circumstances. We would simply respect that, while ensuring we did not create inequities with other provinces in the process.

ENDGAME

ELECTIONS OFTEN TURN ON intangibles. In this election, the biggest intangible was the degree to which Paul Martin and his Liberal Government were already damaged before it began. The Chinese philosopher and military strategist Sun Tzu is credited with saying that every battle is won or lost before it is fought. Paul Martin had largely lost his credibility as a financial manager, a democratic reformer, and a decisive leader during the minority parliament.

The election had moved into 2006, and thus far it had been going the way we wanted it to go. We were getting out our messages for governing, and the Liberals were not. Their usual attacks on abortion and healthcare had gone nowhere, and their attack on the UCCB had backfired. Then they made another critical mistake.

Perhaps it was a Hail Mary pass. Whatever it was, the Liberals reached down deep into their bag of dirty tricks and came up with an attack that focused on our campaign promise to begin rebuilding the Canadian Armed Forces—something you would expect from the Conservative Party. The very nature of this attack made us wonder if we were imagining things. The Liberals charged that I had a hidden agenda to put soldiers on the streets and even hinted that I might impose martial law.*

The Liberals' staunchest defenders among media and policy analysts could not point to anything in our platform that remotely resembled such thinking, even if you took its language way out of context. The result was widespread ridicule of the Liberals. It solidified the impression that we were running a solid campaign and they were not. It also confirmed that we were starting to pull ahead. It made them look desperate.

Still, I can honestly tell you that at no time, short of election day, was I certain we were going to win. I would never be that presumptuous. At that point, I still was not even confident. That began to change, however, with the second English-language debate and yet another Liberal error.

Paul Martin said he would abolish the notwithstanding clause of the Constitution. He then challenged me to say I would do the same thing. Of course, what he was implying was that Conservatives would not defend Canadians' core rights and freedoms. My immediate response was obvious:

---

* I cannot help but comment on the irony of this, given Pierre Trudeau's use of the War Measures Act in 1970 and Justin Trudeau's use of its successor, the Emergencies Act, in 2022.

nobody is interested in opening up the Constitution. In fact, from left to centre to right, from *centralisateur* to federalist to sovereigntist, that was a consensus. The prime minister had just put himself outside it.

I reminded the audience that the notwithstanding clause is there for a reason. Whereas in the United Kingdom, Parliament is the sole arbiter of rights, and in the United States, the Supreme Court is, in Canada, the Charter of Rights and the notwithstanding clause were designed to create a dialogue between the courts and the legislatures on the scope and nature of those rights. Our system is uniquely Canadian.

The fact is that the notwithstanding clause is a vital part of the Constitution. And like "beer and popcorn" and "soldiers in the streets with guns," this was yet another ploy that backfired for the Liberals.

It was in the dying days of the campaign at a rally in Montreal—hardly a hotbed of Conservative support—that I started to think victory was likely. The turnout was far larger than we expected, and security broke down into a wild (and scary) mob scene.

VICTORY

BY EARLY IN THE EVENING of January 23, election night, it had become clear that we were going to win. It was no landslide, and not even a majority, but it was a healthy margin. Mr. Martin had said prior to the vote that he would concede if he did not win the greatest number of seats. So we knew we were headed for government.

When the ballots were fully counted, Canadians had given our Conservative Party 124 of 308 seats. Paul Martin's Liberals had declined to 103. The Bloc Québécois was down slightly at 51. Jack Layton's NDP was up to 29. André Arthur, a conservative Independent, had also won in the Quebec City area. I would become Canada's 22nd prime minister. And the math was good; any one opposition party would be sufficient to carry a vote in the Commons.

It was a crazy time in that Calgary hotel suite that night, watching the results. Some long-time warriors were there with me—Ray Novak, Carolyn

Stewart-Olsen, and Doug Finley among them—as well as some new key players too, like Don Plett and Irving Gerstein, head of Conservative Fund Canada. Irving came from the PC side. He had held the job before with the PC Canada Fund, and he would be a great Fund chairman and source of advice for the rest of my days as Conservative leader. There were lots of others coming and going—too numerous to recount and too blurry to recall. My whole family was there, proud and excited—my mother, brothers Grant and Robert, Laureen, Ben and Rachel, and the in-laws and cousins on both sides.

Through it all, I had to contain my own emotions, stay focused, and get ready to make my acceptance speech. I was both exhilarated and exhausted. Like it or not, next steps were already filling my head. There would be a lot of work, and that would begin in the wee hours of the next day. Still, it was hard not be swept up in the jubilation of the Calgary convention centre that evening.

When I stood on the stage, I saw a big part of my life before me. Family, of course. Friends from my university days. Jim Hawkes was there. Preston Manning too. There were people who had campaigned with me as far back as 1988.* Given my serious and analytical disposition, I always had to be reminded, "You must be elated. You've got to enjoy these moments." I was, and I did, and it was very special. But it was not just my moment; it was that for all the people in front of me as well. They had played their parts in the story and were rightly sharing in the triumph.

TRANSITION TO GOVERNMENT

THE NEXT DAY we headed back to Ottawa, boarding the campaign plane for the last time. Obviously, there was a lot of excitement. However, I was

---

* I should mention Connie and Doug MacRae. They served in senior campaign roles in every one of my local campaigns from 1993 to 2015. There were many people who long supported me, but I think they probably had the record.

more preoccupied with the challenges that lay ahead, and they would be immense. I had a large binder of information from our transition team, and that was just for the next couple of weeks. The transition team was headed by Derek Burney, a former Canadian ambassador to the United States who had served as Brian Mulroney's chief of staff. Derek and the people around him* thus had a good handle on both the bureaucratic and political imperatives around transition. The first decision was to set the date for the swearing-in of the new government. As the standard period was two weeks following an election, I saw no reason to deviate from that precedent. The date was set for February 6, 2006.†

Burney's transition memo had been signed off with "Good luck!" and I was acutely aware of the challenges in front of us. Besides our minority government status, our experience in power was thin. I had never been more than a junior staffer in government, and only a handful of our current employees went back to the Mulroney era. The institutional memory in our ranks was slim indeed.

This deficiency had become apparent to me shortly after I won the leadership of the new Conservative Party of Canada. I had received a congratulatory call from Brian Mulroney. He had not supported me for the leadership, but he had encouraged the merger talks behind the scenes. One of the first things I asked him was whether he could point me to some PC veterans who we might call on when we formed government.

I had hoped to pick up some of that federal experience through the merger, as there was none on the Reform/Alliance side. In truth, there were few who even went back to the Preston Manning era, as most of those had

---

* Other members of the team included Camille Guilbault, Elizabeth Roscoe, Ray Speaker, and Maurice Archdeacon, with Marie-Josée Lapointe as spokesperson. Of course, senior staff like Ian Brodie, Doug Finley, Patrick Muttart, Ray Novak, and others also weighed in.

† Readers may note that this timing was, coincidentally, exactly 54 years after Queen Elizabeth II had succeeded to the throne and my parents had had their first date.

left during the Stockwell Day period. However, Mr. Mulroney pointed out that he had just turned sixty-five, and he had been one of the younger people back when he took office. In other words, the senior people from his era had long been retired.

Experienced or not, we had to proceed. I met early on with senior public servants—my previous exposure to the top echelon had been minimal—and began deliberations on Cabinet selection. There was, of course, the required meeting with the governor general too, and a transition meeting with Paul Martin. The outgoing PM seemed to me to be almost relieved. He had had two very difficult years. Mr. Martin gave some good advice on a few issues.

There were also briefings galore. Briefings on a wide range of existing government files, with particular depth on international issues, military operations, and national security. Detailed briefings on finances—the finance department was starting to make its own assessment of our campaign promises and how they would fit in the existing fiscal framework. Again, all of this was happening in that two-week period between January 23 and February 6.[‡] And people wonder why, during our election-night celebrations, I had other things on my mind!

Although there was some suspicion of the federal bureaucracy within the Conservative Party and among my team, I never started with that mindset. I know people attributed to me a hostility to bureaucrats, but that was not the case. Rather, I arrived with two assumptions I had learned in politics, and which I now applied to public administration. First, people usually do not start with the intention of being your enemy. In turn, you do not assume someone is an enemy or a problem until you see some evidence that they are. The other thing, particularly when I won races, was not to

‡ In comparison, the transition time in the United States is two months. The short time frame in our parliamentary system reflects critical differences. The permanent government is the Crown, represented by the governor general, not the prime minister and Cabinet. However, the Crown requires a "responsible" prime minister to govern, that is, one who can control the legislature to pass budgets and other legislation.

hold grudges against people who opposed you. The better question is not "Did they oppose me then?" but "Will they oppose me in the future?" The truth of the matter is that, when somebody's on the losing side of a race, they rarely want to be on the outs with the winner.

I started from the assumption—mostly correct—that the bureaucrats were there to do a job. Judging from the quality of my early briefings—they were generally excellent—this appeared to be correct. Of course, the public service does have its own agenda and interests. But those are not usually partisan or ideological. In fact, if anything, they tend to be biased to the status quo, whatever that is. I found that the best way to proceed was to set a clear direction from the top. Officials are generally more comfortable responding than leading themselves—as they should be. And we were, after all, a new government; changes were expected and were made.

One additional set of responsibilities you acquire as prime minister, even before swearing-in, is relations with other governments. I received the first congratulatory calls from several provincial premiers. It was clear that federal-provincial affairs were going to be a big part of my job, whether or not there was an "Intergovernmental Affairs" minister. Canada also has a wide range of memberships and relationships internationally. I received dozens of congratulatory calls and even more correspondence. I particularly recall my warm conversation with President George W. Bush, a leader I am proud to have as a friend to this day.

One particularly memorable incident during that transition period occurred early one morning. I walked into my office to find former U.S. president Bill Clinton sitting there waiting to talk with me. This impromptu meeting was a very worthwhile discussion, covering a range of international issues.

Many of the challenges of leadership have little to do with where you stand on the political spectrum. That is especially true in international affairs, where the issues and relationships often transcend the governments of the day. The fact that Bill was left-of-centre made little difference given the common interests, values, and threats that Canada and the United States share in the world. I found President Clinton's perspectives, experience, and advice invaluable, and we kept in touch over the years.

CABINET FORMATION

DURING THIS WHIRLWIND of activity, we also had to start the processes of planning the Government's agenda, preparing a Speech from the Throne, and turning our campaign promises into legislation. Those things were set in motion while I turned my attention to the appointment of the first Cabinet.

I had a relatively free hand in selecting my Cabinet. That was because, in my political career, I had made very few promises of Cabinet spots to individuals and no promise of a specific spot to anyone. I suppose this was in part because I came up mainly through third-party politics, and even as leader of the Opposition, few people had expected me to be prime minister. (For similar reasons, I had surprisingly few in the way of personal relationships with Canada's corporate elite, even in Calgary.)

But I would hasten to add that "freedom" is a relative term when it comes to Cabinet selection. Never overestimate how much freedom a prime minister actually has in that regard. One might think a prime minister can appoint whomever he or she wants if he or she has not made promises. But it is not so, because well beyond the prime minister's personal preferences or assessments of ability, there are many factors that need to be considered.

Regional and urban–rural balances come into play, as well as gender and ethnicity. The latter has become a bit of a proxy for religion, which was once a category of critical significance on its own.* To further complicate matters, each of these categories has "camps" within the party and seniority within

---

* Protestant–Catholic relations played a major role in Canadian political history—and for a long period before Confederation—although most Canadians these days may not be aware of it. From the Quebec Act of 1774, through to the settlement of Western Canada, to education, and to Quebec's "Quiet Revolution," religious issues could be political flashpoints that threatened to bring down governments. Voters closely watched the religious composition of Cabinets, like they do today for race, gender, and cultural diversity.

those groups. In other words, the PM has far more freedom in assigning the individual portfolios than he or she does in picking particular Cabinet ministers. And that was true even for me—a prime minister who had largely created his own party!

There was one way, however, in which I consider myself uniquely privileged in selecting my Cabinet. I was fortunate throughout my prime ministerial career that virtually everyone I had to choose from in my caucus was honest, hard-working, and dedicated, with good professional experience and motivation. I had very few cases where I appointed someone and then fretted about what kind of scandal they might get into. I also had a caucus that, though having a range of opinions, suffered no deep ideological cleavages.

The only person in my first Cabinet who had served in a previous federal Conservative ministry was Rob Nicholson. He was my first House leader, and he had been a member of Kim Campbell's brief government. Rob was a wonderful choice; he was unassuming, but he was highly competent and a source of good judgment for years to come.

It was not as though our people had no Cabinet experience at all. Several ministers had had solid experience in provincial Cabinets. There was Loyola Hearn from Newfoundland (Fisheries); Lawrence Cannon from Quebec (Transport); the Ontario triumvirate of Jim Flaherty (Finance), John Baird (Treasury Board), and Tony Clement (Health); Vic Toews from Manitoba (Justice); and Stockwell Day from British Columbia (Public Safety), a long-time minister during his days in Alberta.

We then looked to people who had relevant career experience generally—not necessarily Cabinet experience, but solid political backgrounds and instincts that could be put to good use. Gordon O'Connor (National Defence) had been a general in the Canadian Armed Forces. Bev Oda (Communications) knew something of the bureaucracy from her days as an industry executive. And, of course, people like Peter MacKay (Foreign Affairs), Jim Prentice (Aboriginal Affairs), Jean-Pierre Blackburn (Labour), Greg Thompson (Veterans Affairs), and Chuck Strahl (Agriculture) had plenty of political (and other) experience.* Overall, despite a small number of caucus members with federal Cabinet experience, I felt satisfied with the mixture of veterans and newcomers appointed to a small Cabinet of twenty-seven.

But no Cabinet is complete without a surprise, and I had two. The first was Michael Fortier. He was a successful banker, former Progressive Conservative leadership candidate, and PC co-chairman of my leadership campaign. I named Michael to the Senate and the Public Works portfolio. I did this simply to give Montreal, our second-largest city where I had no MPs, a seat at the Cabinet table. I was not, as the media alleged, about to fill a bunch of Senate vacancies.

The other surprise came in the form of David Emerson from British Columbia. The story is worth telling. It began when we were having our initial transition team meetings to discuss potential Cabinet appointments. Derek Burney asked me, "Is there anyone not in your party you have seen in the House that you'd like to consider for Cabinet?" David quickly came to mind. He had been a senior business executive of no particularly strong partisan persuasion who had been recruited to government by Paul Martin. This was back when Paul Martin was going to be the conservative saviour, not just the Liberal saviour.

It had seemed to me that, as the Martin Government got less conservative, David was less comfortable. Taking up Burney's challenge, I asked Emerson if he would consider joining our Cabinet. With little hesitation, he said yes. He became minister of international trade. (I will also add that I did not ask him about joining the party, but he likely assumed that was the case.)

In one of those strange twists, some tried to label the Emerson appointment as "unethical." I say "strange" because you constantly hear that political

---

* Other ministers included Rona Ambrose (Environment), Diane Finley (Employment and Social Development), Maxime Bernier (Industry), Monte Solberg (Immigration), Josée Verner (International Co-operation), Carol Skelton (National Revenue), Gary Lunn (Natural Resources), Marjory LeBreton (Senate Leader), and Michael Chong (Intergovernmental Affairs).

parties should reach out beyond their ranks. This is probably one of the rarest and clearest examples of that happening in recent Canadian history.

CABINET STRUCTURE AND GROUND RULES

OVERALL, THIS FIRST CABINET turned out to be very effective, in my judgment. Its effectiveness was enhanced by some ground rules we established from the outset and never strayed from. The most important of these was that members were always to keep their debates and arguments internal, in Cabinet as well as in caucus. Cabinet confidentiality is, of course, a cornerstone of our system of government. After all, it is why those sworn to advise the Crown are called "privy" councillors. Yet this tradition had broken down significantly in the later years of the previous Liberal Government. I believe the nature of Paul Martin's rise to power—his coup against Jean Chrétien—was at the core of that problem.

While on Cabinet secrecy we were restoring past practice, other rules were more novel. For instance, I forbade log-rolling—the practice of ministers doing side deals with one another outside of the Cabinet room. I needed—we all needed—to hear each minister's frank opinions. My message was: "Everything's on the table, and everybody who is at the table is to be involved in the discussion—and the decisions." It was not that hard to spot when ministers were not playing by this rule, which, fortunately, was infrequent.

As well, ministers were expected to bring what I called a whole-of-government perspective to Cabinet. This means simply that ministers were not in Cabinet to represent a narrowly departmental interest. For example, copyright is often a bureaucratic tug-of-war between the Industry and Heritage departments. Military procurement is notorious for the turf wars it generates between National Defence, Industry, and Public Works. That is all fine, but I did not need Cabinet ministers to advocate for their senior departmental officials. Through the clerk of the Privy Council, I would hear about those views. Our considerations were to be a level above that kind of debate. I needed my ministers to discuss the broader policy and political sides of the issues, including, for example, regional or even constituency perspectives. When a minister started acting like a representative of their deputy minister, I frankly discounted their input.

Our initial smallish Cabinet (by federal standards) was aided by a streamlined committee structure—at least compared to the Martin Government. The main decision-making body was Planning and Priorities, which included about a dozen ministers and which I chaired weekly. Full Cabinet met only about once a month for broader discussions. I also had three policy committees—Economic Affairs (chaired by Jim Flaherty), Social Affairs (Tony Clement), and Foreign Affairs & National Security (Peter Mackay)—along with two administrative committees—Operations (Jim Prentice) and Treasury Board (John Baird). They also met roughly once a week, and each minister was typically on two committees. We also decentralized things significantly, by moving roughly 10 per cent of the staff and responsibilities out of the Privy Council Office and into the line departments—contrary to another of those media "perceptions."

I should mention one other ground rule established early on. I learned that something called "unfunded memorandums to Cabinet," or "unfunded MCs," were winding their way through the Cabinet committee system. These were essentially departmental proposals queuing up for the next budget cycle. Going forward, I would have to give sign-off for anything to proceed that was not in ministerial mandate letters (which tracked very closely to our election platforms). Besides making fiscal discipline easier over time, this rule kept the political wing of the Government fully in control of agenda-setting.

SWEARING-IN MEMORIES

THE INITIAL PLANNING PHASES ended with the swearing-in of the new Cabinet by Governor General Michaëlle Jean on February 6. It was an incredibly special and meaningful day for me. All those years of challenge and struggle, the many ups and downs, the joy and grief politics brought now all seemed worth it. We had actually made it! The happy feelings that accompanied the moment were made more precious by the presence of family and friends.

Laureen, Ben, and Rachel were there, of course. So was my mother—it was wonderful that she was able to see this. Both of my brothers, Grant and Robert, attended, the latter with his wife Elan and my two nieces Katie and Lizzie. Two other family friends, Beryl Graham and her daughter Sandy, were also present.

Sadly, one very special person was not there—my father. Dad had passed away in early 2003. He had suffered a massive heart attack at fifty-eight, just after retiring. But he had changed his diet, undertaken an exercise program, and lived seventeen more years, most of them pretty good ones. However, he did not feel well enough to attend my swearing-in as leader of the Opposition. At that point, I knew that his remaining time with us would not be long.

The loss of Dad left and still leaves a hole in my life. He had a tremendous impact upon me—not just as a father but also in the thought processes he had encouraged in me, and even, to some degree, my political thinking. I can honestly say that to this day I have those moments where I want to call him up and tell him something, before remembering that he is not around. At the swearing-in, however, he was with me in spirit.

The day felt all a bit surreal. That was on purpose on my part. Just before the 2006 vote, as winning looked likely, someone had said to me, "Now, Leader, remember, everything you say and do is now significant." There is some truth in that. But it also implies that one should live in a kind of great-man psychodrama. Instead, I resolved that I would view being Canada's 22nd prime minister as just the guy occupying the office for a time. Someday it would end, and I would be back to being Stephen Harper, citizen. That is what would be real. This would be an extraordinary, unusual, and unique adventure, and one that I would never take for granted.

PART TWO

2006–2008

6

—

LAUNCHING "CANADA'S NEW GOVERNMENT"

WITH THE SWEARING-IN DONE, we were in office. Now, it really was showtime. How did I feel? Energized. Exhilarated. But no doubt I was also running on a lot of adrenalin. In less than four years, I had run for Parliament three times, and fought two leadership contests, a party merger referendum, and two national election campaigns. All this was accompanied by non-stop travel across the country as leader of the Opposition—and without the support mechanisms a prime minister receives.

Still, I was in much better shape than an earlier version of me would have been. My "reflective period" of 2003 had led to stronger capacities. I had since learned how to better put things out of my mind, to sleep more soundly, to more effectively control my emotions, and to work hard without exhausting myself. I was beginning to reap the benefits of those better habits. Certainly, I was tired, but I was nowhere near the total exhaustion of those early leadership years.

Around me, though, things had altered dramatically. As the song says, "And now my life has changed in oh so many ways, My independence seems to vanish in the haze."* I was ensconced in a permanent set of security layers.

---

* This lyric is from the Beatles' song "Help!" I was not crying for help, but I was experiencing life at the top, and the attention and intensity that came with it.

Staff and officials were omnipresent. Every significant meeting was being minuted, and every public or semi-public interaction was being recorded by the Privy Council Office. I tried to maintain a degree of "normal" during downtimes by, for example, going to the local movie theatre with friends. But that state really existed just in my own mind. My presence anywhere was noticed, doubly so because of the inevitable security and entourage.

It is hard to describe the combination of authority and celebrity that envelopes the prime minister. It cannot be ignored. In fact, I found it was not ignored even by people close to me. I was shocked in those first few months to find long-time friends and even relatives behaving awkwardly around me, unsure how to speak or act. Of course, I did my best to behave as if nothing had changed, and those interactions returned to more familiar patterns quickly.

But it was more than the level of attention that had changed. I now had enormous responsibilities. I know there are some people who think that, when you get to the top, you are a free agent. After all, you are the boss. In my experience, people who think that way usually fail in those positions. The truth is that, at the top, you have more obligations to more people than ever before. Because you are making decisions for others, your life is not your own, especially when you are "running the country." That is how a responsible leader sees things.

FIRST THINGS FIRST

WE HAD SET THE DATE of the opening of Parliament for April 3, 2006. That gave us two months to prepare the Throne Speech, our first budget, and enough legislation to get us through the session to the end of June. Remember, this was a minority situation, and we were rookies, facing (as always) a largely hostile press. There would be little room for error.

In this planning, we would be guided by the platform that we had been elected on. It was specific and detailed enough to serve the purpose. This approach made great sense because, in the minority situation, we could always say "we received a mandate from the people" for these measures.

Besides, we knew that our core promises were popular, even among many who had voted for the opposition parties.

Another advantage was that our platform had been clear and straightforward, with its repeated emphasis on the Five Priorities. Indeed, that had effectively become a mantra during the election. Those priorities were also, for the most part, reasonably uncomplicated to deliver—a big plus for a rookie minority government.

With that in mind, we made the immediate legislative objectives the accountability agenda, certain tax reductions, the new childcare policy, and some criminal justice initiatives. The wait time guarantees would take more than a few months to negotiate. As for addressing the fiscal imbalance, it would be the subject of intense discussions with the provinces, with the objective of proceeding in Budget 2007.

Just as important was what we decided not to do—what broadly came under the term "machinery of government." This refers to the general configuration of government departments and agencies and their responsibilities. Machinery of government changes are, with rare exceptions embedded in legislation, the sole prerogative of the prime minister (as, otherwise, administrative chaos would be a real danger).

The advice I had received from my transition team and others with government experience was to minimize machinery of government changes unless the rationale, objectives, and benefits were crystal clear and substantial. No one structure is perfect, so there can always be an inclination to undertake such reorganizations. However, they can easily absorb immense amounts of time and resources, detracting from more immediate actions. History will show that I did do some machinery changes, but not a lot. I followed what proved to be a good piece of advice and one I am happy to pass on to those aspiring to lead the Government of Canada—or for that matter any large organization—in the future.

The consequence of that resolution was to change some decisions that had been made during the Martin Government. This meant not just stopping them in their tracks but in some cases reversing them before they went further down the road. Prominent examples were Mr. Martin's actions to separate the functions of Human Resources and Social Development, as well as Foreign Affairs and International Trade. The latter was particularly significant, as I would eventually conclude that further integration, not separation, was required in the area of international policy entities.

THE ACCOUNTABILITY ACT AND ENHANCED OVERSIGHT

ON FEBRUARY 1, 2006, just one week after the election and before our swearing-in, I announced that our government's first legislation would be the Federal Accountability Act (FAA). This surprised no one. The sponsorship scandal, the Gomery Commission, and their fallout had been a central focus of ours when we were in opposition. And, of course, we had promised such an Act during the election.

We wanted the Act to create a clean break from the culture and operating style of the previous government. As we said, we wanted it "to change the way business is done in Ottawa." This critical first task was assigned to John Baird as president of the Treasury Board.

John was both a savvy and combative political operator. It was the kind of leadership that the FAA—a sprawling and transformative piece of legislation—would require. But this was far from the last time John would be entrusted with a big job. He always served in critical ministries over almost the entire length of my Government, including two difficult stints in Environment. His views in Cabinet were always forceful and, privately with me, could be even more so from time to time.

One major set of FAA changes strengthened auditing and accounting within departments. This was a no-brainer. The auditor general had attacked the spending and the scandal as well as the auditing deficiencies that allowed them to take place. We made a point of addressing these shortcomings directly, making them more prescriptive and detailed. That was a better solution than the Treasury Board "web of rules" that the previous government had developed, which officials complained was grinding the wheels of government to a halt.

We also created the Parliamentary Budget Officer, modelled on the Congressional Budget Office in the United States. The aim was to give parliamentarians and Canadians more broadly an "objective" view of Canada's finances.

This was meant to address two kinds of complaints during the last years of the Liberal Government. First were obviously instances of flagrant spending abuse, of which the sponsorship scandal was only one. But there was also a lot of frustration, especially in minority parliaments, around constantly changing, and thus increasingly unreliable, budgetary estimates. Budgetary projections began to fluctuate wildly for unexplained reasons. This had caused us great frustration when we were the Opposition, and it left the public with the sense that the Government either did not really know what the numbers were or was not telling the truth about them.

Another key office we put in place was Office of the Director of Public Prosecutions. We made it an independent office within the Justice Department to deal with decisions on prosecutions. Why was this important? It addressed what many have seen as an uncomfortable reality in our parliamentary system: the minister of justice, a partisan, elected official, decides who gets prosecuted and who does not.

Other independent oversight offices established by the Federal Accountability Act were the Commissioner of Lobbying, the Public Sector Integrity Commissioner, the Procurement Ombudsman, and the Conflict of Interest and Ethics Commissioner.

However, one of the independent offices we intended to establish never got off the ground: the Public Appointments Commissioner. To run this office, I nominated a highly qualified individual in Gwyn Morgan. In fact, Gwyn had just been named as Canada's "CEO of the year." But the Opposition, feeling it needed to inflict a "defeat" on the Government, decided to block approval of the appointment in committee. I felt terrible for Gwyn, whose willingness to serve for virtually nothing had been widely praised. But I was not going to waste time fighting the Opposition over this, especially as I quickly concluded that I could achieve my objectives without actually establishing the commission.

What we did instead was set out clear criteria for nominations within the appointments department of the Prime Minister's Office (PMO). I was always clear about partisan considerations when ministers had to nominate people. I told them that I expected them to appoint people who were on our wavelength and would help the government achieve our objectives. But I did not care whether they were Conservatives, supporters of other parties, or nonpartisan individuals. And I warned them not to assume that a Conservative would be an automatic and co-operative fit. I often quoted the words of our long-time Senate Leader Marjory LeBreton, who had served as the appointments' guru in Brian Mulroney's Government. "You will find out," Marjory would warn, "how easily some appointees conclude that their position is a result of 'immaculate conception.'"

THE ACCOUNTABILITY ACT AND LOBBYING

FIRST, A WORD OF CLARIFICATION about lobbying. While the term "lobbyist" has developed a negative connotation over time, the act of petitioning government is, in and of itself, a completely legitimate activity. In fact, the right to lobby your government is inherent in a democratic society and a mark of democracy everywhere. If you cannot lobby your government, you almost certainly live in an authoritarian state. In today's complex world, more complicated issues do often require more sophisticated representation, hence the rise of professional lobbyists.

The key in our view is transparency. The FAA strengthened the Lobbyist Act and the Lobbyist Register to make sure professional activities were documented. The public could know who is lobbying and why they are lobbying and thus be assured no one was taking secret advantage of the system.

However, we went further. A particularly notorious practice, especially prevalent during the previous Liberal administration, was what had been called the "revolving door" of lobbying. That was where officials (both political and bureaucratic) on leaving the government would immediately turn around and lobby the people they used to work with, to their great profit. Not surprisingly, a lot of money tended to go to people who had those kinds of ties.

That was one of the top concerns people told us they had with lobbying. It was not about the actual process of lobbying someone to make a decision that benefits somebody else. Of course, we assume all that. The bigger problem was conflict of interest—insiders using their connections to benefit themselves.

The most important thing we did to address this was to create a five-year lobbying ban for a range of public office holders. Those in senior, or in some cases mid-level, positions were banned from lobbying for five years after leaving that position within the Government of Canada or the Parliament of Canada. We chose five years as assurance that a person would never be lobbying their own majority government. By the time they are eligible to lobby, they will either be facing a new government or, if a government from the same party is re-elected, they will most likely be approaching different people.

This had enormous public support, and I believe it still does. But I can tell you with great certainty that it did not have enormous support in the world of lobbyists, and we got a ton of pushback.

Not unrelated to the lobbying restrictions were the limits we placed on donations to political parties. Jean Chrétien had started moving in this direction, but our reforms were much stricter and much more comprehensive. Corporate contributions were banned, as were union contributions and those from non-Canadians. For Canadian citizens, we established a limit of $1,000 for donations to a riding and a further $1,000 to a political party, with reporting requirements for donations over $200. This was to assure Canadians that those contributing to political parties were actual voters, using their own money to fund the parties they believed in.

These reforms did two good things for the system. First, the new model took the really big money out of the picture, which could otherwise have undue influence on government or party priorities. Second, it requires politicians and parties to listen to the concerns of large numbers of donors. In other words, it makes them accountable to the political marketplace generally but not to individual donors specifically. It is an inherently democratic model that makes elected officials get out of the "Ottawa bubble" and be responsive to the "real world." For similar reasons, we would later eliminate the direct government funding of registered political parties.

Coming from the Reform/Alliance background, these reforms were a natural thing for me to pursue. The parties I belonged to had long been funded by masses of individual, grassroots members, so I knew it was a feasible system. I had fought and won two leadership campaigns on that model. My Canadian Alliance leadership campaign had raised over a million dollars, while my Conservative Party effort had accumulated well over two million. In both cases, donations over $1,000 had been a small fraction of the fundraising, and corporate contributions were virtually non-existent.

There were some who felt that these reforms to party financing were inconsistent with the positions I took as president of the National Citizens Coalition. Back then, I had continued long-standing NCC litigation to allow private citizens and organizations to use their own money, without restriction, to finance political advertising campaigns during elections. In these legal battles, the NCC was ultimately unsuccessful.

The two issues are, however, logically distinct. The point of restrictions on party donations is not to limit the expression of donors' political views; it is to ensure politicians are not beholden to particular donors. In any case, the "third-party" advertising limits were no longer being raised by anyone when we were pursuing the reforms in the FAA.

GETTING THE ACCOUNTABILITY ACT PASSED

THE FEDERAL ACCOUNTABILITY ACT was tabled by Minister Baird on April 11, 2006, and our Government immediately got to work advancing it through Parliament and promoting it to the paublic. The fact that our ministers and caucus fanned out across the country came as a surprise to many commentators and political pundits. It should not have. This was, after all, a defining piece of legislation for our Government.

But there was more to it than that. A big part of our decision to take the issue outside Parliament was our minority government status. We wanted to put pressure on the other parties to support the bill. We were particularly worried about a rearguard action by the Liberal majority in the Senate to block key measures. Hence, we launched our campaign-style strategy.

This involved a lot of travel for me, but it was only the beginning. We used this approach regularly throughout our time in government. Although previous prime ministers had periodically gone out of Parliament to make important speeches in places like Toronto, Montreal, and Vancouver, I travelled far more often and far more widely. I went somewhere at least once most weeks, and I would eventually visit virtually every part of the country. We were an "outsider" government with a regionally diffuse support base. We needed to constantly touch base with our constituencies and rally our supporters.

As I said, the minority situation also mattered. I never made the mistake of trying to stay in office by making deals with the opposition parties. Yes, I did speak to opposition leaders both on general and specific matters regularly. But I understood that their job is, at heart, to oppose, and their objective is, ultimately, to bring down the Government. So the key to getting any constructive opposition engagement is to keep the public onside. Do that, and at least one opposition party will support you. Fail to do it, and you will invariably be defeated. That is why I ran two of the longest minorities in Canadian history. Besides, I never had a leader of any opposition party foolish enough to give me a Jagmeet Singh–style blank cheque.

The strategy worked in this case, as it would often in the future. In fact, both the Bloc and the NDP had considerable sympathy with much of what we were trying to do in the FAA. As for the Liberal Party, it increasingly wanted the debate, which kept the focus on their scandals, to just go away. The Federal Accountability Act was passed by the Commons on June 22 and by the Senate on November 9. It received Royal Assent on December 12 with few changes to its original form.

EVALUATING THE ACCOUNTABILITY AGENDA

THE FAA WAS A PRODUCT of the shock and outrage of its time, but I believe the measures have held up well overall. The Government's core objective was accomplished. Business in Ottawa did indeed change, quickly and dramatically. My Government was relatively free from scandal, particularly where the expenditure of public funds was involved. The untoward was generally identified and dealt with quickly. Nevertheless, some reflection on these reforms is in order these many years later.

As I noted, the establishment and strengthening of several statutorily independent oversight officers was a key part of the legislation. Such bodies are always created with the best of intentions. However, the nature of them is not always fully appreciated. "Independent" can just as easily mean "unaccountable." After all, once their heads are named, they are extremely difficult to remove, and their operations are separated not only from partisan interference but also from normal government oversight controls. In short, you are naming someone very powerful, giving them the carte blanche ability to, in practice, pursue any matter in their purview.

For those reasons our plans to create these officers were opposed by some in the Public Service, and their concerns were not just theoretical. The bureaucracy had had some previous nasty experiences. Still, in retrospect, I do not regret creating these officers, but I did learn some important lessons along the way.

In particular, I learned that the selection of these officers has to be done with great care. An unelected, unrecallable, unaccountable individual with wide-ranging oversight authority is, in effect, being given godlike powers. If you are naming a god, you had better be bloody sure that person is capable of serving a godly function. Some of our early choices in this regard—ironically often proposed by the Public Service—were not good, but we did develop much better selection processes as time went on.

The creation of one of the independent officers that I certainly do not regret is the Director of Public Prosecutions. That body became relevant when the Trudeau PMO tried to intervene in the prosecution of SNC Lavalin. Such an incident could never have happened in our Government as I forbade any dialogue with SNC Lavalin during its attempts to lobby on such matters.

Our changes to the lobbying rules were also necessary. In retrospect, however, we may have been somewhat zealous in making it a five-year lobbying ban. For instance, some of my former staffers wondered why they were barred from lobbying the Liberal Government after ours was defeated in 2015. There was certainly no "insider" risk there.

I also regret one minor part of the FAA that stripped away the ability of former political staffers to get fast-tracked into the Public Service. At the time, we were worried about the flood of Liberals heading into non-partisan positions. That said, we rarely found these former Grits problematic when we were the Government. On the contrary, political staffers are generally smart, highly motivated young people with a great work ethic. It makes little sense for the Public Service not to take advantage of such experienced personnel.

On the other hand, I do not think we went far enough on preventing potential conflicts within the Public Service, particularly in areas of procurement. And later, other conflicts came to my attention that should be addressed. For example, it has been distressing to find former foreign service officers employed by foreign government interests, including Chinese state interests, after leaving the Government of Canada.

I also believe that the new fundraising rules have held up very well, although the limits have been creeping up over the years. What remains unresolved is creating reasonable rules for private citizens and groups to communicate their views during election periods. The key problem is the necessity of forbidding collusion, so that effectively the contribution limits cannot be circumvented. The failure of Elections Canada to deal with collusion on other kinds of election spending—a growing problem in more recent campaigns—is not encouraging.

That problem has been complicated by the fixed-election-dates legislation that was also part of my Government's reforms. There were already challenges with it in my time—we will get to those—but more have developed. As critics suggested, the law has essentially lengthened the electoral period. Full campaigning can be undertaken very early, given certain knowledge of the election date. That includes high-profile, well-funded, well-coordinated advocacy campaigns by groups strongly aligned with particular political parties.

I have therefore concluded that the fixed election date was the wrong solution to the problem. The problem was governments catching opposition parties unprepared with snap election calls. But that only became possible because of legislation in the 1990s that allowed campaign periods to be as short as thirty-seven days. All that really had to be done to address that problem was to lengthen the minimum campaign period. The shortened option was never a good idea in the first place, as no election should be so brief as to not allow the key opposition parties to get into full gear for the lion's share of the campaign.

BUDGET 2006

IT HAS BECOME a bit of a tradition for incoming governments to declare that the "cupboard is bare" as one of their first acts. That was not true in my case; the books were in relatively good shape. The later Chrétien-Martin Governments were reaping the benefits of the strong budget medicine they had delivered to Canadians in the 1990s. In fact, they were running large surpluses even after the increased program spending and tax reductions of the early 2000s. I am the first to admit that this was a great advantage for my Government. Since John A. Macdonald, most Conservative governments had been elected when times were tough and had to assume the unenviable task of cleaning things up. That was not so when we got elected.

This is not to say that preparing our first budget was a simple matter. Between February and the budget date of May 2, the numbers we received from the Department of Finance kept fluctuating. Often, they appeared better, but still there were way too many surprises. One day it seemed we had a certain degree of fiscal room to work with; another day it was a different thing all together. In other words, the frustrations we had had in opposition—the ones that had helped give rise to the Parliamentary Budget Officer—seemed to be following us into Government.

We came to believe that a big part of the reason for these fluctuations could be found in Finance Department thinking. Ever since the near-crisis fiscal situation of 1995, a departmental culture had taken hold that believed the best way to manage government finances was to portray the budgetary situation as worse than it really was until the very last minute. Perhaps that was necessary with a Liberal Cabinet; however, in my Government, we wanted to operate based on what the numbers actually were. We insisted that the culture shift to this new Conservative realism.

Overall, as we compared the numbers to our campaign promises, we increasingly felt confident we would have the leeway we needed for that first budget. The budget items were as advertised: we cut the GST by the first full point, from 7 to 6 per cent. We also introduced a range of other tax deductions benefitting workers, families, pensioners, students, and people with disabilities. Many of these had been promised in our platform. Additionally, Minister Flaherty launched the Working Income Tax Benefit, which made it easier for the poor to transition from welfare to work. This was classic Jim. Despite his image as a hard-nosed minister—one that was well earned—he was always looking for ways to assist the truly disadvantaged in our society.

We also brought in another significant tax reduction that we had not planned for. On its way out the door, the Martin Government, feeling pressure on the taxation front, proposed a cut to the lowest income tax bracket. They had introduced a lowering of the rate by a full percentage, from 16 to 15, which, because it is paid by most people, would be very costly. However, that had never been enacted in legislation. There was great pressure for us to honour the proposed cut, even though we had never promised it. In the end, we enacted our GST cut but added a half-point cut to the lowest threshold, with the commitment to bringing in the other half-point cut in the future. The upshot is that we actually wound up doing both the Liberal cut and our own.

Budget 2006 also formally announced our new Universal Child Care Benefit. The transition was already underway, and it was proving to be a more complex and messy process than we had hoped. Minister Diane Finley

(Doug's wife) had to wind up hundreds of largely advocacy contracts related to the Liberal's non-existent daycare program. It was a tough job, but Diane did it promptly and efficiently.

The budget also tackled several spending areas. There were a few reductions as well as some important injections. A key priority, right from day one, was infrastructure. While this category grew significantly in future budgets, we made an early commitment to the Asia-Pacific Gateway. We understood that Canada's trade and trade opportunities across the Pacific would continue to expand rapidly. In hand with British Columbia Premier Gordon Campbell, we worked to bolster major trade-related infrastructure on the West Coast. This was one of many areas where Premier Campbell's Government would prove to be a focused and effective partner.*

A lot of the new spending in that budget was not sexy. Our focus had been to work with the Public Service to identify areas that had been underfunded and legitimately required addressing. The message was that, if there were things to worry about, then take advantage of a good financial situation to plug the holes.

It is worth mentioning that one of the areas we identified as deficient was pandemic planning. We recognized this as a major risk in a globalized economy. In that first budget, we put one billion new dollars into that priority. Our Government was fortunate not to have to face anything on the scale of the Covid-19 pandemic, but we were at least cognizant of the risk. The SARS outbreak of 2003 had been a big scare. My health minister, Tony Clement, had been in that role in Ontario when the federal government had stumbled through that crisis. We were determined not to repeat such an episode.

* Gordon Campbell would go on to be Canada's High Commissioner to the United Kingdom in the later years of our Government. In that role, he undertook a reconfiguration of Canada's real estate in London that saved Canadian taxpayers hundreds of millions of dollars.

INCOME TRUSTS

THERE WAS NO PANDEMIC threat that year, but a crisis of sorts did emerge after Budget 2006 in the fall. First Telus and then BCE announced their intentions to convert their corporations into income trusts. There were strong indications that other major financial and commercial institutions were also planning on converting. They were, however, waiting to see what the federal government would do about it.

For any federal government, the revenue implications of this were a big issue. Income trusts took on certain restrictions in their structure and growth, but they got very favourable tax treatment in return. The conversion of a mass of blue-chip Canadian companies thus threatened to create a major hole in our corporate tax base. Longer term, it also risked the emergence of a business environment that was less dynamic and growth-oriented for the Canadian economy.

Against this reality our Government faced two additional, big problems. One was that we had promised not to levy new taxes on income trusts. That had come about during a series of controversial moves by the previous Liberal Government that had shocked the markets. But they had done more than shock the markets. A major income trust tax announcement by then–Finance Minister Ralph Goodale had been preceded by considerable market movement. That had led to an ongoing RCMP investigation into the leaking of confidential information and had become a significant story during the 2006 election campaign.

Under these circumstances, our Government was simply unable to consult widely on options. We had to keep discussions extremely private, restricting the dialogue to myself, Minister Flaherty, and a tiny handful of senior Privy Council Office and Department of Finance officials. It did not help that this group had a long-standing agenda to get rid of the income trust structure.

Whether or not these officials had an agenda, the fact was that they were right. The worst-case scenario was unfolding right before our eyes, with devastating consequences for our fiscal position. I decided to bite the bullet and make an unpleasant decision.

In the end, we brought in corporate-tax equivalent levies not only on new income trusts but also on existing ones. It was a case of in for a penny, in for a pound. If we grandfathered the existing trusts, we would spend years enacting additional anti-circumvention rules, with constant reminders of our about-face. No, we would endure the pain now. Only real-estate trusts, so-called REITs, were spared our measures. In that sector, we judged the structure more appropriate.

The announcement was made by Minister Flaherty—Jim was also one never afraid to make a tough decision—on October 31, 2006. As I am still reminded, it was the "Halloween massacre." Market prices for income trusts dropped as much as one-third the next day.

We tried to soften the blow. Given the impact on seniors' savings—a big reason we had opposed income trust taxation in Opposition—we brought in some tax measures directed at pensioners. The big one was income-splitting on pension income. It was a move that proved extremely popular with the vast majority of seniors.

Of course, that did not remotely compensate those heavily invested in income trusts. Nevertheless, the sudden market response was an overreaction. There were transition rules to be put in place, and Minister Flaherty had committed to extensive consultations to help manage that transition. Besides, the corporate tax burden was also falling. We had taken some important steps in Budget 2006 and would develop a broader approach going forward. Between the transition arrangements and the tax cuts, the eventual losses from moving income trusts to corporate taxation would be a fraction of those incurred by first-day sellers.

Politically, the government was not threated by this move. The NDP supported it on tax equity grounds, and the Bloc would eventually do so as well. But, for me, it was and remains terribly embarrassing. We made a point of tracking and honouring the commitments undertaken in our electoral platforms. This was a rare case where we did precisely the opposite, on something that mattered deeply to some people. Although they were relatively small in number, some never forgave us. I cannot blame them.

But how did this happen? I still believe that breaking our commitment was the right thing to do under the circumstances. But what were the circumstances of the commitment to never tax income trusts? The truth is that it was made in the heat of the moment when we were in Opposition and had the Martin Government on the ropes.

At the time, my Finance critic was Monte Solberg, by now minister of citizenship and immigration. Monte had expressed concern to me that the trust arrangement was simply too generous and that fiscal realities might make my promise unsustainable. Although I had not heeded him at the time, Monte was good enough never to say, "I told you so."

The clear lesson here for a leader is to try to think long-term when making commitments. In opposition especially, it is easy to make popular promises. That is great as long as you never have to make good on them. However, if you are serious about being in government, you do have to think twice before committing yourself.

TACKLING THE JUSTICE PORTFOLIO

JUSTICE LEGISLATION WAS ONE of our original Five Priorities, and, indeed, one of our priorities throughout our time in office. Our approach reflected a core conservative philosophy that both views criminal justice as a central responsibility of Government and emphasizes a particular approach to that responsibility. However, before any legislation would be drafted, we had an important justice-related matter to attend to—a vacancy on the Supreme Court of Canada.

The previous government had done a lot of legwork looking for the right candidate. At the top of their list was Justice Marshall Rothstein from Manitoba—a no-nonsense, by-the-book judge. In one of the very few cases where we saw eye-to-eye with our Liberal counterparts on justice issues, we agreed that Rothstein was perfect for the job. It helped that our justice minister, Manitoban Vic Toews, whose views were highly respected inside our Government, vouched for Rothstein. Then again, we had promised a different approach to naming Supreme Court justices.

During the campaign we had said we would hold transparent, publicly open parliamentary hearings. Justice Rothstein was thus interviewed by an ad hoc parliamentary committee—ad hoc because Parliament had not yet been convened. The hearing went well. Critics of this approach had warned that we risked politicizing the judicial appointment process—potentially moving toward U.S.-style hearings of confrontation, spin, and prime-time theatrics. In the end, that did not happen, and we used a similar process for each Supreme Court nominee.

That said, I would not use such a process again. While the crass politicization feared never happened, some warning signs of it did appear as time went on. More importantly, the benefits of the process were virtually nonexistent. There was wide-ranging questioning that the candidates would not, or could not, answer. Ultimately, there was little scrutiny and little utility to the exercise.

That done, our Government began to develop its legislative and policy program. It would encompass four main themes: making punishment fit the crime (especially for serious, violent crime); ending the notion of "innocent after proven guilty"; putting greater emphasis on victims' rights; and introducing practical measures to improve policing and security.

The bedrock of our conservative approach was responsibility: that offenders are responsible for their actions and that government is responsible to society at large. If people commit crimes, they need to be held responsible. And in administering such a system, the primary responsibility of the government is not to lawbreakers and prisoners but, as I said repeatedly, "to law-abiding citizens, their property, and their families." This was a radical overturning of the previous liberal approach. That had been reflected in the language of senior justice department personnel, who (shockingly, in our minds) often referred to inmates as "clients."

This is not to say that rehabilitation is unimportant or bad for society. Nor do I suggest that many people who commit crimes have not themselves been victims at other times—of horrible upbringings, severe mental health issues, substance abuse problems, and the like. Obviously, in a caring and just society, these factors must be taken into account. But we cannot allow the principle that people are fundamentally responsible for their actions to be overwhelmed. Indeed, I would argue, the internalization of an ethic of personal responsibility is key to rehabilitation, without which that objective is simply an illusion.

Making the Punishment Fit the Crime

IN THE 2005–2006 CAMPAIGN, our pledge to make criminal sanctions fit the crime resonated strongly with voters. Our first target was the violence involving guns, gangs, and the sale of illicit drugs. To bring the concept of individual responsibility to bear, we introduced mandatory minimum prison sentences for gun crimes. Commit a gun crime and you go to prison. This was a day-and-night change from the previous government, whose response had focused on enacting the costly and ineffective long-gun registry.

To this day, I find the Liberals' ongoing obsession with curtailing long-gun use by millions of law-abiding hunters and rural Canadians very hard to explain. Neither this category of weapons nor of demographics makes any appreciable contribution to violent crime. I figure it just comes down to the liberal creed that there really are no bad people and that it really must be the environment—that is, the gun—that ultimately causes the crime. In any case, if, after all manner of gun control, you are still not prepared to seriously sanction somebody when they use a gun to commit a crime, the logic truly escapes me. I believe there is room for rational gun control measures, but gun control alone is not sufficient to tackle the problem; you must also be prepared to deal directly with gun crime.

Tightening bail provisions for gun-related crime was another responsive measure to liberal failure. It had become laughably easy for people accused of very serious criminal offences to get bail. The most shocking cases occurred in Canada's major urban centres, particularly in the GTA. In 2006, the Toronto Police Service reported that 70 per cent of those arrested on homicide charges that year were either on bail or probation, or they were under court-ordered prohibitions at the time of the crime.

For months both Ontario Premier Dalton McGuinty and Toronto Mayor David Miller—no hard-core right-wingers—had been urging action to toughen our bail conditions.

On November 24, 2006, I joined the two of them to highlight our legislation to "rebalance the scales of justice," as I put it. The key feature was the "reverse onus" clause, under which offenders charged with gun crimes would have to show why they should not stay in custody until trial. Previously, rules required prosecutors to demonstrate why gun offenders should *not* be released. It is hard to imagine why this change had not been made years earlier, but in any case, we removed this glaring "get out of jail free" card from the gun offender's deck.

We also applied this principle to those involved in the drug trade. There is a vast difference between drug users, who often require compassion and help, and the drug dealers who prey upon them. It is with that in mind that, in 2007, we sharpened the distinction between toughening penalties for those profiting from narcotics and enhancing treatment and other assistance for those suffering from addiction.

It was inevitable, I suppose, that our critics would raise the prospect of otherwise innocent drug users being jailed for smoking a joint. That is a myth of the modern age. The truth of the matter is that, long before the legalization of marijuana, people were rarely charged for minor possession, unless police had suspicion of wider criminal activity. Our government never set out to prosecute people for having a drug problem—far from it.

On the other hand, it was clear that the courts were becoming progressively more lenient on drug use. That is one of the reasons why, early in the term, we tackled the issue of drug-impaired driving. We could see the day when drug use would be more permissive and, obviously, would lead to many of the same problems as drunk driving.

Of course, we did not decriminalize marijuana. This may come as a surprise, but I was never closed to the idea. I did not entertain legalization, but I had become convinced that the "war on drugs" was a failure. Simply imposing criminal sanctions on the use of narcotics has not and will not deal with all the problems around drugs, at least not in our society.

The upshot is that I believe there legitimately are various strategies and combinations of strategies to deal with narcotics use, the drug trade, and addiction. But I strongly disagree with those who make the argument that it is the illegal nature itself of drug use that is the problem, and that, if drugs were legal, there would be none of the violence and social ills that characterize the drug trade. That is silly and misguided.

Drugs are illegal historically in a whole range of societies because drug abuse is a very bad thing. It invariably causes significant personal and wider social harm. Over time, it ruins health and can lead to death. It rips apart lives and families. It is a factor in far too many other crimes. That is why narcotics are illegal. How the law deals with such drugs is open to many different approaches, but we should not fool ourselves into believing that if you make them legal, the bad effects will somehow disappear. There will still be addiction, with all the ills it generates, and there will be those who profit off addiction, who will never be reputable actors.

I am not for legalization, but what bothers me even more is the idea that drugs should be encouraged. I have been approached on more than one occasion with opportunities to get involved in the marijuana business. The pharmaceutical benefits of the trade are always stressed. But make no mistake, that side of the business is usually trivial. In my view, pharmaceutical companies are likely to dominate that part in the long run, just as tobacco companies will eventually take over the recreational business. Legalization will, over time, prove to be increasingly bad for our society.

Ending "Innocent After Proven Guilty"

CANADA, LIKE ALL WESTERN democracies, upholds the concept of being innocent until proven guilty. But under modern liberal theories of criminal justice, a different concept had taken root—"innocent after proven guilty." In other words, convicted criminals would continue to be treated as if they were innocent. In a system that had clearly lost its way, we sought to restore some balance.

When Pierre Trudeau's Government abolished capital punishment, Canadians were assured that "life would mean life." However, that promise was quickly undermined. The most infamous example was the so-called faint hope clause, which allowed the most notorious offenders to apply for parole and get out of prison early. Even for someone like confessed serial child killer Clifford Olson, life might not really mean life after all.

Earned parole versus automatic release for convicts was another area that cried out for fixing. House arrest even more so. True, incarcerating people in their home instead of in prison can be cost-effective, and it can make sense as a rehabilitation measure. However, applied to those convicted of serious, violent offences, it simply trivializes punishment. We wanted it to end in such cases.

The pardon system was another glaring example of innocent after proven guilty. Most Canadians did not realize that, even after committing the most heinous crimes, there comes a point in time when, under previous legislation, a criminal could receive a full pardon. Not only could they, it was virtually automatic.

This came to my attention in 2010 in the case of the notorious pedophile hockey coach Graham James. In that case, Vic Toews did the finding out, and he had the unenviable task of informing me by telephone. It was during a parliamentary break when he told me that James had received a pardon "from our Government." Of course, it was from parole officials under legislation. Vic would relay to colleagues how he briefed me quickly and then held the receiver far from his ear before my anticipated verbal explosion. In any case, we significantly tightened up the pardon system. It had become a case of the system forgiving and forgetting even in the complete absence of remorse or rehabilitation.

The Graham James incident revealed a disturbing feature of the criminal justice bureaucracy—our Government was almost never forewarned about such things. It was part of a pattern. The system never proactively brought to our attention anything that a government like ours might want to change. We always had to find out ourselves, and we always had to develop our own remedies. We would then invariably discover layers upon layers of interpretations and precedents justifying what virtually all Canadians would see as outrageous abuses of the system.

Innocent after proven guilty covers the worst outrages of liberal criminal justice ideology. Canadians overwhelmingly condemned such things when they heard about them. The real problem was that such abuses were so extreme—for example, prisons paying salaries to their inmate-clients—that it was sometimes difficult to convince people they were actually true. Frankly, I fear the system is yet again riddled with absurdities like those.

Enhancing Victims' Rights and Security

THE JUSTICE I HAVE BEEN talking about to this point is legal, technical, jurisprudential. But real justice is much broader in scope, addressing the needs of the victims who are too often forgotten. We were determined to change that. We introduced several practical measures to better address victims' rights. Of course, our fourth justice theme—enhancing policing and security—was also victim-centric, particularly in trying to reduce the number of victims in the first place.

Victims' rights are not, however, an easy area for the federal government. Ottawa's role in the justice system is focused on the Criminal Code, some aspects of law enforcement, the administration of the senior layers of the court system, and parts of the prison system. The federal government is not primarily responsible for delivering social policy outside the prison context. We found ways to move forward, nonetheless.

Very early on, I met with the families of the victims of Air India Flight 182. That remains the worst terrorist incident in Canadian history, with over three hundred of our citizens perishing on June 23, 1985. Two years later, to the day, the ratification process began for the Meech Lake Accord. That tells you how little the event had penetrated the national consciousness at the time. Canadians heard "Air India" and automatically thought of it as a foreign rather than domestic terrorist act. Of the perpetrators, only one was ever convicted.

As we had promised in Opposition, our Government worked with the families to establish a full public inquiry to get to the bottom of events around the incident. This involved examining subsequent actions, including the investigations and eventual prosecutions, which were widely seen as bungled. Headed by retired Supreme Court Justice John Major, the inquiry also focused on how to avoid similar acts of terrorism in the future.

Although addressing issues like this would seem like common sense and fairness to most, they were almost always fiercely resisted in the bureaucracy. Officials, as I have noted before, often have a long history of defending the status quo, so they are frequently invested in it. As well, such cases can open wounds that are highly indicting of the conduct of various government departments and agencies, leading to unwanted scrutiny and negative publicity. That certainly applied in the case of Air India. Without a doubt, some of those who resisted the inquiry were personally uncomfortable with what we were doing, and not for good reasons. I will leave it at that.

All this was yet another source of resistance to our Government's justice agenda. As well, outside of government departments and agencies, there is a whole legal industry—lawyers, academics, and advocates—who were also frequently (though not universally) opposed to the move away from offender-centric justice. Such voices would receive blanket media coverage for their criticisms of our Government.

Ironically, this publicity almost inevitably helped our cause. What it usually betrayed was a justice establishment wildly out of step with the citizenry. Their attacks helped us to gradually pass most of our measures, even in minority parliaments where, initially, we would often face united Opposition resistance.

The problem with many of the criticisms from the justice establishment is that they were transparently linked to either vested interests or ideological paradigms. The latter is a widespread problem in many areas of so-called social science. Nevertheless, it remains a reality that elites fiercely resist reform in this area regardless of public opinion. It is just one example of the growing disconnect between elite and grassroots perspectives in modern democratic societies—a subject I have written about at length elsewhere.

PROMISES MADE, PROMISES KEPT

LOOKING BACK, I REMAIN STRUCK by how many issues we were able to address—in many cases rather quickly—in our first minority government situation. Our success in doing so, I believe, was that we had religiously followed the straightforward agenda proposed during our election campaign. We were very aware that the clock was ticking and that our government could fall at any time. We were clear in our objectives, remained focused, and, for a new government, had incredible levels of discipline, starting in the PMO under chief of staff Ian Brodie and continuing throughout our Cabinet and caucus.

Still, many are familiar with British Prime Minister Harold Macmillan's response to a questioner about the greatest challenge for an officeholder: "Events, dear boy, events." We had made a good start, but we were going to be exposed to that lesson going forward.

7

—

THE STATE OF THE FEDERATION

A CONSERVATIVE APPROACH TO FEDERALISM

AMONG CANADA'S PRIME MINISTERS, I came to office through the most unusual route. I also had a unique exposure to the country before doing so.

I had family roots in Atlantic Canada, principally New Brunswick, and I had spent some time there as a boy. I had grown up in Ontario, where many of my friends and most of my extended family—both urban and rural—still lived. And I had been based in Alberta for most of my adult life. My staff would sometimes remark that I was essentially claiming three home provinces.

I had become familiar as well with Quebec perspectives over my many years of learning French (and Canadian history). I had also long been a student of Canadian federalism and was well informed on the history, strengths, and weaknesses of the system. During my time as Reform's principal spokesperson on constitutional issues, I had witnessed up close the constitutional battles of the late 1980s and early 1990s, and I had become acquainted with many experts and players in the field.

This cross-country and cross-perspective background was reflected in my view of the country. I see Canadians as having both common national traits and distinct regional cultures. As I have said before, I was moulding the new Conservative Party of Canada to embody three different traditions—Tory, populist, and *nationaliste*—that reflected the diversity of the country. These traditions differ on some axes, but there is considerable common ground. One of the latter is a basic view of federalism.

It was a conservative-led coalition that hammered out the British North America Act of 1867, and that remains the fundamental DNA of our governance to this day. For conservatives of all backgrounds, federalism is therefore not some "bug" in the system. It is its heart—the organ that reflects the country's genuine nature and allows it to be workably administered. Naturally, we conservatives all have things about Canadian federalism we would like to change, but we are neither centralizers nor separatists when it comes to defining Canada.

Federations can, of course, be fractious, and most of my life had been a highly fractious period. Pierre Trudeau's years in power had left the country both economically weakened and emotionally divided. The divisions had culminated in two events around 1982—the patriation of the Constitution without Quebec's consent and the adoption of the National Energy Program without Western support. The Quebec sovereignty movement had persisted since then, having spiked recently around the sponsorship scandal. And Western alienation remained a widespread sentiment, having been freshly stoked by the Liberals in the 2000 election campaign. There might not be an immediate threat to the federation, but these were ongoing fissures that could well up and test national unity at any time.

Obviously, we wanted to tackle these issues. On the other hand, we remembered all too well the attempts of the Mulroney Government to address federal–provincial tensions through amending the Constitution. Whatever its intentions, that had led to further acrimony and had contributed to a devastating fracturing of Canadian conservatism. In our desire to mitigate the challenges left by the past, we were determined to avoid creating new problems in the future.

EARLY FORAYS INTO INTERGOVERNMENTAL AFFAIRS

AT THE CORE of Canadian federalism is the constitutional division of powers between the federal government and the provinces. Conservatives believe that the country cannot, and should not, be governed unilaterally from Ottawa. We thus came to power with the view that the distinct authorities of the provinces should be respected—a premise repeatedly violated by modern Liberal governments. Naturally, we acknowledge some overlaps in jurisdictions and periodic needs for collaboration, but practical governance will focus the federal government on its own areas of jurisdiction. The same, by the way, is true for the provinces.

That was the approach I wished to signal early to my provincial counterparts. Therefore, on February 24, 2006, I met with the premiers of the provinces and territories for the first time as PM. It was an informal dinner at 24 Sussex Drive.* I had spoken to most of the premiers already, and through Conservative politics I knew several of them personally. Our first session together was cordial and useful, but it also pointed to some challenges ahead.

Every province and territory—PTs in Ottawa-speak—believes its problems are the most pressing ones. The big provinces, with their economic clout and large populations, view their concerns as the most substantial and worthy of superior focus. Smaller provinces, on the other hand, see their smaller size as a source of neglect and a cause for special attention. Those who have growing economies want financial programs that stress their rapidly expanding infrastructure and social service needs. Those with declining or stagnating economies want the emphasis on creating employment and bolstering revenues. Large or small, growing or declining, the one constant is the demand for more money. However, not far below the surface lurk deep disagreements on how those funds should be allocated.

---

* Contrary to what some have written, 24 Sussex was a lovely residence to live in during my time as prime minister. It did need a structural overhaul, but these were not noticeable to the inhabitants, that is, until the building was gutted under Justin Trudeau. Unfortunately, the costs of a rebuild are politically unjustifiable. That is why Jean Chrétien and I have offered to raise the money privately.

Senior officials in the Privy Council Office and Intergovernmental Affairs had much advice on the menu to address these matters. Often, it was too *centralisateur* for the tastes of this *autonomiste*. There were, however, some offerings that proved particularly valuable over time.

One piece of advice was to pay little attention to the partisan stripe of a provincial government. I was told the following: "If a provincial government is doing a good job, it will be a good partner for your government, regardless of its partisan makeup. Likewise, if a provincial government is not doing a good job, all its problems will be your fault." That turned out to be devastatingly accurate.

Another useful counsel was to engage the provinces bilaterally, wherever possible, rather than as a group. Given their differences, it was suggested, policy progress would be hard to make collectively; the end result would only be demands for ever-increasing amounts of money. Conversely, one could get more substantive and cost-effective results one-on-one. The wisdom of that was also often borne out.

For that reason, I conducted precious few large, federation-wide conferences. I avoided them for the same reason the media loved them—the unproductive confrontations they were likely to feature. There were times, nonetheless, when we brought the premiers together under one roof. Those would be times of shared mission and an inclination of all to collaborate. That said, we were always cognizant of one critical need in our "bilateral" PT relations: what we would do for one, we had to be prepared to do for all.

Early on—June 2, 2006—I also met the representatives of local government when I gave my first speech to the Federation of Canadian Municipalities. In contrast to the provinces, municipalities have no status under our Constitution. They are solely creatures of the provinces, who can establish them, modify them, and abolish them. Nevertheless, they are an important reality of Canadian political life and of intergovernmental affairs. I met with municipal leaders regularly, and we worked to address their concerns.

Federal engagement in municipal government had increased enormously during the period of the previous Liberal Government, particularly when

Paul Martin was prime minister. Direct federal funding and tripartite agreements around municipal infrastructure had become an ongoing feature of our system. This was a sea change from my early days in federal politics. Back then, no one thought that they should appeal to the federal government for, say, road improvements in their town or city.

This was a new reality that my Government accepted and, indeed, would build upon substantially over the years. That is not to say I was ever entirely comfortable with it. To start with, I have serious doubts about why municipalities cannot fully finance the kind of infrastructure development they once did. My guess is that, over the decades, funds that used to go to capital projects have been greatly diverted to the pay, perks, and pensions of overexpanded workforces. I also fear that federal funding, though undoubtedly improving local infrastructure across the country, has contributed to that trend.

I was skeptical of this development for philosophical reasons as well. It is, after all, a significant and expanded intrusion into provincial jurisdiction, and one got the feeling that the Liberals sought the ability to play the municipalities off against the provinces. Certainly, that is how Quebec saw it. Its view, clearly and frankly expressed, was that the prime minister was always welcome to meet Quebec municipalities, but that giving money to them directly was strictly out of bounds. That had to be done through the Quebec government. That attitude could be a pain, I admit, but it was one I had considerable sympathy for.

THE "NATION" MOTION

FROM DAY ONE, MY APPROACH to the Quebec sovereignty movement had a Hippocratic ethic: "Do no harm." The "don't have another referendum"/"don't open the constitution" creed had emerged both inside and outside Quebec since 1995. Under such circumstances, it had become apparent that separatist flames would diminish when deprived of oxygen. Unfortunately, the sponsorship scandal had reversed that trend. Yet it was evident that the heat was again dissipating from the issue even in the first few months of our new Government.

The Bloc Québécois, which had unexpectedly lost some seats and votes to us in the election, had to do something to reverse the trend. This they attempted on November 21, 2006. Leader Gilles Duceppe signalled that the upcoming Bloc opposition day motion would be: "That this House recognize that Quebecers form a nation." All these years later—and with the sovereignty movement somewhat diminished—some background is required to explain why this was so dangerous for our Government.

In 1987, the Mulroney Government had managed to get the unanimous agreement of the provinces for a package of constitutional reforms. That was hammered out at the Meech Lake government retreat in Quebec, not far from the prime minister's summer residence at Harrington Lake.* The reforms were designed to address Quebec's opposition to the constitutional changes brought about under Pierre Trudeau in 1982.

The Meech Lake Accord was, in many ways, a remarkable achievement. However, it was reached with little public discussion, input, or even anticipation. While quickly endorsed by leaders both inside and outside of politics, opposition began to grow as Canadians became aware of its contents and its omissions. Much of the debate focused on the provision that declared Quebec a "distinct society" within Canada.

The distinct society clause exposed a deep divide within the Canadian population about the nature of the country. There is one interpretation that sees "one Canada," a country indivisible from coast to coast. There is another that stresses the federation's nature as a union of "ten equal provinces." Finally, there is the view that Canada should be understood as an agreement between "two founding peoples." The distinct society clause, in its full reading, endorsed the third version, and it did so unequivocally. Other parts of the agreement reinforced that interpretation.

---

* Laureen and I enjoyed the Harrington Lake residence even more than 24 Sussex. More on that later.

The Reform Party, in the process of being founded just as the accord was coming together, was one of Meech's first opponents. In fact, Deborah Grey was the first MP to speak out against the Meech Lake Accord in the House of Commons. However, contrary to mythology, our principal concern was not the distinct society clause. It was the provisions of Meech that raised additional constitutional barriers to traditional Western demands like Senate reform. Indeed, it rendered them virtually impossible. But it is fair to say that the ten equal provinces view predominant in Reform found the whole thing unpalatable.

Another of Meech's early critics was Pierre Trudeau, whose opposition provided cover for growing Liberal discomfort with the whole project as time went on. That opposition was much more along the lines of the "one Canada" perspective. It feared that the accord weakened the sense of shared Canadian nationhood and the role of federal government.

Regrettably, as opposition to the Meech Lake Accord rose, its supporters repeatedly suggested that the opponents "rejected Quebec's identity" in what was purely "symbolic recognition." I think it is important to set the record straight. The first attack line was simply unfair; the second was untrue.

The distinct society clause was not just symbolic in character. It was to be an interpretative clause applying to the entire constitution. What this meant in specifics was unknowable, but the Quebec government, having been given substantial power over future appointments to one-third of the Supreme Court, would have a big role in shaping that interpretation. The accusation that this was a route to "special status" was thus not without merit.

As for the "rejection of Quebec" argument, the notion that there was an English-Canadian movement to deny the province's francophone reality and pursue an assimilationist agenda was pure demagoguery. Yes, there were voices that were concerned about the future of anglophone and other minority rights in Quebec. That was a sensitive issue in the context of federal legislation that further promoted French outside the province. It largely explains why, when the Quebec government brought in further restrictions on English after Meech was signed, public support for the accord began to unravel outside Quebec.

Whatever one's view of these events, what happened subsequently is indisputable. The Meech Lake Accord ultimately failed. The attempt to revive it in a wider constitutional settlement—the Charlottetown Accord—was defeated in a national referendum. The most stalwart supporters of the accords, including the federal and Quebec governments, suffered electoral defeat. Finally, the Parti Québécois almost succeeded in its near-miss referendum of 1995.

Who would want to go back to all that? Certainly not most Canadians. Certainly not a prime minister who had just pulled the elements of Canadian conservatism back together. Certainly not Quebec's federalist government. A debate about whether Quebec was "a nation" benefitted only one group—Quebec separatists.

I had made my views on this entire subject matter clear. In the 2006 election I had committed that a government I led would not open the Constitution or propose any changes that would require comprehensive constitutional negotiations. I knew the other federal parties were of the same mind. However, soon after the election, the door to this debate was cracked open.

The Liberals gave the issue life in the leadership race that followed Paul Martin's resignation. One of the leadership candidates was Michael Ignatieff—an undoubtedly intelligent and highly accomplished Canadian. He had, however, spent much of the constitutionally tumultuous years outside the country. Ignatieff proposed recognizing Quebec as a nation during the campaign, thus setting off a divisive debate within the Liberal Party.

Part of what made this issue tricky was the different connotations of "nation" in the English and French languages. In English, we use the terms "country" and "nation" virtually interchangeably. For example, anglophone Canadians invariably refer to Canada as both a country and a nation. In French, though, the term "*nation*" tends more to refer to the concept of a cultural or "national" identity rather than a country or "*pays*." Many Quebecers thus see no contradiction in viewing Canada as their *pays* and Quebec as their *nation.* Conversely, the whole notion of Quebec as a nation, to English-Canadian ears, sounds more like a challenge to national unity than a recognition of cultural identity.

What was unambiguous was that the Bloc saw the opportunity to revive the debates that had divided Canadian federalists and had inflamed Quebec separatism. And they had been (inadvertently) invited to do so by a prominent Liberal. But it was not just the Liberals who would be divided. It was our party as well. Indeed, it was the country that would be divided, and this was the risk I saw immediately. In short, the Bloc motion was clever.

But was the Bloc motion too clever by half? As I thought about how to respond, what struck me was that this really was purely symbolic recognition. In fact, Duceppe had probably gone further than he should have on proposing to label "Quebecers" rather than "Quebec" as the nation. Also, this was merely a parliamentary motion, not a constitutional amendment or even a piece of legislation. Perhaps, I started to think, this was an opportunity to put the whole issue of the recognition of Quebec's nature behind us and to do so quickly.

I talked it through with a few advisors and some senior Cabinet colleagues, particularly my then lead Quebec minister, Lawrence Cannon. I decided I would take control of the agenda rather than leave it in the hands of the Bloc. I would table a motion myself. It would be one that I knew could be supported by most of my caucus, including my Quebec caucus, as well as (after consultation) by the other federalist parties.

We had to act quickly, so I made minimal changes to the Bloc motion: "That this House recognize that the *Québécois* form a nation within a united Canada." The use of the French term "*Québécois*" further emphasized the cultural meaning of the motion. It was not "*Québec*" being recognized or even "Quebecers," but only those Quebecers who saw themselves as part of that francophone identity. In other words, nothing even hinted at special constitutional status for the province itself. And, of course, with the last four words, the motion was now an affirmation of Canadian unity.

I took the text to our caucus for approval that Wednesday morning, and then I tabled it and spoke to it in the House in the afternoon. Interim Liberal Leader Bill Graham was fully supportive, as was NDP Leader Jack Layton. Gilles Duceppe came out with guns blazing.

The opposition of the Bloc strengthened my hand in my caucus and outside Quebec. However, even in Quebec, Duceppe came under fierce attack for rejecting what the mainstream of the population thought was completely reasonable. Within twenty-four hours, the Bloc flipped its position. When the vote took place on Monday, November 27, only sixteen MPs opposed the motion. They were mostly Liberals, but also a few Conservatives—generally hard-core "one Canada" advocates.

But I had not expected and did not need unanimity. The result was sufficient to put to bed the myth that there was some fundamental anglophone rejection of the Québécois as a francophone people. In also reminding everyone that the sovereigntist crowd would never be content with such recognition, it reinforced the wisdom of not taking the matter any further.

It had been a good day for Canada.

BUDGET 2007 AND FISCAL TRANSFERS

IN THE MEANTIME, OUR Government's next budget would have big implications for intergovernmental relations. That budget, entitled "Turning a New Leaf," would be tabled on March 19, 2007. It would address the fiscal imbalance between Ottawa and the provinces.*

No budget ever has a single purpose, and Budget 2007 had a range of important initiatives. There were additional tax cuts. There were major environmental announcements. Even with all those things and more, we were able to project large surpluses. We would pay down $14 billion worth of debt in the year just finishing—the largest since the early post-war period—with another $10 billion projected for the year to come.

---

* Peter Van Loan, who had served as the president of the Progressive Conservative Party of Ontario and the Progressive Conservative Party of Canada, was intergovernmental affairs minister as we were developing these budget measures. He was succeeded by Rona Ambrose before the budget.

Still, our commitment to redress the fiscal disparity created by the Liberals in the 1990s was the most important commitment left from the campaign. The measures that involved would have the largest long-term financial impact of Budget 2007's decisions, while also being its most politically significant and difficult part. The focus would be on what are called the "major transfers"—a group of funding policies the federal government maintains for the provinces and territories.

The major transfers include the Canada Health Transfer (CHT) for healthcare services and the Canada Social Transfer (CST) for other social programs, especially post-secondary education. These transfers include both direct cash payments and tax points, where the federal government effectively gives the provinces some of its taxation power. There are also the Equalization payments, which go to less-affluent provinces, and Territorial Formula Financing (TFF), which is a separate equalization program for the northern jurisdictions. Minor transfers include the Fiscal Stabilization Program, various infrastructure initiatives, payments for the judicial system, and others.

To give some idea of the magnitudes, major cash transfers rose from about $40 billion to close to $70 billion over the course of our Government. As a share, they went from roughly one-fifth of our program spending to about one-quarter. The dependence of PTs on these transfers varied considerably. For Alberta it was as little as 10 per cent of the provincial budget, rising to nearly 40 per cent in the Atlantic provinces, and exceeding 80 per cent for Nunavut. Overall, these payments are critical to the functioning of provincial and territorial governments.

Of all these transfers, the Equalization program is the most misunderstood. Most critically, Equalization as a principle is enshrined in the Constitution of Canada. Its purpose is "to ensure that provincial governments have sufficient revenues to provide reasonably comparable levels of public services at reasonably comparable levels of taxation."* The federal

---

* Constitution Act, 1982, s. 36(2).

government is obligated to provide Equalization; it cannot be abolished. However, the specifics of the program have always been decided solely by the federal government acting on its own.

The differences in these transfers are important for one very big reason: the provinces/territories do not have identical interests. We had committed to reform and enhance the payments based on clear principles that, we hoped, would allow all PTs to make their own spending decisions based on their own diverse needs. But therein lay the rub: the provinces did not agree on what those principles should be. And their preferred principles would change with their fiscal circumstances. When a province went from have-not to have status, or vice versa, then it would invariably take a different position on Equalization. Views on how resource revenues should be handled would vary with the scale of its own resource production.

These differences produced four distinct blocs of PTs, each lobbying us for its preferred set of reforms. One group was the have provinces, which wanted to see less money for Equalization and more for CHT and CST. For the have-not provinces, Equalization was the focus. However, they split into two camps, depending on whether they had substantial non-renewable resource revenues. Those that did not—Quebec, Manitoba, New Brunswick, Prince Edward Island—wanted those revenues fully included in the Equalization calculations. Those that had the resources—Saskatchewan, Nova Scotia, Newfoundland & Labrador—wanted such revenues completely excluded. For the territories, TFF was the overwhelming concern.

The last group was the easiest to address. We augmented TFF and the territories were happy. For them, it was a lot of money. For us, it was a small amount relative to our budget. For the provinces, it was not enough to make them grumble.

The have provinces were not pleased with our intention to increase the generosity of Equalization. However, we had a way of bringing them on board. It was to not just increase CHT and CST but also end the "equalization" portion of that transfer. In effect, the formula under the Liberals had deducted some of their CHT and CST cash—a move justified by arguing that the tax-point portion of the transfer was more lucrative for higher-income provinces. The upshot was that the cash transfers for have provinces were less per capita than for have-not provinces.

This was a long-standing grievance—one that I had heard about in Alberta for years. It was not so much the Equalization program that bothered the Alberta government. It was the fact that every other federal program seemed to have an additional equalization component baked into it. We agreed this was unfair, and we committed to end the "equalization deduction" (immediately) for CHT and (later) for CST. We had the have bloc on board.*

The two have-not groups were going to be the most difficult because their interests were diametrically opposed. The argument for excluding non-renewable resource revenues from Equalization calculations was two-fold. One was practical: those revenues were volatile and highly concentrated in Alberta, so it could be argued that they distorted the overall interprovincial revenue situation. The other was philosophical: such revenues permanently depleted an asset, so they could not be viewed as ordinary income. The existing formula was an odd compromise: non-renewable resource revenues were fully included in theory, but Alberta was excluded from the calculations.

Determined to find a more principled, but creative, approach, we settled on what I would call a King Solomon formula.† We decided we would have

---

* There was a brief hiccup with British Columbia when this was announced. A drafting error by officials would not have given B.C. the full benefits we intended. However, we managed to get that corrected before much controversy arose. Unfortunately, we seemed to have many such problems in this area with the Finance department.

† For those unfamiliar with the reference, in Book of I Kings in the Bible, King Solomon is asked to judge between two women, both of whom claim to be the mother of a baby. Solomon offers a solution: cut the baby in half and give half to each. One agrees to that proposition, and the other expresses her willingness to give up the baby, thus revealing herself to be the true mother.

a 50 per cent inclusion of the non-renewable resource revenues. We thought that this was a reasonable compromise and that we would get grudging acceptance from both sides. We did not. Instead—perhaps we should have expected it—we got a King Solomon reaction. One group acknowledged the judgment as fair; the other group went ballistic.

It was the non-resource provinces that supported the changes. In a way, this should not have been surprising. The reform benefitted them substantially, and they needed the money. For the resource provinces, the Atlantic Accord offsets had already put them in a strong fiscal situation. They had nothing to lose from demanding more and fighting with the federal government.

Dealing with the Holdouts

OBVIOUSLY, THIS WHOLE EXERCISE was a complicated business. Still, I was determined to seek "peace in the family." I would do what I could to bring the three holdout provinces onside.

Saskatchewan proved to be the easiest to deal with, as it well should have been. It was growing and was on the verge of becoming a have province. Under these circumstances, no formula was going to offer it any significant amount of Equalization. I tried unsuccessfully the explain this to the province's NDP government. They refused to accept the fact and made an issue of it in their upcoming election.

It was one of the most bizarre campaigns I have witnessed. The incumbent NDP Government ran on a sky-is-falling theme—poor, struggling, desperate Saskatchewan needed more help from the feds. The opposition Saskatchewan Party of Brad Wall ran on the province's new prosperity, promising to make it permanent. It won handily.

That was the end of the Equalization debate in Saskatchewan. The new government did not want it. Under Wall and his successor, Scott Moe, Saskatchewan has become the country's most consistently well-governed jurisdiction, with the Sask Party now having won five consecutive elections.* Saskatchewan has become a truly have province.

Nova Scotia's opposition to the new formula was also as unfortunate as it was unnecessary. My view is that, with the strident opposition of Newfoundland & Labrador, the PC government in Halifax had wrongly concluded that it would look weak if it did not also "take on Ottawa." In any case, it quickly realized a nasty fight with a fellow Conservative government over an already generous package was not in their interest. It was looking for a creative way out.

That opportunity came in the form of a suggestion from Peter MacKay and former premier John Hamm. Hamm had noted that the original Atlantic Accord had a provision for the province to be awarded something called the "Crown Share,"† an entitlement whose value had long been in dispute. Nova Scotia had received nothing from that provision and was threatening to take the federal government to court.

Hamm and MacKay suggested we work with the province to establish an arbitration to resolve the issue. Premier Rodney MacDonald and I were able to agree to this. Nova Scotia then joined the consensus on the new transfer formulas.‡

That left Newfoundland & Labrador. From the outset, Premier Danny Williams was the most vociferous opponent of our new transfer arrangements. He demanded a 100 per cent exclusion of oil and gas revenues from

---

* I would be remiss if I did not mention the Saskatchewan Party's first leader, my former Reform colleague Elwin Hermanson. Under Hermanson the Sask Party came within a whisker of winning its first two provincial elections, in 1999 and 2003, when no one expected it had a chance in the socialistic province. The transformation of Saskatchewan's political culture really began at that time, and it has been a remarkable evolution from the decades of stagnation it endured, mainly under CCF-NDP governments.

† In short, the Crown Share was an amount Nova Scotia was to receive as compensation for giving up its potential ownership interest in offshore projects.

‡ The arbitration panel would largely side with Nova Scotia on the Crown Share issue, so the process ended up being quite beneficial for the province.

the Equalization calculations and quoted past Conservative support for that idea. Of course, that predated the 100 per cent offset provision for oil and gas revenues that the province had received from Paul Martin. That was, by the way, something the province had won in significant part because of the pressure our party had provided for that demand in the minority parliament.

Williams now wanted both provisions—something that would virtually guarantee Newfoundland & Labrador getting Equalization even if it someday became a have province. And Williams wanted even more. He also demanded that my Government give the province the federal government's ownership share and revenues from the Hibernia oil development.

The problem with acquiescing to that demand was that it had nothing to do with jurisdictional authority. The federal government had already let Newfoundland & Labrador have the royalty income. The money Ottawa received from Hibernia was because it had been a commercial investor in the project.

Newfoundland & Labrador had only joined Confederation fifty-eight years before. It had gained some considerable benefits. Yet coupled with the historic sense of separateness was a subsequent series of critical conflicts with the federal government. The resulting emotional scars always came quickly to the surface in any discussion between Ottawa and St. John's.

In short, Danny Williams was plowing fertile ground when he asserted that the new transfer arrangements would screw Newfoundland & Labrador out of untold billions of dollars. The claim was patently false. We even amended the legislation so that any province could opt back into the old Equalization formula if it would be more beneficial. We were making it clear that Newfoundland & Labrador could not possibly be worse off.

Nonetheless, Williams had the clear support of Newfoundlanders for his position. Our attempts to state the facts fell on deaf ears, drowned out by the passions and the history behind them. It was ultimately our people there who paid the political price. We had three great Newfoundland MPs—Loyola Hearn, Norm Doyle, and Fabian Manning—who took the brunt of rising public anger in the province. After the coming federal election, none would still have their seats.

That was a terrible injustice because these men had been real champions for the province. In the previous Parliament, Loyola and Norm had really whipped our caucus into being a battering ram to help extract those Atlantic Accord amendments from the Liberal Government. Norm retired, but I later appointed him to the Senate. I made Loyola our ambassador to Ireland, where he did a top-notch job. I also named Fabian to the Senate, where he continues to be a strong voice for the province.

I felt bad about the whole situation because Newfoundland & Labrador ultimately gained nothing from it. I also hated being portrayed as some kind of federal bogeyman who was out to destroy the province. I love Newfoundland & Labrador, and the truth is that no prime minister was as sympathetic to Newfoundland's historic grievances as this one. I believe that the province's view of Ottawa is, to a large degree, justified.* But, no matter, minds were made up, and I was henceforth to be considered part of the same old problem.

REFLECTIONS ON OUR EARLY FEDERALIST AGENDA

IT IS NOT LOST on me that, in political memoirs, hindsight can be twenty-twenty. Still, looking back on our election promise to repair the country's fiscal imbalance, I believe that it was the fair thing to do and that it needed to be done. Overall, it was a big success. Bringing twelve of the thirteen provinces and territories on board was no small feat. It did not hurt that we were in good fiscal shape at the time and able to spend the money necessary to make it work.

Yet, once again, the lesson was that it is one thing to promise something big when you are the Opposition; it is something completely different to deliver it when you are the Government. That is a polite way of saying we underestimated the complexity of the issue. I suppose a side benefit of wading

---

* As one example, I had no time for federal officials' tendency to hedge over Quebec's claims to Labrador, which are without merit and a clear violation of the terms under which Newfoundland joined Canada.

deep into fiscal transfers is that I came to understand all the complexities and technicalities of the Equalization formula. It has been joked that there are six people in Canada who get it, and three of them are dead. I would add that, for the three of us who are alive, it is not a particularly marketable skill.

The transfer reform was a significant accomplishment, but did we do it right? What we left was better than what we found. Nevertheless, there remain significant problems with Equalization, in my judgment.

On the practical level, our formula ran into difficulty quite quickly. During the global financial crisis of 2008–2009, we decided to limit the growth of Equalization to avoid skyrocketing payments. It was meant to be a temporary measure, but it remains in place.

On the more philosophical matter, I have come to believe that non-renewable resource revenues should be fully included in the calculations, and I regret having once taken a different position. Revenue is revenue. The fact that it is non-renewable is irrelevant. When the resource runs out, revenue will go down and Equalization will go up. That inverse relationship is the way it should be.

Yet these contortions of the formula happened for a reason that needs to be addressed: the incentives in the Equalization program. It makes no sense that a have-not province is as well off leaving its resources in the ground as it is developing them. Whether we are talking about individuals or governments, one should always be better off with higher income.

I recognize that the solutions to these various problems are neither obvious nor complementary. I still hope that someday a wiser, more patient, even more thick-skinned government will address them. But with the horrible mess that is the fiscal position of the Government of Canada today, that is not likely to happen anytime soon.

The "nation" motion, though short and costless, was an even clearer success for us and for the country. We did not solve the Quebec constitutional issue, but we put to bed the notion that the province was being "rejected" by the rest of the country. That symbolic recognition was important.

It is just as important that it stay symbolic. Unfortunately, some have sought to use the nation motion to argue for special status. That, for example, was attempted by the NDP, when they tried to get the formula for Commons representation changed to effectively give Quebec the seats of other provinces. That was certainly not the intent of my motion or of the vast majority of MPs who voted for it. Yes, Quebec has substantive constitutional aspirations that it can legitimately press. But those must be negotiated in good faith, not assumed merely by linguistic difference.

As for the motion itself, in my heart I would like to have designated all Canadian francophones as the "nation," rather than just the Québécois. Such a notion would have appealed to francophones outside Quebec, a large percentage of whom voted for my Government. But time was of the essence, and it would have involved a more thorough re-working of the motion, with no guarantee of a consensus.*

In any case, dealing with these various matters is the heavy work of federalism, and it cannot be ignored in a country like ours. We had brought a new approach to these issues, consisting of a conservative view of the federation, a focus on bilateral relationships, a respect for divided jurisdiction, and a willingness to seek the kind of honourable compromise that could be extended to all partners in Confederation. That had made our first ventures into national unity largely successful—for us and for Canada.

---

* René Lévesque, for example, spoke of three distinct francophone "nations" within Canada: the Québécois, the Acadiens to the east, and the Canadiens-français to the west. His views may not be universal, but in my experience, the Québécois do see themselves as distinct.

8

CANADA'S PLACE IN THE WORLD

NO GOVERNMENT, AND CERTAINLY no incoming government, ever sets its own priorities in all things. I wish that it were so, but, as John Lennon said, "Life is what happens while you're busy making other plans."[†] Much of that unplanned life over the course of my government came from events outside Canada.

It is in the nature of democratic politics, I think—certainly in Canada—that opposition parties rarely make international affairs a priority. The Conservative Party of Canada was no different, although we were not completely unprepared. We did have both members of Parliament and staff who had been entrusted with various aspects of foreign affairs over the years. For my part, I had not travelled extensively, but I had read broadly on global history and geopolitics.

I also had some exposure to foreign affairs and personalities through meetings and conferences during my time as leader of the Opposition. One such personality was Australian Prime Minister John Howard. Howard's people had been in touch with me when he was chairman of the International

† This quote is widely attributed to Lennon from his 1980 song "Beautiful Boy," but it is close to a line first used by the American writer Allen Saunders in a 1957 issue of *Reader's Digest*. It is not known whether Lennon was aware of the origin.

Democracy Union, the global alliance of centre-right political parties.* He and I shared common perspectives on most things foreign and domestic, and he was the closest thing I had to a mentor when prime minister. I had also picked up some useful knowledge when Paul Martin swore me into the Privy Council, so that I could receive security briefings.†

Nevertheless, once in power, the learning curve needed for global affairs has a substantial upward arc. You are rapidly exposed to a wide set of issues, demands, and information. As I have found in all things, the only way to sort and process what you need to know is to develop an intellectual framework. In hindsight, I believe that, with Peter MacKay as our first foreign affairs minister, we did that surprisingly quickly.

A FRAMEWORK FOR FOREIGN AFFAIRS

IN FORMULATING OUR APPROACH to foreign affairs, we began by asking a very basic question: What is the purpose of our foreign policy? Our answer: It is to protect and promote Canada's interests in the world, and we saw that as based around three pillars. Our foreign relations must protect and promote our security, our economy, and our democracy, or, more

---

* Howard long wanted me to succeed him as chairman of the IDU, but for practical time and travel reasons, I was unwilling to do so while in office. I did eventually become chairman of the IDU in 2018. Founded in 1983 under Ronald Reagan, Margaret Thatcher, Helmet Kohl, and other conservative leaders of the era, IDU parties meet regularly to discuss geopolitics, lessons for campaigning and governing, and the promotion of freedom and democracy around the world.

† This was one of Martin's "democratic reforms," yet it was a mixed blessing for an opposition leader. On the one hand, the Government shares some important information and insights you would not otherwise have. On the other, you are sworn to secrecy about what you learn and therefore somewhat restricted in being able to hold the Government accountable for these matters in the House of Commons.

broadly, the values that underlie our national life. I am tempted to say that this is also the order of the priorities, but that would be an oversimplification. Foreign policy is a three-legged stool that requires constant attention and balance. These considerations thus served as guides throughout our time in government in evaluating our opportunities, our risks, and the nature of our relationship with various foreign governments.

It is also important to note our general take on the world. From the outset, but with increasing data, it became evident that the period of complete American hegemony was passing. That era had begun around 1991–1993 with the Western victory in the Cold War and its immediate aftermath. It began to falter after 9/11, when the upsurge in U.S. patriotism, ambition, and military activity led to two major conflicts that were turning into bloody, expensive, long-term engagements. By 2006, the emergence of China as a long-term competitive threat was evident (for those with their eyes open), and Russia's role as a perpetual disrupter was also increasingly clear. A degree of diffusion of global power was taking place, but in a way that would mean a less clear and more risky global order for Canada.

The other consideration that shaped our views was our evaluation of foreign-policy tools. In brief, we believe that influence in world affairs is principally a consequence of the possession of "hard power." Most notable are the size and diversity of the national economy and the strength and breadth of military capability. It is not to say that "soft power"—diplomacy, development assistance, moral advocacy—are unimportant. But the ability to project these is usually linked to underlying hard-power capabilities.

This framework was broadly consistent with the various conservative viewpoints that made up our Government. All Canada's conservative traditions stress the importance of key allied relationships, recognize the realities of a dangerous world, and wish to possess a full range of tools to protect and promote Canada's interests. Not everyone in my Government agreed on everything in international affairs, but our debates on these issues were usually at the margin and not over principles.

However, this framework was generally not consistent with the thinking of Global Affairs—the then–Department of Foreign Affairs and

International Trade (DFAIT)—and that led to periodic conflict. This is not to say that DFAIT had a diametrically opposed or even a single alternative view of the world. Nevertheless, I would describe much of the department's thinking as focused not so much on a Canada-centric view but on a "global community" perspective. At its worst, that meant a go-along-to-get-along approach, where the priority was "good relations with everyone" as an end in itself rather than a clear focus on Canada's interests. That led DFAIT to often badly misread international developments, as I would experience on more than one occasion.

RENEWING CANADA'S MILITARY

ONE OF MY FIRST in-depth foreign-policy briefings was on Canada's role in Afghanistan. Neither our new Government nor the public at large had fully understood the implications of Paul Martin's decision to make Canada primarily responsible for security in Kandahar province. It was the heartland of Taliban resistance, the single most dangerous province, and an odd choice for a military whose capabilities were widely seen as in serious decline.

From Pierre Trudeau's time in the late-1960s, our armed forces had shrunk in size. With only rare injections of resources, their equipment was largely old and rusting. Accompanying this, not surprisingly, was a decline in morale as well. For us as conservatives, this state of affairs was unacceptable. It was also out of line with the realities of Canada's history, which, liberal revisionism aside, has seen Canada as a consistent, forceful, and disproportionate contributor to global security and the defence of democracy for well over a century.

Unfortunately, there is no guarantee that an under-equipped, undermanned, and demoralized armed forces will not be thrown into tough situations—often by the very people responsible for that sorry state. In such a situation, the chances of failure or serious errors rise, as in the difficulties of the Somalia mission in the 1990s. As the member of Parliament for Calgary West at that time, I had regular contact with the Canadian

Armed Forces. Canadian Forces Base (CFB) Calgary—later all but closed by the Liberals—was in my riding, and I became aware first-hand of the severe troubles plaguing our military.

It was against this backdrop that we developed the Canada First Defence Strategy. While some likely thought the name jingoistic, it perfectly described what we wanted to do, which was rebuild our defences from the inside out. In the person of our first defence minister, Gordon O'Connor, a thirty-year army veteran who had retired as a brigadier-general, we had capable hands to undertake this effort. It also helped that the then–chief of the defence staff (CDS), General Rick Hillier, was one of the most energetic and ambitious commanders in years.

Minister O'Connor laid out six very specific capabilities that the Canadian Armed Forces (CAF) had to be able to undertake—simultaneously, if necessary. Four were domestic: the surveillance and security of our vast territory; the conduct of a major international security event in Canada, such as the Olympics; the response to a significant terrorist event; and the engagement in significant disaster relief. Two were international: the capacity to respond to a short-term crisis or disaster outside our borders, and the ability to sustain a long-term military engagement somewhere in the world.

The military we inherited in 2006 would have been hard-pressed to accomplish some of these, let alone all of them. In later years Walt Natynczyk, Hillier's outstanding successor as CDS, put it succinctly: "We need to have a one-hundred-degree military." He was referring to a force capable of operating from Canada's frigid Arctic to the searing heat of Afghanistan, from fifty degrees below zero to fifty degrees above. Given the state of the CAF, this was no small task.

An early decision in our mandate was to make a major investment in heavy airlift capability. This resulted in Canada's purchase of five Boeing C-17s, the heavy-lift workhorses of advanced militaries around the world. For those who have not seen one up close, it is hard to describe the immensity of these giant birds. By length alone, they are more than half a football field.

The purchase of the C-17s began our rebuild in the right place: upping our logistical capacities. What we learned early on was the importance of having top-notch logistical capacities for air, land, and sea. Those are key to all other capabilities. Without strong logistics, it matters little what other offensive or defensive resources you have because first you need to be able to get in and out of places quickly and effectively.

This applies in both war and peace. For example, our enhanced transport capacity allowed us to expand the effectiveness of Canada's famous DART, the medical and disaster assistance unit that we deploy around the world. Whereas before we had had to pay the Russians to transport us—yes, the Russians—we could now deploy our emergency assistance ourselves and do so rapidly. Our newly acquired aircraft brought the added benefit of making Canada more valuable to our NATO allies, who would periodically call upon our support for airlift. Adding the five planes was a brilliant decision, and Gordon O'Connor deserves the credit for it.

THE AFGHANISTAN MISSION

NEVERTHELESS, ANY PROACTIVE PLANS for rebuilding our military were quickly eclipsed by the urgent challenges of the Afghanistan mission. Canada had been part of the international, American-led military mission to that country since the 9/11 attacks, in which twenty-four Canadians had died. Stockwell Day and I had strongly supported our involvement from the outset.

However, in the weeks preceding our Government's arrival in office, the mission had gone to another level. Why Paul Martin chose Kandahar, I can only guess. But even before that fateful decision, Canada's unpreparedness was evident. Many remember the images, seen around the world, of Canadians clad in green camouflage in the arid mountains and desert, where brown was self-evidently required. Revitalizing the Armed Forces was a Conservative preference, but we quickly discovered we would, in any case, have no choice.

Canada had begun to take casualties even before our Government had taken office, and the likely deadly consequences of this mission were clear from the initial briefings. It was also transparent that our army was under-equipped for what would be by far their most difficult and kinetic engagement since the Korean War. Still, it became apparent in just the first few weeks that things were a hell of a lot worse than even those briefings indicated. The Taliban had been in effective control of much of Kandahar, and they were not planning to surrender it easily. The first few firefights proved alarmingly challenging.

Nonetheless, we were there, and worried as I was, I decided to make a virtue of necessity. I told my Cabinet, defence staff, and officials that we had a bad situation in Afghanistan that, while not of our making, we were going to own one way or the other. There was no point thinking twice about Kandahar; there would be no turning back.

As things got really hot, really quickly, I convened emergency Cabinet meetings to start procuring additional resources. One of the first issues was the vehicle fleet. Readers may recall the controversy around Canada's old Iltis jeeps. They were quickly becoming death traps for our troops as the Taliban stepped up the use of improvised explosive devices (IEDs). Therefore, an immediate priority was the purchase of more light armoured vehicles (LAVs), which were newer and better built to resist such attacks. They, in turn, would be progressively reinforced. But we ultimately had to purchase and deploy a tank force as well.

Of course, the dollars were quickly escalating well beyond expectations. This was all before Parliament had even met. It was clear even to the most knowledgeable among us that the military challenge had been grossly underestimated.

All these things explain why I went to Afghanistan so early: to assure our men and women in uniform that the government was firmly behind what they had been asked to do. In fact, my first foreign trip, on March 13, 2006, was to visit our troops and see the situation on the ground in that country. The message was that we may be a new government, but we were not going to back out of our commitment, neither to our allies nor to our own people.

Going there also showed that not all was doom and gloom. My many visits to Canadian Armed Forces personnel abroad were always exhilarating, and this early trip was surely that, as well as substantively encouraging in several ways. Regardless of the many problems our military faced, I could see in Afghanistan the changing face of the Forces. Compared to what I had witnessed earlier in my political career, the personnel were much younger, much fitter, and much more enthusiastic. They understood that the mission was dangerous, but they had a high level of commitment to it. This idealism and dedication were inspirational and infectious.

That is what makes the people who serve in the Canadian Armed Forces special. They want to make a real difference, make a contribution at a level that most people would never make or even contemplate. Those of us who serve in Parliament believe that we make a contribution to the country, but that never involved putting our lives on the line every single day.

Canada's Afghanistan mission was what is known as a "3-D Mission": integrated defence, development, and diplomacy. Defence, obviously, because nothing could be done without establishing security on the ground. Development assistance, delivered through our provincial reconstruction team in Kandahar. Diplomacy, to try to build political relationships with the local population to create support for the new Afghan government institutions.

Once there, I was caught up in the enthusiasm that was in the air. But I also knew that my presence posed practical problems for my military hosts. I wanted to absorb and understand as much of the experience as I could, and they had the difficult task of making sure I was not harmed in the process.

General Hillier asked me early on: "Well, how far do you want to go?" "Forward operating; I want to go out on a patrol," I replied. He responded quickly—masking his alarm, I am sure: "You're not doing that. You're taking enough risk as it is, and we're not putting you out on patrol!" I did as I was told, but regardless, I ventured pretty far "outside the wire," as they put it, and I think I got a good sense of what we were doing. There were some fascinating experiences, including spending a night with the JTF 2, our special forces, at a forward operating base.

It was a true privilege to go to Afghanistan and be able to assure our troops first-hand that their government was behind them. The worst thing for a soldier's morale is to be put in a high-risk mission with uncertainty about whether your country and its leaders support what you are doing. I was never going to let that happen on my watch, and I wanted them to know that, not second- or third-hand, but directly from me on the ground. I believe they appreciated it, as I was told during the literally hundreds of photographs I took with serving men and women on this and other trips to CAF missions.

All that said, I was already feeling uneasy about the broader aims of the Afghanistan mission as a whole. It had had its roots not just in 9/11 but also in the ambitious "nation-building" agenda of the Bush administration. What I saw in Kandahar was a deeply traditionalist, rural, and tribal Muslim society. Yes, it was very old, but it was also, in many ways, very primitive. I did not see how one would build a Jeffersonian democracy there anytime soon. And while I believe the promotion of democratic values is important, I am by nature more of an old-fashioned realpolitik conservative in international affairs than I am an idealistic neocon. My initial skepticism about what was possible was only beginning to grow.

PREPARING FOR PRESIDENT BUSH

NOT LONG AFTER THE TRIP to Afghanistan, I was off to my first summit—that of the North American leaders. It would be on March 31 in Cancun. That was where Laureen and I had gone on our honeymoon, and I had been back with the family since. It was a place of good memories, even if I was approaching it with some trepidation.

This would be my first meeting as PM with U.S. President George W. Bush. The stakes for Canada are always high when dealing with the Americans. They are our only neighbour, our by-far biggest customer, and our indispensable ally. But really on my mind was the fact that my relationship with President Bush had been difficult when I was Opposition leader.

I know this is contrary to the perception that was out there. After all, it was common knowledge that the members of our party, myself included, tended to have a fairly pro-American view. Certainly, you would not find anti-American hostility deeply held in any branch of the Conservative Party.

Plus these were two "conservative" governments, so why would the relationship be strained even before we met?

It traced back to 2004, when President Bush, on an official visit to Canada, had asked to meet with me as leader of the Opposition.* He wanted to follow up on an issue that U.S. Ambassador Paul Cellucci had raised with me previously—the desire to have Canada join their Ballistic Missile Defence system (BMD). Knowing that we were in a minority parliament and that our attitude for this initiative could be important, they brought on the pressure. They urged us to proactively push the Martin Government to join BMD. If we did, they believed, it would clear the way for Liberals to enter the program, likely under the umbrella of the North American Aerospace Defense Command (NORAD).

I was very uneasy about this. I was not convinced of the merits of the case. I did not fully understand the needs, the costs, or the implications of such a decision. More importantly, I smelled a Liberal trap.

After some digging around, it became clear to me that this notion of pre-emptive Conservative support for BMD was something the Liberals had pushed, not just to the Americans but also to some in the media. But was it true? Would the Liberals really join BMD if we urged it? Or would they continue to decline to do so, depicting us as warmongers who were "in the pockets of the Bush administration." They were already publicly shovelling that stuff, even as they privately told others—but not us—that they needed our support on BMD.

Experience had also taught me to be leery. As Canadian Alliance leader, I had supported the American decision to remove Saddam Hussein in 2003. Through Ambassador Cellucci, the U.S. administration had come to me and asked for support from our party. I had told him that, given our view of the

* This was not completely unusual. In some countries it is conventional, and even expected, for there to be meetings between visiting heads of government and leaders of the opposition. In other countries, it is considered optional, and in others still it is a breach of protocol. In Canada, we have left things fluid, tending to opt for the practices of the visitors.

importance of the relationship, our party would never be "against" the United States. However, I had a couple of requests before our support became vocal.

I told the ambassador that I expected the United States to topple the Iraqi regime in less than a month with minimal casualties. I did not buy the more difficult scenarios some were floating. Still, I wanted to know two things, I said: "First, assure me that you will find these weapons of mass destruction. Second, assure me that you have a plan to govern the country after the victory." Ambassador Cellucci pledged both. Neither turned out to be true.

In the end, I decided to take a cautious approach. We signalled that if the Liberal government were to join BMD, we would support it. But we were not going to be proactive in advocating that position. As it turned out, the Liberals eventually declined to join BMD—and continued to attack us as American-puppet warmongers.

The president, I heard through channels, was not pleased with either the Liberals or us. I knew that Ambassador Cellucci never forgave me. And even though George W. Bush's congratulatory call to me after the election had been quick in coming and friendly in tone, I was not sure what to expect going forward.

CANADA-U.S. RELATIONS

IT IS IN THIS CONTEXT that I was seeking guidance on managing the relationship with the U.S. president. To some degree, my views were already out there. I had made it clear as Opposition leader that the United States was Canada's most important international relationship and that it had to transcend partisan divides, personality differences, or individual disagreements. Fortunately, there were a few individuals who could give me useful additional advice.

Derek Burney was one such person. He had headed my transition team, had once been Canada's ambassador to the United States, and had amassed a wealth of broader foreign policy experience. Michael Wilson, whom I would later name ambassador to the United States, was also a sound thinker on these matters, as he was on many things. This was also a period when I had open lines of communication with Brian Mulroney.

As most readers will know, there were many times when Mr. Mulroney and I were not allies and many issues where we were not in agreement. But it cannot be denied that his success in managing Canada-U.S. relations had been unparalleled. He secured both the Canada-U.S. Free Trade Agreement and Canada's entry into the North American Free Trade Agreement. These were not just important steps in their own right; the negotiations gave Canada exceptional terms (which, of course, would later become an issue under President Donald Trump). I know that Mr. Mulroney also became a valued interlocutor for both Presidents Reagan and Bush Sr.

The advice I received from these and others helped me form a more detailed, definite view about our relationship with the United States. It comes down to this: Canada does itself a disservice when our dealings with them are complaint-based, conducted as the little guy with a chip on his shoulder. The opposite is needed: approach the Americans as a confident partner focused on the big picture.

The United States has enormous global responsibilities. They need friends and allies in the world who can be helpful to them. If you want your concerns addressed, do not go whining to them about this or that irritant. Instead, look for ways to be a partner and collaborator on global matters. Do that, and you will get a hearing when there are legitimate and important problems that need addressing. As in so many things, building a foundation of goodwill, mutual understanding, and trust is the starting point.

That is essential because, as with all relationships, there will be disagreements. We will want things from the Americans they will not give, just as they will make requests of us that we must decline. Believe me, that happened several times with both Bush and, later, Barack Obama. In those circumstances, decline respectfully and in private. The Americans, more than anyone, appreciate a frank and straightforward approach. While you can always score domestic political points by being publicly offside with the United States in some way, such advantages are more than offset by the damage it does to Canada's interests in its most important relationship. And the worst thing a Canadian PM can do is be two-faced: play nice with the president in private and then beak off at him in public.

I believe strongly that this constructive approach consistently served Canada's best interests. I would also stress how important it is that good relations with the United States take precedence over partisan or ideological differences. It was obviously the case that politically I agreed more with Republican George W. Bush's domestic policies than I did with those of Barack Obama, a liberal Democrat. But there was no point in weighing in on how either one was running the United States, any more than we would appreciate them pontificating on how Canada should be governed. What matters is that our countries are fundamentally aligned in international affairs on security concerns, economic interests, and democratic values. That is the basis of our enduring partnership and the secret to managing what are, in comparison, minor differences.

LOOKING FOR AN EARLY WIN

IT DID NOT HELP THAT my first meeting with the American president would be in a trilateral context. I served with three Mexican presidents—Vicente Fox, Felipe Calderón, and Enrique Peña Nieto. All were good colleagues—genuine democrats and friends of Canada. But the integration of our relationship with the United States into this new context has not been ideal for Canada. In fact, I consider it the biggest foreign policy mistake our country has made in modern times.

Our relationship with the Americans is special in a way the Mexican one with their neighbours is not. Yes, we are in a three-way trade pact with increasing integration across both U.S. borders. But Canada is bound in perpetual alliance to the United States, whereas Mexico remains a non-aligned nation. Canadian and American society have been integrated far longer and far more deeply than in the American-Mexican relationship, with democratic traditions that, unlike in Mexico, go back almost two centuries. Finally, American-Canadian relations are remarkably irritant free. The U.S.

relationship with Mexico has long been troubled, and many of those troubles continue to this day in terms of security, criminality, the drug trade, illegal immigration, and many other issues.

In short, folding our bilateral talks with the Americans into a largely trilateral partnership, particularly given the emphasis in recent years on border security, has been very unhelpful for this country. How did this come about? It was an outgrowth of 9/11 and the subsequent U.S. invasion of Iraq. The Chrétien Government's opposition to the invasion, though later proven correct, was done in a public and undiplomatic manner that was very injurious to Canada. It put additional space between our countries at just the time when the American instinct was to "thicken" the border.

In fairness, Mr. Martin attempted to fix the situation. It was under his government that the North American Leaders' Summit and the trilateral Security and Prosperity Partnership were instituted, precisely to re-establish a closer dialogue with the Americans. Those new trilateral arrangements were better than what we had, but it was not where we needed to be.

Nevertheless, there was time for a bilateral discussion in Cancun, and it went well. Unlike our earlier meeting, Bush and I hit it off immediately on a personal level. I wanted to improve the tone and substance of relations, and I quickly saw that he wanted the same thing. We started to talk about what we could do to "re-set"—that word had not yet achieved its later, infamous meaning—our partnership.*

I first proposed that we look at ways of deepening our economic relationship beyond NAFTA. Obviously, there was some self-interest in my raising this issue. In a few short years, we had gone from having largely open crossings with the United States to escalating levels of security checks, bureaucratic procedures, and border regulations. If we could deepen NAFTA, this could, besides the potential economic benefits, be a mechanism to re-establish a unique bilateral dialogue and thin the border once again.

---

* I refer, of course, to Hillary Clinton's gift of the "re-set" button to Russian Foreign Minister Sergei Lavrov—a geopolitical blunder for the ages.

This idea, however, was a non-starter. To my surprise, President Bush and his people immediately made clear their view that "NAFTA could no longer pass the United States Congress in either house on either side of the aisle." I had not appreciated the extent of that shift in public opinion over the previous twenty years. Neither, apparently, had our foreign policy establishment, for I had received no briefings to this effect.

While the advent of CUSFTA and NAFTA had been extremely contentious in Canada, that was not so much the case in the United States. Yet Canadians had come to view these trade deals as a great success, which, by objective measures, they have been. Still, American views had become progressively more negative. Remember, this is 2006 I am talking about—a decade before the election of Donald Trump.

The second thing I proposed was more to the point—that we might look at streamlining security across the border, while enhancing co-operation between our two countries. Although President Bush and I would later do some work on that front, the truth is that progress was limited. The problem was the creation of the U.S. Department of Homeland Security in the post-9/11 period.

Homeland Security quickly became a threat-obsessed leviathan that eschewed economics—and sometimes common sense as well. Much of the thinking was a simple "fortress America" mentality, although there were legitimate concerns. In particular, the Americans did not trust that agreements reached with our elected governments would survive challenges in the increasingly unpredictable Canadian courts. So, for the time being anyway, that was a non-starter too.

Then we moved on to another item, one that had been central in post-Iraq tensions: softwood lumber. This issue, the longest-running of Canada-U.S. trade disputes, has vexed our relations almost since Confederation. So much so that it was judged too hot to be addressed in the CUSTA and NAFTA discussions.

In trade disputes and in negotiations generally, I always try to understand the other side's point of view. It ultimately helps in trying to find a resolution. But to put my editorial two cents in, I have never been able to rationalize the American approach on softwood lumber. At its core, their argument has been that because we do not apply the same taxes, i.e., stumpage fees, on lumber that they do, we are therefore subsidizing the industry. As a conservative, it is pretty hard to justify seeing a lower tax as constituting a subsidy, but that is the essence of their position.

I am not alone in this view. Over the years, during periods when the United States imposed penalties on us, and we litigated those measures, we have done well in the eventual trade tribunal judgments. Unfortunately, those cases have dragged on, with the Americans getting angrier and coming up with revised remedies. For Canada, it was often a case of winning the battle but losing the war. In the end, we usually ended up settling for a separate, softwood lumber trade pact to avoid the penalties and further litigation.

This was the case once again. We were getting hammered with American duties, and we were headed back to the international trade tribunals. We would probably win, but what would be the damage in the meantime? To his credit, and to my surprise, when I raised softwood, President Bush said, "Look, Stephen, let's solve this one."

That is easier said than done because Canada's lumber industry has regional differences that point toward contradictory solutions. But Bush agreed early to my request that the various provinces—even the different parts of British Columbia—get their own terms. Without that concession, in which Bush demonstrated both a real understanding of the complexity of the issue and a high desire to get a resolution, a deal would not have happened.

In fact, it was a great deal, which I announced on April 27, 2006—the best Canada had ever had on softwood. Under normal market conditions, Canada would face no penalties on its softwood exports. In tighter markets—which, unfortunately, would occur during the global financial crisis—the various regions would have a choice of tariffs or quotas, except for the Atlantic provinces and the Northern territories, which would be exempted under all circumstances. In the meantime, some 80 per cent of the collected Canadian duties would be returned.

Overall, this was very well received. The provinces and virtually all lumber companies were on board (although the media gave lots of airtime to the one

The Harper home in Leaside, where we lived until 1971. *(Courtesy of the author)*

The Harper boys celebrating Christmas, 1967. Left to right: Grant, Robert, and Stephen. *(Courtesy of the author)*

The Harper family at our home in Etobicoke, 1977. Left to right: Stephen, Joe, Margaret, Robert, and Grant. *(Courtesy of the author)*

Far left: During my short and (memories to the contrary) unsuccessful hockey career, 1972. *(Courtesy of the author)*

Immediate left: My official collector card as a Reform Member of Parliament, 1996. *(Courtesy of the author)*

Top: Sharing a laugh with Preston Manning, 2009. *(Deb Ransom)*

Middle: With an early mentor, former Member of Parliament Jim Hawkes, 2013. *(Jason Ransom)*

Bottom: With Reform's first Member of Parliament, Deborah Grey, 2013. *(Jill Thompson)*

A monumental day as Peter MacKay and I announce our agreement to merge the Canadian Alliance and Progressive Conservative parties, October 16, 2003. *(The Canadian Press/Tom Hanson)*

Election night in Calgary, 2006. *(Deb Ransom)*

Meeting with Michael Wilson, soon to be Canada's next ambassador to Washington, and Peter MacKay, Minister of Foreign Affairs, 2006. *(Jason Ransom)*

Conservative Party of Canada's campaign manager, Senator Doug Finley, 2009. *(Deb Ransom)*

Reviewing budget documents with members of the Cabinet, 2009. *(Jason Ransom)*

Spending a few extra moments in the House of Commons, 2010. *(Jason Ransom)*

Being greeted at 10 Downing Street by Britain's
Prime Minister Tony Blair, 2006. *(Jason Ransom)*

Having tea with former British Prime Minister Margaret Thatcher, 2006. *(Jason Ransom)*

With troops during a tour of the forward operating base Ma'Sum Ghar in Kandahar province, Afghanistan, 2007. *(Jason Ransom)*

Visiting the Kicking Horse Canyon bridge on the Trans-Canada Highway with B.C. Premier Gordon Campbell to announce major infrastructure funding, 2007. Premier Campbell would later serve as Canada's High Commissioner to the United Kingdom. *(Jason Ransom)*

National Chief of the Assembly of First Nations Phil Fontaine responds to the official apology for the Indian residential school system at a ceremony in the House of Commons, 2008. *(Jason Ransom)*

With Governor General Michaëlle Jean during the Remembrance Day Ceremony at the National War Memorial, November 11, 2008. *(Deb Ransom)*

Governor General David Johnston delivers the Speech from the Throne, 2013. *(Jason Ransom)*

Swearing in Parliamentary Secretaries, 2008. *(Deb Ransom)*

With Gary Doer, Canada's Ambassador to the United States and former Manitoba Premier, in New York City, 2013. *(Deb Ransom)*

or two that opposed the deal). It passed easily in the minority House of Commons. The Liberals, however, did quietly vote against it, and they never forgot that opposition. Thus, many years later, when our successors had an opportunity to renew the agreement, they foolishly allowed it to slip away.

MY FIRST FOREIGN POLICY "CRISIS": THE SECOND LEBANON WAR

THE MIDDLE EAST THRUST itself onto my agenda even before I was sworn in. The Palestinian elections, held on January 25, 2006, resulted in a legislative majority for Hamas. It is an avowed terrorist organization, opposed to Israel's existence and supported by Iran.

When the governing Fatah of President Mahmoud Abbas indicated it would form a coalition under a Hamas prime minister, we deemed this unacceptable. We immediately followed Israel in announcing our government would not recognize the coalition and would cut aid. Despite the misgivings of some in Foreign Affairs, the Middle East Quartet—the United Nations, United States, European Union, and Russia—soon took the same position, along with other Western nations.

A more challenging situation arose on July 12 as I prepared to depart for my first G8 Summit in St. Petersburg, Russia. Hezbollah, another terrorist organization, increasingly embedded in Lebanon and its government, attacked Israel with rockets and anti-tank missiles, accompanied by a raid into Israel that killed and captured some Israeli soldiers. By the time I was boarding the government Airbus, Israel was retaliating. I unequivocally backed its right to do so. Within days, the situation morphed into an all-out war.

Given later events, it was fortunate that my first international meeting to discuss the situation occurred in the company of Canada's closest allies. In St. Petersburg the immediate reaction of President Bush and, especially, Prime Minister Tony Blair of Britain was like-minded, unambiguous support for Israel. However, the dialogue was initially restrained.

The fallout from the Iraq invasion was still very much in the air. The social interaction of Bush and Blair with President Jacques Chirac of France was notably limited. Still, once formal discussions got going, all but one leader took a similar stance. Only Vladimir Putin held out, initially being vague in his assessment. I told him point-blank: "You are the host of the G8; you have to decide if you are really part of the G8, or if this is really just the G7+1." On this occasion at least, that argument seemed to bring Putin around.

In the meantime, the human cost of the crisis was quickly escalating. Complicating it all were the tens of thousands of Lebanese with Canadian citizenship who were caught in the conflict. In truth, they ranged from those who were full-time Canadian residents just visiting Lebanon to people who, through a ridiculously loose process, had been able to get Canadian citizenship with only a tenuous connection to the country. Regardless, all of them understandably wanted one thing—to get out.

There we were, on the other side of the Atlantic Ocean with room to spare on our airplane. We decided to help. As officials in Ottawa worked away on a full-fledged airlift, we turned our big, camouflaged military aircraft around and headed to the region. We landed in Cyprus, where we agreed to evacuate some of the initial groups of Canadians who had gotten that far.

That was the right thing to do. We were able to carry back a couple of hundred fleeing citizens, in what was only the beginning of a full-scale humanitarian effort by Canada. Almost without exception, the returnees were deeply grateful. I want to make this point because there were media reports at the time about some evacuees criticizing the conditions and making outrageous demands. With one or two exceptions, nothing could be further from the truth. These citizens were immensely appreciative, thanking me and the country, often with tears in their eyes and, in some cases, kissing the ground when we landed. For someone born in Canada, it is uplifting to see that kind of love of our country.

Despite the G7 consensus, it turned out that we were not done with our position on the Second Lebanon War. In late September I attended my first summit of the Organisation internationale de la Francophonie in Bucharest,

Romania. As is typical at such meetings, a final declaration had been negotiated by all the countries well in advance, and that declaration had "consensus," meaning, in diplomatic-speak, unanimity. Then, just a couple of hours before the official end of the gathering, Jacques Chirac, in league with Egypt, insisted that the Romanian Chair entertain a new statement on the Second Lebanon War.

Re-opening the declaration for a new motion at such a late hour was highly irregular. Even more inappropriately, the French-Egyptian resolution condemned the State of Israel as solely responsible for the conflict—completely contrary to what Chirac had already agreed to in St. Petersburg. The motion was, of course, untrue and unbalanced. Yet no one appeared willing to object—until I did.

I have many weaknesses, but one is not a fear of saying "no." A lot of people do not like saying "no"—even if it is just to a salesman over the phone—and elected office is full of such persons. Not me. This is not a boast, and I do not think I am a contrarian by reflex, but I have no problem disagreeing when I do not feel the argument on the other side has merit. In such cases, pressure is not going to change my view. If you can make a compelling argument, you can move me. But if it is clear that you are badgering me because you have no compelling argument, I am not going to bend. In fact, I am more likely to get my back up.

That was the case here, where I was being asked to attack and marginalize a democratic Western ally on grounds that were plainly and categorically false, not to mention completely contrary to our Government's previous declarations. But the pressure was on, some of it coming from our own officials not wanting to be "offside with the consensus." It began with an effort to tinker with the wording to get me to alter the substance of my position. It culminated in a heated meeting with Chirac, who essentially declared that what France wants at the Francophonie, France should get.

I did not budge—I could not have and retained any foreign policy credibility—and I blocked the declaration. I half-jokingly told my team that "after four hundred years, I have declared Canada's independence from France." But it was no light matter, with international headlines blaring out that I had single-handedly prevented agreement among some fifty-plus francophone nations.

In truth, it was not nearly that simple. Some of the more Western-oriented nations had whispered to me that they agreed with my position. Many developing countries, who were aid recipients of both France and Canada, just wanted the dispute to go away. It was really only a small minority of the organization's members who felt strongly. The rest were, to be blunt, just going along to get along, as some of our officials so badly (and typically) wanted to do.

Two months later I found myself in Riga, Latvia, for my first summit of the leaders of the North Atlantic Treaty Organization. In the company of NATO allies, Chirac suddenly seemed to be back to his position at the G8, and the controversy did not come up again. However, my Government's support for Israel would. I had not intended to make it such a high-profile plank in our foreign policy, but the events in Bucharest had assured that. Fortunately, my position—rooted as it was in support for an allied Western nation—was strongly supported by virtually every member of my Conservative caucus.

MEMORABLE EARLY BILATERAL VISITS

ALTHOUGH I WAS ALREADY RUSHING from summit to summit, there was time for a number of bilateral visits with foreign leaders. Those were always valuable, particularly because of a practice I developed early on. That was my insistence on a tête-à-tête—a private, one-to-one meeting with my counterpart with (if necessary) only a translator present. Such an encounter would usually precede the larger, more formal meetings.

The fact is that there is nothing as good as that kind of a meeting with a fellow head of government. You can connect on a personal level. You can begin to distinguish between the official position and what is really driving it. You get to understand the political thinking behind the stance. What is the *real* calculation? What *really* matters and what does not? Where can a fellow leader deal and where are they up against a wall? And what makes this guy or gal tick? You can read a hundred pages of briefings and sit through a dozen formal meetings, but you will not get the insights you will get from one-on-one interaction.

I also benefitted immensely from sharing the challenges and lessons of leadership in such meetings. Leaders have experiences that are unique to their position. After all, precious few people are, have been, or will be leaders of their countries. These intimate discussions allowed for an exchange of unique knowledge, even if the political situations, cultural contexts, and policy issues often differed. And, of course, you form friendships. In short, these encounters added greatly to my understanding and effectiveness as a national leader.

On the other hand, officials hated this, especially at first. They worried—no doubt based on previous experience—that I might start making commitments in such meetings. I would not. Just the same, diplomats love to be in meetings, like to take notes, and fret when they are out of the loop. At a certain point, they do need to be in it. Yet I saw very early on the tendency of foreign affairs officials to write down literally everything during meetings and then circulate such notes shockingly widely. On more than one occasion, that caused a problem for us (and, conversely, benefitted us when we got similar information from other countries' officials).

There were far too many bilateral visits to list them all. Still, several stand out for me from my early days as prime minister. Often, these coincided with visiting leaders addressing our Parliament.

One of the first was Hamid Karzai, president of Afghanistan, who spoke to the House of Commons on September 22, 2006. It is fair to say that, over time, allied evaluations of Karzai and his administration became increasingly critical. Still, that day, he delivered a deeply heartwarming speech of appreciation for the involvement of Canadians in his country—soldiers, diplomats, aid workers—and for their efforts to secure and improve the lot of the Afghan people. It resonated as genuine and heartfelt, and it was good to hear at a time when the challenges of the Kandahar deployment were becoming all too evident to the public.

Another memorable visit was from Ukrainian President Viktor Yushchenko, who addressed our Parliament on May 26. His time as president proved to be increasingly difficult, with his popular support collapsing at the end. But he was one of the heroes of the Orange Revolution, saving Ukraine from an attempt by pro-Russian elements to undermine its democracy and independence. He was also a heroic figure in the struggle—his sacrifice carved into his face from the skin disfigurement caused by a poisoning attempt by (one presumes) Putin's thugs. Yushchenko's speech was a reminder to us all that freedom comes with a price. Sadly, it would not be the last where Ukraine is concerned.

A week earlier, I had hosted my friend and colleague John Howard, then prime minister of Australia for over a decade. I mentioned John previously as a conservative mentor, and in that regard, his speech to Parliament did not disappoint. Its main theme was that shared Western values matter deeply and that, should like-minded Western democracies fail to stand up for them, the long-term security and prosperity of our societies will be eroded. He put particular emphasis on the alliances Canada and Australia are part of and of the United States' leading role in those alliances. He warned that those who decried American leadership would regret the day when the United States no longer wished to lead. That would become prophetic years later.

In terms of personal experiences, however, there was no topping the meeting I had on July 14, 2006, with Baroness Margaret Thatcher. It occurred on the margins of my travel to the G8 Summit in St. Petersburg. Our delegation stopped in London where we had much on the schedule, including a courtesy call with Her Majesty the Queen—typical for a new Canadian prime minister—and a visit to Tony Blair at 10 Downing Street. You would think that meeting the Queen and the current prime minister would be the highlight—I had already met the Queen as Opposition leader—but the Thatcher appointment was special.

Since I was a young conservative, I had been an admirer of Thatcher as one of the leaders who, with Ronald Reagan, had brought the Cold War to a successful conclusion. She had also turned Britain around economically and politically. I know she remains controversial—consequential leaders always are—but she unequivocally changed the trajectory of Britain for the better. At least since World War II, if not earlier, Britain had been in consistent national and international decline and, worse, had accepted that as its narrative. Thatcher reversed that, so much so that successive Labour Governments never undid her core reforms.

I had been warned that Thatcher's mental acuity was in decline, but I can assure you there were no signs of it on that day. She came into the meeting thoroughly aware of my political career, and well briefed on our platforms, my speeches, and the actions my Government had taken to date. She gave me a grilling about what we were up to, why we did what we did, and offered her frank evaluation of our prospects. As you might expect, her search was for greater clarity, and her advice was always toward greater boldness. She really boxed this young pup around the ears for more than an hour. I might have taken it badly had it not been Margaret Thatcher doing the boxing, but as it was, being schooled by a master was a grand experience and a great memory.

In the fall of 2006, I met with Kofi Annan, secretary-general of the United Nations. I had gone to New York to give my first talk at the UN and was fortunate to be able to spend some time with him. The UN is neither the model of global governance some on the left hope for nor the international leviathan some on the right fear. As my late father said, "the UN is what it is: the sole forum for all of humanity—the good, bad, and ugly."

The UN building itself was a disappointment for a first-time visitor like me. Most parts of it were in shockingly poor repair and stuck in a design time warp. Still, like all Canadian governments, ours was engaged with the UN on multiple levels through its many agencies. That said, a conservative administration like ours would never subordinate the country's vital security, economic, and democratic interests to that organization.

I met Annan with, among others, Ian Brodie, my then–chief of staff. I had met Ian as a graduate student in the early days of Reform, and he had worked for me in increasingly senior positions after I became leader of the Opposition. Ironically, he and I had grown up only a couple of blocks apart in Leaside, but—no one believes it—this was a fact we did not discover until after he became my chief.*

Anyway, Brodie and I were exceedingly impressed with Annan. He was thoroughly briefed, on top of everything, and saw big pictures very clearly. But his term did not overlap with mine for long, as he left office at the end of 2006. However, he did leave behind a consensus on the sharply defined Millennium Development Goals, which would prove critical in the development of our Government's foreign aid policies.

In October of that year, I was privileged to open the Global Centre for Pluralism in Ottawa, where I was joined by the His Highness the Aga Khan IV, Imam of the global Ismaili Muslim community. I had links to that community going back to my university days when Alnoor Lakhani, now a resident of Vancouver, was my roommate. Through Alnoor, we came to have several mutual Ismaili friends. Every Ismaili carries a picture of the Aga Khan, so after all those years, it seemed surreal to be standing in front of the man himself, right in my office.

That visit began a strong and productive relationship that continued until his passing in 2025. Much of our work with the Ismaili Imamat involved philanthropy and international development. The Aga Khan Development Network is one of the world's greatest organizations in terms of improving the lot of humanity in large parts of the world. The Aga Khan IV also had incredible international networks, a deep knowledge of global affairs, and close connections to many current leaders and events. Over time, he became a real source of advice on many matters.

I ended my travels in 2006 when I made an unscheduled trip to Mexico to attend the inauguration of its new president, Felipe Calderón. He had won the election to replace outgoing President Fox by a hair's breadth. His defeated opponent was the radical populist-leftist candidate Andrés Manuel López Obrador. AMLO had refused to recognize the results, and his actions

---

* Ian is eight years younger than me, which means, as kids, we lived in different worlds.

felt increasingly like an imminent coup attempt. Mexico City was essentially under siege for the inauguration ceremony.

Between the Americans and ourselves, we decided we should send a high-level delegation to show support for the democratic transition of power. I went down to represent Canada and was joined on the American side by former President George H.W. Bush and Governor Arnold Schwarzenegger of California. The mood was electric and you could feel the tension in the air. It was positively eerie, the city swarming with military and police and feeling like a powder keg where violence could break out at any moment.

Some fighting actually did erupt in the hall of Congress as the inauguration ceremony progressed. There was screaming and fisticuffs as the factions fought for control of the proceedings. I remember Bush yelling, "Arnie, you've got to get down there and straighten them out," as if Schwarzenegger actually was one of those movie characters who could take on a whole army by himself. Eventually, to our relief, Calderón was inaugurated.

That trip established some useful relationships, but more than anything, it was a graphic lesson in the fragility of democracy and the passions that politics can unleash. As for AMLO, he eventually became divorced from his party—the Party of the Democratic Revolution, Mexico's traditional leftists—establishing his own personal vehicle instead and becoming president in 2018. He left office in 2024 and was succeeded by his hand-picked candidate. AMLO proved to be every bit as worrisome as we feared, with corruption and cartel power reaching new heights and the rule of law and democracy being gradually dismantled.

FIRST BRUSH WITH THE PEOPLE'S REPUBLIC OF CHINA

CANADA'S MOST IMPORTANT RELATIONSHIP by far is the American one—of that there can be no doubt. Our connections to the British and French retain immense historical, cultural, and geopolitical relevance. But by the time I became prime minister, another relationship was pushing its way onto the list of those requiring special attention—that with the Chinese. As many officials and businesspeople would never fail to point out, China not only is the world's most populous country and its second-largest economy but also has become a distinct world power whose influence is destined to grow under all plausible scenarios.

That assessment was one that I share, but it tells only part of the story. Unlike America, Britain, and France, China is not aligned with Canada on the critical axes of foreign policy. It is not simply misaligned on the values around democracy and human rights. It is—and was long before the arrival of Xi Jinping—both an economic competitor and a significant risk in areas of national security. While its growth represents opportunity for Canada, that potential had not been realized in the relationship when we took office. The benefits of both trade and investment had been radically skewed in favour of the Chinese, partly because of the one-sided terms under which the People's Republic of China (PRC) was admitted to the World Trade Organization in 2001.

In view of these realities, few in our new Government shared a desire for the previous Liberal administration's obsequious approach to China. That put us offside most of our officials—security officials were the exception—and much of the corporate community. Yet we had no intention of "confronting China" out of the gate. However, in no time at all, the Chinese decided to confront us.

The occasion was my first Asia-Pacific Economic Cooperation (APEC) Summit, which would take place in Hanoi, Vietnam, on November 17–19, 2006. As I prepared to leave the country for the trans-Pacific voyage, the Chinese announced the "cancellation" of their bilateral meeting with me via the Canadian media. Except that we had not agreed upon a meeting; only preliminary negotiations had been held.

This was clearly a demonstration of typical PRC power games. On cue, a chorus of officials, businesspeople, and journalists quickly engaged—at various volume levels—urging me to undertake symbolic forms of bended knee to "fix the relationship." But what had caused this one-sided spat in the first place? No doubt it was in part Chinese unease with our Government, which did not intend to be the client-state they had become so accustomed to. More specifically, the Chinese were apparently annoyed at my insistence in raising the case of Huseyincan Celil in any initial meeting.

Celil is a Chinese-born Canadian citizen of Uyghur background, that is, he is from the Chinese region of Xinjiang, which has traditionally been dominated by a Turkic people of Muslim faith. Around the time my government came to power, Celil had been visiting family in Uzbekistan. There, he had been seized by police and extradited to China. China then refused to recognize his Canadian citizenship and the rights of Canadian officials to provide him consular assistance.

The case was self-evidently outrageous, and I had a responsibility to raise it, regardless of Chinese bullying. I made it publicly clear that we were not going to be cowed on issues of human rights where it involved Canadian citizens and that I would raise the Celil issue with Chinese president Hu Jintao at the first opportunity. This I intended to do whether or not there was an official meeting.

I am not a confrontational person by nature, but I was not going to let this kind of thing slide. After I arrived at the APEC venue and was escorted into the green room where the leaders gather prior to such events, I sought out President Hu. I proceeded to give him a piece of my mind at great length. I was not subtle. I made it clear that denying Celil's rights as a citizen ensured that his case would stay high on my agenda. I also reminded Hu of the privileged access the PRC had to Canadian markets, and I made it clear that, given our trade imbalances, he had a lot more to lose from an antagonistic approach than I did. But Hu is a tough guy, and he gave as good as he got.

Our rather high-volume conversation must have gone on for a good hour, with other leaders in easy listening range. Frankly, it is the kind of thing that makes the Chinese uncomfortable. Gradually, the dialogue became quieter and more constructive in tone. In fact, it set the stage for many later conversations with Hu, which were always frank and appropriately private, even if we frequently disagreed. The Chinese rarely played any games with me after that.

Unlike our predecessors, we began to actually get some things out of the Chinese. I also raised the Celil matter at every subsequent meeting. The PRC did end up granting our officials consular access, although they never officially recognized his Canadian citizenship. Sadly, he remains in a Chinese prison.

There were some in bureaucratic and business circles who had urged me to forget Celil altogether. One senior official went so far as to suggest that Celil was in fact the Uyghur terrorist the Chinese alleged. Given that he had been granted citizenship, that would have indeed been a revelation. I asked the official to bring me the evidence. None was forthcoming. It was, as I said at the time, nothing but the attempt to abandon a Canadian just to protect the almighty dollar. It was an eye-opener on the extent and power of Chinese government influence in our country.

Given the Celil experience, I was hardly surprised when the Chinese seized the "two Michaels" in an ongoing dispute with the government of my successors. The cynic in me cannot help but note that, because these prisoners were more like our bureaucratic and business elites, concern for their well-being was much higher.

A BUSY START

AS IS APPARENT, THE FIRST YEAR or so in government had produced countless interactions with foreign countries and rapid development of the key elements of our foreign policy. Of course, this was only the beginning, with much more coming into play, and into place, in the years to come. In the meanwhile, there were things to be done at home in terms of shaping Canada's place in the world. Our gaze first turned to the North.

9

—

THE NORTH: CANADA'S CALL TO GREATNESS

BY THE SUMMER OF 2007, we were wrapping up our first session as a government. By then, a sixth priority had already taken shape: our Northern Strategy.

I have always been infatuated with our country, its history, and its geography. Some of that I picked up from my father, who also had those interests, and some from the times I grew up in. I was a boy in the 1960s. Among other things, it was very much an age of Canadian nationalism. There was the new flag, the centennial celebrations, Expo 67, and more. I guess all that rubbed off on me.

To my mind, one of our truly greatest strengths is our geography. There is no nation on earth that has more space and more resources for the size of its population than ours. And if you are talking about that space and those resources, then you are talking about Canada's North. We are a northern nation, probably the most truly northern nation on the planet.

I believe that this is what defines us. The United States also has a geographic narrative. For decades, the call was to "go West, young man," to the American frontier. In Canada the frontier was and is the North. It is one of the reasons that, when I first left home, my destination was Edmonton, southern Canada's "Gateway to the North."

I know I am not alone in my fascination. The North has long had a grip on Canadians' imaginations. For centuries, explorers tried to master it, and readers have been thrilled by their (often deadly) exploits in those attempts. They have consumed the accounts of poets like Robert Service, writers like Jack London, and popular historians like Pierre Burton.

At the close of the 19th century, the Yukon gold rush made Canada's North home for tens of thousands and alerted the world to the massive resources it contained. After World War I, Canadians followed the exploits of bush pilots and others who defied the elements to provide essential services and further exploration. In World War II, vital infrastructure was constructed in the North as part of the global struggle against fascism. Finally, the Cold War drew our attention to the Soviet Union on the opposite shores of the Arctic and made our governments aware that they could not take the North for granted.

THE FIRST NORTHERN TOUR

HAVING A PERSONAL FASCINATION with the North and making it a government priority are two very different things. Interestingly, the North found its way onto our platform almost as an afterthought. We had settled upon the Five Priorities as the backbone of the 2005–2006 campaign, but it was going to be a long race, and we were looking for other issues to augment them. It was then that some of our former-PC friends brought it up: "What about the North?"

The PCs had a proud heritage in the North. John A. Macdonald had brought the lands into Confederation. John Diefenbaker had his famous "Northern Vision"—a key element in his landslide victory in 1958. And Brian Mulroney's Government had created Nunavut.* For the new Conservative Party of Canada, it seemed logical to build on that legacy.

---

* Although Nunavut did not come into existence until 1999, the Nunavut Act had been passed in 1993 as one of that PC Government's final pieces of legislation. While efforts at splitting the Northwest Territories had begun in the 1960s, it was the Mulroney Government that finally drove it to a conclusion.

During one lull in the campaign we went to Winnipeg and announced our intention to have a northern agenda, with a focus on northern sovereignty. We did not want this to sound too Dief-like, but it was a northern agenda, nonetheless. This announcement was merely one of many we made. Yet, to my pleasant surprise, it seemed to capture the public imagination as it had earlier captured mine.

The first step would be a northern tour, which we planned for the summer of 2006.

From August 12 to 17, 2006, I undertook that initial visit. It would be the first of nine annual summer journeys I would take throughout my time in office. These were supplemented with numerous stand-alone visits at other times of the year. We always covered the three territories, with periodic visits to northern Quebec and northern Manitoba as well. Many people do not realize that the northern third of Quebec is an Arctic region, Nunavik, populated mainly by Inuit. And notwithstanding Edmonton's claims, it is Churchill, Manitoba, that is the true Gateway to the North. Sitting at the spot where the boreal region meets the Arctic tundra, it has played that role for centuries.

That first northern tour was a time of personal discovery and great memories, and a template for those that followed. I went to all three capitals—Iqaluit, Yellowknife, and Whitehorse—and I made a major address on our northern agenda at the first. In those and the other communities I visited I was always greeted on the tarmac by the local unit of the Canadian Rangers.

The Canadian Rangers are Canadian Armed Forces (CAF) reserve units stationed throughout our northern communities—hence you will often hear them referred to as the Northern Rangers or Arctic Rangers. They are lightly armed, then using old but reliable Lee-Enfield rifles, supplemented by survival equipment and skills. Canada relies on the Rangers for surveillance over the large stretches of our territory that the regular CAF cannot routinely reach on land.

My visit to Alert, Nunavut, was a particularly memorable part of that first trip. For Canadians who do not know, Alert, on the far end of Ellesmere Island, is the most northerly inhabited place in the world and has been for decades. It was named after HMS *Alert*, a British ship of exploration that wintered nearby in 1875–1876. How a tiny wooden vessel made its way that far north boggles the mind, but the British back then were nothing if not daring.

Early in the Cold War, Alert was established as a high Arctic radar and weather station—functions that continue to this day. The population is transient, with military personnel, government employees, business contractors, and the odd visitor cycling through. At the height of the Cold War, there were about three hundred people there at any given time, but that has since shrunk to about sixty-five due to improvements in technology.

At 82.5 degrees latitude this little settlement is so far north that it cannot receive satellite signals directly due to the radical curvature of the earth. To communicate with the outside world, it relies upon an even smaller settlement, about five hundred kilometres south, called Eureka. From there, signals must be bounced off a series of transmission towers. In fact, Alert is so far north that it is geographically closer to Moscow than it is to Ottawa in absolute distance.* That is as close to the North Pole as you can get on land. (How close? One of the buildings there is named "Santa's workshop.")

This remote community was glad to get visitors, especially of the human type (as there is no shortage of wildlife, some of it dangerous). My trip there took eleven hours by various military aircraft, as only certain planes can land on Alert's gravel runway. As a buff of all things northern, I had always wanted to say I had been to Alert; had eaten at the restaurant, the Igloo Bar; and had slept there overnight. On this trip I did that, sleeping behind blinds that completely blacked out the sun that shines twenty-four hours a day at that time of year. It was a remarkable experience, and I met some dedicated, resilient, and special people, becoming only the second prime minister to get that far north.

* I was able to make this point several times to American audiences during Trump's first term in office when I jokingly noted that Alert being closer to Moscow than to Ottawa was "not unlike your president." Some found that funny, as I intended it to be; others not so much.

THE NORTHERN STRATEGY

BETWEEN THIS TRIP and the second, in August 2007, we worked hard to build a full and ongoing Northern Strategy. There would be no trouble finding things to do. Canada's investments in the most basic northern infrastructure have been small and insufficient compared to other Arctic nations. The reasons for this are rooted in our history and geography.

The Dominion of Canada took over jurisdiction of our northern territories in 1870,[†] but for many decades the Canadian government's presence was minimal and sporadic. That only began to change in the 1950s with the Cold War and easier air travel. Our North is more vast and more inhospitable than that of virtually all other nations—Greenland would be an exception—with the added difficulty of fragmentation. The dozens of islands render a road network impossible and add greatly to the natural transportation challenges.

Given these realities, it quickly became apparent that the North needed a multi-faceted approach. We settled on four elements to the strategy. They would be its sovereignty, economic/environmental, social, and governance pillars.

The first pillar would be sovereignty, for the simple reason that it underpins everything else. We Canadians tend to be people of goodwill, inclined at almost all times to peace. We have therefore not historically worried about our hold over our vast, oft-neglected land mass. True, many decades ago there were periodic issues with the Americans and the Norwegians and, more recently, silly spats with the Danish over a large Arctic rock called Hans Island. But generally, we have been way too sanguine about potential challenges in the North.

---

† I refer to the purchase of the Northwest Territories (that is, Rupert's Land and the North-Western Territory) from the Hudson's Bay Company. They then included not only today's three territories but also all the prairie provinces and the northern two-thirds of Ontario and Quebec. Jurisdiction over the Arctic islands was ambiguous, however, and was not definitely assigned to Canada by the United Kingdom until 1880.

These many years since we left office, something our Government knew back then is now more widely understood: we are in a new Cold War. By 2006, Vladimir Putin had been president of Russia for six years. Even then, he was showing signs of becoming a geopolitical threat. Most important for us, he had renewed Cold War measures like the regular testing of Canadian and American airspace. The Chinese had also begun to establish an unprecedented presence in our Arctic, most notably through the incursions of submarines.

Canada's ability to monitor these challenges, let alone meet them, was minimal. We set out to boost our capacity to project our presence in the Arctic. Key would be the use of enhanced military and other transportation assets, along with annual northern military exercises that augmented those of the Canadian Rangers. This would be the "cold part" of the one-hundred-degree military we were building. It would involve substantial long-term investments to ensure we could surveil the length and breadth of our territory and conduct operations in all weather conditions.

The second pillar would be to create economic development in environmentally responsible ways. This was not without controversy. Some in the South contended that the better thing to do was to leave the land unaltered and the local inhabitants to live as they do. All I can say is that such people have evidently not spoken to many in the North.

The North is not just a region of enormous, untapped resource potential; it is also the home of a young and growing population desperate for opportunity. Yes, we have only scratched the surface of the region's natural wealth. But we have had literally no plan to provide the people who live there with jobs—any jobs. They need development. Such development, we were clear, would have to be pursued in harmony with the fragile northern environment, meaning that greater environmental knowledge and protection would be an integral part of our economic development efforts.

The third pillar would be built around the social needs of the people of the North. As for all Canadians, health and education are critical priorities for Northerners. However, the needs are so much more acute in that part of the country. With its vast distances, harsh climate, long periods of darkness, and thinly dispersed population, the North defies even the best efforts to improve life. There are formidable barriers to the delivery of services and food in the North. Life expectancy is shorter; mortality is higher.

I have immeasurable admiration, mixed with not a little wonder, at how the Inuit were able to survive and flourish in that beautiful, but equally unforgiving, environment. Obviously, some aspects of modern life have made living in the Arctic—or at least surviving there—easier. But it remains a difficult life even today. Still, the people of the North are proud to live there. This was reinforced in the significant time I spent meeting Northerners, listening to their needs but also to their hopes and dreams for the future.

The fourth priority would be the governance agenda. The fact is that for most of Canada's existence, the North has been governed from far away as a virtual internal colony, with local people having little say. True, the people of Yukon have long had limited powers, and the establishment of Yellowknife as the capital of the Northwest Territories in 1967 represented some progress. More was made when Brian Mulroney's Government created Nunavut. Still, in our view, more needed to be done.

PROROGATION AND REORGANIZATION

AS MY SECOND NORTHERN TOUR was underway, so were our plans for the next stage of the 39th Parliament. Since the end of the spring sitting in June, we had been sending signals that we would prorogue. Given the controversies that were to come later, and the resulting sense conveyed by the media that prorogation was somehow illegitimate, let me take a moment to talk about that.

For those not familiar with the term, prorogation is when a government ends a session of Parliament, which terminates all unadopted legislation. But this is not dissolution; Parliament is not over, as when an election is called. Prorogation includes the intention to recall the chambers with the presentation of a new Speech from the Throne outlining a renewed government agenda.

New legislation will be tabled, but often existing legislation—both the Government's and that of individual MPs—is reintroduced. While the legislative processes usually then begin from scratch, sometimes there may be agreement to take up old bills from where they left off. In short, prorogation is not only a normal part of the functioning of Parliament but also an expected part. Since Confederation, Parliament has seen prorogation occur every one to two years.

Given where and how things stood at that point, proroguing made sense. Put simply: our Government had accomplished most of what it set out to do in the Throne Speech of April 2006. From the Accountability Act to the UCCB, to crime legislation, to tax cuts and the fiscal imbalance, we had moved forward significantly. We had to begin to focus on next steps. I summarized all this in my formal statements announcing prorogation and setting the return of Parliament for October 16, 2007:

> I am pleased to report that Canada is united, our government is clean, and our economy is strong. Now it's time to launch the next phase of our mandate. The First Session of the 39th Parliament was exceptionally productive, especially for a Government in a minority situation. We delivered on all the major commitments we made to Canadians during the 2006 election.

We had delivered because, first and foremost, we had survived as a government in the minority environment. Our success had been largely due to a tight agenda built around the electoral platform on which we had received a mandate. It had also helped that we had a relatively small number of ministers, which lessened potential issues to be managed.

Nevertheless, I had already concluded that the small ministry was creating its own challenges and was not sustainable. Thus, earlier in the year, I had created several junior minister positions. These were initially called secretaries of state, later revised to the more appropriate ministers of state. They were not part of the Cabinet, but they were part of the ministry.

They did not hold the legal responsibility for a department, but they were entrusted with some agency or policy area of a portfolio.

One reason for this move was to provide a meaningful training ground for members of caucus who could well be full ministers in the future. That it fulfilled this function is indisputable, as a number of these early junior ministers would become mainstays of the government over time. I think of Jason Kenney (initially secretary of state for multiculturalism and Canadian identity), Gerry Ritz (secretary of state for small business and tourism), Christian Paradis (secretary of state for agriculture, with a focus on Quebec agricultural issues), and later James Moore (secretary of state for the 2010 Olympics).

The greater objective of this change was thus to better use the talents and potential of my parliamentary team. One of the biggest challenges I had as prime minister, as the head of the political side of government, was employing the vast array of abilities and knowledge available among our parliamentarians, particularly our elected members.* MPs and senators, besides representing a wealth of points of view and political perspectives, come with varied and often deep experiences in business or in other areas related to public policy. This was certainly true of my caucus.

The reality in the federal government is that there are just too few jobs for the size of caucus. My first Government was small by parliamentary standards; we never had more than 127 members in the Commons and 25 in the Senate. By the time of our majority Government (2011–2015), we would have 166 MPs and 65 senators. Obviously, it is impossible to have 150 or more full Cabinet ministers. But everyone needs to be engaged and to contribute.

With the creation of the ministers of state, we now had two levels of Cabinet, although one could argue that the Priorities and Planning Committee constituted a third level. This was augmented by parliamentary secretaries (PSs). These are members specifically appointed to help senior

---

* The information that follows largely describes how the Commons' caucus was organized. The Senate caucus had a similar but less-elaborate structure, mainly because ministers do not usually sit in the Senate. Also, the roles there were generally allocated with less input (but not no input) from the PMO.

ministers in their legislative responsibilities. In my government, the PSs were generally younger members identified as having both Cabinet potential and Cabinet possibility in the future.

Unfortunately, there were many MPs who, due to the demographic realities of Cabinet-making, had very little chance of ever being a minister, regardless of their abilities and experience. These are the ones I would typically make the Chairs of parliamentary committees. We had crafted the parliamentary committees so that they would largely mirror the Cabinet portfolios. On those committees, the Chair would be backed by a senior lead member, and the more junior members.

Crafting these tiers was part of our effort to better utilize talent. My office and the whip's office monitored all MPs' performance. That way, I was kept aware of everyone's contributions and could make informed decisions when promotional opportunities came up.

Having an active and engaged caucus not only was beneficial for advancing the government's agenda but also contributed directly to caucus unity. In this, we were largely successful. Over our decade in office and its ups and downs, we had very little in the way of caucus strife.

Because caucus was generally so united, I was accused of having aggregated all the power to the Prime Minister's Office. Such criticisms have been common all the way back to Confederation, and they sometimes have merit. As I have often said, I have seen only two kinds of PMs: those in control and those not in control, and the latter do not last very long.

There is a deeper issue, however, and it is that a significant degree of prime ministerial control is how our system is supposed to work. The Crown entrusts government to the prime minister, who has long been understood to have the leading role in foreign affairs, intergovernmental relations, financial matters, machinery of government, and parliamentary management. In fact, the prime minister is solely responsible to the Crown for all matters.

Believe it or not, there is nothing in our system that requires a prime minister to have any Cabinet ministers at all. In his book *At the Centre of Government: The Prime Minister and the Limits on Political Power*, my former chief of staff Ian Brodie wrote about our earliest conversations with officials, when they asked, "Prime Minister, do you plan to name a Cabinet?" What kind of question was that I wondered. Were they making fun of my reputation for control? Actually, no. It is one of the first questions incoming prime ministers are asked for the simple reason that the prime minister does not have to name *anybody* to Cabinet. Now, having been PM, I cannot imagine how anyone could govern without a Cabinet. Even with one, the workload is crushing.

Yet, at the heart of our system is a tension. On the one hand, our Constitution makes the PM the "boss" of their caucus. Yet the PM can only remain PM with the consent of that caucus. Any first minister that forgets that is in deep trouble. That is one reason why we went to such effort not just to engage everyone but also to build caucus consensus for everything. And our efforts on that front were only just beginning.

PRIORITIES FOR THE NEW SESSION

AS PER TRADITION, the second session of the 39th Parliament opened with Governor General Michaëlle Jean delivering our Speech from the Throne. Entitled "Seizing Canada's Moment: Prosperity and Opportunity in an Uncertain World," the address foreshadowed a range of fiscal actions, further measures of criminal justice, next steps on the Northern Strategy, legislation to limit the federal spending power,* and a commitment to hold a parliamentary vote on the extension of Canada's Afghanistan mission past 2009. Broadly speaking, our government was furthering and deepening its existing agenda.

The government brought in some new criminal justice measures as the session progressed, including a bill to raise the age of consent for sexual relations from fourteen to sixteen. This was proposed in light of increasing evidence of older people taking advantage of those in the fourteen to

---

* This was one promise that never came to pass, as we could not arrive at an agreement with the government of Quebec, despite much effort.

sixteen age range. Conservative backbenchers also introduced their own crime bills, as such private members' legislation had received Royal Assent in the first session. That trend would grow in this and subsequent periods.

Yet it will come as no surprise that the greatest emphasis was on economic measures. Obviously, there were days when other things muscled their way to the front of the queue, but over any sustained period of our time in government, the economy was always our highest priority. The Throne Speech had talked of an "Uncertain World" partly in the context of the economy. Although growth remained healthy, we were aware of stresses in global markets, hence the renewed emphasis.

ECONOMIC UPDATE 2007 AND BUDGET 2008

IN RECENT DECADES, the federal fiscal cycle has been marked by a full budget in the early spring and a more modest economic update in the fall. Under the Martin Government in particular, the update had begun to morph into almost a second full budget. We did not believe that this was a good development, and Minister Flaherty made early efforts to bring the fall statement back to its original function.

As things turned out, however, we made some of our biggest budgetary announcements in that fall's update. We had on this occasion moved back toward the Paul Martin practice for, I suspect, a similar reason—the minority parliament. With the risk of an election through parliamentary defeat always a reality, we did not want to wait to further deliver on our key platform commitments. We especially wished to complete our big tax-cut pledges.

Before I get into the details, a comment on my fiscal philosophy is in order. Even on the matter of lower taxes, I am an "old-fashioned" conservative. By this I mean that the integrity of the fiscal framework is always paramount. I know that there are different views about tax cutting among conservatives around the world. I think particularly of some of our Republican friends in the United States, who make tax cuts the single-greatest priority, giving little concern to their long-term affordability. Thus, even conservative administrations south of the border have lavishly contributed to the spiralling levels of deficit and debt.

In contrast, our test was always whether any tax reduction or program enhancement was affordable over the long haul. Assuming normal levels of economic growth—neither boom nor recession—could we undertake such-and-such a measure and maintain a balanced budget? That was the question we always asked.

Fortunately, we were in a good position in that regard. Even with economic concerns in the back of our mind, we were executing record paydowns of federal debt. That was after our initial round of tax cuts and spending initiatives, including the expensive fix to the fiscal imbalance and the monies set aside for the promised wait time guarantees. In other words, it was time to get the rest done.

The fiscal update was delivered on October 30, not long after Parliament opened. I will not enumerate all its elements in detail, but some deserve particular attention. For one, we finished the cut of the GST—"7 to 6 to 5 per cent"—well ahead of schedule. We also finished the reduction of the lowest personal income tax bracket. It went down to 15 per cent, eliminating that pesky additional half per cent, and we also raised the basic personal exemption. Finally, we launched a systematic approach to reducing business taxes.

We had made broad commitments to reduce the tax burden on business and had already enacted some initial measures. But that fall statement was when we articulated and began to pursue a long-term goal. That would be to gradually lower the federal corporate tax rate from around 22 per cent to 15 per cent. Further, Minister Flaherty would work with the provinces to try and get their level to 10 per cent, yielding a combined federal-provincial rate of 25 per cent. Along with other measures, our goal was to make Canada's taxes on new business investments the lowest in the G7.

We achieved that goal federally, with most provinces coming on board, regardless of partisan stripe. To be clear, I never viewed this as a "gift" to business. We wanted a corporate tax regime that was both competitive and substantial. Critics could always—and they did—project a higher tax rate on existing corporate profits to claim that we were foregoing revenue. That misses the point; such tax rates influence corporate activity. We wanted a rate that would maximize our corporate revenues.* The fact is that, before the global financial crisis of 2008–2009, our new, lower rates were unquestionably leading to higher tax revenues for the federal government.

That fall's Economic Update also launched the Community Development Trust Fund. It was an initiative to respond to troubling developments we were seeing in single-industry communities. This was especially true where forestry was the dominant industry, which is the case in large parts of middle and northern Canada. That downturn was emanating, we were aware, from a dramatic slowdown in the U.S. housing market.

We did survive that fall, and so Minister Flaherty followed the Economic Update with our Government's budget on February 26, 2008. Without a doubt, Budget 2008 will be most remembered for the creation of the Tax-Free Saving Account (TFSA). Jim characterized it as the "single most important savings vehicle since the introduction of the RRSP."

Besides the obvious benefits to taxpayers and investors, TFSAs would have the advantage of creating a new and large pool of savings. Through our financial system, that money would ultimately be made available for wider investment in the economy. It was a terrific innovation that has become a mainstay of financial planning for working people and their families and one for which Minister Flaherty deserves much credit.

---

* I should make reference here to the Laffer curve [https://www.britannica.com/money/Arthur-Laffer]—which has nothing to do with humour. The eponymous theory refers to the American economist Arthur Laffer, who postulated that as tax rates go up, there is a point at which revenue goes down because the higher taxes depress economic activity. The easiest way to understand this is to think about a tax rate of 100 per cent. If tax rates were all that mattered, that would produce the most tax revenues. In reality, a tax rate of 100 per cent would produce zero revenue. There would be no incentive to engage in business activity at all.

THE RESIDENTIAL SCHOOLS APOLOGY

LATER IN THE SECOND SESSION, my Government would return to its justice agenda in a historic way. Earlier I recounted instances when former Canadian governments and their agencies wronged individuals, families, and communities, such as in the Air India bombing. I have also noted that one of our justice priorities was to attempt to right such wrongs and to address the legitimate claims of victims. There was no greater undertaking in this regard than tackling the issue of the residential school system.

From 1876, and continuing to as late as 1997, it was a policy of the Government of Canada to provide a system residential schools for Indigenous children. For many of those years, the intention of that system was to separate Indigenous children from their families and to educate them with the intention of removing their Indigenous identity. The program was farmed out to churches to administer. Even at the time, the failings and abuses of the system were being noted. Over the decades, evidence of these problems and more—poor educational outcomes, inadequate nutrition and health, frequent physical and sexual abuse—grew significantly and led eventually to class-action lawsuits.

In fairness, the multi-billion-dollar settlement of the residential schools lawsuits had largely been finalized by Paul Martin's Government. However, it was not ratified when we came to office, so it was my Government that formalized the agreement with the Indigenous organizations. But interestingly, even though the settlement addressed such a great historical injustice and involved very large sums of money, there was no provision for an apology in the final terms.

I had known something of the residential school system before I became PM. However, in the course of concluding the settlement, I came to a fuller understanding of the perversity, scale, and long-term ramifications of the policy. First, it involved a staggering level of social engineering, taking children from their families, sometimes without their consent, en masse. Second, the premise—that Indigenous culture was hopelessly inferior and needed to be eradicated—was inherently demeaning, almost inviting the mistreatment that would occur. Finally, there was an utter lack of oversight, accountability, and care for the children who had been enrolled. Much research, evidence, and testimony have documented the injustices that followed and resulted in grave damage not only to individual children but also to the social fabric of Indigenous communities and families.

The argument has been made that many students reported good experiences at residential schools. It is also noted that the program began as a response to the appalling economic, social, and health conditions that existed in Indigenous communities at the time. And there is no doubt that many who advocated the policy and worked within the system believed they were doing good and, in fact, did some good. This does not change the reality that the premises behind the system were wrong-headed and arrogant in the extreme and cannot be excused by good intentions. The problems and abuses that resulted from such thinking were, in fact, inevitable.

Reflecting upon what I had learned during my many briefings on the matter, I became convinced that an apology was both appropriate and necessary and that its omission from the agreement had been a mistake. I concluded that it was important for Canadians to fully understand how ill-conceived and damaging this policy was, so they could in turn understand the level of financial settlement we had committed to. I did not want the settlement to be framed solely around the monetary aspect because people might miss the point.

A formal apology was therefore a means of taking the focus away from the money, placing it instead on the policy and its faults, and trying in a meaningful way to promote reconciliation between the Government of Canada, Indigenous communities, and the broader population. I spoke to Aboriginal Affairs Minister Chuck Strahl as well as Jim Prentice, who had been the minister when the deal was completed, and both agreed that an apology would be a good idea for the reasons I articulated.

On June 11, 2008, on behalf of the Government of Canada, I delivered the apology for the system of residential schools in the House of Commons. Many former students were in the galleries, and I had invited the national Indigenous leaders to join me on the floor for the occasion. They included National Chief Phil Fontaine of the Assembly of First Nations, National

Chief (later Senator) Patrick Brazeau of the Congress of Aboriginal Peoples (representing non-treaty Indians), President (later Governor General) Mary Simon of the Inuit Tapiriit Kanatami, President Clem Chartier of the Métis National Council, and President Beverley Jacobs of the Native Women's Association of Canada. All spoke eloquently that day.

It was a powerful and moving experience for all involved. Having the leaders of the major Indigenous organizations on the floor of the House of Commons was particularly poignant. They represented Canadian communities who had by far the longest history in our country and yet a short and truncated history of involvement in our democratic institutions. Indeed, it was only under John Diefenbaker's government, in 1960, that Indigenous people were granted the right to vote—something that helps explain why they were so easily victimized by the government.*

For me (whether others could see it or not), that day was an emotionally draining experience. I heard the same thing from my Indigenous friends. I also was told over the years by many others that it was a meaningful moment that they deeply appreciated.

At its base, my hope in delivering the apology was to move beyond the payments, to promote reconciliation, and to, as much as possible, turn the page on that ugly chapter of Canada's history. I do recognize that this was an immensely painful experience for many Indigenous communities, which could take generations to resolve. And I know that, over the course of our history, Indigenous people have not benefitted from Canadian society in the ways that so many others have.

---

* A historical note is in order here. John A. Macdonald had secured voting rights for some Indigenous men in 1885, so as to "place them on a footing of equality with their white brethren." It is ironic that Macdonald has been singled out by some as the great villain of residential schools, which were first put in the Indian Act under the government of Alexander Mackenzie, and which reached their zenith under the government of Wilfrid Laurier. It was Laurier's government which also repealed the briefly existing Indigenous voting rights.

Still, I wanted to get beyond the pain and the pathologies created, beyond the anger and the grievance, and to raise our sights toward a more promising future together. That was my hope, anyway. These years later, I am not convinced it has really had that impact. But it was a start, at least, and something that was important to do.

THE INTERNATIONAL TRADE AGENDA

DURING THE SECOND SESSION of our first mandate, one of our oft-stated and longer-term policy objectives began to take shape—expanding Canada's global free-trade network. Here again, we were building on a proud Conservative legacy. Indeed, this was an area where Canada had once been a pioneer. Prime Minister Mulroney's Canada-U.S. Free Trade Agreement had been concluded in 1987 with President Reagan. Five years later, negotiations were completed on the North American Free Trade Agreement, bringing Mexico into the fold. These were arguably the first major trade deals of the modern globalization era, helping to inspire a proliferation of regional and bilateral arrangements around the world.

Since that time, however, Canada's free-trade efforts had stagnated. During thirteen years of Liberal rule, further agreements had been concluded with only Israel, Chile, and Costa Rica. They were small in both dollars and scope. Moreover, as our early reviews of the situation indicated, ambition to do more had deteriorated. Although there were many negotiations underway, they were mostly pro forma and going nowhere.

The focus of our trade officials seemed largely on concluding a big global agreement through the World Trade Organization (WTO). Yet, from my very first G8 Summit where I got a full debrief at the international level, it was evident that the WTO talks had no chance of success in the near future. In the meantime, focusing on these negotiations, where Canada was not a major player, meant that our trade negotiation capacity had atrophied significantly. If we wanted to get back into the business of doing trade-liberalization deals, we would have to look beyond the WTO and rebuild that capacity.

It was clear that this was not going to be an overnight process. We started where it made the most sense, with the low-hanging fruit. This ran counter to the advice I was getting from many, both inside and outside of government, who advised hunting the biggest game—the European Union, China, and India being the most frequently mentioned targets. Instead, we asked ourselves, which countries are most ready and prepared to actually do a deal? That is where we would focus our initial efforts.

Such an approach had several advantages. It would test our ability to make concessions and drive deals through Cabinet (where, I was told, previous Liberal efforts had stalled). It would also allow us to have success, which is the only experience that truly builds capacity. Finally, it would show the bigger players that we really were serious.

The first deal was concluded in early 2008 with the European Free Trade Association (EFTA), consisting of Switzerland, Norway, Iceland, and Liechtenstein. These countries are not part of the European Union, but they are a single trade bloc that is deeply integrated with the EU. This was not a trivial deal in scale. Switzerland and Norway are mid-sized economies that immediately became our third- and fourth-largest free-trade countries. EFTA as a whole represented a market double the size of the Liberals' three deals combined.

Still, there were bigger things at stake in the EFTA deal. We saw it as a critical first step to securing a deal with the European Union. Learning EFTA's trade language, understanding their perspectives, and negotiating an agreement would show the EU we were genuinely back in the trade-negotiation business. After all, the EFTA talks had first been announced in 1998, so Canada really did have something to prove. And even though the concessions and trade-offs in this case were not steep, it showed me that our ministers would be willing to incur the costs necessary to drive a deal to fruition.

In May we concluded our second trade agreement, this time with Peru. A smaller market, it was already a growing one for Canada when the deal was signed, and it has proven to be a lucrative one since. Our bilateral merchandise trade has expanded by over ten times in the past twenty years, across a range of products, with Peru becoming an important destination for Canadian foreign investment.*

The Peruvian deal also underscored the wisdom of focus in our trade strategy. We had terminated several stagnant negotiations and, ironically, that led to our success with Peru. Among the existing talks going nowhere were those with the Andean Community—Bolivia, Colombia, Ecuador, and Peru. They were hobbled by a common feature of multilateral trade negotiations everywhere: they will only be as good as the least ambitious country at the table. The truth is that Bolivia, and probably Ecuador too, did not really want an agreement. But Peru, under the leadership of President Alan Garcia, understood that liberalized trade was important for his country's economic growth and, like us, wanted to get a deal done. At a smaller table, it happened quickly, and both our countries have benefitted greatly.

THE END OF THE 39TH PARLIAMENT

WE WERE NOW DEEP into our first term of office and had the longest minority government in Canadian history.† As I have said, we did not replicate the strategy of bargaining with the opposition parties, which had gotten Paul Martin into such trouble. But neither did we govern as if we had a majority. We always kept one ear to the public—that was critical—but we also kept the other one attuned to what the other parties were saying. Our

---

* Canadian exports to Peru include petroleum products, chemicals, plastic, machinery, consumer electronics, telecommunications equipment, and vehicles. Canadian investment in Peru totalled $12.1 billion by 2021.

† Some will claim that Mackenzie King had a longer minority government from 1921 to 1925. But if you look at the record, that Parliament was sometimes a majority and sometimes not. King was either in majority or close-to-majority with the largest opposition party, the Progressives, unable to act as a cohesive unit. So, for all intents and purposes, the 39th Parliament had easily been the longest minority government to date.

Throne Speeches and budgets always contained items they could support, if that is what they wished to do. Of course, if they decided to defeat us, we could point out that they had voted against those measures.

I can honestly say that I learned something every single day of my first term as prime minister. No . . . I would go further: I learned something every single day of the near decade that I held the job. The job is just so big. The reality is that the position is beyond anybody's capacity. There are so many things to do that require so many skills with so little time to do them all in. My approach is you pick your spots, map out a game plan, concentrate on areas of strength, try to shore up your weaknesses and those of your team, while always leaving enough time to deal with inevitable and unanticipated curveballs. Of course, we had had some fortunate timing in those first two and a half years.

We had also made some of our own luck. A journalist once asked me—this was an off-the-record conversation—why I remained prime minister with such a slender mandate when Paul Martin, who had come to office with enormous support, was removed from the scene so quickly. For this I had one overarching explanation—I had come to power by uniting my party, whereas Martin had come to power by dividing his.

The journalist doubted that explanation, given the importance of the sponsorship scandal in undermining Mr. Martin. But in my view, what made the sponsorship scandal so bad for the Liberal Party was that once the story broke, the players turned on each other due to already existing divisions. The lesson we had learned was the importance of people pulling together. After all, in politics there are enough battles to fight with people on the outside without finding ones to fight internally.

Another important lesson we learned was that in this day and age, with the swift pace of change in our society and the world, and the acceleration of that pace in new forms of media, a government can never sit still. It must keep moving ahead. You can never be satisfied. There is always a desire for something new and something different, always new public aspirations and concerns. Like a shark, you must be moving or you die. And at that point in the life of the 39th Parliament, that reality was presenting us with a problem.

The political dynamics in Parliament were getting more difficult as time went on. The reason was very simple: it is very difficult for any opposition party to support the government on a sustained basis. After all, those parties were elected to oppose the government. If they do not do that, or even if they simply cannot defeat the government, they will face increasing push-back from their own people.

Our Government was in its third year in power. All the opposition parties had supported us at one time or another, most often the Bloc or the Liberals. For the latter in particular, internal frustration was growing. And it seemed to me that they were increasingly looking for ways to impede everything we were trying to do. They were developing a pattern of abstaining, missing votes, and slowing legislation down in the House and in committee. Yet they were also not trying to defeat us.

In the spring of 2008, Liberal Leader Stéphane Dion started to say things that confirmed my misgivings. He announced that, with the fixed election date legislation, he, not the prime minister, was in charge of Parliament. The Government could not now call an election, he reasoned; only the Official Opposition could trigger it. In other words, he could block the Government's business without defeating the Government.

Needless to say, that was a serious misreading of how the fixed election date legislation, let alone the parliamentary system, actually works. More importantly, this was not a situation I was prepared to tolerate. Dion was basically saying that the Liberals would render the government ineffective, without having to risk an election. That was an unacceptable situation, made more worrisome by an economy that was beginning to slow. Growth had certainly not stopped, but it was noticeably cooling down.

After the spring session concluded, I decided I needed to do something about this, so I began to fire some warning shots. Throughout the summer, I indicated, in escalating tones, that we were concerned about a dysfunctional Parliament. I wanted to give myself the option of calling an election. Somewhat to my surprise, when the Planning and Priorities committee of Cabinet met for our summer retreat in late August, my ministers were unanimous in their view that the situation was intolerable, that the

Parliament had run its course, and that I should call the election that the public now expected.

That the ground for an election call had been prepared became clear in the sudden and frantic efforts of Mr. Dion to change tack. He began calling for meetings with a tone that became magically positive and co-operative. We can make Parliament work, he proclaimed. However, his new positioning only confirmed to us that an election was in our interest and not in his. We were ready, and so was the country.

On September 7, 2008, I requested a dissolution of Parliament, and Election 2008 was underway.

10

ELECTION 2008 AND ITS AFTERMATH

THE CAMPAIGN AND THE GLOBAL FINANCIAL CRISIS

WE HAD BEGUN THE CAMPAIGN very optimistic about winning. There had been general satisfaction with our Government's performance. On the other side, we knew Liberal Leader Stéphane Dion did not inspire confidence as a potential prime minister. As well, his central campaign plank, the "Green Shift"—essentially a national carbon tax—was both bad policy and bad politics.

Yet, while we thought we could make gains, we were not expecting—and certainly not predicting—a majority government. We sought only a renewed mandate to unblock Parliament and keep moving forward. The title of our platform, "The True North Strong and Free," emphasized a conservative notion of nationalism, conveying a renewed sense of strength and pride in an uncertain world.

Our plan for the election began by emphasizing the "promises made, promises kept" since February 2006. We followed that by rolling out commitments that largely took our existing agenda further—additional tax cuts, some innovative social policy announcements, and important economic development initiatives. We did our best to power through our campaign plan. The reality, however, was that we were increasingly being caught up in events emanating from outside Canada's borders.

On September 15, 2008, just eight days after the campaign began, Lehman Brothers, a major U.S. financial services firm, collapsed. In the complex world of interbank lending, that immediately sent ripples through financial markets in the United States and around the world. With one of the most trusted global financial institutions exposed as unsound, other such organizations quickly became leery about dealing with one another, freezing banking activity.

By September 29, global stock markets were crashing. With a clear panic taking hold, some of the drops in value were ridiculous. That in turn led to gyrations in stock prices in both directions. In fact, on the eve of the election, the stock market recorded near-record gains. Still, the overall mood was one of rapidly growing uncertainty.

Our read was that the extraordinary events during the campaign had two effects. Initially, they hurt our party. The idea that the economy was in trouble, even if no one thought it was our fault, wounded a government that was emphasizing overall good economic performance. However, as the weeks wore on, the focus shifted to which party was best suited for troubled times. At that point, our original lead came back.

We ended up with 143 seats, up from the 124 we had won in 2006. The gains came largely at the expense of the Liberals. We had gone up most everywhere. We were particularly pleased by the breakthrough in Nunavut with the election of Leona Aglukkaq. There were two big exceptions to the upward trend, however. In Newfoundland & Labrador, we were wiped out by Danny Williams' opposition. Quebec was an even bigger disappointment.

We mostly held our seats in *la belle province*, but we did not make the gains we thought we might have. "Culture cuts" and some "technical tax amendments" were successfully demagogued by the Bloc and others, including, to some degree, the Quebec Liberal government. The cuts to a few cultural programs were in fact trivial in scope. We were spending more on the arts and culture in total and would continue to do so. The technical tax amendments were old legislation that dated back to the previous government and which the Bloc had actually supported at one point. But now they supposedly contained a hidden plan to censor artistic productions.

THE CAMPAIGN ENDS, THE CRISIS CONTINUES

THE ECONOMIC EVENTS of the campaign led some to later speculate that I had called the election because I saw the recession coming. My opponents pointed to the fact that I had acted well before the fixed election date. I had also been candid with the public about slowing growth and growing uncertainty in the economy.

Some friends have suspected the same thing. Indeed, a few years later, I was chatting with George W. Bush, and he reminded me that, in April 2008, I had warned him of trouble in the U.S. economy. That was in a private conversation at the North American Leaders Summit in New Orleans.

The occasion was a call I made to George W. on his birthday. He was then long out of office; I was still prime minister. There were the normal conversation topics—family news, the state of world, and the like. In the course of it, I had asked him, "George, what's your take on the economy?" "Harper," he said, "Don't ask me about the economy. You tried to tell me in spring of 2008 that the economy was in trouble. You were right and I wouldn't listen."

Back then, President Bush had been acknowledging that some firms were in difficulty, while insisting that the economic fundamentals were sound. I had disagreed and pointed to the unusual movements in financial markets and other troubling economic developments. That prompted an exchange that became, in diplomatic terms, quite "spirited."

It takes a big man who years later can say, unprompted, "I was wrong; you were right." But President Bush is a man of outstanding character. This is just one small example of that. However, I was simply not as prescient as President Bush or others suspect.

Here is what I knew: in April 2007, the first American mortgage firm failed as the U.S. housing sector began to slow dramatically. The construction impacts were soon hitting our forestry sector. With logging, sawmills, and pulp and paper, that industry is a major player in large parts of rural Canada. The fall in prices started to trigger duties in our softwood lumber agreement and led us to take some remedial action, as I mentioned earlier.

About that time, we also began to see unusual activity in the global banking sector. In August 2007, we had the first, brief, freezing of financial markets. These developments were causing a cooling of the American economy, and then of ours, given that Canada's export sector is so closely tied to the United States.

As I said at the time, we knew growth was slowing and uncertainty was rising. That was all. I was a long way from understanding the scale and depth of the problems in the U.S. subprime mortgage market or the implications of its coming failure on the U.S. banking sector, the entire American economy, and global growth more broadly.

In any case, election night was a strange feeling for me. I tried to share in the party's jubilation after its second consecutive victory. But by that time, I had more than an inkling of the challenges to come. It was obvious we were going to face a recession. Then, in the days that followed, the situation continued to deteriorate far beyond our worst fears.

The wild market swings of the campaign were becoming an entrenched downward trend. It would be a few weeks before statistics would be published, but we started receiving reports of plummeting shipping volumes across all transportation sectors. News of significant layoffs were also starting to trickle in. This was not merely a slowdown; it was an all-pervasive panic.

Behind the panic was the continuing freeze in interbank lending markets. This meant that all banks, even Canadian banks—among the world's soundest—were being impacted. That in turn translated into a drying up of day-to-day credit for Canadian businesses, even the most blue-chip among them. Minister Flaherty was already in discussion with the banks about ways to unblock the system and provide liquidity, but Canada was nonetheless being swept along by global events.

All this meant that most elements of the platform we had run on would be out the window for the time being. As an example, we had promised some measures to deal with the record oil prices that had taken hold in the lead-up to the campaign, whereas oil prices were now spiralling down. In other words, the economic conditions assumed in the platform were now completely unlike the new realities taking hold. A whole new agenda would be required, at least temporarily.

That would be especially true for fiscal policy. Even late in the campaign, I had pledged to maintain a balanced budget. By election night, that was a very dubious proposition. The coming fall in federal revenues would make maintaining balance highly unlikely, even if we did not implement our election promises. However, given the evident economic cataclysm in the days and weeks that followed, I changed course entirely.

To be clear, my view as an economist is that deliberate "temporary" deficit budgeting is generally unwise. It typically leads to sustained and growing deficits along with declining long-term growth. There are very limited circumstances when it should be practised. However, these were precisely the conditions we were then experiencing —interest rates near zero with dysfunctional financial markets. I thus began to prepare the public for unprecedented fiscal intervention—meaning deliberate big deficits—from the federal government.

LAYING THE GROUNDWORK

WHILE I KNEW INTELLECTUALLY what had to be done, the country had to be prepared for the government's coming change of direction. It seems hard to believe now, but Canadians were then strongly averse to deficits, and fiscal rectitude was especially important to Conservative supporters and our caucus. That meant there was groundwork to be laid and plans to be developed—and developed very quickly—at a time when I faced one of my craziest, most demanding schedules ever.

We had committed to bring Parliament back for substantive work before the Christmas period. That meant, we concluded, that we could not wait past mid-November to get back in the House. In the meantime, I had to go from the October 14 election night celebrations to the Organisation internationale de la Francophonie Summit in Quebec City three days later.

An anglophone chairing an international summit entirely in French was perhaps not ideal, but for me it was a great honour to be presiding in "la langue fondatrice du Canada." The meeting was also a critical part of our strategy for the Quebec City 400th commemoration. We had worked hard to ensure the event would be Canada-affirming and not dominated by the separatists.

After that, we started work on the coming late-fall agenda, which would include the Throne Speech, an initial set of legislation, and an Economic and Fiscal Update. But first, there was the job of naming a new Cabinet, along with parliamentary secretaries and committee assignments. Veteran ministers Monte Solberg, Loyola Hearn, and David Emerson had retired, and Senator Fortier had been unsuccessful in his run for an elected seat. Those changes alone would necessitate many others, given the regional and demographic balances essential in all these appointments.

Fortunately, the election results had contained much more good news than bad, and I had many new options. The swearing-in ceremony at Rideau Hall on October 30 introduced several new faces to the ministry who would serve admirably for years to come. There were Lisa Raitt and Gary Goodyear from Ontario, as well as Denis Lebel from Quebec. Keith Ashfield brought government experience from New Brunswick, as did Gail Shea from Prince Edward Island and Leona Aglukkaq from Nunavut. The last two were places where we had not had ministers before. Steven Fletcher from Manitoba made history by being the first quadriplegic to serve as a federal minister.

A fortuitous element in laying the groundwork for fiscal stimulus came on October 22. That is when President Bush announced that he would be convening an international leaders' meeting in Washington the following month to deal with the crisis. This would turn out to be the first-ever meeting of the G20 leaders. For the preceding decade this body had existed as a forum of finance ministers and central bank governors. Paul Martin deserves credit for initiating it during his time as finance minister. However, it was not certain that it would be the basis of the upcoming leaders' summit.

President Bush had consulted me on the format of the upcoming summit. With globalization, the G8 had developed the practice of bringing the O5—the "Outreach Five" of China, India, Brazil, Mexico, and South Africa—into some of our deliberations. Expanding along these lines was a serious option. My advice was that, if we were to make an ongoing change, a larger and more globally representative group made more sense, particularly given the existing economic dialogue of the G20. That advice, which was no doubt heard from other quarters as well, ultimately carried the day.

I used the coming G20 meeting as the rationale for convening a First Ministers' Meeting as part of my preparations. It would be on November 10, which was short notice by any standards. Given what I believed would be an atmosphere of serious and shared challenges, this seemed one of those occasions when a multilateral meeting made sense. I was not disappointed. With one exception, the premiers were focused on solutions rather than on fights or headlines. After all, we were in the same boat, as their economies were collapsing around them as well.

The meeting laid the foundation for the joint economic action that we would take. I indicated to the premiers that accelerated and enhanced infrastructure spending would be a big part of our government's response, and they agreed they needed to be partners in that effort. We would also all continue to emphasize Canada's relatively strong position, particularly given a banking sector that was sound despite the global turmoil. Of course, the message of upcoming deficits was also getting out, as it was in various semipublic meetings that I was holding in Toronto and elsewhere with the business and financial sectors.

The G20 was scheduled to take place only four days later, but before that I had to travel to Winnipeg. It was for the opening of the national convention of the Conservative Party of Canada. Obviously, this timing had been selected long before the election and the financial crisis. It was now far from perfect, of course, but it presented another opportunity to talk about the big shifts coming in our agenda. Not surprisingly, the assembly itself was an odd mixture of electoral victory celebration and heightened economic unease.

THE INAUGURAL MEETING OF THE G20 LEADERS

GIVEN THE ORIGINS OF THE G20, Minister Flaherty and then–Bank of Canada Governor Mark Carney accompanied me to Washington. At such summits, the Canadian team would typically be a couple of hundred people, including advisors, officials, and a range of administrative, logistical, and security personnel. That may sound like a lot, but Canada's delegation would be a mere fraction of those from places like the United States and China.

There was some venting of anger toward President Bush and the United States. Given the origin of the crisis in the U.S. financial sector, that was not without cause. However, for some it was a deflection of attention from similar problems at home, particularly in Europe. But overall, the mood there was very much the same as I had seen with Canada's First Ministers—extremely sober and seeking solidarity.

The leaders had good reason to be so disposed. For while in Canada we were looking at a recession, other countries were in freefall. Balance sheets and banking systems were falling apart in some places, with people unable to get cash for day-to-day use. Rioting had already broken out in many developing economies as a consequence of the strange events leading up to the crisis. In the preceding year, much of the money fleeing bad real estate investment had gone into commodities. The resulting price spikes in those had driven up food, energy, and other basic living costs in many nations.

My major objective at this first G20 was to help shape a collaborative international response to the global economic challenges before us, but one flexible enough to accommodate Canada's relatively distinctive position as an advanced economy with a stable financial sector. The meeting did accomplish that. The governments agreed on a broad-strokes action plan to address the immediate crisis and lay the groundwork for a mid-term recovery. There was a lot of work still to do at the national level to develop specifics around this plan. Nevertheless, there was an understanding that coordination would continue going forward.

The first part of the plan was to ensure stability in the financial sector. Nothing good could happen until that was re-established. Both the United States and the United Kingdom had passed emergency bank-bailout legislation, although in the former only after the initial failure of such proposals in Congress had further shaken global markets. In any case, much implementation of that legislation remained to be done.

In contrast, there was no reason for the Government of Canada to do bailouts, and I was clear with other leaders on that point. That said, there were some smaller institutions in Canada that failed, and a couple of large ones were on our watchlist as a precautionary measure. Still, we had strong regulatory oversight and a conservative banking culture that put us in a good place, notwithstanding our inevitable vulnerability to events elsewhere.

The strength of Canada's financial system was a big part of my message at the summit, and it was heard there and back home. Shortly after, our country was given the co-chairmanship, along with India, of the G20's work on financial sector reform. Tiff Macklem handled those responsibilities for Canada, and he did a fine job.

A second set of action items focused on monetary policy. Countries were urged to implement rapid monetary expansion to help cope with the crisis. Central bank rates in many advanced countries were already heading to near-zero interest rates, but there was still a fear that deflationary conditions were taking hold. That would lead the United States to soon implement quantitative easing. In simple terms, QE is the direct expansion of the money supply by the central bank (sometimes called, in loose terms, "printing money").

Canada would also stand somewhat apart in this area. We were radically lowering our interest rates, but given our relative financial stability, I did not see any reason to implement QE. In fact, I was worried that an unnecessary expansion of the Bank of Canada balance sheet could prove inflationary. Minister Flaherty and I instructed the Bank that QE would not be allowed without our explicit sign-off—not that Governor Carney was urging such action at that point.

What Minister Flaherty did authorize was the exchange of liabilities between the government and the chartered banks. We would engage in temporary swaps of financial assets to enhance the immediate liquidity needs of the banks and their capacity to lend. On these trades, the Government of Canada ultimately made money, which I have joked is one of the few times someone has profited at the expense of the big banks.

The G20 also urged expansionary fiscal actions, i.e., expanded deficit financing, to enhance the prospects of an ongoing recovery. This was, of course, what I had been telegraphing. The agreement on this point solidified the expectations we were building and helped reinforce that message to our reluctant supporters.

Beyond that, many of my interventions were, to be frank, counselling attendees not to overreact and to also think longer term. In such a crisis, it would be too easy for extraordinary government intervention to slip toward protectionism and socialism. The unregulated nature of some financial markets in a largely ungoverned system of globalization was the problem. But this did not mean that the vast gains of the previous generation from global markets and trade liberalization should be ditched for older, failed paradigms.

In short, we did not want to see the response to this crisis shift us back to the 1930s. Despite what some people have claimed, that decade-long depression was not caused by poor fiscal policy; it originated with unregulated financial markets, which led to bank failures and a radically shrinking money supply and, finally, to deepening protectionism and economic autarky. The ultimate result had been World War II.

These concerns, particularly on protectionism, were reflected in the conclusions of the deliberations. Taken with the other decisions, the declaration broadly reflected my evaluation of the crisis and the intended actions I had been communicating to Canadians. Canada would undertake measures that would help the world deal with the crisis, but in a way that was consistent with Canada's differentiated, and frankly better, conditions.

THE OPENING OF PARLIAMENT AND THE 2008 ECONOMIC AND FISCAL UPDATE

SOMETIME BETWEEN PUTTING TOGETHER our new ministry and parliamentary team, my post-election international travel to summits, and my cross-country trips for economic consultations, I had managed to meet with the opposition leaders. This was standard practice at the beginning of any parliament, rendered critical by the reality that we were again in a minority situation. I needed to hear what measures might get their support, or at least lessen our chances of defeat. Besides, we were always looking for ideas from the outside that, if adopted, might strengthen our standing with the public.

This time, however, the meetings were very different. Indeed, they were highly unusual. I met with the three leaders individually in my Langevin Block office. In each case, their approach was the same: they were not communicating their priorities. For Stéphane Dion, that was not strange. He had always been taciturn in meetings with me, and he was clearly smarting from the election defeat. But it was much more irregular in the case of Gilles Duceppe, and even more so for Jack Layton. The NDP leader would normally be brimming with suggestions, anxious to look for some horse-trading. But there was little of that this time. When I pressed them about what was on their minds, on what they wanted from the government, the answer I got from all three was little more than, "We'll see."

I concluded from these meetings that they had already decided that they were going to defeat our Government and force a new election as soon as that was viable. It was not hard to imagine how this would play out. In the first weeks and months of the 40th Parliament, the economic growth and job numbers would be spiralling down. That was now a certainty, given the global developments already underway. Our inability to deliver on our platform commitments would be a further cause for censure. Finally, the coming deficits would be the ultimate proof point that we were both failing and had broken our promises.

Nevertheless, we had to govern, and the first formal indication of how we were going to address the current situation was the Throne Speech of November 19. To ensure that people could not miss the point, we titled it "Dealing with a Global Financial Crisis." We officially reiterated that our agenda was going to be different than what people were expecting in the middle of October. Throne Speeches, however, are just broad statements of the government's intentions. The first real political "meat" would be delivered in the Economic and Fiscal Update (EFU) scheduled for eight days later, on November 27.

Minister Flaherty and I were already huddling on the EFU and the parliamentary situation as we travelled to the Asia-Pacific Economic Cooperation

(APEC) Summit. It was slated for Lima, Peru, just three days after Parliament had re-convened. Jim would provide updates on his measures to keep financial markets operating in Canada, and he would undertake further actions for the financial sector. Most notably, he would announce measures to expand the credit available to Canadians through the government's own financial institutions—the Business Development Bank of Canada, the Export Development Corporation , and Farm Credit Canada. As mentioned, we had already been providing substantial assistance to the chartered banks, but this would further prod them to extend more credit to Canadians. This proved to be a wise decision; the federal financial organizations became effective and important parts of the economic recovery.

Given the large deficits we expected to announce in the upcoming budget, Minister Flaherty also took action to control the longer-term trajectory of the fiscal path. The problem was that events independent of any stimulus measures were threatening our financial position. Although not the only area, the most important one was Equalization. The record oil prices preceding the financial crisis—in the range of $140 per barrel—would radically push up our payments to the provinces just at the time when resource revenues for the federal government—oil was now under $40—were tanking. We therefore limited the growth of Equalization payments to nominal GDP.

One other measure Jim and I agreed on was the ending of the direct per-vote subsidy payments to political parties, beginning in the 2009–2010 fiscal year. It was a relatively small item in our expenditures, but we had concluded that we needed to do it to buy time. If, as I believed—and as Jim had surmised as well—the opposition parties were simply waiting for a moment to defeat us, this would give them pause.

Given the political furor that erupted over this, it is easy to overlook the arguments for it. Our party had always been opposed to this payment, and we had been clear on that. After all, there are lots of ways in which the taxpayers support political parties. These include the generous tax credits that people receive for political donations, as well as the expenditure reimbursements that parties and candidates get from Elections Canada (and which they use as collateral to borrow). The per-vote subsidy, in contrast, was just a gift, unrelated to any actual effort by the parties themselves. In the extreme case of the Bloc Québécois, some parties just stopped trying to raise their own funds altogether.

My colleagues had been urging the removal of these payments for some time, and there was a virtually unanimous view in Cabinet and caucus that we should do so. Indeed, when I told the caucus this was coming, the news was greeted with wild cheering. I urged caution, though, and not just because the measure would not be universally popular. Even though we were the party that was least dependent on the subsidy, we were also its largest benefactors. In other words, this would be a significant risk for us if we found ourselves forced to fight an election in the next couple of years.

The opposition response to the Economic and Fiscal Update was strongly negative. Their position was that it did not go far enough in addressing the economic crisis. To that I can only say, of course it did not go far enough. It was not a full budgetary or economic plan, and even at breakneck speed, we would require a few more weeks at a minimum to produce one. The idea that a full suite of new, unforeseen measures could be implemented immediately after the election was neither promised nor realistic.

We knew that the real reason for the opposition's anger was the removal of the per-vote subsidy: we believed it had upset their intended political strategy. On this, they took a radical position—that the measure was an "attack on democracy." That line was immediately taken up by the press gallery. Frankly, how requiring a political party to raise some of its own money is inherently undemocratic, I do not know. Besides, we knew from polling that the measure (at least in its own right) was widely supported by the public.

I was not surprised by the initial opposition response. I also did not think that this would be perceived by the public as the basis on which to force an election. I believed the opposition, after a lot of yelling, would have to accept that they needed to wait for the public to be ready for an election and prepared to help them finance one.

As it turned out, I had accurately divined the opposition's motives. What I had underestimated was their ambition.

THE ATTEMPTED "COALITION COUP"

THE ECONOMIC AND FISCAL UPDATE took place on Thursday. Friday, Saturday, and Sunday saw growing rumours that the opposition would bring forward a non-confidence motion to defeat the government over the EFU. These quickly morphed into reports that they might try to form some kind of a coalition to replace the government. Things were obviously moving quickly—so quickly, in fact, that I concluded the train had likely left the station well before my unproductive consultations. Only the timetable had moved up.

Yet I still found it hard to believe that political subsidies, regardless of the baying of the press gallery, was an issue they could hang a defeat of the government and an election on. And, in truth, I had never seriously considered the possibility of a coalition. Why not? Simple math. Combining the Liberals and NDP seat count, their number was nowhere near ours. It just did not make sense. I thought this seemed like a big bluff, at least initially.

But over those three days, the real complication was on our side. The party seemed to lose all will to defend the repeal of the per-vote subsidies and the government more generally. This was true in Cabinet, caucus, our communications teams, and even, to some degree, among our grassroots. The view that this was a crisis entirely of our own making was taking hold. That was in turn fuelling the opposition's aggression.

In the face of this collapsing confidence, I know that some close to me thought I had lost the will to fight back. That was a misreading. My demeanour was partly brought on by the fact that I had been unwell. On the way to Peru, I had come down with, to be polite, an all-symptoms flu bug. When my presence had not been publicly and absolutely required, I had been sick in bed, although no one outside my inner circle knew how ill I was.* My seeming

---

* Considering my medical history, particularly when I was young, it was amazing how little work I missed due to illness while PM. I do not have an exact count, but it would not have exceeded a half-dozen days in that near decade.

passivity in the days leading up to the coalition announcement was for medical not political reasons.

What is true is that I was unsure how to fight back, given the turmoil within the party. I bought some time by delaying upcoming confidence votes in the House. Then I called a caucus meeting for Monday, December 1, to gauge the mood. I was largely in listening mode (which likely reinforced a view that I was resigned). At that meeting, the sense of alarm was clear to me but, so too, I believed, was a willingness to fight if we could re-establish a narrative. Fortunately, the opposition quickly supplied it.

Later that day, the other parties made their announcement on the coming coalition. Just outside my office, a few staffers had gathered to watch it. After a few minutes, I stepped out to join them. My jaw literally hit the floor.

There they were, sitting in the National Press Theatre. Mr. Dion, who had just suffered one of the worst defeats of any Liberal leader in history, telling the country he would be the prime minister. Jarring, but what did you expect? Mr. Layton, playing the third-party kingmaker. A bit less jarring perhaps. And Mr. Duceppe, grinning like a Cheshire cat, an apparent co-equal in the grand project. At that point, with that image, I knew this was a fight I could win.

Of course, there had to be some part for the Bloc Québécois somewhere in this. Given the numbers, it could not be otherwise. But I thought everyone understood that relations with the Bloc had to be managed with great care. After all, we had co-operated on a limited basis with them from time to time. Even that limited co-operation had raised accusations of my being "in bed with the separatists."

As it turned out, I had thought this issue through much more thoroughly than my critics. But I had done more than that; over the years, I had also looked carefully at the data. The data showed that the opposition was on a suicide course.

There was one matter on which about 90 per cent of the English-Canadian population was united: a dislike of Quebec separatists. No, not a mere dislike—a loathing. Quebec separatists were not merely people English-Canadians disagreed with; they viewed them as, in essence, illegitimate.

Knowing this was a third rail of politics outside Quebec, I had always limited my interaction with the Bloc to tactic-specific actions. I knew anything general in nature had to be off the table. If, as a mainstream English-Canadian politician, you were ever seen as being in alliance with Quebec separatists, it would be a career-ending move. There was no way you could justify it to the public, and if it became the subject of a fight, there was no way you could survive.

THE GOVERNMENT GOES ON OFFENCE

NDP SUPPORTERS—then almost entirely anglophone—were not as allergic to a deal with the Bloc as the supporters of other parties. The far left was the one group of English-Canadians who had charitable views of Quebec separatists, because they were (then) perceived as good leftists. To these people, left-wing ideology mattered more than anything, including the country (and, frankly, much of the anglophone press gallery would fit into that group).

However, this venture was not riskless for the NDP. Their base might have stayed with them, but any appeal beyond that would have been destroyed. An even greater danger for them was being the junior partner in the coalition. In any democratic system, but especially under first-past-the-post, it is the riskiest position to be in. If people like the government, they tend to vote for the leading party; if not, they will tend to vote for the opposition. Support for the junior partner vanishes. Of course, as it turned out, the NDP never did have to deal with that risk.

In contrast, for the Liberals this was unambiguously bad. Since at least the days of Pierre Trudeau, the Liberals had trademarked themselves as *the* party of national unity. From childhood, I could recall images of Trudeau standing in defiance of bottle-throwing separatists at a Saint-Jean-Baptiste Day event. Here was a Quebecer prepared to stand up to Quebec separatists! It was a brand the Liberals had retained throughout the following decades, as the party always willing to defend Canadian unity. Jean Chrétien had built his national political success on this attribute, despite (or perhaps because of) the reservations within his own province.

Ironically, Stéphane Dion's own willingness to take on the separatists had been instrumental to his rise in federal politics. There was, however, no way for Mr. Dion to rationalize this new gambit. Quite simply, he risked permanently destroying the Liberal Party's most fundamental electoral asset.

Then there was the Bloc. For them, this arrangement was a dream come true. After its initial success under Lucien Bouchard, the Bloc had always struggled to show their relevance in Ottawa. That was a big part of the reason we had been able to pull a base of voters off the BQ's right flank—their "*impuissance*." Now, that problem was solved. The Bloc was not merely relevant; it was the *most* relevant player in Ottawa. It had made itself the potential swing vote in the House of Commons, able to have the government of its choosing.

Apologists for the arrangement tried to highlight that the Bloc was not technically "in" the coalition. But that made it even worse. Yes, Duceppe would not be part of the government. But that only meant that, while being critical to its survival, he would have no responsibility for its actions. He would be, to be blunt, the puppet master. As long as the government did what he wanted, he could support it. As soon as it did not, he could allege betrayal. I had long known that this was Duceppe's ultimate objective. I was just surprised that he found someone willing to actually give it to him.

That evening was the Conservative Christmas Party, where I was scheduled to give the normal seasonal good-cheer speech. By the time it came around, I had resolved to use the scene from the National Press Theatre as my campaign launch against "the coalition with the separatists." My aim would not be to merely defeat it; I would crush it in a way that nobody would ever consider it again. I delivered a rousing and combative address to get the troops ready for the battle to come.

The next day in the House of Commons, Stéphane Dion got up in Question Period (QP) to launch his opening salvo in the plan to remove the government. I suspect I caught him off-guard with the unvarnished, brutal tenor of my reply. Quite simply, I called his deal with the Bloc a sellout of the country's interests.

The "leader's round"—the opening five questions—went badly for Dion. He had no real comeback because what I said was true. He tried to counter by continuing to rise as the QP went on. I just kept pummelling him. By the end of it, our guys were in a frenzy singing "O Canada" on the floor of the House of Commons. The opposition looked like they had been shelled by heavy artillery.

But we did not limit our barrage to Parliament. That very day we began to run a countrywide radio campaign attacking the coalition deal. The next day, I followed up with a national television broadcast.

We knew we were winning at that point. But we were not merely winning. Contrary to the press gallery's chosen narrative of coalition success and Conservative suicide, we were watching Liberal support freefall in real time across the country. Our data suggested that, had an election been called at that moment on that issue, we would have had a shot at winning every single riding outside Quebec. That is how bad it was for the opposition.

Canadians were in an uproar. I received a graphic confirmation of this on Friday, December 5. I was in Kanata, a suburb of Ottawa, taking Ben to a hockey tournament. It was in a Conservative-held riding, but no right-wing bastion. I entered what I will describe as a working-class restaurant to have a bite with the other hockey dads.

On similar occasions in the past, when I was recognized, people might come over and ask for pictures. In this case, the whole restaurant leapt up, spontaneously cheering and singing the national anthem. Our campaign against the coalition had become unstoppable. The only way you could miss it was if you lived in a bubble on Parliament Hill. Or, perhaps, if you lived in Quebec.

Public opinion in Quebec was different, reflective of the very different political reality in that province. Sure, lots of Quebecers are strong federalists and do not agree with the separatists politically. But every francophone has relatives and friends who are Quebec sovereigntists. They are people like any other people. They have been in government. They are respectable.

In short, the issue of sovereignty is seen as well within the bounds of normal political discourse in Quebec. In English Canada, to be a Quebec separatist is beyond the pale, equated with any form of unacceptable political extremism. On this, neither "solitude" really appreciates the depth of the other's feelings.

PROROGATION AND THE COLLAPSE OF THE COALITION

OUR ANTI-COALITION CAMPAIGN UNDERWAY, there were only three paths forward in dealing with the situation. Two of those we deemed unacceptable.

The first would have been to let things play out. If the current session continued, the opposition would have been able to schedule a confidence vote sooner rather than later. Initially, everyone would have thought they would win it and form their new government. However, that outcome was more in doubt with each passing day. Stéphane Dion had followed his disastrous House performance with a disastrous national TV address in an effort to counter mine.* Rumours of a plot within the Liberal caucus to remove him were already beginning to circulate.

Still, we gamed out the prospect of a Liberal-NDP-Bloc coalition. It would come to power viewed not merely as unpopular but also as illegitimate. The hostility against it in a majority of the electorate would have been nuclear. It is hard to imagine that it would have governed either long or successfully. After all, given Duceppe's longer-term agenda, it was in his interests that this Bloc puppet government ultimately fail. So before long, we might have been back in power with a stronger mandate. But who really knows? Would our own party have faced internal strife in the meantime?

The second option would have been to call an election ourselves, given the surge of public opinion and the spectacular polls in favour of our

---

* I will not elaborate here except to say that the production was so poor that it overwhelmed whatever message Dion was trying to communicate.

government. But we quickly took that off the table as well. The public did not really want an election. In fact, they did not want any of this. Canadians were extremely anxious about the economy, and that is what they wanted the focus to be on. There was always the possibility, too, that they could go back to blaming us for the crisis.

While we thought that improbable, given the revulsion demonstrated by Canadians at the very idea of the coalition, the likely outcome was also unpalatable. We would win the vast majority of seats outside Quebec while the Bloc would win most of that province's, leaving the Liberals and NDP with just a smattering of ridings. The result would therefore have been a country completely polarized, with the sovereignty agenda back on the table. We had worked for three years to get rid of that, and we had been making real progress. It was not in the country's long-term interests to have it resurrected, and we certainly did not need that challenge back on our plates during such a perilous time. This once again underscored how the Bloc would be the sole clear winner if the coalition scenario continued to play out.

That left the only viable scenario: to ask Governor General Michaëlle Jean to prorogue Parliament. The idea had come to me first (and virtually simultaneously) from two sources. One was John Baird. The other was a long-time Conservative organizer in Ottawa, my close friend Colin McSweeney.

The rationale for this was compelling. It would delay a confidence vote until we could present our budget. Then, if we were to be defeated in the House, it would be on our full economic plan, on which work was already underway. Defeating us on substantive economic policy would only have strengthened our hand. Added to the ugly motivations of the opposition coalition, it would have put us in an almost unassailable political position.

The logic of prorogation grew with each passing day, as did support for the notion in our caucus. We were already in a position to win this confrontation. Prorogation would give us more breathing room, and let cooler heads prevail on all sides. The Liberals were likely to use the time to extricate themselves from this dilemma, which was in the interests of both our parties. We indicated we would cancel the upcoming repeal of the per-vote subsidies as a way of helping this along.

The meeting with the governor general was on December 4. We planned carefully. Although there was a great media show of drama, we never really had any doubt of being granted a prorogation. Our constitutional position was rock solid on the matter.

Having (I am sure) consulted the same legal authorities as we had, Michaëlle Jean conducted the meeting as we expected. For her, though, it was a no-win situation, so her handling of the matter needs to be fully appreciated. No expert on the constitutional position of governor general when she was appointed, Mme Jean worked hard to understand her duties and to perform them diligently in the best interests of the country. As for the initial rumours that she was supportive of, or at least sympathetic to, Quebec separatism, my experience was that nothing could be further from the truth. She is your typical Canadian immigrant, extremely proud of her country of choice.

The prorogation was granted, with one important caveat—that the government was not trying to indefinitely avoid a confidence vote. On this, Governor General Jean wanted an assurance. "By no means," I said. "In fact, we are going to come back before the end of January, with the first order of business being a budget containing the full economic action plan. That will of course be a confidence vote." Frankly, at that point, I relished having that confidence vote.

Although this turn of events deeply disappointed most of the media, by now the line that we were the ones on a suicide course was quickly unravelling. Only a few days later, on December 10, Dion was forced to resign. His successor, Michael Ignatieff, skilfully slipped into the interim leadership by subtly signalling an unwillingness to continue with the coalition pact. Although its official demise was not announced until January 28, there was zero doubt that the Liberal Party had gotten the message that the coalition was a suicidal political strategy.

The election had officially concluded on October 14. Only now had it finally ended in the minds of Messrs. Dion, Layton, and Duceppe. Yet, while the political crisis was winding down, another chapter in the economic crisis was quickly taking shape.

PART THREE

2008–2011

11

EMERGING FROM THE CRISIS

HAVING SURVIVED THE COALITION coup for the time being, one might have thought there would be a pause to catch one's breath—after all, it was mid-December—but that was not to be. Global economic activity and markets continued to trend down sharply. Several European countries, including Iceland and Ireland, were teetering on the edge of insolvency, and riots had broken out in Greece. Even China's economic engine was experiencing a dramatic slowdown. The looming spectre was mass unemployment, which we economists call a lagging indicator, that is, it is usually the last thing to get worse and the last thing to get better.

Despite the origins of the crisis outside our borders, strong effects were now being felt inside Canada. In short order, they would hit one of the country's largest industrial sectors—the automobile industry. My Government would be forced to make an unprecedented intervention.

SECTORAL ECONOMIC INTERVENTION

DIRECT SECTORAL INTERVENTION into business was not entirely new for our Government. Although we had generally opposed business subsidy and grant programs while in opposition (outside of agriculture), we quickly had to accept the economic realities in some sectors. Most notably in the automotive and aerospace industries, it was standard practice of governments around the world to provide incentives to land major industrial investments, so-called anchor capital.

Those anchors would form the basis of further supply chain development, usually in the same region. For automotive that was Ontario, and for aerospace it was Quebec. In short, you either played the game of attracting anchor investments to some degree, or you would eventually be without an industry in that sector. On the eve of the 2008 election, I had made one such announcement at the big Ford plant in Windsor.

On December 10, we received reports that George W. Bush was planning to step in and implement a massive restructuring and rescue plan for the entire American automotive sector. Given the complete integration of the Canadian sector with our southern neighbours, I immediately recognized the dire implications for our country of unilateral U.S. action. A strictly American restructuring would likely move the bulk of the sector out of Canada. That could mean as many as half a million jobs through the entire supply chain.

Alarmed, I immediately asked senior officials for their assessment of the implications of what we were hearing. Their read was the same as mine. "Then we are going to have to be part of this," I told them. "Figure out what percentage of the overall sector we are"—we guessed it was in the 20 per cent range —"and I'll call President Bush."

My first call, though, was to Ontario Premier McGuinty. Dalton and I did not have the warmest relationship at this point, but I knew him to be someone you could be direct with. Getting right to the point, I said, "The U.S. government is going to bail out and restructure the auto sector. We're either going to be part of this or watch them restructure it right out of Canada. So I'm making a call to President Bush to say we want to be part of what they're doing, and I want to say that the Government of Ontario is with us on this."

There was no doubt I had the premier's full attention. I could also feel his palpable sense of relief, as they were no doubt hearing the same things that we were. "The challenge, Premier," I went on to say, "is that the industry's so concentrated in Ontario that I cannot ask my Cabinet or caucus to do this without the full participation of the Government of Ontario. So you'll have to pay a big part of the bill."

There was a pause. "How much are we talking about?" he asked. "Well," I said, "the Americans will decide the scale, and we'll pay our percentage of the industry, around 20 per cent. On that 20 per cent, I want you to go in fifty-fifty with me. I want you to pay half." Another pause, and then he countered, "How about 25 per cent?" I responded, "How about a third?" His answer: "Done."

Often in government you can spend hours debating whether to spend a few million dollars. In those few moments, Premier McGuinty and I committed to share what would be a roughly thirteen-billion-dollar expenditure. That was the crazy time we were living in. McGuinty came to my office a few days later to sort out some of the technical aspects of the arrangement and plan for the formal announcement.

Up to then, my closest first-minister relationships were probably with Gordon Campbell in British Columbia, Gary Doer in Manitoba, and Brad Wall in Saskatchewan.* I would not have ranked Dalton McGuinty high on the list—nor me on his, I am sure. Different philosophies. Different priorities. Different personalities. From here on, though, it became a productive working relationship. Engulfed in the economic crisis, we were drawn together by the urgency of the moment. Perhaps we made strange bedfellows, but that was fortunate, considering what was on the line for Ontario and Canada.

That weekend, I talked to President Bush. I told him directly that Canada wanted and needed to be part of the automobile sector bailout and restructuring. I said that we would want our people at the table—the Province of Ontario being part of our team—in the negotiations, but I assured him we would not cause trouble. And, of course, we would pay our percentage share of the rescue package. He was both pleasantly surprised and in complete agreement. His

---

* I could add Bernard Lord of New Brunswick to the list, but he had ceased to be premier less than a year after I became prime minister.

quick concurrence was the fruit of our constructive-engagement approach to the United States. Within a couple of days, we had our officials on their way to DC.

Dalton McGuinty and I were able to set the announcement date for December 20—lightning speed for such a sweeping and complex initiative. It came off without a hitch, although not without some degree of shock, particularly in more conservative circles.

I have talked elsewhere of the economic lesson this whole episode should teach us about markets. There are some who have said that the auto bailout should have been sorted out in the financial market. Normally, I would agree. If the issue had been in Canada, it could conceivably have been solved in the private sector. The problem was that, in the United States, there was not, at that moment, a fully functioning financial system. So no private restructuring would be forthcoming. Without government action, the sector would have failed, and the U.S. economy would have faced yet another stage in its downward spiral. The American government thus intervened and, by its actions, forced our hand.

The lesson is that less government is not always the answer in terms of building a strong market economy (although it often is). Healthy markets have some public policy structure. Financial markets especially require some degree of regulation to prevent the boom-and-bust cycles that history has shown they are prone to.* The United States failed to do that and now, in both the financial and automotive sectors, we were facing the kind of massive intervention that free-market conservatives should rightly want to avoid. You can only imagine my contempt when, just a few months later, some executives in these very same sectors started to complain about "government interference."

---

* I believe that this is because financial markets are less "concrete" than other markets, in that their supply and demand curves are built around speculation about an inherently unknowable future. Thus, they are more prone to irrational cycles of greed and fear.

CANADA'S ECONOMIC ACTION PLAN

ON JANUARY 16, 2009, I invited the premiers back to Ottawa as part of the lead-up to the government's budget. The mood was marginally better than in November. The economy had certainly not recovered by then—it had not even started to recover—but at least the decline was no longer precipitous. The worst of the panic had passed, and markets had stabilized, albeit at low levels. Now, within the confines of budget confidentiality, we would outline the stimulus spending that was coming forward and confirm provincial and territorial participation. It was all part of building public support for the plan before it was formally tabled in Parliament.

Minister Flaherty and I had decided to brand the Government's unprecedented response "Canada's Economic Action Plan" (EAP), and as expected, infrastructure spending would be at its heart. Most of that spending would be tripartite in nature—the federal government, a provincial/territorial partner, and a third party. The last would usually be a municipality or municipal utility, but it could also be an Indigenous community, a university or college, or, on occasion, a private-sector participant. It would depend on the specific program and the nature of the project.

The necessary preparations complete, our Government introduced the plan to Parliament on January 27. That was just one day after the Throne Speech and, as promised to Governor General Jean, before the end of the month. Obviously, this was a whole different program than what had been discussed during the election campaign, with a deliberately large, proactive, Keynesian deficit that would clock in at around $60 billion in the first year.

As we had signalled, the backbone of this spending would be on "traditional" infrastructure: roads, bridges, wastewater facilities, and mass transit, as well as federal border and national security assets. We would also invest in electronic infrastructure—items like broadband and electronic health records.

A second part of the plan was directed at labour markets. We upped spending on skills training, created comprehensive work-sharing agreements between the Employment Insurance Commission and individual employers, and made temporary changes to the Employment Insurance (EI) program for first-time claimants. What we declined to do was make permanent enhancements to EI—the one policy on which the Liberal-NDP-Bloc coalition had been agreed. Finally, we looked at ways to stimulate consumer activity. Our big gun on that front was the Home Renovation Tax Credit. It would have the added benefit of bringing these expenditures, often unreported, into the tax system.

Ironically, this last element was as controversial with our officials as it was popular with the public. My own suspicion was that the bureaucratic resistance came because the money was not going into their ecosystem—departments, agencies, academia, the broader research community, and all those in government or tightly linked to it. But Minister Flaherty and I insisted on the program. I was blunt, saying, "We're not going to spend sixty billion dollars and have none of it go to middle-class, private-sector taxpayers. They must see some direct benefit in all of this." In fact, the program proved to be effective, accomplishing all the employment aims we set for it.

THE PARLIAMENTARY VERDICT

IT WAS NOT UNTIL January 28 that the coalition agreement was officially ended, although events in mid-December had left little doubt that it was over. The new Liberal leader, Michael Ignatieff, had made a point of being the last Liberal MP to sign the coalition pact, sending a strong signal that he was in fact against it. When public opinion turned on it with a vengeance, he was vindicated. Runner-up in the Liberal race in 2006, he was quickly made the interim leader and was well on his way to being coronated in the leadership contest to come.

Still, Mr. Ignatieff did not want it to look like his abandonment of his erstwhile coalition partners meant he was giving the government a blank cheque. Thus, the Liberals sponsored a non-confidence motion on January 29. But we never believed there was a serious intention to topple the government. The EAP had the enthusiastic backing of the provinces and other key economic and social stakeholders across the country. Ignatieff was certainly smart enough to know that the budget's popularity, combined with the residual brand damage from the coalition escapade, would put the Liberal Party in real peril were it to force an election at that moment.

We had concluded that Ignatieff simply wanted to show that the Liberals would not now be "bullied" in Parliament by the Government. He would not bring down the Government, but there would be a "price" for letting the EAP pass. His key demand was that the Government report quarterly to Parliament, show our progress on the Plan, and demonstrate that the money was being effectively spent.

This strategy would allow Ignatieff to show he was holding the government to account and keeping it on a tight, ninety-day leash. He could even claim that he was in the driver's seat. Nevertheless, I quickly agreed to his demand, and the budget passed.

I had readily embraced Ignatieff's condition because I saw it as opportunity. It fit neatly in with our government's philosophy of carefully tracking our commitments. We had already noticed that the bureaucracy could be particularly weak at following through on implementation. Having a formal parliamentary reporting requirement would put that issue at the top of the agenda.

In other words, we would try to make the Liberal condition a tool for our own success.

ASSESSING THE EXPERIENCE OF THE COALITION COUP

WITH THE PROSPECT of the government's quick defeat in the rear-view mirror, this is probably a good juncture at which to reflect on that whole episode. Would I have handled the series of events around the coalition coup differently if I had to do it again? Frankly, I have never been big on the should've-could've-would've scenarios, but in this case, let us give it a go.

Though it is easy to say that the whole situation could have been avoided had we not attempted to end the per-vote political party subsidies, I do not believe that really holds up to scrutiny. Our government had won the election, but with our minority—even an enhanced minority—our options were terrible.

The first judgment we had to make was whether or not to call the House back. When we did, we were accused of not having a full program ready to address the economic crisis. But if we had waited to get such a program ready, that would have delayed bringing the House back until after Christmas, followed by the inevitable charge that we had been asleep at the switch.

By the time we were back in Parliament, I faced the realization that the opposition was determined to defeat us one way or another and that the escalating nature of the crisis meant they would have grounds sooner or later. The move on the subsidies was an attempt to buy time. Admittedly, it hastened the crisis instead. Yet I think my real mistake was not preparing the ground for the measure. Despite our long-standing opposition to the subsidies, it caught too many people by surprise, making it easy to demonize.

That was a mistake I should not have made, as I was certainly aware that surprises can easily go sideways. That instinct is deeply engrained in my character. My mother likes to say that, even when I was a small child, she used to warn people, "Never surprise Stephen. Even when it's a very pleasant surprise, he will react badly to anything that is out of the blue. So don't surprise him!"

Perhaps, though, there was more to it. One of my observations in politics is that it is particularly easy to make mistakes when you are convinced you are on the right side of an issue. I saw that happen more than a few times in my Government and others. When your side is completely united on something, the scrutiny of both substance and communications can sometimes be lacking. Without some dissent, things often do not get thoroughly hashed out beforehand. Conservatives were fully united on the per-vote subsidy issue, and our polling had long showed that eliminating it would be popular. The debate about how to roll it out in context had never really occurred.

To be clear, however, there was no dissent. I say this because I would later read how such and such a minister or caucus member was reputed to have been against the measure or had even argued against it. These were, of course, "anonymous source" stories, and one should always question whether such stories are based on anything beyond rumour. But the idea that there was internal opposition to this measure was utterly untrue.

This is where the most important leadership lesson comes in. There is a reason that, as they say, "success has a thousand fathers, and failure's an orphan." Once the per-vote subsidy elimination got the pushback it did, vocal support virtually evaporated. That was partly because our supporters were completely unprepared for the reaction. But it is also human nature.

This is something I warn all who aspire to leadership about, particularly those with populist tendencies. It does not matter how popular a measure appears at first or how much effort goes into developing consensus around it. If a decision turns out to be wrong, you as the leader will be held solely accountable for it (just as you will take credit for it if it is a success). So be very leery about making seemingly popular decisions that you know to be wrong (not that this one was wrong). If the results are bad, nobody will remember that they were also for it. In fact, they will inevitably remember that they were not really for it after all. As someone once told me (and I wish I could remember who): "If you are wrong, your people may forgive you. But if your people are wrong, they will never forgive you."

The irony was that the opposition would repeat my error on a far grander scale. The surprise announcement of a Liberal-NDP-Bloc coalition government dwarfed the surprise of the per-vote subsidy elimination by orders of magnitude. It shocked even me, who already had reason to believe they were up to something. Furthermore, they completely neglected to ask themselves whether their actions were defensible or even popular. They were not—not remotely. The expression "jumping the shark" does not come close to describing where the opposition ended up.*

---

* I grant that some from generations younger than my own may not know the expression. It stems from the 1970s–1980s TV show *Happy Days*. The show's tough-guy hero Fonzie seemed to gain powers with each passing season. But when he jumped over a shark water-skiing—in his leather jacket no less—even the show's biggest fans found the storyline ridiculous.

I have always thought this episode was a particular tragedy for Stéphane Dion. He had long been one of federalism's most vocal and articulate defenders in Quebec. He may have thought that his reputation could justify actions completely contrary to that reputation—a mistake politicians often make. But it is just a fact that the bitterness of political defeat can distort the best people's judgment.

All this makes it hard for me to conclude that the approach was ultimately wrong. Even if we bungled the elimination of the per-vote subsidy initially, it ended up putting us where we wanted to be. We got the breathing room necessary to govern for long enough for an economic recovery to begin to take hold. Yes, how we got there was as unfortunate as it was traumatic. But if we had done nothing, we almost certainly would have been defeated in short order. In the end, the only loss was on the per-vote subsidy itself. I ended up having to delay it until after the next election, when I made it a specific platform commitment.*

THE CORNER IS TURNED

IN 2009, THE NEWLY MINTED G20 Leaders' Summit would occur twice. In April, there would be an interim meeting in London. It was felt that, given the magnitude of the crisis, we should gather to assess progress.

It would be an exaggeration to say that the London meeting was about recovery. The overall picture was still one of decline, particularly on the employment front. However, we were truly past the panic phase. The extraordinary actions in financial sectors and monetary policy were having an impact. So, too, were some fiscal measures around the world, although, for the most part, they were still in the very early stages.

---

* Interestingly, the opposition did not challenge us on it during that campaign, as they knew it was popular. We had delayed it, and to look reasonable, we committed to phase it out over three years. A drafting error in the eventual legislation made the phase-out over four years.

Overall, international co-operation and the sense of shared mission among G20 leaders remained very high at the London meeting. It was also the first appearance of the new U.S. president, Barack Obama. Although George W. Bush had led the creation of this summit and its initial actions, it is fair to say that the change was generally welcomed. Obama was seen as more "multilateral" at heart, that is, more aligned with most leaders on a wider range of issues.

Our international message, especially at the G20, was that Canada should serve as a model for how an economy can be fundamentally market-oriented and private-sector driven, yet also responsibly managed in the financial sector. Canada did not need to purchase bad assets, undertake bank bailouts, or nationalize financial institutions. That was important because, when it came to the discussions around a new global regime for banking regulation, we were concerned with the kinds of proposals coming from the countries that had engaged in such actions.

We advocated Canada's system of regulation, which has been described as "macro-prudential." Our approach was not built on escalating arrays of rules, as others were advocating. No set of rules will ever be comprehensive enough to address all risks, and such an approach can unnecessarily burden the sector and its lending capabilities. Yes, we had rules in Canada. But they were generally light and high-level, with regulators instead dialoguing with the major financial institutions to assess the overall stability and risks in the sector. That dialogue had, in turn, helped create a conservative banking culture that avoided the bailouts required elsewhere—bailouts that, in some cases, had to come from the International Monetary Fund and be applied to entire economies.

By the time of the next G20 meeting in Pittsburgh in September, there were signs of substantial improvement in the global economy. So-called green shoots were beginning to appear in various places, including Canada. By June, our unemployment rate had peaked at 8.8 per cent, well below the double digits that had been expected. In the third quarter, there were clear signs of growth in both jobs and economic activity. Those were the reports we were getting from the business community and others across the country, and they would later be confirmed by Statistics Canada data.

At Pittsburgh, I was able to draw attention to Canada's superior economic performance. I observed that "Canada remains in a very special place in the world. We are the one major developed country that no one thinks has any responsibility for this crisis. In fact, on the contrary, they look at our policies as a solution to the crisis. We are the one country in the room everybody would like to be."

Yes, it was boastful, but it was deliberate. While I recognize that we are not by nature a boastful nation, the speed and scale of the economic crisis had really spooked Canadians over the preceding months. I judged, during that period, that the country needed unusual shots of confidence. That had really hit me early in the global financial crisis during a Chamber of Commerce event. (I think it was in Mississauga, but I am not sure.) I had praised the performance of the Canadian banks and the strength of that sector, for which I received a standing ovation. When small-business people are wildly cheering the banks, I thought, the Canadian psyche really is in an unusual place!

THE OPPOSITION LOSES THE PLOT

AS IN ALL OTHER THINGS, managing our way through the global financial crisis was rendered more challenging by the politics of our minority parliament. However, even on that front, the situation was improving. The failure of the coalition coup had put the opposition on its back foot for a time. With the rollout of the EAP and the gradual improvement in the economy, our Government's own footing got stronger.

On February 17, 2009, shortly after the budget received approval-in-principle from Parliament, I went to Toronto to make a big announcement with Premier McGuinty on expansion plans for GO Transit. In short order, I also signalled major mass transit funding for the Evergreen Line Project in Vancouver. Then there was money for the Sheppard Line, a major expansion of Toronto's subway system. I could go on like this at length, with a growing list of projects that the reader might find tedious. Suffice it to say that my efforts were being multiplied by our ministers, who fanned out across the country doing the same. Every day, it seemed, was a "good-news day" for the government.

The advertising campaigns around the EAP were also kicking in in a big way, along with that distinctive branding and signage. There would soon be hundreds of signs. The commercials would direct Canadians to custom-designed websites with more detailed information.

There is a cynical saying among opposition politicians of all stripes: "Cheer up; things could get worse." However, in this case, they were getting demonstrably better, and thanks to the Liberals' own idea of detailed government reporting, the public was seeing results. To everyone's surprise, the recession was turning out to be a terrible time to be the opposition.

Under these circumstances, it is not surprising that the release of each EAP report became a crisis for the opposition rather than for the government. We would launch the reports with high-profile events across the country. They would demonstrate that the rollout of projects was faster than just about anywhere in the world—way ahead of the expectations of most objective analysts, way ahead of where even we thought we would be. Yet, in a sign of how detached Parliament Hill can be from "real life," the first two reports triggered crises in Ottawa.

Very shortly after the first report in June, Michael Ignatieff had tentatively signalled an intention to bring in a non-confidence vote. When that was poorly received, I made it easy for him to back off by offering to meet and discuss what further measures we could take. As it turns out, we did identify some items of interest to him, including raising the number of Opposition days in the Parliamentary schedule.

The Liberals also wanted a broadening and expanding of Canada's Employment Insurance program, which was more of a problem for us philosophically. Still, I tried to meet Michael halfway: "If there are ways we can work together," I said, "let's look at the system. Where it can be improved, without high work-disincentive effects, we might be able to do something."

We set up a bipartisan panel to privately discuss the issues, but it never got off the ground. It was clear from the first meeting that the Liberal members had instructions not to do anything. Thus, it went nowhere.

Yet the fact that we had made these concessions gave Ignatieff the chance to walk away from his threat. It was the wise thing to do anyway. The reality on the ground was that the public did not want an election—it had only been eight months since the last one—and certainly not one that we all just stumbled into. My move also sent a clear message that our party was trying to avoid such an election. It reinforced our stated position that we were squarely focused on the economy and that any parliamentary dysfunction was not on us. It was a narrative that we wanted to keep driving.

We soon had a chance to do so. In September, the second EAP report came out. Against the backdrop of an improving economy, we were able to document significant and continuing progress. It did not matter. This time Ignatieff was definitive; he would move a confidence motion against the government.

It was a strange development. No storyline had been built to explain why an election was necessary. We had just come out with a positive, fact-based report, and there was no attempt to refute it. Why would Ignatieff drag the country into an election at that moment? Nobody knew.

Regardless of how this played out, we were prepared for an election. That was something on which we never let our guard down. Doug Finley had our election machinery ready to go. Irving Gerstein, chairman of the Conservative Fund, had the financing in place. At this point, I viewed Ignatieff's hard-core stance as, in fact, a sign of weakness, so I went on the attack. I may not have used the phrase, but I described the unfolding scenario as a "Seinfeld election"—an election about nothing. We drove that message hard, and it worked.

In the end, it was the NDP that stepped in to avoid a campaign. On October 1, 2009, Jack Layton's MPs voted with us and against the Liberal motion, leading to its defeat. Ignatieff wound up being severely criticized, even in the liberal media, for a strategy that just seemed to be completely off-key in terms of public sentiment.

I have often wondered why Michael Ignatieff, such an intelligent and accomplished individual, proceeded as he did at that point. Of course, I cannot say for certain, but I do know something about opposition dynamics in a minority parliament, having endured them myself. Following the coalition crisis, it had principally been the Liberals that sustained us in office. That is always a very awkward position for any opposition leader to be in. Recall that I had successfully used the discomfort it creates against Jack Layton's NDP in the fall of 2005.

So I suspect the pressure on Ignatieff came from within the Liberal Party. A rewriting of history had begun—at Mr. Ignatieff's expense. It went like this: the Liberals had me and my Government dead to rights with their coalition plan. Along comes Michael Ignatieff; the coalition ends; I survive. Not only do I survive, I get stronger politically. And now the economy is getting stronger too. Michael is thus urged to do something before it is too late, as in "do not miss another chance; act now."

That is my supposition, and it is consistent with the narrative that many commentators who supported the coalition have long nurtured. The problem is that it is completely contrary to fact. Michael Ignatieff had saved the Liberals from the debacle that was taking shape had it continued to ally itself with the Bloc Québécois. The polling at the time was crystal clear: the Liberal Party of Canada could not survive linked to people whose goal was the destruction of the Canadian state. Any opportunity to quickly bring down the government had already been blown out of the water by Stéphane Dion's action. There was nothing in the short term that Ignatieff could have done to restore it.

The upshot was that our Government survived. Indeed, we had survived for the fourth time. And each ham-fisted attempt to remove us was only strengthening us politically. It was building up our narrative: we were working on the economy; they were playing politics. And the best narratives are true.

FACTORS IN CANADA'S SUCCESS

BY THE TIME of our third EAP report, we had committed 90 per cent of the funds in the Plan via some 7,500 shovel-ready infrastructure projects. Half of them were already underway. As I had said from the beginning,

Canada would be the "last in, least affected, and first out" of the global financial crisis among the major advanced economies. It behooves us to ask why.

For one thing, we had a solid financial system that had no significant problems of its own and required no bailouts. We were also helped by the diversity of our economy, with the rapid recovery of energy and other commodity prices as a particular asset at the time. As well, our strong balance sheet meant we could run a large deficit with little risk of long-term debt problems and without any need for experimental monetary policies like quantitative easing.*

Most of all, our rollout of fiscal stimulus was rapid and effective. Unlike many countries, we did not create new machinery—new bureaucracies, departments, or agencies—to deliver the stimulus. On the contrary, we used the crisis as a way of thinning federal approval, accounting, and auditing practices around project delivery. It helped that the clerk of the Privy Council, Wayne Wouters, had witnessed first-hand the construction of the "web of rules" in the later years of the previous government, so he had a good idea of what needed to be done. In the end, we had virtually no administrative, competency, accounting, efficiency, or corruption issues despite the rapid execution of the EAP.† In fact, the Plan laid the groundwork for permanent improvement in federal approval processes and later, comprehensive, regulatory reform.

---

* Quantitative easing (QE) as a form of monetary policy in which a central bank, like the Bank of Canada, purchases securities from the open market to reduce interest rates and directly increase the money supply, that is, "printing money" in laymen's terms. QE creates new bank reserves, providing banks with more liquidity to encourage lending and investment. In the United States, the Federal Reserve implemented three rounds of QE that lasted until 2015. Even then, it did not significantly pare back its balance sheet.

† There was one small segment of spending around the G8 in Muskoka that raised concerns, but it had been done outside the framework of the EAP.

A GREAT TEAM

AS I SAID, there were a lot of factors—some pre-existing, some created by us—that allowed Canada to get through the global financial crisis far better than most. That success was widely acknowledged, even if the full set of reasons were not understood. But the most underappreciated aspect was the team I had in government overseeing our actions.

Let me start at the centre, with the Privy Council Office and my own organization, the Prime Minister's Office. The Ignatieff reporting requirement made the rapid and effective delivery of the EAP a no-fail mission, and that had to start at the top. A solid relationship developed between two relatively recent appointees: Clerk Wouters and my chief of staff, Guy Giorno‡. Guy is a systems-oriented lawyer who brought solid executive experience from the Mike Harris government. They brought the political and bureaucratic priorities of the EAP into line. Wayne was particularly effective in getting "the system" to rise to the challenge.

This was a big change in image for a federal bureaucracy that had only a few years earlier been defined by a series of failings and abuses, including the sponsorship scandal. I have periodically been critical of shortcomings in the public service, but in my experience, the chance to help improve the country is why most people join the public service in the first place. At the senior levels, they certainly do not do it for the salaries, which are far below their private-sector equivalents. In this case, the public service grabbed the opportunity to do something extremely helpful for Canadians, and they deserve to be recognized for it.

---

‡ Ian Brodie had left in the spring of 2008 to become a Canadian representative at the Inter-American Development Bank. He had spent nearly three years as my chief of staff. Given the demands of the job, that is about as long as one can do it effectively. Wouters, who had been Treasury Board Secretary, replaced Kevin Lynch as Clerk halfway through 2009. Lynch had succeeded Alex Himelfarb, who as Clerk had handled the transition between the Martin government and ours.

Of course, Prime Minister's Office–Privy Council Office co-operation was far from sufficient to do what needed to be done. That had to happen down the line and be led by individual ministers as well. Fortunately, the key ones were, for the most part, experienced players who delivered our programs calmly and expeditiously. These people were all backed by staff members—dedicated, highly competent young professionals—who are too numerous to mention.

Diane Finley was responsible for the temporary but essential changes we made to EI and the related agreements with industry. Hundreds of thousands of Canadians benefitted from these. John Baird held the Transport portfolio, which then included Infrastructure, and was therefore critical to delivering the accelerated, yet virtually flawless, approvals for thousands of projects. Christian Paradis and later Rona Ambrose were largely responsible for efficiently executing the projects under direct federal control. Stockwell Day kept our trade negotiations moving forward while the world lunged from one crisis to the next. And I would be remiss not to mention our then House leader, Jay Hill, who had to keep our agenda moving through the Commons during those tumultuous times in Parliament.

Special mention should also go to Tony Clement, who was ultimately responsible for seeing through the negotiations with the auto industry and the U.S. government, as well as Vic Toews, who, as president of the Treasury Board, kept EAP items moving forward. I mention these in one breath because we were all together on April 30, 2009. That was my fiftieth birthday, but also the day the auto sector agreement had to get final approval from the Treasury Board. Although this action was overwhelmingly supported in Cabinet and caucus, there were members with great reservations about the dollar amounts involved, and we had one final debate.

I cannot deny that I was one of those people with mixed feelings. On that milestone birthday, I was torn between two truths. One was that this was contrary to many of the reasons I had entered politics in the first place. The other was the understanding that, as a conservative focused on dealing with economic realities, this simply had to be done.

I think a word is warranted about the outcome of that undertaking. I sometimes hear it said that "the government made money on saving the automobile industry." That is not the case. We immediately wrote down the value of the subsidies and loans. When we eventually sold our shares, we recovered more than the reduced value, hence the stories that the venture was profitable. However, we were still about three billion dollars in the hole, although that was much less than the thirteen billion the bailout initially cost Canada.

My judgment remains that that money was well spent considering the alternative scenario. Nevertheless, the downside of that period has been the opening of the door to similar, but much less justifiable actions. Our successors have, for example, recently twice committed sums roughly equivalent to the entire auto sector bailout just to get electric-battery plants placed in Canada. It is impossible to imagine how those undertakings will ever justify that kind of expenditure. Besides, those were done without the kind of pressures to act that we faced in 2008–2009, nor with the same likelihood of eventual success.

But I digress, as I have not yet mentioned the most important person by far in Canada's successful response to the global financial crisis, inside or outside of Cabinet. That was my friend, the late Jim Flaherty.

I did not know Flaherty well at all when I became leader of the newly merged Conservative Party of Canada. A Whitby lawyer, he had served in several senior positions in the Mike Harris government, including minister of finance and deputy premier, when he contacted me about exploring a transition to federal politics. Sometime in 2004–2005, he came to see me, and we had lunch in my office.

Jim asked, "I'd like to run, but will you give me anything if I run?" I had never made such a commitment before, but I was prepared to make an exception for him. Even then, I did not promise a specific Cabinet posting. I just said, "Run, and, if you get elected, Jim, you'll be in Cabinet." He responded: "I'd like to get an economic portfolio." And I said, "I can't guarantee it, but that is probably in the cards." We talked about the Industry portfolio, which was his main interest.

After he won the federal seat in Whitby–Oshawa, I named him finance minister, the same post he had once held in Ontario. To my surprise, when I told him he was going to be finance minister, he was not quite sure that was the job he really wanted. Either way, he accepted and eventually came to love it. A couple of years later, when I was thinking of moving him to Industry, he made it clear that Finance had indeed become his first choice. And he just got better and better at it.

There are many things that I can say about Jim, but the most apt is that he was what we call a "smart-smart" guy. He had a great intellect, being remarkably capable of quickly assimilating all kinds of complex material. But he also had common sense, good judgment, an instinct in separating the important from the unimportant, and the ability to distinguish between academic theory and practical reality. Jim was smart in both senses.

Jim had this image as a tough little Irish brawler, and believe me, I had enough of those tussles with him to not entirely dismiss that stereotype. Yet, contrary to that image, Jim was at heart a very empathetic person. Fiscally more conservative than even I am, he was not a hard sell on the need to take extraordinary actions during the financial crisis. He saw people on the ground losing their jobs in large numbers, and he desperately wanted to help them.

One of Jim's most underrated series of accomplishments was in the whole area of assistance for the disabled. He pioneered a lot of our Government's work on disabilities, including the Registered Disability Savings Plan and the renowned Abilities Centre in Durham. This was a huge passion for him, as he had a disabled child.

Jim moved comfortably through Wall Street, Bay Street, and their equivalents elsewhere, but it was not who he was. He was a small-town lawyer, not a big-city financier. Whenever we were considering budget proposals, he would always ask how ordinary working- and middle-class families would benefit from what we were doing. When it came to things like converting capital gains to a Tax-Free Saving Account or making our income-splitting proposals operational, he made sure a broad range of the population would be winners. He was always very sensitive to good community economics, just as he believed we needed to lower the corporate tax rate. He helped create the lowest corporate tax on new business investment in the G7, but he also ensured that our tax cuts had widely distributed benefits. He was a populist conservative in the best sense of the term.

Jim Flaherty was not merely the guy who brought forward the fiscal measures in the EAP. He was the person charged with the day-to-day oversight of the financial, monetary, and banking complexities that arose throughout the global financial crisis. He was indispensable to Canada's superior response.

CANADA'S UNIQUE CHALLENGES

I DO NOT WISH to leave the impression that we had no challenges during the global financial crisis. One was obviously the parliamentary dynamics, which I have spelled out in detail. There were also specific issues around Air Canada and Davie, the Québec-based shipbuilder.

While we never had to bail out our banking sector, problems in these two companies ultimately saw us act. In both cases, we were concerned that their failure could have wider ramifications in their sectors. We also judged that these businesses would be fine with short-term, emergency government assistance. That proved to be true, and Canadian taxpayers were promptly reimbursed.

The most serious issue in the financial sector itself was largely beyond the federal government's scope. That was the crisis in what is called asset-backed commercial paper (ABCP). These are promissory notes backed by other assets as collateral, and they are largely governed under provincial regulatory authorities. In Canada the ABCP market was over $100 billion. The issues emanating from the U.S. sub-prime mortgage market in 2007 began to spook markets in Canada, putting the fulfillment of these significant obligations in jeopardy.

Led by lawyer, businessman, and industry veteran Purdy Crawford, a solution—messy and imperfect but a solution nonetheless—was negotiated. Some $32 billion in liabilities would have to be restructured. That would, at its core, involve lengthening the maturity terms of the ABCP. However, with the escalation of the crisis in the fall of 2008, the ABCP market and the deal were again in trouble. Although it affected the industry across the country, the centre of the crisis was Quebec, with the Caisse de dépôt et placement du Québec and the National Bank of Canada at particular risk.

Premier Charest's government petitioned us to help, which was ironic. Our government, led by Minister Flaherty, was trying to create a national securities regulator—we are the only major economy without one—to better avoid this kind of problem. Now here was the biggest opponent of the national regulator coming cap in hand. Frankly, a side of me wishes that I had I used the opportunity to push Quebec to get on board. However, with the world falling apart late in 2008, I resisted the temptation to complicate what was an already fraught situation around ABCP.

We agreed, along with Quebec, plus Ontario and Alberta, to provide some backstop funding for the maintenance of the negotiated ABCP settlement. The backstop was necessary to get the more reluctant parties to sign on, and in the end, it was not drawn. Unfortunately, however, the opportunity for the national securities regulator was lost. Our first proposal to set one up was rejected as unconstitutional by the Supreme Court. Minister Flaherty then led efforts to create a co-operative regime of willing provinces and territories, of which eight of the thirteen bought into the plan. Some efforts were continued under our successors, but they ceased in 2021.

Minister Flaherty and I also took some time, once the crisis had passed, to contemplate the ones that did not occur. It was an interesting exercise. With senior officials, we did some brainstorming around what risks might exist in Canada or elsewhere that could again trigger the kind of situation we had just been through.

One scenario that started flashing big red lights was the Canada Mortgage and Housing Corporation (CMHC). Under both the previous Liberal government and our own, the CMHC had been radically scaling up its activities but with very little political oversight or understanding. As I recall, CMHC had expanded its balance sheet by an order of magnitude, taking a lot of the overall risks of institutional mortgage lenders onto their books. It appeared that CMHC was well on its way to becoming Canada's version of Fannie Mae and Freddie Mac—the federally backed mortgage companies that had played a significant role in creating the U.S. mortgage crisis.

It was apparent that the expansion of CMHC had not been well considered, so the Minister took several actions. For one, he had a full assessment done on CMHC and required it to develop comprehensive risk-management tools going forward. Efforts were also undertaken to gradually shift mortgage risks back to the banks and other lenders. I believe these changes at CMHC helped the country avoid a longer-term problem. Ironically, it was the difficulties in the United States and elsewhere that alerted us to this potential time bomb in Canada.

Although most of this work on CMHC was never seen or understood by the Canadian public, one set of measures was. Those were the changes to consumer mortgage rules. For decades, CMHC had only been willing to insure mortgages of twenty-five years or less. That had been increased to forty years, with less stringent down payment requirements. This increasingly meant people were paying almost no principal on their monthly mortgage payments. Over time, we tightened those rules and moved the insurable mortgage term back to twenty-five years. However, the terms of mortgages have been creeping back up since we left office.

There is one last item worth mentioning. As Minister Flaherty and I worked through possible future crisis scenarios, there was one for which we had no real answer: a sovereign debt crisis in the United States. Few people talk about this because too many, especially in the U.S., believe it cannot happen. They are wrong.

As with any other institution, a government may someday need to borrow more money than the market is willing to provide at an interest rate that it can afford. There is no law that releases the U.S. government from the tyranny of arithmetic under such circumstances. Unfortunately, what we do know from experience is that the bigger the institution, the longer a debt crisis takes to develop, the longer no one thinks it is possible, and once it does, the faster it moves.

The U.S. fiscal position is far worse today than it was when I was in office. Frankly, its trajectory is now that of a runaway train. If something is not done, a U.S. debt crisis is an outcome that we will eventually have to deal with, and probably sooner than most people think.

REFLECTIONS ON THE GLOBAL FINANCIAL CRISIS

I HAVE OFTEN LOOKED BACK at the global financial crisis and how it was handled around the world. I have thought about it particularly in the context of the turbulent politics that Western democracies began experiencing a few years later.

In 2016 alone, we had two remarkable political events. One was the election of Donald Trump as president of the United States. He was not just an unorthodox candidate in almost every sense; he succeeded by running against both American political parties, including the Republican Party, which he essentially hijacked as an outsider. The other was the vote for Brexit in the United Kingdom. Whatever one thinks of that outcome—I am of two minds myself—it was truly unprecedented.

Such developments have not been restricted to the U.S. and the U.K. Most democracies experienced the rise of new and unorthodox political parties and leaders in the post-crisis period. They came in the form of so-called populists, whether (usually) right-wing nationalist or (in some cases) neo-Marxist movements. All have questioned the post–Cold War consensus around free markets, free trade, and freer migration, as well as challenging some aspects of institutional governance in free and democratic societies.

I strongly believe that these developments are a fallout from the way the global financial crisis was handled in several countries. Two of these stand out: the bank bailouts and monetary policy. In both cases, Wall Street recovered quickly; Main Street not so much.

The U.S., the U.K., and others rushed in with massive emergency bailouts for the financial sector. This essentially meant that the banks had their bad assets taken off their hands at public expense. Yet it seemed like the good life of private jets and corporate bonuses went on seamlessly. While I am sure that was not universally true, there were no stories about the financial-sector rich becoming destitute, while those of ordinary folks losing their homes and jobs were legion.

I believe that the monetary policy effects are especially underappreciated. For years central bankers worried about deflation, pumping more liquidity into the economy through ultra-low interest rates and, in the case of quantitative easing, increased reserves on bank balance sheets. Then they wondered why there was "no inflation."

But there was inflation. It was asset inflation, not consumer inflation. After all, the monetary expansions did not go, for the most part, to consumers. They went largely to corporations, higher-worth individuals, and asset-holders generally. This was probably the largest upward transfer of wealth in history.

I am not saying that all these actions were necessarily wrong under the circumstances. But they were certainly consequential. Add these tales to the generally poor performance of working- and middle-class incomes in many countries in the years prior to the global financial crisis. Frankly, the real question is not why political upheaval came, but why it did not come sooner. Listening to "elite" voices even today, there still seems to be little understanding of why ordinary people would be unhappy.

I am proud that, in Canada, we avoided the worst of the policies and that fallout. We had no bailout of Bay Street. The economy returned to growth, modestly but quickly. Home ownership statistics improved. There was income improvement, again modest, but across a wide range of incomes—a result, in part, of our broad-based tax cuts. Thus, there was no political upheaval. Yes, governments did change (including, eventually, mine), but the alternatives chosen were conventional political options.

Yet there is no law of nature sparing Canada from political turmoil under different scenarios and different policy choices.

12

FOREIGN AFFAIRS DURING THE GLOBAL FINANCIAL CRISIS

THE DAY-TO-DAY of the global financial crisis, the accompanying recession in Canada, and the heightened uncertainty of the parliamentary environment meant that most of our practical focus was domestic in 2009. Some international meetings, especially the G20 Summits, were closely tied to managing our economy during that period. Still, the conduct of foreign affairs beyond the crisis had to continue since much of it happens on a regular, preordained schedule.

THE "SUMMIT CIRCUIT"

BEFORE ASSUMING OFFICE, I did not fully appreciate—I think few Canadians do—the amount of time the prime minister is required to devote to the international travel related to foreign affairs. No amount of experience in opposition really prepares you because foreign affairs are almost exclusively the preserve of the governing party.

Yet, once prime minister, I learned very quickly—almost immediately—how burdened with international travel one really is. It begins with a series of automatic, pro forma international summits that, under all but the most exigent circumstances, cannot be missed. By my count, there were ten on my travel agenda before I even set foot in my office.*

First, there were the meetings that occur annually. These include the G8—later G7, after Russia's suspension—and the G20, which, as mentioned, occurred twice in 2009. There was the Asia-Pacific Economic Cooperation group (APEC) and the North American Leaders' Summit (NALS). NALS was annual at the time, but it became intermittent after 2009 and has remained so. The United Nations also has a yearly High-Level Week, for leaders, which Canadian prime ministers typically attend every two or three years. However, it constitutes an annual exercise because there are usually side meetings in New York and/or Ottawa around it.

Then there are the summits that are less than annual but still regular. The North Atlantic Treaty Organization (NATO) meets every eighteen months. Every two years, there are meetings of the Organisation internationale de la Francophonie and the Commonwealth Heads of Government Meeting (CHOGM). (And, yes, distressingly, CHOGM is used as a word.) Every three years, there was the Organization of American States' (OAS) Summit of the Americas, which is attended by all the leaders of the western hemisphere.

The meeting that then occurred most frequently was the Canada-European Union Summit. I discovered that it would meet every six months, alternating between Canada and Europe. To the extent I wanted to pare back my travel, I identified attending this as a target early on.

In addition to these regular summits are not-infrequent one-off international events. I think of the trips we made to Europe to mark World War II memorials or the travel to South Africa for Nelson Mandela's funeral. And nothing on this long list of meetings includes voyages that prime ministers might want to make for their own specific or pressing foreign affairs priorities.

---

* The Obama administration would eventually add an 11th high-level meeting, the Nuclear Security Summit. It met every two years from 2010 to 2016 but has not been held since.

The prime minister's time is very limited, and success is not measured by how many international organizations we belong to or how many international meetings we attend. These summits are all time-consuming in both preparation and execution. For any voyage beyond Washington, they are also long distances and often many time zones away. All that was very taxing, even for me as a PM who was then in his mid-forties.*

The reality is that these summits varied greatly in value for Canada. The most consistently important was the G7/G8, without a doubt. That is because all the countries represented in those meetings were advanced economies, NATO members or NATO partners, and full-fledged democracies. There were thus great alignment of interests and a frequent desire to act in concert—except for Russia (which I will address later). Because Canada was arguably the smallest party at the table, these encounters were by definition quality time in terms of leader interaction.

Generally speaking, the smaller the cast of players, the more like-minded the countries, and the more focused the summit agenda, the better it was. Many summits could be consistently wanting on one or even all these measures. Frankly, for a trip that could take a week or more of my time when you added it all up, I would frequently wonder why we were there at all.

Our officials argued that there was a lot of value in the bilateral meetings that took place around these summits. That is true to a certain extent, but they did not always justify the trip. Those rushed, frenetic meetings were nowhere near as valuable as a bilateral visit when a foreign leader came to Canada or I went to their country. Those were invariably far more substantive engagements, enhanced by the tête-à-tête meetings and relationship-building that transpired. Yet the sheer volume of summit travel left much less time for more focused trips like those.

---

* Perhaps the most remarkable thing about my travel during my time as leader and prime minister was that we had almost no foul-ups ever with luggage, reservations, or anything else. Credit lies with a superb tour and planning team led for most of those years by Debbie Campbell.

A NEW AMERICAN PRESIDENT

THE MEETINGS OF THE G20 brought about a new intensity to international economic diplomacy, particularly after the first encounter in Washington. Besides the April meeting in London, there were calls and engagements at other summits with my fellow G20 leaders, as we compared notes and hammered out summit declarations. I took a cautious approach to such meetings; I avoided meetings for meetings' sake, only calling other leaders if there really was a need, or unless they wanted to talk to me.

When I did talk to others, even on the phone, I would often try to keep things less formal and structured than they might otherwise be. I would seek to get beyond the policy talking points and into the political situations, which is often what drives most leaders. In those conversations, it was very apparent that other countries were noticing Canada and how much better conditions were here.

Of course, the most important of these bilateral interactions was with the new U.S. president, Barack Obama. Freshly inaugurated, he gave me a call on January 23, 2009. It is hard to describe the public excitement around Obama at that time. He was the first African-American president—a true landmark in a country with long-troubled race relations—and was admired for his soaring, inspirational oratory. As we say, he was truly a rock star.

This call was obviously an opportunity to try to establish a personal, working dialogue with the new president, which would hopefully lead to open exchange and collaboration on bilateral and international issues. As I have said before, I consider this vital for any prime minister. I felt that the call was successful on that score.

For that discussion, I had one big specific matter on the top of my mind: the auto bailout. I wanted to ensure that the working relationship between the United States and Canada-Ontario, established in the dying days of the Bush administration, would move forward. It was critical that the hand-off be complete and seamless and that Canada not get lost in the transition shuffle. The president reassured me in this regard, and he was as good as his word.

We did indeed collaborate with the Obama administration to complete the work on the auto sector. It is also worth noting how that progressed, compared with his predecessor. Although Obama was accused of being in the pocket of the unions and thus likely to go soft in the negotiations with the automobile companies, we did not find that to be the case. If anything, we found that the new team were tougher bargainers.

Only a few weeks later, on February 19, President Obama paid Canadians the honour of visiting Ottawa. As per the (then) long-standing tradition, it was the first foreign trip by the incoming American president. There were good reasons for this. We are not merely close neighbours. We share large and close diplomatic, security, and economic relations in all their dimensions, including the biggest bilateral trade relationship in the world.

The trip was obviously a big opportunity to build on our introductory phone call. Again, I began with a long tête-à-tête in my Centre Block office, which was critical to the kind of working relationship I wanted. It was a wide-ranging and constructive dialogue, surveying the issues we both had on our plates and where we might work together. We then moved into a conversation that was both more political and more personal, comparing the challenges and pressures we were under. This meeting was followed by a long working lunch, which was attended by my ministers and his most senior people.

Over time, I got to know Barack Obama, as I had his predecessor. I have found this relationship, and the one with George W. Bush, to be a matter of intense interest to people, and I get questioned about them all the time. The fact is that I think highly of both. Of course, with each, there were things we held in common, and others where we differed. But I was never at an international meeting where the president of the United States, whether it was President Bush or President Obama, was not one of or the best-informed, best-briefed, and most-articulate people in the room. They are both very impressive individuals and good friends of Canada.

They differed in their personalities. President Bush, who often appeared somewhat wooden in public, is actually extremely outgoing and gregarious. You never had to guess what he was thinking or feeling. He laid it all out there, heart on his sleeve. President Obama is very congenial and respectful, but he is by far the more reserved of the two. While we always had good, substantive exchanges, he tended to keep his cards close to his chest.

Throughout the Ottawa meetings with Obama and his team, two broad subjects dominated: the world economic crisis and the war in Afghanistan. On the first, we compared notes, which made it evident that Canada was in much better shape. We explored the measures we were taking to get through the "panic phase," for lack of a better term, from which we were just beginning to see the faintest signs of emergence.

In both our countries, it was hard to separate dealing with the economic challenges from managing our political situations. Obama had his fair share of political problems, maybe even more substantial than mine. He had been abruptly thrown from the campaign into an economic crisis and was struggling to complete financial sector and auto industry bailouts. Like my post-election situation, he faced instant and fierce opposition from the other side of the aisle.

Sometimes partisanship matters in international relations and sometimes not. While I might have, from a different perch, sympathized with conservative Republicans who were resisting what many did see as genuinely bad policy, as prime minister, much of that now looked to me like opposition for its own sake. Such dynamics can be found in all democratic countries. Those out of power will sometimes seek to oppose beyond the bounds of common sense, constitutional obligation, political consistency, or even the public interest.

In Obama's situation, he was discovering very quickly the profound differences in our two systems of government. Despite Democratic majorities in both the Senate and the House of Representatives, there was no guarantee of progress on his key initiatives. I, on the other hand, with minorities in both chambers, was making progress. A parliamentary government requires that of the prime minister, or both the government and the opposition will face the consequences in an election.* As I ironically observed to Barack,

---

* This, I might add, was one of the reasons the Liberal-NDP-Bloc coalition proposal was so objectionable. Including the separatists was bad enough, but the underlying purpose was to defeat the government and yet avoid an election—an election that the new government could not possibly have won.

"Look, the truth of the matter is that I am in a better position to get things done with a minority in both of our houses than you are with a majority in both of yours."

On our other big topic, Afghanistan, we had a long, frank exchange, but we also brought two very different perspectives to the table. When Obama came into office, America was fighting two wars—in Iraq and Afghanistan. Iraq, started on faulty intelligence, had descended into deadly internecine fighting. It was a sinkhole for the American military and required massive financial resources. Obama saw it as a "bad war" and was determined to end American involvement. By contrast, he considered Afghanistan a "good war," to which he intended to commit additional troops, materiel, and money. Yet, when he asked my opinion, he was surprised at the answer.

Everyone in NATO was aware that Canadians were doing our part in the Afghan mission. It was a fact sadly highlighted by the growing number of motorcades bearing our honoured dead down the Highway of Heroes between Trenton and Toronto. We were there for reasons that Canadians generally supported, including eliminating terrorism, advancing democracy, rebuilding civil society, and providing humanitarian aid and education for Afghan citizens, especially for the women who had been so harshly treated during Taliban rule. There were many good things being done on all these fronts. However, I had become increasingly concerned about America's war aims—these were the coalition's objectives by definition—and I used the opportunity to be candid with Obama.

Afghanistan, unlike Iraq, had been a necessary undertaking, but I still saw both as ill-conceived in ways that had produced ongoing and unresolvable difficulties. Both had been sold as nation-building exercises intended to turn repressive and backwards countries into modern, Western, democratic, secular nations.

That would have been a tough mission regardless, but in neither case had a full military victory been attained, and the time to do so had passed. True, the Taliban regime had been toppled and driven from Kabul and other major urban areas. But as Canada had seen first-hand in Kandahar, insurgents remained deeply embedded and often in firm control in the large, rural areas. The new Afghan governance structures, despite the best Western intentions, were superficial, fractious, and notoriously corrupt. And any effort to create religious freedom and toleration in a state that called itself the "Islamic Republic" was a pipe dream. In short, I told Obama that in my view, this mission, defined as a nation-building exercise, had already failed. Any attempt to salvage it would need new and more limited objectives.

Given Canada's commitment to the mission, President Obama was clearly surprised—perhaps taken aback—by my assessment. But he appreciated the frankness, and he listened. And this initial conversation kicked off a dialogue that would be continued. We were already engaged in a debate in Canada, both in public and inside our Cabinet and caucus, and I promised the president that we would stay in touch on that.

There was one other subject in that initial Obama meeting worth mentioning. Unprompted, he complained to me about the upcoming burden of his summit travel. He had many of the same summits we did, and some others. He did not see how he could set a proactive foreign travel agenda with so much pro forma travel. As I say, there are perspectives that all leaders inevitably share!

BUILDING CANADA'S PROFILE

DURING THIS PERIOD, I did not limit my U.S. relations to the new administration. Canada was getting good publicity in the United States on both sides of the aisle, especially around our economic management. In my view, this was an opportunity to build our profile south of the border.

I went to the States, especially Washington and New York, to meet political leaders and business leaders, as well as to do interviews with American media. During all that I had to walk a fine line between drawing attention to Canada's performance and not saying anything that could slight my hosts. I did not want to look cocky or seem to challenge the efforts that American leaders were making on the crisis. I certainly wanted to nip in the bud any notion or conspiracy theory that Canada was doing well at the expense of the

United States. That narrative could potentially be very damaging. I think I avoided those pitfalls, but it helped greatly that I was a known friend and admirer of America and did not have a history of anti-American rhetoric.

The truth was, of course, that any improvement in the American economy would be unequivocally good for Canada. Still, the circumstances in 2009 and for the next few years created fertile ground from which to pitch investors on Canada. The reverse was also true to some extent. As I observed, particularly to Canadian financial institutions, their relative strength was a real opportunity to build up their position in American and global markets. Some did take up that challenge.

NATO AND AFGHANISTAN

APRIL 2009 WAS A VERY BUSY TIME on the summit circuit. The London G20 meeting concluded on the second, and my next summit—NATO in Strasbourg, France—would begin the following day. This was already my third NATO Summit. Despite my long and strong support for Canada's role in the trans-Atlantic alliance, I had come away from the earlier meetings with mixed impressions.

It seemed to me that NATO consisted broadly of three camps, each holding very different ideas about the purpose of the organization. The first group, which included Canada, was the Anglosphere and Nordic countries, which saw NATO as a robust, globally oriented alliance. The second, the Eastern Europeans, still looked at NATO through a Cold War lens, with deterring potential Russian aggression as their principal concern. The third, comprised of some of the Western Europeans, seemed to view NATO more as a vehicle through which they could pressure or constrain the United States by pushing it in a more multilateral, more pacifist, and less robust direction. Those countries also tended to be the least likely to commit to NATO missions, especially in a kinetic sense. That is, of course, a generalization, as France, then under President Nicolas Sarkozy, was far more engaged and collaborative than under many of his predecessors.

This debate over fundamental purpose was on display in Bucharest, Romania, in 2008. That is where and when we debated NATO membership for Georgia and Ukraine. While there was a large majority in favour of proceeding, particularly in the case of Ukraine, progress was blocked by a group of Western Europeans. It was a fateful decision, not just for Ukraine but also, as we would eventually come to understand, for the entire world.

NATO's divisions were also reflected in widely divergent contributions to the Afghanistan mission. Given that reality, we were not going to defer to the alliance on what to do about our own mission there. In any case, my options were somewhat limited by developments in the minority parliament back home.

I have already described the immense challenges the mission faced on the ground—all stemming from Canada's ill-prepared entry into Kandahar in late 2005. But the politics were getting progressively more difficult as well. That began as early as May 2006, with what we thought was a routine vote on extending the Afghan mission for a year. Despite the support of many prominent Liberals, including Opposition Leader Bill Graham—in my experience, a fine individual who always put the country's interests first—many in that party voted against the motion. It passed by just four votes.

What was happening? To be charitable, there were probably Liberals who had never really signed off on Paul Martin's Kandahar commitment in the first place. Now that the human costs were becoming apparent, they chose to express their disapproval. Nevertheless, it is clear there were some who simply saw this as an opportunity to damage or embarrass our Government.

The argument they used was that we had changed the mission, militarizing it in some novel manner. That was nonsense, of course, and they knew it. Afghanistan had always been a military mission, and it had become a significantly more dangerous military mission by virtue of the Martin Government's deathbed escalation. But brassy and cynical as it was, that was their line.

Since leaving Kandahar at the drop of a hat was not a viable option—at least, not if Canada was to have any credibility at all internationally—we knew we would have to have a plan for managing Afghanistan going forward in our minority situation. As a start, we approached the former Liberal deputy prime minister, John Manley, and asked if he would be willing to chair a group to take a thorough look at the mission and provide recommendations on the future path. Our intention was to take the issue out of the day-to-day politics in Parliament and give it the careful analysis it deserved.

Manley led a group of prominent, qualified, serious Canadians of mixed partisan backgrounds.* They worked intensely for four months, delivering a quick but thoughtful report on January 22, 2008. Their recommendations broadly paralleled our Government's thinking, but they went further. They emphasized the need to continue to upgrade the equipment and capabilities of our Forces in the Kandahar theatre, as we were already doing. They also stressed that we should give higher profile to the non-security or non-military aspects of the mission, that is, the development and diplomacy components of our three-legged strategy.

However, what really broke new ground was the panel's recommendations about the future. They advised that we gradually reshape the defence part of the mission from a security mission to a training mission. Under this scenario, we would focus on training the Afghan armed forces and police, have them conduct operations with us, and gradually increase their operational independence. This would provide a mechanism by which Canada's military involvement would not be open-ended.

We accepted the recommendations, and as we had hoped, the report smoothed the political waters for a time. It allowed us to put greater focus on what we were doing in Afghanistan, why we were doing it, and what we were hoping to achieve. A highlight for me was when we brought several prominent Afghan women, including elected parliamentarians, to meet

---

* The Independent Panel on Canada's Future Role in Afghanistan also included former Mulroney Cabinet minister Jake Epp, former clerk of the Privy Council Paul Tellier, former journalist and Liberal-appointed consul general to New York Pamela Wallin, and Derek Burney, whose wide experience in government has already been noted.

with their counterparts in the House of Commons. These were remarkable women who had entered public life in the face of grave threats from extremists. They were taking their lives into their hands every single day. It was something that gave Canadians a greater sense of the gravity and importance of our mission.

All these things contributed to the passage of a motion on the further extension of the mission in March 2008. Key to that passage was the inclusion of a sunset clause. We committed to transition the mission from direct defence to training by 2011. This could be extended by Parliament before 2011, of course, but by that point, Canada would have been in Afghanistan for a decade, having greatly improved security through enormous sacrifice of money and lives. That effort was never intended to be indefinite, so a transition plan was more than reasonable. The Liberal Party did the responsible thing and supported the motion. Sadly, but unsurprisingly, the Bloc and the NDP did not.

I had already communicated our intentions to NATO in 2008 and to President Obama in our first meeting. But by the time of the Strasbourg summit, another year had passed, and our planning for the transition had begun in earnest. While I expected to get some pushback, I received little. Furthermore, I went on the offence, making it clear that we had a plan and why. The mission could not be indefinite, and I urged NATO members to similarly evaluate their own plans. Many, I suspect, were doing just that. In any case, I was not really open to the input of the many countries whose engagement had been minimal.

ANOTHER TRIP TO AFGHANISTAN

NOT LONG AFTER the Strasbourg summit, I returned to Afghanistan, visiting Kandahar in May 2009. This was my third "surprise" visit to the country, labelled as such and always shrouded in secrecy beforehand. Afghanistan was a war zone, after all, and enormous operational security procedures were required to ensure maximum protection to visitors.

Notwithstanding these concerns, I kept up my visits to the troops throughout our mission there. While we were making clear-eyed assessments back home of how the deployment needed to evolve, the reality was that our troops were still there, putting themselves in harm's way. It may not have been my Government's mission to start with, but it was ours now, and it was my responsibility to support them. They also deserved to hear our thinking on these matters in person from the top. In any event, our military personnel on the ground were, for the most part, under fewer illusions than anyone back home.

In short, my trips were made to ensure our troops, diplomats, and aid workers of their country's support, regardless of the debate in Parliament. The people in this extraordinarily dangerous mission were extremely dedicated, making great sacrifice, and my trips helped to bring attention to the good work they were doing. We travelled not just to the main encampments but also to the front lines and forward operating bases, taking photos, giving speeches, and breaking bread with our personnel.

We also met with senior commanders, Canadian and allied, to get comprehensive security briefings on the situation on the ground, the capabilities of the enemy, and the progress we were making. We shone a spotlight on Canada's development efforts and made a point of visiting projects, including schools, health facilities, and the Dahla Dam, which was one of our major infrastructure initiatives. We engaged in important diplomatic work, meeting with senior officials in Kabul and Kandahar to assess their progress and exchange views on how the situation was evolving.

While our first trip was largely confined to only need-to-have attendees, once we got comfortable with our ability to secure the areas we visited, we started to bring special guests with us to rally the troops. Most of our people on the ground were young men and big sports fans, so we made a special point of bringing celebrities from the athletic world. Among those who came on my trips or my ministers' separate visits were Jarome Iginla, captain of the Calgary Flames; Brian Burke, president of the Toronto Maple Leafs; Don Cherry, the high-profile hockey coach and personality; Gord Miller, the popular TSN broadcaster; and Jayna Hefford and Marie-Philip Poulin of the national women's hockey team. A highlight for our people was getting to play road hockey—there being no ice, of course—with bona fide stars.

Despite the dangers and the political pressures around the Afghanistan missions, these visits were always special and meaningful times for me. I was especially appreciative of the efforts these celebrities made in coming with us. Remember, nobody was getting paid or was compelled to do this, and the hazards were real. They did it because they wanted to support the troops and serve the country, yet received very little in the way of wider recognition for their efforts.

I distinctly remember the heat during some of our visits. The hottest I have ever been in my life was at Camp Mirage—a small air force base we maintained for a time in the desert of the United Arab Emirates. For obvious reasons, we were not going to fly the conventional RCAF1 aircraft, unarmed and with little defensive capability, into Afghanistan. We would stop over at Camp Mirage and transfer planes.

I kid you not that on one occasion it was 54 degrees Celsius at that air force base. What is 54 degrees like? It is like putting your head in a hot oven and holding it in there for as long as you can. That is the only way I can describe it. When I got off the plane and headed for my cabin, which was about two and a half minutes away, I was not sure I could stand it for even that long. It seemed like an eternity. Those who served in this furnace were accorded a few side benefits, like all-you-can-eat ice cream, which seemed meagre compared to the heat.

Once we arrived at our destination, further high-security transportation was necessary whenever we went off base—via helicopter or armoured vehicles. Everywhere we ventured required special security under typically scorching heat. Afghanistan has virtually no amenities and is terribly underdeveloped.

My purpose in describing these conditions is to emphasize the fact that I was only on the ground for a couple of days now and again. Then I would get on a plane and leave. For those deployed, this was daily living month after month, with threats to life a constant reality.

When one discusses our military and debates their funding, their size, and the merits of their various missions, this is the context we should remember and keep front of mind. As prime minister, I have been in some awfully difficult places in the world with our military—Afghanistan not being the worst, by the way. But these locations are where our men and women in uniform go to serve, and they deserve tremendous respect for doing this. They are extraordinary people doing extraordinary things, and they always deserve our support, not only from their prime minister and government but also from the entire country.

RELATIONS IN THE HEMISPHERE

BEFORE MY BRIEF HOP to Afghanistan, I had attended my third big international leaders' meeting in April 2009. That was the Summit of the Americas in Port of Spain, the capital of Trinidad and Tobago. It was my first time at this summit, and I had gone there with Minister of State Peter Kent thinking it would bode well for one of our Government's early foreign-policy priorities—our "Americas strategy."

The emphasis on the Americas came from our belief that Canada needed to broaden relationships within our own "neighbourhood." The truth is that we do not really have a neighbourhood in the sense that most countries do. That is not all bad. As Benjamin Netanyahu said to me, "Canada has the most ideal neighbourhood in the world—oceans on three sides and the United States of America on the other." He was quite jealous.

For decades, Canada had been diplomatically detached from much of Latin America. We only became a member of the OAS in 1990 under the Mulroney Government. We did have long-standing ties to the Caribbean region, principally through the Commonwealth, but even those relations had become more distant in recent years. In short, it looked like there would be fertile ground in the hemisphere for our strategy. I began going there regularly from our first days in government. I even took a few Spanish lessons to help me feel more at home.

The Trinidad meeting would bring together all the sovereign countries of the western hemisphere except, at the time, Cuba. It sounded like an auspicious occasion for the advancement of our strategy. And it was, until it began. Then reality hit.

As we quickly learned, the Summit of the Americas is utterly cacophonous. Of all those eleven summits I attended, this was the one where member states were least likely to agree on anything. Not only were there deep divisions but also much of the deliberation consisted of heads of government pontificating endlessly, talking entirely past one another, largely oblivious to whether anyone was listening.

The main drivers of this dysfunction were the members of the Bolivarian Alliance for the Peoples of Our America. Led by Hugo Chávez's Venezuela, the Alliance was a group of far-left populist-socialist countries. Their agenda consisted of opposing anything the Americans were trying to do and then blaming the United States for everything that did not get done. There was rarely a constructive voice to be heard in this group. Although its vocal members were a tiny handful of countries, Chávez had bought the lower-key acquiescence of several others through generous oil subsidies. Their one perennial agenda item was the reinstatement of Cuba as a member.

Despite my distaste for everything Hugo Chávez was and what he stood for, he was not a person without abilities. He was a tremendous, if completely demagogic, speaker, with a great sense of humour. A larger-than-life personality, he left me with one of my better, if stranger, PM stories. It took place at that very summit.

At the opening reception, Chávez spotted me across the room and came over, pulling me aside. I had been warned that something like this might occur, as Chávez apparently thought I might be a potential ally. That notion stemmed from his experience at the previous Summit of the Americas in 2005. There, Paul Martin had apparently—and uncharacteristically, I might add—gone after Chávez. He had called out his disruptiveness quite bluntly, aggressively, and publicly. Thus, when I defeated Martin in the election just a couple months later, it was posited to me that Chávez believed the revolutionary Canadian people had risen up and thrown out the American imperialist lackey, Paul Martin, in favour of a potentially more Chávez-friendly prime minister in yours truly.

Lowering his voice, Chávez explained to me that we had a historic opportunity. If I would join his Alliance, we would potentially have the Americans encircled. He had his growing following to their south, and I would cut them off in the north. And who knows, someday there might be an opportunity to move against them.

Was Chávez serious? Was he just joking? Was he trying to size me up? Who knows—he was funny, crazy, and wily all at the same time. As dryly as possible, I explained to him that Canada and the United States had gone to war some two hundred years ago, and while we felt we had done reasonably well, it had since been Canadian policy to avoid that happening ever again in the future.

The only contribution I can think of that Canada made through my attendance at the Americas Summits was on the issue of the Falkland Islands. Argentina had virtual unanimity for its claim over the British territory, that is, except for me. In a venue where nothing would be decided anyway, I frankly relished blocking its baseless, jingoistic aims.

Of course, as per the world of diplomacy, much of the room, including the United States, was going along to get along on the Falklands issue. I would not. I made it clear that Canada's position was that it was for the people of the Falklands to decide (and why, pray tell, would they want to join Argentina?). Anyway, it did score me some useful points with the U.K. and a nice reception when I visited the islands several years after leaving office.

The upshot of that Summit of the Americas was our realization that a multilateral approach to the hemisphere was a non-starter. We were, however, discovering several bilateral relationships worth deepening. In fact, for reasons that are not entirely clear, we found that hemispheric countries on the Pacific rather than the Atlantic offered consistent opportunities for deepening relationships. There would be more to come on that front.

EXPANDING INTERNATIONAL TRADE

AMID THIS FLURRY of international meetings, I had a clear priority that went beyond the day-to-day management of the global financial crisis—expanding Canada's free-trade network. Despite the crisis, we continued concluding trade negotiations. Two of these were broadly part of the Americas strategy. A deal with Colombia was announced in November 2008, and one with Panama was unveiled in August 2009. We had also concluded an agreement with Jordan in June 2009.*

Thus, by the end of 2009, we had five trade agreements with eight countries under our belts. We had built up our negotiating capacity and developed the political will to make the necessary compromises. Yet we had a long way to go in terms of expanding our trade network in a large-scale sense.

That would be the purpose of the summit I had jammed in between NATO and my journey to Afghanistan. On May 6, 2009, I went to Prague for the Canada-European Union Summit. As I noted earlier, of all the summits, this was the most frequent. It was also among the most useless.

The EU meetings are with the Brussels leadership, not the member countries. Although led by often impressive people—like European Commission President José Manuel Barroso, with whom I worked for many years—the agendas were thin, passive, and repetitive. At every meeting we would go through a list that never seemed to change and that had no action items. "Did we discuss the seal hunt?" "Did we exchange views on climate change?" "Did we review the trade relationship?" As I looked to thin my pro forma travel schedule, these semi-annual encounters were an obvious place to start.

Early in my prime ministership, I took the (apparently unprecedented) step of cancelling my trip to one of these summits. It had me going all the way to Finland just to roll through the checklist. "It is off," I said to my staff and officials. "I am not going. It is not worth my time." European officials were up in arms, but so were our officials, because officials seem to love these box-ticking exercises. But I went further. I indicated that I had no intention of hosting the next summit either.

In fact, I had a plan. It was apparent to me that these meetings, unsubstantive as they were, were nonetheless very important to Brussels. So I put

---

* These were all during Stockwell Day's time as Minister of International Trade.

out an option. "I can have another summit," I said, "when we have a major agenda item on which we are taking significant action. For Canada, that is one thing—the development of a free trade agreement. We've been talking about it since the 1970s. Show me some progress toward it, and I'll be at the next summit. And, by the way, I'll only be at the summit after that if there is further progress."

The tactic seemed to work. In 2007, it was agreed that Canada and the EU would announce a joint "trade complementarities study," which is essentially a pre–free-trade negotiations phase. By the time I reached Prague, this work had us at the next step. In the Czech Republic, we were able to announce that Canada and the EU were beginning negotiations on a full-scale trade agreement. This was a very big deal. No Canadian government had gotten this far, and an agreement with the European Union would transform our global free-trade network.

We were under no illusion that this would be difficult and take considerable time. But I had a degree of confidence, built up through the early successes, particularly with the European Free Trade Association. Yet I also knew that we would not get a deal just through a strategy of meeting boycotts.

UNINTENDED PROPHESY AT THE G8

ON JULY 8–10, I attended the G8 Summit at L'Aquila, Italy. Naturally, the world's financial health was the focus, but the mood was decidedly better. The global economy had stabilized, and there were some indications of recovery. Yet the future of the G8 itself was in some doubt.

There appeared to be some risk that the G8 would be completely displaced by the G20. There were rumours that the G8 was a target of President Obama's desire to thin his summit obligations. The G20 had become the pre-eminent global economic forum during the financial crisis, leading to debate over the G8's ongoing utility.

We did not see things that way, and we launched a stout defence of the regular G8 meetings. We had an immediate goal—to preserve the next G8, which Canada was scheduled to host. With our desire to continue highlighting "the Canadian way" of managing through the crisis, we were very averse to any cancellation. We ultimately avoided that by successfully lobbying to host the G20 in 2010 and promising to schedule the two summits back-to-back.

My defence of the G8 went beyond our narrow hosting interests. In my view, the G20, because it reached beyond the security-economy-democracy allies that constituted the G8, could not displace the unique value of the smaller body of like-minded countries. Besides, I wondered how long the G20's unity of purpose would last beyond the crisis. That concern would prove to be well founded in the decade to come.

One of the distinctive features of the G8 is its international development agenda—the G20's emerging economies generally not being big foreign aid donors. Those parts of the G8/G7 meetings usually include representatives from low-income countries, particularly in Africa. Host Silvio Berlusconi had gone further at L'Aquila, inviting many African and Arab leaders, some of whom he had close personal relations with. It led me to make a quip that turned out to be an unintended prophesy.

As the summit proceedings began, I was sitting at a table with members of our delegation. One of our officials—a woman . . . I wish I could remember who—said to me, "You know, Prime Minister, you're one of the most senior leaders at this summit." "Really?" I responded. I had been PM for only three-and-a-half years, less than a typical term of office in most countries. It seemed hard to believe.

Sure enough, as I looked around the room, it was true, at least among the democratic countries. In the world of the global financial crisis, elected leaders had been dropping like flies. At that summit, one of the few more senior was Germany's Angela Merkel, who had become first minister less than three months before me. In fact, we were two of the very few elected leaders anywhere to survive the crisis. I do not think it is a coincidence that the two countries boasting the best economic and fiscal management were the ones whose leaders stayed in power.

The official's observation may have been true of the G8 and other elected leaders, but it was certainly not so when it came to all the summit's invitees, many of whom were long-serving dictators. Most notable were Libya's Muammar Gaddafi and Egypt's Hosni Mubarak, who had been in power for forty and twenty-eight years, respectively. Struck by the contrast, I responded to her, "You're right. But look at some of these other people around the room. Many of them have been in office for decades." "Prime Minister," she responded, "in all fairness, I don't think you'll live long enough to be in office as long as those people." To which I said, "Well, I don't think I'll live *in* office as long as those people, but I bet I will live *out* of office a lot longer than they do." Two years later, my joke proved to have more than a bit of truth to it.*

There is more to this story than a prophetic joke. Despite our constant criticism of our democratic systems—which is a right in such systems—we often forget that there is an enormous, qualitative difference between a democratic and an authoritarian state. Democratic leaders enter and leave office because the people choose them and the people remove them. In autocracies, leaders are in office because they successfully jail and/or kill their opponents.

We should never trivialize this difference or close our eyes to the kinds of leaders these different systems produce. Democracies may be messy, but they are fundamentally free societies. Autocracies may appear highly ordered, but they are at heart far more violent systems. Democracy is always something to be cherished and guarded, and we forget this at our peril.

There was more travel yet to come in late 2009, although its nature and the issues it raised would be a little different. First, however, I want to take a little time to reflect on some of the personal highs and lows during that year.

---

* In 2011, Ghaddafi was summarily executed by rebels after a brief civil war. That same year, Egypt's Mubarak was overthrown in a revolution. He spent the rest of his life in confinement, dying in a military hospital in 2019.

13

DAVE BATTERS, MEMBER OF PARLIAMENT

JULY 4, 2009, was one of the saddest and most haunting of my days in office. On that day, I attended the funeral of former Conservative member of Parliament Dave Batters. Dave had captured the previously NDP-held riding of Palliser, in Saskatchewan, in the 2004 federal election. Two years later, he won it again by a comfortable margin. His first victory always stuck out in my mind because he ran on his own local slogan. The Conservative Party's national English-language motto in that election was "Demand Better." Dave modified it in Palliser to "Demand Batters." I always like clever deviations from orthodoxy.

The Dave Batters I came to know in that election and afterward was the kind of person you wanted to be around. Those who dealt with him on a day-to-day basis knew him as the most energetic, enthusiastic, and optimistic MP in the House of Commons. He was just a bundle of energy, and he made everything seem like fun. He could be a fighter when he needed to be, but only in the sense of being the classic "happy warrior."

However, as 2008 wore on, I began to learn that things were not well with Dave. It came into focus one day when he had uncharacteristically dropped the ball on something (I certainly cannot remember what). When I mentioned it to Jay Hill, then our caucus whip, he said that Dave had recently been acting erratically. Dave was in considerable emotional turmoil, Jay said, and he believed that our normally lively MP was struggling with anxiety and depression.

The comment floored me. But as we learned more about Dave's condition, it became clear that his ebullient persona was a classic example of coping through overcompensation. He had long suffered privately and quietly with his chronic mental and emotional difficulties.

Recall that in the summer of 2008, I was steadily ramping up the expectations for a fall election. One day that August, I was at Harrington Lake, enjoying some downtime when I was informed that Dave would be calling and that I needed to speak to him. At that point, he had been away from the House for several months. In a sombre voice, Dave said to me, "Prime Minister, I'm not going to run in the election. I really need to give more attention to my mental health. And that's what I'm going to do."

We spoke for a few minutes more, and I understood his decision, which he was strongly wedded to. It was clear that Dave felt he was not in a place where he could continue as a member of Parliament. On that, his mind was made up. Dave made the announcement and publicly indicated the reasons for his decision.

Less than a year later, Dave died by suicide.

AS I PREPARED to go to Regina, I knew that this funeral would be difficult. Dave's death had occurred just five days earlier, and it had been an emotional gut punch for everyone who knew him, including me. Of course, no funeral is easy, but the younger the person, the greater the sense of tragedy. And when suicide is the cause, the emotional range extends far beyond grief, because suicide invariably exacts enormous collateral damage on loved ones.

Being prime minister (and now a former prime minister), I am asked to attend and speak at many public events. Unless there is a clear reason for me doing so, I often resist such invitations, as I find my presence often detracts from the purpose of the gathering. But in this case, I wanted to be there to speak. My colleagues wanted and needed to hear from me, and Dave's family needed and deserved all the support we could give them.

But what was it that they needed to hear? I do not believe that the role of a leader on such occasions is simply to express personal emotions. It is certainly not to be the highest embodiment of the audience's emotional reactions. Of course, the leader will express and share some degree of the emotional ambience of the event. But I regard the leader's role as fundamentally different. It is to go beyond his or her own emotions in order to provide solace and perspective to others.*

I put a lot of thought and effort into my speech. This was a traumatic experience for all touched by it. Given that reality, I had my office consult widely with mental health professionals to ensure the messages that I would deliver were helpful and appropriate. I began by reflecting on Dave Batters the person, and I want to repeat that here:

> We are gathered together to remember Dave, to lament his passing, and to comfort each other. Dave held a place in all our hearts.
>
> To his wife and family, he was a loving—and beloved—husband, son and brother. To his friends, he was unfailingly loyal, generous and caring. And among his colleagues in Parliament, myself included, he was greatly admired for his dedication to his constituents, our party, and our country.
>
> In my experience, no one, on either side of the aisle, ever had a bad word to say about Dave. His passion for the causes he embraced was matched only by his respect for his opponents. Dave was always excited about whatever issue

---

* Usually that includes providing humour as well. I have always said that the best speeches, including eulogies, will "make them laugh, make them cry, and make them think." However, given the circumstances of Dave's passing, humour was out of the question.

> or initiative he was working on. His energy and enthusiasm were infectious. He lifted spirits and inspired others.
>
> I used to tell my staff that I wished I could match Dave Batters' liveliness and optimism.

I followed that introduction by talking about Dave's reasons for entering politics—the senseless murder of a friend—as well as his contributions to public life and the backdrop of his struggles with anxiety and depression throughout it all.

PUTTING DAVE'S STRUGGLES IN PERSPECTIVE

THAT STORY WAS TOLD not just to fill out a portrait of Dave. It was also to provide an understanding of the circumstances of his passing because, ironically, this was an opportunity to draw attention to an issue dear to my heart and to our government's agenda—the challenges around mental health.

The first point I made was that mental illness is shockingly common. At any given moment a significant percentage of the population—up to 20 per cent according to some research—is suffering from some type or degree of mental illness. The truth is that *most* people will at some point in their lives face mental health challenges.

Second, mental illness afflicts all kinds of people. It is not simply a phenomenon of those in sad or tragic situations. It is not just something that afflicts the vulnerable or the poor or people experiencing tremendous problems or stresses in their lives. Mental illness is common at *all* levels of society, for people in *all* phases of life. There are lots of well-known examples of high-performing and highly successful individuals who suffered from chronic mental illness. Two of the most influential political leaders in Western history—Abraham Lincoln and Winston Churchill—were among them.

My final lesson was to convey that mental illness is, in fact, an illness. It is not merely an extension of mood or of character or an indicator of personal strength or weakness. In many, if not most cases, it is a disease of the brain, of physical or chemical problems in the brain itself. It is like having a bad knee or a bad shoulder or problems in your guts. It is a medical problem. The most tragic thing is that, in most cases, it can be readily and effectively treated. Yet often it is not.

If these points are, as one of my editors suggested, now well understood in our society, then we have come a long way, and for that, I think our government can take some credit. Unfortunately, I believe that there still exist tremendous taboos and stigmas surrounding mental illness. The result is that too few people will seek proper medical treatment.

Just as unfortunately, it is common for people with mental illness to turn to alcohol or narcotics. Ironically, they are seeking treatment. But the treatment they seek is self-administered and medically unsound, even though prescribed and supervised treatment regimens are available. This was in part the case with Dave, who became addicted to the pharmaceutical drugs he had been prescribed.

Dave himself was open and honest about these things. While there are few silver linings in a tragedy like his, one of them was the public attention that Dave bravely brought to his situation.[*] When he announced he would not seek re-election, he was frank. And he was not afraid to speak about his challenges. Dave ultimately lost his fight with anxiety and depression—that also remains all too common—but his was a courageous battle that drew much-needed attention to the wider struggle.

CONTINUING DAVE'S FIGHT

EVEN BEFORE DAVE'S PASSING, this issue was a priority for my Government. In my life, I have had an unusual set of experiences, from living in low-rental accommodations with the unemployed to walking the halls of

---

* Recall that Dave's public disclosure of his battle with depression occurred two years *before* Bell Canada's "Let's Talk Day."

power, money, and fame. I have seen how frequent, how universal, and how misunderstood mental illness is. When we were looking at healthcare and where we would focus our attention, this was a logical place. We sought a role consistent with federal jurisdiction, that is, where the need for research and education, as opposed to just service delivery, would be a crucial element.

As early as 2007, we began by launching the Mental Health Commission of Canada. We named as our initial Chair long-time Liberal Senator Michael Kirby, who had a keen and abiding interest in this field. A few years after that, we launched a full-blown mental health strategy. The idea was to pull together the most experienced and cutting-edge professionals to share best practices, to conduct top-line research, and to make education the emphasis. There remains a long, long way to go and the effort continues.

One of the ways I was able to ensure that Dave's tragedy was not forgotten was by naming Dave's wife, Denise Batters, to the Senate in 2013. Denise is a lawyer who had long been politically active in our party. I had watched her live through the previous four years with exceptional courage. It was both heart-wrenching and inspirational to see her experience life with a suicidal partner, suffer his departure, and then emerge as an articulate and heartfelt proponent for the cause of mental health.

Denise has since been one of the most active and energetic senators across a range of issues, including mental health. She has been particularly effective on many pieces of legislation in the justice portfolio. I could not have made a better appointment.

MANY YEARS LATER

TO SOME READERS, the Dave Batters story may seem peculiar. I have gone from talking about a hectic domestic and international agenda to this emotionally traumatic event, after which I would be right back to a packed schedule—almost as if the in-between had never happened. I grant that it may all seem emotionally jarring. It is. But that is simply the nature of the life attached to the job of prime minister.

That does not mean that the impact on the prime minister of highly emotional events is as transitory as it appears. The greatest stress, in my view, is the constant need to rise above and, in very short order, move beyond one's own emotions in the service of one's greater responsibilities. Where others celebrate, you start to plan for the next challenge. Where others worry, you lay out a path. Where others become angry, you must focus on solutions. And where others grieve, you provide comfort and reassurance.

In such a life, your own emotional experiences inevitably end up stunted. Some of the best and worst moments, so quickly passed through, stand still in emotional time, leaving a lingering imprint of triumph or tragedy. Which is why this case, especially my last conversation with Dave Batters, has left me, many years later, with a haunted feeling.

When Dave told me of his decision not to run, I was not entirely at ease with it. It was clear what Dave *was not* going to do—political life was clearly not the best thing for him at that point. But it was not clear what he *was* going to do. And what *purpose* would his life have going forward? Detachment from excessive stress—like the life of a member of Parliament—does make sense for dealing with mental health challenges. Yet emotional attachments and, above all, purpose are critical for emotional health.

But Dave's mind was made up. As uneasy as I was, I was in no position to cast doubt on his choice. Still, that does not change the brutal reality that this is one life that simply never should have ended the way it did. I will always wonder if there was something I could have said or done.

14

WITH A LITTLE HELP FROM MY FRIENDS

WHILE 2009 HAD ITS SHARE of sad and stressful moments, I came away with many good memories as well. In fact, one of my most enjoyable days as prime minister happened that very year.

Cameras and microphones were not a particular attraction of public office for me. For some, they are truly the raison d'être of a political career. For those who have the desire to be in show business, but who lack the talent, the political stage seems to be a desirable, if ultimately bizarre and unfulfilling, substitute. By contrast, I think most people know that I stayed out of the limelight for a surprising amount of my time as prime minister. Part of that was because I had concluded, watching my predecessors, that overexposure carried large risks. Part of it was because I am naturally introverted.

Still, I admit that, from time to time I had some fun doing the things that "show people" do. For instance, I had a couple of cameos on Canadian television programs.* However, most of my ventures into pure entertainment were connected to my passion for music.

---

* I recall appearing on *Murdoch Mysteries*, *Corner Gas*, and *Rick Mercer Report*.

REDISCOVERING THE PIANO

I HAVE TALKED ABOUT my interest and my progress in piano playing as a youngster. That phase of my life more or less ended after I left home. My lifestyle as the years went on saw me rarely around a piano, and any practising was out of the question.

That changed when I became leader of the Opposition. Stornoway had a piano, although it had to be one of the most consistently out-of-tune versions of that instrument on the planet. Still, put a piano player in the vicinity of a piano, and he is bound to try to play it.

Not long after, my son Ben started showing musical interest, particularly in the guitar. He is naturally musical—much more so than me—and I encouraged him to pursue it. I began to accompany him on piano and teach him some of the concepts. Still, at this point, I practised only rarely and made little effort to regain dexterity in my fingers. I mostly played chords, but that was generally sufficient for my purposes.

The next phase of the journey started when I became prime minister and moved to 24 Sussex. It had a very good (and well-tuned!) baby grand piano in the living room. It also came with a superb staff, led by butler and later residence manager Roger Charbonneau. Roger is exceptionally musical, and he would pull out a guitar or fiddle at family or other residence gatherings. Sometimes I would play along with him, and I even started singing a bit. I had rarely done that before, but Roger thought I could carry a range of tunes, so he encouraged it.

As often happens, one thing led to another. For these family and friends' gatherings, we would encourage those who played to bring their instruments and to sing along. Colin McSweeney was usually there—he has an exceptional singing voice—and he eventually brought some local semi-professional musicians he knew. Thus, before too long I had a regular band that got together every few weeks to jam, in the process preparing a few numbers we would plan for those gatherings.

For me, playing music while in office was about getting into a different headspace. I was often asked, "What do you do for fun? What do you do for relaxation? What do you do for vacations?" In fact, I took almost no real vacation as prime minister. The way I figured it, the job was a once-in-a-lifetime opportunity; there would be time for vacations later. But music was different. With the nature of my personality and the degree to which I focus and get wrapped up in stuff, it became a much-needed way of taking my brain completely out of the job for a few hours.

Of course, music was not the only thing that did that. Spending time with my children, particularly when they were little, would help me refocus. As would a couple of my hobbies (which I will talk about later). But music is special. It takes your mind back and forward, to special moments and to greater possibilities. In my opinion, it is the most unique feature of human life.

BEATLE FOR A DAY

WHEN I WAS IN LONDON in 2009 for the G20 meeting, my family joined me. They did not come on many of these trips, but every so often they would, depending mostly on the school year calendar. The timing of the summit was only four weeks prior to my fiftieth birthday, and it turned out they had set up a surprise for me.

Knowing all too well my life-long love of the Beatles, Laureen suggested we all go to Abbey Road and take that iconic shot from the album cover of the same name with the four of us crossing the road. "Why not?" I said, "I mean, people are doing that all the time there, so it should not seem too abnormal." Right? Wrong. Being prime minister meant that security insisted on clearing the intersection. It was a little embarrassing, but it did get us a better photo. Ben took his shoes off, so he really got into the vibe.

With the picture taken, and us standing in front of the studio, Laureen said, "Why don't you go knock on the door and see if anyone's there?" "I'm not just going to start knocking on their door for no reason," I told her. At that, she revealed that she had arranged a full studio tour, and they were expecting me.

Things have changed radically in the music industry with the advent of digital formats. One of those changes has been the displacement of the traditional, large studios by much smaller ones. In fact, many artists do much of their recording in home shops. While many of the older studios have therefore closed, Abbey Road has stayed true to form: a huge working studio, capable of laying down tracks for outfits as large as orchestras or choirs, using state-of-the-art sound technology. For me, it was like being a kid in a candy store.

Our hosts took us through the facility. They demonstrated the use of the best modern recording equipment. They also shared a few stories. When someone in our group tried to use their cellphone but discovered there was no connection in the place, which seemed a little odd, our host laughed and said, "I can tell you that last week Keith Richards was here recording something. I'm not making this up," he said. "He was running down the hall yelling, 'I can't get no cell reception!'"

As I have said, being PM does come with some very good perks. Well, this was right up there with the best of them. When the official tour was over, they took me to the famous Studio 2, where the Beatles did almost all their recording. Our hosts pulled out all the various pianos and keyboards that the members of the Beatles had used for composing and performing—some of these instruments had the ivory almost worn off the keys—and let me try out the pianos and keyboards. This fanatic was in heaven!

When we were finished and heading out the front door, the Abbey Road people said, "Oh, Prime Minister, we have a gift for you." They handed me a CD—a recording of my playing at Abbey Road Studio 2. Unfortunately, I never really tried to play anything properly as I was just hacking around. So this is a recording of me doing nothing in particular. To this day, I wish I had known I was being recorded. I would certainly have tried to properly knock out a couple of Beatles tunes.

A NIGHT AT THE GALA

THE PRESSURE TO TAKE this revived interest in playing music to another level came from none other than Laureen. Like many prime ministers' spouses, she involved herself in a number of charitable and non-profit activities. In this capacity, she had become honorary chair of the annual gala at the National Arts Centre. Five weeks before the event, out of the blue, she said, "I think you should play at the gala."

I assumed she was joking, or maybe just thinking out loud. "What are you talking about?" I asked, stunned at the suggestion. "You should get up on stage with your band and do a number," she said. Still rather taken aback, the best I could come up with was, "Are you kidding me?" She was not. "You're actually pretty decent, and you can do it." But she was as insistent as I was hesitant, adding the hard to dismiss, "Please do this for me."

I agreed to consider it, but with a fair bit of misgiving. "The only way this is going to work is if we keep things very quiet," I told her later. The best way to have a chance at success was to make it a surprise and thus keep expectations as low as possible. After all, the prospect of failure or embarrassment was real, and I did not want this to become a (negative) defining public moment, like Joe Clark losing his luggage or Robert Stanfield fumbling a football.

A few days later, I brought the band over and ran the idea by them. Called Herringbone, they were a Celtic-rock group used to playing in front of live audiences in Ottawa and on the road. However, this would be their biggest gig to date, with orders of magnitude greater attention than they were used to. Yet they were keen on the idea.

The next question was, "What would we play?" Naturally, this being me, Beatles tunes came to the fore. The guys suggested relatively easy numbers, to play it safe. They first proposed "Eight Days a Week," which I could do, although it is not one of my favourite Beatles songs. We ended up settling on, "With a Little Help From My Friends," which was perfect for all kinds of reasons. In preparation, we worked up to two or three practices a week to tighten up the band, finding time later in the evenings.

Meanwhile, my closest staff were busy doing their job, worrying about how this might come off politically. One day we were at a morning department heads meeting, and Doug Finley happened to be there. When we discussed what I intended to do, he said, in his gruff Scottish accent, "Prime

Minister, you've got to think twice about this. You say you can do it, but what about these band members?" When I told him that they were semi-pro, he countered, "Semi-pro could also mean that they aren't very good. I insist on coming over and hearing this."

Doug dropped by the house that night, heard us play, and the next day delivered his verdict on the group: "They're okay. They're good enough to perform." We had passed our first audition. Before you start wondering why Doug Finley's opinion mattered so much, it should be noted that, in his younger days, he had been involved in the British music scene, booking acts for various clubs. Over the years, he had collected an incredible collection of recordings and had, literally, an encyclopedic knowledge of popular music.*

On the evening of the performance, October 3, 2009, it would have been an understatement to say that I was nervous. While I was routinely in front of crowds, I had not performed musically before strangers in more than thirty years. I was particularly worried about the old problem of the shaking hands. We managed that with a little trick. If you look at the photos of my performance, you will see that the piano—a truly magnificent Steinway—is positioned in a way that prevents the crowd from seeing the keyboard. In any case, the band had my back. My piano part was rather incidental, so they suggested that I concentrate solely on singing if my hands shook, and they would carry off the playing just fine without me.

We sneaked into the National Arts Centre early that Saturday for an onstage rehearsal. Besides me, there was Richard Linke on guitar, Andre Van Schyndel on bass, Phil Nolan on drums, and Colin McSweeney, who acted as our "manager." Colin also sang with us occasionally, but not on that night. When we got there, Colin told us, "We have a surprise for you. Yo-Yo Ma

---

* Doug liked to tell the story that when he was working clubs in the U.K., he actually booked the original five Beatles—John, Paul, George, Stuart, and Pete. It was a classic Doug Finley story. However, when I was writing my eulogy for his funeral, I decided that I should probably double-check it. As it turned out, if this story were true, Doug would have been all of thirteen or fourteen years old at the time!

is going to sit in with your group." Apparently, he had been at our sound check, heard us, and wanted to play.

Having worked to really nail this tune as a group, my first reaction was, "Does he know the song?" McSweeney stopped me short, saying, "Prime Minister, cut it with the artistic temperament. It's Yo-Yo Ma, for crying out loud. He'll learn quick." It did not hurt when later Yo-Yo came running up to me to introduce himself saying, "I'm Yo-Yo Ma. Are you Paul McCartney?"

When I got on the stage that night, there were a range of reactions, but mainly bewilderment. What was the prime minister doing on the National Arts Centre stage? Was he going to give a speech? In the middle of the concert? However, as we launched into the song, it became obvious I was there to play, and the crowd got into it too. They did get a laugh at me singing "I just need someone to love," which, admittedly, did not quite fit my image. In the end, the performance was very well received, with a long standing ovation to top it off. Yo-Yo stood out in obviously having a lot of fun. And my hands never did shake. A little help from my friends, as the song says.

Personally, I think we were helped by the fact that the audience had just sat through two hours of fairly dry classical music before we took the stage. Our appearance provided a perfectly timed diversion and lightening of the mood. Besides being some of the best publicity I ever got as PM, the performance went viral on the web and was viewed by people all over the world. That included some of my fellow world leaders, which made for interesting comments during future meetings.

WHAT'S NEXT?

BY THE TIME THE BAND and I got back to 24 Sussex that night, all memory of the nervousness had been forgotten. We were on an incredible high. I have spoken to some very large and enthusiastic crowds, but that does not compare to the experience of giving a musical performance in front of a big, excited audience. It was truly unique.

Almost immediately, we started talking about doing it again. Quitting our day jobs for musical careers was certainly not an option, but this was a blast, and we wanted to do some more of it. Besides, the longer we played together, the larger our repertoire got and the better we sounded.

We decided to keep up our periodic rehearsals and look for another opportunity to perform. That turned out to be another surprise appearance, this time at the 2010 Conservative Christmas party. It was a much more ambitious undertaking; rather than just a single song, we committed to a whole set, basically a mini concert. After all, these people worked for me and were a captive (and paid) audience!

We opened with Neil Diamond's "Sweet Caroline," for which I actually wrote a verse. The song has only two verses, and I wanted it to be a longer. I also did it as a tribute to Laureen.* Among our other numbers, we played The Proclaimers' "I'm on My Way." Doug Finley loved the Scottish group and the song, and it was performed in his honour. By then, Doug was well into his long fight with cancer and sadly could not be there that evening.

This gig led to others, and in the end, we performed a couple of times a year. One was usually at our private Canada Day party at Harrington Lake, which would have two or three hundred friends and close associates.† The

---

* Nobody seemed to notice at the time that the third verse was novel. A couple of weeks later, my office started to get questions about it. For the record, here it is:

Open my eyes with every dawn that wakes me
Seeing your face I feel the sun
And as I take
Every shot life throws at me
Here by my side you are the one
Hearts, touching hearts
Reaching out, touching me, touching you

† Performers then in the area, sometimes from the Canada Day show on Parliament Hill, occasionally joined us. Barenaked Ladies, Corb Lund, and Andy Kim come to mind.

other would be in a public venue. Although they gradually got less publicity, the performances were always a lot of fun and a huge hit with our audiences. With one exception, we always prepared beforehand and set out to sound professional.*

Herringbone performed with me until 2013.† After that, I created my own band, with a little help from my chef at 24 Sussex, Tim Wasylko, who also knew a few good local musicians. We called the group the Van Cats, a word play on 24 (*vingt-quatre*) Sussex. It consisted of Brady Moffatt (rhythm guitar), Dave Milliken (lead guitar), Jon Coote (bass guitar), and Mary Gellner (drums). They were also good vocalists, and the extra musician made it a better band. But it was a different experience. Unlike Herringbone, this group was a generation younger than me, and their music was the eighties and nineties, rather than the fifties-sixties-seventies stuff I usually played.

Mary had been a professional musician at one time, so it was interesting to see her reaction to it all. (She has written an interesting memoir about the experience.) Entering the PM's world—not only the celebrity and entourage but also the unique security arrangements—was a real revelation to her, even for someone with a bit of background in show business. When you are in that world as I was, you sometimes forget how weird it can be, including getting to know real-life celebrities who, whether positively or negatively, have high but inevitably two-dimensional public profiles.

---

* The exception was during my 2014 trip to Israel, where I was at an event hosted by Prime Minister Benjamin Netanyahu that had a band. They ended up pulling me on the stage to do a couple of impromptu numbers. It was certainly not my greatest performance, but the circumstances made it impossible to say no. Still, it was a big crowd that was wildly enthusiastic.

† Herringbone broke up tragically. Drummer Phil Nolan, an award-winning schoolteacher, was charged with sexual offences related to events some fifteen years earlier. He was convicted. To this day, those of us who knew him remain totally shocked by the revelations.

I refer here to the Van Cats in the past, but the group still very much exists. Although, alas, not with me in it. They play as the Retrogrades for crowds of their generation in the local Ottawa music scene. We do get together occasionally, but of course, I live in Alberta now.

I recorded a couple of numbers with both of my bands, but we never released them.‡ Those years, as it turned out, marked the high point of my musical career, such as it was. My post-2015 business life keeps me on the road regularly, and even though I have various electronic keyboards at home, I have had little time to play. I honestly do not know when, or if, I will get the chance again.

But it was great fun while it lasted.

‡ One will be released as part of my archive project with Library and Archives Canada. It is a number I wrote (around about 2014) called "Now Comes the Time."

15

MOVING BEYOND THE GLOBAL FINANCIAL CRISIS AT HOME AND ABROAD

MOST OF THE FRANTIC PACE of 2009 had been devoted to the global financial crisis. That had started domestically with the Economic Action Plan launch in January, followed by the subsequent parliamentary challenges to the plan's rollout. Internationally, it had been the dominant subject matter of the summit circuit for much of the year.

However, as the year wound down, there was a sense that growth was resuming. This began to shift the focus of international summits to other matters, especially climate change. It also led me to pursue foreign priorities beyond the normal summit meetings.

OFF TO INDIA

ON NOVEMBER 15, I departed for Singapore and the annual Asia-Pacific Economic Cooperation (APEC) Summit. Its agenda was typically weak, although there were the usual bilateral meetings and exchanges on global economic developments. Nevertheless, it provided an opportunity for strategic engagement in the region. After APEC, I took that opportunity by heading directly to India for a bilateral visit, with plans already in place for a subsequent trip to China and South Korea in early December.

The decision to go to India before China was deliberate and strategic. It was a symbolic shifting away from the preferred priorities of the Department of Foreign Affairs. The voices for maintaining the previous Liberal policy of obsequiousness toward the People's Republic of China (PRC) were numerous and loud. By contrast, their tone toward India was genuinely cool, lacked vision, and was highly distrustful.

Why was that? My only explanation is that it was a holdover from the 1970s and India's secret use of CANDU technology in its first atomic bomb. That, to my mind, was ancient history. The more relevant evaluation was its contemporary standing on the critical axes of foreign policy. By those measures, India is arguably a better opportunity for Canada. It is certainly a less risky one.*

India is partially, though not fully, aligned with Canada on matters of security and values. That makes it unlike China, which is by the same criteria, and to a significant degree, an opponent. I also admit that I like the longer-term bet on the Indian economy.

India's economy is clearly not as large as China's, and both are difficult places to do business. Still, I believed then—and continue to believe—that India's fundamentally free and democratic environment will create more stable development and more compatible partnership opportunities for Canadians in the long run. India appears chaotic, but democratic systems, in my view, are more robust over time and circumstance. China appears more ordered, but authoritarian structures like it are more fragile and more prone to sudden divergences from apparent trends.

The visits to both emerging Asian economic powers were driven principally by our longer-term focus on international trade. No big trade negotiations were about to be launched, but trips to these countries are occasions to push individual commercial deals over the line. Signing ceremonies are

---

* I write this subsequent to Justin Trudeau's accusation that the Indian government murdered an innocent Canadian citizen on Canadian soil. However, at the time of writing, no charges have been laid, and no public evidence has been provided. Prime Minister Mark Carney has thus normalized the relationship.

an important aspect of such voyages, as is door opening and the resolution of economic disputes.

The delegations on bilateral trips like these were always large, and the spots relatively few and highly sought after. It was a priority for me to include business and cultural delegations on bilateral trips. These were important opportunities to develop lasting business and personal relationships that would build on our Government's efforts. There was always great interest from the educational community as well since Canadian institutions were eager to create academic linkages and to recruit foreign students and their highly lucrative tuitions.*

Foreign Affairs Minister Cannon and I made stops in Delhi, Mumbai, and Amritsar, with official meetings that included President Patil, Vice President Ansari, Opposition Leader Advani, External Affairs Minister Krishna, Congress Party President Sonia Gandhi, and, of course, Prime Minister Manmohan Singh. PM Singh is an economist by training, and he played a major role in India's economic reforms and progress from the 1990s forward. Through my many meetings with Dr. Singh over the years, I developed a very high regard for his intellect, his wisdom, and his accomplishments.

Our talks with the Indian government covered a range of bilateral and global matters. The focus was obviously on economics, but enhanced security co-operation also began to take shape. We shared not just global security concerns but domestic ones as well, including the need to guard against local jihadist, Khalistani, and other extremist elements. One significant item was our desire to secure uranium exports to India and their

---

* After years of promoting this flow of overseas students, I think we should think twice about the degree to which this is really in our interest. We as governments subsidize Canadian universities to teach Canadians. It is great that foreign students bring in additional money, but does this really benefit Canadian students, or does it just take away slots while providing the institutions higher budgets and salaries? I think the facts need to be researched thoroughly and the broader benefits weighed much more carefully.

desire to develop a nuclear co-operation agreement. On both these fronts, we expected resistance from officials.

FIRST FORAY INTO CHINA

ON DECEMBER 2–6, 2009, I made my first official visit to China. I had been criticized for the delay in going, but there were important reasons beyond just prioritizing India. Canada to that point had a terribly one-way relationship with China—all their way—and I was not going to visit unless we would be able to deliver some concrete benefits for the country. On the Chinese side, they were reluctant to extend an invitation until I would commit to not raising Celil and to not again meeting the Dalai Lama.[†] Since neither commitment was ever going to be made, the Chinese eventually relented.

With over one hundred cities of a million-plus people, there is no shortage of places to visit in China, especially from the perspective of economic opportunity. That first trip targeted three: Beijing, Shanghai, and Hong Kong. The first would feature the key political meetings, and the second is the largest commercial centre in the country. As for Hong Kong, it has long been a special place from a Canadian perspective.

There are some 300,000 Canadian citizens living in Hong Kong, and its Canadian Chamber of Commerce is one of the largest in the world—larger, in fact, than most inside our country. With its fascinating mix of Chinese and British cultures, Hong Kong long served as an important gateway for the West into China. Unfortunately, much of that value proposition has since been undermined by Xi Jinping's administration.

It is hard not to be impressed by the age and scale of Chinese society. It is one of the oldest—if not *the* oldest—of civilizations in the world. Whereas

---

† My recollection is that I met the Dalai Lama three times—once as leader of the Opposition and twice as prime minister. It was truly an experience to be in his presence. I was always clear that I was meeting him as a spiritual leader and not in any political capacity.

we measure our history in decades that add to a few centuries, the Chinese measure theirs in centuries totalling a few millennia, with the rise and fall of multiple empires and dynasties.

Despite big regional differences over an immense territory, there is an essential cultural unity, with the Han Chinese constituting some 95 per cent of the population. They may use multiple regional dialects,* but Mandarin serves as a common one. When I speak of regions in China, note that many of these have populations greater than all of Canada, with secondary centres that are larger than Toronto.

The dynamism of modern China is also striking. The Chinese have an enormous entrepreneurial class. They are ambitious, disciplined, and optimistic in their outlook (which, frankly, is quite a contrast with the West these days). They make things happen quickly and on an astonishing scale. The skyline of places like Shanghai changes radically in the space of only a few short years.

This entrepreneurial energy and size of China is comparable only to the United States. As different as they are in their cultures and governance, this is one thing these two great powers have in common. Their uniquely large entrepreneurial classes have created and will sustain their global importance. As in America, every Chinese city has thousands of enterprising families who have built fortunes. In China, virtually all this has occurred in just the past forty years.

Outsiders might find this dynamic entrepreneurial culture a strange contradiction to China's authoritarian communist governance. However, this is not inconsistent with much of Chinese history. It has long been a country of entrepreneurs under the authority of a single leader in a one-dynasty (now one-party) system. I will admit, though, to long believing that the dynamism and wealth creation of the economy and the rigidity and Marxist ideology of governance will eventually come into conflict.

---

* What the Chinese call dialects would be considered separate languages by Western standards.

Each of my trips to China provided moments that highlighted both our differences and our similarities. No one embodied this fascinating mix more than a Canadian named Mark Rowswell, who accompanied our delegation on this first trip. Who is Mark Rowswell, you may be asking? Well, he is probably the most famous Canadian in the world, although his name is virtually unknown in his own country. Not so in China, however, where he is known and loved as Dashan by nearly one-fifth of the world's people.

In the 1980s, Rowswell went to China, learned the language—a kind of slangy local dialect—and got his own television comedy show. As famous there as Seinfeld here, he played a white guy trying to fit into Chinese society. The Chinese find him hilarious, and he is a cultural phenomenon. His fame was immediately apparent when I walked the streets of Shanghai with him. Things quickly developed into a mob-like scenario, with literally thousands of people clambering to see Dashan. Extremely affable, Dashan is a great ambassador for our country and did great work for us on these trips.

If the photo ops and cultural talks were the garnish on our trips, it was the senior-level political meetings that furnished the meat. They were the focus of all my trips to China. In fact, our agendas were filled with meetings between members of our delegation and Chinese political figures at all levels. But the "big show" was reserved for China's top leadership.

On the 2009 trip, our hosts were President Hu Jintao and Premier Wen Jiabao. I always found the top Chinese leadership to be impressive people. They would have to be to make their way upward in such an immense and competitive political system. But each leader I met was unique in approach and manner.

Hu Jintao was a product of the "collective leadership model" that Deng Xiaoping created. He was a cautious consensus-builder, in some ways like senior officials in our systems. However, the "tough guy" was not far below the surface. He was also very, very straitlaced. Someone in caucus once asked me, "What is Hu Jintao like?" I said, "If you were going to have a wild party, and you had to invite me or Hu Jintao, you'd invite me." I was not exaggerating. Nonetheless, we gradually developed a decent working relationship.

Wen Jiabao was much more open and spontaneous by nature, which led to an interesting incident on that first trip. At the media photo op that typically led off official meetings, he committed what would usually be regarded as a diplomatic breach by stating, "This is your first visit to China, and this is the first meeting between the Chinese premier and a Canadian prime minister in almost five years. Five years is too long a time for China–Canada relations, and that's why there are comments in the media that your visit is one that should have taken place earlier." My response was equally pointed, but briefer: "I agree with you, Premier, that five years is a long time. It's also been almost five years since we had yourself or President Hu in our country."

This kind of political jousting is not uncommon with the Chinese leadership, and they watch carefully what kind of response they get. If it is met with deference, silence, or apology, they will take that as weakness and act accordingly. Back home, the Liberals reacted with their typical submissiveness, demonstrating why our relationship was so one-sided.* But in this case (and in other such incidents), the Chinese were not met with any backing down.

On occasion, I would even initiate such jibes. Stockwell Day likes to remind me of the time Chairman Wu of the National People's Congress tried to say his one-party, rubber-stamp, 3,000-member parliament was more complex to manage than mine. "That's interesting," I replied. "The difference is that among my three hundred people about half of them are against me and actually say so." We were not going to play along with the charade of PRC democracy. And they were not going to have hurt feelings; these are tough people. Anything that smacks of being xenophobic or broadly anti-Chinese will genuinely trouble them; disagreement itself will not.

In fact, we were gradually developing a constructive rapport with our

---

* The rhetoric from the Official Opposition was even more over the top than usual. Liberal Foreign Affairs critic Bob Rae said: "Mr. Harper's provocative refusal to engage with China for four years comes with a price, which Canada is paying for, and which this incident reflects." When we were in opposition, the media tried to claim that protocol required us to show a common front with the Liberals where international affairs are concerned. Frankly, I do not remember that *ever* happening on the part of the Liberals when we were in government.

Chinese counterparts. We had increasingly frank exchanges with fewer games and more concrete progress. The secret is not to try to always agree. That is neither responsible nor expected. The secret is trust. Do not surprise your interlocutors. Do not grandstand, especially in merely symbolic ways. Do not talk differently in public than in private. That is what works, not only with the Chinese but also with most foreign governments. And it must have worked, since Chinese officials continued to seek my views even years after I left office.

Of course, part of that first trip was the long, pro forma, joint statement issued by our two governments. On this occasion, however, we were able to point to something other than diplomatic language. We had successfully dealt with blockages to Canadian exports of beef, pork, and canola. We also got Approved Destination Status from the PRC—something very important for the growth of Chinese tourism to Canada. In other words, for once, Canada was actually getting something from the PRC.

COP15 IN COPENHAGEN

ALTHOUGH IT HAD BEEN driven from public consciousness, or at least relegated to the back burner, by the global financial crisis, climate change was now coming back as a top issue with a vengeance. The turn really began in September. I had gone to New York for United Nations Leaders' Week, where this was an increasing focus of discussion. That included a private dinner on the issue, hosted by Secretary-General Ban Ki-moon, between a couple of dozen heads of government. From there, great anticipation began to build around the Conference of the Parties (COP15).

In truth, that is an understatement. Leader after leader began announcing their intention to attend COP15, even though it was not normally a leaders' event. Finally, President Obama announced that he would also participate. With that, I confirmed plans to go as well.

While I could not avoid the rising tide, I was far from enthusiastic about making the trip. To be clear, it was not that I believed the issue to be unimportant. It was then and is now very important. Our government had been intensely involved in the international negotiations, the goal of which was proclaimed to be an all-countries agreement to legally binding targets for greenhouse gas emissions. Yet it was for that very reason that I was apprehensive about going to Copenhagen.

Any smart leader wants to be part of success and to avoid being part of failure. Unfortunately, all the signs pointed to COP15 becoming an epic failure. As leaders continued to announce their intention to make "historic" journeys to Copenhagen, I kept checking with my officials. "What progress is being made on an agreement?" I would ask. The answer, repeatedly and definitively, was, "None." Frankly, I wondered exactly why any of us were planning such a trip at all.

It got worse from there. Leaders, especially European leaders, not only reiterated their intention to attend but also began to ratchet up expectations. This was, apparently, our last chance to save the planet, and so an agreement was both essential and inevitable. Still, at the negotiating table, no sign of any such deal was remotely on the horizon.

This was a strange way to try to reach an accord. The plan was apparently not to find common ground; it was simply to raise the temperature. I have had some success as a negotiator over the years, and I can tell you that, as a strategy, that is never sufficient to attain a successful conclusion. In fact, what was occurring was just plain dumb.

It got even worse once I arrived in Copenhagen with Environment Minister Prentice and our delegation. Present were delegations of the close to two hundred negotiating countries. There were some 115 world leaders heading those delegations. There were thousands more stakeholders, interest groups, and self-appointed climate change gurus. What was not there was even the framework for a potential agreement. Worse yet, there was no clear process by which these two hundred parties could reach such an accord.

It all hit a new low as the conference kicked off. With an unprecedented world stage, many could not resist seizing the microphone. One of the first speeches was delivered by Hugo Chávez, whose remarks, while highly entertaining, focused on the need for a world revolution against American domination. Other leaders followed, most of whom played to their domestic audiences, further raising the stakes and expectations to levels as high as the negotiating progress was low.

The speechifying continued hour after hour. I lost track of how many—they all seemed to blend into one enormous rant about both imminent apocalypse and upcoming, historic achievement. In the hallways and conference rooms, delegations and leaders, me included, talked endlessly with one another about what we wanted and, increasingly, if there was any way of getting there. It was turning into a pointless talking exercise, a quagmire, and was so inanely boring that even the protestors began to leave. Very soon we leaders would have to go as well. This was, to be blunt, a couple of days of my life I will never get back.

Still, something had to be done to demonstrate success. Finally, the biggest players—the United States, China, the European Union, a couple of others—released a broad statement. They would pledge to fund climate initiatives around the world. After all, climate finance, not emissions reductions, was all that most developing countries were willing to talk about. There were also to be voluntary, aspirational emissions targets, to be achieved over any time period, defined and implemented by each country at its own discretion.

The goal of binding, legally enforceable targets was nowhere to be found, despite the soaring rhetoric delivered by world leaders who had declared such as a minimum necessity. The results, compared to expectations, were underwhelming, to say the least. We all agreed and made the best of it, but the global reaction was near-unanimous criticism.

For years, leaders had been under pressure to have this kind of big "world-saving" gathering, and leaders had steered clear of it. I suspect this time the inauguration of Barack Obama had convinced some that an agreement was doable. But, candidly, the most positive development from that 2009 failure was that we set out to avoid such a situation in the future. For the rest of my time in office, there was no pressure for leaders to rush to some COP conference and pull an agreement out of a hat.

The lesson learned was expectations management. When this exercise was tried again, in 2015, a modest agreement was in the works, and, with expectations met, leaders more plausibly heralded it as a historic achievement. Yet the

Paris Accord, for all the attendant hype, imposed not a single legally binding responsibility on any government in the world. It may have been a better constructed deal, but it is really nothing more than Copenhagen 2.0. More importantly, it has, once again, resulted in no discernable progress on the emissions front.

THE FAILURE OF INTERNATIONAL CLIMATE CHANGE POLICY

THE CONFERENCES AT COPENHAGEN, Paris, and since are just a continuation of a pattern I have witnessed for the past thirty years. A cry goes up about the importance of stopping the increase of greenhouse gas emissions. The world sets targets, but without any idea how to achieve them. After a few years, with the targets not met—not remotely met—the world sets even more ambitious targets.* The next failure is assured.

On top of this, the invariably voluntary nature of the targets means that the most ambitious efforts to address them are in affluent countries. This drives the production of emissions to poorer economies with far laxer environmental standards. The result—we are seeing this once again with the Paris Accord—is that emissions not only grow but also can accelerate.

What is to be done about this? I know that I was often depicted as opposed to action on climate change. That was simply untrue. What was true is that I believe that action on climate change is very difficult. As Bill Gates has said, the biggest problem in climate change is not those who think that it is not an issue; it is those who think that dealing with it is easy. Pretending it is easy—and proclaiming targets without measures is easy—may make some environmentalists feel very proud of themselves, but that approach has failed and will continue to fail.

---

* It is now apparently supposed to be the total elimination of all emissions by 2050, so-called net zero.

The reason it is difficult to reduce emissions is that energy use is largely essential in nature, being directly tied to economic activity. It is that simple. What do people use energy for? To keep warm or cool, depending on the environment, or to keep objects warm so that they live, or cold so they do not spoil, like food or vaccines. We use energy to run almost everything, from power plants to factories to offices. We need energy for transportation and distribution—of people and most everything people use.

In fact, if you think about it for a second, almost nobody burns or uses energy just for the sake of it. It is not a lot of fun to turn on a generator or an engine and watch it burn fuel away. That only costs money. People almost always use energy for things they consider vital. So, in the short term, if you are going to reduce emissions, it is almost impossible to do it without reducing economic activity.

Therein lies the dirty little secret of the global emissions game: no country will significantly depress real economic activity to achieve some notional target. At least, no sensible country will. Especially when an individual country doing that will achieve absolutely nothing in terms of global emissions reduction.

That is just as true of affluent individuals as it is of advanced countries. For all their virtue-signalling, wealthy elites do little to reduce emissions. They instead look to buy carbon credits, that is, to try to talk poorer people into taking the emissions hit. Or they try to get the less wealthy to pay carbon taxes—more on that in a minute. In fact, they actually benefit financially from emissions-reductions schemes, like subsidies for high-priced electric vehicles or expensive home retrofits.

If wealthy people will not pay the price of emissions reduction, then it is understandable that poor societies like China and India will not either. For the last decade or so, China has been the world's largest greenhouse gas emitter, yet its emissions are still growing. Publicly, they will say this is a tremendous problem, and something must be done. But what they will tell you privately is that a climate change goal achieved decades from now is not remotely as big a concern as generating more jobs and more wealth for their people today. Hence their demand for astronomical amounts of climate finance from the developed world. It is, in fact, the only thing that would make reducing emissions worth it for them.

CANADA'S APPROACH TO EMISSIONS REDUCTION

IN THE LEAD-UP to Copenhagen, I had spoken to several world leaders about trying to get off the path of ambitious-yet-actionless targets. I pointed to the Montreal Protocol. A 1987 international agreement to reverse ozone depletion, it had been successful by prescribing particular actions. There was, however, no getting leaders off the course we were on at that point.*

Given the inevitable failure of international climate change policy, we would remain on our own with the difficult question of how to approach this issue. Unfortunately, Canada had already dug itself a massive hole on this front before we even arrived in office. It stemmed from the previous government's adherence to the Kyoto Protocol.

The Kyoto Protocol had been negotiated in 1997, although it was not ratified by the Chrétien government until 2002. The accord was deeply flawed from the outset. It committed only developed countries to binding targets, which the United States subsequently refused to ratify. This meant only about a third of global emissions were covered, and that proportion was rapidly shrinking. In short, Kyoto was a recipe for the flight of economic activity to higher-emitting jurisdictions. That is what happened, and global emissions grew, predictably and strongly.

Canada had accepted targets that were unattainable even at the outset—a reduction of 6 per cent below 1990 levels by 2012. Yet even after the delayed ratification, next to no actions were taken, beyond flowing money to pro-government environmental groups. That may have been politically shrewd—the Liberals could have an abysmal record and still be praised—but

---

* Some such actions have been agreed to since 2015, but the "targets" approach remains largely in effect.

it certainly did not lessen the production of hot air. Thus, by 2006, we found ourselves some 30 per cent over the target. The only way of reaching the target would have been to shut down a third of the economy, literally. That would have been truly insane.

Fortunately, my Conservative Party had opposed the Kyoto Protocol categorically from the beginning. We were clear that we would not approve it, and we would not adhere to it. However, that was not going to make the problem of Kyoto go away.

Because Canada's commitments were legally binding, the country faced potentially significant (but still undefined) penalties for failing to achieve its targets. The most likely would have been a requirement to buy carbon credits from what were, frankly, dubious sources of emissions reductions elsewhere. That would have been grossly unfair to the Canadian taxpayers—although I would have happily considered it if sending the bill to the Liberal Party had been an option!

In the end, what we did was simply withdraw from the Kyoto Protocol before the commitment period expired. This reasonable response was met with howls of anger and indignation. Some accused us of "breaking" the Kyoto Protocol. But that was nonsense. The Protocol contained a provision, which we used, under which you could exit completely legally. It was, after all, the only sensible provision where Canada was concerned.

After Copenhagen, we set our new target in line with the American one. It was still ambitious—in truth, too ambitious—but it was only aspirational. We did this because aligning with the United States was a minimum criterion for any measure that would not unduly hurt the Canadian economy (although all actions invariably have some degree of negative economic impact).

In any case, both before and after these events, we were undertaking climate change measures. We brought in regulatory measures that set technical standards to gradually reduce emissions intensity over time. The most well-known of those were in the vehicle sector, where we worked hand in glove with the Obama administration to set North America–wide emissions standards. These occurred in stages, allowing industries and consumers to adapt in a way that we believed was affordable.

We also mandated biofuel requirements in the country's energy system. That was one method of incentivizing the development of either non-fossil-fuel alternatives or at least less intense emissions from such fuels. As well, we funded two major carbon capture projects, which are considered to this day to be a big piece of the emissions solution. We also supported considerable research into other new, emissions-reducing energy technologies.

One of the most important steps we took was addressing coal-fired electricity. This is one of the largest sources of greenhouse gas emissions in the world (and, in the case of China, still growing). We were able to work with the provinces to plan for the virtual elimination of coal-fired electricity in Canada. No new dirty coal plants would be built after 2015, and all but a couple would be offline by 2030. To be fair, this was only possible because, unlike many parts of the world, we had readily available, far less carbon-intensive options, like hydro, nuclear, and low-cost natural gas.

Critics have said that changes such as these only make a difference at the margin. But that, given current technological options, is the only way that any progress has been made or is going to be made on such a difficult issue. The reality is that changes that go beyond the margin will impose enormous costs that will be deemed unacceptable, even in the wealthiest societies.

WHERE SHOULD WE GO FROM HERE?

I HAVE NEVER SEEN a public policy issue play out like climate change. I have never seen so much rhetoric expended in proclaiming an objective with so little actually achieved. This will continue until we face some fundamental facts.

One such fact is that energy systems are extraordinarily difficult to transition. Fossil fuels have become and remain the dominant world energy source because they have very strong attributes of reliability, efficiency, and high density at enormous scale. Unless new technologies can replicate these attributes, they will not replace fossil fuels. That is not even remotely true of renewables today,* and asserting it does not make it so. This is a genuinely "inconvenient truth."

This is why it is useless to set targets without means. One viable, though still challenging, means of transition is nuclear power, and it is good that some environmentalists are coming around to this. Beyond that, only much greater technological innovation can achieve ambitious emissions reductions. Otherwise, we are left with pursuing adaptation measures, which, given present realities, we should be putting much more focus on.

Governments, including mine, have been pouring trillions of dollars into new energy technology with some, but limited, progress. In recent years, more private money has also been flowing in. To have a greater chance of picking "winners," government money should start following, not leading, that private money. These public funds can help scale and de-risk initiatives, but they should not be in the form of pure subsidy, and there should be insistence on a return for such investment.

I suggest this approach going forward as a far better path than the other alternative frequently advocated—carbon taxes. Carbon taxes are a bad idea, and they are advocated for bad reasons. Their impact is largely limited to those who struggle to afford energy in the first place.† Beyond that, they are simply a dead-weight economic cost. Frankly, in the hands of virtually any government, carbon taxes will invariably become about tax revenue not carbon reduction. If energy transition is good economics, as is often asserted, then the right policy is to earn money for taxpayers, rather than costing them more.

---

* This is in part because of their intermittent nature, which cannot be ignored in calculating cost.

† This is because energy is what economists call a highly "inelastic" commodity. People use what they must—neither much more nor much less—regardless of price, and it is a higher percentage of the budget the less affluent one is. Carbon taxes thus massively shift the tax burden to the poor, which is one reason why large corporations and social elites often advocate them.

PROROGATION, DECEMBER 2009

IN DECEMBER, I DECIDED to ask the governor general to prorogue Parliament for a new session in 2010. This she agreed to on the thirtieth. The reason was straightforward: we needed time to plan for the next session of Parliament.

Recall that we had found it necessary to ditch our platform after the October election and quickly bring in a whole new agenda in response to the global financial crisis. Those measures—Canada's Economic Action Plan—were being successfully executed, with the country's economy getting back on its feet. However, from a legislative standpoint, the work was essentially done. We needed to start to put together a longer-term agenda for governing.

A secondary consideration was the upcoming 2010 Olympics (February 10–28) and Paralympics (March 12–21) in Vancouver and Whistler. These events had been years in the making, and naturally, the world's eyes would be on Canada. As prime minister of the host country, I was expected to attend multiple events and meet leaders and dignitaries coming from around the world.

Governments at all levels had put enormous resources into this, with our Government contributing over a billion dollars toward security arrangements alone. That was on top of record athletic funding. This was a big undertaking, to put it mildly, and we were bound and determined to showcase Canada.

Of course, we thought there would be objections to prorogation, but the howls of outrage really were over the top. Democracy itself, the opposition and their media allies claimed, was being threatened. Our Government was said to be once again avoiding imminent defeat. This was news to us. Even if we were trying to avoid defeat, prorogation would not accomplish that. In fact, in this case, the delay in the return of Parliament was a mere three weeks.

The more important question was what, pray tell, was the Opposition planning to defeat us over? The previous year, there had actually been an issue—the desire to form the Liberal-NDP-Bloc coalition—and defeat over the economy, remote though it had become, was at least a possibility. But now the economy was recovering.

In short order, however, they had an answer. The issue was apparently the mistreatment of Afghan prisoners, something that had heated up late in 2009. It is an issue that warrants some commentary.

AFGHAN PRISONERS CONTROVERSY

TRUTHFULLY, I CAN BARELY REMEMBER how this controversy even arose. I remember that the *Globe and Mail* ran some articles alleging mistreatment of Taliban prisoners—the source being the Taliban itself. I think some left-wing professor somewhere made similar claims on the flimsiest of evidence. This was seized upon by various media outlets and, of course, the opposition parties. What was clear was that they wanted to report a Canadian version of Abu Ghraib—the infamous U.S. prisoner abuse scandal in Iraq. Whether there was any evidence of such was secondary.

But how would they deal with the lack of evidence? This, they would claim, was itself the proof. The lack of evidence could mean only one thing: a systematic cover-up. In other words, where there is no smoke, there must be fire!

Next, they moved on to how to discover the cover-up. Evidence for this iniquity would surely be found in the vast trove of documents currently classified as secret. Never mind that national security–related document classification decisions were made by justice department lawyers with no reference to the government of the day. That fact also had to be part of the vast cover-up conspiracy. Thus, given the minority parliament, a motion was passed by the opposition parties demanding public release of all these documents.

There were serious problems with this demand. First, the government actually does have strict legal obligations to protect much of this information. Second, national security documents are designated secret for many compelling reasons, including the safety of Canadian personnel or their associates and our obligations to our allies.

To be clear, while we were concerned with the ramifications of the opposition demands, we were never worried about the underlying issue. The biggest reason for this confidence was that we had been alive to this risk from the beginning. After the Somalia prison abuses of the 1990s, we were certainly aware that they *could* happen.

Early in our Government's first term, then–Defence Minister Gordon O'Connor had taken action to revise our prisoner transfer protocols. This was done to be doubly sure there would be no such abuse issues. To be clear, there had been no evidence of abuse to that point, but we were not prepared to tolerate even the *possibility* of abuse.

But, for argument's sake, let us suppose we had become aware of abuse. Indeed, if it had happened, we probably would have become aware. Does one really think the government would have then made itself complicit in something like that by covering it up? Not a chance—why would we do that? Instead, we would have thrown the book at the abusers and held them fully accountable under the law.

Still, we had to decide what to do about the parliamentary motion. Frankly, there was a side of me that would not have minded being defeated over this issue. It might not have been as big an opposition error as trying to form a governing coalition with Quebec separatists, but forcing an election over unsubstantiated allegations against Canadian soldiers by the Taliban would have been up there. The data we had on this was clear; it was neither what Canadians were focused on nor what they wanted to hear.

Yet, my calculation was the same as before. If there were to be an election, it would have to be strictly because of the opposition parties, not us. We would have to have been as reasonable as possible in avoiding that outcome. With this in mind, we made the opposition a take-it-or-leave-it offer. A representative from each party could review the documents in private, after having been sworn to the normal secrecy requirements for viewing such material. Obviously, these documents could never leave the room.

The opposition wisely accepted the offer. Notwithstanding the ongoing media advocacy, they had to know that an election over this matter was another suicide mission. On our side, I chose Laurie Hawn from Edmonton Centre as the representative.

Laurie was a great member of Parliament who served as parliamentary secretary for National Defence. That was after serving his country for many years as a lieutenant-colonel in the Royal Canadian Air Force (RCAF). Laurie was a perfect example of the dilemma PMs often face—someone well qualified to be in Cabinet but, for regional and demographic reasons, destined to serve in lesser, supporting roles. In any case, I knew I could count on Laurie to do a top-notch job in what would be a long, tedious, and thankless task.*

A HUMANITARIAN CRISIS IN HAITI

THE PARLIAMENTARY BREAK proved fortuitous when we were hit with an unexpected event demanding significant attention and quick action. A magnitude 7 earthquake hit Haiti on January 10, 2010. Given our place in the Americas, Canada had a responsibility to help in any way we could. There is a large Haitian community in Canada—its most prominent member being Governor General Jean—and many Canadians have family in Haiti. I knew the importance of quick action, and I was immediately on the phone with the defence minister Peter Mackay, chief of the defence staff General Walt Natynczyk, and the clerk of the Privy Council Wayne Wouters to authorize the mobilization of an immediate and significant response.

The Canadian Armed Forces provided the backbone of our efforts. RCAF CC-130 Hercules and heavy-lift CC-177 Globemaster aircraft deployed within hours along with our Disaster Assistance Response Team (DART), and the Royal Canadian Navy destroyer HMCS *Athabaskan* and frigate HMCS *Halifax* sailed within days. We had designated disaster relief as one of the essential capabilities of the military under the Canada First Defence

---

* An example of an Alberta MP in a similar situation was Rick Casson, the longtime MP for Lethbridge. I asked Rick to serve on the Permanent Joint Board of Defence with the United States and named him a member of the Privy Council as a consequence. Laurie Hawn succeeded him in that role.

Strategy, and these investments paid off. We were able to deploy people and assets to assist Haiti more quickly than just about anyone.

In mid-February, I was one of the very first Western leaders to go to Haiti. I toured the disaster zones from the air on an army helicopter, met with Haitian leadership, and spent the night on the HMCS *Athabaskan*. On the ground, I saw Canadian government personnel delivering aid, working with our citizens and refugees, making connections with relatives back home, and ensuring that basic embassy services were functioning. This was the Canadian public service—military and civilian—at its best. The effort was a whole-of-government achievement, with these Canadians making the kind of difference they got into public service to make. In a way that often distinguishes us from the Americans, our departments and agencies worked collaboratively with each other. In short, it was a tremendous effort to witness up close.

Public sentiment rallied as well. While we are sometimes accused of looking too inward, Canadians do care deeply about what happens in the world. In this case especially, it struck a chord that brought out tremendous generosity. Our Government established a matching fund for humanitarian contributions—a practice that would become standard for us—and it ultimately raised well over $200 million in aid. On a per capita scale, it was far beyond almost every other country.

Though the dysfunction and corruption of Haitian institutions would limit (and continue to limit) the country's ability to recover in the years since, I remain proud of Canada's response to the 2010 disaster—proud of our system and our people.

THE 2010 OLYMPIC WINTER GAMES

NOTHING WAS BETTER THAN the Olympics, because the focus was on the country, not on me. As I have said, I never really enjoyed the cameras, the microphones, and the celebrity of being PM. So the Olympics, where I would become, in effect, Canada's number-one cheerleader, was going to be great fun for me. It turned out to be even more successful than we had ever imagined.

Canada's Olympians stepped up big time, and by the final day, we had won a record number of gold medals. I cannot say I ever got tired of attending gold medal ceremony after gold medal ceremony. I especially enjoyed meeting and talking with the athletes, who were genuinely inspiring young Canadians—true role models.

Our performance at those Games was transformational for Canada. Despite our climate, we had not been a Winter Olympics power. In the past, our gold medals were so rare that their recipients became national icons for life. A perfect example was Nancy Greene Raine, our sole champion in 1968. (Nancy was now a Conservative senator and able to join me at the Games.) But "owning the podium"—our pre-Olympic objective—like we did in Vancouver was something entirely unprecedented.

How did such a transformation occur? The effort had begun under the previous Liberal administration, with increased funding for high-performance athletes and with improved results to show for it. Our Government really kicked that up to another level. During the tenure of Peter Van Loan and Gary Lunn as our sports ministers, additional specialized support for world-class athletes was provided. My friend Gordon Campbell, then premier of British Columbia, was instrumental in bringing the Olympics to Canada and his Government invested heavily in establishing top-tier venues.

Much of these new resources went into psychological coaching. In the top echelons of a sport, skill levels are often close to the maximum. It is the mental toughness that then makes all the difference. These are people in incredibly high-pressure situations, beyond what any of us will ever experience. A lifetime of training comes down to a few minutes. Watching athletes at the speed-skating events, for example, made it abundantly clear to me the fractions of seconds involved between getting a medal or not.

The last day of the 2010 Games featured the men's gold-medal hockey game. It was the pinnacle and could hardly be scripted any better than it was: we would face the Americans, our "archrival." To add even more drama, it was not just the gold in hockey (and the accompanying bragging rights!) but also the chance to win an all-time Winter Olympics' record of fourteen such medals.

Going to that event would have been a treat no matter what. It was made that much more special when Ben and I were joined by Wayne Gretzky. The Great One, whom I have had the pleasure to get to know and stay in touch with, is not just a great hockey player; he is a truly Great Canadian.

Before the game began, I said to Wayne, "These guys must be under enormous pressure. Nothing short of gold ever satisfies Canadians when it comes to hockey. On top of that, they will now either win or fail to win the record fourteenth gold medal. Literally the entire country will be watching. Streets will be deserted. The stress must be unlike anything even a professional athlete has ever experienced." Wayne listened patiently and then said to me, "No, Prime Minister. These guys have done this their whole lives. This is what they live for."

Nevertheless, Team Canada began the game very tentatively. They did not look at all on in the first few minutes. Wayne turned to me and said bluntly, "You were right. The guys are nervous."

Team Canada started to get back on track and eventually took a 2–0 lead. Then they became tight once again and fell into a defensive shell. (This was not the strategy, the coaches told me later. They guys were just nervous.) The Americans came back to tie it up.

We went into overtime, and the play continued to be close. Nevertheless, Sidney Crosby got the winner on a set-up from Calgary Flames' captain Jarome Iginla, his off-balance shot catching the U.S. goalie off guard. It was one of those iconic moments, on par with Paul Henderson's winning goal against the Soviets in 1972. To be in the building to witness that was the experience of a lifetime.

Lest you think my attendance at the Olympics was all fun and games, I did have some work to do as well. The Olympics attracts reasonably high-profile political delegations. Countries often send their head of state or their head of government, or at least a very senior official. Hence there are numerous receptions or quasi-diplomatic events to attend, including the opening and closing ceremonies.

Top: A game of cribbage with Rachel en route to Toronto, 2008. *(Deb Ransom)*

Middle: Racing with Ben to the puck on Harrington Lake, 2009. *(Jason Ransom)*

Bottom: Crossing Abbey Road where the Beatles were pictured for the cover of *Abbey Road*. After, we toured the recording studios as a 50th birthday surprise from Laureen, 2009. *(Jason Ransom)*

Meeting with Queen Elizabeth II at Buckingham Palace, 2009. *(Jason Ransom)*

At the American Cemetery at Colleville-sur-Mer in France with Allied leaders and Prince Charles to mark the 65th anniversary of the D-Day landings. *(Jason Ransom)*

Being welcomed to the White House by President George W. Bush, 2008. *(Jason Ransom)*

With President Barack Obama in the Oval Office, 2009. *(Jason Ransom)*

With the Prince of Wales, and the Duchess of Cornwall, attending Remembrance Day at the National War Memorial, November 11, 2009. *(Jill Propp)*

Cheering on Team Canada at the 2010 Olympic Winter Games with former Prime Minister Jean Chrétien. *(Jason Ransom)*

Celebrating Canada's win with Wayne Gretzky during the women's hockey gold medal game at the 2010 Vancouver Olympics. *(Jason Ransom)*

Taking Rachel to meet Taylor Swift and watch her concert was a highlight for me as a dad! *(Deb Ransom)*

Hamming it up with the Carnaval de Québec's Bonhomme, 2010. *(Jason Ransom)*

Laureen and I meeting a baby panda at the Chongqing Zoo in China, 2012. *(Jason Ransom)*

Top: Watching a pair of CF-18 Hornets and a CC-150 Polaris fly past during northern sovereignty exercises in Resolute, Nunavut, 2010. *(Jason Ransom)*

Right: Meeting Canadian Rangers in York Sound for Operation NANOOK during my ninth annual tour of Canada's Northern Territories, 2014. *(Jill Thompson)*

Bottom: Touring CFS Alert, Nunavut, the most northerly inhabited place in the world, 2006. *(Jason Ransom)*

A turning point in Question Period during the "coalition crisis," 2008. *(Jason Ransom)*

Chatting with NDP Leader Jack Layton in the House of Commons, 2011. Despite our different perspectives, he was a man I genuinely respected. *(Jason Ransom)*

With Finance Minister Jim Flaherty before delivering the budget in the House of Commons, 2012. *(Jason Ransom)*

Top: Her Majesty Queen Elizabeth II arrives on Parliament Hill to celebrate Canada Day, 2010. *(Jason Ransom)*

Middle: Sharing a laugh with Her Royal Highness The Duchess of Cambridge, on Parliament Hill during Canada Day celebrations, 2011. *(Jason Ransom)*

Bottom: With His Royal Highness The Prince of Wales, at the Fort York Armoury in Toronto marking the 200th anniversary of the War of 1812. *(Jason Ransom)*

Of these, my most memorable meeting was with the American delegation headed by then–Vice President Joe Biden. I developed a good relationship with Biden over the years. He is extremely personable and very candid, which I like. He also happens to be a great friend and admirer of Canada. We had a long conversation on a range of bilateral issues and international affairs. On these matters, Joe is very well-versed and often has strong opinions.

A NEW SESSION OF PARLIAMENT

SHORTLY AFTER THE OLYMPICS, we were back in the House for a new session. Despite all the activity of the previous few weeks, the planning had been completed. The Throne Speech had been prepared, and it was delivered. Then, the day after, Minister Flaherty unveiled Budget 2010.

This budget was to signal a change in direction. While there was still a year to go in delivery of the fiscal stimulus, planning was now focused on deficit reduction. This was important to me, to our party, and, back then, to Canadians more broadly.

The country had experienced the harsh austerity of the late 1990s, and no one wanted to be in that situation again. Our Conservative MPs, some of whom were even more fiscally conservative than me, wanted assurance that we were not headed to chronic borrowing. That is not why they had come to Ottawa. For my part, I was determined not to create the legacy of structural deficits that usually plague governments after Keynesian "short-term" borrowing.

Our approach to deficit reduction would consist of three elements. First, we would stop "emergency" stimulus spending on schedule. That would get us at least halfway to our goal. Second, we would limit spending growth over the next five years so that revenue could catch up but, critically, without tax increases. Finally, we would have to face the fact that some expenditure cuts would be needed.

The reason for the third element was that the recession had permanently knocked the revenue growth track down to a lower, long-run trend line.

However, we would aim to focus spending reductions on the costs of bureaucracy rather than services to the public. And unlike in the Chrétien-Martin years, we were clear that major transfers to the provinces for health and education would not be cut.

This approach would not be harsh, but neither would it be easy. For up to five years, it would require sustained financial discipline throughout the government. That started with Jim Flaherty, who I knew was up to the job. Important roles would also be played over time by the ministers of state for Finance, Ted Menzies and later Kevin Sorenson, as well as Treasury Board president Tony Clement, especially on the negotiation of labour contracts.

I would note that the pressure to keep the stimulus money flowing was often intense. Every single agency and organization that received funds was lobbying for the spending to continue "for just one more year." Jim, true to his word, said no to all of them. The only flexibility he showed was in some of the infrastructure projects that, if at least underway before the end of the second year, would be allowed to finish somewhat later.

Ironically, some of the most severe battles were with our conservative constituency. The biggest single early battle was over the Home Renovation Tax Credit—the program we had deliberately tailored to middle-class taxpayers. Ultimately, a lot of Conservative voters had used it and liked it, and, through our caucus members, let us know very loudly they wanted to see it continue.

I was not completely deaf to the appeal, and I discussed it with Jim, but he was immovable. He understood the pressure and the appeal, but countered that if we continued it, it would become an expectation, and then a permanent program. He was right, of course, because the program was very expensive, and for the integrity of our deficit reduction efforts, we needed it to stop on schedule. Jim could be moved by arguments of real compassion, but not by those of mere expediency.

While deficit reduction was core to our budget planning, we had a broader emphasis on economic growth. The budget's title, "Jobs and Growth," signalled to Canadians that we had not forgotten our overall focus. That is why refusing to raise taxes was so important.

In fact, we began to introduce the tax-cutting measures that we had promised before the crisis. One important additional measure was the elimination of almost all tariffs on manufacturing. We made Canada the first virtually tariff-free manufacturing country in the G20. That was a big step forward. Another area we emphasized to encourage jobs and growth was research—both for the business and academic communities.

We also laid the groundwork for thinning government, by launching the Red Tape Reduction Commission. Begun under Stockwell Day, this program was taken over by Tony Clement, who became its champion. A streamlined regulatory state would be an important tool in our arsenal, both to reduce the costs of government and to encourage economic growth.

THE TRUTH REVEALED

HOW DID THE OPPOSITION respond to all this? When we prorogued Parliament, the air was thick with accusations. Yet, when we reconvened, we heard crickets. The budget gave the opposition an immediate golden opportunity to bring us down. Instead, all of it quietly passed.

In truth, I think the opposition was starting to learn some lessons from their previous attempts to overthrow us. With a rapidly and noticeably improving economy, their efforts had not endeared themselves to the public and would likely have failed anyway. So why appear to be disruptive? The irony was that, following the worst economic crisis in half a century, our Government was at less risk of defeat than at any time since our election in 2006.

And what about that tale of the widespread abuse of Afghan prisoners and its subsequent cover-up? For months on end, the opposition privately pored over the documents—finding nothing. The issue slowly evaporated.

There is a side of me that remains angry about this episode. All I can say is that, while it went on, Canada's soldiers, out in the field and suffering terrible casualties, continued steadfastly on their mission. In stark contrast to their critics on the opposition benches and in the press gallery, they showed what professionalism and integrity really mean.

16

INTO THE INTERNATIONAL SPOTLIGHT

THE WORLD WORKS in funny ways sometimes. In a minority situation, following one of the worst downturns in recent economic history, our Government found itself in a strong political position. There seemed to be no immediate prospect of our defeat well into the second year of our second minority parliament. This was just as well, because much of my focus in the upcoming months would be once again on international matters.

I would be chairman of both the G8 and the G20 Summits in Canada. The first would be in Muskoka on June 25–26, 2010, and the second immediately after in Toronto on June 26–27. The arrangement had been agreed to as part of our effort during that period (mercifully brief) to preserve the G8 when its relevance was in question in some allied capitals.

PREPARING FOR THE G8 AND G20 SUMMITS

OUR INITIAL THOUGHT was to host both summits in the cottage country of Muskoka, north of Toronto. Given the positive experience around the G8 Summit in Kananaskis Country west of Calgary in 2002, we felt that the security challenges would be better managed in a rural area. The summits would also be more welcome and less disruptive to economic life there. It soon became apparent, however, that this was not going work for the G20. Given the newness of the forum—three previous summits, but in just a year and a half—it took us some time to get our heads around the scope of the arrangements required.

The big issue was size; between all the delegations, including security and media, the total attendance at the G20 would be well into five figures. There was no way this crowd could be accommodated within a reasonable distance of Muskoka. A large chunk would have to stay in Toronto anyway, so the decision was made to move the event to the big city. We knew that this would mean additional security complications, but there was simply no choice.

Hosting any summit is a big undertaking. Still, scale matters, and the bigger the summit, the bigger the challenges. Some organizations, like the Commonwealth, the Organisation internationale de la Francophonie, and the Organization of American States, have their own secretariats, which can help with planning such events. That was not the case for either the G8 or the G20, despite the former having been in existence for four decades. In these cases, as the host, you assume full responsibility for all aspects of the event organization.

Thankfully, this was not left to me and my office alone. Canada's Foreign Affairs Department has people who have long specialized in this sort of thing, and they are very good at it. Then–Assistant Deputy Minister Peter McGovern headed up the Summit Management Office that oversaw the logistics for both summits, working directly with the Privy Council and my team in the PMO. Peter was a skilled professional, and I had regular reports noting the excellent collaboration in support of this unique situation where we were hosting back-to-back summits.

With logistical matters in hand, the most important elements of chairmanship are development of the agenda and any declaration that would follow from it. This always involves extensive consultations, often carried out by telephone, but also including trips I made to talk to world leaders individually. Sometimes they came to see me, to raise their individual concerns or even to lobby for an inside track on the program.

Building an effective agenda is more art than science. It starts with recognizing that as chairman, you are only a presiding officer, not a CEO. You must find the topics that most want to talk about and then try to build consensus around the declaration that will conclude the event. This being international relations, it is certain that people are not going to agree on everything all the time, but you generally want to avoid situations where disagreements could cause a crisis or even a breakdown in the summit itself. Sometimes this means lowering some leaders' expectations beforehand regarding what they think they might achieve at the summit.

The chairman does have has some room to shape the agenda to his or her priorities and outcomes. This, however, must be done with care. If you cannot carry the room, then you risk your chairmanship becoming a failure.

THE G8 SUMMIT AND TURKEY

THE TWO SUMMITS have very different feels. The G8 is obviously much smaller than the G20, and it is a long-standing institution composed, for the most part, of trusted allies and partners. Its declarations are thus much simpler to develop, and as chairman, you want to encourage intimate, free-flowing conversations with a genuine exchange of views. There is limited need for scripting. This approach, I believed, would remind our allies of the G8's ongoing relevance in the face of the G20's rising prominence.

Yet I also knew there was a real constraint on our deliberations—the presence of Vladimir Putin. That was a consequence of the 1997 G7 decision to admit Russia as a member. After the fall of the Soviet Union, there had been growing confidence that Boris Yeltsin was taking Russia in a democratic, free-market, pro-Western direction. Contrary to Putinesque myths, this was welcomed and encouraged. Far from "humiliating" Russia, the West had wanted Russia to become a critical pillar of its alliance, and there were strong reasons to believe that was happening.

By 2010, it was clear that Russia was headed in a very different direction. Russian democracy under Putin was being progressively dismantled. Its post-Soviet economy, which had always been a kleptocracy, was dominated by organized crime, in which Putin was its biggest don. And Russia was increasingly an opponent in international affairs.

At least, those were my views. They were shared in part, though not yet fully, by most others. But they were sufficiently appreciated as to inhibit conversation on some critical items—China and North Korea come to mind. In any case, Putin would not be at Muskoka. The president of Russia for the time being was Dmitry Medvedev, who was a younger and more constructive interlocutor. While I was under no illusion that he reported directly to Putin, his presence made the conversation at least tolerable.

Ironically, the sharpest exchanges of the summit did not involve Russia in any significant way. They revolved around Turkey, specifically the question of whether Turkey should be admitted to the European Union. This was not on the agenda, and I cannot really remember how its intensity ramped up so quickly.

On the pro side, some G8 leaders asserted that membership would help consolidate Turkey's development toward the West and our values and that rejecting it was pushing it in the other direction. On the con side, some argued that Turkey was clearly headed away from the West and that its admittance would undermine EU cohesion. All I can say is the discussion got extremely heated and surprisingly personal. In fact, I have never seen a discussion among world leaders that got so heated and so intense.

I had a view, but as chairman, I kept it to myself on this occasion. I thought it was better to act as a referee. There were more important issues G8 members needed to focus on at this time. But privately, I did have a view.

This is another one of these areas where the views of our Government and those of Foreign Affairs were offside from day one. Turkey then had a rapidly growing economy and its prime minister, Recep Tayyip Erdoğan, had started out as an economic reformer. Officials described his political vehicle, the Justice and Development Party (AKP), as the "Islamic equivalent of Christian Democrats," that is, essentially the Muslim version of a centre-right conservative.

That was the Foreign Affairs position—yes, they cultivated their own positions—and it came with an ask. It was not just that I make Turkey a high-priority relationship. It was that I should disavow a parliamentary resolution, passed during Paul Martin's Government, that recognized the

Armenian Genocide of World War I—which our party had supported at the time. This demand came up repeatedly, and I rejected it each time. The deaths of close to a million and a half Armenians is an incontrovertible historical fact. To be blunt, I was not about to become a genocide denier, and the fact that Turkey's leader was such a strong one was not reassuring.

I had other reasons for suspicion. From the outset of his regime, it looked to me like Erdoğan was moving Turkey away from Kemalism—its long-standing secular, Western orientation in both foreign and domestic affairs—and toward what has been called neo-Ottomanism. The latter would see Turkey once again rooted in the Islamic world, attempting to provide Sunni leadership to the areas once controlled by the Ottoman Empire. There were more than a few signs of this, not least of which were Erdoğan's anti-Israeli views and past antisemitic utterances.

My encounters with Erdoğan at various international summits fed my misgivings. In comportment and attitude, he came across as an authoritarian and nationalist in the Islamist sense. I certainly got no sense of Western identity, at least not in any non-opportunistic way. To me, he was only keeping a foot in the West for the purposes of convenience.

I declined to make Turkey a foreign policy priority, and sadly, it was the right decision. Erdoğan has systematically moved his country in the troubling direction I saw from the outset. Yes, he has won elections, but that has been for the purpose of consolidating power and dismantling an emerging, Western-oriented, free and democratic society. He has created an executive presidency for himself and pursued the mass incarceration and purges of civilian and military officials, especially after the convenient, poorly organized "coup attempt" of 2016. He has made life increasingly difficult for Kurds, Christians, and other minorities in Turkey. As his political objectives have clashed with Turkey's financial interests, he has turned away from reform and runs a troubled, inflationary, devaluation-prone economy.

This is more than a tragedy. For a member of NATO, it is a travesty. Erdoğan continues to benefit from NATO membership even while actively opposing NATO allies and undermining many NATO priorities. These range from funding the Muslim Brotherhood and its extremist allies throughout the Arab world to provoking conflicts in the Aegean and the Caucasus. He even plays both sides with Putin's Russia.

Erdoğan is not, as some once wishfully thought, a Western ally with a foot in the Islamic world. He is a political Islamist and Sunni sectarian leader using the West when it suits him to do so. And, frankly, this is what he always was. We can all be grateful Erdoğan's Turkey was never admitted into the European Union.

THE MATERNAL, NEWBORN, AND CHILD HEALTH INITIATIVE

AS IS CUSTOMARY, we wanted to put a Canadian legacy stamp on these summits. One way to do that was to focus on the G8's unique development agenda. Our choice did not come out of the blue. My foreign affairs advisor in the Privy Council Office, Christine Hogan, led an extensive review of the issues with a range of development organizations. We ended up identifying two of what were called the Millennium Development Goals—a sharply focused program initiated by Kofi Annan when he had been secretary-general of the United Nations. These were to reduce child mortality and improve maternal health, hence the "Muskoka Initiative on Maternal, Newborn, and Child Health," which inevitably took the bureaucratic short-form MNCH.

Why these? For one, we did not anticipate the objectives would be controversial. After all, who can argue with improving the lives of children and mothers around the world? It also became very apparent that the possibilities of success were very promising. Health outcomes for young mothers and their children in developing countries could be substantially improved on a significant scale and at reasonable cost. This was quite literally a chance to save the lives of millions of people and to better the lives of millions more.

The Initiative would fit well into our evolving foreign policy. As a government, we believed in developing free and democratic societies, but we also saw that there were real barriers to achieving such advancement. Just toppling a dictator and holding an election were, we had witnessed, often completely insufficient. Deeper changes had to be made in these societies. The elevation of the rights and welfare of women became one of the key pillars we would focus on.

It turned out that the G8 was an ideal launching pad for this Initiative, as other G7 countries and organizations quickly bought in. The Gates Foundation showed early interest, as did Prime Minister Erna Solberg of Norway, a great friend and generous supporter of these causes. Soon the World Health Organization was also on board. Its main contribution was to set up an Accountability Commission, which I co-chaired with President Jakaya Kikwete of Tanzania. This would carefully track outcome metrics for the monies committed, starting with the seven-and-a-half billion dollars pledged at Muskoka.

Beyond involving the global development community and, of course, Canadian development organizations, MNCH was also supported by regular Canadians. We were able to secure the contributions of tens of thousands of private citizens.

By any measure, this was a successful launch to the Muskoka Initiative. But one pall hung over it—the issue of abortion. This became an obsession in media coverage, although to most participants, the discussion was seen as bizarre. The inclusion of abortion would not only destroy private funding—the Gates Foundation and others made that clear—but abortions are illegal or highly restricted in many of the jurisdictions that the Muskoka Initiative targeted. That alone could have rendered the Initiative inoperative.

The Liberal Party, always looking for an opportunity to put the abortion debate back on the public radar, actually moved a motion on this in the House. It was defeated, leading the journalists who had goaded Michael Ignatieff into pursuing the issue to then condemn him for failing. But many Canadians, even if they supported a right to choose abortion, did not necessarily want their tax dollars to pay for abortions overseas.

As a government, we refused to get drawn into the weeds on the abortion question, and we took a pragmatic approach. We were not going to fund organizations whose principal purpose was to provide abortions. However, we supported those that delivered general health services, even if abortions might be done in hospitals under certain circumstances.

We never viewed MNCH as ending with the Muskoka G8. This would be an ongoing priority for our Government. Going forward, Minister Bev Oda and later Christian Paradis would provide leadership in Cabinet, while Jeremy Hunt in my office played a key role with outside stakeholders.

THE "GLOBAL BANK TAX" CONTROVERSY

THE CHALLENGES OF THE G20 were very different. Being a much larger body, there could never be the level of trust and intimacy of the G8. In fact, numerous rivalries and distrust surrounded the summit table. Any of those could erupt, become public, and undermine the success of the forum. Getting too far off script could mean courting disaster.

The backdrop to the summit was a mixed bag. By this time in 2010, the global economy was certainly improving. The panic had clearly passed, and in many countries, genuine recovery was underway. This was certainly true in Canada, although the U.S. economy remained sluggish. The big emerging economies like China were further ahead. More significant challenges remained in Europe, but the situation there no longer appeared critical.

Yet, in an odd way, the recovery made things more difficult. As countries emerged from the economic abyss, the profound level of international consensus of the previous year and a half was beginning to unravel. I was not entirely shocked by that—different circumstances in various countries would invariably mean different priorities—but, still, it was a reality that had to be managed.

Unfortunately, there was one bad idea being pushed hard by some countries in the lead-up to the summit—the so-called global bank tax. This was most vigorously championed by the members of the European Union, who wanted a special levy on major financial institutions around the world. Its stated purpose was to be a source of financing for bank bailouts and, therefore, insurance against taxpayer burdens in the future.

There was certainly no unanimity around this, and some countries were strongly opposed. Of these latter, Canada was near the top of the list. We had not done taxpayer-funded bank bailouts, so there was no apparent need for such a policy. Plus, my Government's agenda was not about raising taxes and certainly not about imposing surtaxes on business. Our priority remained to drive down Canada's tax rates and to make them more globally competitive.

But I had an even more important objection: I was suspicious of the motives behind this trial balloon. I do view modern Europe as a great force for good in the world, yet I am also aware of the tendency of European leaders to sometimes cloak self-interest in the guise of high moral purpose. We had just experienced a global financial crisis where European and American banks had to be bailed out or fail. But Canadian banks were solid and now in the best internationally competitive position in their history. In fact, their valuations were placing them among the largest banks in the Western world. I was not about to apply a tax that would in effect socialize the costs of European and American bailouts and thereby erode a competitive advantage that we had gained by superior performance.

Far from looking to restrain our banks, I was encouraging their CEOs to become more aggressive (though certainly not reckless) in taking advantage of the situation. Now, I thought, would be a real opportunity for them to expand their global holdings and footprints and help raise Canada's status—Toronto's status in particular—as a global financial centre. Some did just that.

Fortunately, we were not alone in our opposition. And my chairmanship was a fortuitous position from which to diplomatically head off this initiative—at least on this occasion. However, this was not the last we would hear of the European agenda on these matters.

THE G20 DELIBERATIONS

WHILE IT WAS INEVITABLE that G20 discussions would not be as free-flowing as the G8, I wanted to do something to enhance the proceedings. Many leaders would, believe it or not, simply read their interventions from prepared notes. There was nothing I could do about that. But there was a bigger challenge.

The problem was with a couple of the leaders, who will remain nameless. Their interventions were very likely to be excessively long. These were not quite the endless rants that I had witnessed at the Summit of the Americas, but experience indicated these participants could be expected to take three to four times the allotted duration.*

This is something I have never quite understood in politics, particularly when you are dealing with people at the level of international leadership. There is rarely an upside to speaking for too long and seldom a downside for being succinct, whatever your audience. I have given a lot of public speeches in my life, and no one has come up to me after and said, "Your speech was too short."† Probably the best political speech ever in the English language—Abraham Lincoln's Gettysburg Address—was a mere 272 words. Over one hundred and fifty years later, people are still quoting it and writing books on its significance.

After consulting with various leaders beforehand, I decided to experiment with a lighting system to limit comments at the plenary sessions. Right off the bat, I said to the leaders, "I'm going to give you so many minutes. During your allotted time, you will see a green light, right in the middle of the table. When you are drawing to the end of your time, you're going to see a yellow light. And then, at so many minutes over your time, it will hit red, and I actually will cut you off."

And you know what? It worked. The leaders quickly settled into the allotted time. I never did cut anyone off, and only one speaker went over and then only briefly. The interventions became sharper and more focused throughout the sessions.

In terms of the general deliberations, we attempted to build consensus around what was essentially the Canadian model for recovery. Where the financial sector continued to be problematic, that should be dealt with. And,

---

* After the first three summits, the culprits were well known by everyone attending.

† Truthfully, I have heard that comment—twice in my entire lifetime. The exceptions prove the rule!

by all means, fiscal stimulus should continue, if required. Canada, after all, was still pumping stimulus money into our economy, even though we were beginning to wind it down. The stated policy of a "freeze" against protectionist actions, which had generally been respected, was reiterated. However, the next phase needed to be "fiscal consolidation," that is, a medium-term plan for getting deficits under control and debt-to-GDP ratios down.

We were marginally successful in getting some language into the summit declaration around those general parameters. But the truth is that many of those countries never made fiscal consolidation a priority in practice. The consequence was that, when the pandemic crisis hit a decade later, deficit and debt burdens skyrocketed, leading to the inflation and sustained slow growth the world then experienced.

This was a disappointment for me, even if it was inevitable. It was simply a consequence of the growing differentiation in various countries' economic situations. However, it foreshadowed a pattern that has continued unabated since that time—a steady diminishment in the common purpose and effectiveness of the G20 as an organization.

This reality does not render the G20 Summits unimportant, however. In the modern global economy, with its ongoing integration, it is very important to have the world's leading economies, as different as they are, around the same table, discussing these issues. No matter what some of my libertarian friends think, markets are not spontaneous. They are structured by policy, and without sound governance, they fail. And the closest thing we have to governance in the global economy is the G20 and the more specialized forums it has spawned. In the meantime, however, its commonness of purpose has all but vanished, and the world is poorer for it.

THE SECURITY FAILURES IN TORONTO

ONE OTHER MATTER NEEDS to be addressed about Canada's leadership of the G20—the cost and execution of security. The reality is that the government of the day simply has no control over those things. There is a long history in Canada of governments staying out of the day-to-day operations of police, prosecutors, and other security officials.

Under most circumstances, this is exactly as it should be. When governments try to intervene, as we saw in the SNC-Lavalin affair, enormous controversy can ensue. And rightly so. Such actions put the quality and reputation of the justice system at risk. We do not want politicians trying to manipulate the actions of police or prosecutors.

Some explanation for the high price we paid for G20 security is still in order. A significant part of this went to pay for physical infrastructure. Miles of fencing and other installations to channel crowds and protect the visiting dignitaries are not cheap. These were hard and unavoidable costs. So too were the vast personnel costs. Having tens of thousands of police on the job for twenty-four hours a day was also hugely expensive.

Of course, it was not just the costs that were criticized; it was the results as well. Well-planned demonstrations by a wide range of interest groups targeting the G20 had begun the week before the Toronto summit got underway, and they continued throughout the event itself. While many of these were peaceful, some were populated by thugs. There was growing violence, a riot, and major damage to downtown Toronto businesses.

The police were criticized in some circles for what were depicted as the brutal suppression of gatherings. The nightly international news featured images of officers tear-gassing and arresting protestors while police cars burned in the streets of Toronto. Police ended up conducting the largest mass arrest in Canadian history. In the end, ninety-seven officers and thirty-nine protesters were injured.

I wish I could tell you that this was a shock to me. It was not. While security had gone well for the G8 at Muskoka, there had been warning signs almost from the moment we shifted the G20 venue to Toronto. We as a government had our concerns from the outset with the leadership of the Toronto police, who would have primary responsibility for security.

In my conversations with the RCMP and other federal security officials, we felt the police department was not taking the risks of deliberate protest violence seriously. Other forces around the world had experience at similar gatherings, and they had learned that proactive steps must be taken. In Toronto's case, the attitude of the leadership seemed to be about building bridges with the protestors, giving them as much latitude as possible and, once they realized what good guys the cops were, believing all would go well from there. That may or may not be an entirely fair assessment, but it was certainly our impression. In any case, the willingness to listen to other experiences was not there.

This, by the way, has been a pattern evident in many of the summits held in Canada. I am thinking of the Asia-Pacific Economic Cooperation Summit in Vancouver in 1997 as well as the Summit of the Americas in Quebec City in 2001. Police began their operations with a very passive approach. Then, when things spun out of control, they were seen as being excessively heavy-handed—necessarily so as a consequence.

Whether my read of what went wrong is correct or not, from that point forward I ruled out hosting any further such summits in Canada while I was prime minister. For whatever reason, law enforcement in Canada seemed not to be learning from past situations. I simply did not need to spend hundreds of millions of taxpayer dollars for bungled security that only embarrassed the country and risked injury to front-line law enforcement—especially when I had no control over it anyway.

That is a dilemma for any government. Even if you are not responsible—even if you should not interfere—you take the blame for this kind of problem. After all, as the elected people, you are the only ones who can be held accountable.

FROM THE SUMMITS TO STATE VISITS

ONE OF THE SIDE BENEFITS of hosting summits is the opportunity for bilateral visits with those present. With a couple of dozen leaders making a rare journey to Canada, it was inevitable that many would request a stand-alone visit before or after the event. I chose to host Chinese President Hu before the summits and Indian Prime Minister Singh immediately after.

Both visits included large welcoming banquets, along with the standard bilateral meetings.

Immediately following the Indian bilateral visit, I would welcome Her Majesty, Queen Elizabeth II and HRH Prince Philip to Canada. This nine-day tour, Her Majesty's twenty-second tour of Canada, began with a fleet review ceremony in Halifax to mark the 100th anniversary of the Royal Canadian Navy. I will not forget that beautiful day in Halifax Harbour, joining the Queen and Prince Philip aboard HMCS *St. John's* to mark the historic legacy of service and sacrifice that is Canada's proud naval heritage.

I had by now met the Queen privately on several occasions, beginning during my time as leader of the Opposition. I always found her well briefed and engaging, with a charming, dry sense of humour. She genuinely loved Canada, and though leaving Canadian Crown affairs fully in the hands of the governor general, she was always broadly aware of developments here.

The Queen's most interesting attribute was her read of people. She had met everybody who was anybody everywhere in the world for decades, and she was a shrewd judge of character. If you developed a trust with her, she was a valuable source of insight into some of the people you would have to deal with as prime minister.

The Queen's stamina during this visit was incredible. She undertook events from Nova Scotia to Manitoba, including an unforgettable Canada Day celebration on Parliament Hill in Ottawa. I recall in particular the banquet we had in Toronto, where the eighty-four-year-old monarch stood for hours for individual photos with hundreds of guests. And that was just one event.

However, as Laureen and I with the assembled guests at the Royal York Hotel sang a hearty "God Save the Queen" in the presence of Her Majesty, I had a sense that this would likely be her last visit to Canada. It was a premonition that sadly turned out to be true. I am grateful to the Canadian secretary to the Queen, Kevin MacLeod, and the dozens of officials he worked with for planning this unforgettable final tour for Canada's Queen. It made for memories that I, along with so many Canadians, will long cherish.

THE UN SECURITY COUNCIL CAMPAIGN

IF HOSTING THE G8 AND G20 was the international highlight for me in 2010, the low point was the campaign for a seat on the United Nations Security Council (UNSC). It would come to a head in the fall. Unfortunately, I was probably one of the least-surprised people at the time when it failed.

Almost the moment we took office, the ground for this campaign shifted on us. The Liberals had launched it prior to our election in 2006. At that point, it was just Canada and Portugal in the running for the two open spots. As we were coming to power, the Germans jumped into the race, changing the situation dramatically. Right then, we should have asked ourselves some hard questions about why we were running and what we hoped to achieve.

It was not as if I did not raise these matters with officials over time. In fact, I had asked two really basic questions: Why were we running for this seat? And what was our strategy to win it? They may sound like reasonable questions. But the truth is that the answers were never satisfactory.

The first time I asked why we were running for a seat, I received a version of "that's how we've always done it." By that, they meant that Canada had been on the United Nations Security Council about one term per decade since the UN's founding in 1945. By that logic, 2010 was our time to seek a seat again.

Of course, the great weakness of any that's-how-we've-always-done-it argument is that it often means the original reason something was done has been completely forgotten. I pressed harder, but I did not really get much beyond something about Canada's "prestige" on the world stage, which a UNSC seat would supposedly either demonstrate or at least recognize.

The important thing is this: at no point did I receive a concrete reason why this was in Canada's interests. What exactly would Canada gain if we won this seat? What would be jeopardized if we did not? Frankly, the arguments I heard were never compelling.

It goes without saying that the Security Council is a very important institution of the United Nations, probably even more important than the General Assembly. It is where the big and meaty issues of peace and security are discussed. But here is the reality about the UNSC: there may be fifteen members, but only five really matter.

Those five members—United States, United Kingdom, France, China, Russia—have permanent spots and veto power over any matter they choose. Nothing can pass without them. On the other hand, if all five are behind something, it is hard to conceive of something not passing. The Council is thus utterly controlled by the five major players. Yes, the ten temporary members will get a bit of the spotlight, and they will be wined and dined by other UN members seeking to get their positions adopted, but the reality is that they are bit players at best.

Our strategy to win the seat also felt flimsy to me. It hinged on our standing as a "great global citizen," that is, a strong contributor to almost all major international efforts, whether they be security or developmental or economic. The problem with that approach, however, was that this was a political campaign, not a branding exercise. This would be a real election. As in any election, the voters—in this case, the countries of the UN—would ask what was in it for them to cast their votes for us?

I made clear that, as a government, we would not tailor our foreign affairs policies (or offer other inducements) for the sake of this campaign. Our foreign policy was principles-based, not popularity-based. And it was certainly not based on seeking popularity at the United Nations, which, bluntly, consists of virtually every state—the good, the bad, and the ugly. Of course, if our foreign policy was not popularity-based, why were we in such a popularity contest in the first place?

But there was an even more fundamental weakness to the campaign—the great global citizen argument itself. I think it is, to a significant degree, true. However, the reality is that many UN members do not believe it to be true. There is a reason for this: Canada's policies are often designed in a way that ensures we get neither visibility nor credit. More on this later, particularly as it relates to development assistance.

For all these reasons, I was very skeptical that we could win an intense contest at the UN. Unfortunately, by the time this campaign was thoroughly reviewed by Cabinet—it was not one of our initial priorities—many had bought into the Foreign Affairs' pitch that it was necessary to continue it and win it. By then, the prestige argument had been turned on its head. If we were not successful in the race, or abandoned it outright, then this mythical prestige was something we would lose.

Despite my overriding doubts about the whole exercise, I did my bit. I promoted our candidacy in speeches at the General Assembly and elsewhere. When I travelled around the world, I raised it with numerous leaders. I even called some other leaders—a few of them dubious characters indeed—to pitch them for their support. I gave it a shot, but down deep, I never believed we had a winning strategy.

So it was no surprise that we did not win. In the UN vote, Canada came in third behind Germany and Portugal, which many in our foreign affairs community and commentariat labelled a humiliating defeat. Our successor government undertook another failing effort. Despite their willingness to take any position necessary to get support—maybe, in fact, because of that—they lost again and by an even bigger margin.

It is impossible to say definitively why we or they lost these races. The votes are cast by secret ballot. Most countries are smart enough to promise their ballot to every contestant, so your candidacy will always get fewer votes than you think you will.

Some suggested—sometimes as praise, sometimes as criticism—that we lost because of positions we took, particularly our staunch defence of Israel. That did move a few votes, but as our successors proved with far less principled Middle East behaviour, probably not very many. A far bigger problem for us is that Canada is in the Western European group in the voting. That is a serious structural disadvantage in an era of European unity and integration, as it renders us an outsider in our own group.

It is perhaps an overused phrase to say that when you are the leader, the buck stops with you. So feel free to blame me for the loss of this campaign. But the blame should be not that I lost per se, but that I allowed it to proceed against my better judgment. This, by the way, is key to some advice I give new conservative first ministers everywhere: shut down every campaign, committee, or activity that you did not create, if you can. Make your own evaluations of your own needs, and do not allow pre-existing agendas to become entrenched before it is too late.

On this matter specifically, let me be clear about what I tell those I advise: serious countries do not seek prestige; they seek clout. And they never put their image on the line when their hard interests—their prosperity, their security, their democracy—are not at stake. The search for prestige is a diplomat's game, played by foreign affairs offices around the world, including Canada's. But that does not mean this game is in the interests of the countries they serve.

THE "ARAB SPRING"

IN OCTOBER 2010, we began to witness a series of events that became known as the Arab Spring. The first protests took place in Tunisia and quickly spread throughout the region. On December 17, a Tunisian street vendor named Mohamed Bouazizi set himself on fire to protest the confiscation of his wares and ongoing harassment by Tunis officialdom. This extreme and gruesome event immediately went viral. It was a dramatic demonstration of the emerging power of social media to transform political discourse and human life. It also became a symbol of the frustrations of people whose lives were economically fragile, corruption-riddled, and violated regularly and arbitrarily in ways that go way beyond anything we complain about in the West.

The growing turmoil caused Tunisian dictator Zine El Abidine Ben Ali to step down on January 14, 2011, ending twenty-three years of despotic rule. By then, protests had taken place in most Arab countries. In some cases, they turned from mass demonstrations to violence, then to organized violence, and finally, in Syria, Yemen, and Libya, to armed rebellion and civil war.

The most serious situation was in Egypt, simply because it is the largest Arab nation by far and thus vital to geopolitics in the Middle East and North Africa regions. Its peace treaty with Israel in 1979 has since been a critical pillar of global security. Yet by February 25, its three-decades-long dictator, Hosni Mubarak, had also been forced from office by escalating protests and disintegrating authority.

To many Western democratic leaders and the media, this seemed a sure sign that Jeffersonian democracy was about to burst forth in the Arab world. In fact, some of these leaders had pressured Mubarak and others to surrender power. By contrast, I was distinctly unenthusiastic about what was taking place, particularly in Egypt, and I was criticized for it. So why was I leery? To be blunt, an opponent of an existing dictatorship does not, in and of itself, a champion of democracy make.

My unease was not because I was in any way a supporter or an enthusiast for the Mubarak regime. In fact, when I hosted the G20 in 2010, I was lobbied by officials and other G20 attendees to invite the Mubarak government to attend as a special guest. I refused, for the same reasons I had argued against G20 membership for Egypt when the group was being put together in 2008. Egypt was authoritarian and corrupt, with an appalling human rights record and a long-troubled economy. Besides, I did not want a repeat of what I had seen at the L'Aquila G8, with its collection of dictators and thugs invited to observe the proceedings.

Nevertheless, I was alarmed by what was happening in Egypt. I saw little evidence that the opposition to Mubarak was motivated by the values of freedom and democracy. It was, in large measure, Islamist, that is, theocratic and extreme in character and dominated by the Muslim Brotherhood.

Now, with Mubarak gone, elections were to be held. I spoke to Benjamin Netanyahu about the situation. The Israelis invariably have not only the best, but sometimes the only real, intelligence on what is going on in the region. "Stephen," Bibi said, "if they have an election, the liberal democratic forces will get seven per cent of the vote." He was pretty much dead-on.

In June 2012, Mohamed Morsi of the Muslim Brotherhood was elected president of Egypt. Immediately, he began supporting extremists on the border with Israel and escalated persecution of Christians and other minorities. Within months, he was consolidating power and on the path to creating an Islamist regime.

This was a replay of what had occurred in Iran in 1979, when the West had welcomed the overthrow of the Shah, leading to the Ayatollah's regime. However, in this case General el-Sisi led a countercoup that removed Morsi a year later and, for all intents and purposes, re-established the old regime. It remains in place to this day.

LIBYA

OF ALL THE ARAB SPRING uprisings, it was ultimately the one in Libya that would be most consequential for Canada. Events in that country followed the same trajectory from peaceful protest to violence that had been seen elsewhere. In this case, however, things escalated very rapidly—within a matter of ten days—as the government of dictator Muammar Gaddafi began firing at masses of unarmed protestors from the outset.

As multiple armed uprisings began to take hold across Libya, Gaddafi and his sons made it clear that they intended to slaughter any segment of the population that had rebelled against them. That was not unexpected from Gaddafi, who had ruled with an iron fist for forty-two years and was widely regarded as one of the most psychotic dictators in the world.

I had met Gaddafi only once, at the L'Aquila G8, where I had to shake his hand and stand beside him for a photo. He was a frightening individual to be around; he truly looked and seemed like a madman. He also had a history of international terrorism. Indeed, he continued to encourage celebration of the infamous Pan Am Flight 103 bombing over Lockerbie, Scotland, in which three Canadians had died.

For that reason alone, I had refused to roll out the red carpet when, late in 2009, Gaddafi indicated he planned to land his plane in St. John's while returning from UN meetings in New York. In fact, I made it clear that Foreign Minister Lawrence Cannon would meet him to raise various concerns. Gaddafi then cancelled his trip, much to the annoyance of some in the department, as well as Canadian corporations that did business in Libya.

The Gaddafis' show of naked brutality did more than shock the world. It quickly underscored how few friends the regime had in the international community. It was not just the West that was appalled. Gaddafi was widely seen as unstable and was not trusted anywhere. The League of Arab States, whose members had long worried about Gaddafi's desire to foment turmoil in their countries, called for the United Nations to implement a no-fly zone over Libya. On March 17, 2011, that proposal passed the UN Security Council, with Russia and China, which had been silent as Gaddafi sought support for his crackdown, abstaining.

In short, the world had concluded that events in Libya could not be regarded as merely the "internal affairs" of that country. This led to an urgent conference on March 19, hosted in Paris by the French and chaired by U.S. Secretary of State Hillary Clinton. By then, a consensus had developed among most Western allies on limited military intervention, and the French had already initiated air sorties over Libya to prevent the mass slaughter of civilians. The British were actively planning to do the same.

Though technically not a call for regime change, one would have to be naive to think that bombing Gaddafi's forces would not inevitably bring about that result. It was thus an odd intervention in that it was clear where it was headed even though nobody was willing to spell it out. Making it even odder was the fact that it was Hillary Clinton—a capable secretary of state—who was chairing the conference rather than her boss, Barack Obama.

We soon learned the reason for this: it was to be the famous—or infamous, depending on how you look at it—policy of "leading from behind." The United States was not going to take formal leadership of this action. After all, it was the French and the British who were proactive in Libya, pushing the United States and others into intervening.

That said, you should be under no illusion: the United States was the single biggest contributor to this campaign, providing a whole range of satellite and intelligence assets to the coalition. The mission could not have been executed with anything resembling its level of effectiveness and sophistication without the United States as the backbone of the operation. Still, the U.S. was saying, in effect, "We do not want to own this. We will help, but you (the British and French), this is your mission—you lead it."

That immediately led to a complication—the natural rivalry between the British and the French. The British were never going to accept a Frenchman leading the mission. And the French were never going to have a Brit in charge. So who could France and Britain agree on to lead it? Well, why not Canada, the daughter of both?

Suddenly, we found ourselves making a unique contribution. It was agreed that Canadian Air Force General Charles Bouchard would assume formal leadership of the allied effort. We may have had nowhere near the largest forces deployed, but this was a real feather in Canada's cap.

Charlie did a great job. He capably managed a U.S.-dominated mission where the U.S. was in the background and an official NATO operation that oddly included non-NATO countries while excluding some alliance members. Yet the coalition lost not a single plane in months of bombing.

For Canada, the Libya mission was a different experience in other ways as well. While our Afghanistan engagement was principally focused on the army, this one centred on the air force. There was, in fact, no intent to use large-scale ground troops, although small elite units were involved from time to time when needed. There was also limited naval engagement between Canadian and Libyan forces, our first such encounters since the Korean War.

Given the international consensus on military action, we had not referred this deployment to the House of Commons at first, as was our policy. When we did so on March 22, 2011, it was approved by a vote of 294–1. This was a remarkable moment of unanimity in an intense and turbulent Parliament, whose divisions had often centred around military matters. Ironically, a mere four days later, the opposition parties voted non-confidence and brought down our government.

REFLECTIONS ON LIBYA AND THE ARAB SPRING

I THINK IT IS WORTHWHILE to jump beyond the turbulent spring of 2011 and offer a few thoughts on their broader significance. The events of that time provide cautionary lessons that remain relevant today.

In Libya, after a seven-month bombing campaign and relentless progress by rebel groups, Ghaddafi's government collapsed. The dictator himself was captured and killed in Sirte on October 20, 2011, effectively ending the struggle. I wish I could say peace followed for that troubled country, but that has emphatically not been the case.

At the time, NATO forces were quick to declare the mission a success. In fact, Nicolas Sarkozy and David Cameron visited Libya in September 2011, before the conflict was officially over. They received heroes' welcomes in Tripoli and Benghazi.

Given Canada's high-profile role, we began to plan for our own trip to Libya not long after the end of the conflict. However, it soon became apparent that peace and order were not taking hold. While the Libyans expressed keen interest in my visit, our officials were concerned.

Every few days, senior military and security people visited my office to announce greater deployments of personnel and assets to manage my time on the ground. Finally, about a week before we were to make the journey, they came in and said, "Prime Minister, you just cannot go. No matter what assets we and our allies deploy, we simply cannot guarantee your safety." So that was that.*

The situation in Libya would continue to deteriorate. From 2014 to 2020, the enduring factions from 2011 threw the country into a second civil war. While today there is a government that is generally recognized by the international community, the reality is that it is largely split between two competing administrations in the west and the east of the country.

In this context, many have retroactively branded the Libya mission a failure. And it is undeniable that it did not bring peace and stability to the country. In that sense, the revolution that NATO enabled was ultimately unsuccessful.

Yet I believe that the criticism is unfair in very substantive ways. First, the mission was explicitly not about nation-building. It was not even about setting up a new regime. Its purpose was to prevent slaughter on a massive scale. In that, it was clearly successful, as the worst (and likely) scenarios around Gaddafi's fall were avoided.

---

* For me, that was that. You can imagine my thoughts when U.S. Ambassador Christopher Stevens was killed while undertaking a lightly secured visit to Benghazi. That was a year later, when the situation was infinitely worse than when I had cancelled my trip.

In fact, the revolution was not merely far less bloody than had been probable; I would also argue that the aftermath was no worse. There is zero evidence to suggest a more stable Libya would have emerged if NATO had not intervened. The country was already descending into a multi-sided civil war. Once fighting broke out and Gaddafi went over the top with his clear intentions of slaughter, arms began pouring in from all sides, particularly from the Arab and Muslim world. Without friends, Gaddafi's fall would have been inevitable. So would have been a Libya carved into ongoing, violent factionalism.

I think the more valid criticism of the NATO mission is that it could have done more to shape post-rebellion Libya. For instance, NATO might have tried to develop a plan to create a unified security force. Those who were arming insurgent groups—the Turks and Qataris funded the most radical—were part of the coalition. Perhaps they could have been leaned on to coordinate on a plan? There was time to do this. After all, it took three full years of internal rivalry for post-Gaddafi Libya to completely fall apart.

Could NATO have executed such a plan? The answer, at best, is maybe. That almost certainly would have required some coalition presence on the ground following the conflict. After Iraq and Afghanistan, there was no allied willingness to do that. Unlike those other missions, the problem in Libya was under-ambition by the United States, NATO, and our allies. In the end, far less—a tiny fraction—was expended in blood and treasure in Libya compared to Iraq and Afghanistan, with results that were certainly no worse and, in some respects, actually better. The bottom line is that NATO had limited aims, and those were achieved.

As for the Arab Spring more broadly, my initial pessimism was sadly but largely borne out. Only Tunisia emerged as a fledgling democracy, but that achievement has been systematically dismantled since 2021. The talk, as early as mid-2012, was of an Arab Winter. In other words, in a little over a year, wildly optimistic assessments of the region had been replaced by the realities of violent chaos or renewed repression.

For those who had their eyes open, who had taken any time at all to examine the facts on the ground, this should not have been a shock. But as is too often the case in the Western world, even "experts" were quick to see things through rose-coloured glasses. And they were just as quick to completely, if belatedly, revise their analysis.

In the case of Yemen, that reassessment took way too long. In the meantime, the Houthis became ensconced in power, leading to much additional violence and instability in that corner of the Arabian Peninsula. The assurance I heard from officials that this Shia group would not be an Iranian ally was self-evidently wrong from the outset. Fortunately, similar prognostications that Morsi's Muslim Brotherhood might be genuine reformers were ignored by the Egyptians themselves.

This does not mean that things in Egypt turned out well. From advancing democracy to transforming the economy, today's Egypt leaves much to be desired. But from the standpoint of regional and global security, the counter-revolution was a salvation. Had Morsi stayed in office, we would have had a dictatorship anyway. In fact, we would have had a Sunni version of Iran, which is already one of the most evil and dangerous regimes on the planet. That would have quickly become a truly dire situation for the region, as well as for our allies and ourselves.

Yes, the options in Egypt were not good. But this outcome was the far better one. I state this because, if in the future we are to avoid the continuing debacles that Western foreign policy has created, our leaders must make choices in international affairs between real options, not rainbows and unicorns. That is what pragmatic conservative foreign policy is about. It is not about dispensing with ideals; it is about learning the facts and choosing between realistic alternatives.

In most of the Middle Eastern dictatorships that came under pressure in 2011, the liberal-democratic alternatives were weak or even non-existent. Their opponents were, more often than not, theocratic, as well as sectarian, ethnic, or tribal. Those were the brutal realities. They would later lead to some important disagreement with our allies around the ongoing civil war in Syria.

As these events unfolded, I was left with one interesting, though troubling, side story about it all. In January 2011, as events in Egypt continued to spiral out of control, we had to think about how to aid Canadian citizens, particularly those trying to exit. I went to the Lester B. Pearson Building, the headquarters of the Foreign Affairs Department, to give a press conference to explain to Canadians in Egypt, and also those who had family there, what aid they could expect from their government.

Officials had set up the room in a manner appropriate for such an occasion. On the wall that was to be my backdrop, there was a map of the region. It was a logical visual. But there was one problem. Courtesy of our Foreign Affairs Department, the map did not have Israel on it. It was as if it did not exist.*

I kept that map. It is in my office at Harper & Associates. We kept it to remind ourselves of the kind of deep ideological opposition we repeatedly experienced in our Foreign Affairs Department to any kind of positive relationship with Israel. This view was by no means universal within our public service, but there were many corners where this hostility was deeply entrenched.

Why is this? My explanation is relatively straight-forward. There are two dozen Arab states, some fifty Muslim states, and one solitary Jewish state. With any anti-Israeli initiative in the international community, the easiest thing is to go along to get along. It is as pragmatically easy as it is morally wrong.

---

* I am reminded that Melissa Lantsman, then a political staffer, was the first person to catch this. She would later become a deputy leader of the Conservative Party in the House of Commons.

17

THE PARLIAMENTARY SESSION OF 2010–2011

AS BUSY AS MY international calendar was in 2010–2011, we still had a full domestic agenda to pursue. Once Budget 2010 had cleared Parliament without a non-confidence vote, non-financial matters became our focus. Foremost among those would be our next steps in criminal justice reform.

PRESSING AHEAD ON CRIMINAL JUSTICE

JUSTICE REFORM STOOD OUT as both an area where much had been accomplished and where much remained to be done.

In our first Parliament, Justice Ministers Vic Toews and Rob Nicholson had managed to pass two major pieces of justice legislation. The most critical was the Tackling Violent Crime Act, a collection of previous individual bills that had toughened penalties and bail conditions for gun crime, started reform of the pardon system for dangerous offenders, introduced a new regime for drug-impaired driving, and raised the age of consent.* It had received Royal Assent on February 28, 2008. Prior to that

---

* Passed as Bill C-2 in the 39th Parliament, 2nd Session.

we had successfully passed legislation to reform conditional sentencing.†

In our second minority, Minister Nicholson and his colleagues were able to pass several additional pieces of legislation under the rubric of "making the punishment fit the crime." These were all amendments to the Criminal Code. They included matters related to organized crime,‡ white collar crime,§ foreign corruption,¶ and auto theft.**

Laws pushing back on the concept of "innocent after being proved guilty" were introduced and passed as well. One of note was the Truth in Sentencing Act. It dealt with the outrage of inmates receiving credit for time spent in prison before trial—at two and even three times the amount! This meant that criminals effectively had their penalty reduced the moment they were convicted. This "sentencing discount" had even applied for cases as notorious as multiple murder.†† We were also finally able to get tough action on the pardon system. The Eliminating Pardons for Serious Crimes Act applied to infamous inmates, like sex offender Graham James, who were pardoned automatically even if they were unremorseful and likely to reoffend.‡‡

We also took some concrete steps to strengthen policing and security. The most prominent of these was to tighten up the laws related to sex offenders, establishing a National Sex Offender Registry to allow law enforcement agencies to keep better track of those who were a danger

---

† Passed as Bill C-9 in the 39th Parliament, 1st Session.

‡ Passed as Bill C-14 in the 40th Parliament, 2nd Session.

§ Passed as Bill C-21 in the 40th Parliament, 3rd Session.

¶ Passed as Bill C-61 in the 40th Parliament, 3rd Session. This bill was sponsored by Lawrence Cannon in his role as Foreign Affairs Minister at the time.

** Passed as Bill S-9 in the 40th Parliament, 3rd Session.

†† Passed as Bill C-25 in the 40th Parliament, 2nd Session.

‡‡ Passed as Bill C-23A in the 40th Parliament, 3rd Session. This legislation came under the Minister of Public Safety. Stockwell Day, Peter Van Loan, and Vic Toews served in this portfolio and pursued these reforms in our first two terms.

to reoffend.* We also brought in the mandatory reporting of child pornography on the internet.†

The rights of victims also received some attention. During this Parliament we passed reforms that toughened the laws on crooked immigration consultants—those who abused the system and preyed upon thousands naively paying them to get admitted into Canada.‡ We also generally tried to raise the profile of victims' rights and the organizations that worked to address them, while preparing future legislation in this area.

Throughout our efforts, the reality faced by victims of crime was top of mind for me. One can get lost in the statistics and the slow grind of advancing legislative change through the system. But the jarring emotional and physical cost paid by innocent Canadians victimized by criminals drove us forward. I participated in dozens of events throughout our time in office where I met personally with victims of often horrific crimes. I was often in awe of their resolve to engage with political leaders and share their tragic stories in the hopes of preventing others from suffering as they had.

The above constitutes only a partial list of our legislative actions, which were often supplemented by private members' bills from Conservative MPs. However, I must confess that our progress in all these areas was less than desired. It was becoming readily apparent that our justice reform efforts were a drop in the ocean of what needed to be done. The system had become so offender-centric in all its aspects, so off kilter philosophically, that we were only touching its very worst aspects.

But the bigger challenge was the minority parliament. All the other parties were deeply opposed to the general direction of our legislation. Since they were offside with public opinion on these matters, their opposition

---

* Passed as Bill S-2 in the 40th Parliament, 3rd Session.

† Passed as Bill C-22 in the 40th Parliament, 3rd Session.

‡ Passed as Bill C-35 in the 40th Parliament, 3rd Session. This legislation came under the Hon. Jason Kenney as Minister of Citizenship and Immigration.

was often in the form of guerrilla warfare. They would not express disapproval but instead aim to slow the bills at every stage of the parliamentary process in both chambers, sometimes adding problematic amendments along the way. Our legislation usually had to be debated in at least two sessions—sometimes even more—to ultimately be passed. Our successes came through mobilizing public opinion—the pardon system reform was a perfect example—without which the opposition would rarely move.

I do not believe that most Canadians understand the degree to which we and the other parties disagree philosophically on matters of criminal justice. As conservatives, we believed that the role of a criminal justice system is to protect society and hold criminals accountable for their actions. But those ideas have been largely rejected by the modern left.

At the core of their position is a complete rejection of the notion of personal responsibility, substituting instead the idea that people are powerless over their circumstances. Taken a step further, the criminal is only such because of circumstances for which society, not that person, is ultimately responsible. Society thus becomes the perpetrator, and the criminal becomes the victim. Everything is turned on its head.

With this kind of thinking, legal extremists on the left cannot care about real victims. In fact, if anything, victims of society are just a part of that society—the one that bears the real guilt. Obviously, such thinking runs completely opposite to the conservative view that individual responsibility is at the core of well-functioning societies. We were determined to challenge this approach to criminal justice.

As this idea of criminal as victim has been put into practice even more widely in the past decade, particularly since the pandemic, we are witnessing the growing lawlessness and disorder it is creating. It needs to be fought at every stage. But the first challenge is for the public to understand that such noxious nonsense really is at the centre of the criminal justice problems we are facing.

TIMES OF COMMEMORATION

IT IS HARD TO IMAGINE earlier generations straying into the kind of criminal justice nonsense we are now dealing with. That would certainly be the case with John Babcock. Not long before Parliament resumed in 2010—on February 18 to be precise—we learned of the passing of this 107-year-old Canadian. Babcock was our last living veteran of World War I. With his death, the generation who had won that struggle had departed from this earth.

To mark the occasion, we planned a special event on Parliament Hill for April 9, 2010—the 93rd anniversary of the Battle of Vimy Ridge. That engagement had been a special moment in Canada's effort in the conflict. For the occasion, sixty-five doves—one for every one thousand soldiers Canada and Newfoundland had lost during the war—were released into the sky.

This was not the first time we had commemorated Vimy Ridge. In 2007, we had marked the 90th anniversary with a major ceremony in France at the Vimy monument. Soaring twenty-seven metres, that memorial, created with six thousand tonnes of Croatian limestone, features two massive towers, symbolizing Canada and France, as well as symbolic carved figures representing peace, justice, truth, knowledge, gallantry, and sympathy. It is visually stunning, and I would recommend that all Canadians see it. So impressive is it that, when the Nazis overran the area in World War II, Hitler ordered it preserved despite it being a symbol of German defeat.

The Battle of Vimy Ridge was a seminal moment in Canadian history. A Canadian army from all parts of the country under a Canadian commander won one of the most decisive battles of the war. It was, in retrospect, a critical step to our eventual and complete independence from the United Kingdom. Yet the loss of nearly four thousand men—in what is considered a great victory—says much about the scale of the carnage in World War I.

That 2007 commemoration had Her Majesty Queen Elizabeth II and some thirty thousand Canadians in attendance, many of them schoolchildren. My daughter had the opportunity of presenting the Queen with flowers (and Her Majesty recognized Rachel immediately). While the number on that occasion was truly impressive, it is also part of a trend. For the past generation at least, there has been a noticeable increase in people attending Remembrance Day ceremonies. For years, the crowds seemed to be getting smaller and smaller, but then they began to grow once again. I believe that is important—important for us to remember our past, particularly those times of enormous sacrifice and achievement.

Such remembrance was of a different character when I attended commemorations of the Korean War and World War II. At those events, I would still have a chance to meet with living veterans. The 65th anniversary of the liberation of the Netherlands by the Canadian Army, which we marked there in May 2010, was one very memorable example. That uniquely Canadian contribution to World War II has been the basis of incredibly close relations between the Dutch and us ever since.

Another unforgettable occasion was the 65th anniversary of the D-Day invasion on June 6, 2009. As part of the commemorations, the "war leaders" walked along Omaha Beach—President Obama for the United States, President Sarkozy for France, Prince Charles and Prime Minister Gordon Brown from the United Kingdom, and me, representing Canada. The membership of this group really showed better than words can describe the league we were in at that time. Canada played a disproportionately significant role in the victory over fascism in World War II, and this part of the commemoration was an acknowledgement of that. This is what it looks like when a country truly punches above its weight.

From that occasion, I particularly cherish the recollection of joining some of those who had earned our country that stature. During the visit, I walked along Juno Beach with three Canadian veterans of that day sixty-five years before, one each from the Army, Navy, and Air Force. Their ages ranged from eighty-eight to ninety-one. They all moved strongly, even though one required a walker to make his way. They were all alert, with sharp memories, and we enjoyed a great conversation together. Yet within a couple of years, they were gone.

This is perhaps why Remembrance Day ceremonies have swelled over the years. We are running out of chances to express our thanks to the Greatest Generation, and we know it. These were the Canadians who won the hot war against fascism and the Cold War against communism. They built the incredible prosperity of the post-war period that my generation, the baby boomers, had the good fortune to be born into but, if we are honest with ourselves, appreciated far too little.

Sometimes, though, it is not clear how we should honour our wartime heroes. That reality came before our Cabinet as we approached the 100th anniversary of the start of World War I in 2014. There was a proposal before us that all the participating countries project the names of all the fallen—one at a time as I recall—on a wall or screen of some sort in their capital city. On the surface, it seemed like a way to recognize sacrifice.

However, we soon realized that each country was to project the names of all the fallen of every country, including of enemy combatants. As someone asked, "Would we be putting our soldiers on the same list and in the same category as the Germans and the others who fought us?" Well, that opened a can of worms and provoked quite an impassioned debate.

On the one hand, it was a hundred years later, and the participants have long since buried the hatchet. The principal combatants of World War I, even the principal combatants of World War II, are now some of our best friends and allies in the world. But were we really prepared to honour the German war dead in the same breath as the Canadian soldiers, sailors, and aviators who gave their lives?

In the end, we decided not to do it. It was emotionally difficult because there were compelling arguments on both sides. In the end, we asked, "Would our grandparents' generation have been comfortable with us doing this? Would they have understood a decision to do this? Would they have agreed with it?" In my own experience, and in that of the majority around our Cabinet table, it would have been a bridge too far for them.

MOVING FORWARD ON THE NORTHERN AGENDA

EVERY YEAR, INCLUDING THAT tumultuous 2009, I looked forward to my northern tours. By the end of our second term of government, there had been five of them. Each was designed to add to our presence in the North and our service to the people of the North, according to our four pillars of sovereignty, sustainable economic development, social progress, and governance.

On the sovereignty front, we executed annual military exercises of constantly greater size, scope, and capability, which I usually made a point of attending. From the beginning, we also committed to expanding our permanent presence up in the Arctic. This included establishing an Army training base in Resolute Bay and a deep-water Navy facility at Nanisivik. In 2007 we committed to build a fleet of Arctic and Offshore Patrol Ships, and in 2014, I announced that the lead ship of this Canadian-built class would be the HMCS *Harry DeWolf*.* The fleet has since been completed.

We spearheaded important and far-ranging initiatives on the northern economy. We were improving roads, airports, and port facilities, most of which had invariably lagged far behind those of other Arctic countries. We also unveiled a major initiative to create comprehensive geological mapping of the North, which would help in the longer-term development of mineral resources. As well, we invested in northern research and development, aimed at areas like agriculture, to help make human life and economic activity more feasible in those extreme climates.

As I have said, our commitment to economic development in the North was matched with a determination to protect the environment. One of the more memorable of those initiatives was our 2007 expansion of the Nahanni National Park Reserve in the Northwest Territories, which is a great legacy of Pierre Trudeau. I visited its iconic Virginia Falls to make this announcement, an incredible experience I will never forget. We also extended the enforcement of Canada's environmental laws offshore, to prepare for the likelihood of greater shipping and naval transport through that part of the world. And in 2010, we committed to establish a Canadian High Arctic

---

* Admiral DeWolf was a Royal Canadian Navy hero of World War II who once commanded the HMCS *Haida*. I made the announcement during a visit to the HMCS *Haida* in Hamilton. The HMCS *DeWolf* launched in 2018.

Research Station (CHARS), to be located in Cambridge Bay. Every major northern country has a world-class, cutting-edge northern research facility in its Arctic area, and we did not, so remedying that was a priority.

On the social front, we implemented dozens of programs spanning the entire range of the North's needs in healthcare, education, sport, and other social programs. Some of those involved the building of specific infrastructure. Also, as mentioned earlier, there were big increases in territorial financing to assist in delivering some of those services.

We also made substantial, longer-term efforts to deepen the North's governance capacity. Most Canadians do not know it, but almost one-third of Quebec is in the Arctic—the Nunavik territory north of the 55th parallel. In 2008, I was in Kuujjuaq, the capital, where we announced the settlement of Nunavik land claims—an achievement our Government was especially proud of. In 2009, we held a Cabinet meeting in Iqaluit to demonstrate our presence there, to support the seal industry, and to promote other economic activities. It certainly helped that the local MP, Leona Aglukkaq, was now a minister in our government. Leona was a staunch advocate for the issues and people of the north and without her work our Government simply would not have delivered the impressive list of projects and programs for northerners. In 2010, Minister Flaherty made a point of holding one of the preparatory finance ministers' meetings for the G8 in Iqaluit. And discussions continued about how we might devolve more power, currently retained by the federal government, to the Northwest Territories and Nunavut.

Going back to the CHARS for a moment, that announcement turned out to be a real-life demonstration of how challenging Canada's North can be. On August 23, 2010, we had been in Churchill, Manitoba, to initiate upgrades to the airport as part of that summer's northern tour. Before our departure, I ran some errands and saw a few of the sights, including the local museum. Then, for some reason, we headed down to "the beach" on Hudson Bay—which is about as far from bathing suits and sunscreen as can be imagined.

As we approached the shore, a very early winter storm started to blow in. I got out of my vehicle and was still about fifty yards from the water when the wind started to whip off the Bay, bombarding me with fast-moving (and painful) ice pellets. Deciding this was not a congenial environment, we returned to our hotel, where we quickly learned we were going nowhere. Nothing flies in these nasty winter storms, not even prime ministers.

We were stuck there, in August, in a winter blizzard. There was nothing to do but hunker down in our hotel—the Lazy Bear Lodge—where we were held "weather prisoners" for a couple of days. As the hours passed, I became so desperate for company that I even went and had a meal with the media!* Being stranded like that vividly demonstrated the harsh realities of the North.

A CRITICAL VICE-REGAL DECISION

BECAUSE OF MY ATTENTION to matters of the Crown, people assume that I am a monarchist. That is true, but perhaps not to the extent some think. I like to say that I am "a monarchist, not a royalist." Unlike some in our Prime Minister's Office (PMO) and our party, I had no fascination with the royal family or royalty generally. I am not one to buy royal magazines or to follow all the gossip around the royal family.

I consider myself a pragmatic monarchist. I support the institution of the monarchy principally because it works. It provides the parliamentary system with a constitutional head of state that effectively rises above politics, representing the continuity of the system regardless of the party in power. In Canada, the system is maintained with extremely modest cost—mostly around the maintenance of Rideau Hall and the functioning of the vice-regal offices. By contrast, the alternative suggestions offer no significant improvement and non-trivial risks. As a conservative, I do have a bias against change for change's sake, especially when something has served its function well.

---

* The whole experience could not have been that bad because two of my three official photographers, Deb and Jason Ransom, ended up returning to the lodge to become permanent workers after we were out of government. I like to joke that they would rather be trapped in the Lazy Bear Lodge than keep working for me!

If anything, the relatively smooth functioning of the Crown in Canada has often obscured its importance. The office of governor general is the oldest and the highest in the land. The king (or queen) may be the head of state, but they are rarely present in the country and seldom exercise their authorities. That is done by the governor general, in whose name senior appointments are made, laws and regulations are adopted, diplomatic relations are conducted, and the Armed Forces are issued commands. It has been this way since 1608, when Samuel de Champlain became governor (informally to begin with) at Canada's *ancienne capitale*, Quebec City.

This position is the foundation of our constitutional, legal, and institutional polity, and in state terms, the governor general outranks the prime minister. It is certainly true that the prime minister is the head of government and possesses most day-to-day power. But it is the Crown, normally in the person of the governor general, who represents the permanence of the state as an institution. The office possesses critical residual powers, including, most importantly, the responsibility of ensuring the country has a prime minister. That is why the governor general and the prime minister never travel together.

In this regard, the governor general is the ultimate arbitrator of disputes if the power or the hold of the prime minister on the office is in doubt, as was highlighted during the attempted coalition coup. In those circumstances, the governor general must select a path forward, whether that be an election, a change of government, or latitude for the incumbent. The governor general 's decision is definitive. For that reason alone, there are great risks to the country if the position is not handled properly.

In those decisions, the governor general must, according to precedent, minimally impact politics and, at all other times, avoid intervening in its day-to-day affairs. This is made easier because Canada's first-past-the-post electoral system usually delivers a majority or at least a very small number of options for government. If, God forbid, we ever adopt a proportional representation system, then the governor general would be called upon to execute these functions much more regularly. In my view, that would make the governor general's vocation of rising above politics considerably more difficult.

Because the role of governor general has functioned so smoothly, some have suggested that it (or provincial lieutenant governors) could be dispensed with entirely. Why not, some have asked, just let the prime minister (or the premier of a province) handle the function? That is not merely a naive suggestion but also a dangerous one.

The prime minister occupies their position by virtue of their control of the legislative process and the day-to-day executive business of government. By contrast, in an American-style system, the president is the head of state, with executive authority but without legislative control. A combined governor general–prime minister would thus represent the state as a whole, carry all its prestige, and simultaneously control all its important executive and legislative functions. The holder of such an office would have such immense authority that they could easily place democracy itself in jeopardy. In fact, there was somebody who did this very thing, who combined the office of president with that of prime minister in a parliamentary system. I hesitate to prove Godwin's Law, but his name was Adolf Hitler.* That is not an advisable precedent.

The Evolution of the Office

OVER THE YEARS, THE TYPE of person chosen for this important role has changed dramatically—and not always with a lot of thought. So has the office. From Confederation up until the Statute of Westminster in 1931, the governor general performed the dual roles of representing both the Crown within the Canadian political system and the British government. The latter retained residual authority for Canada's defence and foreign affairs, although that was declining almost from the beginning. In those days, the British government appointed people of tremendous experience, accomplishment,

---

* Godwin's Law maintains that if any political discussion continues long enough, someone will almost certainly compare someone else to Hitler.

and stature, who had usually played senior roles in the British government or British military. By and large, those appointments also served Canada well.

Despite the legal changes of 1931, it was not until 1952 that our governments became convinced that the office of governor general should be held by a Canadian. After that, the type of person appointed evolved, and three stages of that evolution can be identified. During the first phase, about twenty-five years in duration, we appointed people who were more or less similar to those the British appointed: of high rank within the system, accomplished, but with largely non-partisan, independent stature. Then things began to change.

For the next twenty years, we named people who had explicitly partisan backgrounds, often related to the governing party. This is not to cast aspersions; these governors general were well-regarded individuals who generally rose to expectations of a non-partisan role. This was, however, a significant departure with potential downsides. In particular, it risked creating situations like we have seen with many of the lieutenant governors of the provinces. Historically, those appointments were long partisan in nature and, being federal, often resulted in considerable distance and mistrust between the appointee on the one hand and the premier and his Government on the other.

During the third phase—much of the last generation—those appointed were prominent Canadians, not from partisan backgrounds but from more diverse cultural and professional ones. This has some risks of its own. At least with partisan appointments, whether you liked its appointees or not, they came to the role with high knowledge of how the system worked. They would, therefore, be unlikely to overstep their conventional authority. But when you start to appoint people from outside politics and without long-standing institutional government experience, you run a real risk that you could appoint somebody who does not understand the system or is simply ill-suited for the role.

The latter arguably happened with Julie Payette (despite her clear qualifications). But the former would be a very serious problem for our parliamentary democracy. Imagine a governor general exercising their "formal" (that is, in name only) authorities, getting involved in day-to-day politics, trying to frame or veto legislation, making independent appointments, issuing orders to the military, or perhaps even opposing the prime minister of the day. The damage someone without the necessary wisdom, contextual knowledge, or personal restraint could inflict on our polity would be substantial. Things could go off the rails very quickly, and we would have a very serious constitutional crisis on our hands.

The Search for a New Governor General

WITH THE ABOVE VERY MUCH in mind, we decided to institute a serious vetting process. Part of what convinced me to do this was the experience of the Michaëlle Jean appointment when I was Opposition leader. I thought she did a great job, by the way. Still, at the time of her announcement, there were reports that she was a Quebec separatist. More importantly, the government of the day did not seem to know whether that was true or not. Clearly, we had to do better.

As referred to earlier, after the demise of our proposed Public Appointments Commissioner, I gave all authority to the Appointments Secretariat in the PMO. I also outlined the general criteria for government appointments. Beyond that, I limited my involvement in the process to constitutional offices—my own Cabinet and roles within caucus (obviously), plus appointments to the Senate, the Supreme Court, and the vice-regal positions.

By "vice-regal," I mean the positions of governor general, lieutenant governor, and territorial commissioner. The last is technically not vice-regal, because they represent the federal government rather than the Crown. However, they are functionally the equivalent in the territories to a lieutenant governor within a province, so we treated them as vice-regal appointments.

With the looming appointment of a governor general, a search committee was struck. Sheila-Marie Cook, secretary to the governor general, was named its Chair. The other members were Kevin MacLeod, the Canadian secretary to the Queen and Usher of the Black Rod (the Senate's equivalent to the Commons' Sergeant-at-Arms and Parliament's top protocol officer); Christopher Manfredi, dean of the Faculty of Arts at McGill University; Rainer Knopff of the University of Calgary; Father Jacques Monet of the Canadian Institute of Jesuit Studies; and Christopher McCreery, historian and private secretary to the lieutenant governor of Nova Scotia. The committee had a wealth of expert knowledge and was drawn from across the country.

My instructions to the committee were to reach out far and wide, assemble lists of potential candidates, assess their fitness and willingness to serve, and ultimately provide me with five names of people who were fully qualified and vetted from which I would choose. This they did, which presented me with a good news/bad news scenario. The good news was they found five exceptionally qualified candidates to choose from. The bad news was that this made my choice very difficult.

The Selection

IN THE END, as now known, I picked David Johnston from the list of five. He was broadly known to Canadians because he had been the moderator of national leadership debates going back to the 1980s. Political parties trusted him to be a fair adjudicator.

I came to know David in the 1990s when, as president of McGill University, he was the host and moderator of a PBS program called *The Editors*. It was filmed in Montreal, and I was one of the frequent panelists in my role as president of the National Citizens Coalition. By the time we came to office, David had moved to the presidency of the University of Waterloo. He was also the chairman of the Council of Presidents of the Canadian University Association. I would usually meet him once a year in that capacity, along with the other heads of the major universities. It was evident at those meetings that he was highly respected by his peers.

David also possessed a strong ethic of public service. He believed that when an independent advisor was required, it was a reasonable public expectation that academics, especially those heading major public institutions like his, could be called upon. On various occasions, he responded in this way, but one sensitive and thankless task in 2007–2008 stood out for me especially.

I had called on David Johnston when it came out that former prime minister Brian Mulroney appeared to have had private dealings with German-Canadian businessman Karlheinz Schreiber while he was still in office. That was a real pickle for the Government. While it obviously had nothing to do with us, almost any course of action we chose could draw us into it, being interpreted as either a vendetta or a cover-up (depending on how one assessed my relationship with the former PM).

Clearly, we had to be uninvolved in any decision on how to proceed. I asked David if he would review the matter and give the Government his recommendation, whatever that might be. Frankly, he made no bones about the fact that he wanted the assignment like a hole in the head, but he agreed that I was choosing the only way to proceed under the circumstances. As he said, "When the prime minister asks someone in my position to do a public service, you say yes." In the end, David did a good job on a very messy and delicate matter.

In light of that, I was already favourably disposed to appointing him. It turned out that the committee was too. I asked each member to consider the five short-list candidates, all of whom would have been excellent, and give me their top-three rankings. Most ranked David as their top choice. In fact, having talked to hundreds of prominent Canadians from all regions and all walks of life, they told me they did not find a single one who did not know who David Johnston was or did not think well of him. As far as I was concerned, that made his appointment very safe and quite inspired.

David Johnston fully validated the confidence of the committee in his subsequent splendid service to Canada in the role of governor general. He did what all good governors general do. First, he was a cheerleader for the country, travelling everywhere to meet people and honour those whose work and lives made Canada a better place to live. Second, he was also a superb advisor. While the governor general's principal constitutional responsibility is to make sure there is a prime minister, they also have the constitutional right "to be consulted, to encourage, and to warn" that prime minister. There are not many people a PM can talk to in confidence, but David was certainly one. He had more than enough knowledge and experience to be an excellent sounding board.

David Johnston's most underappreciated skill was in his role as an ambassador. The governor general is the country's highest-ranking official in diplomatic protocol. When there were important events that I could not attend or travel that I could not undertake, for whatever reason, David Johnston would go and represent the Government of Canada. He would always return with detailed reports on what he had learned, and as I would hear later, he had invariably left a very good impression of our country behind. He was, in short, the best diplomat, the most effective diplomat, this country had.

APPOINTING GOVERNORS GENERAL IN THE FUTURE

GIVEN THE SUCCESS of the process in identifying candidates for governor general, I made it permanent by creating the Advisory Committee on Vice-Regal Appointments.* This committee performed its task admirably while it lasted. As in the case of the governor general, it would generate a short list of five candidates from which it was (invariably) hard to choose. The appointees all proved to be exemplary office holders.

The Vice-Regal Appointments Committee would have, without a doubt, quickly discovered Governor General Payette's unsuitability for office. Why then did my successor abandon the committee and return to a haphazard approach? I suspect there was a belief that this was "Harper's committee" and somehow either a partisan body or an attempt at control "from the grave."

If so, that was simply wrong. The committee acted on instructions from the prime minister and would have done so for the incoming one. Besides, the prime minister had the right to change the membership of the committee if they did not trust the motives or loyalty of any member. Water under

---

* I named Kevin MacLeod as Chair. Two permanent members were added—Jacques Monet (francophone) and Robb Watt (anglophone), the former chief herald of Canada. They would be joined by two others, who would rotate in on a short-term basis from the jurisdiction we were seeking to appoint.

the bridge, I suppose, but the concept served Canada very well and could be re-established in the future for the same purpose.[†] In the meantime, a series of events occurred that I believe represent substantial risks to our constitutional system of government.

On January 21, 2021, following the resignation of Payette, Canadians found themselves without a governor general. Richard Wagner, chief justice of the Supreme Court, was sworn in to fill the position temporarily, which he did until July 26, when Mary Simon was appointed. This alone should concern Canadians. The extended occupancy of the governor general position by the chief justice presents real risks of (further) politicization of the Supreme Court. Remember, this six-month tenure occurred during a minority parliament, with its heightened risks of constitutional crises.[‡]

The circumstances of Payette's resignation are also concerning, especially the suggestion that the prime minister effectively "fired" the governor general. Constitutionally, that would be a complete violation of our system. In fact, it is the governor general who has the authority to fire the prime minister (under certain carefully defined circumstances). The reverse would remove a critical check on the PM's already massive authority. In fact, the PMO appointing an inquiry into the governor general's conduct in office was itself a violation of that office's independence. Payette, had she understood her role better, could have and should have refused it (although this is not meant to condone the alleged behaviour).

---

† I note that there was an ad hoc committee established for the process that selected Mary Simon as governor general. However, that ad hoc process, while better than the one used for Julie Payette, is still a move backwards from where we were in 2015.

‡ When Beverley McLachlin was chief justice, she had raised concerns with me about the fact that Supreme Court justices frequently exercise the governor general's responsibilities on a temporary basis, as in giving Royal Assent to legislation. This situation exemplified that concern times a hundred. But frankly, so does the chief justice's role as Chair of the Order of Canada committee. Judges should not be delivering judgments outside their judicial roles.

In short, the authority and the independence of the office of the governor general have been severely undermined by this series of events. Reinstating the Vice-Regal Appointments Committee might help avoid these problems in the future. But to my mind, what has happened raises the question of whether the prime minister's control over the appointment needs to be replaced.

The importance of these issues is very much underappreciated. The Crown is not an anachronism or vestige of a long-gone imperial system. It is a living expression of our heritage and a vital protection of what has been an extremely successful constitutional order. We ignore or dispense with it at our peril.

MOVING INTO 2011

WITH A BUSY YEAR, both domestic and foreign, winding down, we began to cast our minds to 2011. The economy continued to improve, with Canada clearly emerging from the pack better than others, and public support for the government seeming robust. Nevertheless, we began to plan for the reality that a parliamentary defeat was increasingly likely.

We were now the longest-serving minority government in Canadian history, and yet the opposition—all philosophically on the other side of the spectrum—had never actually defeated us in a vote of confidence. For that reason alone, the situation seemed unlikely to continue.

Where exactly would we get support going forward? Since the coalition confrontation, support from the Bloc was off the table. In the past year, the Ignatieff Liberals had moved away from sustaining the government, even though their methods of doing that had been ham-fisted. That left the NDP. Its ongoing support for a Conservative government was inherently improbable.

With that landscape in mind, I gave a speech on January 23, 2011, marking the 5th anniversary of my Government's election. It was an opportunity to celebrate our successes, emphasize our values to our supporters, and begin to frame narratives for a possible election. Clearly, our successful response to the global financial crisis, including its large-scale stimulus spending, had been key to the government's support. Yet our Conservative base needed to be reassured that the big deficits we had needed to run were only temporary and would not evolve into long-term structural shortfalls.

Part of that reassurance was reminding Conservatives that our fiscal policy had not been about an expansion in government. Even then we were cutting taxes, not raising them. We had collaborated with the provinces on stimulus spending, rather than inserting ourselves into their jurisdictions. In fact, we had largely resolved the fiscal imbalance issue, to the point where it had disappeared from the public radar. Provinces were getting permanently higher levels of cash for their core health and education responsibilities. On the childcare front, we had provided unprecedented financial support directly to Canadian families instead of developing a state-run daycare agency.

We were also working hard to fulfil our promises on the justice front and had some notable successes. That was despite the seemingly bottomless problems of the system and the hostility of the justice establishment. Our legislation, focused on protecting society and making punishment fit the crime, was a clear departure from previous Liberal and even previous PC governments.

We had passed the Accountability Act. It made a lot of concrete changes in the way things worked in Ottawa, particularly the lobbying business. Through all that, we had managed to remain pretty much scandal-free for five years. Given the enormity of the previous government's problems, particularly the sponsorship scandal, this was an accomplishment to be celebrated.

This was more than just a list of achievements. It was also a contrast with what a Liberal or coalition government would look like. Canada was no longer a second-tier performer. Our Government had demonstrated effective administration of its fiscal and economic programs, and our financial sector's position in the world was rising. Divisive issues like Quebec separatism and Western alienation had receded, and there was a greater sense of national unity than there had been for some time. We had also seen unprecedented success in international sports.

Beyond our borders, Canada was again making a difference through our principled engagement internationally. Ours was not a go-along-to-get-along administration; this was a government standing strong in defence of freedom, democracy, human rights, and the rule of law. We were aligned with like-minded countries and robustly engaged in opposing the world's bad actors. We were engaging on the big questions of global peace and security and making unique contributions to global development assistance. We were particularly proud of the investments we had been making in the Canadian Armed Forces, and the consequent restoration of their capacities, their global role, and their traditions, profile, and respect among Canadians. This was no longer just Liberal virtue-signalling; it was a substantive role in the world.

All these things had been done while retaining the caring and compassionate values Canadians rightly held dear, as well as the programs and services that embodied those. To my mind, and those around me, all these things were cause for celebration. And Canadians, we believed, were responding positively to this Conservative incarnation of Canada.

Not all Canadians, mind you. In fact, some were developing a passionate hatred for the government. Why? It certainly was not because we were cutting everything in sight; in fact, our spending at this point was unprecedented. But, still, this was not a government focused on serving what might be called "rent-seeking interests." Those are the groups and organizations whose real concern is just getting more government money, preferably (and usually) with as little accountability as possible. We were clearly not their party, and yes, if you do not cater to those interests, they hate you.

Neither were we going to be loved by those who see the country as deeply, historically flawed and needing to be deconstructed into some kind of post-national state. That was not us either. Without ignoring the real failures of the past, we wanted to celebrate our country and its accomplishments. As Conservatives, we believe that is the only way a society stays healthy and moves forward.

As has been said, "You can't please all the people all the time." I made this point frequently to Cabinet and caucus. People have divided views. It is impossible to advance some without alienating others. Effective governance is about making those choices.

Although there is a tendency in academia and the media to over-analyze things, usually making them morally grey, politics really boils down to a few essential truths. There are those who naturally support you. You give them much of what they want (although you cannot give them everything), and you never betray them. There are those who can go either way—the ones critical to election campaigns—and you always work to get and keep them onside. Then there are those who will never support you, no matter what. Still, you treat them fairly and hope that someday they will come around. You should not cater to them, but in a democratic society, you do not punish them just because they have different partisan loyalties.

READYING FOR ALL SCENARIOS

I ENTERED 2011 with a new chief of staff. Guy Giorno had returned to the practice of law. His was a very successful tenure, which saw our staff ranks mature and our processes for decisions and communications become much more refined.

Guy was succeeded (at his suggestion) by Nigel Wright. I had known Nigel for about a decade. He was a sharp, Harvard-educated lawyer, who had a very successful career at Onex Corporation, which had made him independently wealthy even when we first met (he being four years younger than me). Nigel had supported me in the leadership races and was already serving as a volunteer for Conservative Fund Canada. Having worked in the Mulroney government many years before, public service was not new to him, and he did not mind the enormous pay cut.*

Nigel's biggest challenge would be dealing with the turnover of veteran staff. These veterans were not old—seldom much more than 30. But, once they got married, especially if they had children, it was almost inevitable that they would look for more secure, less demanding, and better paying jobs outside of politics. That meant we had to be constantly moving people up the ranks.

---

* Given the later controversy around Nigel, the reader should know that he never charged a dime of expense to the Government of Canada, even those clearly allowed. He covered hotels, meals, and everything else with his own funds.

We thought our first political test of the year would be Budget 2011. It was our sixth. While we believed the risk of a parliamentary defeat was rising, we did not desire it. We were getting things done as a government, and at this point, governing was certainly my personal preference. I had fought three general election campaigns already. They were a tough grind, and any thrill from them had long since worn off. Besides, it was important that we try to keep Parliament going. The public, we knew, did not want another election.

The challenge for this budget would be to make ongoing progress on deficit reduction while offering some concrete reasons for the NDP to support our plan. To that end, we purposefully included several measures that we believed the NDP could and should support. The most important were an increase in the Guaranteed Income Supplement, which goes to the lowest-income senior citizens, and a renewal of the ecoENERGY Retrofit – Homes program to reduce home heating costs. These had long been NDP asks.

On the substance of the budget alone, we should have been in good shape. Even with the "goodies" added in, the deficit was falling sharply, and the improvement in the economy was projected to continue. When the document—"The Next Phase of Canada's Economic Action Plan"—was tabled on March 22, we were confident that Canadians would respond well to both the proposals and the economic backdrop. The opposition parties must have felt the same way because, although all three said they would oppose it, it quickly became apparent that this was not the reason they would use to defeat the government.

Instead, they went back to their earlier cry that "democracy itself is under threat!" This, by the way, is an increasing tactic of the political left everywhere. Any government that is not left/liberal, it is argued, must be undemocratic by definition. Voters cannot have freely chosen something on the right—now typically labelled the "far right." They must have been systematically cheated or deceived. In our case, how such an "undemocratic" government could have been elected twice and then kept in office for over five years, despite its minority status, was not explained. Instead, three arguments were advanced.

The first was related to budget: that the government was not providing adequate financial information about its activities or its plans. I never quite grasped the logic of this reasoning. Through the Accountability Act and our quarterly Economic Action Plan reports, we were providing more detail on the financial activities of the Government of Canada than any administration ever had.

What was really driving this idea, I suspect, was the opposition's hope that, in our Government's long-term plan to balance the budget, they would find a whole bunch of spending cuts to run against. The truth of the matter was, though, that we had no such plans at that time, and spending constraint was only one relatively small part of our long-term plan. In effect, they were saying ,"Let us know what your budget will be in three years, and we'll let you know if you can stay in government." Absurd.

A second line of attack was on International Cooperation Minister Bev Oda's decisions on various grants and contributions in her portfolio. There were several cases where officials had recommended expenditures that the minister had rejected. Frankly, that was her prerogative. There is a reason why the minister is the signatory: in the end, it is the minister's decision.

In fact, Bev was extremely conscientious in reviewing grant proposals to make sure they were appropriate from the elected government's perspective—something I had instructed all ministers to do. This was particularly necessary with the entity under her authority: the Canadian International Development Agency (CIDA). As I will discuss later, CIDA had particularly troubling grant policies. In any case, it boggles the mind how democracy is threatened when an elected person makes decisions on how public money is spent. That is actually the essence of democracy.

Their final argument was to return to a dispute between the Conservative Party and Elections Canada that went back to 2006. This had to do with interpretations of the allocation of spending between the national and riding campaigns. There was nothing secret about it; all the spending had been reported. Ultimately, we lost our argument in court on the apportionment of $50,000 in spending. This was on a thirty-million-dollar budget. It was laughably trivial. Still, the opposition argued this was a case of electoral fraud that undermined the entire 2006 election.

Thus, on March 25, the opposition parties bundled their complaints together and passed a contempt of Parliament motion against us. The vote was 156 to 145. While they tried to make it sound like some special judicial finding—"the first time ever in a Commonwealth country," they proclaimed—it was simply a non-confidence motion passed against a minority government.

They had made their choice. On our side, although Doug Finley was by now very ill with cancer and had been succeeded as campaign manager by Jenni Byrne, his election machinery remained in place. We were ready to go.

18

ELECTION 2011 AND ITS AFTERMATH

WE FELT VERY GOOD going into the campaign. It was not just that our polling numbers were healthy. We believed that we had effectively managed to avoid any responsibility for an election the public did not want. The plan we put before Canadians was titled "Here for Canada—Our Low-Tax Plan for Jobs and Growth." This was our overarching theme, as it had been for the previous two years: we were focused on the economy, while the opposition was playing politics. We had an Economic Action Plan that we were successfully executing and a well-received budget that we were ready to pass. The election—the fourth in seven years—was unnecessary and irresponsible. We Conservatives simply wanted to get back to work.

On the other side, we judged that the opposition narrative of various threats to democracy had little traction. We felt they had so little, in fact, that we essentially refused to even address them. On the contrary, we launched a counter-narrative to explain their behaviour: they were willing to reassemble the odious liberal-socialist-separatist coalition to get into power.

We did not anticipate that our counterattack would go far. We expected the opposition to downplay or deny the possibility of a coalition because they knew it was so unpopular. And we expected the media to play along with them. But then, lo and behold, early in the campaign, Michael Ignatieff mused about this very possibility, certainly not ruling it out.

That was, in my view, the most significant turning point of the campaign. While we never would have concluded that the election was already over, it was, for the most part, smooth sailing after that. We had won the argument about the framing of the election—the economy—and we had a ready-made platform—the budget—that embodied that narrative. We had also successfully created a negative narrative for our opponents. The Liberals never got out of that box. On top of it all, we were effective in casting Michael Ignatieff as someone detached from Canadians' concerns and even the country itself—"just visiting," as the ads said.

THE CAMPAIGN UNFOLDS

THERE WAS A BIG DIFFERENCE between this election and my earlier ones: I was explicitly asking Canadians for a majority government. I had avoided that in the past. That was just sensible expectations management; you either win or you lose, so why raise the stakes on yourself? Take the win; see anything better than that as gravy.

The reality, however, is that this election was different. To start with, our narrative demanded a majority. If the opposition alternative was, in fact, a coalition—being well behind, it was their only alternative—then the one way to stop it would be to elect a majority Conservative government. It was simple arithmetic. Hence our phrase, which became my mantra during the election: Canada needs "a strong, stable, national, *majority* Conservative government."

Privately, I had another reason for asking for a majority. I had already fought three elections, done better each time, and won the last two. Politics being politics, you are either going up or you are going down. The nature of the game is to not just tread water.

We had won 143 seats in 2008, which left us 11 or 12 from a majority.*

---

* I equivocate on the number because one of the non-Conservative MPs was the Quebec City independent André Arthur. Arthur almost always voted with us, so much so that we did not run a Conservative candidate against him. On the rare occasions when André broke with us in the House, I would

In this election, if we went up, we would be in majority territory. But if we went down, that would be it for me. I had made a promise to Laureen—and to myself—that I fully intended to keep: if that happened, it would be time to move on to post-political life.

There was no choice: we had to go for a majority. In short, the stakes for me were as high as they could get.

That said, I cannot tell you that this campaign felt different—at least not for the first half. There were the daily announcements, the rallies, the debates, for sure, and they had their moments of adrenalin overload. But strangely, this extraordinary life was becoming routine for me.

This was my fourth national campaign as leader. I knew what I had to do. I was disciplined enough to generally avoid getting too high or too low, and I quite consciously did not allow my mind to dwell in a psychodrama. I also understood that much of the ultimate outcome was out of my hands.

That did mean there was more time to genuinely enjoy spending time with people across the country during the course of my travels. I got special energy from meeting the supporters who, from coast to coast to coast, were giving us their time, their money, and their prayers. Maybe it was a sign that we had our narrative and campaign in order, but the two specific memories that stand out from the first part of that campaign were largely of a non-political nature.

The first was a return to Leaside, with a campaign event being held at the Leaside Memorial Community Gardens. Although I had been away from Leaside for forty years, I was going back to the rink where I played my hockey. In the upstairs office were pictures of all the greats who had come through Leaside. The most prominent were the Mahovlich brothers, Frank and Pete. Their father had long been the skate sharpener at the Leaside rink.

---

make a tongue-in-cheek threat, telling him that "if you don't vote with us, I'll force you to join our caucus!"

To my great surprise, there on the wall, alongside the greats, was a picture of me in the jersey of my Leaside Lions house league team. It gave me quite a laugh. My time there had been three excruciatingly humble years that saw me score just one goal each season from the right wing! The joke has cropped up over the years; I cannot tell you how many times I met people from Leaside who remembered me as a great hockey player. Needless to say, I do little to correct their version of history!

Another event I attended was memorable because it showed me first-hand the inroads that we were making in Canada's immigrant communities. It was the premiere of the Bollywood film *Thank You* at a Brampton movie theatre. Attending was the Indian cinema icon Akshay Kumar. The packed crowd was going absolutely nuts, as Akshay is a huge figure in the gigantic world of Bollywood cinema.

The event was arranged by a friend, supporter, and businessman, Cargojet CEO Ajay Virmani. His son, Vinay, is an actor and entertainer who was promoting his Canadian film *Breakaway*. It certainly helped push up our already-rising profile and support in the Indo-Canadian community. The event also led to a relationship with Akshay and his wife, the former actress Twinkle Khanna, who was one of the producers of *Thank You*. I found them down-to-earth—in my experience, the big stars usually are—and they have been active promoters of good relations between India and Canada ever since.

Through all these events, our lead in the polls was significant and holding up well. Then, without warning, halfway through the campaign, the landscape began to change. Indeed, except for the Kim Campbell implosion of 1993, it would be the most remarkable series of campaign events I have ever witnessed.

LA VAGUE ORANGE

IN 2008, WE HAD hoped we could gain some seats in Quebec, but in the end, we were fortunate to have held the ones we had. In 2011, well into the campaign, it seemed even more likely that we would gain seats.*In the Saguenay–Lac-Saint-Jean area, for example, two strong Conservative MPs—Jean-Pierre Blackburn and Denis Lebel—held two out of the three seats. Halfway into the election campaign I visited there, and it looked like we had a good chance of taking the third seat from the Bloc.

Then everything in Quebec started to change. It began with the French-language debate, where Jack Layton was seen to have performed well. He then had a couple of very good interviews, particularly on *Tout le monde en parle*, Quebec's most-watched public affairs show. Jack had been raised in Montreal, spoke good colloquial Quebec French, and had an engaging personality in both languages. Moreover, the Layton name was not unknown; his father (federal Progressive Conservative) and grandfather (provincial *Union Nationale*) had both been Quebec Cabinet ministers.

Suddenly, the NDP just took off like a rocket across Quebec. It would soon be called *la vague orange*—the orange wave. As it continued to rise, our chances of gains disappeared. Then our core ridings became threatened.

The campaign hastily sent me to Montmagny–L'Islet–Rivière-du-Loup, the riding of Conservative MP Bernard Généreux. Bernard had won a by-election in 2009 in this riding just east of Quebec City, and he was proving to be a solid MP. But now I was being told that "Bernard's in trouble." I flew into the riding, drove around the area, and did a couple of events.

The strange thing was that everything looked okay. Our signs were plainly and widely visible, as were those of the Bloc, our presumed opponent. The odd Liberal sign could be seen too. But there were no NDP signs anywhere. So I asked, "Why am I here? I don't see any NDP campaign. Who's the candidate?" Their answer surprised me: "We have no idea who the candidate is, nor does anyone else. But at the doors, voting NDP is all people are talking about."

On election night, Bernard lost by nine votes. The result was verified by multiple recounts. Meanwhile, back in Saguenay–Lac Ste. Jean, only Denis Lebel survived, with the NDP taking the other two ridings. Along with Blackburn, Cabinet ministers Lawrence Cannon and Josée Verner were also defeated, as were stalwart MPs Sylvie Boucher and Daniel Petit. All were beaten by largely unknown NDP candidates.

It seems hard to simply attribute this to Jack Layton's campaign skills. After all, this was his fourth campaign as a national leader. He was anything but unknown. Yet his three earlier campaigns had produced a grand total of one seat in *la belle province*, with only the last one cracking past 10 per cent of the vote. There had to be something else going on.

There is no question that Jack's stoicism in the face of serious health challenges brought an emotive quality that energized his campaign. Jack had been suffering from cancer for some time, a struggle made visible by his increasing use of crutches to get around. But his difficult health situation by no means slowed him down; he campaigned hard, with his courage shining a light on his personality. It is hard to forget Jack, on election night, proudly raising his crutches in the air in celebration of the NDP's historic performance. As I said in my victory speech that night, "I think I can speak for the entire country in recognizing the determination and tenacity of Mr. Layton and his remarkable campaign." Emotion is inseparable from politics, and the image of Jack fighting on with a smile on his face certainly struck a chord with voters, especially in Quebec.

The one benefit in this voter shift was that the Bloc was devastated—reduced from 47 seats to a mere 4, losing Official Party status in the House. I think the explanation is obvious. Originally created for the election of 1993 as part of the push for sovereignty after the failure of the Meech Lake Accord, the Bloc had instead become a permanent fixture in Ottawa. But its mission had become ever vaguer. Almost from the day of Lucien Bouchard's departure, the composition of the Bloc had narrowed. It had originally included MPs of the left, centre, and right, with both Liberal and Conservative MPs leaving to join the new entity. Over the years since then, Mr. Duceppe had moved the party dramatically to the left, alienating both his right wing and centre.

The turning point was the coalition attempt. The Bloc had largely buried its sovereignty message before it gambled everything to go for the brass ring. That strategy failed spectacularly. In effect, their message was: "We're no longer about sovereignty. We're about providing a left-wing alternative to the Harper government." Quebec voters replied: "If that's what it's all about, aren't you making a case for the NDP rather than for the Bloc?" My view was always that, had the coalition coup succeeded, the big winner would have been the Bloc, and the big loser (as the junior partner) would have been the NDP. Ironically, the failure of the coalition completely reversed their fortunes.

The fall of the Bloc was good for the country, even though we ended up losing seats in Quebec too. On the other hand, there was a side effect in the rest of the country that helped us. Because of its rise in Quebec, the NDP began to overtake the Liberals in national polling. That prompted commentators to start musing about an NDP federal government. That sharpened the election choice around our issue—economic management. At that point, an important block of voters we call "Conservative-Liberal switchers," "Blue Liberals," or "business Liberals" began to move to us. They rightly believed that the last thing the country needed in these challenging times would be a rookie NDP government.

THE DEATH OF OSAMA BIN LADEN

ONE OF MY LAST STOPS of the campaign was in Abbotsford, B.C. That final rally was overshadowed by the news that Osama bin Laden was dead.

I immediately issued a formal prime-ministerial statement. I expressed my feeling of "sober satisfaction" over this development. I was trying to convey agreement with the action, but without any sense of joy or triumph. My emotions were not conflicted, but they were nuanced.

It is hard for me to be elated over the killing of anyone. It is God who will render the final judgment on each one of us. But that does not relieve us of the responsibilities of making our own judgments in our own time. And if we have any moral sense at all, it is hard to see how Osama bin Laden did not deserve to come to such a brutal end. This was an individual leading a violent, nihilistic, evil movement that brought nothing but death and destruction to this world.

In my time as prime minister, I had come to know the families of the twenty-four Canadians murdered on that terrible day, 9/11, including Maureen Basnicki who lost her husband and father of their two children, Ken, in the World Trade Center. Maureen channelled her grief into action by co-founding the Canadian Coalition Against Terror, an organization that assisted the government quite actively in a series of anti-terrorism initiatives and legislation. Sharing their pain as they did helped me to understand and feel, at least as much as possible, the agony of such senseless loss. Of course, ending bin Laden's life would not bring their loved ones back. Still, it was some measure of justice, a case of the punishment fitting the crime, as they say. And so I was looking at it through their eyes too.

President Obama and his administration deserve full credit for executing the complex operation. But the very fact that bin Laden's death occurred some ten years after 9/11 said a lot. The reality that we were still fighting the Taliban and al-Qaeda said even more. The fundamental flaws in the Afghan mission were only becoming more manifest with time. It was "sober satisfaction" indeed.

ELECTION NIGHT 2011

IN THE END, it turned out Canadians were receptive to our proposition for the country. On election night, May 2, 2011, we won 166 seats,* with the NDP at 103 forming the Official Opposition and the Liberals' 34 seats being their worst showing ever.

There was indeed much to celebrate. Outside Quebec, we had won a broad-based majority, with almost half the popular vote. We won most

---

* Of course, this included my riding in Calgary Southwest, where the campaign had been led by Curt Bruggencate. Besides voting, my only appearance in the riding during national elections would be a single visit to our local campaign office. I could rely on the team in Calgary Southwest to take care of everything on their own.

of the seats in the Greater Toronto Area, including the elusive 416 and 905 suburbs outside Toronto's central core. We took the most seats of any single party in Atlantic Canada. In fact, we almost swept New Brunswick, my ancestral home province, and we even won a seat in Newfoundland & Labrador. Our candidate Ryan Leef won the seat in Yukon, which conservatives had not held since the famous Deputy Prime Minister Erik Nielsen. Even in Quebec there was something to cheer about. Despite retaining just five ridings, we were establishing a dependable regional base—something we had not had in almost a century.

We were encouraged that Canadians had given us this victory after looking at how we had performed and what we had on offer. This Conservative majority was neither a single-issue mandate nor some throw-the-bums-out coalition that might quickly break up. It had been built from our base out.

The growth of the party under my leadership had happened in three phases. Beginning in 2004, we consolidated the traditional conservative ridings that had been lost during the years of Progressive Conservative–Reform/Alliance vote-splitting. Starting in 2006, we established a beachhead in Quebec among the traditional *bleus* of that province, and we had similarly added conservative francophone voters outside Quebec. In 2011, the most notable gains were in the Greater Vancouver Regional District and, especially, the Greater Toronto Area. Those gains were concentrated in "cultural communities."

Adding "ethnic" voters had been a clear strategy since my Alliance leadership days (and, in fairness, had begun in earnest under Stockwell Day). It had not been a scattershot approach. We had concentrated on groups where our conservative values—entrepreneurship, law and order, faith, family, democracy-oriented foreign policy, and the like—were strong, with additional focus on the subgroups that most embodied those values. In the words of Jason Kenney, we were simply "turning small-c conservatives into big-c Conservatives." He and the late Deepak Obhrai were the two MPs most critical in these efforts, although many had played a role.

It is important to mention what this strategy was not. We were not focusing on affluent white liberal voters. Sure, their parents and grandparents may have been staunch Conservatives, yet oftentimes they are anything but. Some may be "kind of conservative" on economic issues, but in my experience, they will always find some reason why the Conservative Party is "too right-wing" for them. Romancing them is not merely a waste of time; it can also jeopardize our support among base conservative voters and, for that matter, among the kind of New Canadian voter we hope to attract.*

It is hard to properly describe the feeling on election night as I took the stage in Calgary to address the packed room of elated supporters. The celebrations continued afterwards, with Laureen, Ben, Rachel, extended family, friends, and long-standing political associates. I was also buoyed by the knowledge that thousands of others I had worked with over the years were similarly rejoicing across the country. These are wonderful but fleeting moments, so I tried to enjoy and appreciate every minute of it.

Yet I felt a sense of relief more than anything. For one thing, I now knew I would have some real runway to govern, without the need—and the constant energy drain—of trying to plan election contingencies. I know my entire team and staff felt the same. More importantly, I would be continuing in office. Securing the majority meant there would be no thought of leaving (for the next three years anyway). After all, I still wanted the job, and no part of me was ready to depart, despite my intention to do that in the case of a less favourable outcome.

We knew we would be back to the grind within days, but Laureen and I still marvelled that this moment of "strong, stable, national, majority Conservative government" had arrived. Ten years earlier, when I promised her that I would leave Ottawa whenever things turned downward, we never really believed we would get so far. But we had.

---

* In my not-so-humble opinion, that is what happened in 2021. The Conservative campaign on issues like the carbon tax failed to pick up new voters and lost old ones, mainly to the People's Party.

BACK TO WORK, TO PARLIAMENT, AND TO THE PARTY

THE RETURN OF PARLIAMENT was set for June 2, exactly one month after the election. It was important for the government to pass our budget and continue implementing our economic plan. In the meantime, however, there was urgent travel to be undertaken.

In late May I joined fellow G8 leaders in Deauville, France, for our annual summit. Peace and security matters related to the Arab Spring were on the agenda. I also took the opportunity to discuss progress on Canada's Muskoka Initiative for maternal and child health that we had launched the previous year. After Deauville I made a bilateral visit to Greece, a country with significant people-to-people ties with Canada that was grappling with its own financial crisis.

During this trip, Laureen and I visited a monument in the mountain town of Kalavryta, west of Athens, to pay our respects. Kalavryta was the site of a horrific atrocity in 1943, when Nazi soldiers executed one thousand men and boys, virtually the entire male population of the town. One of the men murdered was the grandfather of my director of communications, Dimitris Soudas.

This sobering reminder of the heavy price so many countries have paid for freedom was in my mind as our RCAF jet lifted off from Athens and turned, not west for home but east toward Afghanistan. It would be for my third and final visit. Our combat mission was due to end in July, and the transition to a focus on training would soon begin. On the ground in Kandahar, I visited a forward operating base and an agricultural area called Tarnak Farms that had been a Taliban stronghold. I also attended a memorial service for our fallen. Our men and women in uniform had paid a heavy price for their efforts on the ground, and it remained important for me to demonstrate that our Government was fully behind them.

On May 18, the governor general had sworn in a new Cabinet. Since 2006, my Cabinets had evolved from deliberately small—due in part to the lack of Cabinet experience—to a larger one with ministers of state. The idea was to help engage the growing caucus and to identify the next generation of talent.* Looking back on my appointments, I was surprised to see how much change there had been. After just five years, less than half of my original ministers were still in Cabinet. That was mostly due to election churn and the normal course of retirement. Regrettably, 2011 had been the first election where sitting ministers were defeated at the polls. Despite our overall success, that had been a major disappointment to me and the team.

With Parliament's return, we presented our first majority Speech from the Throne, entitled "Here for All Canadians: Stability, Prosperity, Security." It laid out three broad priorities for the coming year and beyond. The first priority was to pass the budget presented just before the election. When he introduced the budget on June 6, Minister Flaherty employed his typical wit and understatement by beginning: "And so, as I was saying in March . . ." A second plank of our program going forward would be to enact many promises that had been backlogged or impeded by the opposition during the minority parliaments. We now had the votes, so there could be no excuse for not getting them done.

Within a week of Parliament's return, we hosted the national convention of the Conservative Party of Canada in Ottawa. Because of the timing and circumstances, it also turned into a huge election victory party. It was a great opportunity for me to get the troops revved up and lay out our agenda for the months and years ahead.

In the next hundred days, I told party members, they could look forward to seeing an omnibus crime bill, an end to the Canadian Wheat Board monopoly, a reform to enact better representation-by-population in the Commons, the repeal of per-vote subsidies for Canada's political parties, and Senate reform legislation. In the fall, we would finally put an end to the

---

* New ministers were Steven Blaney, Ed Fast, Steven Fletcher, Bal Gosal, Joe Oliver, Peter Penashue, Tim Uppal, Alice Wong, and Bernard Valcourt, Valcourt, who was returning to Parliament after many years, having been a minister under Brian Mulroney. John Duncan, Julian Fantino, Peter Kent, Ted Menzies, and Rob Moore, who had joined the ministry later in the previous Parliament, were also reappointed.

hated long-gun registry. The future seemed boundless in these happy days, and we had every intention of enacting these promises into law in the new parliamentary session.

In my address, I also identified our third priority: to reach out to Quebec—even though those voters had gone overwhelmingly to Jack Layton's NDP. I always took the view in my political career that we should look for opportunities to grow our party. While commentators were busy writing stories about the demise of the Conservative Party in Quebec, I was in fact optimistic about our prospects. Our focus groups showed it was far from clear that the NDP had any staying power in Quebec. Further, for three elections in a row, we had hammered out a small but durable Conservative base in part of the province, so we felt there was something to build on going forward.

RESOLUTE BAY

ALTHOUGH THE SUMMER SCHEDULE was less hectic, we always made a habit of not standing still during the time away from Parliament. I would typically do at least one foreign trip, and that summer we focused on Latin America. During this trip, we concluded a free trade agreement with Honduras. It was our eighth free-trade partner in the Americas. We also formally brought the Colombia deal into force during my visit to that country. As well, we sought to deepen our trade relationship with Costa Rica. The Liberal government had struck an earlier, less-comprehensive deal with that country that we wished to build on.

I also undertook my sixth annual northern tour. This year, however, it was overshadowed by one sad, unrelated event.

On August 20, First Air Flight 6560 crashed on landing at Resolute Bay, killing twelve of the fifteen people on board. This tragedy slightly delayed a trip I had planned to take to the region. When we did get there, on August 23, we found a community in shock and mourning. Because I had been there three or four times already as prime minister, I had come to know many in this community of two hundred. One is Aziz (Ozzie) Kherai, an Ismaili

Canadian originally from Tanzania. Ozzie is the leading businessman in the town and was an early member of the Reform Party, hence the long-standing connection. He and virtually everyone in the community was touched by the crash, and we did what we could to console the residents.

This tragedy visited upon Resolute seemed doubly cruel given its unfortunate history. If you look at a map of Canada and the northern islands, right in the middle lies a huge east-west waterway called the Parry Channel, named after the explorer William Edward Parry. Inuit had traditionally not lived north of the channel, but that all changed in 1953. That was when the federal government forcibly relocated Inuit from northern Quebec and Baffin Island to two new communities in the High Arctic: Resolute Bay and Grise Fiord. The purpose was to demonstrate Canadian presence and sovereignty, but the result was that the displaced Inuit were long neglected afterward.

On one of my previous visits to Resolute, I was able to meet with the elders in the community to acknowledge the hardship the government had caused them, to apologize, and to thank them for what they contribute to Canada. At this point, although the families had been there for sixty years, some of the original transportees were still living. This meeting, and others like it, left an indelible impression upon me.

These citizens were pleased to receive the acknowledgement of their injustice and hardships. What struck me more was that these residents had chosen to stay, even when eventually given the opportunity to return to their original land. This was now their home, and they had embraced their community's role as the gateway to the High Arctic.*

Meeting with and getting to know these remarkable people, I learned first-hand about their concerns and unique way of looking at the world. Among First Nations, there are differing views about their relationship with Canada. In the Arctic North, the perspectives, at least in my experience, are

* I never had the opportunity to travel to the even more remote community of Grise Fiord on Ellesmere Island, to transmit the same apology in person and to have similar conversations. It is one of my regrets from my days in office.

much less nuanced. The Government of Canada has had a sustained presence there only since the 1950s. Yet, despite the High Arctic relocation and some sad experiences in residential schools, the Inuit generally view themselves as proud Canadians.

That is because, despite the things that have gone wrong, life is, in living memory, much better than it was. The Inuit today have access to modern accommodation, heating, transport, medicine, and communications. My most vivid recollection of the Inuit perspective came from the former premier of Nunavut Paul Okalik. He recounted how, one hunting season, his grandparents went inland for the annual caribou chase. They did not find any animals in time, and they starved to death. "That doesn't happen anymore," Okalik said. That is no small statement.

Still, life in the Arctic remains harsh, and the provision of modern amenities is difficult and extremely costly. The move from nomadic to sedentary life has brought its own considerable challenges. On top of that, cultural influences from the South to a people long self-sufficient have not always been benign. Yet I remained wholly impressed at the Inuit's commitment to the land, their quiet strength, and their loyalty to Canada. I know I spoke for the Government and people of Canada when I told them we would do everything we could to improve their lives and the lives of their children.

Doing this starts with listening to them and understanding what their needs are, not what others think their needs should be. A perfect example of that occurred on August 24, when I toured the massive Agnico Eagle gold mine. It is 100 kilometres by road to the predominantly Inuit community of Baker Lake. Afterwards, I was able to sit down with the leaders and the elders of the community to hear what was on their minds. Our conversation was fascinating.

I observed that, at the mine itself, the infrastructure was very good: housing, roads, and even an airstrip. "Wouldn't it have been better," I asked them, "if all this infrastructure were located in the town itself?" The response was quite candid. They said they had asked for it to be the way it now was because they were not sure how the development would affect life in the community. It was a decision they very much regretted.

Why? Because, given our Southern environmental regulations, when that mine eventually winds down, they will rip up the road, take all the housing away, eliminate any vestige of the airstrip, and literally return the mine area to a state of nature. There will be no long-run benefit to the community whatsoever. Their view now? Obviously, as they told me, if they could have a do-over, they would want to integrate the mine infrastructure into the community. They also asked that I change the general federal approach to resource development to ensure that the infrastructure created provides long-term benefit.

I certainly took this message to heart and set out to change the policy, but with constant resistance from the regulatory departments in Ottawa. Any permanent change in the North has long been contrary to the policies of the Government of Canada.* A deeply held view within the Environment, Fisheries, and Indigenous Affairs bureaucracies has been that infrastructure must be temporary. This is not only clearly contrary to the best interests of our Indigenous people but also exactly the opposite of what they want. Of course, it is important to them to preserve their environment, but like Canadians in the South, they want to have economic development as well. And, Lord knows, they have the room to do it in!

Such development is badly, desperately needed in many communities. The population is often young and growing but with severely limited opportunities. Serious social pathologies—substance abuse, crime, suicide—are everywhere and frequently visible. The idea of a state-of-nature North is little more than cultural imperialism—an uninformed utopian view on the part of Southern city dwellers that they have the power to impose. In my experience, the Inuit hunger for economic development—environmentally responsible economic development for sure, but economic development nonetheless. This, they deserve.

---

* I believe that these "return everything to a state of nature" policies were restored by our successors.

HARRINGTON LAKE

ALTHOUGH MY VACATIONS were few and brief, summers were generally relaxing, and they centred on what was, to my mind, the real perk of the job—the prime minister's summer residence on Harrington Lake. It is about thirty kilometres outside Ottawa in Gatineau Park. The main facility is a rustic seven-bedroom cottage, located on fourteen acres of cleared land and a six-kilometre-long lake. For all its privacy, it is barely a half-hour commute to the office when the need arises.

Our family would move out to Harrington Lake when the kids were done school in June and live there until Labour Day. We also spent the New Year's period and a few weekends there. The visits to Harrington were always something Laureen and I looked forward to. There is nothing like it. As I would tell Ben and Rachel, the richest family in Canada would not be able to buy anything like this. (I had to tell them that as they never fully appreciated it, especially as they got older and wanted to spend more of the summer in the city with their friends.)

I have mentioned that one special tradition Laureen launched at Harrington was our own private Canada Day celebration. Following the official event on Parliament Hill, we would head to Harrington Lake and be joined by friends, staff, some political associates, and occasionally a few celebrities from the Parliament Hill celebration. My band and I would have rehearsed a long set for entertainment later in the evening and be prepared to back any of the professionals who wanted to perform. In the meantime, before a big barbeque, people would have great fun in the water, including going down a long slip-and-slide from the high embankment on which the main cottage sits.

Over the years, a variety of guests joined us at Harrington Lake. They were mostly extended family and close friends, but John Howard, Felipe Calderón, Benjamin Netanyahu, and David Jacobson were official visitors. Jean Chrétien and Brian Mulroney were among those who came for dinner. These would often bring their spouses or even their families. Others sometimes came to fish. Governor General David Johnston came a couple times, as did his predecessor Michaëlle Jean. David was the only guest I remember who accomplished the unheard-of feat of not catching a single fish. The lake is teeming with them and even I—no fisherman indeed—could catch them. Other notable—and successful—fishermen were then–Toronto Mayor Rob Ford and later-Premier Doug Ford.

On those Canada Days, we would have fun all afternoon and evening and then top it off by gathering near midnight around the large stone inukshuk that I christened "Pierre." It was a play on words,* but it was also the first Trudeau who put it there. Anyway, we would have a big fireworks show and end the night by singing "O Canada." These are great memories, for which Laureen—and the household staff—deserve the credit. Laureen always prioritized time with family and friends, being sure to create a rich family life in the midst of this crazy whirlwind we were living.

One summer night, Ben, Rachel, and I were watching a movie on the television in the main floor living room, when suddenly something whizzed over our heads. It was a bat loose in the house, which happened from time to time. We decided to close off the various entrances to the room and to open the outside door to the adjacent sunroom. The idea would be to chase the bat outdoors.

We tried this for a few minutes, but we just could not direct the full-of-energy bat. I suggested Ben run down to the boathouse and find a fishing net. I thought maybe I could trap the bat in that and take it out. However, moments after Ben left, a raccoon spotted the open door and decided to join us in the living room.

Now I had two problems. I did not want to tangle with the raccoon, as they can sometimes be nasty. So I quickly exited the room with Rachel, and we watched through the glass door, waiting for Ben to return. Fortunately, the raccoon left shortly of its own accord. I went back inside and shut the sunroom door behind it.

Just then a panting Ben reappeared, looking traumatized. "After I came out of the boathouse, I was being followed by a bear!" he exclaimed.

---

* Pierre, besides being a name in French, is the word for "rock."

Fortunately, he did have the fishing net. I spent the next fifteen minutes or so chasing the bat around the room with the net. When it finally tired enough, I was able to snag it and release it out of the sunroom. All's well that ends well.

Ben's bear encounter was no surprise as black bears are common near the Harrington Lake property, and I ran into them more than once in the woods nearby. The first time was when I was with an RCMP officer, who pulled out his weapon and chased the bear away. It was the only threat that ever required my security to draw a gun! But his aggression was instructive because later, when I met up with a black bear alone, I used a similar aggressive posture to avoid an attack.

ROYAL VISITORS

THE HARRINGTON LAKE PROPERTY is owned by the Government of Canada; "The Queen in Right of Canada" is the technical language. Thus, it was fitting that on Canada Day 2011 we were privileged to host Prince William and Princess Kate, then the Duke and Duchess of Cambridge, as our special guests. They had come to Canada for an extended visit, before and after Canada Day, and Harrington Lake proved to be an ideal retreat for them. They stayed in the little guest "cabin in the woods" about a half mile from us that we reserved for special visitors. I am sure they found it a welcome break from the paparazzi madness that always attends their travels.

I was hugely impressed by both. They were a pleasure to spend time with—down-to-earth, very personable, and warm. In every setting, from the Canada Day celebrations to their time in Quebec and their visit to the Calgary Stampede, they seemed effortlessly at ease at various events and with different people.

Those worried about the future of the monarchy need not be. Elizabeth II was a great monarch and left an amazing legacy. Charles III, in my experience, is intelligent, engaging, quite humorous, and more than up to the task. Although we had met briefly before, this was my first opportunity to really size up William. William and Kate and I talked a bit about their life as royals. They were, of course, newlyweds, and this was all new for Kate.

They were both clearly enjoying all the positive attention they were then getting. Yet, the royal couple were well aware of two things: that there would be the inevitable ups-and-downs in news coverage of them and that this was forever. There could be no turning back; being in direct line to the throne is a lifetime role and no other opportunities will be open to you. I know they found that daunting—decades of repeat appearances and meetings—but both seemed reconciled to and accepting of their futures. I came away confident William will make his own special contribution to the monarchy when his time comes.

This was not our first brush with royalty at Harrington Lake. In the summer of 2009, Emperor Akihito and Empress Michiko of Japan came to Canada for a visit. We had had an opportunity to meet with them in Tokyo, and we hit it off immediately. When they came to Canada, we offered Harrington Lake to them. We cleared out so that they could stay at the big cottage along with their large entourage, and the grounds and trails were set up to accommodate their advanced age. The Japanese royal couple reported having had a wonderful and relaxing time, and we were so glad we were able to share our special retreat with them. They particularly enjoyed seeing all the wildlife.

There was one other aspect of this visit that warmed my heart. After I became prime minister, I had had a small upright rental piano brought to Harrington, so I could play when I wanted to. Apparently, the Empress, an accomplished pianist I am told, saw one of my Beatles songbooks on the piano and started playing. She must have liked what she heard, because she took the book with her back to Tokyo. We later got a note from her offering to buy us a replacement. Needless to say, I wrote back, "Don't worry about it—it's yours!" That was certainly one of the more fun "official gifts" that I was able to present while prime minister.

FAREWELL TO JACK LAYTON

ON AUGUST 22, 2011, NDP leader Jack Layton died of cancer. Death is never fair, I suppose—nor is politics—but it seems that Jack's death at this time was especially unfair. Consider his recent accomplishments: a massive breakthrough in Quebec, winning second place nationally for his party, and becoming the Official Opposition—the first time in the NDP's long history. He now seemed set to stamp his influence on Canada's legislative chronicles. His joyful, energetic, and enthusiastic campaigning won many hearts, and not just in Quebec. His passing occasioned a genuine outpouring of grief across Canada, including at 24 Sussex Drive.

Nothing brought the seriousness of Jack's illness more into focus for me than an interaction we had in the Commons in late June 2011. We were debating back-to-work legislation for Canada Post workers. Jack and the NDP were putting up a spirited defence against this action, and we had marathon votes and sittings. At one point I think we went fifty-eight hours of vote after vote, debate after debate. Jack attacked with his usual vigour and appeared to be in his element—the consummate happy warrior.

At some point during that debate, we had a pull-aside meeting to discuss something, as is not uncommon for leaders to do. I walked across the aisle—the two swords' length of historical repute—and we sat down together. Being that close, I was shocked to see how gaunt and pale he had become. While I cannot say I was surprised by his death, I certainly can say that he died with his boots on. May it be so for us all.

After consultations with Clerk Wayne Wouters and senior people at Canadian Heritage, I decided that we would hold a state funeral for Jack. It was set for August 27. This was a departure from protocol as state funerals are normally only held for former governors general, former prime ministers, and sitting Cabinet ministers. The only other leader of the Opposition to have died in office was Wilfrid Laurier in 1919, and he was, of course, a former prime minister.

In other words, this was a novel situation, and my judgment was that we could make an exception without creating any long-term dilemmas.

Plus, given Jack's prominence in Parliament, and the emotional impact his untimely passing was having on the country, it just seemed like the appropriate thing to do. At the funeral, Olivia Chow, his wife and a member of Parliament (Trinity–Spadina), expressed the appreciation of Jack's family. It was one of those rare occasions when parliamentarians from all the parties were drawn together. I believe Jack would have been pleased.

One last word on Jack: we shared a love of music. He was reputedly an excellent guitar player, and his genre, I was told, was classic rock. We talked a number of times about getting together to jam but never did. The reason it did not happen, honestly, was my lack of confidence that I had the ability to play at his level. It is one of those things I wish I had done but never did. If there is rock 'n' roll in heaven—I know I am being presumptuous here—maybe we will get a chance to correct that one day.

ON PARLIAMENTARY RELATIONS

THE RELATIONSHIPS BETWEEN politicians in our system are often misunderstood. People see the loud verbal battles in Parliament, with the parties rallying around their leaders, and they often assume that is the full reality. On the one side are teammates in battle, on the other side sworn enemies. The images of certain leaders going hammer and tongs at each other not only sticks in people's minds but also often defines the Canadian political life of that era.

However, the reality is much more nuanced than that. Two or more parties will often agree on particular items of parliamentary business. Unfortunately, that very reason often renders those lower-profile. And the party leaders and/or their delegates frequently meet each other for various purposes. Those meetings are almost always professional, and sometimes downright friendly.

Notwithstanding media perception to the contrary, I genuinely respected, and even liked, most of the other party leaders I served with. As already mentioned, Jack Layton and I always had a good relationship in private. Another example is Jean Chrétien, whom I duelled with as his last leader of the Opposition. We had and still have our political differences, but there was never any personal animosity between Mr. Chrétien and me. On the contrary, we have become genuine and longstanding friends.

Cynics might say that the cameras turn on, you insult one another, and then it is all chummy-chummy afterward. But it is not like that. Our debates and disagreements are, for the most part—periodic grandstanding aside—real enough. Parties and their leaders have genuine, divergent, strongly held views on what is in the best interests of the country. Yet we are there because we fundamentally all believe in the country and want to serve its best interests. Even the Bloc, in its own way, believes in the best interests of the country, as it defines it. That is the way I always looked at it: we are opponents, not enemies.

I have known leaders who intensely dislike, and even hate, anyone they have ever run against or crossed swords with. I saw that when I was young. It is a terrible way to live, and I was determined I was not going to let that happen to me. Of course, sometimes I felt that I had been genuinely wronged by some opponents. I also have no doubt that there are some who genuinely feel I have wronged them. Since I have won more than I have lost, they might feel more intensely about it than I do.

By and large, I put all this down to the combative nature of politics and tried not to nurse personal grievances. I looked in the mirror every so often to keep this in perspective. Politics is a rough game. Do not pretend that the other guy is evil and you are pure as driven snow. Although I am a very flawed practitioner, I do try to follow the words of my divine teacher: "Forgive us our trespasses, as we forgive those who trespass against us."

Just as relationships between the members of various parties are not always bad, those between members of the same party are not always good. There is a story about Winston Churchill, probably apocryphal, that illustrates this best. He was showing a young Conservative MP into the British House of Commons, and he pointed out the seats occupied by the Labour Party and its leader. The young fellow said, "Ah, there's the enemy," to which Churchill is purported to have replied, "No, I told you that's the Opposition; the enemy is all around you."

That is too dark a view, I think, but there are often deep animosities within parties. In my experience, they usually have one or two origins. A common one is in fights over positions early in political careers—usually in the youth wings of political parties. It is amazing how some battle for power in a youth wing thirty or forty years earlier can lead to people literally not talking to each other for the rest of their lives.

The second big generator of long-standing political animosities are leadership contests within political parties, and the way people are lined up in those battles. I had two leadership races. In the first one, my opponent was Stockwell Day. My second contest was against Belinda Stronach, essentially a non-Conservative outsider who did not stay.

The result of these contests was the Conservative Party of Canada. It was a genuinely new party, which had relatively few tribal animosities. I joke that we had so many factions in each of the two legacy parties that they were all too small to matter once we were inside a genuinely big tent. It also helped that I had won both leadership races by large margins and made the effort to bring the defeated onside. Leadership opponents Stockwell Day and Tony Clement, for instance, became two of my most trusted colleagues and later friends.

I have never tried to add it up, but I would bet that in my parliamentary career I served with some four hundred MPs and senators in various caucuses. I can honestly say that I liked almost all my colleagues. They were overwhelmingly good people, of good motivation and good work ethic, who made real efforts to contribute positively to the team and to the country. Once in government, I rarely worried that someone might have their hand in the cookie jar or behave in other awful ways.

My style was probably different than many other leaders in terms of dealing with colleagues. I made real efforts to have professional relationships with almost everyone in my caucus through various meetings and dinners at 24 Sussex. Since I met Cabinet ministers the most, those were invariably closer relationships. On the other hand, I did not try to build personal friendships in my caucus. I felt that a leader being the friend of some but not others would create more problems than it would solve.

I did have some pre-existing friendships. Probably the best was Scott

Reid, a great MP whom I had known since my days when we were both Reform Party researchers. Peter MacKay and I had obviously become close during the merger process. The list was short, but this has changed since I left office. Many relationships have subsequently deepened as several dozen of my former colleagues have become friends, business associates, or ongoing confidants.

THE ESSENCE OF DEMOCRACY

ALL THAT SAID, there are many who criticize the level of animosity often on display in Parliament. People ask, "Why can't they just be polite?" Or even, "Why can't they just get along?" I admit there is some justification for them to feel that way. As I mentioned, one of the achievements of the Reform Party was ending desk thumping in the House of Commons. It was loud, juvenile, and deplorable, as have been many other behaviours and shenanigans of elected members.

Parliamentarians do, too often, go over the top in their rhetoric and get personal when they should not. There is also too much heckling in the House of Commons. It is sometimes clever and even appropriate, but too frequently it creates a boorish din that turns the average person off.

Still, we must never forget that disagreement in politics, even intense disagreement, is a fundamentally positive thing. It is, after all, what being a democracy is all about. The essence of a democracy is that there are choices to be made about what direction the body politic takes. There is no one irrefutable Truth on which all citizens must agree. The very premise of democracy is that people not only can disagree but also have every right to do so and should not be afraid to.

It is through that clash of ideas and choices, of competition and options, that we believe the body politic will arrive at better decisions. Show me a country where everyone "agrees" politically, and I will show you a nasty place to live, where people's most basic human rights are not respected and where those losing political contests are not merely defeated but jailed and/

or murdered. That is what it is like when people "agree," because people do not just naturally agree.

My father would often argue that the strength of our Westminster-style institutions was, in fact, their loud and cacophonous nature. "We elect people with conflicting views," he would say, "so that they can go to Parliament, sit close together, and fight over their differences. They express not only their intellectual positions, but the emotions—the hopes and the hostilities—underlying their views. That's the place to get it all out. They do it for us, so that, outside Parliament, citizens largely get on with their lives and interact civilly despite our differences."

As my dad wisely observed, "you'll see a lot of places in the world where it's all very stately and cordial, even consensual, in the legislature. People seem to agree there, but they are fighting in the streets over their political differences. That's the genius behind the British system, because it developed through trial and error over many centuries."

In the past couple of decades, it has been fashionable in some circles, especially business circles, to be impressed by how quickly, how decisively, and how correctly authoritarian systems can make decisions. China is often cited. Our delays, divisions, and deviations are pointed out in contrast.

I would argue that democratic systems have proven far more resilient over time. When things go wrong in a democracy, new leaders eventually come along to address the problems and try different solutions. When dictators go wrong, they go really wrong. Then they double- and triple-down on their mistakes to prove their claims of infallibility (which is, after all, the only basis on which such leaders can claim power). For a few years of a Deng Xiaoping, there is a full generation of a Mao Zedong. Even at its best, the Chinese model has yet to create a society even remotely as desirable a place to live in as the free and democratic world. There is a reason why Winston Churchill said, "Democracy is the worst form of government, except for all the others."

PART FOUR

2011–2015

19

A MAJORITY GOVERNMENT'S DOMESTIC AGENDA

WITH THE 2011 BUDGET finally passed, we returned to Parliament in the fall with the new mandate and renewed energy. These were heady days. For the first time, we had four years ahead of us with little prospect of a parliamentary crisis or an election. We were determined to use these years to get as much done as we could. This was the opportunity to implement the governing agenda Canadians had endorsed in May.

But we wanted to go further. Now was the time to secure Canada's long-term economic success by building on the strong foundation we had laid. We also had significant outstanding commitments to rebuild defence capabilities and complete our justice reform agenda. At the same time, as I had committed to my party, we would be fulfilling a number of important five-year-old promises that the minority parliaments had stalled. Ours was a full and ambitious agenda, but never one we viewed as a blank cheque. We would always seek to build consensus for our initiatives with caucus and the broader public.

ENCOURAGING SCIENCE, TECHNOLOGY, AND ACADEMIC EXCELLENCE

ONE OF OUR FIRST economic announcements that fall was part of a long-under-reported government priority: science, technology, and academic excellence. I went to McMaster University to announce the latest winners of the Vanier Canada Graduate Scholarships, named after the former governor general. This was an excellent initiative, which also served as an opportunity to stress the much wider strategy of our Government. Although there had been attention to our investments in university and college infrastructure through Canada's Economic Action Plan, our more expansive commitment to research and development remained largely unappreciated.

This was not, contrary to media myth, because the academic and research communities were hostile to our Government. On the contrary, those responsible for implementing our programs in this area—the universities, the granting councils, the research institutes—were very supportive. After every budget, they regularly spoke out in favour of the government's initiatives. Why would they not? Their budgets went up every single year that we were in office.

Our strategy was, however, ultimately focused on economic performance, rather than just academic funding. It had been initiated in 2007. Titled *Mobilizing Science and Technology to Canada's Advantage*, it aimed to address the low levels of private-sector funding relative to other advanced economies. Business funding contrasted markedly with public funding in Canada, which had been reasonably generous by global standards.

This had long been a complaint of governments in Canada, but as near as we could tell, they had not really asked themselves why these levels of commitment differed so dramatically. One explanation should have been blindingly obvious: very little research conducted on the public side was of any direct interest to the private sector. Government was largely focussed upon so-called basic research. That is certainly important, but it is of mostly limited utility to business, which is, after all, focused on commercial opportunities.

Thus, *Mobilizing Science and Technology* was geared toward generating private-sector buy-in through a more targeted approach aimed at commercialization. It had four priorities: to encourage partnerships between research institutes, academia, and the private sector; to focus on areas most consistent with Canada's natural advantages; to attract the best global talent in those areas; and to ensure better accountability for what were very significant expenditures. The fields of specialization, identified with the assistance of the Council of Canadian Academies, were: natural resources and energy; environmental science and technology; health and related life sciences; and information and communications technology.

Unfortunately, but also predictably, this strategy attracted some criticism. It came from a vocal minority and was cheerfully amplified by a media anxious to promote their stereotype of conservatives as anti-science. I say "predictably" because, while the research and development community as a whole were supportive of our actions, this new approach was indeed goring some oxen.

We would not be focusing on everything, which is, of course, equivalent to having no focus at all. We would also be aiming for world-class results. The previous pattern had been regular grants in many research areas, which had turned into virtually automatic renewal of the same funding to the same people every year. Our view was (and remains) that reform to that approach was essential. Only more competitive processes would produce better results. Hence the gored oxen.

Examples of this strategy could be seen throughout my Government's tenure and in the bones of every single budget. It was not just about individual research programs. Our initiatives funded major healthcare research; automotive and aerospace innovation; large components of our northern agenda (like the High Arctic Research Station); climate change research; and major investments in IT, quantum computing, and laboratories. The list was as long as my arm. Suffice it to say that it was a major and ongoing thrust of our Government.

RED TAPE REDUCTION

REGULATORY STREAMLINING was another area we targeted to improve long-term economic performance. On January 18, 2012, the Red Tape Reduction Commission, which I had commissioned a year earlier, released a wide-ranging report. We then launched an all-out effort to implement its recommendations through the government-wide "Red Tape Reduction Action Plan."

The Commission called for fifteen systemic changes and ninety department-specific solutions to reduce or remove regulatory irritants. President of the Treasury Board Tony Clement took this up with a passion. It was a major initiative, a fulfillment of our promises, and an important undertaking by our Government.

One of the most significant elements of our plan was the "one-for-one rule," which required regulators to offset any regulation they imposed with a cut to another one of matching impact. To my knowledge, this made Canada the first country to give such a rule the weight of legislation.*

Other elements included implementing a "small business lens" on the actions of regulators; mandating departments to publish "forward plans" outlining upcoming changes; setting service standards for the issuance of high-volume licences; and compiling an annual scorecard on our actions for Canadians. By all accounts, our Action Plan was received well by the business community. It led to the repeal of thousands of unnecessary regulations to the benefit of our communities and our economy.†

---

* They say that imitation is the sincerest form of flattery. So I suppose I was duly flattered when, in 2017, the Trump administration famously took up the one-for-one rule and applied it with even more vigour than we had. That is credited with playing a big role in the pre-Covid "Trump boom" in the U.S. economy. I know Americans like to claim everything they do is the best and greatest, but in this case our government can absolutely claim original ownership!

† The one-for-one rule alone produced a $21-million annual reduction in administrative burdens, representing over 260,000 hours saved dealing with red tape. A simple example was a new rule enabling the transfer of prescriptions by pharmacy techs as opposed to only pharmacists. This alone led to savings of $15 million. The small-business lens contributed savings of $75 million for over 5,000 businesses. A set of thirty-four new service standards assisted over 320,000 annual transactions.

"WESTERN WEALTH IS NOT A GIVEN"

I DID NOT VIEW our push on the economy as a series of measures, but rather as a determined effort to change the long-term trajectory of the country. That was my thinking when, in late January 2012, I travelled with Ministers Jim Flaherty and Ed Fast to Davos, Switzerland, to address the World Economic Forum (WEF).

There was great interest internationally in how Canada had made its way so effectively through the global financial crisis and its aftermath. I viewed this as a chance to underline the reasons for our success. It also gave me an opportunity to demonstrate to Canadians and the world's financial community that our majority government had a long-term, forward-looking plan for the country. Most importantly, it was an occasion to deliver a message of caution—that our success to date had been far from adequate and could not become a reason for complacency.

I had decided to give this speech outside the country because of a conversation Barack Obama and I once had. Our shared observation was that, if you want to draw serious attention to your government's policy, you needed to do it outside your capital city and its press corps. Their coverage will invariably fixate on the "strategies" and "real meaning" of what you are saying rather than the substance.

Besides, the WEF had been regularly praising Canada's economic performance, so I knew I would have a receptive audience. It had observed that Canada had the strongest, most stable banking system in the world, and *Forbes* magazine had just said that Canada was the best country in the world in which to do business. The International Monetary Fund and the Organisation for Economic Co-operation and Development, both major international financial institutions, had predicted that Canada was going to lead the G7 growth for the next couple of years.

We had set the lowest tax rate on new business investment in the G7. We also had the lowest debt-to-GDP ratio in the G7, which was also one of the lowest in the developed world by a wide margin. This was at a time when much of Europe was still wracked by the debt crisis. We were leading on international trade as well. We were cutting tariffs and even eliminating them in many cases. We were signing trade deals. And we had all but wrapped up our emergency stimulus programs, having executed them far quicker than most countries. With all that, the Canadian economy was now at a point where we could take a longer-term focus. That included making future-oriented investments and eliminating our deficit without raising taxes.

The real message, though, was in the second part of my speech, when I stated that "Western wealth is not a given." The truth was that, notwithstanding Canada's strong performance in relative terms, the developed world was not doing very well overall economically. To sustain our standards of living and generous social programs, we needed to do better going forward, especially given the new, rising giants in the world.

I had a long-standing concern that in our advanced democratic societies, we had come to casually assume that our comparative wealth was some kind of birthright, that no matter what we did in terms of economic policy or performance, we would remain the wealthiest in the world. That is not true. Countries in Asia—like Singapore, for example—were already approaching, if not surpassing, us. Complacency simply could not be an option. Our comparative wealth was earned through many decades of superior policy and superior productivity, and if we ceased to deliver on both those fronts, our wealth would gradually wither away.

Needless to say, my speech received a range of reactions, with those on the left predictably and precisely reflecting the "entitlement to wealth" mentality that I was worried about. Nevertheless, those were my very real concerns. Writing this nearly a decade and a half later, my worries are exponentially higher, and the West's comparative standing is, in fact, slowly slipping away.

I used the Davos speech to signal one important change that was coming in terms of our fiscal sustainability. Our plan, already approved by Cabinet, was to gradually raise the age of eligibility for Old Age Security (OAS). This was not about doing something that would in any way benefit or serve any immediate interest of my Government, as the impacts would be long after I left office. It was about fixing a serious long-term financial problem for the country.

Here is the problem: OAS, unlike the Canada Pension Plan (CPP), is a non-contributory program; it has no fund and has not had one for decades. It is also virtually universal at age sixty-five (although a small portion is clawed back through the tax system from those with very high incomes). In this way, it is different from the Guaranteed Income Supplement (GIS), which is also non-contributory but is paid only to poorer seniors. The bottom line is that OAS is an unfunded pension plan that was, and remains, the single biggest federal program in any given year. Our analysis was that it would continue to grow relative to our economy for the foreseeable future.

How did we get into this mess? When sixty-five was made the universal age of eligibility for OAS in 1967, the average person only lived to seventy-two.* Today that number is eighty-two, meaning on average we pay the pension two and a half times longer. And we pay it to a lot more people. Less than 8 per cent of the population was over sixty-five in 1967; today it is nearly 20 per cent. That means the relative cost of OAS is over six times what it was in 1967, with a shrinking percentage of the population paying for that cost. These numbers are only going to deteriorate.

We legislated a rise of the OAS eligibility age to sixty-seven—something many other countries had already done. We also allowed for earlier receipt at a reduced amount (and later receipt at an increased one). But this higher age threshold would only begin to take effect in 2023—over a decade later—and it would not be fully phased in until 2029. This would ensure that future generations had lots of time to plan for the adjustment. Neither GIS nor CPP were affected by this reform.

We knew this would be fodder for opposition demagoguery, and they did their best. Yet, with present OAS recipients and the next generation untouched by the changes, we figured the public would accept it once the dust settled. That is what happened. That was partly because most

* When the original old age pension was first introduced in 1927—it was only for the poor then—the age of eligibility was seventy. That was at a time when life expectancy was fifty-eight years!

mainstream policy analysts found this a prudent measure for long-term fiscal planning. Left on its own, this adjustment would have benefitted the nation's finances and increased the security of the country's pension system going forward. Sadly, and foolishly, our successors repealed the plan shortly after coming to power.

That was, by the way, my second and last appearance at Davos. I had first attended in 2010 to see what it was like, as the WEF always offered the opportunity to have a wide range of bilateral meetings in one place, given the global attendance.

Davos has gradually moved from being a forum to becoming a club and from being a place where ideas are exchanged to a platform where an agenda is pushed. That agenda increasingly reflects only the narrow interests of its globalist, elitist attendees. It is not merely divorced from the interests of ordinary working people; it is increasingly contemptuous of them. And it is just as contemptuous of democratic institutions, urging the use of central banks and other unelected transnational bodies to impose its thinking on electorates.

While, in many ways, I admire what Professor Schwab achieved in setting up the WEF, if I were the prime minister today, I would remove the Government of Canada from participation at Davos.*

"RESPONSIBLE RESOURCE DEVELOPMENT"

ON MARCH 29, 2012, Minister Flaherty delivered the first (new) budget of our majority government. We titled it "Economic Action Plan – Jobs, Growth and Long-term Prosperity." Even though the original Economic Action Plan had been wrapped up for almost a year, we decided that this branding remained useful for telling people what we were doing.

---

* In fact, as board chair of AIMCo, the Alberta government's pension and sovereign wealth investment agency, I have removed that organization from the World Economic Forum.

Our "Deficit Reduction Action Plan" (DRAP, an unfortunate acronym) clearly signalled that deficit reduction was moving to centre stage. But our approach, as I have said before, was by no means all about cutting budgets. In fact, our plan was to hold the line on spending overall, while putting the emphasis on getting the economy to generate new growth, jobs, and tax revenues over time.

An even more critical initiative in this budget was our plan for "Responsible Resource Development." This involved a comprehensive streamlining of regulations across a range of departments and processes related to the resource sectors. Our goal was to attract investment and kick-start this critical component of the Canadian economy. It would be a massive effort, requiring the amendment of fifty pieces of legislation. It was also a shining example of what we could now do in a majority parliament, given that the combination of left-wing opposition parties had made such changes impossible before.

These reforms were desperately needed. It was increasingly obvious that the previous Liberal governments had, for thirteen years, added layer upon layer of regulatory requirements and processes to any kind of natural resource project. These truly Byzantine rules virtually ensured that determined opponents could hold something up for years, preventing a decision being rendered in any kind of timeline required by investors. That was unreasonable, and it was giving Canada a bad name in the international investment community.

We already had the experience of drastically streamlined regulations during the stimulus phase of the original Economic Action Plan. Those regulatory processes had created precisely zero problems, demonstrating that far lighter evaluations and faster decisions were possible. Here was a golden opportunity to apply those learnings to the major resource projects the country needed to see done.

There were the expected critics among the opposition to this initiative, anti-development "environmentalists" and the like. They included those professionals who earned their livings from the long and burdensome processes. They argued that our new approaches were designed to circumvent proper scientific and regulatory scrutiny and that projects would be rubber-stamped. That was nonsense.

In fact, our government regularly turned down projects on the basis of good environmental science and expert recommendations. What we did do, though, was ensure that the review processes could reach a science-based decision, whether positive or negative, within two years. This was intended to give some form of certainty to resource investors. Judging by the uptick in major resource project applications, during our time in office things started to flow.

A HOCKEY STAR BRIDGES TWO COUNTRIES

ON JUNE 15, 2012, our Government announced yet another major economic initiative and one of Canada's largest infrastructure projects ever: a new bridge connecting Windsor and Detroit. This was a very big deal.

We did not invent this idea. The previous government as early as 2003–2004 had recognized the need for another major Canada-U.S. crossing and kick-started conceptual studies on the project. The necessity of actually getting it done was crystal clear to us, but its importance was little recognized by our neighbour to the south. I had several conversations with President Bush before he truly grasped the significance of the project and the enormity of the obstacles it faced.

The Windsor-Detroit crossing is the largest individual trade corridor in the world. Every single day, dollar-wise, more trade goes between these two cities than almost at any other international trade crossing in the world. Yet it is mostly done through one connection, the Ambassador Bridge, privately owned by one Manuel (Manny) Maroun.

This was a major problem—and a major economic threat to Canada—for several reasons. First, the bridge had been allowed to deteriorate to a significant degree. Second, any failure of the bridge, whether through structural compromise or terrorist attack, could effectively throttle much of the total volume of Canada-U.S. trade in an instant. Finally, we had to deal with the reality of a determined owner who, over decades, had made it his business to block any proposals that would cut into his lucrative ownership.

Maroun had become very adept in his objective, using every means he could. He lobbied complex U.S. decision-making processes at the municipal, state, and federal levels. He engaged in extensive court action and regulatory challenges against rival proposals. And he funded deceptive media and public relations campaigns.

I concluded early on that there was no reasonable price at which Maroun would make a deal. In effect, he appeared to take the view that he did not just own the bridge; he believed he was the owner of the Detroit-Windsor crossing itself. That was something unequivocally contrary to Canada's national interests. I thus decided that, on our side, come hell or high water, we would do whatever was necessary to break Maroun's quasi-monopoly.* We would open our wallets, use every option, and dig in for a long war.

Fortunately, there was no doubt of the need for this bridge on our side of the river. Nor were there any illusions about the massive effort that would be required. In fact, even before our announcement, the McGuinty Government at Queen's Park had proactively begun building the major connector roads to where we hoped to build the new bridge.

Key to our efforts would be neutralizing influential American political figures or even getting them on our side. That is why I continually raised the issue with President Bush. But the most important breakthrough was with the governor of Michigan, Rick Snyder. More a businessman than a politician, Snyder was close enough to the situation to understand the importance of a new bridge, but he was far enough away not to be ensnared in Maroun's Detroit political operation.

Snyder knew that Maroun's tentacles in the legislature would make it impossible to pass new-bridge initiatives in the near future. He had, however, plenty of executive power over regulatory matters. Thus, we made a

---

* Technically, the bridge is not a monopoly because other bridges make the crossing, though at far greater distance and much lower volume. There is also a tunnel, jointly owned by the cities of Windsor and Detroit. However, all these combined comprised only a fraction of the trade crossing the Ambassador Bridge.

deal. If he cleared the regulatory path, the Government of Canada would be solely responsible for the bridge authority. We would, on both sides of the river, build the bridge, operate the bridge, and collect the tolls that would pay for our investment.

On that day in June, the governor thus joined me on stage for the announcement. Given the complexities on his side, it was a bold decision. The next year, when the federal baton passed to the Obama administration, we got an equally strong ally in Washington. We soon received a critical permit from the president, and at every step U.S. Ambassador David Jacobson, a great friend of Canada, did solid work to coordinate with us on myriad aspects of the project.

The right to set up the bridge authority now allowed us, over the next few years, to buy the necessary land on both sides of the river. After that, there would be a process to pick construction consortiums to do the actual building, and every step of the process would require years of environmental and mechanical approvals. Of course, the old bridge owner would do what he could legally and politically to obstruct us. But it was now all just a matter of time and money; we had the allies and the tools necessary to eventually grind Maroun into the ground.

By my last year in office, 2015, it was obvious the bridge would eventually be built, and so we started to think about its name. I do not mind stating that the name was my idea.* As I said earlier, branding is not my speciality. But I understood enough to know that the working name for the structure—the Detroit River International Crossing or DRIC—was uninspiring Ottawa bureaucratese at its finest.

I asked myself, what connects Canada and Detroit? It hit me—one of the greatest players—some think the greatest player—our national winter sport has ever known. Gordie Howe was Canadian, born in Floral, Saskatchewan,

---

* I gather the idea had appeared earlier in the media, but I was unaware of it. Transport Minister Denis Lebel also suggested it at about the same time. In short, the idea may have been mine, but I was not alone in thinking it.

but he spent the lion's share of his career, including his four Stanley Cup–winning seasons, with the Detroit Red Wings. I picked up the phone and called Governor Snyder. He loved the name! We decided on a second joint public appearance.

On May 14, 2015, the governor and I formally announced the soon-to-be-started "Gordie Howe International Bridge." Sadly, Mr. Howe was not well enough to attend the event, but his family came and reported that he had been informed and was pleased about the announcement. The name has really taken hold. Completed by our successors, the bridge will do for our two countries economically what Gordie had done athletically for hockey with his skill, his stick, and his strength (plus his elbows and fists).

CANADA NEEDS SHIPS!

ON JANUARY 12, 2012, I travelled to Halifax to announce a major milestone in our efforts to rebuild Canada's military and enhance our sovereignty. It was an agreement-in-principle with Irving Shipbuilding Inc. to lead our National Shipbuilding Procurement Strategy.† For years, a large part of the Royal Canadian Navy had essentially been rusting out. Even compared to the Canadian Army and Royal Canadian Air Force, it had been underinvested in for decades. We were at the point where a large percentage of the Navy fleet would have to be replaced. The same applied to the Coast Guard.

Major military procurements of this sort, as I discovered in conversations with other national leaders, are always tricky propositions, inevitably plagued by government infighting. There are three sets of interests in play. First, there is the taxpayer, represented in Ottawa by the Public Works Department and,

† The National Shipbuilding Procurement Strategy was announced in Ottawa on June 3, 2010, by Rona Ambrose, who, as minister of public works and government services, had the lead on this initiative. She was joined on that occasion by Peter MacKay, minister of national defence, and Gail Shea, minister of fisheries and oceans.

to some degree, the Treasury Board. They are looking for the best quality at the lowest prices, and they believe that a competitive process is the best way to get what they want. Second are the users, usually elements of the Canadian Armed Forces, who want the best equipment possible plus interoperability with our key allies. Cost is not a significant concern for them; they have a strong idea of what the best option is, and they want it sooner rather than later. Their view is generally that competitive processes delay procurement, making them time-consuming and cost-increasing. Finally, there are the interests of the Industry department, representing the Canadian economy more broadly. They prefer options that see production, or at least parts of it, done within the country to provide jobs and regional economic benefits.

While all these considerations are important, reconciling them is extremely difficult. Indeed, within government, they often result in war (mostly figuratively speaking) between the various departments and the interests they represent. To manage the procurements and their conflicts, governments will typically have three options: hold a genuine competition, do a sole-source contract, or—what happens far too often, in my opinion—proceed with a "fake competition." That is where technical requirements are exhaustively spelled out, bidders are encouraged to apply, and their proposals thoroughly examined. There is only one small catch: in the end, it is all designed so that only one company or supply chain can win. But governments have at least covered their behinds and can claim that there was a competition.

By comparison, our Shipbuilding Procurement Strategy was unique. Because almost the entire Navy and Coast Guard were being rebuilt, the amounts involved would be huge—some $35 billion over a couple of decades.* These procurements were thus not one-offs or even a series of one-offs. Given the unprecedented nature of that reality (at least post–World War II), we concluded that rebuilding our national industrial and shipyard construction

* These numbers have continued to grow under our successors. A 2021 Parliamentary Budget Office report estimates that construction costs have since ballooned to $84.5 billion, with total operating costs over the lifetime of the fleet of $306 billion.

capacity had to be a priority of the initiative. It was a sector that had shrunk considerably over the preceding decades.

Under our process, we invited Canada's major shipyards to engage in a competitive bidding process. Irving Shipbuilding of Halifax won and had been awarded the biggest single package—the "Combat Package"—which consisted of the major naval elements. Vancouver's Seaspan was picked second for the "Non-Combat Package"—the core of the Coast Guard's needs. There would also be work on smaller vessels outside the Royal Canadian Navy and Coast Guard (such as for Fisheries and Oceans) and myriad subcontracting opportunities, all of which would go to the remaining Canadian shipyards[†]. Halifax was thus the first of many announcements to come.

A distinctive feature of our shipbuilding strategy was the built-in capacity for broad and ongoing oversight. We assembled a supervisory committee consisting of the Privy Council Office (PCO)/Prime Minister's Office (PMO), the relevant departments, and the major contracting interests to monitor the work. Gathered around one "big table," this committee was designed to move beyond the usual bickering and finger pointing to identify issues early and hash them out before they became large, expensive, and potentially existential problems. This strategy was largely successful in keeping budgets and timetables within reasonable limits.[‡]

Ironically, scandal did arise in the shipbuilding strategy, but very strangely and only after our successors took over the program. I am referring to the saga of Vice-Admiral Mark Norman. It was a truly shameful serious of events, in which the role played by the Liberal Government has never been fully revealed.

Here is how that scandal unfolded from my point of view. In 2015, near the end of our Government, we found ourselves without either of our two joint support ships, which are essential for any navy's overseas operations.

† As I recall, three other shipyards were of sufficient size to bid on parts of the work. There are other, much smaller operations.

‡ My understanding is that, since 2015, this advisory committee has vanished, and we are back to the old, one-off approach that has bedevilled governments—since the Phoenicians, I suppose.

One was overdue for retirement, and the other was suddenly destroyed by a catastrophic fire. We arranged to get short-term assistance from the United States, but this was untenable over even the mid-term. To make matters worse, Canada's major shipyards were already totally booked (and already behind schedule) in executing the Shipbuilding Procurement Strategy.

This situation was as dire as it was embarrassing. To the rescue sailed the Davie Shipyard of Quebec City. On its own initiative, it proposed what appeared to be a cost-effective plan to convert some existing civilian ships into military support ships that they would then lease to us for a period. It not only looked like a reasonable deal, it was the only deal on the table. As this was a full-fledged crisis, our government decided to execute a sole-source contract outside the shipbuilding program. It is highly ironic that, of all the shipbuilding projects we worked on, this sole-source project was the only one that came in on time and on budget.* Full credit is due Davie for this accomplishment.

But that is not where the story ended. Some three years later, on June 27, 2018, Vice-Admiral Norman was removed from command by the Liberal Government, accused of breach of trust for ostensibly leaking sensitive information related to the government's purchase of the interim supply ship from Davie.† Norman was later charged—a "prediction" made on two occasions by Justin Trudeau. Norman's career was wrecked, and for three more years, his name and reputation were dragged through the mud.

---

* When I look back at some of the most effective military contracts that we undertook in terms of getting things done on time and on budget, it seems that emergency, sole-source contracting was usually involved. Our procurement efforts in those cases invariably involved getting off-the-shelf products, thus avoiding significant customization. So much for careful planning!

† On November 19, 2015, the CBC revealed details from a Liberal Cabinet committee meeting that discussed the Trudeau Government's decision to delay approval of a $668-million contract that my Government had concluded with the Davie Shipyard. The RCMP investigated the leak for nearly two years before Norman was charged with breach of trust and relieved of his position.

From the outset, I had found this peculiar. I do not recall Vice-Admiral Norman being a terribly vocal proponent of the sole-source strategy when it was first suggested. He was certainly not the moving force behind the Davie proposal. In any case, his defence in court was hindered by the Government of Canada invoking Cabinet Confidence privilege over its own documents.

Through what we believed were PCO and PMO channels, the Trudeau Government told media that they could not release documents because I was refusing to disclose any Cabinet confidences of my Government. This was not true; my view had never been sought. However, I had already indicated informally to PCO that I would not block disclosure of relevant material if asked. After all, our Government's private deliberations on the matter were no different than our public statements; we had nothing to hide. Yet, in court, government lawyers falsely claimed that my Government had blocked access to Cabinet records.[‡] I thus prepared a statement for Norman's lawyer, Marie Heinen, contradicting the Government's claim, to be read in court.

With the Liberals then faced with having no credible reason not to release their own Cabinet confidences, the government dropped the charges. Suddenly we were told that there was "no reasonable prospect of conviction" of Mark Norman. He later received an apology and a settlement. Still, there remains much for my successor to explain in this regard. Maybe he will do so when he writes his own memoirs.

JUSTICE

WE HAD ACCOMPLISHED a lot on criminal justice reform. Still, in the first two parliaments many things had been either blocked by the opposition

‡ To be clear, while the statements of the government lawyers were false, I am not saying that they were lying. It is quite possible that they were not told by the PCO that I would consent to the release of relevant material.

or slow rolled. We had a substantial backlog in the legislation we had previously introduced.

On March 12, 2012, we sent out a strong signal that this would not continue. That was the day we introduced Bill C-10, the Safe Streets and Communities Act, a comprehensive bill that addressed a substantial part of our backlog. It was the "looking back" portion. As for moving ahead, we introduced measures throughout our third Parliament that reflected how seriously we took criminal justice reform.

We addressed "making the punishment fit the crime" by establishing mandatory minimum sentences for certain crimes, including specific types of child sex offences and drug trafficking offences. We also toughened up sentences for a small but growing element of the criminal youth population who were serious, repeat, violent offenders. Later, we introduced measures to protect children from internet predators and cyberbullying, and we strengthened penalties relating to elder abuse.

On "innocent after proven guilty," we established a guiding principle in legislation for Corrections Canada and for the National Parole Board—that the protection of society was to be the paramount consideration. You would think this would be obvious but, at the time, was not. We also ended a lot of the conditional sentencing around child sex crimes and ended parole for those who committed new serious offences. (Believe it or not, prior to our legislation you could commit an offence while on parole and stay on parole!)

In subsequent legislation, we cracked down on illegal drugs inside prisons. I found it hard to believe there would be as much tolerance for the drug trade within prison as there was. Surely, if the system claimed to be concerned about rehabilitation, you would be worried about drug abuse within prisons. Another undertaking was tightening the definitions around the "not criminally responsible" defence. The principle that some people cannot be held criminally responsible for their actions for reasons such as mental illness goes back centuries. However, in our judgment, the definitions had become far too broad.

We also paid heed to improving the administration of justice, clarifying how foreign criminals should be dealt with, and making it less complicated to transfer offenders internationally. You obviously cannot transfer people to places where they would be tortured upon arrival. However, that only applied to a tiny subgroup of offenders. We also made it more difficult for certain types of suspected foreign criminals to work in Canada and easily integrate into society.

Later, we invested in additional tools to deal with the commission of crime online. We had had a lot of pushback when we originally tried to address this. Some of the concerns were legitimate, but there did appear to be a widely held view at the time that the internet should be a completely free space, devoid of any rules or law. But the internet was never such an ungoverned space. Various internet companies ran it and were using it to mine and sell personal information from day one. My view was always that what was illegal outside the net should be illegal on the net. What we did was make it easier for the police to investigate criminal conduct online.

Finally, we enhanced victims' rights. These were some of my proudest initiatives as they often followed from meetings with real victims and hearing their stories. I will never forget being in Burnaby, B.C., in early 2013 announcing changes to the Criminal Code to toughen restrictions on those found not criminally responsible for their actions. There I spent time with Darcie Clarke, whose three children had been murdered by her ex-husband Allan Schoenborn in 2008. The magnitude of her loss is unthinkable. Yet, by 2012, Schoenborn was eligible for day passes. We simply had to do better. We had to put the rights of victims first.

In April 2014, I travelled to Mississauga to announce the Victims Bill of Rights, a series of legal changes to codify the rights of victims, making it easier for vulnerable witnesses to testify and access information about cases. Joining me that day was Justice Minister Peter MacKay, Public Safety Minister Steven Blaney, and Senator Pierre-Hugues Boisvenu. Senator Boisvenu had suffered the horror of having a child murdered and had thereafter been a fearless advocate for the rights of victims and a powerful voice within our team to keep moving our agenda forward.

We also ensured that victims had the right to give impact statements at parole hearings. Of significant relevance even today, we introduced measures to allow victims of terrorism to sue the sponsors of terrorism. That was inspired by the experience of Canada's 9/11 victims' families who, unconscionably, had to fight for that right against foreign affairs and legal establishments determined to look the other way.

In subsequent legislation, we strengthened protections around citizen's arrest and the right to engage in self-defence. The legislation was inspired by a ludicrous case in Toronto where store owner David Chen was prosecuted for apprehending a thief at his establishment. The case caused great public outrage because it created the impression that the police were more interested in protecting perpetrators than victims. (Unfortunately, sometimes police do see citizens defending themselves as a challenge to their own authority.) We also strengthened the right of victims to go after their assailants for costs.

As extensive as this list is, it does not cover everything, for our Conservative MPs were eager to introduce private members' bills (PMBs) to address crime issues that were important to their local constituencies. Their right to do so had been championed by the Reform Party. Its pressure had helped change parliamentary rules so that it was easier for backbenchers to advance legislation without having the support of the government. Thus, from the 1990s, we began to see PMBs pass. That had rarely occurred previously.

With a majority, we now took steps to make that process even smoother. It resulted in many PMBs making their way through Parliament and being signed into law. Almost all of these were introduced by Conservative members, who had in most cases negotiated with the relevant minister for support. The same right applied to all members from all parties. In fact, justice-related PMBs became so popular and numerous that successive justice ministers pled in caucus for fewer of these, as they threatened to overload the government's broader legislative agenda.*

---

* Nonetheless, some very good work was done on this front. Notable examples were: PMBs by David Sweet and the late Mark Warawa toughening conditional sentencing rules; Blake Richards's legislation around the deliberate concealment of identity during public disturbances (which now seems somewhat quaint after Covid-19); Joy Smith's important

Even taking all this additional private members' legislation into account, we did nowhere near what was required in terms of criminal justice reform. We left an awful lot of unpassed legislation on the agenda when we were defeated in 2015. On top of that, as I have said before, decades of misguided philosophy (not to mentioned wrong-headed court rulings) have made the need for additional reforms virtually bottomless.

ENDING THE LONG-GUN REGISTRY

ANY DISCUSSION OF CRIMINAL justice reform would be incomplete without talking about our elimination of the long-gun registry. Introduced by the Chrétien Government in 1995, it had experienced unrelenting opposition from law-abiding hunters, farmers, and gun owners across the country ever since. In fact, the slogan "Remember C-68 when you vote!" had become a rallying cry for successive Reform/Alliance, Progressive Conservative, and Conservative candidates ever since, especially in rural ridings.

Of course, I had been raised in urban Canada, and despite spending much time on my grandparents' farm, I had never fired or even handled a gun in my life. Nor had I given the issue much thought before joining the Reform Party. In fact, when the Liberals introduced C-68, I initially thought it did not sound like a totally bad idea. After all, we already had a handgun registry. I was taken aback at the vehemence of the opposition initially expressed by some of my colleagues.

Consistent with Reform policy, I did a survey of my constituents on the issue. I found that a very clear majority agreed with the registry in principle.

---

work on human trafficking; Roxanne James's bill restricting the right of prisoners to bog down the justice system with endless complaints; Parm Gill's legislation on gang recruitment; Earl's Dreeshen's initiative to criminalize impersonating a peace officer; and long-time Reform-Alliance-Conservative colleague Dick Harris's PMB barring prisoners from receiving Employment Insurance while in prison (yes, that really was happening).

As a result, I voted for Bill C-68 at second reading. I was the only Reformer to do so, and although I was never treated disrespectfully by my colleagues in any way, I admit that I felt very uncomfortable being in that position.

I also felt uninformed. Therefore, I set out to learn more about the issue. I read material from the advocates on both sides. Frankly, little of it was very persuasive. I attended several of the committee hearings, and I was even occasionally placed as an alternate by the party on the committee. The testimony I heard was eye-opening.

The more I listened to the evidence, the more it became clear that the bill's proclaimed purpose—to prevent crime—made no sense. Statistics show that, without a doubt, most firearms crime is committed using handguns, the vast majority of which are smuggled into our country (usually from the United States). It is possible that registration might assist police in investigating some felonies, but long guns—hunting rifles and the like—are just not common weapons of choice for the commission of crime.

The further problem was the sheer number of long guns out there. They would count in the millions. Moreover, many of them did not have serial numbers or easily identifiable markings. That meant that even the registry's utility as an investigative tool would be extremely limited. This also suggested that the costs of implementation would be enormous.

On the other side, as I listened to gun-control advocates address these issues, I became increasingly concerned about their real motives. I soon concluded that the use of the registry for eventual confiscation was not some "gun-nut conspiracy theory." In fact, it was the only real purpose that a long-gun registry could possibly have, given the objectives of gun-control advocates. As a conservative, I found the notion of such broad state action against personal property for such vaguely defined purposes unjustifiable.

Armed, so to speak, with my better understanding, I undertook another survey of my constituents prior to third reading. To it I attached a covering letter stating the reasons why I had come to personally oppose Bill C-68. Prominent among those was my prediction that the registry would eventually cost at least $50 million, some twenty-five times what the Liberal Government was estimating it would cost.

A few of my constituents thought I was exaggerating wildly. But the ultimate cost was literally over one thousand times the government's estimates at roughly two billion dollars. In the end, my constituents let me off the hook and concurred with my opposing the bill. I was pleased by that, because otherwise my second reading vote would have been my record, and that was one of the worst votes I ever cast in the House of Commons.

I was even more pleased when, on April 5, 2012, our Government's bill scrapping the registry passed the Senate and received Royal Assent. But I went further. I brought in technical experts to make sure the registry's data was deleted and irretrievable. I did not want a future Liberal government bringing the registry back in through the back door—something that, in numerous ways, they have been trying to do since 2015.

Given my own spotty record on the long-gun registry legislation, most of the credit for its abolition is due to other people. Many members of our caucus were dogged in their pursuit of this issue from the beginning. I think, for instance, of Jack Ramsay, the Reform MP from Crowfoot, who was our earliest official spokesperson on the issue. Lee Morrison later carried the torch for Reform. Over time, the charge was increasingly led by Garry Breitkreuz of Yorkton–Melville. Garry argued passionately about the issues of cost and effectiveness from day one and never dropped it. If there was ever an example in politics of a guy sticking to his guns, figurately and literally, and eventually getting his point through, it was Garry on the issue of the long-gun registry. Fittingly, when the vote finally passed, the ovation that he got was very moving. Credit is also due Candice Bergen (Portage–Lisgar), who was a very effective spokesperson during the final debate and, of course, would eventually become interim leader of our party. Finally, I would be remiss not to mention Justice Minister Rob Nicholson, who guided this important legislation to completion. Rob was a stalwart throughout our Government—a workhorse, a team player, and always a thoughtful source of advice.

Unfortunately, while the gun registry per se has not returned, anti-gun legislation today has gone well beyond Chrétien-era extremes. The great irony, of course, is that those who impose more gun control invariably reduce the penalties for actual gun crime. That has also happened. Consistent with the left-wing notions of criminal justice I have talked about, their view is inevitably that guns kill people and that people do not really kill people. Therefore, get rid of the tool, and the violence will disappear. Once again, it is that deeply rooted delusion that people are not responsible for their actions; "societal" things are. In this case, inanimate objects apparently are.

The reality is that a lot of people use guns for legitimate reasons. Besides sport, they are used in hunting, agriculture, and other rural occupations for predator control and animal husbandry. In many rural and remote areas, a gun may well be necessary for personal security as well. Particularly for Indigenous people, many make their living using firearms. Taking their guns essentially means removing their livelihood, their ability to support their families, and their right to live according to their culture.

This reminds me of an amusing story. It goes back to the summer of 2011—July 11 to be precise. That was the day when, at Stand Off, Alberta, I was inducted into the Kainai First Nation (the Blood Tribe) as an Honorary Chief. It was mainly for having delivered the residential schools apology. Many were curious what the medicine man had said to me privately while ritually painting my face. It was: "Now, promise me, Prime Minister, that you will keep your word, and you really will get rid of that long-gun registry!"

My personal views on guns have continued to evolve. Since leaving office, I have taken the required gun training courses and am now the proud owner of a Possession and Acquisition Licence (PAL). It permits me to own a gun, should I choose to. I have no intention of ever hunting. Although my Government supported the hunting industry—it is a big business in rural Canada—I personally do not believe in killing animals for sport.

I do believe, because it is people who commit crimes, that the screening and licensing of gun owners is very important. I also supported and still support a handgun registry. It was relatively inexpensive to run given that handguns are far less common than long guns. They are also easily concealable and the main weapons used in gun crime. But I do not support banning them, although I think it is reasonable to limit the types of weapons people can have, in line with the legitimate private uses of firearms. No one would suggest you should be able to build an atomic bomb in your backyard, and following that logic, I do not know why ordinary citizens would need military-grade weapons.

My views are consistent with conservative principles, based on common sense and experience, demonstrated by history and tradition, and not limiting personal freedom without good reason. Perhaps, however, in this sense it is different to be an American conservative than a Canadian conservative. Many Americans believe that their freedoms are protected by being able to take up arms against the state, whereas our history is that it is the state that has been needed to preserve our freedom from violent elements. In any case, when some argue that a wide range of personal weaponry is needed to build a private militia, that is where we part company.

MARKETING FREEDOM FOR WESTERN GRAIN FARMERS

ONE SPECIAL MEMORY from the summer of 2012 occurred at the family farm of the late Art Walde near Kindersley, Saskatchewan. That was the day we brought together hundreds of Western Canadian grain farmers to celebrate their marketing freedom. It was a fight many of them had been involved in for decades.

Back in 1968, Pierre Trudeau had asked some protesting Western farmers, "Why should I sell your wheat?" To the average Eastern urban listener, including this nine-year-old boy, it sounded like a reasonable question. But it was not—not in the least. The federal government, through the Canadian Wheat Board, had made itself the only legal seller of Western grain. The farmers were not allowed to sell it themselves.

The Canadian Wheat Board (CWB) had long been wrapped in a web of such misperception and misinformation. It was claimed it had been introduced to get higher prices for farmers. It was not. The monopoly was introduced during World War II to keep grain prices down. The CWB was said to have delivered huge benefits to the country through Cold War wheat sales to the Soviets and the Chinese. In fact, those sales had been subsidized by federal taxpayers. Some dairy and poultry farmers believed that the Wheat Board helped protect their system of supply management. That was also false. The CWB, though a compulsory seller, did not manage supply. And the Wheat Board itself contended that its monopoly power allowed it to command price premiums. The reality was that its ability to deliver large-scale, high-quality product at low prices is what gave it marketing power.

Among Western grain farmers there had always been opponents of the Wheat Board's monopoly position. Still, for many decades, when the industry was dominated by small producers with little understanding of global grain markets, many found the CWB to be a reasonable arrangement. But in the 1990s, a new generation of younger, better-educated, larger-scale producers, with computer access to real-time marketing data, began to seriously challenge the status quo.

To prove they could get better prices on their own, some farmers staged symbolic protests by taking individual bags of grain over the Canada-U.S. border to sell. These farmers were charged, hauled into court—literally in chains—convicted, fined, and jailed. Their equipment was seized and their livelihoods threatened. (Once again, this was a demonstration on how much more seriously the state often treats trivial acts against itself than violent crime against private citizens.)

As the battle went on, the CWB also tried some "carrots": the Wheat Board would be "democratized." Farmers could be elected to positions. The only problem was that the elections were a sham—slanted in numerous ways to make it extremely difficult for "marketing freedom" candidates to win. When one did, he would invariably be threatened by CWB attorneys against speaking out in favour of ending the monopoly.

Despite my urban background, this is how I became involved in the issue. Even before I became its president, the National Citizens Coalition had assisted farmers charged under the Canadian Wheat Board Act. Under my leadership, with the financial assistance of pro-freedom farmers, we ran ads in Western Canada pushing for an end to the monopoly. That led, on one occasion, to a call from a CWB lawyer, threatening to charge me with violating the Wheat Board's rules limiting farmers' ability to spend money on the issue (yes, the Wheat Board really had such rules!). I did not stop, and the CWB wisely decided not to follow through on the threat.

Over the years, the CWB's monopoly power steadily lost support. By the time we had a majority government, it was virtually non-existent among full-time producers. The only bastion for the Wheat Board was Winnipeg, where its head office was located. It was another example of how the only real clientele of a government program had become the people who worked for it.

Our Liberal successors have never contemplated bringing back the monopoly. As I predicted at the time, no one would ever want to go back to that arrangement once it was repealed. The subsequent benefits have been substantial—not just for primary producers. As PM, I was able to announce more than one secondary food processing business that started up in the West after the end of monopoly arrangement.

Ironically, though, the CWB had one very important legacy—the diversification of Western agriculture. From canola to organics to pulses, farmers sought to develop other crops to get out from under the Wheat Board monopoly. Talk about the law of unintended consequences!

While a couple of generations of rural Western MPs fought the monopoly, I must single out a few for special mention. Charlie Mayer, a Progressive Conservative Cabinet minister under Brian Mulroney, was the first politician to begin to loosen the monopoly. The late Jake Hoeppner was the most vocal among Reform MPs, raising the profile on the issue back in the 1990s among those of us who did not understand it. My former Reform colleague Elwin Hermanson—the first leader of the Saskatchewan Party—was also very effective. Of course, Gerry Ritz was the agriculture minister during most of my Government. The most successful federal ag minister in a century, he not only got the Wheat Board legislation through Parliament but also developed the plan that allowed us to successfully privatize the CWB (which we had initially thought was worthless without the monopoly). He was ably assisted by his parliamentary secretary David Anderson, who was a backbone of our Saskatchewan caucus during all my years as leader. Finally, farmers Jeff Neilson, Henry Vos, and especially Jim Chatenay continued to advocate for marketing freedom as CWB directors, despite the ongoing legal threats they faced.

That day at the Walde farm was memorable for another reason. I announced the pardoning of the farmers convicted under the Wheat Board monopoly. I was able to do both agricultural reform and criminal justice reform at the same time. It was truly a day to celebrate. I will not forget it.

20

FOREIGN AFFAIRS, TRADE, AND INTERNATIONAL ISSUES 2011–2012

AS IN DOMESTIC AFFAIRS, the new majority mandate offered us the opportunity to advance our priorities in international relations more deeply. Without immediate electoral distractions, our highest objective was to aggressively advance our trade agenda. Our international aid policies also got attention. Still, there would be the inevitable "events," such as those impacting global peace and security. And the global financial crisis was having a very long tail in Europe.

THE EUROZONE CRISIS

DURING THE SPRING and summer of 2011, just as the threat of a world economic meltdown seemed to be receding, another Hydra-like threat began to appear. This was the Eurozone Crisis, also referred to as the European sovereign debt crisis. From 2009 onward, a number of EU countries—most specifically Greece, Portugal, Ireland, Spain, and Cyprus—would face severe stresses in the repayment or refinancing of their government debts.

A major sovereign default in Europe would clearly have very negative implications for the global economy as a whole. The matter had thus been discussed at the G8 Summit in Deauville, France, in May, with an increasing focus on Greece. Coincidentally, I would be travelling to that country immediately following the summit.

The visit to Greece aimed to strengthen the cultural ties between our countries. That would be reflected in a strong Greek-Canadian delegation, featuring key caucus members like Minister Tony Clement, Senator Leo Housakos of Quebec, and MP Costas Menegakis of Ontario. We concluded a youth mobility agreement to strengthen those ties and discussed matters of trade and investment. However, the heaviest dialogue was during my private time with Greek Prime Minister George Papandreou. He was now the man at the centre of the gathering debt storm.

I found Papandreou, a third-generation prime minister, to be intelligent, thoughtful, and pleasant. I felt we hit it off, despite our obvious philosophical differences, he being the leader of the centre-left Panhellenic Socialist Movement (PASOK).* Newly elected, neither Papandreou nor his party had created Greece's debt crisis, but it was quickly becoming their problem. Greece's public debt was an astounding 300 per cent of GDP and rising rapidly. Privately, he indicated to me an understanding of the severity of the measures that would have to be employed and his willingness to lead them.

The situation only deteriorated in the months following my visit. It is worth noting here a big part of the reason things were getting worse: European inaction. In the turmoil of late 2008 and early 2009, the Europeans had been very vocal about America's role in the global financial crisis, essentially assigning the U.S. all blame for the situation. The truth was, of course, that the EU had problems deeply embedded in its own financial systems. But regardless of one's view of U.S. culpability, at least the Americans dealt decisively with the problem and moved on.

---

* Papandreou was later president of the Socialist International, a historical grouping of centre-left socialist and social democratic parties. He is, in effect, one of my counterparts on the other side, as I am chairman of the centre-right International Democracy Union, which unites conservative and Christian democratic parties.

Two years later, Europe was in worse shape than ever, and it would be so for years to come.

With growing turbulence in European financial markets, a troika stepped in to negotiate a resolution with Greece. It consisted of the European Commission (EC), the European Central Bank (ECB), and the International Monetary Fund (IMF). They put together a rescue package to calm the markets. Any such bailout, of course, would come with very tough austerity measures for the Greeks, but at least it looked like a solution had been reached.

Just before I left for the G20 Summit, scheduled to start at Cannes, France, on November 3, Papandreou announced he would be putting the troika package to a national referendum. In doing so, he may have just been trying to get the public to face the reality of their limited choices. But this was interpreted (not entirely unfairly) by the Europeans as Greece either pulling out of the deal or trying to renegotiate it. All hell broke out in European financial markets as a consequence.

The pressure on Papandreou both within and without quickly became unbearable. Within a matter of days, he cancelled the referendum. A week later, he was kicked out of office. His replacement would be Costas Simitis, a technocrat, who managed to survive for a few months before being forced to call an election. This resulted in PASOK—one of Greece's two major parties since the end of military rule in 1974—being virtually wiped out. To this day, PASOK has not fully recovered and may never. It was certainly a stark example of the impact that financial mismanagement can have upon political leadership.

Papandreou's absence at the G20 was noteworthy. But there were other countries attending that were in the same boat, for the contagion had spread. In very short order, while we were in Cannes, Italy's bonds came under enormous pressure, with its interest costs spiking accordingly.

To my astonishment, the other European leaders began to openly call for Italy's prime minister, Silvio Berlusconi, who was sitting there with us, to resign. This message was amplified in public and private meetings with him. While Berlusconi was never popular among his fellow European leaders, I had never seen intervention like this in the politics of another sovereign country. Within weeks, Berlusconi was gone too, also replaced by an unelected technocrat.

THE CRISIS AND EU GOVERNANCE

THERE ARE A COUPLE of ways of interpreting the remarkable events that occurred around the time of the Cannes summit. While it is easy enough to characterize them as a straight-out assault upon democracy, they were more complicated than that. In effect, we had countries so badly governed that they had lost control over their own economic and financial decisions. If you must borrow more than markets are willing to lend you—unwilling at any rate of interest—then your options are limited, and your democratic independence is lost. The numbers in the case of Greece were clear, and no amount of demagoguery could make them otherwise.

Surely the lesson for democratic governance is that there are limits to incompetence, beyond which the system itself is undermined. As a conservative, I believe that democracy has, over time, proven to be the best system of government. But this is not an axiom, and what has been demonstrated by the lessons of the past can be undone by the errors of the future. As I look around the world, I am not greatly reassured that one lesson—the need to implement modest, voluntary austerity early to avoid deep, imposed austerity later—is fully understood today. If not relearned in time, this can indeed undermine democracy itself.

On the other hand, there truly was an assault on democracy going on here, particularly in the case of Italy. That has not proven to be a one-off, with unelected technocrats reappearing as Italian prime ministers a couple of times since. In some ways, this betrays a fundamental weakness of the European Union for, at its centre, it is really a technocracy, not a democracy. Hence the tendency of European leaders to easily opt for technocratic solutions during times of crisis.

This, I believe, was ultimately part of what led to Brexit. With its centuries-long development of the system of responsible, democratic governance, the United Kingdom and its people were never truly at ease in the Brussels model. Some think the British ignored possible economic pain when they exited the EU. I am not so sure. I think they accepted the notion of some modest, immediate pain as the price of having full democratic control over their future.

Today, many on the conventional centre-left betray a preference for technocracy over democracy, particularly in their incessant demand that unelected judges, "independent" officials, and assorted "experts" overrule the decisions of mere "politicians." But where is the evidence that such people, in dealing with messy complex realities (versus tidy academic models) are any more correct over time in their decision-making? By contrast, what is not debatable is that elected politicians can be held accountable, while such experts almost never are.

CANADA-EU TRADE CONSIDERATIONS

THE EUROZONE CRISIS WOULD continue, and it was still very much alive when I visited Paris the following spring. I tell people that after the United States, Canada's two closest and most important allies in the world remain the mother countries, Britain and France. For the latter, my principal interlocutor was France's new Socialist president, François Hollande.

On domestic economic policy, Hollande and I would agree on little—his initial economic actions were disastrous—but he was an individual I came to like very much. He was pleasant and respectful, and he turned out to be particularly strong on international affairs. He was a shrewd observer on matters of global peace and security, and he was exceptionally decisive on those things. While less outspoken, he also continued his predecessor's strong friendship with Canada.

Nicolas Sarkozy deserves to have something written about him on that subject. Sarkozy was no ordinary friend of Canada. In 2008, after the Organisation internationale de la Francophonie Summit I hosted, he insisted on going to Quebec's National Assembly to deliver a strong message of French support for Canadian unity. French presidents had been friendly to Canada before, but none had truly rectified the damage Charles de Gaulle wreaked in 1967 on the trust between our countries. That was when he publicly expressed support—on Canadian soil, of all places—for the then-fledgling Quebec independence movement. It was a despicable act by an otherwise remarkable leader. It was Sarkozy who finally made it right.

With the air cleared on that past history, my discussions with Hollande were largely economic on this occasion. That was because our number one priority in Paris was the Comprehensive Economic and Trade Agreement (CETA), that is, the Canada-European Union trade deal. Negotiations had been underway since 2009, with Steve Verheul as our lead negotiator.

Considerable progress had been made in the talks. As is always the case, the negotiations had addressed the easiest issues first. Most of these had been resolved—maybe some 80 or 90 per cent—but now we were coming to the more difficult ones, like agriculture, automobiles, and a couple more. I was there to push the Canadian point of view, obviously, but also to hear what the French and others were thinking. Influencing the perspectives of the new government was important, because we knew the French were among the more hesitant countries about a free trade with Canada, often pressuring the EU behind the scenes to go slower on negotiations.

It was not by happenstance that I knew this. In any negotiation I have ever been involved in, I have made it my business to find out what motivated the other side and what they were thinking. In this case, I commissioned our system to use all the tools at their disposal to get me intelligence on the European position. I needed to know what their bottom lines were in order to distinguish grandstanding from real dealbreakers. This knowledge was especially important to us as the smaller party at the table.

What I learned very early on was that the real priority for the Europeans was getting a free-trade deal with the United States. This I never forgot and used at key moments of stress in the negotiations. I made the point—I believe convincingly—that the EU would never get a trade deal with the United States without getting one with Canada first. For one thing, the key issues for them (more on those below) were far easier to resolve with us. For another, enhanced trade access between Canada and Europe would at the very least put some pressure on the Americans to level up their market position.

The reality was that Canada, while the tenth-largest national economy in the world and by no means a trivial market, was a small prize for the EU. The big catch would be the United States. In effect, a trade deal with Canada was an unavoidable trial run for the EU to attain its larger goal with the U.S., much as our negotiations with the European Free Trade Association had been an entry point with the EU for us. That was the argument I made, which had the added benefit of being true.

Beyond this, our intelligence revealed that there were two very specific things the EU needed from us, as they would be critical for them in talks with the United States down the road. The first was what is called "geographical indications." The second was "subnational procurement."

Geographical indications refer to products that are in essence known by their geographical origin. Champagne, for example, comes from that region of France, and the French insist that it can only come from that area. There were many other products that fell into this category in the minds of the Europeans, including, for example, Greek feta cheese. What the Europeans wanted was for us to recognize geographical indications as basically a form of copyright.

Given its importance to the EU, we allowed geographical indications to go onto the agenda. That was certainly going to create issues for us with some of our own businesses, but it was worth the risk. In American eyes, however, geographical indications were nothing but a form of protectionism. Thus, getting the matter into our talks was an important victory for the Europeans.

On subnational procurement, it is one thing for one country to make a deal with another—the reality is that states/provinces and municipalities sometimes have considerable powers of their own and, most importantly, their own procurement processes for goods and services. The EU has the authority to act as a trade negotiator for all its member states on these issues. However, in Canada (and, of course, the United States), much procurement, especially related to major infrastructure development, is handled exclusively by lower levels of government.

Compared to geographical indications, subnational procurement was a much more difficult issue. Ultimately, it meant that we had to bring the provinces directly into the negotiations. This was something our officials, based on their own experiences, were reluctant to see, but they would eventually concede it had to be done.

It helped that our party had a principled approach to federalism to start with, and that had been reflected in a campaign commitment to consult our provincial counterparts on any proposed trade deals. Thus, from the outset we fully involved the provinces and territories in these negotiations, and their officials worked closely with our federal negotiating team. It was federalism at its best and boldest, which, with one exception (which I will discuss later), created a true Team Canada approach.

The uninitiated will often ask me about Quebec in this regard. In fact, Quebec was not only co-operative but generally the leader among the provinces and territories during this process. This may appear counterintuitive, given Quebec's well-known jealous defence of its provincial authority. But Quebec's trade relations with Europe, and with France in particular, were (and still are) very strong, and the province had a keen desire to expand that footprint. Those offensive interests compensated many times over for Quebec's understandable defensiveness on supply management, whether under Jean Charest's Liberal or Pauline Marois's Parti Québécois government. Both were strongly supportive of our negotiations.

One interesting fact about Quebec's involvement was the ongoing and pre-eminent role, through both governments, of its lead negotiator, former PQ Premier Pierre Marc Johnson. This underscores the unique pro-trade consensus that crosses the Quebec political spectrum. There is virtually no ideological opposition to the concept of liberalized trade in Quebec, even on the left. That consensus was a big reason why the Mulroney Government was able to drive the original Canada-U.S. Free Trade Agreement to a successful political conclusion, despite the then-big division of opinion in much of the rest of the country.

AN EU BAILOUT?

AS I ROLLED THROUGH PARIS and other international meetings in 2012, my biggest focus would remain on trade, especially on getting a deal with the European Union. Unfortunately, our interlocutors in these discussions increasingly had their own immediate priority as this period wore on. It was one completely at odds with our interests.

Throughout the spring, our Government was getting reports that the EU was floating the idea of what was innocently called an "international facility." This would be a pool of money, to be administered by the IMF and designed to financially backstop the EU, that is, to bail out European countries "if necessary." The EU's aim was to get approval of this at the upcoming G20 Summit in Los Cabos, Mexico, on June 18–19.

The proposal took our breath away with its scope, scale, and sheer audacity. First, it was completely unprecedented. Following World War II, a safety net had been built for countries facing economic distress or needing economic advancement. This involved a web of transnational organizations like the IMF, the World Bank, the regional development banks, and others, which provided funds largely from advanced countries to developing ones under a range of circumstances. This had been modestly successful. But the suggestion that the IMF might bail out the European Union or some very prosperous portion of it would turn the whole system on its head.

From the very first reports, I was against this concept. Regardless of our desire for a Canada-EU trade agreement, I did not see how, as a matter of principle, we could possibly go to Canadian taxpayers with a proposal to bail out some of the biggest and richest economies in the world. Jim Flaherty was, if anything, even more vehement in his opposition. In fact, this was a big part of the reason he had opposed the selection of France's Christine Lagarde as the IMF's managing director in favour of Agustín Carstens, governor of the Bank of Mexico. Jim had believed we should break from the tradition of a European IMF head precisely because of the risk that the EU would try to use that position to "globalize" responsibility for its debt problems.

In short order, an international lobbying campaign began to ratchet up the pressure to make this the centrepiece at Los Cabos. The leaders of the EU itself began the effort, followed by government heads of the major European countries. Other leaders chimed in, particularly the G20 host, Mexican President Felipe Calderón. They all called me personally.

I was resisting the pressure, with the United States appearing to be our ally on the matter. Then, lo and behold, the Americans started to shift ground too. At first, the Obama administration had begged off with the argument that such an arrangement would never pass Congress. Then they began to soften their rhetoric, suggesting at least notional support for the idea. Real momentum was taking shape behind the EU-bailout proposal.

Los Cabos G20

DESPITE THE CAJOLING, I never had any hesitancy in opposing the EU's scheme. But I really crossed the Rubicon in my phone call with Calderón on the issue. He claimed that we needed unanimity on the matter to make the G20 Summit a success. I told him that, in my books, unanimity on a bad idea was not a success, and that I expected zero pushback from Canadians for opposing such a proposal.

I like and respect Calderón a great deal, and we have remained friends over the years. However, the exchange again underscores how powerful the go-along-to-get-along ethic can be at international meetings. There is this notion that somehow everyone not agreeing on everything amounts to "failure," regardless of the substance of the issues. The notion is nonsense, but it is a reality.

I was comfortable at being the odd man out. For one thing, letting the EU foist their debt problems on the rest of the world was a truly dangerous idea, especially for Canada. Even after the recent IMF reform, advanced

Western countries were still shouldering a high burden of IMF obligations. If European nations could become net beneficiaries, the number of disproportionate contributors could become very small indeed, and we would be one of them.

Worse still, there was, in my judgment, a serious risk for Canada in the U.S. position. The U.S. Senate would never ratify the EU proposal. While that meant it could never be officially adopted, given what was effectively a U.S. veto, it did not mean our acquiescence would be meaningless. If we had gone along, with the American administration agreeing in principle, then it was predictable that the Europeans would pressure us to "fulfill our moral obligation" when they put future bailout arrangements together.

The position I was taking was not without risk. It would irritate the EU while we were in the middle of our trade talks. However, I observed that they had never raised a bailout obligation at the negotiating table itself. They knew that such a demand would be so unprecedented as to risk a breakdown in the discussions. For that reason, I had already calculated that this spat would blow over quickly.

I had other reasons to think that might be the case. In the calls I received from world leaders, a few had gone soft when I pushed back with my reasons for opposition. That led me to suspect there were several doubters about the wisdom of this among the governments that had appeared to jump on board. Again, as is the case in these go-along-to-get-along situations, there was likely a "nudge, nudge, wink, wink" expectation that somebody else would block consensus for them. The United States was probably their hope, but my reputation by then was such that they knew Canada would do so if we had to.

In the days preceding the Los Cabos meeting, controversy began to emerge over Canada's firm rejection of any bailout fund for the EU. European leaders openly resented my contention that they needed to get their economic house in order before appealing for handouts from the world community. The pre-G20 atmosphere was so tense that some pro-EU-fund countries held their own press conference, accusing us of "lecturing" them and threatening the free-trade talks. I pushed back diplomatically, but firmly. The table was set for a confrontation.

Yet, when we met on June 18–19, 2012, no big fight took place. The proposed fund basically disappeared from the discussions. With it being clear that Canada would not agree, the rest apparently decided that they did not want the appearance of "failure." The truth, I believe, is that, while everyone else had nominally agreed to the EU proposal, very few really wanted it to happen.

Recall that electorates around the world were then in a foul mood, with incumbent governments falling everywhere. In what country would a leader want to go back home from this summit and brag that their "achievement" had been to agree to take citizens' money and bail out some of the wealthiest countries on the planet? Had they actually done that, they could have bashed me all they wanted. I would have come off as the good guy in that story.

The EU never did raise the prospect of a global bailout again. Instead, it managed through its debt problems, mainly due to the willingness of Germany's Angela Merkel to make the tough decisions when called upon. But you can bet that, had the international facility been set up, the EU would have used it.

JOINING THE TRANS-PACIFIC PARTNERSHIP TALKS

THE GREATER IRONY of the Los Cabos G20 was that it turned out to be a big win for us on the trade front: we were admitted to the twelve-country Trans-Pacific Partnership (TPP) negotiations. It was something we had been trying to achieve for some time.

The TPP had begun as a trade agreement between four very open but relatively small economies—Singapore, Chile, New Zealand, and Brunei. The stakes were upped dramatically, however, when the United States was admitted toward the end of George W. Bush's presidency in 2008. President Obama took up the charge, particularly in his second term, and hammering out a wider deal became an American priority.

The Americans had two objectives. The first was the same as for all the other parties: to get a free-trade deal and grow market access and commercial relations between countries on both sides of the Pacific Ocean. The other, and maybe overriding, American objective was geopolitical: to establish a robust, liberalized, rules-based trading order in the Asia-Pacific to offset China's growing influence. Who was involved in these negotiations became very important to the Americans, with the Obama administration decidedly cool on admitting Canada.

There were a couple of reasons for this reluctance. The one we feared most was that the Americans intended to create what is called a hub and spoke trading map, where, instead of being fully integrated into the trade relationships of our most important partner, we would become a just one spoke. Canada had joined with the United States in negotiating NAFTA with Mexico precisely so that would not happen in North America. Our suspicion was aroused because the Americans were also resisting the presence of Mexico at the TPP negotiating table.

However, it turned out that the American resistance was driven by an even more problematic position: they were unhappy with their trade relationship with Canada. A view had gradually taken hold in Washington that the Mulroney Government had gotten far too good a deal when the original Canada-United States pact was signed. If you look at it objectively—whatever my differences were with Mr. Mulroney—he *did* get a very good deal. Canada got pretty much everything it wanted in terms of access to the American market. Plus, we got to protect an awful lot of key Canadian sensitivities, from supply management to cultural industries. So it turned out that if we wanted into the TPP talks, the Americans were going to want some special concessions.

It was not like there was nothing in this for Canada. True, we already had trade deals with the TPP countries on our side of the Pacific—the United States, Mexico, Chile, and Peru. What these talks promised was additional free-trade access on the fast-growing Asian side, with Malaysia, Singapore, Vietnam, and Brunei. There were also Australia and New Zealand, long-standing allies but with whom we could use much closer commercial relations.

Still, the real prize was Japan, the third-largest economy in the world. Canadian governments had wanted to get a trade deal with Japan for decades. Canada did have a bilateral negotiation going on with the Japanese when we took office. But it was another one of those pro-forma tables. The real action in terms of getting a deal was going to be in the TPP.

Despite the opportunity offered by the TPP and the risk of not being in it, I simply could not open the Canada-U.S. trade deal to grant unilateral concessions. That was a political non-starter for us. We could try to work with the Mexicans to get in, but it was clear that their path was going to be easier. In short, I was running out of options—until Sebastián Piñera entered the picture.

Piñera was then the president of Chile, and one of the smartest, best-educated leaders I ever dealt with.* I was with him and a couple dozen others in Honolulu in November 2011 for the Asia-Pacific Economic Cooperation (APEC) Summit. As my staff and officials knew, I had a low opinion of APEC and was often musing about passing on its annual meeting. It would always be a long trip, with a thin agenda, and at the closing press conference, I would usually find myself hard-pressed to explain exactly what I had dragged myself and the media all that way for.

The weakness of APEC was underscored by the TPP itself. One of the prospective benefits officials touted for APEC was that it would eventually be the basis of an Asia-Pacific trade deal. Yet the TPP negotiations had grown up outside APEC, and we were not part of those despite attending all these time-consuming summits. In fact, in Honolulu, President Obama held an entirely separate TPP meeting for the select countries that had been invited in.

At that same APEC, I had a bilateral meeting with Piñera. Canada and Chile have had close relations for many years for various reasons, including a trade deal going back to the previous Liberal Government.† During our conversation, Piñera expressed surprise that, given our focus on free trade,

---

* I stayed in touch with Piñera for many years. He was tragically killed in a helicopter crash in 2024.

† The Canada-Chile Free Trade Agreement (CCFTA) was concluded in 1996. My Government negotiated an expansion of it to include financial services in 2012. It was further modernized by our Liberal successors in 2019.

we were not trying to gain admission to the TPP. Taken aback by his apparent assumption, I quickly disabused him of it. He then confided that, at Obama's TPP meeting, the U.S. president had told the other countries that he wanted Canada to join but that we were reluctant.

I assured Piñera that that was certainly not the case. More importantly, I had my opening. Obama, having told everyone he wanted us in the TPP talks, would now have his credibility with his counterparts at stake if he continued to categorically block our admission. The United States quickly conceded this, but they still made it difficult by seeking to impose some preconditions to our joining the talks. Specifically, they sought assurances that we would be prepared to negotiate some matters, like supply management, that were already part of NAFTA.

I took this to our Cabinet for discussion, where there was a long, robust, and divisive debate. This was unusual, because most of the time we had a generally consensual government. There were some strongly held objections to the American offer, with some even suggesting that we should just tell the Americans to stuff it and walk away. Others felt we simply had to engage at any price, given the longer-term stakes.

After going around the table multiple times, I laid out my thinking. I pointed out that, if we said no to any precondition, that would be the end, and we would be out of the process. But if we agreed to the preconditions, a lot of which were very high level in nature, we could at least get to the table. At the table, we could defend our interests. Yes, we might have to make concessions, but they might not be as bad as we thought. If they were really bad, we still could drop out at that point. In other words, it was best to keep our options open.

Fortunately, my argument carried the day. We were able to satisfy the Americans and were admitted to the TPP negotiations.

So, here we were, negotiating trade deals on two major fronts—with the European Union and the Trans-Pacific Partnership. We had already expanded Canada's free-trade network from five to fourteen countries, with access to a large part of the Americas. We had a lot of work yet to do, but we now had the possibility of transforming this into a truly global set of relationships.

SECOND TRIP TO CHINA

TRADE WAS ALSO top of mind back on February 8–11, 2012, when I made my second trip to China. We could not ignore the country and its huge population, burgeoning economy, and growing global political clout. At the same time, my skepticism of China's governance, particularly its human rights performance, was also part of the public record and had been communicated forcefully and personally to China's President Hu Jintao. Mr. Hu and I understood each other pretty well, which served as a foundation for frank discussions about what was possible in our relations.

Hu was very much in the tradition of Deng Xiaoping. Deng assumed leadership in 1978 and is credited with bringing elements of capitalism—formerly anathema to the Chinse Communist Party—into its economic system. "It doesn't matter whether a cat is black or white, as long as it catches mice," he would say, referencing his pragmatic approach to raising the Chinese people out of poverty.

It was Deng who, by unleashing the natural entrepreneurial energy of his nation, transformed China into an economic powerhouse. But unlike Mao Zedong, who ground China's economy into the dust, leaving it one of the poorest countries on the planet, you do not see pictures of Deng everywhere in public. That is because Deng created and fostered a collective leadership style, stripped of the cult of personality. Those who followed him, like Jiang Zemin and Hu Jintao, were of like demeanour. Yes, internal Chinese Communist Party politics remained very tough, but rivals were sidelined and retired, not, as in Mao's time, persecuted and imprisoned (or worse).

Since my first visit in 2009, our Government had sent a steady stream of ministers, officials, and business representatives to China, and Governor General Jean had also made an official visit. It was time for me to re-engage as well. I held all the normal high-level meetings with senior leaders, exchanging views on a range of matters, and looked for ways to improve the bilateral relationship. Specifically, I wanted to see more balanced Canadian trade and investment access to China while also better protecting us from the security risks it presented and not ignoring the human rights abuses that (as mentioned earlier) sometimes affected us directly.

My visit concluded with a broad leaders' statement, outlining a range of actions to "strengthen the Canada-China strategic partnership." Much of this was diplomatic bland-speak, but the comment that "the leaders also agreed to bring the economic partnership to the next level by improving the bilateral investment regime" was more than that. Here we were noting our intention to conclude a bilateral foreign investment protection and promotion agreement. At the same time, we were being very cautious with respect to the desire of China to be added to Canada's list of free-trade negotiations.

The wisdom of combining continued caution with this renewed engagement was underscored by a dramatic and disturbing series of events that occurred during that 2012 trip. They revolved around my scheduled meeting with Bo Xilai. He was the governor of Chongqing, the huge interior port city that we visited.

As Chinese internal politics then went, Bo was considered a rising star in the hierarchy—a charismatic figure who might someday be president. Our officials were proud of the fact that they had managed to get me a private audience and dinner with him. Given his status, this was considered a real coup—an important connection for me and a symbolic manifestation of our embassy's clout.

However, before reaching Chongqing, we stopped in Guangzhou. There, we began to hear strange news reports and rumours about Bo and his inner circle—the defection of his police chief and the possible arrest of Bo's wife, Gu Kailai. Our officials were dumbfounded as to what was happening and what it might mean.

I arrived in Chongqing and was greeted by Bo at his official residence. He was as advertised—photogenic, energetic, and extroverted. However, once the cameras went away and we proceeded to our meeting and private dinner, his disposition went from at ease to on edge. Bo actually had televisions wheeled into the room so he could watch Chinese news reports as we ate. Throughout the meal, he cast nervous glances at the screens, where his name was being mentioned and his picture broadcast. He became increasingly distracted during our conversations.

Not long after, it became clear that Bo and his entourage had fallen afoul of the central authorities. He and his wife were soon arrested and imprisoned. He is still there, serving a life sentence on bribery and embezzlement charges, his wife doing the same for murder. Basically, our meeting went from being a great diplomatic coup to spending time with a non-person.

Suffice it to say, this only reinforced our vigilance in dealing with this growing power. It also coincided with the rise to the presidency of Xi Jinping, to whom Bo Xilai had been rumoured to be the principal competitor. Few realized at the time to what an extent this episode was a warning about the future.

RETURN TO INDIA

MY TRADE AGENDA ALSO took me once again to India later that year (November 4–9), although we were not blind to the challenges our ambitions faced. India still has significant elements of protectionism and other barriers to doing business. Its development also remains spotty; while some areas of the country are indiscernible from advanced Western economies, others have barely progressed at all technologically. Such radically different levels of development can sometimes be seen in proximity.

How successful were we in advancing Canadian interests in India? To be honest, it was a mixed record. Trade and investment flows did grow substantially. Most important in my view was our conclusion of a nuclear co-operation agreement, which offered us all the safeguards we needed (despite being fought at every stage by Foreign Affairs). Since then, Canada (more specifically Saskatchewan) has become a significant supplier to India's increasingly important civil nuclear power system.

We also concluded a social security agreement and some bilateral contracts, but as I recall, that was about the extent of our success on the business front. For years, we pursued a Foreign Investment Promotion and

Protection Agreement (FIPA) with India, in the hope that it would be a stepping stone to a free-trade pact. We seemed close to getting it done many times, but it never happened.*

I do not think there is much more we could have done to deepen our economic relationship at that time. The Indians (at least back then) simply did not have an ambitious free-trade agenda. In fact, when the Association of Southeast Asian Nations began to negotiate the Regional Comprehensive Economic Partnership to deepen their trade flows, India dropped out before the signatures.

Where we were unequivocally successful was in re-establishing strong, high-level political bonds between our two countries. This was true through two different prime ministers and two very different governments. I was personally close to both. The late Manmohan Singh predated me in office, and I have already talked about my high regard for him. If anything, those leader-to-leader ties strengthened after 2014. I will leave until later my reflections on relations with the government of Narendra Modi.

THE SUMMIT CIRCUIT 2012

THESE TRADE-FOCUSED TRIPS were interspaced by a flurry of pre-scheduled summits in 2012. They kicked off in March with the Nuclear Security Summit in South Korea, to which I added visits to Thailand and Japan. In April, continental trips had me in Washington for the North American Leaders' Summit and Cartagena, Colombia, for the Summit of the Americas. May's G8, held in Camp David, Maryland, was billed as an

---

* Another name for FIPA is a Bilateral Investment Treaty (BIT). In essence it is an agreement establishing the terms and conditions for private investment by national companies of one state in another state. It usually includes guarantees of fair and equitable treatment, protection from expropriation, and free transfer of means and security. It also typically includes a dispute resolution mechanism whereby companies have recourse to international arbitration.

"emergency summit" due to the ongoing Eurozone Crisis, and it was immediately followed by the NATO Summit in Chicago. On June 3–7, I was in London and Paris for a range of meetings. I also hosted Israeli President Shimon Peres and Prime Minister Benjamin Netanyahu as well as Polish Prime Minister Donald Tusk during this spring period.

Of all my travel that year, my trip to London ranks as one of my best memories during my time in office. I was there for the Queen's Diamond Jubilee, which combined various political, economic, and cultural engagements. I participated in a range of memorable events where the focus was rarely on me. Laureen, Ben, and Rachel were also able to join me for some of the festivities.

One occasion stands out. It was a star-studded Diamond Jubilee concert held just outside Buckingham Palace, for which dignitaries like my family and me had special seating. Many of the biggest stars of British music, from Paul McCartney to Tom Jones to Elton John and Ed Sheeran, performed. Now where in your life are you ever going to get a ticket to a concert like that? And for free?

It was a magical evening. At the end, they played a video montage of Queen Elizabeth's life, built around her family and decades of service. It was very apparent that the crowd, especially the older members, were seeing the story of their own lives and their own families reflected in the national life of this remarkable queen. It was the monarchy at its very best as the embodiment of the British nation. Truly a powerful evening, it finished with Prince Charles delivering a moving tribute to his mother.

Shortly after—the next day, I believe—I had my audience with Her Majesty. A number of the meetings I had attended featured the Queen, but it was still always a highlight to meet her in private and hear her latest take on Commonwealth and world affairs. She was especially pleased with her new Canadian portrait—a large, vivid rendering that, in the style of artist Phil Richards, subtly captured many aspects of her life.*

---

* I was so impressed by this work that I commissioned Richards to do my own official portrait, unveiled in Ottawa on February 3, 2026.

My conversations with Prime Minister Cameron over the course of this visit also proved useful, as they always did with David. As well, I made a special point of visiting with our High Commission staff, both Canadians and local employees. While I certainly had my disagreements with the Foreign Affairs mandarins, I have always admired our overseas staff who labour day in and day out to carry on Canada's business abroad. Most everywhere I went, I took the same opportunity to meet them, to thank them for their diligent service to our country, and to pose for photos with their families.

THE FRANCOPHONIE AND HUMAN RIGHTS

CANADA HAS RIGHTLY BEEN long praised for its work on human rights through international diplomacy. In October 2012, we found ourselves furthering that mission at the Organisation internationale de la Francophonie Summit in the rather inaccurately named Democratic Republic of the Congo (DRC). Our host was strongman Joseph Kabila, who had succeeded his father, the brutal dictator Laurent Kabila, after elections nobody believed were clean and fair.

I have talked previously of the many wonderful places I have visited as Canada's prime minister, but the DRC capital of Kinshasa was not one of them. For starters, the country was awash in human rights abuse, civil war, torture, arbitrary detention, and endemic civil strife. Fear was everywhere. When our motorcade drove down the streets of Kinshasa,[†] often through areas of extreme poverty, people just froze. They would do so for any official-looking vehicles, clearly afraid that, if they moved,

---

† I am told that the road from the airport to Kinshasa had been completed only days before the summit—by the Chinese! In fact, the Chinese had built much of the summit infrastructure, including some of the hotels. That rendered conversations within them problematic, due to potential bugging. However, the dangers outside meant leaving the hotel for such discussions was also not feasible.

someone might shoot them. This was hardly the ideal location to hold a summit, but I suppose there was some benefit in seeing for myself how dark the world can be.

At the summit itself, Kabila had packed the hall with supporters, many of them thuggish-looking military personnel. The atmosphere was vaguely threatening, with people roaring and jeering at the various leaders' comments. Decidedly not typical protocol at these events.

In my opening speech, I delivered some comments about good governance, human rights, and the rule of law, which, clearly, were not well received by this intimidating crowd. Still, I tried to not mince words. "We are here, not to excuse the things that are happening, but to spotlight them," I said. I gave notice that the Canadian government was examining many human rights issues in the DRC, especially violence against women. "Canada will be supporting additional initiatives to combat the barbarous acts of sexual violence against women that are occurring in the [eastern] part of the DRC." I do not want to exaggerate, but after finishing my speech, I did not feel entirely safe. I did, however, get through it and lived to fight another day—all for a good cause.

Beyond the oppressive atmosphere of the summit, however, there was an interesting Canadian domestic political angle. This being the Francophonie, Quebec and New Brunswick attended as "participating governments." Leading the Quebec delegation was newly elected Premier Pauline Marois of the Parti Québécois, whom I had not yet met. At home, the PQ had been trying to provoke a war of words, which I had been ignoring.

There was much speculation about what would happen at this meeting. Certainly, there was the potential for embarrassment for Canada in this international arena. In the end, though, Marois and I had a cordial, frank, and productive meeting in Kinshasa. In fact, this proved to be the norm for my dealings with the premier and the PQ at international events we attended. When it came to our government-to-government dealings in these global venues—or in domestic venues, for that matter—Premier Marois was always very professional.

Some might see an irony here; after all, the PQ's goal was to break up the country. But there was another factor at play. New Brunswick, in this case represented by Premier David Alward, always conducted itself impeccably at the Francophonie. Acting differently—as radicals, trouble-makers, and disruptors—would not cast the PQ and their independence cause in the best international light. They took pains in such situations to do everything they could to look like responsible actors, worthy of sovereignty. And to be fair, they did so successfully.

IRAN, SPONSOR OF INTERNATIONAL TERRORISM

WE HAD NEVER BEEN afraid to take strong foreign policy positions, so our majority standing was not going to cause us to be any less outspoken. In that vein, on September 7, 2012, our government announced an action that made a bold statement to the world: the suspension of diplomatic relations with Iran and a declaration that both Iran and Syria were state sponsors of terrorism. Many in the Foreign Affairs Department had deep reservations about this, of course, but within our Cabinet there was very little debate. Iran was and still is the world's largest sponsor of terrorism, period. This move was thus a logical consequence of our Justice for Victims of Terrorism Act, passed earlier that year. It was also the right thing to do.

We shuttered our embassy in Tehran and the Iranian Embassy in Ottawa. This was a long-overdue, pragmatic action. The Ottawa operation was a nest of spies and disruptors that no one in our capital would miss. Persian Canadians generally understood and supported our action.* Closing our embassy in Tehran was a more significant step, but

---

* A comment on terminology is in order here: Iranian Canadians generally refer to themselves as Persian Canadians, partly to avoid any association with the regime in Tehran.

I had pressing reasons. In the proceeding weeks there had been a ransacking of the British Embassy in Tehran, which we believed—on good evidence—that the Government of Iran had tacitly endorsed. Given our Government's position on the regime, particularly my public statements, I was no longer confident that we could guarantee the safety of our embassy and its personnel.

I would hasten to add that the closing of both embassies did not mean we gave up on international diplomacy regarding Iran. In fact, Canada's diplomatic mission to the UN had sponsored a resolution in the General Assembly every year condemning Iran's human rights record. Each time it passed with increasing majorities. To give credit where credit is due, this is an area where Canada's Foreign Affairs people did good and effective work.

21

CELEBRATING, PRESERVING, AND PROTECTING CANADA

THE HIGHEST RESPONSIBILITY of any prime minister and government is to preserve the country's unity and sovereignty for the benefit of Canadians. The year 2012 threw up some important challenges in this regard. One was the election of a Parti Québécois government, once again focusing attention on the serious challenge of Quebec separatism. Another revolved around some controversial foreign investments, which raised real questions about the role of our national government in a globalized economy.

However, for conservatives, just as the future is about decisions in the present, the present is about the achievements of the past. Our country cannot be understood only through the perspectives of our age, but through our forebears' journey and what they left us to take forward. These are legacies that need to be honoured by all Canadians, and they should leave us, first and foremost, with a strong sense of pride in our great country and its future.

Allow me to confide that I despise the alternative way of looking at our past—the "black armband history" that has been practised by some (though certainly not all) Liberal governments. It is nothing more than deconstructing the country. It is done so that Canada can be conveniently described as some kind of post-national phenomenon whose only virtue rests in the individual prime ministers who express it. It is self-serving, arrogant, and historically baseless.

Yes, we need to acknowledge our failures. But far more than that, we need to celebrate how we have overcome our failures and achieved our (enormous) successes. This great country been built and given its character through countless extraordinary acts by many previous generations. Cut us off from those roots, and we will wander aimlessly into a dangerous future.

That is why, in 2012, we focused attention on a milestone of enormous historic significance.

COMMEMORATING THE WAR OF 1812

I AM PROUD of how our government marked commemorations around Canadian contributions to World Wars I and II, along with the Korean conflict. Part of the reason for these was to make clear to Canadians the importance we placed upon those fellow citizens, especially our remaining veterans, who had put their lives on the line. It is imperative that a society never forget those individuals who served it and who paid the price of that service.

In our time in office, we put no less emphasis on recognizing sacrifice in the contemporary conflicts in which we were involved. That was why, in 2008, with casualties mounting in Afghanistan, we introduced the Sacrifice Medal. It recognizes those who were killed or seriously wounded in the Canadian Armed Forces and among the civilians and allies working with them.* We also held a big event on Parliament Hill in 2011 to celebrate the successful conclusion of the Libya mission, including the leadership of General Charles Bouchard. Of course, honours and commemorations were not the only thing we did to recognize sacrifice. Very large additional resources were expended on the welfare of the veterans of those actions, particularly those who had been injured.†

---

* The Sacrifice Medal replaced the old "wound stripe"—a historical medal used by Commonwealth countries.

† On more than one occasion, the military returned the favour, presenting me with special tokens of their esteem, like military jackets, badges, and insignia. I also collected plenty of the so-called challenge coins, common among

Beyond the heroism and sacrifices that war brings out, there are even bigger reasons to commemorate military engagements. Societies are often profoundly shaped by such conflicts. Enduring boundaries will be drawn. Constitutions of government will take shape. National values and symbols will be permanently embraced or scorned.

It was in large part because of a war that began two hundred years earlier to the day on June 18, 2012, that our own country began to take shape. That was when the United States declared war on the United Kingdom, with the specific aim of conquering the British colonies to its north. Thus began the War of 1812—a two-and-a-half-year struggle that unquestionably ranks among a small handful of the most critical events in Canadian history. It is that for two big reasons.

First, the War of 1812 is a fascinating war story in itself—a tale of nothing less than Canada's improbable military survival against massive odds. With Britain bogged down in the Napoleonic Wars and the northern part of the continent sparsely populated by small, isolated, and diverse peoples in numerous jurisdictions, few in the United States believed victory would be anything other than quick and complete. At the outbreak of the war, former President Thomas Jefferson opined that conquering Canada would be a "mere matter of marching." Not so, after four initial American offensives were turned back on every front. From there the struggles went back and forth, with the Americans claiming their own periodic successes. Yet Canada survived. Indeed, our side did more than that, as many of those later U.S. victories—take Baltimore and New Orleans—underscore the degree to which the American invasion had deteriorated into a defensive struggle.

The second reason the War of 1812 is so important is that it laid the seeds for Canadian nationhood. Of course, historians caution against

---

Canadian and Allied forces, which mark various missions, accomplishments, or units. Yet by far the biggest military recognition given to me was my 2013 induction as an honorary member of the Royal 22nd Regiment in Quebec City. The "Van Doos" are the most famous French-Canadian regiment, counting among its celebrated members Governor General Georges Vanier.

simplistic cause-and-effect tales and rightly so. Still, it is indisputable, in my view, that the War of 1812 took a bunch of distinct groups that had settled disparate areas for different reasons and gave them the beginnings of a unique identity—common in many ways, yet diverse in others, both pan-continental and non-American.

Our Government's recognition of this historical struggle included many elements. For example, partnering with the Royal Canadian Geographical Society, we created educational awareness programs that teachers or students could take advantage of, and many did. A series of documentary films were developed too, which are still well worth watching. And we sponsored a competition for a monument commemorating the war to be placed on Parliament Hill, where it stands proudly today.

The distinct military aspects of the War of 1812 were also commemorated. From as early as 2010, we began to hold events that marked key battles and the local histories of those who fought in them. A particular pleasure for our Government was to present battle honours to several local militia units that, for two hundred years in some cases, had sought recognition for their predecessors' role in the defence of British North America.

Ironically, this was one of most pitched battles I ever had with the bureaucracy. In this case, the Department of National Defence and their historians argued adamantly that no militia units could be recognized prior to the Militia Act of 1855.* The position was so entrenched that it bordered on insubordination, to the point where I literally had to threaten to fire senior people to get this initiative approved. Approved it eventually was, and it was wildly popular with the affected communities and their regiments.

One commemorative event held special meaning. On October 25, 2012, Governor General David Johnston hosted a recognition ceremony on behalf of the Crown for the First Nations who had contributed to the British/

---

* They argued that such an interpretation of history risked the creation of a "bad precedent." But a precedent for what? I never could get an answer to exactly what the risk was.

Canadian cause during the War of 1812. That included almost all Indigenous nations, on both sides of the border, in almost every battle fought. Special medals and banners were presented to some fifty of them, several of which had fled north to settle before, during, and after the war.

It is true enough that the lives of these Indigenous peoples since then have too often experienced disappointment and tragedy. Yet their ancestors were under no illusion of how unlikely survival would have been on the American side of the border. And their descendants were clearly appreciative of the renewed recognition that was part of our efforts at ongoing reconciliation. This event was not, by the way, the first acknowledgement by the Crown of the contributions of their Aboriginal allies. At Rideau Hall, several of the First Nations brought with them and proudly displayed the medals presented to them by the government of George III two hundred years earlier.

There was one other important aspect to this Canadian commemoration: while celebrating Canada, it did not denigrate the United States. The end of the war marked the beginning of the long journey through which Canadians and Americans would become the closest friends in the entire world. Indeed, their Ambassador to Canada, David Jacobson, was a big fan of what we were doing—particularly in how it demonstrated the extraordinary fullness of the reconciliation that has taken place between our two countries.[†]

THE ELECTION OF THE PARTI QUÉBÉCOIS

WHILE THE WAR OF 1812 was the first time Canadians began to walk the path of history together, the forces that can pull us in different directions

---

† Sadly, this verdict may have to be somewhat revised as I write this, during the initial year of the second Trump Administration. However, I still believe that, in the long sweep of history, today's tensions will be an incident rather than a trend. I am also pleased to note that, in 2026, Prime Minister Mark Carney once again highlighted the critical role the War of 1812 played in the evolution of Canada as a country.

remain two-hundred years later. That is certainly true in Quebec. In my lifetime, much of Canadian political life has been preoccupied with the threat presented by the Quebec sovereignty movement. However, that threat appeared to be gradually receding for nearly a generation, particularly during our Government's time in office.

That perception was challenged on September 4, 2012, when Quebecers elected the Parti Québécois (PQ), led by Pauline Marois, as their new government. Many in the media and the public policy "commentariat" were quick to label this as a renewed threat to national unity. For my part, I was not complacent about this result—no prime minister can afford to be—but I was also much more sanguine about the situation.

The election of the PQ seemed to have little to do with sovereignty. In fact, Marois had indicated that she would not hold a referendum in a first PQ term of office. Even if she were so inclined, the new premier had only a minority legislature. The balance of power rested with François Legault's Coalition Avenir (CAQ) and, like its predecessor, Mario Dumont's Action démocratique du Québec (ADQ), it was opposed to a third sovereignty referendum.

Clearly, the election had more to do with the unpopularity of Jean Charest's governing Parti libéral du Québec (PLQ). After three terms and nearly a decade in office, it was the victim of what I call the Murphy's Law of Politics, that is, "friends may come and go, but enemies accumulate." In other words, after almost ten years lots of people could easily recall things the PLQ had done that they disliked, but no one could remember the stuff they had supported. Even at that, the PQ had won less than one-third of the vote—hardly the basis on which to launch a referendum campaign.

I also felt some comfort about the generally positive mood toward federalism in the province, which I believe our Government had helped create. It is true that our Government was not wildly popular, but through our "*fédéralisme d'ouverture*," we had addressed several long-standing Quebec asks and grievances. Besides the "*nation*" motion, we had arranged for Quebec representation at the United Nations Educational, Scientific and Cultural Organization. We had harmonized the federal and provincial sales taxes, allowing Quebec to administer the joint system within the province. We had given Quebec the land on which the National Assembly was located (and, yes, that had actually been federal property before). Most of the expropriated Mirabel lands had been returned to their previous owners. We had also steered clear of interventions in provincial jurisdiction, addressing such irritants as the Millennium Development Scholarship Fund. And, of course, we had substantively addressed the "*déséquilibre fiscal*."

We also made sure we did a reasonable share of federal announcements in *la belle province*, and I went there regularly. I took particular care to visit the Conservative beachhead we were establishing in the greater Quebec City region. I appeared regularly at such things as the Carnaval de Québec—an important cultural event in Calgary's sister-city.* Our national commemoration of the city's 400th anniversary celebration had been quite popular there.

In short, while not compromising our agenda in some un-conservative manner, we had gone out of our way to address Quebec's concerns. We were particularly careful not to create any perception that Quebec was being treated unfairly in Confederation and not to pour gasoline on any fire the sovereigntists tried to start. With the PQ now in government, that approach was sure to be tested.

It was—on November 15, 2012, to be precise. I was in Quebec City for a previously scheduled event to announce our support for the reconstruction of the landmark Manège militaire, the historic Quebec City Armoury, which had been destroyed by fire. Shortly before I got on the plane to fly there, the PQ announced their intention to remove the flag of Canada from the Quebec National Assembly. As the previous Liberal Government had brought the flag in, this was obviously a provocative move designed to get a reaction.

Once in Quebec City, I made the announcement to a large crowd, including journalists from the provincial press gallery. I gave my statement about rebuilding the Manège, but the first question, from a French reporter, was

---

* To the surprise of my staff, I had even mastered the famous Bonhomme Carnivale's kick!

about the flag's removal from the National Assembly, challenging me to, in effect, "stand up for Canada."

This was precisely the kind of fight that I had decided not to engage in, notwithstanding some doubts in both the Prime Minister's Office (PMO) and the Privy Council Office (PCO). I paused, gave a bit of a smile, and then shrugged. The crowd erupted in laughter.

At that moment, my instincts had been confirmed: Quebecers did not want to go back to debates about sovereignty and referendums. Those had been highly divisive experiences in most Quebec families. Therefore, I had not taken the PQ bait and had refused to play "Captain Canada" when the PQ expected it. This underscores a key political maxim: always be careful when you are being part of someone else's agenda. The fact that the PQ wanted me to react meant that it was absolutely not a good idea.

The sovereignty agenda never did get traction when Marois was in office. Indeed, the PQ did little to push it. In any case, within a year and a half their minority collapsed, and they were out of office.

THE FUTURE OF THE QUEBEC SOVEREIGNTY MOVEMENT

THERE IS A QUOTE, attributed to Napoleon, that goes: "Never interfere with an enemy while he's in the process of destroying himself." There was an element of truth in that where the PQ was concerned. Beyond a long-term secular decline in its election results, its coalition was unravelling.

People often forget that the Parti Québécois was founded by three distinct elements. René Lévesque had brought together his own centrist group from the PLQ, the Mouvement Souveraineté-Association, and combined it with two others—the right-wing Ralliement national and the leftist Rassemblement pour l'indépendence nationale. From 1995 on, the ADQ/CAQ split away from more conservative nationalists from the PQ, while Québec solidaire gradually ate into its more ideologically left supporters.

We did not just observe these developments; we also did regular polling on Quebecers' attitudes. Three trends stood out during our time in office. First, there was a gradual decline in support for sovereignty, although that option still appealed to as much as one-third of the population. Second, there was a more precipitous decline in the number of Quebecers who believed sovereignty would ever happen. That certainly explains why "soft sovereigntists" like Dumont and Legault abandoned the cause. But the third trend was not reassuring: there was only a slight rise in support for federalism itself. A greater percentage of Quebecers were simply becoming agnostic on the whole question of Quebec's constitutional status.

As I said, we were not complacent about this during the PQ's time in office. I assembled small teams in the PMO and PCO to track the sovereignty issue, in the event that referendum planning proved to be necessary. I also developed a clear strategy in my mind on how I would deal with such a referendum, should one come to pass. It was informed by the public opinion trends we were observing, the work I had done for Preston Manning in 1995, and the near-fatal flaw in the federal government's strategy back then.

That fundamental error had been pretending that a vote for sovereignty was unthinkable. That was, quite simply, a denial of reality. One consequence of it was complete ambiguity about how Ottawa would respond to a Yes vote. That had effectively encouraged wavering Quebecers to believe they could vote Yes for "leverage" with the rest of Canada without really risking separation. (Of course, while PQ Premier Jacques Parizeau encouraged a similar view, he had every intention of treating a Yes vote as a clear mandate for sovereignty.) An even bigger problem with "unthinkability" was that it resulted in an utter lack of preparation in the event a Yes vote occurred. (Again, Parizeau was many steps ahead of the federal government on that one.)

At the core of my strategy, had it come to that, would have been the original "Clarity Act" I had proposed back in 1996. I would require a clear question. Failing that, the federal government would hold its own vote on a question of its own. I would also demand a clear result. The separatists would have to get a majority of all votes cast—no more attempting to win by invalidating votes, as happened in 1995.

Presuming a clear question, my approach to the campaign itself would be a radical departure from previous federal governments. Yes, we would appeal to Quebecers' sense of Canada and the overwhelming desire of Canadians to see Quebec remain in the country. We would convey our strong belief that separation would be a tragedy for all of us. That said, there would be no ambiguity permitted in the choice.

I would make it clear that, if Quebecers voted Yes, sovereignty would be inevitable. There would be no turning back. This was not a threat; it was a promise. As prime minister, I would respect the result and make Quebec sovereignty happen—happen as quickly as possible—thoroughly protecting the interests of Canada in doing so. I had no intention of spelling out this scenario in detail, but I would have prepared all the contingencies necessary to maximize our leverage in the subsequent negotiations.

This does not mean, by the way, that I would have sought to impose punitive conditions on an independent Quebec. Good relations between Quebec and Canada would be desirable going forward for both sides. Quebec's continued prosperity, which separation really would jeopardize, was in our interests as well as theirs. Some joint institutions would likely be put in place. But there was a range of issues on which post-independence would not look much like the rosy scenarios the separatists promised, and which invariably assumed that Quebec could unilaterally set the terms of its departure and its place in the global community.

Thank goodness, of course, that we did not have to go there. I say this not for the reason that many believe. At the time, some analysts claimed that my Government's hold of power would be jeopardized if the sovereignty threat became real. That was a complete misreading of how public opinion had changed outside Quebec since Canada's near-death experience of 1995. Had a referendum taken place, our conviction was that "English Canadians"* would

---

* I put "English Canadians" in quotation marks since the term, while still used by many Quebec political analysts, seems anachronist outside Quebec, and even in the "English" parts of Quebec. Only a minority of these populations are "English" or even "British" in their ethnicity. While almost all do

Top left: Australian Prime Minister John Howard addresses the House of Commons, 2006. *(Jason Ransom)*

Top right: Hosting Shinzo Abe, Prime Minister of Japan, on Parliament Hill, 2013. *(Deb Ransom)*

Bottom right: Welcoming Petro Poroshenko, President of Ukraine, to Parliament Hill, 2014. *(Deb Ransom)*

Bottom left: Hosting Narendra Modi, Prime Minister of India, in Toronto after a multi-stop tour of Canada, 2015. *(Jason Ransom)*

With my mother, Margaret, and brothers, Grant and Robert, during the annual Calgary Southwest Conservative Stampede Barbeque, 2014. *(Jill Thompson)*

Enjoying the Calgary Stampede breakfast tradition, 2015. *(Jill Thompson)*

Touring Lac-Mégantic in the aftermath of the horrific disaster that claimed forty-seven lives, July 7, 2013. *(Jill Thompson)*

Pausing for a moment of reflection at the Western Wall in Jerusalem, 2014. *(Jason Ransom)*

Top: Performing "With a Little Help from My Friends" with Yo-Yo Ma at the National Arts Centre, 2009. *(Jill Propp)*

Middle: Signing a copy of *A Great Game*, 2013. *(Jason Ransom)*

Bottom: Sailing across the Northwest Passage aboard the HMCS Kingston in search of Sir John Franklin's lost vessels, 2014. *(Jason Ransom)*

With Finance Minister Jim Flaherty during a cabinet meeting at Willson House in Chelsea, Quebec, 2009. *(Jason Ransom)*

Hosting former Prime Ministers Mulroney, Campbell, and Chrétien en route to the funeral of Nelson Mandela, 2013. *(Deb Ransom)*

Our government's first Cabinet at Rideau Hall, 2006. *(Jason Ransom)*

The 2008 Conservative Caucus. *(Jason Ransom)*

Laureen and I hosting a caucus BBQ at Harrington Lake, 2009. *(Jill Propp)*

Swearing in a new Ministry at Rideau Hall, 2011. *(Jason Ransom)*

Posing with the new Cabinet beneath the Diamond Jubilee portrait of Queen Elizabeth II, 2013. *(Jason Ransom)*

On the ice in Frobisher Bay, Iqaluit, Nunavut, 2012. *(Jason Ransom)*

have strongly preferred a prime minister from outside Quebec. Only such a PM would not allow the ambiguities that had cost the federalist side so dearly the last time and left it totally unprepared if defeated.

Frankly, after the coalition fiasco of 2008, such analysts should have understood that, outside the province, public opinion on Quebec issues had shifted radically in the past generation. Our reason for wanting to avoid another referendum had nothing to do with partisan survival. It was about the broader interests of the country.

Another separatist referendum would have been, at best, an enormous distraction for our Government. At worst, it would have undercut much of what we had done during and since the global financial crisis to present Canada as one of the most stable economies and investment climates in the world. International investors had already been noticing the decline of the sovereignty threat and were reacting accordingly. We were fortunate that they did not read the PQ's victory as a genuine revival of that threat.

Does the PQ's abject failure in 2012–2014 mean that the risk of Quebec separation is gone? I am undecided. On the one hand, the numbers for separation are just not there today. And, yes, the PQ could still disappear at some point if voter orientations continue to move to a more conventional left-right spectrum. On the other hand, Quebec political opinion and its political system remain in flux, with five significant parties having a range of orientations on the province's future.†

The bigger geopolitical reality is that most democratic systems are moving away from conventional politics, with the rise of populism, nationalism, and unconventional parties on both the right and left. As well, there is still a large minority of the Quebec population who believe in

---

speak English, a sizable proportion of those use it as a second language. This contrasts with Quebec, where francophones are still overwhelmingly French in ethnic and linguistic background.

† As I write this, the PQ has been leading the polls in this five-party setting, having finished a very bad fourth the last time. Yet support for the party and for sovereignty is not much more than thirty percent.

sovereignty, with less than half the population strongly committed to federalism. After a decade of declining income performance and increasing political upheaval, who knows?

I especially worry about the trend over the past decade of deconstructionist wokeism in much of Canada outside Quebec. This has been reflected both in reckless immigration policy and the widespread labelling of all Canadian cultural narratives as automatically racist. There is the potential for—indeed, there is already evidence of—a backlash to these trends in Quebec.

In Quebec, such historical narratives are foundational. There may be much in the province's legislative approach to its linguistic and cultural identity that many outside, me included, are uncomfortable with. But the underlying motivation—to preserve the French language and culture—is non-negotiable for Quebecers. Given its central place in the founding and identity of Canada, it must be so for any federal government as well.

A CONTROVERSIAL FOREIGN INVESTMENT: CNOOC/NEXEN

AS WE DREW TOWARD the end of the year, our Government was faced with a major and controversial decision that involved both domestic economic policy and international relations. I refer to the application by the China National Offshore Oil Company (CNOOC) to buy the Canadian energy company Nexen.

Our Government was generally encouraging of foreign investment in Canada, just as we were of Canadian corporate investment elsewhere. These were pragmatic positions consistent with our general support for international trade, tempered by our assessment of Canada's national interests. They were not ideological positions.

We had inherited a foreign investment policy that had been largely unchanged since the early days of Brian Mulroney's Government. That administration had, in its efforts to undo Pierre Trudeau's disastrous economic management, overhauled foreign investment policy. Gone was the

Foreign Investment Review Agency (FIRA), which discouraged foreign investment across a wide range of activities, replaced by the Investment Canada Act. It was part of a series of policies aimed at unravelling an anti-business environment and liberalizing the economy.

The Act prescribed reviews for transactions of a certain size and allowed the government to impose conditions on individual takeovers. Governments did that on a number of occasions; however, neither the Mulroney Government nor those of his successors—Campbell, Chrétien, or Martin—blocked or turned down a single foreign investment. There had, indeed, been a sea change. From a regime that was suspicious of foreign investment, Canada had gradually become almost laissez-faire in practice.

From our earliest days in office, we sought to adjust the foreign investment regime. This was by no means a wholesale change. In some ways, we sought to further loosen the rules. For instance, we raised the thresholds that would trigger reviews of foreign investment transactions. We also relaxed specific thresholds in some industries, like telecommunications. In other ways, however, we tightened the regime.

The most substantive legislative modification we enacted was the insertion of a National Security Review of Investments clause (NRSC) into the Investment Canada Act. It was high time, as Canada was one of the few countries that did not have explicit criteria along those lines. These new security reviews could be initiated regardless of the size of the transaction.

It is true that some countries have abused such clauses, turning them into thinly veiled protectionism. We had no such intention—which is why these reviews would be conducted by our national security agencies and officials, not trade or industry departments. The main reason for doing this was the new realities of economic globalization. Potential problematic actors from places like Russia and China were now investors in a way they could not have been in the 1980s.

We made good use of the NRSC. There were several occasions (but less than a dozen) when we declined foreign investments for national security reasons. This was done quietly, well outside the public eye (although, occasionally, a disappointed applicant went to the media). None of the transactions we disallowed were even remotely borderline. They were blatant examples of foreign governments attempting to acquire assets through which they could compromise Canada's national security.

We also provided some additional guidance for reviews in a couple of areas. For example, we made it clear that we would not allow Chinese take-over of Canada's rare earth mineral resources. China held a virtual monopoly on these vital industrial materials, and it was beginning to use that control to bully or intimidate countries that needed access to them.

Another area we began to watch closely was information technology, specifically the roles of the Chinese firms of Huawei and ZTE Corporation. It was the unanimous view of our security officials that these companies were, in practice, extensions of the Chinese state and its security architecture and, as such, represented serious risks to our national security interests. We developed a plan to gradually exit these technologies from Canada, starting with the federal government itself. Interestingly, while there is a widespread consensus on this today, we were alone when we were doing this, even among our Five Eyes partners.

Invoking the Investment Canada Act

THE MOST DRAMATIC CHANGES we made in the foreign investment space were arguably not in law but in practice. We became the first government to ever disallow a transaction as "not a net benefit" to the country under the Investment Canada Act. That occurred in 2008, when we blocked the sale of the space division of MacDonald Dettwiler and Associates (MDA) to an American company.

Our main reason was because the company had some proprietary technology that we believed important to the industrial capacity of the country. It was technology that the Government of Canada itself had invested in in the past. We also suspected that the purchase by American interests was intended to force Canada out of the business, which, of course, was not in the national interest. After Minister Jim Prentice blocked the sale, there seemed to be relatively little controversy around the decision, either within or outside federal government.

The second time we did this, near the end of 2010, was much more contentious. It was for the proposed hostile takeover of the Saskatoon-based Potash Corporation by an Australian firm, BHP Billiton. Potash is an essential resource for agriculture around the world, and Canada is the world's largest single producer of it. The Potash Corporation was the largest single miner, and Canada's position in the industry gave us significant market power in a strategic resource. Potash Corporation had begun as a Crown corporation of the Government of Saskatchewan, which recognized this strategic value many years ago.

In this case, there was a wide range of opinion pressing the government on the matter, although the vast majority was opposed to the deal. That included Saskatchewan's current government—a conservative, trade-oriented administration under Premier Brad Wall. It was joined in its opposition by virtually the entire business leadership of Western Canada.

It is not hard to figure out why this was, and it went well beyond a typically nationalist (or provincialist) argument about "keeping head offices." This one transaction could have real impacts on our global market position. Overnight, Canada would be reduced from a major participant with influence over world markets in a key industry to a marginal, bit player. After due consideration and consultation, Minister Tony Clement laid out a series of very tough conditions, which the company ultimately (and appropriately) rejected.

This time, however, we met with very serious bureaucratic resistance to this decision. At times, it seemed almost fanatical. When we rejected their arguments that this was simple protectionism, or at least opening the door to it, officials went much further. At one point, they tried to argue that the takeover could not be legally rejected at all. They also tried to claim that no one on the political side of government besides the Minister was even legally allowed to discuss the matter. (Apparently, unelected officials were not similarly prohibited.)

I emphatically disabused them of that notion, but the situation was sufficiently alarming to me that I brought our ministers together for discussion before Minister Clement took the final decision. I knew that his intention was to negate the takeover, and I was seriously worried that government lawyers might try to strong-arm him if they were able to isolate him at the last minute. We already understood their advice clearly enough, and I would not permit further interventions. Thus, with the Cabinet review completed, the Minister publicly announced his decision.

This episode was clear evidence of just how firmly a laissez-faire view had taken hold within the bureaucracy. That is not to say I had no understanding of their position. There could indeed be a slippery slope into a general protectionist approach or a general opposition to moving any Canadian head office. Naturally, our Government was not sympathetic to that view, and we were not going to do anything to systematically discourage foreign investment. We were simply being pragmatic on this transaction, which, if it had gone through, would have been a net negative for the Canadian economy. Subsequent events have confirmed that it was the right decision.

The Final Decision

GIVEN THAT HISTORY, it was clear that the proposed Chinese takeover of Nexen would be no less controversial. Internally, there was a strong impulse to rubberstamp the transaction, because of both the ideological orientation of the Industry Department and the hyper-pro-China bent of the Foreign Affairs bureaucracy. Outside the government, however, the controversy was precisely because of the nature of the proponent. The ultimate reason for rejecting BHP Billiton had little to do with the company, which was not held in any disregard in Canada. By contrast, the Chinese state-owned enterprise (SOE) raised suspicions quite widely.

There were additional aspects of the transaction that were troubling. For example, CNOOC's proposed purchase price for Nexen—over $15 billion—was well above any reasonable market estimate of the value of the company. It came on the heels of a series of Chinese investments and takeovers in the oil and gas industry, particularly in the oil sands. There was a growing concern that this was part of a Chinese strategy to gain effective control of that portion of the Canadian economy.

Unlike the federal bureaucracy, everyone else—the industry, the public, and my Government—was very divided on the CNOOC/Nexen deal. This immediately became a complication because of another transaction. Petronas, the Malaysian state-owned enterprise, was proposing to take over Progress Energy, a mid-sized natural gas producer operating in northern Alberta and B.C. We had no serious concerns about Petronas; it had a reputation as a genuinely commercial enterprise operating independently of government. Still, we knew it raised some of the same issues, at least conceptually. When the Industry bureaucracy tried to quickly ram the Petronas transaction through—a clear attempt to tilt the field toward CNOOC—we were forced to step in to delay any approval.

Once again, the industry minister, now Christian Paradis, was solely responsible for making these decisions under the statute. However, given that we were now looking at bigger policy questions, we had a full discussion in Cabinet. This was one of the rare times when we did not come to anything resembling a consensus. Views ranged from quickly approving and applauding the CNOOC application to blocking it without recourse.

That left the Minister and me to make the decision, and we agreed on a two-pronged approach. The Minister would approve the transaction, but I would announce a policy change going forward, that is, we would not approve future takeovers in the oil sands by state-owned enterprises under normal circumstances. In part, we adopted this approach because opinions were deeply split, and my political instinct was to offer something to both sides. But there was more to it than that.

The reason I did not reject the proposal was that, in and of itself, CNOOC taking over Nexen was not going to give the Chinese government undue influence over the oil sands. Turning it down would have badly blindsided the Chinese. When I had attended the Asia-Pacific Economic Cooperations Summit in Vladivostok in July 2012, this matter was raised with me at the highest diplomatic level by President Hu. The Chinese were clearly very anxious about this and found themselves in the middle of a controversy they had not expected. From my exchange with Hu, my suspicions were further raised that the Chinese had received indications from our bureaucracy that the investment would be automatically approved.

That said, we were genuinely worried about the Chinese desire to gain greater state control over the development of the Canadian oil sands. The factor we examined the most closely was the SOE element. In many cases, state-owned enterprises operate truly commercially, like Petronas. Certainly, nobody thinks Statoil in Norway functions as an arm of the Norwegian government. In this case, however, there was little doubt about Chinese state supervision of the investor, and the proposal certainly did not look like a normal commercial transaction. While we did approve the sale, we added some conditions to address our concerns.

The more general "conditionality" I laid out regarding future SOE transactions had a broader purpose. Increasingly, I did not believe that our economic relations with China served Canada's longer-term interests. I am referring to the fact that their access to our markets and assets were largely unfettered, whereas the Chinese carefully screened and limited every single trade and investment opportunity in their country. I hoped this new approach would help give us some leverage the other way, allowing us to bargain for a long list of Canadian investments that were being delayed or blocked in China.

REFLECTIONS ON FOREIGN INVESTMENT POLICY

WHEN WE ANNOUNCED the approval of both the Nexen and Petronas takeovers on December 7, 2012, there were strong reactions across the board. Of course, left-wing, the-state-knows-best nationalists were ideologically opposed. But there was some opposition on the other side as well, some of which was also ideological.

That was certainly true of the more libertarian, laissez-faire crowd. I must admit that I had little time for them. Market-oriented conservatives had long opposed government ownership in Canada's energy industry, and we had succeeded in getting Petro-Canada privatized. How could one be against Canadian government ownership, but in the name of the free market, defend Chinese state control—by a communist government no less? That was a real head-scratcher.

There was more pragmatic, self-interested opposition in the business community. Some in the Alberta oil patch had seen the price of the Nexen takeover and, hoping to be next in line, had big-dollar figures dancing in their heads. Others objected to the fact that there were now different approaches to private versus SOE transactions, and they decried the ambiguity in the new approach to the latter. This was especially true among some of the professionals who helped facilitate foreign merger and acquisition activity. They warned that our new approach would "chill investment."

That take was missing the whole point. We did, in fact, want to restrict SOE takeovers, unless we could get reciprocal access for Canadian investment. To get that reciprocal access, ambiguity is essential. It is that ambiguity that would encourage the Chinese to engage in discussions. Any set of fully clear-cut rules meant that the system could be gamed, and Canada would have no leverage.

The even bigger reason why the chill argument made no sense was, of course, that our government had taken much broader steps, both taxation and regulatory, to create a good environment for business investment, both foreign and domestic. The results bore that out. For the opposite reasons, foreign investment in Canada fell steadily after 2015. It certainly had nothing to do with any spillover chill on private investors. In fact, BHP Billiton, the one private company whose foreign investment proposal was rejected, is now a major greenfield investor in Saskatchewan.

Once again, I saw the nuanced decision on CNOOC/Nexen and other foreign takeovers as a reflection of our conservative philosophy of government. Yes, we have broad principles, but unlike ideologues, we do not allow these principles to become completely detached from an assessment of the facts. Investment flows are generally a very good thing for an open, trading economy like Canada's. My Government's record in promoting trade and investment is unmatched in Canada's history. We concluded a record number of free trade and foreign investment agreements. We subjected far fewer foreign investments to reviews and approved all but two of them. Yet we also understood that some investments, carefully analyzed, might not be in Canada's national interest. That position, not liberalized markets, was the ultimate principle at stake.

The most interesting thing in all this was that the Chinese clearly understood what I was doing. In the period following the Nexen decision, they began to come to us with specific investment ideas, seeking dialogue on how they would fit into our new approach. They also agreed to take our requests back to Beijing. This process was, unfortunately, still in the early stages when we left office.

I also later became aware of fallout in Beijing from the Nexen decision. Apparently, comments I had made at my press conference—especially my concern about the "non-commercial nature of the transaction"—went to the highest levels of the Chinese government. That led to some serious questions about the price that had been paid and, I understand, greater reverberations at CNOOC itself.

I got a taste of those reverberations a couple of years later during a private business trip to China. At one meeting, I was welcomed by a high-level official who opened his remarks with a two-pronged set of comments. He spent his first few minutes praising me for my contributions to Chinese-Canadian relations, singling out my role as the prime minister who approved the Nexen purchase, one of China's largest foreign purchases and certainly the largest ever in Canada. He then spent the next few minutes cursing me (somewhat in jest) for having allowed the transaction because it had proved to be one of China's poorest global investments ever! What could I add to that?

22

ECONOMY, WORKFORCE, AND IDENTITY

AS WE ROLLED INTO 2013, economic issues remained at the top of our agenda. We were now spending significant time on deficit and expenditure reduction, but contrary to some perceptions, that was never the first item on our economic agenda. Our priorities were economic growth and strengthening the revenue side of our finances.

FACILITATING VENTURE CAPITAL

THE BUDGET FOR 2013 contained many growth initiatives, the largest of which was renewal of the Building Canada Fund. This was the major infrastructure program that we initiated in 2007—distinct from the 2009–2011 stimulus spending—and we extended its life by ten years, adding significant cash.

One major initiative was launched even before the budget—the Venture Capital Action Plan (VCAP). Minister Flaherty and I announced this in Montreal on the set of *Dragon's Den*—the prime-time investor-contest show. The announcement was intended to address, at least in part, a significant problem within the Canadian financial system.

Many early start-ups in our country are successful in attracting angel investors. These are non-institutional backers, usually wealthy individuals, who will put seed money behind a promising entrepreneur with a good idea.

However, at the next stage, the "venture" or early-growth stage, institutional money in Canada had been hard to attract.

Our banking system, while strong and stable, is dominated by six large banks that are increasingly global in nature. Venture is just not their end of the market. Governments have tried to fill some of the gap—federal regional development agencies are an example—but the truth is that their financing is limited, and they are not that great at picking winners. Consequently, entrepreneurs who have passed through the early stages of business development will often move elsewhere, particularly to the United States, where venture capital markets are well developed.

Minister Flaherty was aware of this systemic economic weakness from day one and looked for ways to address it. In 2007, we had made tax changes to facilitate investment into the venture capital sector, but we needed more input on next steps. Two studies on R&D investment and venture we commissioned—by Tom Jenkins, formerly of OpenText, and by Bay Street entrepreneur Sam Duboc, respectively—contributed greatly to the VCAP. It created four funds of funds, that is, four big pools of cash aiming to invest in various sectors, which would be endowed by the federal government, some of the provinces, and other large private-sector participants.* A lot of money was generated in that initial process, and it gave the project a much-needed kick-start. Our purpose was straightforward: to create a thriving Canadian private sector–driven venture capital hub.

A little over a decade later, I believe we can say that this initiative was a success. Although VCAP cannot be given all the credit, it played a critical role in achieving our policy aims. As a result, the venture capital industry is now very real in Canada, and it has grown significantly. It is also true that much more remains to be done.

---

* The four funds were the Northleaf Venture Catalyst Fund, the Teralys Capital Innovation Fund, the Kensington Venture Fund, and the HarbourVest Canada Growth Fund.

TACKLING SKILLS SHORTAGES: THE CANADA JOB GRANT

ANOTHER MAJOR UNDERTAKING in terms of encouraging economic growth was our attempt to tackle skills shortages, especially in the trades. This was an area we had been concerned about from the beginning. It was why we had earlier created the Apprenticeship Completion Grant, which is self-explanatory and, as it happens, a real challenge for many. We also made thirty Red Seal trades fully eligible for the Canada Student Financial Assistance Program, which (unbelievably) they previously were not.

This priority was also pursued via infrastructure funding. When we made major investments into post-secondary infrastructure, particularly through the Knowledge Infrastructure Program, we had ensured that community colleges and technical schools were fully eligible. That meant these institutions got a much greater share of federal funding than they had in the past. We also undertook periodic advertising programs to make people more aware of the opportunities in trades education.

Even with all these previous efforts, we had barely made a dent in the problem. New enrolments in trades programs were not filling the gap created by tradespeople retiring. All the evidence suggested that this would only get worse. Unfortunately, the barriers to fixing this problem were very serious.

The first roadblock was policy. Jurisdiction in this area is largely provincial, and provincial priorities had long encouraged young people to go to university. Not only were trades rarely considered, but there was a growing trend of phasing out shops and related education in high schools.

I saw the consequences of this when I toured trade schools, which I did to see how our efforts to expand their capacities had progressed. What I found was stunning. Two-thirds of the new enrollees in these programs already had university degrees. After four or more years, at great cost to themselves and taxpayers, they graduated without marketable results. Only now were they pursuing much-cheaper, much-quicker education that was far more likely to lead to a job.

The second problem is society-wide: a long-standing and deep social prejudice against blue-collar work within the middle class. I suppose this goes back to the post–World War II generation, who saw getting a university degree as the preferred means to social advancement in almost every case. Other countries, like Germany, are way ahead of us in addressing this problem; getting a trade there is regarded as being on equal social footing with studying to get a university degree. That has been a key part of Germany's post-war resurgence and its rise as a global manufacturing giant.

The third problem is misinformation. I suspect if you ask parents of almost any age in Canada, you will find a widespread belief that a university degree will result in better economic opportunities for their kids. But that generalization is simply untrue. The data on a range of university degrees shows that many graduates will experience below-average earnings for life. Trades and technical training are often far more sophisticated than is believed, and tradespeople today often earn six-figure salaries from a young age with little risk of sustained unemployment. Given the developments in AI and other changes in the workforce, these trends are likely to accelerate.

As we approached the 2013 budget, our desire to deal with this problem grew stronger, in part because we felt there was an opportunity to do so. We were due to renew various labour market development programs with the provinces. These were monies beyond the no-strings-attached Canada Social Transfer, which helps fund post-secondary education. They were historically linked to programs tied to Employment Insurance. EI is a clear federal jurisdiction, but the related training programs had been delegated to the provinces through these labour force agreements many years earlier.

The plan was developed with Human Resources Minister Diane Finley and later with Jason Kenney when he moved to the portfolio. It was centred on the Canada Job Grant. We would tie a portion of federal funding to matching grants from the provinces and the private sector to create jobs based on labour force needs.

Canada being a federation, getting the provinces' buy-in on the Canada Job Grant was always going to be difficult. They most certainly have their own views about how to spend such money. They also tend to bristle when the feds become involved, particularly when the plan involves more conditionality than they are used to. Minister Kenney was tasked with nailing down the agreements. We eventually got them with all the provinces and made various announcements around the country. This represented some progress in the direction we wanted to go, but it was quite limited.

The provinces' resistance had gone beyond jurisdictional turf arguments. While some, particularly Quebec, claimed they were already doing what we were proposing, that was, in most cases, quite dubious. Certainly, when I met with premiers, their opposition was deeper. It was clear that the provinces generally believed that we were trying to address a problem that did not really exist.*

How could this be? The truth is, I believe, quite disturbing. The provinces have largely farmed out post-secondary education policy to the post-secondary institutions themselves. Not surprisingly, those institutions then create policy strictly in their own self-interest. For most, labour force consequences are of little consideration. They just want to fill their facilities with as many students bringing in as much money as possible. So when the provinces sought advice on the Canada Job Grant, these institutions advised them it was unnecessary.

The result is that our post-secondary education system—high-quality though it is—predictively produces tens of thousands of graduates every year for whom there is woefully insufficient market demand. At the same time, key occupations are just as foreseeably facing growing labour shortages. This is true not just for the trades and technical jobs, but also for most occupations requiring high levels of numeracy—scientists, engineers, mathematicians, and the like. Still, the universities keep growing, and their salaries keep rising, so there is little problem as far as they are concerned.

If I sound frustrated by this, I am. The problems we saw developing in the labour force were not imaginary; they were as plain as the nose on my face. Having failed to address them when we still had a chance, the Canadian

---

* One premier went so far as to repeat social prejudices about how university degrees produced "better people," even if the job opportunities are not there. However, it would be wrong to suggest that the provinces all responded that way.

labour market is now facing critical shortages in many areas that will seriously impede our economy for many years to come. The coming AI revolution is only going to make this much, much worse.

I know I have raised this before, but this is another example of why elected governments should set public policy and never leave matters entirely in the hands of autonomous technocrats. At best, their focus will be excessively narrow—witness how the Covid-19 pandemic was handled. At worst, it will be self-interested. Most importantly, it will always be unaccountable.

THE TEMPORARY FOREIGN WORKERS PROGRAM

GIVEN CANADA'S INABILITY to replenish its skilled workforce, it is inevitable that the country would increasingly turn to recruiting workers through immigration. A growing number of those workers would be temporary in nature. This gave rise to some embarrassment for my Government—an episode that still gets me upset when I think too much about it.

The Temporary Foreign Worker (TFW) program has a long history in Canada. It has allowed some types of workers, who are presumably not available in the domestic labour market, to be brought into the country for a relatively short period to fill a company's needs. Typical uses would be for major development projects in the construction, energy, and mining sectors, where particular skills are needed, but only for the duration of the project. When these projects are finished, it is expected that the workers would return to their country of origin. There have long been similar programs for seasonal work in the agricultural sector. It has been argued that these farm workers are needed because it is impossible to recruit enough Canadians—at least that is the claim.

All that said, the TFW program was subject to a major change under the Martin Government. It expanded the program to bring in unskilled or low-skilled temporary foreign workers for a wide range of occupations, particularly in the service sectors. We inherited this program and continued it.

TFWs, particularly in the unskilled category, began to mushroom from the earliest days of our Government. I had misgivings about this from the start. The program was a departure from the Canadian model, which had prioritized permanent immigration, with a path to citizenship, to fill critical employment needs. On several occasions, I asked officials (and occasionally ministers) about the rising numbers of TFWs.

I was told that this was due to an overheated labour market, both in the pre-financial crisis and later recovery periods. The oil and gas sector was usually cited—the booms in Alberta and Saskatchewan were said to have put pressure on not just the supply of skilled workers but the labour force generally in those areas. With a hundred things on my plate at any given time, I did not dig deeper. Besides, I was assured that comprehensive "labour market assessments" had demonstrated the need for the growing number of TFWs.

That all sounded good—except that it was not true.

The first indications that something was amiss surfaced in several media stories about individual instances of abuse in the TFW program. Initially, these involved some TFWs being brought in to do jobs in areas where there was, in fact, high unemployment. Then we became aware of employers requiring TFWs to stay in the low-end housing they provided, presumably to increase their profit margins. It had a sweatshop feel to it.

Even more troubling was a reported case where a company had brought in TFWs to help them move Canadian jobs overseas. It involved bringing in temporary foreign workers, training them on jobs staffed by Canadians, and then shifting those jobs and their workers offshore. The former TFWs, now back in their home country, resumed their "Canadian" jobs at a lower wage. While I can understand why this might benefit the company, it was plainly not in the interests of Canadian workers or the Canadian economy more broadly. Yet when I raised the matter with officials, their initial response was to defend the use of TFWs for this purpose.

Now I was alarmed. I tasked the Policy section of the Prime Minister's Office, then led by Rachel Curran, to do a deep dive into the administration of the TFW program. She was ably assisted by Katelin Everson and Phil Harwood. The results were, to say the least, simply astounding—far worse than anything that had appeared in the media.

Abuses exist in any large-scale government program. But in this case, the abuse ran systemically through the entire program. Most critically, the labour force assessments were a sham. They were little more than a company telling the federal government that it needed temporary foreign workers, approval for which was automatically granted. Given that low bar, things got much worse from there.

In effect, whole companies were transitioning their businesses to make the employment of low-wage TFWs their preferred model. Not only were they not searching for Canadian workers at all but also in some cases they were refusing to even accept applications from them. To our deepening dismay, it also turned out that these temporary foreign workers were increasingly not temporary. Their employment was just being rolled over from one application period to the next. Furthermore, these practices were beginning to go beyond unskilled, front-line workers. Some companies were starting to claim that they needed their supervisors and managers to be TFWs as well. Why? Because they now had no Canadians with experience!

Given the irresponsible nature of the program's administration, I suppose this abuse was not that surprising when you think about it. One of the toughest parts of any business, especially in the low-wage service sector, is recruiting, interviewing, and retaining staff. If the federal government is prepared to do this for you—and to do it for free—why not take them up on it? And why not prefer temporary foreign workers anyway? They are usually grateful and hard-working, even if paid less than minimum wage. They are also a captive workforce—essentially a form of indentured servant. If they want to leave to take another job, or even express unhappiness, you can just threaten to send them back to where they came from.

Now, as bad as all this was, it got even worse—with an incident that I still find dumbfounding. As we were reviewing the program, it came to light that a Chinese-owned mine in British Columbia had received the go-ahead from federal officials to employ an entirely Chinese workforce for the duration of the project, without ever having to even look for Canadian workers. How could this be? Well, it was simple. They had agreed to the company's assertion that every job at the mine required Chinese-language proficiency!

This was the very thing I had told other leaders, especially in emerging economies, that we did not do. They had had bad experiences with mining projects, especially Chinese-owned ones. In essence, the Chinese buy a mine, seal off the operations, bring in an entirely Chinese workforce, and ship out all the production. There is virtually no benefit for the host country, save for local officials getting paid off. When the project is completed, the Chinese take all the profits, all the wages, all the minerals, all the skilled workers, and they leave.

I was just stunned that officials would sanction this Chinese "African model" of development in Canada. When they tried, once again, to justify it, I became irate and told departmental officials we were shutting it down.

I tasked Minister Kenney—lucky guy!—with cleaning up the mess. He proposed a series of measures that went to the heart of the program's problems.

The first thing we did was ensure that real labour market assessments were done. Companies would have to first scour the local workforce to demonstrate that they actually needed foreign workers. Second, there would be no free recruitment services from the federal government. We would require companies to pay a reasonable amount for the assessing and processing of workers. Finally, companies bringing in workers would have to meet fair, market-based wage requirements.

These modifications, which were nothing but reasonable, dramatically slowed the pace of TFW applications. Ideally, we would have phased out the unskilled TFW program entirely, but we wanted to first try the new rules to see how things unfolded. In fact, TFWs dropped over 80 per cent within a year, mainly in the low-skill category.

Reflecting on the TFW Experience

I HAVE KICKED MYSELF for long ignoring my misgivings about the TFW program. On reflection, I feel I may have been a bit too hard in my self-evaluation. After all, our Government had not changed existing policy in any significant way, which is why there was never a formal discussion.

And I did ask the right questions. No prime minister should need to assume that the answers he gets are broadly misleading or that the administration of policy is devoid of common sense.

So how and why did that happen? The answer, I suspect, is that both the political and bureaucratic wings of the government were being given very positive feedback about the evolution of the TFW program. It was serving the needs of business widely. That was true not only for big business. Small, retail, and service businesses—often strong Conservative supporters—were using and abusing the program just as much, if not more so, than the corporate sector. And, of course, for the longest time, nobody seemed to be complaining.

The truth is that a temporary foreign worker program, as problematic as it can be, will, at any given moment, have plenty of political support. That does not make it good. In fact, I would argue that the excessive use of TFWs is very bad for both society and the workers involved. This was always the basis of my quiet misgivings.

Where temporary foreign workers have been used to excess, effectively as a business model, deep social pathologies develop. A permanent underclass takes shape. It is defined not just by its low wages but by its non-citizen status, as many of these workers and their employers inevitably ignore the "temporary" nature of their presence. These people are then vulnerable to unscrupulous employers and landlords, not to mention human traffickers, drug dealers, and gang recruiters. Large communities develop outside the law, with little or no stake in the society they live in. There is little effort at integration on either side.

Compare this to the history of Canada. Our country is about people with hopes for a permanent new life, leaving behind deep roots to pursue a dream. This has fuelled the millions of big and small success stories that have helped make our country what it is. That includes being, despite our incredible ethnic diversity, one of the most harmonious societies ever.

I feel very strongly about this. I wrote about the subject in my 2018 book *Right Here, Right Now*. Once we travelled down this route of low-skilled temporary foreign workers, we were developing a model I believe to be fundamentally un-Canadian. The Canadian experience has been about the path to citizenship, to belonging, and, hopefully, to success, for both immigrants and society as a whole. It has not been about creating a cheap underclass partly or wholly outside normal economic life. That is not the Canadian way.

And it is not just un-Canadian; it is also un-conservative. The reason conservatives support (or at least should support) market economics is twofold: they are better over the long haul in producing growth and a competitive market will ensure that the benefits of that growth will be widely spread. A hot economy raises profits, leads to new opportunities, and pushes up the wages of labour.

That is why in the oil boom of the late 1970s and early 1980s, this high-school graduate was able to become a professional computer programmer in Alberta. It is also why there was no need for the job to be filled by a temporary foreign worker. Back then, no one would even have suggested that. In short, it is the broader market that conservatives need to support, not business interests narrowly.

We should be under no illusion. The explosion in temporary foreign workers was really about one thing and one thing only: paying lower wages. The data we reviewed was very clear on this. Whenever there had been any market pressure pushing wages above the minimum, the demands for unskilled TFWs would start to flow in. Effectively, the growth in TFWs had been a policy to deliberately push down market wage rates.

In truth, there was a view developing among some that this was actually the job of our Conservative Government! I remember on one occasion talking with an individual who said he was planning to open a whole chain of restaurants in Western Canada. He had been very happy with his low-wage workers—TFWs largely from the Philippines—and said that, if he could not get more, he would not be opening any more restaurants. To which I responded, "Well, maybe you should think about opening your restaurants in Manila." My point was this: if you are a business and you are not interested in employing Canadians as a matter of principle, why do I as prime minister care whether you open the restaurants here or not? The reason our Government wanted to encourage a good business environment is for the broader benefits a stronger economy brings to society, including good paying jobs for Canadians.

The situations under which a government should consider importing foreign workers temporarily are very narrow. There must be a clearly higher demand for well-defined skills than the market can provide, as well as reason to believe that such demand is truly short term in nature. Beyond that, a fluid labour market and widespread educational opportunities should be capable of managing these issues.

In the end, we did effectively stop the abuse of the program, and the full elimination of unskilled TFWs was in sight. However, our successors started expanding the program once again. It was slow at first, but its scale has now surpassed even our worst numbers. Our country and those workers are the worse for it.

IMMIGRATION, CITIZENSHIP, AND MULTICULTURALISM

THE TFW PROBLEMS ASIDE, we maintained a strong and vigorous immigration policy, along the lines of its three traditional elements: the economic component, the humanitarian commitment, and family reunification stream. To be sure, we made improvements in the humanitarian and family reunification areas, but our central focus was to restore the priority of the economic component. This brings the most direct benefit to Canadians and generates the underlying political support for immigration. When this emphasis is lost or ignored, or immigration becomes largely irregular or illegal in nature, backlashes will occur that undermine all immigration policy. We have unfortunately seen that in many Western countries in the past couple of decades.

I will certainly not claim that our immigration programs were entirely problem-free. However, we made real efforts to deal with abuses quickly and directly where we encountered them. We cracked down on crooked immigration consultants and took measures to stop human smuggling. This has been a major problem elsewhere in the world and was beginning to rear its ugly head in Canada as well. We made it easier to deport foreign criminals from Canadian soil. All these actions went a long way in sustaining public support for immigration in Canada in an age where opposition to it was rising almost everywhere else.

Of course, there are those who will claim that any tough measure on immigration is proof one is anti-immigrant or even racist. But problems in such a large and complex system are as real as they are inevitable, and as with any other program, the public at large expects its government to deal with them. If you do that, you will sustain and build support; if you do not, you will nurture a backlash.

In our case, we not only managed to sustain public support for the system but also did something unprecedented in Canada: we maintained immigration levels during a recession, specifically the recession provoked by the global financial crisis. We were able to do this because we had a system increasingly focused on long-term economic needs. There was therefore no reason for a short-term downturn to cause us to scale back the program.

In line with our philosophy, we also made changes in our laws to reinforce the value of Canadian citizenship. In recent decades, there had been an explosion in the number of "dual citizens" living outside Canada. In many cases, these were people who had little attachment to Canada, either now or in the past.

Officials would frequently cite these hundreds of thousands, perhaps millions—we really did not know the number—of "Canadians abroad" as a bragging right. Yet they were not able to articulate what concrete benefits such a policy, which I called a "citizenship box-top giveaway," provided. On the contrary, since, unlike other countries, we did not require hefty fees or even tax payments to maintain such citizenship, the arrangement provided no revenue. On the other hand, periodic needs for consular services or even evacuation of these citizens from foreign countries could be very costly for the federal government. Thankfully, the fix—at least the fix going forward—was relatively easy and was accomplished by tightening residency requirements before citizenship was conferred.

Our Government also brought in a modified approach to multiculturalism. We started from the premise that multiculturalism is an important concept that brings much good to our country. We should not try to deny that people who come here from different cultures will, to some degree, change the nature of our broader culture. That is part of what happens. New citizens will want to preserve elements of their culture and heritage. These are realities, and they are, for the most part, good.

But we should not deny the other reality, which is that the vast majority of those who have come here, come to be Canadian. People do not take lightly the momentous decision of leaving a place where their ancestors have long lived and are buried. They do not make that decision so they can live in an enclave that looks exactly like their world back home. They want to be part of our broader society; they want to belong; they want to become Canadian.

This being true, we adapted the multiculturalism policy to emphasize both components. Our idea was closer to what is called in Quebec "*interculturalisme.*" The English equivalent is rarely used, but the term implies that immigration is about creating not just a diversity of cultures but also a dialogue between those cultures. The ultimate objective is not cultural deconstruction, fragmentation, or segregation, but rather cultural integration. To be clear, our view was that such integration is, by its very nature, a two-way street.

Along these lines, we enhanced the citizenship guide to give a greater understanding of Canada's institutions, heritage, and history. Some of these amendments were perceived as controversial. However, our goal was to recognize the complexity that immigration adds to the culture and to pursue it in a way that brings new citizens fully into the mainstream of Canadian life.

I felt that New Canadians generally responded well to this concept. Of course, like any other group of Canadians, such people have a range of opinions on everything. Our opponents tried to promote the view that there were monolithic New Canadian perspectives on these issues, which would somehow automatically align with liberal views. However, we saw little evidence that they ever asked the people they were talking about whether that was true. For example, regarding cracking down on immigration abuse, it turns out that no one supports that more than people who were recent immigrants and came through the system legally.

I believe our approach was validated in part by the tremendous growth we saw in support from New Canadian communities during my time as leader. I also believe our opponents devoted so much time and vitriol toward us and our policies because these outreach efforts were, in fact, successful. I recall one of the debates during the 2011 election, when the Liberals (and the moderator, for that matter) attacked us for "targeting" New Canadians in our election campaign. Well, of course we were targeting New Canadians, just as we were targeting any group of voters that we thought we could persuade to vote for us.

And it worked. Part of the reason it worked was that the traditional Liberal Party approach was condescending. What they were saying was, in effect, "We let you in . . . and now you owe us your vote," as if it were wrong for anyone to get them to vote otherwise. The premise is dubious from the outset because, in reality, a large percentage of Canada's immigrants arrived under Conservative governments. The difference is that Conservatives have never asserted that such immigrants are beholden to us. They were, after all, admitted because of choices they made under the law, and it was the law, not a political party, that deemed them qualified. As Canadian voters, they can choose their party preference like any other citizen.

The bottom line is that the policy stances we took on issues of Canadian identity—on immigration, multiculturalism, and citizenship—were based upon talking and listening to New Canadian communities, finding out what was most important to them, and representing those views in our policies. Contrary to what some white Liberals think, you will not find out what immigrants believe by asking white Liberals. You find out what New Canadians think by asking New Canadians. That is what we did. By and large it was effective.

TAX LOOPHOLE WHACK-A-MOLE

WHILE WE WERE FIRMLY against general tax increases, our objective was to close our deficit gap chiefly by revenue growth and not by expenditure reduction. That involved more than just pursuing the various economic growth measures I have outlined. It also included maintaining the integrity of existing revenue streams by closing tax loopholes.

This is a perennial activity of governments, and it was so for us. As I have mentioned before, dealing with "technical" tax amendments—much of which involved eliminating loopholes—had long taken up the bulk of the time that I personally spent on the budget process. Budget 2013 made this a special focus, with Minister Flaherty and me closing nearly a billion dollars in tax loopholes. This would have ongoing benefits in government revenue for years to come.

This raises an obvious question: If there are so many loopholes, which effectively deny revenue to governments, why not just close them all and get it over with? Why even allow them in the first place? I believe such questions reflect a common misunderstanding of what a tax loophole is.

Many probably assume that a loophole is a deliberate government policy, created to benefit wealthy or special interests. I do not believe that is normally the case. It would just be better not to tax in the first place. Rather, a loophole is a tax measure that is being used differently than the way the government intended.

Most Canadians, whose experience is limited to completing a basic personal tax return, probably do not understand how complicated the tax system is. But trust me, it is.* The people and entities governments tax are inherently diverse and often complicated in their economic activities. So, too, are the objectives that governments are trying to achieve through taxation. Certainly, raising revenue is the major one, but there are many others, like encouraging investment, redistributing income, supporting

---

* I have some special insight into this. Besides coming from an "accounting family" and having spent many hours on tax policy in government, I now own several businesses, created through the growth of Harper & Associates and its associated firms—the enterprise I have built since 2016. These businesses, which have dozens of employees, along with clients and holdings in various parts of the world, have shockingly complicated tax affairs. Even though, considered together, this is still just an enterprise of "medium" size at most.

charitable causes, and helping people create savings and financial security. That is why governments, in developing their tax policies, distinguish between levels of income, types of income, definitions of income, and the entities that earn such income.

By way of example, let us take life insurance. Life insurance is purchased to give Canadians and their families greater financial security in a highly uncertain future. For that reason, life insurance income is not taxed. Life insurance can thus be used to avoid taxation. That is not a loophole; it is something governments clearly intend.

Nevertheless, any such tax avoidance measure can be "creatively" employed. There is a whole industry of smart accountants and lawyers who are paid a lot of money to minimize the tax obligations of individuals and businesses. Granted, 99 per cent of this activity will minimize tax in ways that the government intends, even if it did not think of the specifics at the time of enactment. However, tax advisors will also use the complexity of the system to figure out methods to minimize taxation in ways that, while clearly legal, the government did not anticipate and considers undesirable. This leads to a loophole that a government may well want to close.

On occasion, such professionals will also encourage tax avoidance schemes that the government believes are in fact illegal. This is where "tax avoidance" crosses the line into "tax evasion." But the tax department in a rule-of-law society like Canada does not have the final word on this. There are special Tax Courts designed to rule on whether the government's or the taxpayer's interpretation of these complex laws is correct. The government will often lose such cases. In such circumstances, the government will almost certainly consider how to change the law to deal with the situation.

The end result? No matter how many loopholes you close, more always pop up. No one understands this better than a chartered public accountant, the preferred career choice in my family. That always leads me to talk about a humorous encounter I had with the Canadian Institute of Chartered Accountants (CICA).

It was during a question-and-answer session at one of the CICA's big meetings. The organization had generally been very supportive of the government's policies—with one exception, and I was asked about it. The moderator wondered why tax simplification was the one thing that the profession wanted that we had not done. My response was: "Because of you." I said it was them, in that room, practising tax accountants, who were constantly making the tax system more complicated and forcing government to further complicate it in response. I got no argument in response. In fact, the crowd laughed along with me. They knew what I was talking about. Tax simplification would do little more than re-introduce all the loopholes governments have already closed. It is maddening, I know, but that is how it is.

So, is tax simplification impossible? No, but to do it, one would have to face some realities. Is one ready to say that all income should be taxed exactly the same? Whether it is earned by a business or an individual? Whether the business is huge or tiny, or whether the individual is rich or poor? Whether the income is spent, saved, re-invested, or given to charity? Whether the income is profits, wages, dividends, capital gains, or a gift? There are a hundred questions like this, and as soon as your answer to one of them is "No," you have created complexity in the tax system. The more "Nos," the more complex the system will be.

THINNING THE COST OF GOVERNMENT

AS TIME-CONSUMING AS CLOSING tax loopholes was, our work on thinning the cost of government more than matched it. It was just as painstaking and as little fun. It was only partly coincidence that we called the multi-year effort the DRAP (Deficit Reduction Action Plan). Mostly led by Treasury Board Minister Tony Clement, it involved long and substantial efforts by many ministers.

The first challenge was to understand the real effects of any expenditure reduction. This had been underscored for us when, in our first year in office, we had drastically cut the summer student employment program. This was prior to the global financial crisis when student unemployment was hitting record lows. Why would students need that assistance?

Students did not. But the cut was still controversial. It turned out that students were not the real beneficiaries of the program. In many cases, those were non-profit employers who, in a booming labour market, needed some assistance to draw those seasonal workers away from the for-profit sector. We got attacked by those organizations, not by students. We did manage to fix that problem quickly by eliminating only subsidies for the commercial sector. Still, it was an early eye-opening lesson.

The second challenge was to ensure that our public servants, whose assistance we would need every step of the way, were fully aligned with our objectives. This involved restructuring the incentives of senior officials. That meant tackling the public service system of "conditional pay."

This is an area of government expenditure that is often misrepresented. Senior public servants have two levels of conditional pay—an at-risk portion of their salaries and a bonus supplement. It is true, as was reported, that most eligible officials were getting the maximum amounts when we took office. That was based on evaluations that seemed to automatically rank everyone very highly each year regardless of performance. I changed that system almost immediately.

In essence, I bell-curved ratings for officials. Under our Government, only about 10 per cent of the highest performers—certainly no more than 20 per cent—would be considered in the top category. They would receive the maximum pay. All others fell into four lower categories. The lowest category was rare—no at-risk or bonus pay at all—because a senior official performing that poorly was not likely to be retained. While almost all top bureaucrats got some bonus pay under our Government, very few got it all.

That was only the first reform. The next one was to begin coordinating the ratings with the government's objectives. This was done for some departments during the Economic Action Plan. The speed and efficacy of officials in getting our stimulus programs done was factored into deputy minister evaluations. But it was really with the DRAP that we began to comprehensively restructure incentives.

In short, we made a considerable portion of a deputy minister's (DM) conditional pay dependent on our DRAP objective—reducing the cost of delivering public services *without* reducing those services for the public. That was not the sole objective, but it was the overarching one. I felt we generally achieved it. Yes, there were a few controversies, but we did significantly lower the costs of the federal government with only small impacts in most areas.

Under Clerks of the Privy Council Wouters and Janice Charette,* my senior officials responded well to the incentive structure. This should not be surprising. Men and women who join Canada's public service and who get to the top of it are typically people who want to get things done for the country. A prime minister who gives them direction, pays attention to what they are doing, and evaluates how it is being done is something most want.

Early in the DRAP, I met with the deputy minister community. It is some fifty-plus officials of DM or agency-head rank. In fact, I met with this group on a roughly quarterly basis. On this occasion, I made it clear that reducing employment levels was to be a major focus of their efforts and that the government would be generous in encouraging exit from the public service. But this was not to be a typical buyout plan; I did not want the most senior people to depart. Rather, they were to focus on the poorest performers.

I told the DMs to thin bureaucracy and to do it by reducing the number of people. While I admitted that I did not know their departments intimately, I was certain that they had some very poor performers. My own experience was that, if you got rid of those, not only would you save money but also productivity would likely go up. As it turned out, that is exactly what generally happened. By the time it was done, we had reduced the size of the public service by thirty thousand. Interestingly, there was very little public awareness of this.†

I have no idea how Canada's senior public servants are being evaluated and paid today, but I can say that having proper incentive structures at the

---

* Janice became Clerk in 2014 when Wayne retired after nearly five years in the position. She would go on to serve as Clerk for Justin Trudeau in two separate stints.

† Of course, it is well known that the numbers of public servants ballooned by over one hundred thousand under our successors. Were your services any better?

top is as important for the federal government as it is for any other organization. We economists know that incentives *really* matter. Show us the incentives, and we will show you the behaviour. People are people, and it never fails to motivate them when they are rewarded or penalized for how they perform against measurable objectives.

In dealing with public service costs, we did not just reduce head counts. We also dealt with some outrageous benefits that no private-sector taxpayer could ever enjoy. For instance, we ended sick leave without evidence and the banking of unused sick days. That was nothing more than additional paid vacation for a workforce that already had generous vacation benefits. We also required public servants to pay half of their (top-of-the-line) medical expense plans.

However, the biggest savings were in reforming public service pensions. The inflation-indexed, defined-benefit plans that dominate in government are, in and of themselves, an extraordinary benefit virtually unparallelled for other workers. We simply required federal employees to pay half the cost, up from roughly one-third.[‡] This alone was a saving of some two billion dollars per year.

That change was only possible because our Conservative caucus agreed to do the same thing for parliamentarians. As they had been paying less than one-fifth of their eventual pension value, this was a big increase. No one was exempt—not even the prime minister.[§]

---

‡ An exception was made for the Canadian Armed Forces and the Royal Canadian Mounted Police. Because they are usually required to retire early, paying half would have imposed higher premiums. We kept theirs at the same rate as for the typical public servant.

§ A PM who had served four years was eligible for a large additional pension at age fifty-five, for which they paid virtually nothing. I cut that by 75 per cent, raised the entrance age to sixty-seven, and required a half-share payment. I should also add that, in 2002, when I returned to Parliament, I had a one-time opportunity to opt back into the pension plan for my 1993–1997 service, which almost all Reform MPs had later done (at very little cost). I did not.

These various actions on our revenues and expenditures, as well as our earlier decision to end the stimulus measures on schedule, had broken the back of the deficit. It had been some fifty-five billion dollars in 2009–2010. By this point in 2012, our expectation was that it would be less than twenty billion dollars for 2013–2014 and falling. It ended up at well less than ten billion dollars. It was already clear that the national government would be left with no structural or permanent deficit following the global financial crisis. That really set Canada apart.

23

ROUNDING OUT THE YEAR AT HOME

TRANSITION TO SUMMER

IN OTTAWA, THE TRANSITION between ending a parliamentary session and moving into summer tends to follow a roughly similar pattern each year. It was no different in 2013. June is the month where Parliament focuses on wrapping up the government's priority legislation. This often necessitates longer sitting days both in the Commons and the Senate.

For many MPs, the end of House sittings means heading back to the riding. In theory at least, they might wrestle a few recuperation days from their schedule before embarking on the hectic "barbeque season" in their constituencies. Not so for the prime minister. First, there were a series of Cabinet meetings where we would review the session that just ended and then, during the summer, hold further sessions to map out what we intend to accomplish for the rest of the year. That year I was also preparing a significant Cabinet shuffle.

I would also regularly tour around the country during summers. It would all start with the Fête Nationale (also known as Saint-Jean-Baptiste Day), Quebec's major provincial holiday, on June 24. This was always a time for me to celebrate with Quebec friends, and it typically involved a gathering of the Conservative clan in the province. This year we went to St-Lazare de La Chance, located in MP Jacques Gourde's riding (Lévis–Lotbinière), just outside Quebec City. Jacques was one of our best constituency MPs in the country, and we could be sure he would organize a great event.

Exactly one week after Saint-Jean-Baptiste is Canada Day. It typically meant an extremely busy sequence of events, though the passion and patriotism on display were always infectious. The highlight was speaking at the noon show on Parliament Hill in front of tens of thousands of Canadians celebrating. As I have mentioned, July 1st was also the beginning of my family's annual Harrington Lake stay, kicked off, of course, with the big Canada Day party that we enjoyed so much.

However, for me this was merely a temporary respite from a busy summer schedule. The Calgary Stampede, celebrated as "The Greatest Outdoor Show on Earth," opened the first week of July. For a Calgary MP, missing Stampede was unthinkable, and for a Calgarian prime minister, doubly so. There were always a fair number of public functions, including the ubiquitous pancake breakfasts with their obligatory photo ops.

By far the most important of those Stampede events was my annual Calgary Southwest Conservative Association barbecue. I do not think it is too presumptuous to say that it was highly anticipated by my constituents. It was the one time of the year that their prime-ministerial MP could be counted upon to be in the riding and approachable. It was always an opportunity to press the flesh and renew old acquaintances with the many who worked so hard to get me elected.

This event attracted folks not just from my riding but also from across southern Alberta, as well as a surprising number from elsewhere in the country. The Calgary Southwest Stampede Barbeque was a tradition that went back to the days of Preston Manning, and it was a major fundraiser for my constituency association and the party. My speech at this boisterous event would always be a recap of our Government's accomplishments over the preceding year, and it would set the tone for the summer speaking tours carried on by me and my Conservative caucus colleagues throughout Canada.

If I was lucky, there might follow a few days of downtime to spend with my family at Harrington Lake. But an engaged national leader never escapes his responsibilities. Spring and summer 2013 were no different. For example, massive and highly destructive flooding on June 19 had occurred in Calgary and Southern Alberta, which necessitated multiple official and non-official tours.*

Another unexpected episode was the Idle No More protests within Canada's Indigenous communities. To be honest, it was never really clear what exactly these demonstrators were seeking. However, they did pre-occupy Indigenous leaders, and meetings with them, particularly with National Chief Atleo of the Assembly of First Nations, were useful in cooling the temperature and reviewing ways forward.

DISASTER AT LAC-MÉGANTIC

OF ALL THE EVENTS in the summer of 2013, nothing registered so indelibly on my mind as the infamous Lac-Mégantic rail disaster that occurred in the early hours of Saturday, July 6. I got up that morning at our home in Calgary and flipped on the television news. What I saw was a scene from hell. A towering fireball engulfed this small Quebec town, with massive explosions periodically adding to the conflagration.

I had a busy day ahead of me that included some Stampede events and meetings with ministers for the upcoming Cabinet shuffle. I was scheduled to return to Ottawa early the next morning for a pre-scheduled event in the evening. It was immediately clear that my plans would have to be altered.

While there were tragedies and disasters of many kinds during my tenure as PM, this was far and away the most awful. Experts tell us that major catastrophes like this are rarely a single occurrence. Rather, they involve a series of "cascading failures," when one mishap results in even bigger ones in rapid succession. That is exactly what happened at Lac-Mégantic.†

---

* Laureen went to High River, near her hometown of Turner Valley, to help out with the huge task of cleaning up.

† Later, of course, the Safety Board and other agencies assessed the disaster in minute detail, producing multiple lengthy reports and making numerous recommendations, including the re-routing of the tracks outside Lac-Mégantic.

The story is that a Montreal, Main and Atlantic Railway train loaded with thousands of tons of highly flammable crude oil from the Bakken region of North Dakota experienced a fire on board. It was the result of previously inadequate maintenance. This caused the train to stop about eleven kilometres from Lac-Mégantic. The engineer then left the train but did not properly apply the brakes.

The railway track to Lac-Mégantic was at a 1 per cent downward grade. As the air pressure left the brakes, the train began to edge down the track. It was slow at first, but as it moved closer to the town, the unmanned train's inertia kept building to the point where it was travelling over 100 kilometres per hour. That was 80 kilometres above the speed for safely negotiating the level crossing in Lac-Mégantic, which involved a turn in the track. Raw physics took over, and the train flew off the track as it entered the town. Sparks ignited the cargo, leading to a series of explosions and a raging inferno.

What I saw when I got there the next day, I could only describe in terms reserved for the most brutal war zones. The heat of the explosions had literally incinerated a considerable portion of the town. That section looked like it had been carpet bombed. Forty-seven people were dead or presumed dead. In many cases there were no remains of any kind to recover from the charred aftermath.

I did what I could do, conscious that an extended stay would complicate the urgent work of the disaster crews on the scene. I met emergency workers, firefighters, other first responders, Mayor Colette Roy-Laroche, and, of course, families of the victims, which was gut-wrenching. I promised any assistance my Government could offer. I was joined by Conservative MP and Minister Christian Paradis, as this was his riding.

This quick, traumatic visit would be merely the first of many. I attended funerals, infrastructure restoration announcements, and visits to support the town residents as they carried out the grim work of rebuilding their lives and their community.* All told, it was a dreadful day, the memories of which I will never get out of my mind.

---

* The fallout also engulfed the railway, which went bankrupt before the year was out.

THE EMOTIONAL WHIPLASH OF OFFICE

JULY 7, 2013, was an extreme example of what a prime minister often experiences. Your life is a roller coaster. Leaders must pivot from dealing with one event to another in rapid succession. When I am asked about things that happened as prime minister, I would often respond: "I can remember most of what transpired, but I have lost all sense of the timing and order in which things occurred."†

But it is not just that events occur quickly; it is that the substance and personal impact of them varies so enormously. The prime-ministerial roller coaster is an emotional roller coaster, and you have to learn to live through it without becoming either overwhelmed or numb. You must live in the moment almost all the time, and then reset your mind for the next thing.

I can remember days that began with a national security briefing about a plot to assassinate me followed immediately by meetings with industry groups, campaign planning with staff, and working with Finance officials on the budget, with all its hundreds of tax changes. Did I mention Question Period, Cabinet meetings, media availabilities, and the day-to-day issues that capture everyone's attention? One moment you are trying to get opposed Cabinet colleagues on the same page, the next you are dealing with bureaucratic resistance, and then you are smiling for schoolchildren visiting your office.

There are two main strategies for navigating this frantic world. The first is to prepare as much as humanly possible for scheduled events. Walking into a meeting unprepared, either substantively or emotionally, is a recipe for disaster. The second is learning a degree of emotional control—the ability to be in the proper mindset for the moment and to change that quickly for the next one. That does not mean being unemotional. I could get very

---

† However, I do have to say that this exercise of writing my memoirs, which was preceded by extensive recorded interviews on my time in office done for Library and Archives Canada, has forced me to go through my ten years as PM in great detail. My memories are now sufficiently reordered!

excited; I could feel quite down; I might lose my temper. There is nothing inherently wrong with any of those things, as long as the moment requires it, and you can move on as soon as you need to.

Some may think that this was easy for me, given my reputation for emotional detachment. There is some truth in that, as I wear my emotions on my sleeve infrequently. But I am often far more emotional than I let on, although I know that colleagues, staffers, and political opponents alike can testify that my emotional state was often not easy to read. The extent of that opacity, by the way, was something I did not fully realize about myself until I got into politics.* For me, trying to adjust the display of my emotions was as much a struggle as altering my actual mood.

That July weekend was an example of when all these things came into play. Attendance at the disaster scene was very tough, but you have to keep your emotions under control. You must, for example, share in the grief of those who have suffered loss, while also conveying encouragement to those who are hard at work. And you have to shift moods between these encounters, and during the drives and the flights to the next event. It is draining, but it is the life.

PAUL MCCARTNEY CONCERT

MY EVENING RETURN to Ottawa from Laç-Mégantic was just such an occasion because I was headed there for (what I believed to be) a completely unrelated reason—to attend a concert by Paul McCartney. I do not mind admitting that I was looking forward to it. My bandmates were coming as my guests, and it had been a challenging week—the hectic events of Stampede, some challenging meetings with ministers around the upcoming

* A few people who know me very well can always accurately read my moods. My mother is one. When I was very young, she would tell people if I was happy or upset or whatever. They often had no idea.

Cabinet shuffle, and the traumatic events in Quebec. I had also previously agreed to a private meeting with Sir Paul before the concert.

Meeting with musicians or actors before or after a performance is actually pretty standard for a prime minister attending a concert or a play.† Indeed, it is usually expected, if not requested outright. But this one was different—and not just because I was meeting with the most successful popular artist ever.‡ It was also because I was surprised that Sir Paul wanted to meet me at all, given our history.

In 2008, when Paul McCartney was touring in North America, he had a concert in Quebec City to celebrate its 400th anniversary. During that time, he had appeared on television with his then-wife Heather Mills attacking the Canadian seal hunt—a fashionable cause for celebrities at that time. But this annual harvest had worked hard to adopt more humane killing measures over the decades, and my Government strongly supported it as a critical industry in parts of Atlantic and Northern Canada, especially among the Inuit. Frankly, I was fed up with affluent celebrities looking to burnish their social activism credentials at the expense of these Canadian workers.

So when Ray Novak came into my office one day saying he had, of all people, Paul McCartney on the line and that he wanted to talk with me,

---

† Meeting pretty much whomever you wish is a perk of being prime minister. I had the opportunity to meet many celebrities of the music world during my time in office—Bryan Adams, Jann Arden, Randy Bachman & Fred Turner, Barenaked Ladies, Justin Beiber, Blue Rodeo, Bono, Paul Brandt, Michael Bublé, Burton Cummings, Deadmau5, Celine Dion, Howie Dorough (of the Backstreet Boys), Don Felder, David Foster, Andy Kim, Ludacris, Corb Lund, Yo-Yo Ma, Beverley Mahood, Sarah McLachlan, Kenny Munshaw, Nickelback, Mike Plume, Jimmy Rankin, Bob Seger, The Sheepdogs, Gene Simmons, Taylor Swift, The Tenors, Jim Vallance, and Pinkus Zuckerman come to mind. So does Katy Perry, although she is apparently better known by Justin Trudeau!

‡ I do not say this just because I am a huge Beatles fan, with a pretty extensive knowledge of McCartney's decades of solo work. In sheer sales, his lifetime career widely outpaces everyone else in the business.

I asked him what it was regarding. "I think it's about the seal hunt," Ray said. "Well, then, tell him I won't take the call," was my immediate response. Stunned, Ray asked, "Really? Are you serious?" "Yeah, just tell him I'm not taking the call," I responded.

Ray went back to his office and delivered the message, making me, I suspect, the first person since Decca Records refused to sign the Beatles in 1962 not to take a call from Paul McCartney.* I felt terrible about it, not just because I am a huge Beatles fan but also because, as a McCartney watcher, I could see that this out-of-character, abrasive activism was the product of a doomed marriage.

All that said, it was not a hard decision. As prime minister, I took seriously my foremost duty to represent the interests of the Canadian people. On this matter, I was defending those interests, and the views of a foreign celebrity were irrelevant.† Besides, I have always been careful about my relationships with celebrities. Given the publicity-seeking nature of their careers, such associations can be a dangerous thing.‡

However, this meeting with McCartney did have an ulterior motive. It had been facilitated by representatives of the Canadian music industry as

---

* Decca's decision has come to be known as the most infamously bad decision in music business history.

† Actually, I had the same opinion on Canadian celebrities when it came to this issue. Among the many I refused to meet was Pamela Anderson. My wife was very supportive of that decision!

‡ Paul Martin had cultivated a relationship with Bono during his rise to power. However, in 2005 he was booed at a sold-out U2 show by thousands at Bono's instigation for failing to raise Canada's spending on foreign aid. That was one reason why, despite many requests, I long refused to meet with Bono. I had taken that position despite his genuine contributions to the causes he advocated for and his very positive assessments of my government's record. When I finally did meet Bono, near the end of my time as PM, we kept it low-key at 24 Sussex, and he was very gracious in meeting and taking photos with all my household staff.

part of their efforts to influence the government on copyright policy. As we were, in fact, examining the issue of expiring copyrights on 1960s music, this was pertinent. McCartney's office had been clear that he wished to raise "issues related to the music business" with me. We had indicated that I would listen but make no commitments.

I met Sir Paul about a half hour before he went on stage. He was cordial in introducing himself, but instead of bringing up anything about the music business, he started asking me about my trip to Lac-Mégantic and if I could share some of the things I had seen and witnessed on the ground.

From his demeanour, it was clear that the event had shaken him. He paid careful attention as I spoke and at the end asked, "Is there anything I can do?" I responded that I would be going back to Lac-Mégantic, probably several times in the near future for funerals and memorials, and I would certainly pass on his condolences. McCartney never did raise the business issues.

After our meeting, Sir Paul proceeded to put on a magnificent show. He played for three hours. At seventy-one years old, he took no breaks, although his much younger bandmates did. Obviously, I enjoyed the evening, and so did my band members. It was wonderful to see McCartney doing what he clearly loved as if he were still a teenager.

Two weeks later, when his tour took him to Quebec City, Sir Paul paid to bring a thousand fans from Lac-Mégantic to the concert. Further, he offered free concert tickets for all those willing to go to Lac-Mégantic to help with the recovery. Only sometime later did I receive a short letter from him on the copyright issues.

As a politician, I have a sufficiently cynical side about the things that people say. However, in this case, Sir Paul showed how genuine his sympathies for the people of Lac-Mégantic were. He did not have to do what he did. For me, it was refreshing to meet somebody you admire for something and find them to be worthy of that admiration in other areas of their life as well.

PLANNING FOR THE FUTURE

THERE IS RARELY a single reason for changing the Cabinet. Of course, there is the odd resignation that requires moving one or two positions. Any more than that means going back to the drawing board to ensure a balance between regions, gender, abilities, and the "chemistry" factor. This was one of those times, as I had broader, more strategic reasons for making changes.

My Government had now been in office for seven-and-a-half years. We were halfway through our third term, and I knew there would be a tough road ahead. I wanted to start to set our Government's agenda for the final stretch. I also wanted to make some qualitative changes to my ministerial team.

For one thing, I wanted to try to address the gender imbalance that had characterized all the caucuses I had been in throughout my career. We had started electing a larger number of strong and capable women, and I wanted to begin promoting them more systematically. While I do not label myself a feminist, and I have certainly never been for quotas,* the under-representation of women in our system and my party did bother me. I have always felt that it will be a great day when women play a genuinely equal role in the governance of our country. This was a good time to do more work in that direction.

Another, even more pressing, objective was to focus on younger caucus members. In this context, I was increasingly thinking about the party's next generation. As someone who saw himself as an institutional leader building a permanent organization, I believed this was imperative. Among the steady

---

* I did encourage my ministers to try to make women at least one-third of their appointments. In the public service, almost half of my senior public service positions were assigned to women. In neither case were these quotas; they were simply examples of looking for opportunities to push solid female candidates forward. In my experience, this is necessary as women are often less likely than men to promote themselves.

stream of new MPs who had been coming to Ottawa over my four national election campaigns were some very talented people. It was time to push a number of them forward.

There was another consideration in my Cabinet-shuffle thinking: I knew my time as prime minister was finite. This consideration, I hasten to add, was breathed to no one, not even my closest advisors. When you are prime minister, you are prime minister until the day you say you do not want to be prime minister anymore. The day you utter that thought, you are finished.

This reality is built into the institutional structure of our system. It is simply not true, as some academics allege, that the advent of the Prime Minister's Office under Pierre Trudeau exalted the power of the prime minister in some unique way. For centuries, the Crown has entrusted the prime minister, and the prime minister alone, with the day-to-day governance of the country. This authority is granted on the assurance that he or she is in control at every moment—of the Commons, the Cabinet, and the party.

Any prime minister who lets that assurance slip away is in trouble. This, by the way, is the reason why every prime minister who has been in office for any length of time is accused of being a control freak. The reality is that if you are a prime minister and you are not in control, you do not survive as prime minister for very long. Feel free to check the record on that!

I had witnessed these lessons, both successful and unsuccessful, in many places and over a long period of time. Anyone at the top who signals retirement lets loose the political jockeying of ambitious lieutenants, which rapidly erodes organizational coherence, especially in a parliamentary system. If and when you decide to step down as prime minister, you do it in one step, not several. Thus, I would never have sent that kind of signal. But I was thinking about it. And the truth is that I had not decided whether I was going to run again.

In any case, on July 15, just a week after my visit to Lac-Mégantic, I announced my Cabinet changes. The new women ministers were Candice Bergen (Social Development), Shelly Glover (Canadian Heritage and Official Languages), Kellie Leitch (Labour and Status of Women), and

Michelle Rempel (Western Economic Development). Kerry-Lynne Findlay was promoted to National Revenue. There were also newcomers in Chris Alexander (Citizenship & Immigration), Pierre Poilievre (Democratic Reform), Greg Rickford (Natural Resources), and Kevin Sorenson (Minister of State for Finance).*

Several of these people have played significant roles in Conservative politics since 2015, so I consider this generational shift to have been one of my wiser later-day moves. I had cleared the path for a number of these new ministers when I made some changes in the parliamentary secretary ranks in 2011. Likewise, in 2013, I would also promote a fair number of new faces into those roles.†

As desirable as all of this was, it came with a price; some veteran performers had to be moved out. There was no choice. I had set the size of the ministry at forty, that is, Cabinet plus ministers of state, so there was no room for expansion. While some older ministers were not expected to run again, these demotions (of very competent, hard-working individuals) were not all voluntary. Yet they all understood and handled matters as professionally as I could have asked for. Diane Ablonczy, Keith Ashfield, Peter Kent, Ted Menzies, Gordon O'Connor, and Vic Toews (headed to the bench) deserve gratitude for the fine service that they rendered to our country.‡

---

* These were the last new ministers I appointed, save London's Ed Holder. He joined the ministry in March 2014 as Minister of State for Science and Technology.

† In 2011, the new parliamentary secretaries had also included Paul Calandra, Cathy McLeod, and Susan Truppe, as well as some of the names above. This year, promotions would go to Dan Albas, Scott Armstrong, James Bezan, Kelly Block, Peter Braid, Parm Gill, Roxanne James, Costas Menegakis, Erin O'Toole, Mark Strahl, Bernard Trottier, and Jeff Watson.

‡ Let me add to those names some solid, long-serving parliamentary secretaries who had been dropped for similar reasons back in 2011—Laurie Hawn, Ed Komarnicki, Dave MacKenzie, and Mark Warawa.

CANADIAN ENERGY FOR THE WORLD

ON AUGUST 2, I journeyed to Saint John, New Brunswick, to announce that our Government would, conditional upon an environmental assessment, support the Energy East pipeline. This was TransCanada PipeLines Limited's proposed $12-billion project to carry Western Canadian oil to the East Coast for refining and shipment to customers around the world. Among the many energy export projects seeking approval, this one was conceptually exciting because, for the first time, Canada's oil would travel across the country. This would allow Irving Oil, the largest refiner on the East Coast, to become an exporter rather than an importer, finally rendering our country self-sufficient in this vital resource.

Over recent months, in Malaysia and other countries, I had become more vocal about the potential for making Canada an "energy superpower," that is, a trusted supplier of oil and gas (and other energy products) to the entire world. In contrast to most other major oil producers, we are a transparent, rule-of-law jurisdiction, with high human rights and environmental standards, far removed from conflict zones. In short, we are, by any measure, the world's ideal supplier of this still indispensable resource. The revenue we derive from it supports countless high-paying jobs and high-quality social services.

Energy East was just one part of Canada's great potential as an energy supplier. There were also the massive Northern Gateway, Keystone XL, and Trans Mountain pipeline projects, along with a number of liquid natural gas proposals, the most advanced being West Coast applications by LNG Canada and Petronas, the Malaysian national energy company. For our oil and gas, these projects would access global energy markets in a big way, ending our captive-market status in the United States and the huge price differentials we were losing on our resources.

I was aggressively pursuing this at the time because our Government had just recently completed the hard work on responsible resource development. We had now enacted comprehensive changes to the regulatory process for major projects. Before, under the old Liberal system, these major project proposals would have been stuck in review processes almost indefinitely.

From our Government's point of view, it was thus high time to make progress here. Pipelines are the safest way in the world for transporting energy—the safest of all forms of transportation, for that matter. We were confident that our new processes would protect Canadians and the environment while realizing Canada's economic potential.

We were also aware that the prospect of actually getting these projects done was attracting well-funded advocacy groups determined to stop resource development. Much, if not most, of the money for these organizations was coming from the United States. This was in some ways a peculiar development, given what was happening in the competitive landscape.

The biggest change was the growth of the oil and gas sector in the United States. During my time, the U.S.—then under Barack Obama—had been expanding its oil and gas production to record levels. In fact, under Obama the U.S. went from being a net importer of oil to one of the world's major exporters, which reduced American demand for our products. Our lack of direct export capacity threatened any future access to overseas markets. In short, this was a serious, long-term economic threat to the Canadian economy.

In my mind, this always raised questions about the volumes of American dollars that were flowing across the border to propagandize against Canadian oil and gas export projects. True, lots of American environmentalists think Canada should be turned into one giant, northern, U.S. national park. But were these dollars really all "green"? Might there have been considerable money thrown in by U.S. energy interests to keep our oil and gas flowing only south, into their hands? Much of it being dark money, we will probably never know.

Still, it is a valid question to ask why environmentalists have been so antagonistic and vocal against Canadian energy development in particular. Our industry is environmentally sound by any comparison. Our Government was always successful in demonstrating that fact before American and European tribunals that evaluated the science around these claims.

In any case, it is my view that a clear majority of Canadians have always supported and continue to support our oil and gas industry. They know they need these products, at affordable prices, in their own lives. They are skeptical about facile claims of "green jobs" magically replacing those in the oil and gas industry.* And they understand that "peak oil," so long predicted, remains a fantasy. Even climate fanatics are rapidly learning that there is no such thing as "energy transition by decree." Energy transition will come, but at scale, it is (sadly) a very long way off.

So why did Canada become the only major oil-producing country in the world trying to dramatically scale back its own industry? It was certainly not because of the wider world. *Everywhere* I have gone outside of Canada, I have been told that others want to buy and invest in Canadian oil and gas—if we are prepared to give them the opportunity. They have been mystified that we seem unwilling.

The biggest problem, of course, has been our own national government. Sometimes, it has been the provinces, who can block development in their own jurisdictions, although, to be clear, they have no power to stop the interprovincial movement of energy resources. Occasionally, it is the courts and activist judges, impeding projects based on the excuse of a "duty to consult" Indigenous peoples. However, that duty seems not to include Indigenous groups that want resource development—which is the vast majority of them, provided they have a stake in it (which all proponents are more than willing to provide).

A quick survey of cancelled energy projects over the last decade tells the story. Petronas LNG was shelved by Malaysia after they tired of B.C.'s NDP Government putting roadblock after roadblock in their path. Approval for the Northern Gateway project was rescinded by the Trudeau Government, with no scientific basis for doing so. It deliberately raised regulatory barriers high enough to get TransCanada to shelve the Energy East project as well. And then there was the Keystone XL pipeline.†

---

* My brother-in-law Darryl, a tradesman in the oil and gas industry, has a great line on this: "Where do I apply for my new 'green' job?"

† While I will give credit to the Justin Trudeau Government for completing the TransMountain pipeline expansion, those kudos need to be severely qualified. Ottawa did this only after buying out the private sector proponent and completing the job at nearly six times the original cost of the project. Perhaps someday we will find out why this strange route was taken.

While President Obama had withheld approval of Keystone (contrary to the U.S.'s own environmental assessments), he had not rejected the project while I was prime minister. He understood that would cause a major problem in his relations with Canada. That changed with the 2015 election. Within days of the Trudeau Government being sworn in, Obama rejected Keystone. The Liberals' opposition was perfunctory.

Ultimately, the real losers have been the people of Canada and the Canadian economy. Our energy resources and our energy industry had for decades been among our country's greatest strengths and core engines of the national economy, under both Conservative and Liberal governments. More than that, they had been, until the Justin Trudeau Government, one of the main reasons that Canada had not seen the erosion of working-class incomes like in other countries around the world. Losses of traditional manufacturing jobs had been offset by the blue-collar opportunities provided in the resource sectors and related industries. It is no coincidence that the decline of real per-capita living standards in the past decade coincided with Trudeau's desire to "phase out" our energy industry.

PROROGATION

CONSIDERING OUR LENGTH of time in government, and with the addition of many Cabinet newcomers, it seemed like a good moment to ask the governor general for a prorogation of Parliament until the fall. That I did on August 19. This Parliament had endured two years, and it was time for a refreshed agenda. We had spent a very busy couple of years of the majority mandate completing promises we had not been able to deliver on in a minority situation. We had also done the heavy lifting on deficit reduction. A lot of these actions were controversial, but they needed to get done.*

---

* In total, eight-three bills received Royal Assent in the 1st session of the 41st Parliament. Government bills included C-27, First Nations Financial

At this point, we were going to be facing an election in two years. This required governing with a forward-looking election mindset and an eye toward building another majority government. As such, our new Cabinet ministers would need some time to learn their portfolios, their legislative agendas, and the politics of their positions. This time, I was slightly bemused to note that the media did not conjure up another "Prorogation-as-a-threat-to-democracy" narrative. They had finally flogged that tired old horse to death and were now storing up their venom for other opportunities.

A GREAT GAME

ON NOVEMBER 5, 2013, I released my first book. I certainly was not the first prime minister to write and publish a book while in office. However, unlike others, it was not in any way autobiographical or even political in nature.

I have always had an ability to focus my mind intensely for long periods. For the same reason, I have always needed hobbies and side projects to give my mind a rest. Those needs became more acute when I became a national political leader. They certainly continued during my prime-ministerial days as we worked through all the domestic and foreign challenges on our plate. They are responsible for producing *A Great Game: The Forgotten Leafs and the Rise of Professional Hockey*.

Canadians were aware of my passion for our national winter sport but were probably surprised that it extended beyond mere fandom. I had been interested in both hockey and history—and therefore hockey history—since

---

Transparency Act; C-43, Faster Removal of Foreign Criminals Act; 2013; C-26, Fighting Foreign Corruption Act; and several wide-ranging budget bills: C-3, C-13, C-38, C-45, and C-60. Private member's bills like C-293, An Act to amend the Corrections and Conditional Release Act (vexatious complainants), and Bill C-309, Preventing Persons from Concealing Their Identity during Riots and Unlawful Assemblies Act, had also been passed.

boyhood. As I freely admit (see Part One), my athletic inability turned my interest in hockey into an intellectual pursuit.

The idea of writing a book about hockey only occurred to me many years later because of my role in politics. As leader of the Official Opposition, amid struggles with issues of confidence and competence, I was working tirelessly to become better known to Canadians. That is the bane of any Opposition leader's existence. Many suggested that writing a book might help, something outlining my stances on various issues and my life journey thus far.

Certainly, there was plenty of material, but I was not sure how to approach such a task. Then somebody suggested I could build a book about the engineering of the CA-PC merger, an idea that intrigued me enough to do some preliminary work, which amounted to a few nights assembling an outline and pulling together documents.

Then it hit me—I do not want to do this! I am spending all my waking hours, six to seven days a week, living and breathing politics. What I need is a *break* from politics!

Casting about for an alternative, my father's historical research projects came to mind. He had written a couple of books on military history, flags, and insignia, which, despite a successful professional career, he always maintained to be his most enduring accomplishment. At that time, I thought, I am leader of the Opposition, but I may never—in fact, I probably will never—be prime minister. So why not pursue an endeavour I enjoy, while hopefully achieving something concrete and lasting?

I had recently been reading some hockey history in my area of interest—early professional, pre–World War I hockey—so my focus naturally gravitated there. Adding in my interest in the Toronto Maple Leafs since childhood, the idea for *A Great Game* began to emerge. I started in 2004 and literally spent fifteen minutes a night—some nights less, some nights more—for nine years, plugging away on the research, writing, and editing. Then, at last, there it was—a serious book, quasi-academic, well-documented, and thoroughly researched.

The original manuscript followed the development of early Toronto hockey to its first pro team—the aptly named Toronto Professionals—which existed from 1906 to 1909 and had a near-miss in a Stanley Cup challenge on March 14, 1908. The drama mostly revolved around the controversial notion of paying hockey players. It is hard to imagine now, but so morally contentious was professionalism in athletics that it tore Canadian society apart for a time—to the point where the country almost failed to enter the Olympic Games in 1908.

After I signed a contract with Simon & Schuster, veteran sports journalist Roy MacGregor entered the picture to help produce a more "marketable" product. Roy was a pleasure to work with, and his ideas helped me produce a much-improved book.

The journey in producing the book fulfilled its purpose—a thoroughly diverting project that helped keep me sane in moments when I needed it most. I also share my father's sentiment of seeing lasting value in it. After all, I may turn out to be the only serving prime minister to write a book about something other than himself!

To the surprise of many, including me, *A Great Game* quickly became an instant national bestseller. As these matters had ethical implications, I had first talked to Ethics Commissioner Mary Dawson, for whom I have great respect. She ruled that any money this book made was legitimately and ethically mine.*

I did not expect much to come financially from the project, but again, this was another pleasant surprise. I donated all the royalties—the amount was well into six figures—to the Military Families Fund, a great and worthy organization. I have autographed thousands of copies of *A Great Game,* and I expect to do so for the rest of my life. (They do not tell you this when you first write a book!)

---

* I would not have guessed that. I suppose it is just the quirky nature of life in Ottawa. After all, I could not use a picture of me in my office, but I could profit off a book written as prime minister. Maybe someday I will understand the rationale. Some restrictions did make sense, like not participating in Cabinet policy discussions regarding the publishing industry. Those were theoretical, however, as I do not recall the topic ever arising.

24

FOREIGN AFFAIRS, TRADE, AND INTERNATIONAL ISSUES 2013

THE YEAR 2013 had been a busy one on the international front from day one. In fact, foreign affairs was an important piece of the budget that Minister Flaherty had tabled back on March 21.

Budget 2013 contained, as usual, a range of economic and fiscal proposals. However, it was unusual in containing a major item involving foreign policy. That was the decision to merge the Canadian International Development Agency (CIDA) into the Department of Foreign Affairs and International Trade (DFAIT).

REFORMING CIDA

I DID NOT TAKE the merger decision lightly. As I indicated earlier, I was averse to significant changes in the "machinery of government." Restructuring departments and agencies can be time- and resource-consuming and should only be undertaken for clear and compelling reasons. One of the first things I did in office was stop the process of separating Foreign Affairs and International Trade that the Martin Government had begun. I saw no particularly clear rationale for that machinery change.

In fact, my early thinking was that, if anything, the opposite approach was likely required. Surely Canada would be better served by a closer integration of diplomacy and trade. Subsequent experience showed that our instincts on this were correct. Beyond that, however, our interactions with CIDA gradually convinced us of the need for even further integration.

Our very first review of CIDA's activities uncovered an organization that lacked focus.* When we asked about CIDA's "development partner priorities," for instance, we got a list of nearly 100 countries. That list showed precious little alignment with our Government's foreign policy priorities. We quickly insisted on a more targeted approach.

Unfortunately, there were problems with CIDA's programming that went well beyond its lack of focus. This became sharply evident when I visited Tanzania in November 2007, following the Commonwealth Heads of Government Meeting in Uganda. Tanzania had long been viewed with pride as a close development partner of Canada and a priority target for CIDA funding. It was, I had been told, a shining example of Canada's aid efforts in the developing world.

As planning for the visit to Tanzania got underway, we decided we wanted to do a photo op at one of the projects that CIDA was leading. However, our CIDA folks came back to us a few days later saying they could not identify a specific target. Our money went through a range of other organizations and causes; therefore, they could not place a flag on any one thing.

I was incredulous. I sent the public servants scrambling under orders to find something (or else). I was going to visit a so-called key development partner, and it did not seem unreasonable to find somewhere that our money was going. We ended up at a particular school that CIDA said was "most likely" a recipient of Canadian aid. That was the closest they could get.

The problem this incident revealed, as we would discover, was the nature of CIDA's funding practices. The bulk did not go to projects in developing nations but rather to outside organizations that worked in those countries.

---

* Josée Verner was the minister of international cooperation when we first began examining CIDA. Bev Oda transferred to the portfolio in 2007 and was there for the next five years as this saga unfolded.

This was what CIDA called its "core funding" model. Those entities that got the money could spend it on their own priorities.

This became a serious problem in our ill-fated campaign for a seat on the United Nations Security Council. I became increasingly aware of it through my attendance at various international summits as I promoted Foreign Affairs's argument that Canada was a great global citizen. At these meetings, it was clear that the international non-governmental organizations (NGOs) that filled out the sides and back of the rooms thought that Canada was truly great. Why would they not? These were the bodies that got CIDA's core funding. But at the table itself, where national leaders sat, it was clear that many developing countries thought Canada did next to nothing for them. Of course they thought that. They had probably never heard of Canada's contribution to anything in their countries.

Most of the organizations CIDA funded were large, credible, and experienced. That was beside the point. Canada had no profile, and Canadian taxpayers got no credit. More importantly, CIDA's "blank cheque" approach gave Canada no discernable leverage to ensure that our contributions furthered Canada's values in the developing world. In fact, our donations had come to be seen almost as an entitlement. We outsourced our "share" of advanced economies' donations (which was a fixed ratio) to international causes, and others spent it for us.

Some might object to my equating "core funding" with the notion of a blank cheque, as they are not necessarily the same thing. In this case, however, it increasingly felt like that. The more we looked, the clearer it became that CIDA's failings went beyond Canada's lack of profile, credit, and leverage. The truth was that it did not really know if our money was being spent effectively by the organizations it funded.

With our impressions of CIDA continuing to decline, pushback from the agency began to rise. That brought to the fore CIDA's prevailing view that it was an "independent" agency, operating at arm's length from the government and its "political" (i.e., foreign policy) agenda. No doubt this attitude was behind the phoney "scandal" that had erupted in 2011 when it was "revealed" that Bev Oda had rejected some of the recommendations from officials on how international development money should be spent. These revelations had most likely come from CIDA officials themselves.

By now I had concluded that CIDA had to be seriously reformed. I also believed that those reforms would involve changing its status and better integrating it into broader foreign policy. When we investigated how this could be done, it turned out that CIDA had no independent status in law. Indeed, it had no statutory basis at all! CIDA had been established through an Order in Council in 1968. That was it. CIDA was a creation of Cabinet alone. As a branch of the federal government, its status could not have been less.

FROM DFATD TO GLOBAL AFFAIRS

THIS IS AN EXAMPLE of another lesson I learned about bureaucracy over my tenure: bureaucracies will often try to exaggerate their independence. True enough, in our system, the bureaucracy is separate from the political wing of government. However, it is not truly independent of it, like the court system—a constitutionally separate branch of government—or the auditor general—who by law reports to Parliament rather than the government. Most agencies of the federal government report directly to elected ministers and are responsible to them, plain and simple.

As I have noted before, the independence argument is a dangerous and too-frequent invitation to non-accountability, pure and simple. Elected governments in our system must beware the idea, often expressed, that "ministerial accountability" means that ministers bear the responsibility for any bureaucratic failures but, at the same time, are somehow not allowed to direct their department. My advice to future governments is to quickly investigate all claims of legal or functional independence that come from departments and agencies. Good ministers will quickly figure out that, in almost every case, officials should provide only advice, while ministers should provide direction and hold officials accountable for execution.

Having clarified that CIDA's independence claims were entirely spurious, we at last made the decision to integrate the foreign aid function into the broader international affairs department. Thus, DFAIT took in CIDA, becoming the Department of Foreign Affairs, Trade, and Development (the awkward DFATD, pronounced D-FAT-D). The reaction of the foreign policy commentariat to this was quite interesting. Despite their general hostility to us and CIDA's own opposition to the merger, the move was welcomed.

This action was taken formally in Budget 2013 under International Cooperation Minister Julian Fantino. A non-nonsense former police chief, Fantino got to work right away. Yet government mergers being what they are, the integration process was still underway when we left government. Has it been successful? Frankly, I doubt it. Our successors renamed the merged department "Global Affairs." This was not a trivial change. It suggests that their job is not to fight for Canada's interests in the world, but to represent the "global community" in Canada—a view all too common in the department.

OFFICE OF RELIGIOUS FREEDOM

ANOTHER IMPORTANT foreign affairs–related initiative of our Government was the Office of Religious Freedom, established on February 19, 2013. These days, with the constant refrain "separation of church and state," I suppose that the creation of this agency requires a little explanation.

In the post–Cold War era, we had witnessed a growing number of cases where high hopes for democracy had not been realized. Elections had often not led to free and democratic societies but to strongmen, corruption, sectarianism, and renewed oppression. I think of Afghanistan and Iraq, the Arab Spring, some of the former Soviet republics, and others.

What was increasingly clear to us is that merely having an election will not create a democracy. There really are social conditions that must exist to sustain a free and democratic polity. Hence, we began to increasingly put the emphasis in our foreign policy on what fundamental things needed to be done to create the conditions necessary for a democracy to take hold. Our reflections led us to identify two areas that are critical in this regard but are often not adequately addressed by the world community.

The first of these was the rights of women and girls—not of one particular right or another, but essentially the recognition of their personhood and basic human dignity. This concept is still fundamentally challenged in many parts of the world. Yet the evidence demonstrates that societies where women have zero or limited status have stunted social development. The reason is rather simple.

Women—in particular, mothers—are critical for the nurturing and developing of the young. Also, where women are considered non-persons, violence is a much more common social and political tool. Therefore, enhancing the status of women and girls is one of the best ways to benefit societies over the long term, including in creating an environment more conducive to freedom and democracy. Obviously, our G8 Summit "Muskoka Initiative on Maternal, Newborn, and Child Health" was in part a manifestation of this priority.

The other area we identified was freedom of religion. If anything speaks to the development of our democratic political culture—certainly from the history of Anglo-American constitutional development—it is freedom of religion and worship. They are fundamental to freedom of conscience, freedom of thought, and freedom of expression, without which a free and democratic society is simply unthinkable. If you are a country or a political culture where a particular set of religious views are interpreted as the mandate of God, it becomes nearly impossible to have anything resembling free expression and open debate. This applies to all peoples everywhere, all religions and every state, without exception. In short, it can be said: no freedom of religion, no democracy.

With that in mind, we established the Office of Religious Freedom within the Department of Foreign Affairs—clearly *not* as an independent agency. Its role was to help coordinate foreign policy within the department on matters religious. To head it, we chose Dr. Andrew Bennett, dean of Augustine College and a former public servant, and assigned him ambassadorial rank. He was eminently qualified, and his appointment was received well by virtually every faith group, most of whom were there when we made the announcement.

One of the first criticisms of the Office was that its agenda was only to promote and/or protect Christianity. That was simply false, as the Office's record showed. Some of the most important work we did was in defence of Muslim minorities. Muslim minorities, including in Muslim countries, are some of the most discriminated against and endangered peoples in the world. Groups like the Ahmadis in Pakistan and the Ismailis in Syria stand out. The Yazidis in Iraq are a similarly threatened (though non-Muslim) religious group. Of course, our Government's determined opposition to antisemitism at home and around the world was well known.

As for Christian groups, there are those communities that are targeted and discriminated against in many parts of the world, so naturally they would also be included in our mandate. However, any argument that this was exclusively or even primarily focused on Christians was not true. Indeed, it was insulting. We were not promoting any religion; we were promoting the right of people to believe in and practise their own religion. The distinction was obvious to anyone who wanted to see it.

The second criticism—from the same critics, incidentally—was not merely anti-Christian; it was more deeply anti-religion. It was from what I call the "freedom from religion" crowd. This term can easily be misunderstood. Certainly, people have every right to be non-religious, which was affirmed and defended by Ambassador Bennett himself. But the freedom-from-religion view, increasingly common in our public policy commentariat, is not only that the state should not endorse a particular religion but also that the entire public square must be singularly devoted to secular humanism with any expressions of faith eradicated from it. One could call it "atheists only need apply."

Being a convert to faith, I both understand and reject that perspective. Over the course of my life, I have also become convinced that religious belief is hard-wired into humanity. This is, of course, a different question than whether any particular religion is true or not true, but I do think that people have a fundamental need for religion. And when people do not have a formal religion, they will transfer that part of this deeply held need into some kind of non-religious ideology as a substitute.

This has been vividly demonstrated in the past couple of centuries, as communism, fascism, and many other isms, even things like radical environmentalism (or atheism itself), have become articles of faith rather than just ideas or goals. I have also observed that these "religions without God" are prone to a type of pseudo-scientific fanaticism. Borrowing from some scientific ideas, they—Karl Marx was a great example—attempt to wrap their ideologies with a claim of scientific proof. The corollary is that those who doubt their views somehow "reject science" and must be silenced. Of course, that is not how real science is supposed to function.

I do not think we should minimize the dangers of this humanist/atheist fanaticism any more than those of religious fanaticism. True, the belief that one speaks for God has generated many wars and great human suffering over the centuries. But does it really compare to the scale of slaughter perpetrated by those (like twentieth-century communists and fascists) who, rejecting God, substituted themselves in his place?

A milder version of this freedom-from-religion mindset is the superficial view that many modern liberals ascribe to the concept of freedom of religion itself. In effect, they reduce the idea of religion to a set of cultural practices—a way of dressing, lighting candles, breaking bread, or some other set of apparently quirky traditions. This is not at all the same as the conservative understanding—that religious beliefs and their associated practices are the authentic expressions of how we see our place in the universe and, thus, of our basic human worth. These beliefs cannot be dismissed, suppressed, or condescended to without denigrating their adherents as people. This is not to say, of course, that these rights are absolute. But they must be given serious consideration when our leaders are talking about human rights. Where they have not been, free and democratic societies do not exist.

Like all rights, freedom of religion can give rise to conflicting claims about rights. Freedom of religious worship is not the same as an unrestricted right of practice. We do not, for example, allow animal sacrifice in Canada. During the Covid-19 pandemic, restrictions on gatherings for reasons of public health impacted religious services, and even if some of those restrictions may have been unnecessary, it is certainly conceptually possible that such cases can arise. On the other hand, conservatives understand that if we only accommodate religious differences that are trivial, or we refuse to acknowledge that freedom of thought and expression may indeed represent fundamentally different worldviews, then we will not have a free and democratic country for very long.

I do not know why our successors scrapped the Office of Religious Freedom. The Office was an important contribution to our promotion of Canadian values around the world. As such, it needs to be reconstituted.

CELEBRATING BARONESS THATCHER

I WENT TO THE UNITED KINGDOM twice in 2013. The second occasion was pre-scheduled with the summit circuit's G8 at Lough Erne, Northern Ireland. The first came up suddenly when Margaret Thatcher passed away.

Thatcher was a figure whose influence and inspiration reached well beyond her country and her generation, and I was in both categories. As the reader will recall, I met Prime Minister Thatcher only once, but it remains a vivid memory. I was in awe of this lady who had done so much to turn Britain around and set the global agenda. Her funeral was on April 17, and I attended along with scores of other world leaders past and present. It was a moving memorial full of dignity and gravitas. No one does grand ceremony like the British, although I suspect Thatcher would have wondered what all the fuss was about.

However, the real highlight of the trip was my attendance at a much more intimate affair hosted by Prime Minister David Cameron. David and I developed a close bond during our five years as colleagues. We consulted regularly on a range of issues and have remained in touch ever since. Although there is much we differed on, we were particularly close on key economic matters. At my invitation, he gave an outstanding speech on these and other issues to Parliament in 2011.

On this occasion, David was kind enough to add me to a private dinner of about fifteen people closely connected with PM Thatcher. The list of attendees was stellar. Among the dignitaries were former American Secretary of

State George Shultz, former Australian Prime Minister John Howard, and Brian Mulroney, Thatcher's main Canadian contemporary. Also attending were former Thatcher ministers and long-time senior staff and confidants.

Each attendee was asked to share a story or an anecdote about their interactions with Margaret Thatcher. During the next couple of hours, we heard fifteen intimate portraits of Thatcher the prime minister, Thatcher the political colleague, Thatcher the boss, Thatcher the campaigner, and Thatcher the mother. My great regret from this wonderful evening was that nobody recorded and transcribed it. If it had been done, it would have given the world about as clear a picture of a person as you could ever ask for. What came out was how profoundly multi-dimensional Thatcher really was, how completely at ease she was in her own skin, and how acutely she was aware of the people around her. Little of this would be understood if you read most conventional analyses of Thatcher.

I was back in London in June before the G8. I made the by-now customary stop at Buckingham Palace to see the Queen, which always occasioned good conversation and advice. From there, I was scheduled to speak to the British Parliament on June 13. It is always a great personal honour to address the parliament of another country, as I have done in South Korea, Israel, Jamaica, and Australia. But speaking in the Parliament of the United Kingdom felt of a different order, it being the wellspring of our Canadian democracy.*

Uppermost on my mind that day, and the theme of my speech, was our shared heritage,† our ongoing partnership in the world, and the common challenges we face going forward, both domestically and abroad. My various messages were warmly received. However, there was no louder applause than when I reiterated my Government's unequivocal support for the Falkland Islanders' right to determine their own destiny.

---

* It was also a rare honour. Mackenzie King was the only other Canadian prime minister who spoke to the British Parliament.

† Included in that shared heritage is former British prime minister Andrew Bonar Law. I reminded the British parliamentarians that he was born in pre-Confederation New Brunswick.

I also felt it important to point toward a future where the joint history and values we share might see a renaissance:

> Now is not the time . . . to doubt our values or our friends, or, indeed, ourselves. Rather, now is the time to re-discover our values, to reaffirm their importance, and to fall back upon them. Britain and Canada may not be today the largest economies in the world, nor the biggest military powers, nor the greatest in terms of population. But I believe we share things that are more lasting—800 years of constitutional order and evolution that has allowed us to achieve what others wish for: to choose our governments and to hold them accountable; to worship God in our own way and to live in harmony with neighbours who do so differently; and to enjoy standards of living once considered unimaginable, while aiding our fellow citizens in their times of illness, unemployment and need.

That was my message then. And it is even more relevant today.

CALLING OUT VLADIMIR PUTIN

IT WAS AT THE G8 where my growing animosity toward Vladimir Putin would start to become public.

I had been accused of having a Cold War mentality and bringing that to Canada's relations with Russia. The charge was simply not true. My view is that Russia's natural long-term gravitation should be toward the West, not against it. I believe the Russian people, especially the young, want to be part of the wider Western free and democratic civilization. I thus began my time in office very supportive of efforts to integrate Russia and its leadership into Western diplomatic and strategic circles.

While hard to believe now, I also gave Putin the benefit of the doubt in my early days as prime minister. Following the collapse of the Soviet Union,

Russia had come through a decade marked by political, economic, and social turmoil that was unparalleled in any advanced country in recent history. At the end of that decade, Putin had come to power, restoring order and overseeing renewed economic growth. We had some reason to be hopeful about that.

Of course, there were also warning signs long before I came to office. The resumption of military incursions into our airspace—part of the reason for the Northern Strategy—and the growing restrictions on the opposition and civil liberties could not be fully ignored. I would also soon learn from Canadian companies about the deterioration of the Russian business environment and the strengthening of criminal organizations under Putin's rule.

In short, within a couple of years I had heard enough about Russia and seen enough of Putin myself to reassess any optimism I had had. Still, I kept relations with him business-like for several years, particularly at international events like the G8. Our allies were clearly still keen to try to cultivate the Russian leader. Besides, Putin became prime minister in 2008 (due to then–term limits in the Russian constitution), with President Dmitry Medvedev representing him indirectly (and more amicably) at various summits.

My approach began to change after the Arab Spring in 2011 and Putin's return to the presidency (and thus our leaders' meetings) in 2012. As the situation in many countries, particularly Syria, continued to deteriorate, we and our allies searched for ways of addressing the situation. However, any hint of co-operation from Russia vanished when Medvedev left office. It became plainly apparent—at least to me—that Putin was largely focused on undermining any Western coherence and effectiveness.

Our first open clash took place at a bilateral meeting in Vladivostok, on Russia's far-east coast, where the Asia-Pacific Economic Cooperation Summit was being held in the fall of 2012. I took issue with Putin's ironclad support for Syria's dictator, Bashar al-Assad, and I questioned his motives for doing so. Losing his cool, Putin shot back and, in the middle of his rant, accused me of being a Trotskyite.

I suppose he meant that I was some kind of careless exponent of revolution. My usual response to name-calling is to say, "I've been called worse things by better people," but, on this occasion, I just said, "You know,

Vladimir, I have been called every name in the book in my political career, but this is the first time someone ever accused me of being a communist." It was just crazy, but it was also a watershed for me. I said to some of my delegation, "I'm just tired of playing along with this guy's bullshit. I am fed up with it, and I'm not going to do it anymore, because this is just ridiculous."

I was true to my word at the G8. A blow-by-blow report of the meeting is not necessary. Here we were, a group of seven allied countries, trying to have meaningful, constructive discussions—and then there was Putin. I became very blunt with him, both alone and in front of others, giving unvarnished views about what he was saying and his motives for saying it. With other leaders, I made it plain that I did not think Putin belonged in the G8, and I began publicly referring to the G8 as the "G7-plus-one." I had dropped any pretense of diplomacy and became as frank as I thought was necessary.

Those who said that Vladimir Putin and I developed a real antipathy were absolutely right. But I do not want to exaggerate. At no time did I think Putin should be dismissed or taken lightly. He is a formidable and, in many ways, very impressive individual. He is intelligent and extraordinarily disciplined. He comes to international meetings extremely well briefed and knowing exactly what he wants. He is also very manipulative, no doubt part of his background as an intelligence officer, appearing soft-spoken, almost shy, while being quick to spot weaknesses in others and exploit them. I suppose it was that veneer that I was most eager to puncture.

Of all the famous people I have met, I still get asked more about Putin than about any other. I guess it is because he is a real-life Bond villain. And make no mistake, for all his strong attributes, he is a truly evil individual. He has knowingly and deliberately inflicted great and avoidable harm in his country and around the world. As it turned out, I would soon have more to say on that.

SYRIAN CIVIL WAR

IN THE LATE SUMMER OF 2013, the growing problems in Syria created a major international issue. Syria was, of course, one of the countries swept up in the Arab Spring of early 2011. The first major protests against the government occurred in March 2011. These quickly devolved into killing by security forces, escalating rounds of violence, the intervention of militias on both sides, and by July, a full-fledged, multi-sided civil war. It has continued ever since.

However, unlike Libya, there was no international military intervention in Syria. Why not? Because, unlike Muammar Gaddafi, President Bashar al-Assad had important allies, including Russia and Iran, which were committing major resources to keeping the regime afloat. Confrontation would have led to a broader regional conflict, one nobody—except maybe Iran—wanted to see.

Furthermore, the internal situation in Syria was quite different. This was not a simple case of a tyrant and his family or tribe against the vast mass of the population. There were profound divisions within Syrian society. Roughly three-quarters of Syria is Arab, of which three-quarters of those are Sunni Muslim. Their opposition to the Assad regime is deep and longstanding. Much of the other 40 per cent, especially the various groups of Shia Muslims, supported Assad. Even those that did not, like the large Kurdish population, did not necessarily align with the Sunni Arabs either. This made it very difficult for an intervention to have a clear objective.

Because of our read of the nature of this conflict, our Government's position began to diverge from some of our allies. For instance, when Barack Obama declared that "Assad must go," I only begrudgingly agreed in public. I certainly did not want to appear to support Assad; the reader will recall that we had already unilaterally shut down our relations with Assad because of the brutality of his regime. On the other hand, I was very worried about calling for the overthrow of the Syrian government with no idea what would replace it.

This situation became more uneasy for us when many of our allies moved to formally support the Syrian opposition as the "sole legitimate representative of the Syrian people." While we met with the Syrian National Council (SNC), it was clear to John Baird and I that it was overwhelmingly Sunni Arab in character, with little support from the country's large minority populations. For that reason, we did not join in recognizing it. More than that, I was alarmed that an outright victory by the SNC might expose those minorities to genocide. Those fears had been raised with me by the Aga Khan and other representatives of those groups.

Of course, military intervention was discussed. I attended several international meetings where the subject was on the table. Our Western allies were anxious to try and shape outcomes toward something positive in this conflict, and there can be no doubt that some were covertly aiding various rebel groups. Unfortunately, some countries, like Turkey and Qatar, were supporting extremist elements of the Sunni Arab opposition, rendering clear objectives for allied intervention even more difficult. This was another matter on which I clashed with President Erdoğan. My concerns were well founded, as this was to have severe consequences down the road.

We had long been at an impasse when things shifted dramatically on August 21, 2013. Assad used chemical weapons against the opposition-controlled suburbs of Damascus. This clearly flouted a "red line" Barack Obama had publicly laid down almost exactly a year earlier. As such, it demanded U.S. intervention.

Not long after, on September 5–6, Obama and I, along with many of our allies, met for the G20 Summit—at St. Petersburg, Russia, of all places. Chairing the meeting was our host, Vladimir Putin. As always, he was very well briefed and articulate. Although he had been on record opposing the use of chemical weapons, he suddenly had a million reasons why nothing should be done about this.

Putin's concerns, coming from anyone else, would not have been without merit. However, at this point I had no use for him and understood his real motives—to run interference with any American or Western strategy and to support his thug ally, Assad. The G20 descended into a free-for-all over the situation, and eventually we split right down the middle. Eleven of the countries committed to support American action; the others did not. We naturally sided with our American allies. I was also genuinely concerned that opening the door to chemical warfare would be a descent into something the planet had not seriously seen since World War I.

As it happened, an air campaign against the Syrian government's chemical capabilities never occurred. Why? Initially, our American, British, and

French allies had agreed to undertake it. But Prime Minister Cameron, for reasons of coalition politics, unexpectedly presented a motion before the British Parliament on the issue. It was defeated, suddenly taking British involvement off the table.

Then, for reasons I still do not understand, President Obama decided to present an intervention resolution to the U.S. Senate for approval. This strategy also went sideways, and very quickly. The Senate Foreign Relations Committee just barely approved a very watered-down version of the Obama resolution. Then, as each day went by, opposition to this resolution grew—in both parties, in both chambers, and in public opinion. Obama's political position was eroding by the day.

Observing Obama's predicament, I did something unusual in this circumstance: I decided to call the president about the situation. Calling the U.S. president was not unusual in itself; I had more than three dozen interactions with Obama over our joint time in office. The difference here was that I was calling to give him advice. This I rarely did, for reasons I described earlier; advice is best offered when asked for, and the U.S. president always has a lot of things on this mind. However, on this occasion, I demanded to speak to him on an urgent basis.

Once on the line, I urged Barack *not* to proceed with the resolution. The information I had—I am sure he had the same—was that this resolution would not just lose, it would lose very badly. My view was that this would not merely be a defeat for the action against Assad but also a serious blow to Obama's credibility as a leader on the world stage and to that of the United States more generally. Neither of those did I judge to be in Canada's interests. Withdrawing the resolution was not great, but it would be making the best of a bad situation.

I think Obama appreciated the call. He listened very carefully, and we had a constructive conversation about the situation, which was as much as I could ask for under the circumstances. The White House was obviously wrestling with what to do, and they were probably already thinking along these lines. The resolution was ultimately withdrawn.

This situation could have been a real political pickle for us too. As I said, we had also indicated support for the intervention, but there were divided opinions in Canada. Lucky for me—and totally coincidentally—Parliament was prorogued, which meant there was no prospect of me taking this vote to the House of Commons. Thus, the on-again-off-again intervention was history by the time Parliament returned.

The French were not so fortunate. President Hollande had acted decisively, and he had his forces ready to go. With neither the Americans nor the British at his side, he had to do an embarrassing reversal. I never spoke to Hollande personally about the affair, but I have no doubt that this was a blow both to him and to French pride. With the French having only recently, under President Sarkozy, fully re-engaged with the North Atlantic Treaty Organization (NATO), this was bound to affect their military co-operation going forward.

In an unexpected twist, the day after the U.S. administration withdrew the Syrian resolution from the Senate, Obama and Putin announced that they had come to an agreement to force the Syrian government to eliminate its chemical weapons capability. In effect, this was a gracious climbdown for everybody. On the one hand, Obama in theory got what he wanted—the end of Syria's ability to make chemical war—without serious armed escalation. On the other hand, Putin's reputation as a regional player—even peacemaker, absurdly—was enhanced.

I cannot say that this looked very good for Obama and NATO, but it was the best outcome of a tough and complicated situation. However, it would not be the last time the situation in Syria was on our plates.

COMPLETION OF THE CETA NEGOTIATIONS

IN ANY LIST of my Government's accomplishments, October 18, 2013, was a very big day. Along with Trade Minister Ed Fast and Chief Negotiator Steve Verheul, I had travelled to Brussels for a joint press conference with the president of the European Commission, José Manuel Barroso. We would announce that we had reached an agreement-in-principle on what we called the Canada-EU Comprehensive Economic and Trade Agreement (CETA).

There really is no way of overstating how important this agreement was for Canada's trading posture in the world. It increased our free-trade network by twenty-eight countries (to forty-two) and was widely recognized as the future gold standard for trade agreements. Its scope was quite unprecedented. It went well beyond the removal of virtually all tariffs, with comprehensive provisions for services, investment, procurement, and more. In short, it was a great feather in the cap of our Government and the country.

This was *the* major step in the process, but it was not the final one. By the time we were done, it would be the culmination of seven years' work—two years of pre-negotiation and complementary studies and five years of negotiations proper. These had followed the typical course in getting all the least contentious stuff out of the way first. As you come down to the most contentious issues, a deal will invariably look like it is about to fall apart. That is when things go to the leaders themselves, eyeball-to-eyeball. Not surprisingly, agriculture dominated those final talks between Barroso and me.

The next step would be translating the agreement-in-principle into a detailed legal text. As a legal contract, it was understood that there would still be some shouting and waving of arms, but we also knew that this more-technical process would not derail the agreement. Indeed, on September 26, 2014, Barroso and European Council President Herman Van Rompuy undertook an official visit to Ottawa to celebrate the conclusion of the negotiations of the legal text and thus of CETA. The ratification process now lay ahead of us.

Of much satisfaction to me and my team was how this process had strengthened Canada's capacity for negotiating trade deals and bringing stakeholders onside. The first had been built up from 2006. International Trade had accumulated a record of success at the various bargaining tables, while synthesizing the views of other departments. Its head, Ian Burney (son of Derek),* would eventually be given an outstanding public servant award for this work.

---

* Ian served as assistant deputy minister in the Trade Agreements and Negotiations Branch at the Department of Foreign Affairs, Trade, and Development.

Yet the real advancement had been in our external consultations. Through various staff members over the years, including Bill Hawkins, Andrea van Vugt, and Jeremy Hunt, we had built a real expertise at connecting with stakeholders. We talked to other levels of government, industry associations, labour, community groups, activists—everyone who wanted to have a say. Some of these had great hopes, while others had fears to be allayed or managed. The process gave us a wider sense of what our flexibility was at the table and the concessions we could afford to make. Most importantly, it allowed us to know who was going to be on board, who might be on board, and who was never going to get on board, no matter what.

In making these evaluations, we were very successful. When we announced this (and other) trade deals, we knew exactly what all stakeholders were going to say, whether positive, cautionary, or negative, without exception. We therefore already knew that we had enough political support to get any deal through before it was announced. In this case, except for a relatively small number of ideological opponents, CETA would be overwhelmingly backed by Canadians.

As I mentioned earlier, in these negotiations there had been a high involvement of direct provincial participation. All thirteen provinces/territories were on board, but there had been occasional hiccups along the way. The most serious had been—par for the course—with Newfoundland & Labrador. It was around the issue of fish. St. John's concerns had been focused on regulations in Newfoundland that required a certain number of fish caught to be landed at a local port for processing, so-called minimum processing requirements (MPRs).*

We were not convinced that Newfoundland & Labrador had much of a leg to stand on with this issue. Our view was that their regulations were

---

* Quebec had a similar, but much smaller, program. Loss of MPRs was not an issue that mattered for Quebec.

already vulnerable to an international legal challenge through the World Trade Organization, with or without CETA. Still, we were anxious to make sure everybody was on board, so we finally agreed that we would compensate the province up to a maximum of $400 million in the event MPRs were lost and there were identifiable economic impacts.

Things went sideways very quickly. Premier Kathy Dunderdale decided to announce that the province had received a $400 million "signing bonus" for agreeing to be part of CETA. You could hear the alarm bells going off in every other provincial capital. Why is Newfoundland & Labrador getting a signing bonus?!

Over time, the dispute escalated. Dunderdale's assertion was taken up by successive Newfoundland premiers, who demanded their $400-million unconditional cheque just for being a part of CETA. Of course, that was never the deal, nor could it have been. It would have blown every other province's support out of the water. Our assertion remained the same from the beginning: if you lose MPRs, we will be there for you. We worked through scenarios with the province to show we would apply broad criteria in measuring the impacts on workers and communities. Our numbers never came to more than $280 million, and frankly, neither did theirs.

But this had now become a matter of principle for them. They were not agreeing to some lesser amount for actual economic impacts; they wanted that unconditional cheque for the full amount of $400 million. Given that that was impossible, we just proceeded without them. We considered the MPRs in significant jeopardy in any case, so Newfoundland & Labrador could decide whether they wanted what they had originally agreed to or take their chances. If push did come to shove, the EU was not going to leave the deal if that province did not co-operate on the procurement side. They were simply too small a percentage of the Canadian market.

Years later, as CETA was being implemented by my Liberal successors, Newfoundland ultimately ended up agreeing to an "Atlantic fish fund," amounting to $100 million. If they had stuck to the deal with us, they would have done much, much better. Too bad.

THE RATIFICATION PROCESS IN EUROPE

GIVEN THE SIZE and complexity of the European Union, the ratification process on their side was always going to be more challenging. One of the problems was general in nature: the growing opposition to trade deals in principle. As I discussed at length in my book *Right Here, Right Now*, from the second decade of the twenty-first century we have been witnessing the rise of populist, nationalist, and unconventional political forces of different kinds in virtually every Western country. Challenges like this in Europe would be real, but we did not believe they could sink the deal. The EU simply had too much of its credibility at stake to let CETA fail.

There were bound to be specific challenges as well. The issue that arose in 2015 was around "Investor State Dispute Settlement" (ISDS). This is essentially a regime for allowing investors to sue when they believe that a state has undertaken actions to effectively deny them the equal access to the market that the trade agreement promised.

CETA had novel provisions on ISDS that went further than previous agreements. That was largely at the insistence of the German government. We had been reticent. It was not our issue, but ultimately, we conceded on strengthened ISDS provisions to reach the final agreement.

However, the ISDS provisions soon became a lightning rod for opposition to CETA within Europe. Ironically, the government that started pushing for a change to the agreement was none other than Germany. Politics in that country were roiling with populist sentiment, amplified by parties like the Greens, the Left Party—an outgrowth of the communist East German state—and the rising Alliance for Germany on the nationalist right. The German government was clearly worried that these parties and their anti-trade inclinations were increasingly drawing mainstream support.

The Germans' demand was essentially that we rescind the new ISDS rules and go back to the clause that we, Canada, had originally wanted in CETA. Not too hard, right? Wrong. Because the agreement had already been concluded, any proposed changes at this point—even if we happened to agree with them—risked twenty-seven other countries coming forward with their own concerns and demands for change. So, while we privately agreed with this demand, we waited for the European Commission to be able to assure us that this would be the only one.

This issue remained unsettled in 2015 when my Government was defeated. It became one of the key pieces of advice I gave my successor, Justin Trudeau, during our transition meeting after the election. The agreement was done, I said. The EU wants it through; we want it through. The Liberal Party had supported it in opposition. The ISDS change is easy to agree to, but it is a serious potential complication. Do not agree to this until you are certain the EU will come forward with nothing else.

Thankfully, that appears to be what the Liberal Government did. They stuck to the strategy, even as other EU countries began to throw knuckleballs, as I had feared.

We were very fortunate to get CETA done. A lot of people deserve credit for the long, complex, and successful exercise that I consider to be one of our biggest achievements. That includes my successors for seeing the final stages through.*

NELSON MANDELA FUNERAL

ON DECEMBER 5, the world lost a great international leader and human rights icon. I did not know Nelson Mandela personally, for he had left public life before I became prime minister. But his passing was a major international event, as was befitting his extraordinary accomplishments.

Mandela had championed both an end to apartheid as an activist and reconciliation between South Africa's peoples as the first post-apartheid president. For his efforts, he was a Nobel Peace Prize laureate with former

---

* Ironically, even as I write this a decade later, CETA has still not been formally ratified by the European member states. It thus remains merely "provisionally" in force by the European Union.

President F.W. de Klerk, who deserves considerable credit as well. Upon the news of his passing, I gave a statement in the House of Commons, joining a chorus of leaders around the world who expressed grief at this great loss and admiration for a truly remarkable life.

On December 8, I led a Canadian delegation to Johannesburg for the state funeral. While this was not the largest delegation I had taken abroad, it was certainly the highest ranking. I had invited all the living former prime ministers and governors general. I did this because Canada, through governments going back as far as John Diefenbaker's, had been at the forefront of the fight against apartheid. Except for John Turner, Paul Martin, and Ed Schreyer, they were all able to accept. Joining us on the plane were Jean Chrétien, Brian Mulroney, and Kim Campbell,* plus former governors general Michaëlle Jean and Adrienne Clarkson,† as well as several sitting premiers and the national chief of the Assembly of First Nations Shawn Atleo. This was probably the most high-powered Canadian delegation of all time, as I am unaware of anything similar being done in the past.

It was an event-filled few days. We were treated to some fascinating tours of the history and legacy of the apartheid era. There were several official events around Mr. Mandela's passing, obviously including the funeral ceremony. Unfortunately, that event was excessively long and poorly organized, noticeably enough for the media to comment on it. But that did not diminish the importance of the occasion nor the chance we all had to meet other leaders and exchange stories.

On the flight there, I had dinner with the three former prime ministers who had joined the delegation. Having attended this high-profile and solemn event, and being together far from home, we dropped our partisan

---

* Joe Clark also attended, but he made alternate travel arrangements.

† I did not invite the current governor general, David Johnston, because I thought it most appropriate that I lead the delegation on this occasion. As the governor general outranks the prime minister diplomatically, David would have led the delegation if he had been on it. David thus agreed to stay behind for this one.

and political guards and engaged in a long conversation about our experiences in the country's highest elected office. We had a great dialogue about how the country had changed. We even jokingly rehashed some of our old political battles.‡

I have often been asked by my American counterparts whether there is such a thing as a Canadian "Prime Ministers' Club" like the so-called U.S. Presidents' Club. My joking response has always been, "No, because we all hate each other!" This is an exaggeration, of course. The real reason is somewhat more nuanced.

U.S. presidents serve sequentially and are thus often not direct rivals. By contrast, Canadian prime ministers have usually faced off against each other regularly in Commons, frequently in national elections, and, perhaps most importantly, in intraparty leadership battles as well. The rivalries are thus more intense and the animus longer lasting. There are exceptions, of course, such as the friendship between Mr. Chrétien and me. In any case, I suspect that the advent of Mr. Trump has made the Presidents Club a thing of the past!

---

‡ Arthur Milnes, then one of my speechwriters and Canada's unofficial prime-ministerial historian (and someone we all trust), made a recording of the conversation.

25

MAJOR DOMESTIC INITIATIVES

THE FIRST NATIONS CONTROL OF FIRST NATIONS EDUCATION ACT

ON FEBRUARY 7, 2014, I travelled to the Kainai First Nation in Southern Alberta (where I am an honorary chief) to make a very special announcement: the First Nations Control of First Nations Education Act. This was a major initiative of our Government, and it was years in the making.

I had spent some time with Shawn Atleo, then–National Chief of the Assembly of First Nations (AFN) and found him to be a different kind of leader, a new generation leader. He wanted to move beyond the politics of grievance. This is certainly not to say that grievances are unwarranted in many cases where Indigenous Canadians are concerned, but Chief Atleo wanted to focus more on what he called the politics of progress.

Atleo had identified education reform as one of the key issues, if not *the* key issue, to ensure progress and prosperity for future generations of Canada's First Nations people. He had initiated this very early on in his term as national chief. Our Ministers of Aboriginal Affairs John Duncan and later Bernard Valcourt were enthusiastic participants in this initiative. The announcement was to be a big step.

The defining characteristic of this legislation was the transfer of jurisdiction for education from the federal government to the First Nations (FN) themselves. This federal role in education has always been a bit of a historical anomaly, as education is generally a provincial responsibility under our Constitution. But with First Nations' treaties and relationships with the British Crown often predating Confederation (1867) and certainly the Constitution Act of 1982, the federal government was assigned the role of managing "Indian" education as an agent of the Crown.

Arrangements like this have usually not worked well. I would make a general observation that, whenever the federal government has some role in what is typically provincial jurisdiction, it has often done a poor job. Things like Indigenous education and veterans' medical care are two examples. These delivery services are just not Ottawa's specialty.

As I said in my announcement speech, federal education policy for Indigenous Peoples had, for nearly a century and a half, veered wildly from "arbitrary decrees to benign neglect." As an example, everyone now knows about the government's Indian residential school policy. That was symptomatic of the fact that the affairs of First Nations' communities were long exercised through the largely untrammelled power of federally appointed Indian agents. What First Nations people themselves wanted or, in some cases, had been promised was beside the point.

That was the arbitrary decrees part. Later, as some authority was devolved to individual First Nations, the benign neglect element came in. In the case of First Nations' education, this had come to mean no standard curriculum, no provincial equivalency, and, consequently, no portability of the education between jurisdictions. If you had graduated from an Indigenous school, what exactly were your credentials? Problems were legion with a system that had five hundred different standards of varying quality. Furthermore, as the chiefs had argued for years, the system (such as it was) was also underfunded. Clearly, a comprehensive overhaul was required. Working closely with Chief Atleo, this is what we set out to do.

There were five major elements at the centre of the First Nations Control of First Nations Education Act. The first was to establish a core curriculum based upon provincial teaching, making the education standard and portable. Second, within that curriculum there would be ample room for local cultural- and linguistic-appropriate education, reflecting the unique history and character of First Nations communities. The third element was the establishment of a national governance body—emanating from the FN themselves—responsible for supervision, as well as accountability for resources and results. Fourth, there was to be a significant infusion of cash to support the new system—two billion dollars—which was already allocated in our upcoming budget. Finally, we would formally repeal the provisions that allowed the Government of Canada to establish Indian residential schools. After all these years they still existed in law!

Initially, our plan was well received. I believe most people recognized that there were deep problems with the existing system and that this was a legitimate effort to address those shortfalls. It was timely, as First Nations were paying a lot more attention to the many opportunities for their youth in expanding resource and energy development near their communities. This could provide great employment opportunities to the FNs not just near major urban centres but in all parts of Canada, including the most remote.

That is why there was a range of stakeholders there that day to support the initiative, from business to the education sector. Chief Atleo had played the largest role in the effort to get that far, and he had secured the endorsement of his AFN executive. It was a great day, and everything appeared to be headed for success.

Despite how positive we felt about the Act, we still expected resistance from within some Indigenous communities. The reality of Canada's Indigenous Peoples is that their governance is very highly decentralized. There were bound to be FN that did not want to transfer responsibility to any central body, even an Indigenous one, or to have their autonomy in any way infringed. With the large financial component in play, some local chiefs and councils would also oppose measures that might affect their ability to do whatever they wanted with the money.

There was, however, a second and more troubling issue that we in the Prime Minister's Office had become aware of. As we waded into these negotiations with Atleo and his lieutenants, we became suspicious that several senior AFN people were not supporting the chief. In fact, we worried that they were looking for an opportunity to undermine his leadership. Still, this was Chief Atleo's organization, and we were not about to embroil ourselves in politics we did not fully understand.

As it turned out, our misgivings were correct. Having given their go-ahead, some of these individuals began looking for the first opportunity to pull their support from the agreement. We can speculate as to why, but my guess is that Chief Atleo's attempts to shift the paradigm from eternal grievance to future progress was not popular with some, especially those who had made their careers on the former model.

Ultimately, this coup was successful, and the AFN executive dropped its support. Chief Atleo resigned soon after. He had staked his reputation upon dealing with the government on this matter. He is an honourable man, and he did the honourable thing in stepping down.

For all intents and purposes, that was the end of the First Nations Control of First Nations Education Act. Although it stayed on the order paper, there was no way we were going to proceed under the current scenario. While I thought we had a great agreement for the future, without the support of the AFN and the leading FNs, passing the Act would have amounted to us imposing this upon them—exactly the opposite of the entire intent of the Act.

Ironically, not long after, some senior AFN folks were in touch with me. To my surprise, in a meeting with one prominent leader—an Atleo opponent—I was told that First Nations' education remained high on their agenda. I responded that we had signed an agreement with the AFN and remained anxious to move ahead as well. That clearly was not what he meant, though. He said, "Everyone knows we can't really fix First Nations education—it's just not possible. But I've got a group of Chiefs who will support you; just give the Chiefs the money, and we will all be on your side." I indicated that I was committed to reforming FN education, not to buying people off. I would not separate the money from reform. That was where we left it.

Later, the Liberal Party promised the same players that, if they were elected, they would give the money without the reform. This they did. The result, I suspect, is that we have a more expensive First Nations' education system with all the same problems we had before.

I still grieve over this. It was all so cynical and sad. This is to take nothing away from Chief Atleo, however, and the people working with him. They were serious about making progress, and they acted with considerable boldness and courage to move their initiative forward. I will always admire Shawn, who pursued the absolute best for his people, despite the ultimate failure.

SPECIFIC CLAIMS AND OTHER PROGRESS

THERE *WERE* AREAS of our Indigenous policy where we did have success. Of course, as I already noted, our Government completed the Indian Residential Schools Settlement Agreement that the Martin Government had negotiated, and I delivered the formal apology in the House of Commons (which went beyond that agreement). Another, less-known area where we had great success was in what is called Specific Land Claims.

With the exception of British Columbia, most of Canada's First Nations concluded historical treaties with the Government of Canada or its predecessors, which included the ceding of lands. However, it is a sad part of our history that, in many cases, those agreements were broken—often blatantly. The federal government, acting on its own or on behalf of railways, developers, and others, had simply seized portions of a reserve without consultation, negotiation, or compensation. Instances of this have run literally into the thousands.

A tribunal had been set up by previous federal governments to deal with this. However, very little progress was made—in some cases for generations. It is a shameful story, and we determined to do something about it.

We reviewed the situation through various ministers and departments. We concluded that many of these claims were fully justified and that we should act to get them resolved. Working with Phil Fontaine, Shawn Atleo's predecessor as AFN national chief, we streamlined the process, gave the Specific Claims Tribunal more resources, put aside a large amount of money, and set out to resolve those claims. A lot of them—not all of them, by any means—were addressed in fairly short order.*

I consider these to be silver linings in some dark storm clouds. Yet, as is often the case in politics, even the nice puffy cumulus ones come with black lines, and so we began to experience real pushback on the new process. This came mainly from lawyers and consultants involved in the specific claims process. Many had been running their clocks for years on these various negotiations, and now their work was ending. Their general tenor was to claim that the new process really was not working, so we needed to slow it down! Frankly, I consider that a sign of its success.

The specific claims process may have been the most concrete progress we made on Indigenous issues, but it was not the only one. We also made some strides on the broader, so-called comprehensive claims—settlement of larger issues around land and sovereignty, some of which still trouble our relations with Canada's Indigenous Peoples. During our tenure, we concluded and brought into Parliament at least a dozen pieces of legislation around either comprehensive claims or similar major agreements with various Aboriginal peoples.

We also made major investments in infrastructure in Indigenous communities—schools, water systems, housing, and public buildings—through both our Building Canada plans and the Economic Action Plan stimulus programs. Many of these were also tied to our Northern Agenda and implemented in the lightly populated communities of the North.

Additionally, we undertook regular interactions with First Nations, Metis, and Inuit leaders nationally, regionally, and locally, where we did our best to understand their main concerns. As a rule, we did not promise big transformational change, because such promises in the past have been

* On March 17, 2013, Minister Bernard Valcourt announced that the Government of Canada had cleared up a backlog of 541 claims at the assessment stage, doubling the number of claims in negotiation and settling 84 through negotiated agreements, with many more on the way.

too often broken, fuelling immense disappointment and cynicism. Better to promise what you can deliver and then get those commitments fulfilled.

On Indigenous matters, our general approach was to look for straightforward ways that we could make concrete progress on the ground. We did that in many areas. Still, I am under no illusion about how much more needs to be done.

FIRST NATIONS FINANCIAL TRANSPARENCY ACT

MOST OF THE THINGS we did do were not controversial and were accomplished largely under the radar. That was not so with the introduction and passage of the First Nations Financial Transparency Act. It originated as a private member's bill by Saskatchewan MP Kelly Block, but it ultimately became a government bill. The Act made it a requirement for First Nations chiefs and councillors to publicly disclose their salaries and remuneration.

The rationale was that this would bring FN administrations in line with basic standards of government transparency throughout Canada and, for that matter, with all other transparent jurisdictions in the world. This was a way of trying to ensure local accountability within Indigenous communities. That was our core objective. The beneficiaries of this accountability for FN would be their own people.

For years, politicians had been saying that the way forward in Canada's relations with its FN was to devolve authority (and money) for the lives of Indigenous people away from the bureaucracy in Ottawa and give it to local organizations and communities. In fact, this has largely been done. The problem is that the accountability mechanisms have been unusually weak. Our bill was intended to change that.

When it received parliamentary assent on March 27, 2013, the new law was met with a decidedly mixed reception. By and large, most FN had no difficulty with such accountability, and even in most places where they were not happy with the law, they complied. However, the law was not well received by a relatively small group of chiefs and counsellors, who went vocally on the attack.

Let us remember that this Act imposed no standards of pay on chiefs or councils. The level of their remuneration remained entirely up to them. The only requirement was public disclosure, so that members of the FN could ultimately have their say as well. Although our opponents cloaked their criticisms in language of autonomy and control, the only real reason to oppose this was to ensure that such information was not revealed.

This opposition never subsided, and when the Liberals took power in 2015, repealing the Financial Transparency Act was an early priority. This may have made sense for the Liberals' political calculations, but I fail to see how this helped the average Indigenous person. Somehow ensuring Indigenous people never know how their money is being spent is supposed to be a good thing. It is but one more cynical and sad example of the federal government's policy in this area.

WHERE TO FROM HERE?

I HAVE TALKED ABOUT how federal policy on Indigenous matters has veered over the many decades between arbitrary decrees and benign neglect. The early decades of Confederation were generally marked by the first. I have concluded that in our era, things have moved to the other extreme.

In my experience, our Department of Aboriginal Affairs—historically Indian Affairs, now Indigenous Affairs—sent money to First Nations with very little idea of how it was spent. It was transferred, and it was gone. This is not to deny that some FN had great leadership, which was using the money wisely and producing good results for their people. But the truth is that we really did not know.

The most vivid example of this was the controversy related to Attawapiskat, a community in Ontario's far north. It had terrible living conditions, bad water, decrepit infrastructure, and few services. This horrendous situation hit the nightly news when local representatives, in particular Chief Theresa Spence, came to Ottawa and staged a fifteen-day hunger strike.

However, the truth was that, in the preceding years, the Government of Canada had transferred some ninety million dollars to the community. That was for a FN with an on-reserve population of only about 1,500. When we asked what it was being used for, we simply could not get any clear answers from the department. What was certain was that all that money did not seem to have improved the lives of the people of Attawapiskat.

I do not know how much money has gone there since, but I would bet that it is a lot more. Yet, in 2016, a wave of youth suicides in the community prompted the chief and council to declare a state of emergency. Years later, Attawapiskat was still lacking promised mental health services. In 2019, the community still lacked drinkable water.

I do not have an easy or comprehensive answer—you should not trust those who say they do—for how to resolve situations like these. Such remote communities often have a dearth of economic activity and opportunity. They also frequently lack the skills to maintain what infrastructure and services are provided. As well, they are usually cut off from the mainstream of our society, and there can be deep social and familial pathologies that go back decades.

That said, is the solution total local control? If it is, should this really come without any standard accountability mechanisms? It is obvious, I think, that Ottawa should not be running the daily lives of these communities. The federal government has seldom demonstrated any such skill. However, governments should insist on basic standards of transparency in the ultimate use of large amounts of public dollars.

In short, I believe the pendulum has swung way too far toward benign neglect. We fundamentally need local control under FN administration, but with the same accountability standards we expect in any other system of governance. We have to be able to know whether the help we are providing is actually helping the people we are trying to help.

We never did make satisfactory progress on this while I was in office. In our first order of business—the Federal Accountability Act of 2006—we wanted to give the office of the auditor general authority to audit our FN transfers. To be blunt, the then–auditor general wanted nothing to do with the file. I was disappointed by that decision, but I can understand the rationale in Ottawa. To take on such responsibility would come with massive risks of criticism and a dubious likelihood of making progress.

We are now treating Canada's Indigenous Peoples in ways we would never consider treating the non-Indigenous population. We have gone from arbitrary decrees to not just benign neglect but also empty virtue signalling and performative acts that are all talk and no action. These communities deserve better, and I pray that someday we will find a way to make real, demonstrable progress in improving their lives and prospects.

RETURNING TO BALANCE: BUDGET 2014

ON FEBRUARY 11, 2014, our Government tabled its annual budget, *Economic Action Plan 2014*. With it, we reached an important milestone for my Government: the deficit was eliminated, one year ahead of schedule. The budget projected a deficit of a little under three billion dollars, but using very conservative estimates, we thought there was a very good chance that we would be in balance or better. In fact, when the books were closed in 2015, the budget clocked in at a surplus close to two billion dollars.*

This objective had been championed by Minister Flaherty. Although not an economist or businessman—he was a small-town lawyer—nor steeped in the same kind of economic theory that I was, we shared a rock-solid commitment to fiscal responsibility. In his bones, Jim knew that government deficits, if not controlled when there is a chance to do so, will *always* morph from small and temporary to big and permanent. Once that happens, it takes austerity to get back to balance.

---

* Some years later, changes to accounting methodology revised the figure to a deficit of five hundred million dollars (which is virtually in balance by federal standards).

Austerity is not just some technical word accountants use. Nor is it the kind of tight expenditure discipline we had been practising since the end of the global financial crisis. Austerity means serious reductions in public services, like the big healthcare and education cuts enacted by the Chrétien/Martin Government. That was extremely painful, and it happened when Jim was a minister in Ontario. It was difficult and unpleasant enough that he was determined that that was not going to be his legacy. And that is what he achieved.

THE PASSING OF JIM FLAHERTY

FOR A COUPLE OF YEARS, Jim had been wanting to move on. He was now in his early sixties, and he wished to get into the private sector and, frankly, make some money. That he would be successful was pretty much a sure thing, as our Government's reputation and his strong economic management had raised his stature in global financial markets immensely. There would be all kinds of good, lucrative opportunities waiting for him when he chose to leave office.

There was also another reason. Unknown to most, Jim had been quite unwell. Some years earlier, he had contracted a serious skin disease. The ailment caused significant discomfort, for which he was prescribed heavy medications, with considerable and numerous side effects. People had noticed his weight gain, which was one of those. In fact, he was having increasing difficulty with the challenges and demands of one of the toughest and most stressful jobs in government, and it was taking its toll. All that said, while leaving was part of the plan, Jim would not do it until he was convinced that the deficit dragon had been well and truly slain.

With Budget 2014, that goal was now effectively done. A month after it was tabled, he came to me to officially resign. The announcement was made on March 19. This move was in Jim's best interests, and we all wished him a less-stressful, more-lucrative future in private business.

Sadly, that was not to be. Less than a month after leaving office, Jim had a massive heart attack at his Ottawa home and died instantly. The news shocked me to my core. I was in the middle of an official visit from Peruvian President Ollanta Humala when Ray Novak slipped me a note saying that "the Minister has passed." This was one of the rare occasions when I had trouble not showing my emotions in public, which were apparent to everybody in the room. I was devastated and could not go on. We cut short the meetings with the Peruvians. They fully understood.

It was a very sombre caucus that met after Jim's death. I am not going to tell you that he was a universally loved guy. Finance ministers say "no" an awful lot, and Jim had no trouble being tough when he needed to be. But I can tell you that, in our caucus, Jim was universally respected. (And I believe the opposition benches held him in the same regard.) It was just a very sad day.

Afterwards, I left the office early, went home, and did something unusual: I flipped on the Canadian news channels and just watched the tributes. What struck me most was how visibly his health had deteriorated in the previous two years. We knew he was dealing with some serious issues, but working with him day-to-day, I had not really noticed how dramatic a toll the illness was taking on his physical appearance over time. At that point, I began to question myself. Should I have noticed sooner? Could we have done something different? There are rarely any good answers to such rearview-mirror questions. All I know is that, to this day, I miss him.

Over Jim's long career, he had developed an incredible network of friends and colleagues, and it sure seemed like they were all there to bid him farewell at his funeral. During my remarks, I delivered the following words about my dear colleague and friend:

> I do not grieve for Jim Flaherty. I know that for Jim, the Lord has prepared a place where he can be free from the afflictions of recent times, loved, and in joy. No, my friends, when a good one leaves us, grief is for those who are left behind.

Beyond the grief we all shared, it might just be that the Irishman Flaherty got the last laugh. He was famous for wearing green ties. And he was always bugging me to wear them too, especially on St. Patrick's Day.

I would remind him that to the extent I have an Irish heritage, it is on the orange (i.e., Protestant) side, not the green (Catholic) one. But guess what? As it turns out, James Michael Flaherty had, in fact, long been a Protestant. And in death, his funeral was at Toronto's Anglican Cathedral, of all places!

Later that year, on October 15, we named the new Department of Finance building at 90 Elgin Street the James Michael Flaherty Building. It was a fitting tribute and legacy for a man I believe to have been Canada's greatest finance minister.

FINAL TRIP TO THE NORTH

IN THE SUMMER OF 2014, I undertook the last of the nine summer tours I made to Canada's North. I have written earlier about the principles behind the Northern Strategy I announced in 2006: promoting sovereignty, environmentally responsible economic development, and social progress, and strengthening governance for Northerners. Those were the things on which we persisted over the course of the decade. Looking back on our Government's approach to the North, there is much to be proud of, a bit to be worried about, and an awful lot more to do if we are to realize the true potential of this vast land mass.

I outlined earlier some of our major long-term investments to boost Canada's security and sovereignty in the region. The emphasis, as I learned, needs to be on the "long-term" side, due to several factors. First and foremost are the extremes in temperature. These render transportation and construction options very limited seasonally. The geography—both its vastness and its island nature—also make the costs of everything extremely high. These are further complicated by the fragility of the unique Arctic ecosystem. In short, almost nothing gets done overnight—literally and figuratively.

These factors were evident in the decade-plus-long fulfilment of some of our defence and security commitments in the North. Early in our mandate we announced several sovereignty-related initiatives. These included putting an army training centre in Resolute Bay, building a fleet of Arctic offshore patrol vessels, and constructing a major refuelling station for the Royal Canadian Navy at Nanisivik, Nunavut. The army training centre has been operational since 2013. Work on the naval refuelling station was abandoned in 2026.* The real message here is that governments need to remain committed to the initiatives undertaken by their predecessors. That is the only way major projects will get done in the North.† Other northern countries like Norway, Sweden, Denmark, and Russia have managed to sustain high investment levels in the Arctic. Canada's record has been hit and miss, and we need to do better to maintain and develop ourselves as a truly polar nation.

The fact is, we are less and less alone in our North. It can sometimes feel that way when you are up there with so few people and the limitless expanses of land and ocean. But countries like Russia and China are ramping up activities that have direct implications for our sovereignty. Canadians must not let what we have slip away.‡ And it will if our governments and diplomats do not "stand on guard"—as our national anthem proclaims. This vigilance will need to take place at every level, and sometimes in the most obscure areas, as I was reminded in late 2013.

One of the international treaties governing the Arctic is the United Nations Convention on the Law of the Sea (UNCLOS). Through that treaty, extensive mapping of the Arctic Ocean floor was being undertaken to establish continental

---

* The site will apparently be returned to a state of nature, indicating that the southern "no permanent development in the North" philosophy remains alive and well in Ottawa.

† There were some continuities in northern policy between our government and our successors. For example, the extension of the Dempster Highway from Inuvik to Tuktoyaktuk, begun in 2014, was completed in 2017. This finally extended our national highway system to the Arctic Ocean. I am very proud of this initiative, and I hope to drive on it someday.

‡ Since I first wrote this, the second Trump administration has made comments about both Canadian sovereignty and Danish sovereignty in Greenland that should raise additional concerns for all of us.

shelves, which would serve, among other things, as a basis for Arctic claims. I do not know why we did not just pursue a sectoral approach to claims, but nonetheless, the research being done is certainly valuable from a scientific and exploratory point of view. However, as Cabinet was reviewing our 2013 submission to UNCLOS, we discovered that mid-level officials in Foreign Affairs had cut a deal with the Danish government to essentially abandon Canada's hundred-year-old claim to our territorial waters up to the North Pole.*

We were stunned. Obviously, for a government that emphasized Arctic sovereignty, this would be inexcusable. In this case, things were remedied relatively quickly, but not without a dose of embarrassment. Cabinet authorized Minister Baird to renege on that agreement, which he did. Bureaucratic missteps also scuttled a reasonable settlement with the Danes on the Hans Island dispute, which was not resolved until 2022.

I wish I could say that I left office convinced that our sovereignty in the Far North is fully secure, but I cannot. The activities of our geopolitical opponents worry me. So does the go-along-to-get-along mode that often sees Canada being as unambitious as possible in the cases we make to the world.

I am also concerned—I said so at the time—that there are corners of our foreign policy community who desire to see the Arctic go the way of the Antarctic. Antarctica has become an international territory, stripped of its competing national claims. That works there, but it is not appropriate to the Arctic. Our North defines our country, and Canada's sovereignty must be asserted, defended, and developed.

THE FRANKLIN EXPEDITION

ON SEPTEMBER 9, we made an exciting announcement. At least, I found it exciting, and international news coverage confirmed that it was: the

---

* Recognition for noticing this is due to the late Shaun Webb, who handled much of the work in the PMO around northern issues and the northern tours.

discovery of HMS *Erebus* of the ill-fated Franklin expedition of 1845–1848. The whereabouts of this ship and its sister vessel, HMS *Terror*, had been a mystery for almost 175 years.

Multiple searches had been carried out by the British from the 1840s to the 1880s. These had attracted significant resources and huge public attention. Still, only fragmentary evidence had been found. We had made it a priority to take another stab at the search.

During my northern tour in the summer of 2014, we actually had a flotilla of four vessels—some governmental, some private—involved in the search. Finally, on that fateful day in September, using modern sonar scanning technology, the searchers discovered a wreck. Incredibly, HMS *Erebus* had been found in just eleven metres of water at the bottom of Wilmot and Crampton Bay, in the eastern portion of Queen Maud Gulf—a location that confirmed the oral history of the local Inuit. The ship was virtually intact, but it was so overgrown with barnacles and marine debris that without this advanced technology it would have been invisible to anyone standing directly above it.[†]

† The search had involved an incredible range of people and organizations that deserve to be recognized. Marc-André Bernier and Ryan Harris were the leads of the teams that did most of the actual diving. They worked under the leadership of CEO Alan Latourelle and SVP Andrew Campbell of Parks Canada. The Royal Canadian Navy and the Canadian Coast Guard provided vessels and support to the search. John Geiger of the Royal Canadian Geographical Society was the key voice advocating for a coalition of private-sector partners and philanthropies to be involved. He helped bring to the table Andrew Prossin (One Ocean Expeditions), Geordie Dalglish (Garfield Weston Foundation), and Jim Balsillie (Arctic Research Foundation), all of which contributed combinations of finances and platforms. Jeremy Hunt and Shaun Webb did most of the legwork in the PMO, aided by Andrew Moore in Environment Minister Leona Aglukkaq's office. Leona's personal intervention ensured everything came together. She was also very close to the late Louie Kamookak, the Inuit historian who insisted on searching the area that proved to be the *Erebus*'s ultimate destination.

For Canada, the expedition is deeply imbedded in our history and cultural lore, and it represents part of our constitutional and sovereignty claims in that region of the world. The search and discovery of the *Erebus* was a truly big deal, and I took great pride in being personally involved.

A DEADLY ASSAULT ON CANADA'S PARLIAMENT

WHILE CANADA HAS LONG been a contributor to the fight against international terror, political terrorism has been rare, though not unknown, in Canada. Father of Confederation D'Arcy McGee was assassinated by a Fenian terrorist, as was Quebec provincial minister Pierre Laporte by the FLQ. The 9/11 attack in New York claimed twenty-four Canadian lives. Of course, the worst terrorist attack in our history was the 1985 Air India bombing.

Terrorist attacks were often foiled during my time in office. The best known was a planned jihadist terror attack by the so-called Toronto 18. It was uncovered in 2006 by Canadian intelligence services, with assistance from their American counterparts. They were planning to detonate truck bombs, open fire in a crowded area, storm the Parliament Buildings, take hostages, and cut off my head. Charming crowd.

But in late October 2014, Canadians saw for themselves how real the risks are. That was when Canada was hit on two bloody and intense days. It began on October 20, when Air Force Warrant Officer Patrice Vincent died after being deliberately run down by a terrorist in Saint-Jean-sur-Richelieu, Quebec. In this case, the terrorist was pursued by police, caught, and shot dead in the confrontation.

Two days later, a gunman approached from behind, then shot and killed army reservist Corporal Nathan Cirillo in Ottawa. He was standing honour guard at the National War Memorial, just steps from Parliament Hill. The terrorist then crossed the lawn and entered the Parliament Buildings, where he shot and injured a parliamentary security officer who tried to stop him.

The terrorist proceeded to run down the (central) Hall of Honour and engaged in a gun battle with police. People scrambled for whatever cover they could find as bullets flew. Finally, after two terror-filled minutes, the intruder was shot and killed by Sergeant-at-Arms Kevin Vickers and the RCMP. The whole parliamentary precinct was locked down for hours as police searched for any additional attackers.

Those of us in the building that day should consider ourselves lucky. When the terrorist ran down the Hall of Honour, shooting as he went, he passed right by rooms occupied at that moment by both the CPC and NDP caucuses. Had he known the layout of the building and planned accordingly, this event could have been much, much worse. In fact, with a multi-round weapon or a colleague or two, he could have wiped out Canada's entire government that day.

I was at the podium speaking to about 200 CPC caucus colleagues when, at 9:53 a.m., the first gunshots rang out. At first, as is often the case in armed attacks, it took us all a few seconds to realize that what we were hearing was actual gunfire. Once that understanding was clear, however, I instinctively followed the protocol for such circumstances.

The RCMP had put me through a series of robust training exercises for terrorist incidents that might involve me.* It was essentially a three-step process, with an implied fourth. The first step—important above all others—is to exit the scene, preferably with your security detail. (The security detail's own instruction, their highest priority, is to exit with the PM.) If one cannot do that, the second step is to conceal yourself, if possible. If it is not, the third thing you are taught to do is to fight like hell, using whatever weapons you can fashion, until you can escape or are killed. The unthinkable (fourth) alternative is to be taken hostage.

I was in the middle of the room, at the podium, with the doors that face the Hall of Honour right in front of me. Clearly, the gunshots were coming from the Hall. I immediately scanned the room for my parliamentary security detail, so they could guide my exit. But none of them were there. To

---

* For this training and his extensive public service, I am grateful to RCMP Superintendent Ret. Bruno Saccomani and those who served under him for the leadership and professionalism that they delivered through the Prime Minister's Protective Detail.

my left was a door, about twenty feet away—a non-public corridor with easy exit from the building. I walked over, opened the door, and looked out. Gunshots were ringing through the halls, and it was clearly not safe to exit. Staying in the room it would be. I had arrived at step two.

I knew then that if a gunman entered the room there would be little possibility of survival. It was a uniquely chilling moment. I said a little prayer and prepared myself to die, if things were going to come to that. With that prayer came a strange, peaceful acceptance I cannot describe.

Then, after a couple minutes, the shooting stopped. Silence, in such situations, can be a good thing or a bad thing. We knew nothing, so were forced to consider the possibilities. Were we being hunted? Was the gunman dead, or had he left? Or were the security people dead? Was help coming? What do we do now?

After a couple of perplexing minutes of silence, we started to think that this was probably a good sign. It afforded us time to take whatever countermeasures we could contrive. Several of our caucus members with police or military backgrounds took charge and began systematically barricading the doors and combing the room to find things that could be turned into weapons.

At one point, I was asked to take cover in a small utility closet. I was the number one target, without a security detail, and, as step two instructed, needed to be concealed. Until this time, I had not known that this closet even existed. It was in a tiny corner of the room, with the door covered by the same wood panelling as the walls. It was thus easy to miss.

I was in there for just a couple of minutes before the RCMP arrived on the scene and came to the front door. Initially, our former police and security caucus members were reluctant to admit the officers. A call from Myles Atwood, my executive assistant, assured them of their legitimacy. Once admitted, they quickly ushered me and my chief of staff, Ray Novak, out of the building. Myles was a young guy, who looked even younger and was constantly teased for it. But on that day, he was cool as a cucumber.

From start to finish, the whole episode lasted approximately thirteen minutes. But I can sure tell you that it seemed like a lot longer. As per protocol, we were driven to 24 Sussex. It had already been turned into an armed fortress, inside and out, on full alert, swarming with security personnel. I was relieved to find Ben and Rachel there, who had been pulled from school.

Laureen happened to be in Toronto. She was accompanying the recent Nobel Peace Prize–winner Malala Yousafzai, herself no stranger to acts of terrorism, as she travelled to Ottawa that day.* They had been secured, and Laureen returned later in the afternoon. Sadly, the events surrounding Malala's historic visit were all cancelled. I remained at 24 Sussex for the remainder of the day, getting briefed and trying to stay on top of the situation, which remained confusing for far too long.

Regrettably, this uncertainty extended to my caucus colleagues. They remained locked down in that parliamentary caucus room for hours after the event itself. It was not until 7 p.m.—nearly ten hours after the attack—that the RCMP allowed them to leave. Things had become intolerable during their confinement.

That situation bothers me to this day. By the middle of the afternoon, it had become clear that there were no ancillary threats. But there the caucus stayed, seemingly part of the RCMP security strategy for the building. In retrospect, one of my great regrets about the whole event was that I did not override the RCMP and order them evacuated. I apologized to caucus the next day for not ending their lengthy confinement sooner.

Hindsight, as they say, is 20/20. In real time, when events are occurring, especially those involving life-and-death situations, there is often an absence

---

* Sometimes, as on this day, public life offers up uniquely poignant quirks of timing. Of all people for my wife to be accompanying that day, could there be one who could better relate to the day's terrible events? Malala Yousafzai is a Pakistani female education activist and the youngest ever winner of the Nobel Peace Prize. In 2012, she and two other girls were shot and very nearly killed by a Taliban gunman, in retaliation for her activism. Her cause became an international one, and upon her lengthy recovery, she continued her mission promoting education for women and girls around the world.

of clarity. The RCMP were adamant that the MPs should remain secure. Of course, in an extraordinary situation like October 22, 2014, I was very reluctant to overrule those whose expertise it is to keep people alive and safe. What happens if the prime minister does override them and happens to be wrong? What if there were mass casualties, as the security people clearly warned you there might be?

Whether or not I personally disagreed with the RCMP, they had their reasons for caution. Remember, we had just had the attack in Quebec on Warrant Officer Vincent two days earlier. The security folks feared that these two events were connected and that more bloodshed might be planned. After all, security people by nature assume the worst-case scenarios when things start to go south, which they appeared to be doing in this case.

Also in the background were rumours of multiple gunmen all around Ottawa, including some supposed sightings both near and far from the Hill. As it turned out, not all those reports were the product of people's imaginations. An urgent call had gone out to Ottawa's police and security forces for officers to report to work. So there were police in civilian clothes all over the city packing their firearms and heading into downtown Ottawa.

All things considered, it was a terrifying and confusing day. Still, a ten-hour lockdown of the caucus felt unnecessary, and I should have pulled rank. Let us hope future prime ministers are never faced with the same circumstances.

NECESSARY SECURITY CHANGES

MY GOVERNMENT COLLEAGUES and I were determined to send a strong signal that the events of October 22 would in no way impact the functioning of Parliament. Therefore, the next day I rose in the Commons to reassure Canadians that their government remained at work, and to thank people around the world for their expressions of concern and sympathy.

We did our best to return parliamentary life to normal and get back to work. I attended the funerals of both Warrant Officer Vincent and Corporal

Cirillo, and I spoke at each. What I said of Cpl. Cirillo applies to both of them—and everyone who puts their life on the line for all of us:

> As Canadians we stand [at the National Cenotaph on Remembrance Day] humbled and grateful. . . . These monuments remind us that freedom is never free. It has been earned by the soldier and then donated to all of us. Most of us can never truly the understand the significance to a soldier of the simple act of standing reverently on guard at that place.
>
> But those chosen for this sought-after assignment, this vigil of the National War Memorial and over the unknown soldier's grave, they understand. . . . He knew what he was protecting and what he was preserving. He died protecting and preserving. And I'm pleased to know that only after a brief interruption, on Friday past, the honour guard at that sacred place officially resumed its duties.

Still, there was important work to do to directly address this attack. In that regard, it would be an understatement to say that I was not at all happy with the way the police response was handled. It called attention to what I had long known to be a huge weakness in my security: the ongoing jurisdictional issues between the RCMP and the parliamentary security force.

In numerous security briefings, I had been told that the greatest danger I faced anywhere in the world was when I was in the Parliament of Canada. I know that seems hard to believe, but it was a fact. I was at more risk there than in places like the Cité Soleil slum in Haiti, a forward operating base in Afghanistan, the violence-torn Democratic Republic of the Congo, or even the Green Zone in Baghdad (more on that later).

Most Canadians do not understand that the government does not manage the affairs or the budgets of Parliament. That is done by the two Speakers, aided by all-party boards. This independence of Parliament went even further on the issue of security. The RCMP, as the police force of the government, was not allowed to even enter the Parliament Buildings.

The rationale for that dated back to Charles I and the events leading up to the civil war between him and the English Parliament in the 1640s. During that time, the King's soldiers were used to intimidate and suppress Parliament, posing a direct threat to the independence of the legislature and the very notion of constitutional government. In response, Parliament came to manage its own security. This security independence applies, by the way, not just to Britain and Canada but to many other legislatures around the world, including that of the United States and many Commonwealth countries.

No one is disputing that there are many good and brave people in the Parliament Hill security force. However, the truth is that they did not have the resources, capabilities, or training to deal with anything resembling a serious armed attack. They are just not built for that. A further weakness was that the security force was not even unified; the Commons force and the Senate force were two separate entities, policing different parts of the parliamentary precinct.

This situation bordered on farce. Everywhere else I went, in Canada or abroad, I was escorted by an RCMP special security detail, who had the responsibility of interfacing with other security entities. But when I went to Parliament, I was literally handed off at the door to the House of Commons Security Services, and the RCMP departed.

Such jurisdictional problems proved far greater than we had feared on October 22. There had been four police forces involved: Commons Security, Senate Security, the RCMP, and the Ottawa Police Service. These forces could not even communicate with each other because they were on different radio bands.

If there was a silver lining to the attack, it was that, notwithstanding all previous arguments and impediments, I now felt I could do whatever was necessary to address these issues. We promptly brought in legislation that amalgamated the Commons and Senate Security into one single force, the Parliamentary Protective Service. We also fixed the protocols so these organizations could communicate, and we clarified the circumstances under which they could enter each other's turf. Finally, we made it clear that full co-operation between them would be expected in the future.

In terms of my personal security situation, we simply told the Speaker and the parliamentary security folks that things would change immediately. In future, with all due respect to MPs in the era of Charles I, I would be entering the Parliament Buildings with my regular RCMP security detail; we would not be asking permission. Apparently, they got the message because I had no further issues in that regard.

We also took legislative steps to help prevent terrorist attacks more broadly. The first piece of legislation was Bill C-44, the Protection of Canada from Terrorists Act, which had been in the legislative pipeline beforehand. This bill strengthened the Criminal Code provision on terrorism and the ability of the Canadian Security Intelligence Service to investigate threats, both within and outside Canada.

The larger piece of legislation was Bill C-51, the Anti-terrorism Act, 2015. It dealt with unnecessary and egregious prohibitions on information sharing between government departments. It also strengthened anti-terrorist protocols around travel. As well, we improved some of the Criminal Code definitions and procedures around terrorist activity, including explicitly defining the advocacy of terrorism as a crime.

Considered together, these bills did not constitute sweeping change. We were largely trying to fill legal holes in ways that made it easier to identify threats, neutralize them, and punish perpetrators. These Acts have succeeded in preventing several attacks by identifying them and breaking them up before they reached their objectives. They have been of immense benefit to Canada.

26

FOREIGN AFFAIRS, TRADE, AND INTERNATIONAL ISSUES 2014

THE YEAR 2014 saw a serious uptick in global upheaval. It would prove to be a precursor to the coming decade. For my part, I kicked off January with one of my most memorable trips—a visit to Israel and the surrounding region.

A HISTORIC VISIT

GIVEN MY OUTSPOKEN SUPPORT of Israel since my earliest days in office, it might seem odd that it took me so long to visit. Well, it turns out that, no matter how strongly one supports Israel, timing an official trip to that country is not easy.

The first problem is the constant political turmoil in Israel. People often talk about the "pizza parliaments" of Italy in the context of the fractious, multi-party systems sometimes created by proportional representation voting. In truth, Italy has not been that bad in recent decades. The worst illustration of this model is, in fact, Israel.

Israel has a proportional representation system with a very low threshold (3.25 per cent), making it easy for small splinter parties to be elected to Israel's parliament, the Knesset. This is complicated by the overlay of that system on a society that, contrary to much perception, is highly diverse.

True, it is united by its largely "Jewish" identity—some 75 per cent of the population—but that is a surprisingly superficial commonality.

Besides the large Arab minority, Israel is divided by what can only be described as a "multicultural Jewishness." The long-scattered diaspora returned from all over the world with different languages, customs, and worldviews. It is common to hear not just Hebrew, Arabic, and English in the street but also Russian, French, Amharic, and many other languages. A general division between Ashkenazi (broadly Western) and Sephardic (Eastern) Jews is one particularly deep social cleavage. Even Judaism itself is diverse, with adherents ranging from the totally secular to the most fundamentalist.

Given these social and political realities, parliamentary turmoil can often go on in Israel for extended periods. A visiting dignitary will obviously want to avoid being drawn into these political conflicts, which have the potential of being diplomatically contentious. We were constantly trying to find the right moment to visit—a period when neither my minority governments nor Knesset politics would present a challenge.

The other big problem—evident to anyone who watches the news—is the state of security in the region. There are constant conflicts either brewing, underway, or wrapping up. There were the hot wars in Lebanon in 2006 and in Gaza in 2014, but intermittent violence broke out pretty much regularly while I was in office. In these circumstances, flying into affected airspace and burdening different countries with managing our security seemed an imposition at best and a danger at worst.

Notwithstanding the complexity of official state visits, I found ways to meet regularly with Israeli leaders—certainly by phone, and at multilateral meetings like the UN General Assembly. Overall, I was very impressed with the quality of those in charge of the Jewish state. In fact, I have retained relationships with several Israeli leaders since I left office in 2015.

Benjamin Netanyahu was the prime minister of Israel for most of my time. We became very close and have remained so ever since. He is probably the smartest, best-read, most-articulate foreign leader I have met. He has presided over profound changes to the State of Israel, beginning with his role in the economic modernization of the 1990s and, more recently, the conclusion of the Abraham Accords. He is the most consequential Israeli leader since the founding of the modern State. Love him or hate him, my prediction is that no matter who is in power after Netanyahu, they will deviate little from the course Bibi has charted on a range of domestic and foreign affairs.

Given the closeness of the Canada-Israel relationship, and the various high-profile battles I had already waged on Israeli issues, I was confident that it would be a good and productive trip. I was not disappointed. Israel is a fascinating country, and everyone should experience it.

The first thing that struck me is how small the country really is. You can drive its entire length in several hours. It is never more than 114 kilometres wide and as little as 15 at its narrowest.* Enemies on the Golan Heights could easily bombard the northern part of the country, as the Syrians regularly used to do. For basic security, Israel must never relinquish control of that area.

Given my closeness to the Jewish community in Canada and its own deep connections to Israel, I was accompanied by a delegation numbering in the hundreds. That included both Christian and Arab delegates, as well as my parliamentary colleagues, MPs Mark Adler and Joe Oliver (soon to be finance minister) and Senators Irving Gerstein, Judith Seidman, and Linda Frum (all among my best appointments). In any case, capping the number of delegates and managing their movements were no small feats. That was executed by my very capable tour staff, then led by Jeremy Hunt. It included David Belous, Anna Tomala, and Shiv Raj, among others, and they had honed their skills over many years.

I think that, for all of us, the biggest highlight was my speech to the Knesset on January 20. I was the first Canadian prime minister to ever address that forum, and my speechwriting team, led by Nigel Hannaford,

---

* Israel has surprising geographic diversity. I would be remiss if I did not also mention the Hula Nature Reserve in the north—the largest bird migration location in the world. Through the efforts of the Jewish National Fund of Canada, an interpretative centre there is named after Laureen and me.

spent a lot of time putting that speech together. I dwelt upon the many bonds Canada and Israel share through our peoples, history, trade, and diplomacy. As I had done elsewhere, I unconditionally affirmed Israel's right to exist, to defend itself, and to ensure its security. This is not trivial, as Israel is the only present-day nation—democratic or otherwise—that many have long vowed to wipe off the face of the earth. I also urged Israeli lawmakers to help build a "just and secure future for the Palestinian people . . . committed to living peacefully alongside the Jewish State of Israel."

In closing my speech, I praised Israel's relentless determination to survive and thrive, despite all the challenges that surround it:

> I believe the story of Israel is a great example to the world. It is a story, essentially, of a people whose response to suffering has been to move beyond resentment and build a most extraordinary society, a vibrant democracy, a freedom-loving country with an independent and rights-affirming judiciary, an innovative, world-leading "start-up" nation. You have taken the collective memory of death and persecution to build an optimistic, forward-looking society—one that so values life you will sometimes release a thousand criminals and terrorists to save one of your own. In the democratic family of nations, Israel represents values which our Government takes as articles of faith and principles to drive our own national life. And therefore, through fire and water, Canada will stand with you.

The speech was extremely well received, although, as with all things in Israel, it also attracted its share of criticism. In that vigorous and fractious democracy, there is no such thing as unanimity, ever. The day I was going to give my speech, my staff showed me some document—I believe it was a newspaper ad—where a far-right Israeli group attacked me for not being supportive enough of Israel—essentially for not advocating for a one-state solution—and for being a Christian. Later, when I spoke in the Knesset, they had to remove several of the far-left members, mostly Arab, who were anti-Israel and had tried to shout me down. Only in Israel could one give a wholly pro-country speech and still be condemned by significant segments of public opinion!

TRIPS TO THE PALESTINIAN AUTHORITY AND JORDAN

THIS WAS NOT, nor was it intended to be, a one-sided trip to the Middle East. After all, those of Palestinian origin were also represented in our delegation, and an important bilateral meeting was to be held with President Mahmoud Abbas of the Palestinian Authority (PA).

Much to the disappointment of the liberal media, no fireworks occurred. That was because Canada's relationship with the PA was based on the same upfront, straightforward principles that we applied everywhere else. For one thing, we were a big supporter, financially and otherwise, of the PA. That was notwithstanding our Government's cuts to the United Nations Relief and Works Agency, whose antisemitic activities are probably better understood now than they were then. In any case, while President Abbas certainly did not agree with all my views on the region and its conflicts (nor I with his), he did not interpret them as attacks on the PA or on legitimate Palestinian aspirations.

Often lost in all the diplomatic dust was the fact that our Government was supportive of a two-state solution. We may have had some different views on what that would look like and how it might come about, but we believed that the Palestinians should someday have their own sovereign, independent state. I always remind Israeli and Jewish leaders elsewhere of my support for that. In fact, in my meeting with Abbas, I was in the odd position of pushing him to pursue that agenda by returning to the negotiating table. I believe that the Palestinian strategy of the *chaise vide* will not serve it well in the long term.*

---

* "Empty chair" is a reference to the ongoing refusal of the Palestinian Authority to come to the bargaining table with Israel. Sadly, this does seem

On January 23, we moved on to Jordan, hosted by Abdullah II. I have already talked about our Government's good relations with Jordan, the king's visits, our free trade agreement, and our regular dialogue—and of course, our ongoing friendship. This visit focused on the major pressures the post–Arab Spring world was bringing to Jordanian society. Canada had been a long-time supporter of Jordanian development, and during that trip we announced increased aid to help the country deal with the large influx of Syrian refugees, as well as additional funds to bolster Jordan's security. I also acted as a conduit to emphasize the king's concerns to our allies. I believe I was effective in that role and that those efforts were appreciated.

My trip also involved a visit to the Syrian refugee camp at Zaatari. It was indeed sobering. We were then well into the Syrian civil war and literally millions had fled the country as refugees. The hundreds of thousands that came to Jordan imposed—and continue to impose—huge financial, demographic, and political challenges for the Jordanian government.

This is a cumulative problem for Jordan. After successive waves of Palestinian, Iraqi, and now Syrian refugees, the Jordanians have become a minority in their own country. Our trip to the camp made it plain to see how serious and desperate the situation was. The sheer scale was overwhelming; the tragedy heartbreaking; the determination and hope of the refugees, and those caring for them, inspiring.

We also gained great insight into the security situation in briefings from Jordanian and UN officials. All this prompted our enhanced aid commitments, which escalated in the years that followed. As I have said before, it is in the world's interests—and therefore in Canada's interests—that the Hashemite Kingdom of Jordan survive and move forward.

---

to be getting the PA increased concessions from some in the international community, including the present government of Canada.

THE FUTURE OF ISRAEL AND THE REGION

I AM TODAY WRITING in the years following the bloody October 7, 2023, Hamas attack on Israel and the subsequent war with Gaza, Hezbollah, and Iran (at the head of it all). These events have taken anti-Israel and antisemitic narratives to new depths (at least in my lifetime). That said, they do not fundamentally change my view of the region.

I am sometimes asked whether being anti-Israel is the same thing as being antisemitic. In theory, no. As some say, it is possible to be opposed to the policies of the government of Israel and not be antisemitic. After all, opposing the government of Israel is a legitimate activity in Israel itself, as a democratic society. But being anti-Zionist, opposing the right of the only Jewish state to exist because it is Jewish, as do the Boycott, Divestment, Sanctions (BDS) movement and many other critics, is unequivocally antisemitic, full stop. And advocating the elimination of Jews in Israel "from the river to the sea," as the slogan goes, is genocidal antisemitism. It is on par with Nazi thinking—nothing less.

Antisemitism has always been with us, and we are all familiar with far-right views on this. But such thinking is at least widely condemned as unacceptable. The problem, for the past couple of generations, has been the effort, in parts of academia and the media, to make antisemitism acceptable by couching it in far-left ideology. It is every bit as much extremist Jew-hate as its cousin on the far-right.

I am therefore not surprised by the kind of open Jew-hatred we have seen recently. I saw this growing during my time as prime minister, and I was often subjected to it. After my speech in the Knesset, it was particularly sharp, and it was even given licence through a cartoon in the *Montreal Gazette*. The messages we would get at my office, as vile as they were, were sometimes amusing. Some of these antisemites clearly did not realize that I am not Jewish!

The wars that have raged following the October 7, 2023, attacks, the wide-ranging condemnation of Israel, and the fractiousness nature of Israeli society, which is worse than ever, have Israel's friends worried about the future. I am much less so. I believe the strengths that have built Israel from almost nothing to one of the wealthiest, most-innovative, and freest nations in the world in just three generations will continue to drive it forward.

I also believe that the motives that have caused a growing number of Arab states to normalize relations with the Jewish state will resume in time. These are led by a new generation of Arab leaders who want their countries to be economically dynamic and successful, as well as socially progressive and tolerant (though not democratic). They have looked across the Persian Gulf at the alternative—a medieval jihadist basket case—and they do not want that as their future. In fact, they want to be in an ironclad security alliance with Israel against that alternative. If only our current crop of Western leaders—ironically, other than Donald Trump—saw the realities of the region so clearly.

What about the Palestinians? The truth is, if they want to understand the real barrier to their becoming a sovereign state, they need to look in the mirror. On every occasion since 1947 that they have had to make peace with Israel, they have refused, because they remain committed to a one-state solution, that is, one Arab state, "from the river to the sea." Even the Palestinian Authority restricts its recognition of Israel's right to exist to a "right of return," that is, to an Israel that would have to become Arab. Today, there is no Palestinian leader who will go to the bargaining table and negotiate a two-state solution, that is, agree to the permanent existence of a Jewish state. They would have little chance of surviving if they tried to do so.

That must change. When someday, some such leader comes forward, they will be backed by Israel's Western and Arab friends and, ultimately, by most Israeli public opinion. Then and only then will this be resolved.

Here at home, the Conservative relationship with the Canadian Jewish community continues to be very strong. This was not always the case. Traditionally, the bulk of Jewish voters went to the Liberals. This began to change under Stockwell Day's leadership of the Canadian Alliance. But the major shift got underway when I was prime minister, for a couple of reasons.

The first was my principled support for Israel, obviously. But a second reason was that many in the community were shocked by the vitriolic Liberal attacks upon me for that support. Whatever the reason, in the elections since 2008, we won the polls in almost every neighbourhood in Canada with a significant Jewish population—including in ridings where we were not close to winning overall. I have been blessed to have forged many lasting friendships with members of Canada's Jewish community. These have only deepened since leaving office, for which am very grateful.

THE (INITIAL) INVASION OF UKRAINE

IF I WAS AHEAD of the curve in supporting Israel, I was even further ahead in warning the world about Vladimir Putin's Russia. But the world began to catch up—too slowly as it would turn out—when, on February 27, 2014, Putin sent soldiers into Crimea. This led to its quick annexation by Russia. It was accompanied by agitation and similar tactics in the eastern Ukrainian region of the Donbas.*

The one small silver lining in this was the expulsion of Putin from the G8, as I had previously been seeking. The next G8 meeting was scheduled for Sochi, Russia, and we were obviously not going to have it there. At the initiative of President Obama, the meeting was moved to Brussels, and the organization returned to being the G7.

During our meeting in Brussels, it became clear that the expulsion of Russia was permanent. Believe it or not, some European leaders wanted this to be a temporary state of affairs until the dust settled in Ukraine. Obama was having none of that. In our meeting he made it clear that he and I would never tolerate Putin returning to the G7. Whether it

---

* In the last couple of decades, this has been a common tactic from the Russian playbook: to use Russian minorities as a pretext for military action and then turn their areas into puppet states. Prominent examples are Transnistria in Moldova, as well as South Ossetia and Abkhazia in Georgia.

did under some other leader was an open question. However, given the unlikely exit of Putin in the near future, Barack was emphatic that Russia was effectively out for good. Although that ended the discussion, the different views of some European leaders would lead to greater problems down the road.

The truth, sadly, is that the conditions for the invasion of Ukraine, which began in 2014 and accelerated in 2022, were created back in 2008. That was at the NATO Summit held in Bucharest, Romania. President Bush made a hard push to have Ukraine admitted. He had my support and that of probably a good two-thirds of the membership. But a few Western European countries strongly resisted and blocked Ukraine's accession.

What made them do that? All I can do is recall a conversation I had with one of those leaders in 2014. They said to me, "Aren't you glad we didn't admit Ukraine, because if we had, we would now be at war with Russia." To which I responded, "No. If we had admitted Ukraine, this invasion never would have happened in the first place." In short, the opponents utterly failed to understand the basic concept of deterrence—the fundamental reason for which NATO exists in the first place. Unfortunately, that failure continued even after 2014.

Nevertheless, Putin was expelled, which had been an important objective for our government. Immediately, the G7 discussions became franker and more intimate than they had been with him present. That was true on a range of issues in 2014 and became even more obvious at the G7 meeting in Germany in 2015. I was aware that Putin's presence caused our allies some reticence in the discussions. Just how much he had inhibited the conversation only became clear once he was gone.

Putin's expulsion was only the first of our actions. The G7 then announced a range of sanctions on Russia. Ours were by far the toughest and most lasting. For all practical purposes, we severed the Canada-Russia economic relationship in 2014–2015. Most of our allies would not do so until 2022. A couple of Canadian companies did get caught up in this, but that was too bad. These are the risks you take in doing business in a place like Putin's Russia, and it was not as if they were unaware of those risks.

The sanctions apparently made Putin angry, because he retaliated. He sanctioned a bunch of Canadians, including the president of the Ukrainian Canadian Congress, which was just bizarre. He also lashed out by sanctioning various Canadian government officials and people in my office, which remains a point of pride for them and me.

All this did not mean, however, that I would never have to deal with Vladimir Putin again. I would and I did, and that story will come.

A FREE TRADE AGREEMENT WITH SOUTH KOREA

ON MARCH 11, 2014, I visited Seoul to announce the conclusion of a free trade agreement with the Republic of Korea. Being our first such agreement in the Asia-Pacific region, this was a very important milestone in our trade agenda.

South Korea is a large market. It is one of the world's most advanced countries, with a GDP roughly comparable to Canada's. Given the closeness of our countries since the Korean War and some obvious complementarities between our economies, you might have thought this would be a relatively easy deal to arrive at. In fact, our talks had a long and difficult history.

Negotiations had begun under the previous government, but they had stalled early on over the South Koreans' refusal to give us terms comparable to the deal they concluded with the United States in 2007. That deal had never been ratified, given the opposition of the Detroit's Big Three automakers, and it appeared dead in the water. And so, our talks sat in limbo.

Very suddenly, in late 2011, the Obama administration decided to proceed with the original deal, and it successfully pressured the automakers to come onside. There was an almost-immediate negative impact upon our traditional exports, given the preferential trade access that the Americans now enjoyed. Still, the Koreans appeared to be unwilling to budge on giving us similar terms.

South Korea would soon be undergoing elections and a leadership transition. When it became obvious that the new administration did not change its attitude, we took off the gloves.

My first bilateral meeting with the new president, Park Geun-hye,* was on October 7, 2013, at the Asia-Pacific Economic Cooperation Summit in Bali, Indonesia. After the formal introductory pleasantries, I bluntly stated our Government's position that, given our deep and historical relations, the Korean attitude in our trade talks was unacceptable to Canada. I outlined the situation, indicating that, from this moment forward, there would be serious repercussions on all aspects of our diplomatic and economic relations until such time as we concluded a trade deal on terms like those of the United States. With that said, Trade Minister Ed Fast and I led our delegation in rising from our seats and leaving the room.

I believed that the new president had listened carefully and that she had clearly heard the message. The backdrop, as I stressed to her, was that our trade relations were highly favourable to the Korean side (which, of course, gave us considerable leverage). Without going into details, we then undertook a series of economic measures to leave no doubt in the Koreans' minds that we were serious in our threats.

In short order, South Korea returned to the negotiation table with good faith offers. Within a matter of weeks, we concluded a tentative deal. However, the fight was not over, because the Koreans were not the only impediment to finalizing an agreement.

While the Big Three automakers had acquiesced to Obama's deal in the United States, they were against Canadian ratification of a similar deal. We were thus facing the prospect of a major industrial group opposing one of our free trade agreements. This was something we had never faced before.

---

* Madame Park was Korea's first female president. She was also the daughter of former president Park Chung Hee, a military dictator from 1963 until his assassination in 1979.

We ultimately dealt with this one car company at a time. Chrysler and General Motors had, of course, been bailed out by us during the global financial crisis, and we still held shares in the latter. Given that leverage, and our willingness to use it,* they decided that a fight with us would not be worth it. Ford Canada, however, decided to publicly oppose our trade agreement.

When they did, I labelled Ford's behaviour as the height of corporate irresponsibility. Here was a branch plant company opposing trade access for Canada that its parent already had in the United States. We not only needed the agreement but needed it *because* Ford's parent company had supported it. My condemnation must have stung, because Ford Canada went dark very quickly.

That brief public skirmish concluded, yet another of our government's free trade agreements sailed through smoothly. Given the original U.S. concessions to Korea, this was not our strongest agreement. Still, it has been successful, with trade flows increasing significantly since our agreement went into effect in 2015.†

FINAL THOUGHTS ON AFGHANISTAN

ON MAY 9, 2014, Parliament Hill was the venue for an important and solemn event: the National Day of Honour to mark the formal end of Canada's Afghanistan mission. I found it deeply moving, as I know a lot of Canadians did. However, my feelings were decidedly mixed.

We had made a major contribution in blood and treasure to the cause. Canadian families had sacrificed their children to this war—something we can never forget and must forever honour. Yet, on that day, and certainly

---

* Nigel Wright conveyed this to the leadership of General Motors on my behalf.

† Three years later, under President Trump, the U.S. strengthened its free trade arrangement with the South Koreans. Canada's government did not.

in the years that have followed, I have had time to assess the mission and Canada's contribution to it. It seems that many other Canadians have as well, judging from how often I am asked whether it was all worth it.

First and foremost, it is important to remember that, following the enormity of the 9/11 attacks, the United States and its allies had no choice but to undertake the war in Afghanistan (unlike Iraq) and remove the Taliban from power. This was achieved, and Afghanistan ceased to be—and has not been since—a security threat to people outside its borders.

I discussed my reservations about the overall war aims of the U.S. earlier. This should never detract from our real accomplishments. Canada's military had been unprepared in the beginning—certainly at first when the Martin Government had committed us to lead security in Kandahar. But the military made great strides, in part due to our investments in equipment, and far fewer Canadian lives were lost than might have been. Afghan lives were also improved, through our contributions to economic and social development, infrastructure, education, human rights, and the promotion of the status and welfare of women. These are all reasons to be proud of what we accomplished as a country.

Still, it is also important to understand the reasons why the international mission to Afghanistan fell so short of the mark. It was not just that the war aims were too ambitious and the democracy promotion agenda too incomplete. It began with the fact that the Taliban was never thoroughly defeated. It was allowed to retreat into the hills (literally), regroup, and control significant parts of the country. On top of that, a decision was apparently made by the United States to tolerate the active collaboration of Pakistan—a supposed ally—with the Taliban. This it did, providing safe haven for everyone from foot soldiers up to bin Laden himself.

The big lesson is that the decision to invade a country should never be undertaken without a long and deep commitment. That commitment must be to complete both military victory and ground-up governance reconstruction. As in post–World War II Germany, structures must be built from the local level, purged of extremism and corruption, before ultimate authority is turned over to new, capable, proven national authorities.

The international alliance, by contrast, failed to undertake any of the groundwork necessary to make democracy take hold in Afghanistan. We pretended that quick elections and a hastily formed national administration would equal democracy, somehow immediately infusing such values and norms into a society that had no prior exposure to them. As that project faltered, we poured vast amounts of money and effort into achieving what was unachievable. The result was predictable: despite the courage and probity of many Afghans, the government quickly became rife with incompetence and corruption. And we did not have the power to change it, even though it was failing.

I believe Canadians should always be proud of the role our military and development people played in Afghanistan. I also continue to believe that our decision to end our military mission in 2011 was the right decision. We certainly did not anticipate the collapse of the regime in 2021. Even with the flaws in the mission—and I hope I have made clear how deep those really were—the complete collapse of the regime and the return of the Taliban were not inevitable. It only happened, in the end, because the Biden administration literally seemed determined, for whatever reason, to make the effort a failure.

In any case, what was the alternative? To stay forever? That was an option Canadians simply would not have supported.

LEADERSHIP ON MATERNAL AND CHILD HEALTH

A VERY DIFFERENT ASPECT of our international agenda was highlighted a couple of weeks later. From May 28 to 30, 2014, delegates from around the world came to Toronto to attend a high-level conference entitled Saving Every Woman, Every Child: Within Arm's Reach. This was another major step in our Government's Maternal, Newborn, and Child Health initiative (MNCH).

The Muskoka Initiative on MNCH, announced at the 2010 G8, had really taken off. I was joined in Toronto by President Kikwete of Tanzania, my co-chair on the World Health Organization panel. Queen Rania of Jordon was also in attendance; maternal health had been a personal priority of hers for some years. Ban Ki-moon, secretary-general of the United Nations was there, as was Melinda Gates of the Bill & Melinda Gates Foundation. They were joined by the heads of the World Bank, the World Health Organization, the United Nations Children's Fund (UNICEF), and the Aga Khan. It was a very powerful gathering. The aim was to continue to mobilize the global community to complete UN millennium goals four and five, that is, to dramatically reduce the incidence of child and maternal mortality in the developing world.

While the conference was a critical milestone for the initiative, our Government had been highly active on this issue in the four years since it had been announced. I was involved in UN-sponsored seminars, forums, and conferences of various kinds almost every single year. In 2011, the World Health Organization had held an "accountability exercise" in Geneva to keep the momentum going. I had also frequently raised the issues in various international forums and bilateral meetings with other leaders. All this effort yielded fruit. Altogether we raised almost twenty billion dollars U.S.—all new money—toward these important causes. This was something all Canadians could take pride in.

But the importance of a policy is never about the money; it is about the difference it makes on the ground. In this case, in addition to reducing child mortality by 45 per cent, we saw great progress in reducing HIV transmission to newborns. Along with making big strides in rehydration therapy, we also successfully promoted exclusive breast-feeding and vitamin supplementation during the critical early years. There was less progress—but still important progress—on the development of pneumonia vaccines, where we secured major funding from the Gates Foundation to enhance global vaccine programs around MNCH.

Our combined efforts mobilized thousands of people and all the major humanitarian and related health agencies. Canadians were instrumental when it came to the scientific aspects of the initiative, and individual citizens also significantly increased our charitable giving. During my prime ministership, there had been few efforts that were as personally and professionally satisfying. Proudly, the work lives on, as many in the global community have carried forward this essential initiative in the years since.

A NEW TERRORIST THREAT EMERGES

TERRORISM IS A MANY-HEADED HYDRA. Just as Canada's military involvement in Afghanistan was winding down, a new terrorist threat emerged with a vengeance—the Islamic State in Iraq and Syria (ISIS). This deadly new entity was born of two Middle East developments: the U.S. withdrawal from Iraq and the ongoing civil war in Syria. By early 2014, it was emerging as a very significant challenge for the global community.

ISIS's Iraqi provenance stemmed from the governance debacle that followed the American invasion of Iraq. As in Afghanistan, the invading coalition never got full control of the country. Likewise, quick elections were held in the belief that they would usher in a Western-style democracy. Instead, these two things resulted in the country's three major groups—the Sunni Arabs, the Shia Arabs, and the Kurds—retreating into their own areas behind heavily armed militias.

Under Saddam Hussein, the minority Sunnis were the privileged ones, but no longer. Increasingly, the Shia, armed and abetted by Iran, flexed their military muscle, while the Kurds simply tried to run their own show in the north. As the Obama administration continued its drawdown of troops, ISIS appeared to fill the vacuum in the Sunni areas. Emerging from al-Qaeda with alarming speed, it captured the major city of Fallujah in western Iraq on January 4, 2014.

At first, Western security agencies all but ignored this development. This was epitomized by Barack Obama's quip dismissing ISIS as "the JV [Junior Varsity] team." In Ottawa, I recall my own officials' initial assessment: Fallujah was a mere setback and ISIS a temporary phenomenon. The Iraqi Army, I was told, would be recapturing the city in due course—give it a couple of weeks at most. They were all fantastically wrong. Every couple of weeks, I would raise the question, "What about the imminent recapture of Fallujah?" Not surprisingly, the topic had a habit of dropping down the list in the briefings.

Meanwhile in Syria, the ongoing civil war had seen the government lose control of most of its territory. By then it was clearly a four-cornered conflict—the Government, the main Opposition (the Syrian Free Army), the Kurdish forces, and the extremist jihadists—although there were more than a few sub-factions within these. The jihadists in the form of ISIS emerged as the dominant element in the eastern city of Raqqa after the Government lost control in 2013. Some Middle Eastern interests, as I previously mentioned, had been supporting such radicals but, ironically, so was the Assad Government. It was then on the ropes and hoping to divide the opposition.

In any case, ISIS, now in control of both eastern Syria and western Iraq, declared itself to be the headquarters of a new transnational caliphate. Soon it was on the move, launching attacks in Diyala, Salah al-Din, Ninewa, and even northern Baghdad. Far from retaking lost territories, the Iraqi Army was on the run, surrendering tons of ammunition and equipment as it fled ISIS forces.

I do not think most Canadians can get their heads around how radical ISIS and groups like it really are. Too start with, ISIS considered al-Qaeda far too moderate, if that is even comprehensible. I have read some of the speeches and propaganda of ISIS leaders, and it is incredibly blood-curdling stuff—apocalyptic in tone, advocating mindless ultra-violence. There is the use of Muslim language and terminology, but this cannot be remotely considered a theology; it is more akin to what I would call "Islamic anarchism." Fittingly, in areas where it took control, ISIS's governance was not about building or running anything; it was about massacres and nihilistic destruction as an end in itself. It resembled the Taliban at its height—only even more fanatical. However you define ISIS, it was very, very scary.

By mid-2014, the situation was reaching a critical stage. With ISIS consolidating its caliphate—indeed, threatening the very existence of the Iraqi state—it began to undertake a deliberate genocide against a monotheistic people there called the Yazidis. This brought home to everyone the very real human risks of allowing the continued growth of a terrorist state with regional and even global ambitions.

THE ALLIED MISSION AGAINST ISIS

WITH A NATO SUMMIT scheduled for September in Wales, President Obama called me in June and again in August to discuss the ISIS situation. He was preparing to provide some assistance in extracting the Yazidis, but he was also developing a broader plan to stabilize the region. It would involve shoring up the Iraqi Army, pressing the Iraqi government to become more inclusive of the Sunni population, and assisting the Kurds in northern Iraq. The last were proving to be the one element effective in slowing the advance of ISIS. Obama wanted Canada and its other allies to make meaningful contributions to these efforts.

At the NATO Summit there was a fair degree of agreement on Iraq and support for Obama's "Plan of Action." But that left Syria, where the allies continued to lack a consensus on the way forward. However, the original issue of whether the Syrian Opposition constituted a palatable replacement to the Assad regime had been overtaken. The question was now: Which is the bigger threat, Assad or ISIS?

Many of our allies did not want to make that choice. However, I was clear—ISIS was the threat we needed to focus on. Despite our repugnance of Assad, I said, his regime represented no security threat to my country or, frankly, to most of the countries around the table. Not so with ISIS, which had regional and global terrorist ambitions. In Syria itself, further ISIS expansion would surely lead to genocide against the large religious and ethnic minority populations. Better to deal with the *real* threat in ISIS.

This position, firmly stated, led to a clash with Turkish president Erdoğan. I have talked earlier about Erdoğan's philosophy and aims, which were clearly on display when it came to Syria. For most of us, the prevention of a wider terrorist threat and genocide were the priority. Not so for Erdoğan, who saw Assad as the principal evil.

Make no mistake on what motivated Erdoğan: his real priority was the advancement of the Sunni cause. He was prepared to risk a bit of extremism, provided it was of the Sunni Muslim Brotherhood variety. His soft talk was backed by a big stick—he was funding, supporting, and arming those elements in Syria that made Assad's overthrow the goal. Most in NATO were hoping for the creation of a moderate, broadly inclusive Syrian government. Erdoğan's wish, by contrast, was to see the Shiite Assad removed and replaced by a Sunni regime.

This sectarian agenda had an ethnic dimension as well—Erdoğan's hostility to the Kurds. Turkey has had a long and troubled relationship with its large Kurdish minority, and hence Erdoğan viewed the growing Kurdish autonomy in Syria as a threat. The rest of us, in contrast, viewed the Kurds as helpful. They were anti-Assad but not extremist. They were more willing to coordinate their efforts with the West than any other faction in Syria. My strong view was that the Kurds (and their cause) should be embraced by NATO. Although I did not say it to Erdoğan, the solution to his Kurdish problem was to treat them better in Turkey.

The military implication of Obama's plan was a NATO air campaign against ISIS positions in both Iraq and Syria, along with the provision of support, training, and munitions to both the Iraqi Army and the Iraqi Kurdish forces fighting ISIS. We agreed to participate, taking a NATO lead in supporting the Iraqi Kurdish forces. We would also participate in the air campaign, but with an important caveat.

We would be involved in the bombing campaign against ISIS in western Iraq, but we decided *not* to participate in the Syrian portion of the campaign. For us, the lack of a clear political objective in Syria would be problematic for the parliamentary debate we would have on the issue. In Iraq, our intervention was at the request of the sovereign government and, in the north, at the behest of the autonomous Iraqi region of Kurdistan.

This was not the case in Syria, where we had no relations with the Syrian government. We not only had no legal pretext for bombing Syrian territory but also did not know how the Syrian government and its air defences might respond. This could have serious complications if we ever had a Canadian plane shot down there.

There is an additional footnote to this murkiness—the attitude of the U.S. government. It was unclear to what the extent they wanted us involved in parts of this mission. We received mixed messages at different times from the president, the White House, the American military, and, especially, the American embassy in Ottawa. We did eventually conduct some limited sorties in Syria, once we had tacit assurances of no resistance from the Syrian government. Nevertheless, these conflicting signals had real implications, which I will discuss later.

In the meantime, the Turks pursued their own agenda and have done so ever since. In effect, they played both sides. Yes, they backed the mainstream Syrian Opposition, but they also continued to play footsie with the jihadist elements. Most importantly, they turned their guns on the Kurds at every opportunity. This had the ironic effect of eventually pushing the Kurds into a non-aggression arrangement with the Syrian Government.

All this just underlines what I have said earlier about Erdoğan's Turkey: it may still be a member of NATO, but it is no longer an ally.*

---

* A decade after Western leaders had said, "Assad must go," he was overthrown by opposition rebels on December 8, 2024. These were fairly radical elements backed by Turkey, among others. While they have been trying to moderate and broaden their administration, Erdoğan did eventually get his way.

27

FOREIGN AFFAIRS, TRADE, AND INTERNATIONAL ISSUES IN THE FINAL YEAR

THE LONGER I WAS PRIME MINISTER, the more time I spent on international affairs. Over the years, I built up a web of global relationships and became involved more deeply in the ongoing global issues in which Canada had a stake. As such, other leaders, both veterans and those newer to power, became more likely to seek my views.

As 2014 ended and 2015 began, the pace of my international travels and hosting of foreign leaders continued to accelerate. Many of these encounters would be, of course, my last while prime minister.

ADVANCING OUR AGENDA IN CHINA

IN NOVEMBER 2014, I led a delegation on my third and final official visit to China. Canada's trade and investment with China had been growing strongly, and many of the initiatives we had agreed to over the past years appeared to be bearing fruit for both our countries. This trip was intended to find out how far this relationship could be pushed. Although China retained its dynamism, its restless industrial creativity, and manufacturing might, in other respects it had changed markedly. Hosting this visit was a new generation of leaders—President Xi Jinping, with his premier, Li Keqiang.

Like the predecessors I had met, President Xi was clearly an impressive person. In some ways, he was much more in the mould of a Western politician—charismatic, socially at ease, and outgoing. At least it seemed that way on the surface. In fact, Xi was a very closed personality and was not nearly as frank with his views as those who came before him. He always watched and listened carefully, but he would add little. He was clearly a master at getting his interlocutor to believe he was agreeing when he was, in truth, committing to nothing.

Where Xi really diverged from his predecessors was in his leadership style. Almost from day one, he made returning China to one-man-rule-for-life his principal objective. He did this through his "anti-corruption" campaign. Yes, he was addressing a real problem and, yes, my Chinese contacts have told me that Xi did make progress. However, the real purpose was the removal of anyone from the hierarchy on down who did not support his absolute rule.

Along with this consolidation of domestic control came a far greater assertiveness internationally. Chinese leaders from Deng to Hu had tended to understate China's power and ambitions, partly due to the nature of collective leadership. Xi, however, made no secret of China's desire to eventually become the world's pre-eminent power.

At the time, I was proud that our government's approach had achieved results in Canada's interests. On each trip we made to China, we had significantly advanced the economic relationship. In this case, more than two billion dollars' worth of deals were signed, including the announcement of a new Chinese currency hub in Toronto. We managed to get the Chinese to lift several restrictions that had been levied against Canadian products, especially in the agricultural sector, like B.C. cherries and Quebec blueberries. Concrete gains were registered in commodities like lumber, wood products, and seafood. These all added to the Approved Destination Status designation (announced in 2009), which significantly expanded Chinese tourism to Canada.

After my 2012 trip, we had finalized the arrangement for China to loan two beautiful pandas to Canada's zoos. One may laugh, but this was highly symbolic. The world recognizes the immense symbolism of China allowing pandas to travel to foreign zoos. The Chinese, in turn, use the pandas as leverage. They would not dream of sending their pandas to countries that were in their "bad books," for whatever reason. Obviously, that was not the case here, and as we expected, this was a major story in the media. I must admit that Laureen and I were particularly smitten. Having a little panda come and sit on your lap is quite a memorable event!

Trading with China

WHILE MY APPROACH showcased the strengths and greater possibilities in the economic relationship, they also demonstrated the limits of trading with China. At the centre of those are the huge imbalances that the Chinese rack up in their dealings with us. Those stem from the rules under which China was admitted to the World Trade Organization (WTO) in 2001.

Once accepted into the WTO, China invoked the right to claim the "special and differential treatment" accorded to developing countries under WTO rules. I can tell you what that means in practice: China has wide and free access into our markets, unless and until we specify otherwise. But we have no access to their markets, unless they specifically authorize it. They authorize the quantity and the time frame, and they reserve the right to terminate such access at any point. This is highly unsatisfactory, but it is the relationship we have. So it is not surprising that, under such circumstances, the trade balances of countries like Canada, the United States, and others with China have been grossly disproportionate. These imbalances cannot be attributed merely to "competitiveness" or other economic forces.

Beyond the imbalance problem, China practises widespread trade abuse, not merely controlling market access but also engaging in intellectual property theft, industrial espionage, cyber warfare, capital controls, and currency manipulation. These are not issues restricted to Canada.*

---

* On November 21, 2021, at the WTO's twenty-year review of China's accession, over fifty international delegations took to the floor to criticize China's trade practices.

The trade imbalances have meant the loss of millions of jobs in the West without reciprocal access to Chinese markets for our workers. It is true that economic theory indicates that a poorer country like China will run a trade surplus with a richer country like Canada. But it also says that those surpluses should shrink as China becomes wealthier. Instead, they have grown. They have done so because we do not have free trade with China; we have "managed trade," managed solely by China in its own interests. That is the situation the WTO accession established.*

When I was in office, there was little we could do about this, except try to get improvements around the edges. We did, somewhat. Our trade balance went from roughly one-half of theirs to two-thirds, although it has since returned to the old disproportion. We also looked at what we could do on the structural side.

One thing we did accomplish was the conclusion of a Foreign Investment Promotion and Protection Agreement (FIPA) with China. For us, this was relatively easy. China already had substantial protections for its investments in our rule-of-law environment. For Canadian business, this could not help but enhance our safeguards in that opaque marketplace. Whether it did or not in practice was something I did not have a clear answer to when we left office. The truth is that our investments in China are still modest compared to theirs in Canada (which is, once again, the opposite of what economic theory tells us should be the case in a liberalized trade scenario).

For the Chinese, however, the real goal was more ambitious. It was to use the FIPA as the starting point for the launch of free-trade negotiations. But by that point our Government had decided that we would never conduct an actual free-trade negotiation with China. The reason was simple: we lacked sufficient leverage in any such potential talks. Given the imbalances, the WTO framework, and the alignment of much of Canadian business and

* This arrangement was put in place during the terms of Bill Clinton in the United States and Jean Chrétien in Canada.

officialdom with Chinese interests, it would have been impossible for us to get a good deal. In fact, I expected that, from the moment we launched trade negotiations, we would have faced all kinds of new restrictions on our existing exports. The Chinese would have made us bargain for what we already had, while they forced us to give them more. This was clearly not going to work, and thus we did not pursue it.

Perhaps someday a comprehensive trade deal with China may make sense. However, due to a clause it inserted in the United States-Mexico-Canada Agreement (USMCA; the renegotiated NAFTA), the Trump administration has made it virtually impossible for now for Canada to negotiate a trade deal with China without American approval.† While this can be decried as a restriction on Canadian sovereignty—which it is—it is also in our own interests. Besides preventing us making the mistake of entering bilateral free trade talks with the People's Republic of China (PRC), it opens the door to coordinating policy with the United States. Although that is far from a possibility with the Trump administration today, it is something we could consider in the future.‡

In the meantime, my own view remains that Canada must engage with China in a manner that clearly preserves and promotes our interests, as our Government sought to do. This is even more important at a time when our trading relationship with the United States is uncertain. One aspect of this should be moving to a fully managed trade relationship. Doing as the Chinese already do, we should scrutinize every import and every inward investment for value to Canada and/or reciprocity, and we should subject every one of them to approval or disapproval (or delay). This may reduce the scale of the economic relationship, but it will better protect our own economic interests in the long term.

---

† It appears this was discovered *after* the agreement had been signed.

‡ One thing for sure is that Canada must avoid being offside on trade with both the Americans and the Chinese at the same time!

WHITHER CHINA?

I AM A CHINA SKEPTIC. And my views have become considerably more pessimistic in recent years because of the governance of Xi Jinping. Still, the most important thing to understand is that China has *not* changed fundamentally under President Xi, as many "China experts" today argue.

It is true that, under Xi, there has been a change in degree. China under Xi is both more outwardly aggressive and more internally repressive. But the country's ambitions have always been global and hegemonic. Their economic liberalization never had any purpose other than the strengthening of the Chinese Communist Party's internal control and the outward projection of its power.

Because China is less overtly destabilizing than Russia, Iran, North Korea, or other global bad actors, many tend not to think of it in that category. The PRC can even be helpful if (and only if) its own interests are at stake, as in the global financial crisis. However, its challenge to the democratic world is as bold in ambition as any of those others—and superior in execution. It is thus more dangerous in the long term.

China before Xi was already engaged in a fundamentally predatory, neo-mercantilist economic strategy, along with all the other bad economic behaviours I have cited. Its trade surpluses have long been building its armed forces, militarizing the South China Sea, and underwriting its ally, North Korea, in its nuclear threats against the West. The PRC's political system, even at its most benign, remained a highly centralized authoritarian dictatorship that could have, at any moment, reverted to a Mao-style of leadership. Nor has China been content to restrict its governance to its own country. The PRC has long actively intervened and interfered in the domestic politics of Canada and other Western countries, even if Canadians have only recently come to be aware of the extent.*

---

* These actions have long been pervasive, and they go well beyond the PRC's business interests. Let me give one example. In 2008, I was informed by some friends in the Chinese-Canadian community that Falun Gong, a kind of quasi-religious spiritual movement, had been excluded from involvement in Ottawa's annual Tulip Festival by local authorities due to PRC lobbying. Really? Tulips?

In short, on the key foreign policy axes, the PRC is, and always was, a security threat, a dangerous economic competitor, and a democracy adversary. Xi Jinping did not create this situation. The "experts" simply chose to ignore these facts. Consequently, they were grotesquely and irresponsibly wrong in their previous assessments.

One reason for this was economic interest. When an enterprise or interest has significant investments and markets in China, they are effectively in business with the Chinese Communist Party. They will soon realize that they must adapt their wider political and social positions so as, at a minimum, not to run afoul of the PRC. Otherwise, the risk is the termination or even the expropriation of one's enterprise. Some businesses adapt cautiously, while other corporations become enthusiastic proponents of the PRC line. A medieval saying is, "If you sup with the devil, you had better have a long spoon." There is no spoon long enough with China, as organizations like the National Basketball Association have found out.†

Another reason for such faulty analysis of China was simple hubris. Some of this was deeply cultural in the West, as the triumphal optimism of Francis Fukuyama's "End of History" thesis took hold after the fall of the Berlin

---

We contacted the organizers and made it clear we considered that unacceptable. While it was reversed, this sort of the thing has been occurring regularly in many parts of Canada.

† This case began in 2019, when Daryl Morey, an executive with the Houston Rockets, posted an image supportive of pro-democracy protesters in Hong Kong just before an exhibition game between the Los Angeles Lakers and the Brooklyn Nets was about to begin in China. The NBA has a huge following in China, and broadcasts are worth millions in royalties to the NBA. Morey's post provoked a strong reaction from Chinese broadcasters and sponsors; programs were pulled from the air, and sponsorships withdrawn. This prompted the NBA to backpedal quickly: it issued a statement citing Morey's "regrettable" post. NBA owners harshly criticized Morey—all of which was duly portrayed by the Chinese press as an official apology. Since then, the NBA has been a textbook example of spineless corporate pandering to the PRC.

Wall. There was, in short, a conceit in our societies that everyone, including the PRC, inevitably had to become more like us.

The failure of Western experts to accurately assess Xi Jinping is particularly unforgivable. Nothing he said when coming to power indicated that he was a reformer. From day one, his actions were clearly directed at the consolidation of power. The first volume of his book *The Governance of China*—which I read—showed little interest in further economic liberalization and absolutely none in political reform. In short, the direction was all there to see for any serious analyst who wanted to see it.

The great irony, of course, is that ordinary people understood these things. The divergence between elite opinion and the attitudes of ordinary people on China was extraordinary during my time in office. No grassroots opinion pressed us to get closer to the PRC. If anything, it wanted us to be even less friendly. The same was true, in many ways, of Chinese-Canadian opinion. My China skepticism did not prevent the Conservative Party from gaining and holding the Chinese vote during our time in office. After all, there are reasons these Canadians prefer to be Canadians!

What does this mean for China's future? I am afraid that the overall direction is not positive. Xi started out wanting to combine Mao politics with Deng economics, but he is progressively ditching the latter. The costs of running afoul of him have become increasingly severe. The problem with such a strategy, of which dictators around the world are uncomfortably aware, is that once you imprison and kill your opponents, you cannot go anywhere. To retire or otherwise leave office is an invitation to your many enemies to exact their revenge. Xi Jinping seems to have taken careful note, and he governs accordingly.

Hong Kong has been a perfect example. Xi has largely destroyed its autonomous governance, which provided real benefits to China. He did so simply because he wanted greater political control as an end in itself.

As Xi's policies slow the Chinese economy, he is ever more inclined to blame the business sector. He is also increasingly paranoid that anyone commercially successful is a threat to him. "Disappearances" are now being extended beyond those who publicly disagree with him to those who have privately expressed negative views, whether real or imagined.

One-man-rule-for-life almost always ends in a combination of tyranny and stagnation. China is now clearly headed in that direction. It is only a question of how long Xi lives and stays in office—the two things being identical. This does not, however, change the underlying strengths of China's entrepreneurial class, its action-oriented society, its well-educated, proud, and ambitious young people, or its industrial base. But it may be some time before those forces are fully liberated.

However, it is our own performance, rather than Chinese rivalry, that will really determine what kind of governance system ultimately triumphs in the world.

SUPPORTING UKRAINIAN SOVEREIGNTY

OUR GOVERNMENT HAD a clear record of not just caring about the sovereignty of Ukraine but also doing something about it. Shortly after the Russian invasion and annexation of Crimea, I travelled to Ukraine. Only weeks before, there had been fighting in the streets of Kyiv during the Maidan Revolution in which the populace had risen to fight President Viktor Yanukovych's attempt to align Ukraine with Russia. The signs of the violence were still visible.

I was the first G7 leader on the ground. I wanted to demonstrate support for the bravery of Ukrainians in resisting the Russian assault upon their independence and territorial integrity. After meeting with then–Prime Minister Arseniy Yatsenyuk, I affirmed that "it is for Ukrainians and for Ukrainians only, to decide their future. In this principle, Canada will not waver. And, to help the Ukrainian people peacefully secure a bright future of freedom, we shall spare no effort."

That trip was not without danger. Security briefings alerted us to Russian agents deeply embedded in Ukraine, and even in the Ukrainian government itself, that might wish to do us harm. We ultimately decided that it was a manageable risk. I repeated the visit just three months later, when I attended the swearing-in of newly elected president Petro Poroshenko in Kyiv. That showed our firm commitment to Ukrainian democracy. I followed that up by inviting Poroshenko to address our Parliament on September 17, where he received a powerful welcome from all sides.

Our Conservative Government's record on Ukraine went back further. When I visited Ukraine in October 2010, I had raised my misgivings about Yanukovych's suspected pro-Russian, anti-democratic leanings both privately with him and in public remarks. The latter had been edited out by state broadcasters. In fact, the whole trip was a cautionary experience. Yanukovych's people were clearly thugs, who at times physically manhandled our delegation. One of my advance people, Stephen Staley, was even the subject of an attempted robbery at gunpoint—by two policemen![*]

Of course, we had invited Yanukovych's predecessor, President Viktor Yushchenko, to speak to Parliament in 2008. Yushchenko was one of the heroes of the Orange Revolution that took place in 2004 after attempts to rig the national election. Conservative Member of Parliament Peter Goldring, a staunch defender of Ukraine, had travelled there to help uphold democracy.

Also in 2008, MP James Bezan had put forward a bill recognizing the Holodomor—the great Ukrainian famine engineered deliberately by Stalin in 1932–1933—as genocide. It unambiguously was, killing some four million Ukrainians.[†] The bill was rapidly passed by Parliament and received Royal Assent.

In typical style, recognition of the Holodomor was opposed by our Foreign Affairs Department. It had a long history of prioritizing relations with Russia over doing the right thing. That was probably no more on display than back on December 2, 1991, when Prime Minister Brian Mulroney made Canada the first country to recognize Ukrainian independence. As Department of Foreign Affairs and International Trade (DFAIT) types were fretting over the possible collapse of the Soviet Union—most

---

* Fortunately, Stephen was with an RCMP liaison officer at the time. When he flashed his credentials—a presidential security business card—the policemen quickly left rather than risk identification.

† I serve on the board of the Holodomor Museum in Kyiv.

Western foreign affairs departments were at the time—Mulroney clearly saw a moment to be on the right side of history.

ENCOUNTERING PUTIN AT THE G20 IN BRISBANE

ON NOVEMBER 15–16, I was in Brisbane for the G20 Summit hosted by my good friend Australian Prime Minister Tony Abbott. Summit arrivals are invariably a long and choreographed process. To start with, there is a diplomatic pecking order. Monarchs outrank presidents, who in turn outrank prime ministers, since PMs are not heads of state. However, this list is often reversed, especially for summit arrivals, as it is typical to have the highest-ranking arrive last.

While this pageantry plays itself out, those arriving first are shuffled to a Green Room. It will typically house only the leaders, perhaps one assistant for each, and any necessary translators.

Sometimes we would talk business, even serious business, as in my confrontation with Hu Jintao at the 2006 Asia-Pacific Economic Cooperation Summit in Vietnam. However, it is often just normal social chit-chat—our travel to get there, the weather, sports events, how one's family is doing.

I had been in the Green Room in Brisbane for some time when Putin finally arrived near the end of the process. By then, there were about forty of us in the room, and it was not designed for many more than that. The Russian leader began to walk around the space, as one typically does, greeting each attendee.

Inevitably, Putin made his way to me and stuck out his hand. Being Canadian—that is, not being inclined to be outrightly rude to anybody—I just said what came into my head: "Well, Vladimir, I'll shake your hand, but I have only one thing to say to you. And that's get out of Ukraine."

The whole thing might have ended there, but the story quickly made its way to the media. The Russians apparently confirmed that it was true. More surprising was that they seemed to have not spun the story in any particular way. In any case, it quickly became headline news internationally.

I seldom talk about private conversations. I especially do not tend to reveal what others may have said privately . . . but in this case, I will make an exception. The conversation with Putin did not actually end at that point. After our handshake and my blunt statement, Putin just smirked, with, as I have often said, that look he has when he has been accused of poisoning someone. Then he said, "I'm not in Ukraine." To which I responded: "Well, that's why it's a waste of my time to talk to you." And that was that.

It was Teddy Roosevelt who was purported to have said that the problem with Russian leaders is that "they will lie to you even when they know that you know they are lying." Of course, I had long passed the point when I was prepared to play along with Putin for the sake of appearances. He typically counts on Western leaders being conflict-averse and uses these occasions, with their handshakes and backslaps, as propaganda for the rest of the world. It was not so in this case.

Even though our interaction was not loud, in that small room everybody saw it and heard it. You could see the political calculations at work, particularly for the democratic leaders: "Oh boy, if this is a story, and there are pictures of me and Putin smiling and shaking hands, how is that going to look?" So for the rest of the conference, Putin largely ate by himself and was often photographed sitting alone.

I have never been big on the soft power narrative used by some Canadian politicians. Soft power rarely means anything unless it is backed by hard power assets and the will to use them. But sometimes, just telling the truth, just being frank, can make a difference. I suspect many G20 attendees were prepared to pretend that this guy who had just invaded Ukraine, killing innocent Ukrainians, and whose proxies had shot down a Malaysia Airlines Flight 17 killing 298 people a month prior, was just another one of their colleagues. On this occasion, that proved not to be the case—just because someone said something.

FURTHER SUPPORT FOR UKRAINE

MY COMMENTS WERE by no means our last word on Canada's response to Putin's aggression. In April we announced further military aid, which was in addition to the military trainers we had provided since the outset. We also supplied specialized military hardware where we could. This was a great help and was appreciated.*

I would note that this and other military aid was given *before* it was fashionable to do so. The truth of the matter is that, although the United States condemned the Russian invasion and promised support, in my judgment, they did the bare minimum. Within that context, our Government pushed the envelope about as far as we could (and with some pushback from the Americans).

Our assistance went beyond the military side. In June 2015, before the G7 in Germany, I visited Ukraine yet again—my third visit in little more than a year. I wanted to deepen our relationship, as well as to confer with President Poroshenko and Prime Minister Yatsenyuk prior to my interventions at the summit. In July, Yatsenyuk followed that up with a visit to Ottawa, and at Willson House on Meech Lake, we were able to announce the conclusion of negotiations on a free trade agreement. Although Ukraine was, and continues to be, a challenging place to do business, this agreement was an important addition to the free-trade network that my Government was creating.

We made Ukraine a priority for the same reason we made Israel a priority—these are two democratic allies that face existential threats. However, I believe the Canadian reasons for supporting Ukrainian independence run deeply in our culture.

There is probably no place on the globe where the day of Ukrainian independence was more celebrated than in Canada. That is because no country in the world is as close to Ukraine as Canada. We have the largest Ukrainian diaspora in the world outside that region—even more in absolute numbers than the United States. That Ukrainian community in Canada is long

---

* President Poroshenko told me, for example, how much our night vision goggles had helped them win some tank battles with Russian forces in eastern Ukraine. Our assistance went well past those kinds of capabilities.

established and well connected. They have made significant contributions to Canada in all areas of our national life, beginning with their role in pioneering agriculture in the West and all the way up to the office of governor general (Ray Hnatyshyn, 1990–1995).

There are few Canadians who do not have Ukrainian friends, business associates, colleagues, or relatives. Through them, most Canadians were long aware of the dark cloud that hung over our Ukrainian-Canadian citizens for so many decades. That protracted and viciously brutal period of Soviet repression in their homeland was something many of us understood all too well.

Unlike almost any other issue I can think of, I can honestly say that there was no division of opinion in Parliament on supporting Ukraine and precious little among Canadians during my political career. The opposition, while no strangers to playing political games, lined up strongly behind our Government's position on this matter. And, with only a few exceptions, our successors upheld our firm support for Ukraine's sovereignty and territorial integrity.

All that said, the Western world's more general failure to understand the threat from Russia and the danger to Ukraine is something we are all now living with. To my mind, it is almost incomprehensible how, after 2014, Western leaders did not seem to understand the potential for Putin's subsequent invasion. Even now, I occasionally see Putin apologists who blame this on the eastward expansion of the EU and NATO after the fall of the U.S.S.R. This is unfathomable stupidity. These countries are not, and never were, a threat to Russia. They wanted to be in the EU and NATO—as is their right as sovereign nations—because they understood Russia remained a threat to them. It is in our failure to embrace them that these threats have come to pass.

Understanding these realities is far more important today than even during the Cold War. At its height, the Soviet Union did not want to take on the United States and NATO in a ground war. Putin's Russian Federation is a shadow of the former U.S.S.R. Putin is a tough guy, but he is a classic bully. He never takes on anyone who can even remotely fight back, and in

2022, he did not think the Ukrainians could. Indeed, if Putin had thought NATO would provide the kind of support we later decided to give Ukraine, the subsequent full invasion would never have taken place.

HOSTING PRIME MINISTER NARENDRA MODI IN CANADA

MANY OF MY INTERNATIONAL COLLEAGUES made visits to Canada in 2014 and 2015. German Chancellor Angela Merkel, NATO Secretary General Jens Stoltenberg, and (as mentioned) Ukrainian Prime Minister Yatsenyuk came to confer about the war between Ukraine and Russia.

Others came to build upon good, long-standing national relations between our countries. They included King Abdullah II from Jordan, King Willem-Alexander from the Netherlands, President Benigno Aquino III from the Philippines, as well as the Aga Khan. However, the most memorable trip was probably the one undertaken by the new prime minister of India, Narendra Modi.

Modi's visit to Canada lasted from April 14 to 16, 2015. We spent time together in Ottawa, Toronto, and Vancouver. Elected the previous year, his personal energy and his party's formidable political machine were fully on display. It was able to organize massive, arena-filling rallies across our country. Frankly, no Canadian political party could have staged three gatherings of such scale in such a short period of time.

We had already been very successful in re-establishing strong, high-level political bonds between our two countries under Prime Minister Singh. This was something we wanted to do with Modi also. Modi would be, however, a different prime minister from a very different government.

Our Government paid close attention to what was happening politically in India. Modi had been the chief minister in the state of Gujarat, where he had led a government focused upon vigorous economic reform and the encouragement of investment and trade. His was the most effective and energetic administration in the country, with a political machine to match.

Consequently, we had concluded early on that there was a strong likelihood that Modi would eventually become India's prime minister.

To be candid, however, this foresight was no thanks to Foreign Affairs. DFAIT's explicit policy was to shun Modi. The department seemed to believe the unproven allegations that he was behind communal riots in Gujarat in 2002. That was an unfortunate part of its pattern: seeing all evil in India while turning a largely blind eye to the widespread and systemic human rights violations of China.

Despite the opposition of DFAIT, we decided to cultivate a relationship with Modi, principally through the work of Minister Jason Kenney and MP Patrick Brown. We were well ahead of other Western nations in doing this, and Modi has never forgotten it. One of the first calls he took after taking office was from me, and we have remained in contact ever since. In fact, under our Government and Prime Minister Modi, Canada-India relations grew even stronger.

LOOKING AHEAD ON INDIA AND OUR RELATIONSHIP

ONE ONGOING CHALLENGE to Canada-India relations is the Khalistan movement in our country. The Khalistanis are Sikh groups whose aim is to create a separate state, called Khalistan, in India's Punjab state. While this idea has practically zero support in that state, Canada has come to be seen as the global headquarters of the Khalistan movement. Although many who support Khalistan do so peacefully and democratically, elements of this cause have been associated with terrorist acts against both Indians and Canadians.

During my time in office, I was very clear: my party had no toleration for Khalistanis, and my Government quashed anything we saw as outreach to the Khalistan movement.* This is not just about Canada's relationship

* I find it outrageous that there are periodically parades in Canadian cities with floats celebrating the murder of Indian prime minister Indira Ghandi, and we were clear with our MPs that we expected them to stay away from such displays.

with India; it is also good politics. The Khalistan movement is a political loser; it is all but dead in India itself, and it will gradually die elsewhere. Most Canadian Sikhs are not Khalistanis, and of course, no non-Sikh Indo-Canadians are. In other words, there are plenty of Indo-Canadian votes—witness Modi's rallies in Canada—without playing footsie with Khalistanis. That is something most Indo-Canadians find abhorrent.

Today, I give my party and others the same advice I did in the speech I delivered in Toronto on June 23, 2010, at the 25th anniversary of the Air India bombing: "It is incumbent on all of us, not to reach out to, but rather to marginalize, to carefully and systematically marginalize, those extremists who seek to import the battles of India's past here and then to export them back to that great and forward-looking nation."

ON THE GROUND IN IRAQ AND KUWAIT

IN MAY 2015, I made an unannounced visit to Iraq and Kuwait. The purpose was to highlight our support for the campaign against ISIS and to visit Canadian Armed Forces personnel who were carrying out the mission. We travelled to Baghdad and did a second leg to Erbil in Iraqi Kurdistan before going on to Kuwait.

Of these, the most intense was certainly the visit to Baghdad. This trip was probably the most dangerous one I ever undertook. Much of Baghdad remained a series of armed camps. After we arrived at the airport, we had to make our way to the Green Zone, where Iraq's governmental institutions and diplomatic compounds were located. What lay between us and the Green Zone was a swirling cauldron of violence between various militias, much of it well outside the control of the Iraqi government.

We were given a choice of traversing this deadly terrain either by motorcade or by helicopter. It did not take us long to decide on the latter. It was better to be above the fray than in the thick of it. Accordingly, we were loaded aboard an American helicopter-gunship, already loaded with ground suppression weaponry and specialized military personnel.

Nobody could fully guarantee our security against some militia member on the ground with a MANPAD,* a rocket-propelled grenade launcher, or even a heavy machine gun able to bring a short and nasty end to our flight. We crossed our fingers, made peace with our various makers, and set out on a ten-minute journey.† Those ten minutes were among the longest of my life.‡

I met with Prime Minister Haider al-Abadi and members of his government. During the visit, we were able to announce significant increases in aid and assistance to Iraq specifically and to the region more generally. We also wanted to compare notes on how the fight with ISIS was going.

The main purpose of this encounter, however, was diplomatic. In line with allied messaging, we wanted to press the Iraqi government to be more inclusive—to especially reach out to Iraq's Sunni population, whose alienation from Iraqi politics was one of the reasons for the rise of ISIS in the first place. We also wanted the Kurds to be brought more firmly into Iraq's power structures. Both our assistance and our advice seemed to be well received by our Iraqi interlocutors.

The subsequent visit to Iraqi Kurdistan had a couple of purposes. We had sent Canadian Army trainers to assist Kurdish forces in their fight against ISIS. From our first moments on the ground there, it was clear that this was a much more secure environment. I say this even though the fighting was

---

* MANPAD stands for a man-portable air-defense system, which is essentially a portable surface-to-air missile.

† Because of the risk, I undertook this part of the trip with a skeleton staff. My recollection is that it included my then–executive assistant Stephen Staley, advance lead Aliya Mohamed, and photographer Jason Ransom. I took a photographer with me almost everywhere. There were three of them—Jason, his wife Deb, and Jill Thompson. They would take 15,000–20,000 portrait photographs of me per year with the various people (mostly Canadians) that I met.

‡ The only similar time span I can compare this to was when my daughter Rachel was born. There were some complications in the delivery at the end, and those last few minutes were highly stressful and prayer filled.

not far outside Erbil. In fact, we were given a tour that came within a few hundred yards of the ISIS positions.

Yet, in Erbil itself, things felt relatively normal and safe. This confirmed what we had heard, and it reinforced my perception of the Kurds as a remarkable people. More than being allies with us in the war against ISIS, they were among the best fighters too. They were great partners during our training mission as well, despite one tragic incident.[§] I was also able to visit some other minorities there—the Yazidis and Christians most prominently—who had previously suffered the wrath and attempted genocide of ISIS.

What we saw with our own eyes confirmed that the Kurds were a progressive, Western-oriented, humanitarian community who fought bravely and well for their freedom and the freedom of others. Amid all this chaos and warfare, the Kurds had managed to carve out a safe zone. I had a great meeting with Masoud Barzani, then-president of the Iraqi Kurdistan Region and other leading Kurdish officials. I came away impressed.[¶]

I believe it is a tragedy that the Kurds do not have their own sovereign state. In Iraq, for example, both the Kurds and the world would be better off if they had full control of their affairs, rather than being under the ultimate authority of the dysfunctional state in Baghdad. The problem, of course, is that would raise the spectre of the potential breakaway of neighbouring Kurdish areas in Turkey, Iran, and Syria (where the Kurds

---

§ On March 6, 2015, one of our trainers, Sgt. Andrew Doiron, was mistaken at night for an ISIS fighter, and shot and killed by Kurdish forces. It was a very sad and unfortunate event, which did put a damper on our trip. As quoted by *Valour Canada*, "Sgt. Doiron's death is a poignant reminder that in war, there is always an element of risk. There are no 'safe' zones, and unlike the Western Front in World War I, the front line is not clearly defined either, no matter how much we like to impose such deeply ingrained concepts of war onto modern conflicts."

¶ Canada's ambassador to Jordan and Iraq, Bruno Saccomani, capably led the organization of this trip on the ground. He built deep personal relationships with Kurdish leaders and was respected for his kinetic approach and eagerness to visit the front lines.

are already de facto independent). Thus, those countries also oppose any such move, even if it would make the Kurds in their own countries and the rest of us all better off.

When we travelled to Kuwait, I visited with Emir Sabah, although the principal reason for the trip to that country was to visit the logistics base from which the Canadian Air Force was executing its sorties against ISIS.* On this trip, we had been joined by former Edmonton Oilers' stars Paul Coffey and Ryan Smyth, who were kind enough to give of their time and were a smash hit with the troops. On the stopovers in Erbil and at the hot and dusty base in Kuwait, I was again filled with respect and admiration for our men and women in uniform who undertake such missions.

On the Kuwait visit, I did, however, have confirmation of some earlier, troubling reports about the mission. While the advance of ISIS on the ground had been halted and even reversed—more due to Kurdish forces than the Iraqi Army—the air campaign was making only marginal progress. The mixed messages we had earlier received from the Obama administration about this mission were playing out in the theatre. The air campaign had been subjected to high levels of restriction, blocking anything even vaguely resembling collateral damage.† The upshot was that a large majority of Canadian and allied sorties were doing no damage to ISIS at all.

After I had left office and President Trump became commander in chief in 2017, the United States quickly adopted a far more aggressive position. The result was that the ISIS presence in Iraq and (especially) in Syria were degraded in a matter of months. In fact, for all intents and purposes, the ISIS

---

* Readers may recall that we had earlier had our regional Air Force base at Camp Mirage in the United Arab Emirates. An unfortunate dispute between Canada and the UAE in early 2010 on renewal of the arrangement resulted in my decision to move the base to Kuwait.

† One example, given to me by our military commanders, was the refusal to authorize the dropping of payload on an ISIS convoy that might have had a civilian driver, even if the individual was almost certainly being paid by the terrorist organization.

caliphate was eliminated. That is not to say that the fanatical beliefs of ISIS have disappeared or cannot appear again, but this does show that they could not withstand any serious military effort by the West.

IRAN AND THE JCPOA

SYRIA WAS NOT the place in the Middle East where allied policy (or the lack of it) caused complications for our Government. That summer, our American, British, and French allies signed a deal with Iran known as the Joint Comprehensive Plan of Action (JCPOA).[‡] Ostensibly designed to stop Iran's development of nuclear weapons, it was met with immediate Israeli outrage and equally vehement (though much quieter) opposition from the West's Arab allies.

All these various countries had lobbied us to support or oppose this agreement in the months leading up to its conclusion. Given their strong differing reactions and our own deep misgivings, this was a very awkward moment for us. This led my staff, somewhat tongue-in-cheek, to remind me of the "Harper Doctrine." This was my stated view that Canada should try to avoid finding itself offside with all three of our most important allies at the same time. I doubt this term will go down in the rhetoric of global diplomacy, but it accurately reflected our strategy in this situation.[§] We

‡ Three other signatories were Russia, China, and Germany, making this a group of six the "P5 + 1," that is, the permanent members of the United Nations Security Council plus Germany.

§ This internal term had first been coined when our government supported the independence of Kosovo in 2008. Personally, I thought that was a bad idea for a few reasons. It was, however, strongly supported by our American, British, and French allies, and we had little at stake in the matter. Also, the previous government had been going in this direction with our partners for some time, so it would have been inappropriate for us to shift position at the last minute.

congratulated our allies for achieving the agreement, while cautioning that our final judgment on it would be based on how Tehran responded in the months and years to come.

The premise behind the JCPOA was to limit Iran's progress to a nuclear weapon. Through it, the Obama administration hoped Iran would rejoin the community of civilized nations and gradually normalize its behaviour. Given the understandable unwillingness of our allies to remove the Iranian nuclear program militarily, this approach was a reasonable option. However, even conceding these things, the deal was a very weak one.

To start with, Iran was only pausing its advance toward nuclear weapons for ten years. In the meantime, the allies' ability to monitor this was quite weak. Furthermore, Tehran remained free to develop weapons delivery systems. It would also receive billions of dollars from the deal, the uses of which were not constrained.*

Iran went in the opposite direction from what our allies had wished. The Iranian regime interpreted the agreement as a massive concession by the West. It immediately became even more belligerent and used the monies gained from the deal to further support its terrorist network throughout the Middle East. Frankly, given its constant fighting with inspectors, there is little reason to believe it slowed its nuclear program in any meaningful way. In short, the JCPOA was an unmitigated disaster.

The truth is that Iran is an energy-rich country that has zero need for a civilian nuclear program. The clear objective of the Islamic republic's nuclear activities is and has always been the development of nuclear weapons, and it is farcical to pretend otherwise. My own view, communicated to our allies, was long that the Iranian nuclear program should have been taken out militarily before it got so far down the road.

---

* For these reasons, the French were very reluctant signatories, but they did sign and urged us to support the deal in the end.

ADVISING A FUTURE PRESIDENT

CONSIDERING THAT AN ELECTION was just around the corner, I had a surprising number of meetings with foreign leaders in the last few weeks of our Government. Canada's hosting of the Pan American Games and the FIFA Women's World Cup led to some high-ranking visitors coming to our country. I travelled to Vancouver to attend the World Cup final on July 5 between Japan and the United States. I did so in no small part because it would offer an opportunity to spend time with the American vice president.

I met Joe Biden several times while I was prime minister. We always had a good relationship. I found him very open and easy to talk to. We always had candid exchanges, whether they were what I wanted to hear or not. This meeting was no different. In the end, Biden walked away happy, celebrating the U.S. victory.

After I left office, I crossed paths with the former VP on a few occasions. A particularly long and memorable one was in 2018 at an Alliance of Democracies conference in Copenhagen. It was put on by our colleague, former Danish prime minister and NATO secretary general Anders Fogh Rasmussen, and we were both speakers. After the proceedings, Biden asked me if I could come up to his room to chat about something that was on his mind.

Joe got down to business quickly, telling me he was contemplating a run for president. He knew I followed U.S. politics closely, and he wanted to get an outside perspective. He thought hearing from someone who was both non-American and conservative would be useful.

The Joe Biden I met that day was seventy-five. Physically and mentally, he could have passed for twenty years younger. He seemed remarkably energetic. The issues that arose later—as early as the 2020 campaign—were nowhere on the radar, so that was not a matter of discussion.

For what it is worth, I told Joe that my view was that he would win the Democratic nomination if he chose to contest it. That was what really mattered, if he wanted a shot. Given the state of the Trump presidency and the division of his country, his chances at winning as the Democratic nominee in the general election would be at least fifty-fifty. I thought they might be better.

To be clear, I was not stating any personal preferences. I was just giving Joe my "objective" analysis, one long-time political guy to another. Needless to say, a lot of history has transpired since then.

In any case, let us go back to 2015, when I would soon have an election of my own to fight.

28

THE FINAL CAMPAIGN

I SUPPOSE YOU COULD SAY that my preparation for the 2015 election began in the summer of 2014. If I was not going to run for a fourth term, then, for the sake of the party, a leadership race would have to be underway by fall at the latest. I knew I had to decide that summer.

SHOULD I STAY OR SHOULD I GO?

ALTHOUGH I HAD NOT GIVEN the matter a lot of prior thought, I had been inclined not to seek another term. The reason was rather simple: by the time of the fixed election date, we would be fast approaching ten years in office. My observation over many years had been that, in our era, it is rare for a government to surpass a decade in power. Whatever your standing, the public is by then usually ready for a change.

I remember having this very conversation with Gary Doer in 2009. He had been Manitoba premier for ten years and appeared to be well ahead of his opposition. Still, we both thought that asking the public for more than a decade was risky. That led to the discussion that resulted in him becoming my ambassador to the United States—a decision I never regretted.*

---

* My appointments of Michael Wilson and Gary Doer as Ambassadors to the

A few conservations with my closest confidants and family got me thinking differently. No body of opinion in the party was pushing me to go, and I was in no hurry to do something else. On the contrary, despite all its stresses, I still loved the job.

The longer I was prime minister, the more comfortable I felt in the role. Yes, it had been extraordinarily demanding, but far from feeling physically or mentally exhausted, I felt there was much work to do. After all, it was only in this majority mandate that we had been able to get large parts of our agenda through.

What I wanted was a bit more time to deepen the country's more conservative direction. Having done the heavy work of getting through the global financial crisis and then balancing the budget, we had the opportunity to solidify Canada's position and make us much more competitive longer term. Our strong balance sheet, streamlined regulatory environment, and new network of trade deals could, properly implemented, make us far more of a global (and less U.S.-dependent) economic player.

That was my state of mind, but I also asked myself what was in the party's best interests. Our polling showed that we would have an uphill, but far from hopeless, battle to be re-elected. There was also no data to indicate that the party would do any better with another leader. On the contrary, 30 per cent of the electorate* would vote for me no matter what. A change of leader risked that, with no obvious upside.

United States were two of the very best personnel decisions I ever made. I could add to that list naming Gordon Campbell to the United Kingdom and Lawrence Cannon to France. Although I had many good ambassadors and high commissioners provided by Foreign Affairs, a prime minister has an unfettered right to name people from outside the department to these high offices. I would recommend doing it more frequently than I did, depending, of course, on the availability of qualified candidates.

* We had then, and I believe still have, the highest base vote of any federal party. That is, under any normal circumstances, our minimum vote is the largest. This was a change that occurred during my time as leader, especially after the creation of the new Conservative Party of Canada.

Done with mulling it over on my own, I called my campaign chairman, former chief of staff Guy Giorno, along with my present chief, Ray Novak,[†] up to Harrington Lake one sunny afternoon. They agreed with my perspective, and the decision was made. We would take a stab at a fourth consecutive term, even though no one had managed it since Wilfrid Laurier in 1908. We had a shot. If we lost, at worst, the party would be a strong Official Opposition.

However, if we won, my intention would be to serve only until just after the 150th anniversary of Confederation on July 1, 2017. That meant I still had three years left to get things done. After that, a leadership race would take place with an even stronger bench of next-generation candidates.

THE SEARCH FOR A NEW MINISTER OF FINANCE

FOR NINE YEARS, our government had made its mark on management of the economy. Over any appreciable period, the economy was always our focus. It was the economy that was fundamentally the reason we had been given our mandate, and if we were going to get re-elected, it was going to hinge on that issue.

In 2015, this was reinforced by a steady stream of announcements related to economic and job growth. Whether infrastructure, technology and research, skills and labour, or tax measures, all were intended to demonstrate our competence on the economy. Canadians were financially better off than they had been when we were first elected—far better off than most others post–global financial crisis—and we intended to remind them of it every chance we got.

---

† With his many years of increasingly senior experience, Ray was more than ready for the new role. I had to replace Nigel Wright in May 2013 after it was revealed he had re-paid Senator Mike Duffy's dubious expense claims out of his own funds. While this was an act of considerable generosity—Nigel was an extraordinarily generous individual—he had not informed me nor reported the transaction. Nigel resumed his private-sector career, and we stayed in touch until his sudden passing in October 2025.

A good example of this occurred in March, when we announced that Honda would be making huge investments in their Alliston, Ontario, plant. It would be manufacturing North American cars for export to the European market. This was now possible because of the Canada-EU trade agreement, and it was another reminder of what we were doing to create jobs. We wanted to make the lesson hard to miss: Conservative government equals more jobs, more prosperity, and better lives for Canadians.

Obviously, Budget 2015 was a major element in that plan. However, the biggest budget decision had occurred a year earlier, when I had selected the new minister of finance. In Joe Oliver, the choice had been an obvious one.

I say it was obvious because, by experience, conviction, and circumstance, Joe fit the bill. A veteran of the Toronto financial industry, he had been executive director of the Ontario Securities Commission and CEO of the Investment Dealers Association of Canada. In addition to these professional credentials, he had demonstrated political ability. As the minister of natural resources from 2011 to 2014, he had steered through the privatization of the commercial operations of Atomic Energy of Canada Limited. That Joe was able to realize value for an enterprise that had lost the government billions for decades was no small feat.

While Joe Oliver was clearly the best choice for the job,* I think it fitting that I address an issue that has occasionally cropped up in the media. It is that I first offered the position to Mark Carney. That story relates to events that occurred while Carney was governor of the Bank of Canada.

Mark Carney had been in the financial world before entering the public sector in 2004. He first served as a deputy governor of the Bank of Canada and then as associate deputy minister in the Department of Finance. In 2008, Minister Flaherty recommended him to be David Dodge's replacement as governor of the Bank.

---

* There were some other strong potential candidates for the job, most notably Vancouver's Andrew Saxton, the parliamentary secretary for finance. However, my political preference, as a prime minister from the West, was to have a finance minister from the East.

In our system, the role of the governor is to execute the monetary policy set by the government.† Governor Carney was highly effective in his responsibilities and, in addition, provided the Government with solid advice on broader macroeconomic matters. Nevertheless, Minister Flaherty increasingly brought concerns to my attention. These mostly revolved around his belief that the governor was nurturing political ambitions, including the possibility of running for leader of the Liberal Party.

As you can imagine, this was a serious concern for us. As it became evident there was something to it, Nigel Wright and I discussed the matter. Nigel had known Governor Carney for many years. He suggested that the way to deal with this was to offer Mark the possibility of joining the Conservative government instead.

The idea was inspired. If Carney accepted the offer, it would be good for the government. But, if he refused, he would have to say it was because the governor should not enter partisan politics. Indeed, he could not expect to maintain Liberal aspirations and remain governor for our government.

I raised the issue in one of my regular meetings with Governor Carney in mid-2012. Obviously, I did not offer him the post of minister of finance, as it was then not available. However, I indicated that, if he chose to join the government, he would be the leading candidate should the post come open. Mark took some time to reflect on the opportunity, ultimately declaring that he should stay out of partisan politics.

Carney would soon depart for the governorship of the Bank of England. In this case, the rest really is history!‡

---

† It is the Government, not the Bank, that sets monetary policy in Canada. This matter was litigated in the Diefenbaker-Coyne dispute over monetary policy in 1961. While Coyne may have been right on the substance of the issue, the result was the Government's assertion of ultimate control over the Bank of Canada.

‡ History will also record that, on the recommendation of Minister Flaherty, I named Stephen Poloz, head of Export Development Canada, to succeed Carney as governor. Poloz served the full seven-year term under our government and our successors.

BUDGET 2015

JOE OLIVER'S BUDGET was presented on April 21. With $290 billion in expenditures,* it obviously contained a wide variety of initiatives. Still, this one could be narrowed down to three themes.

First was to continue encouraging long-term growth through job-creating announcements. Second, as this was the last budget before an election, we wished to put some things in the window that showed the benefits from our economic management. And third, we wanted to keep the budget in balance. We knew we would likely be in a small surplus in the year that was wrapping up, and we did not wish to undermine our Herculean accomplishment of returning to balance after undertaking a massive stimulus program.

However, accomplishing these three objectives would not be easy. The reason was a rapidly slowing economy. This was not, however, a generalized phenomenon. The downturn was largely restricted to the energy industry and the regions dependent on it.†

In any case, we faced a much tighter budget situation than we had expected even a few months before. Nevertheless, some margin remained. We used some of this room to assist families with children. We would fulfill our commitment to introduce income splitting for families with children, as we had earlier done for seniors with their pensions. We used our discretion on this, modifying the promise to ensure most of the money went to middle-class families.

To ensure we were not withdrawing liquidity from the economy, we also made specific, targeted infrastructure investments. This included the Canada 150 Community Infrastructure Program, designed to help communities

* This will sound like a lot, but a decade later, federal expenditures are closing in on double this amount—and were even briefly above that level during the Covid-19 pandemic!

† From June 2014 to January 2015, the benchmark price of oil went from roughly 106 to 46 USD per barrel. It bounced around after that, but still with a downward trend that saw it hit 26 USD by January 2016.

across the country refurbish their aging hockey rinks and recreational facilities. It was modelled on a similar program for Canada's centennial in 1967, which had been the last big infusion of money into such facilities.

We also announced major spending on federal infrastructure assets around the country. We were able to do so without risking a deficit: when you spend on your own assets, that spending is amortized over the life of the asset and has only limited impact on the bottom line in any given year. By doing this, we were effectively ending the "infrastructure deficit" at the national level.

A DEFENCE OF DEFICIT REDUCTION

WHILE I BELIEVE THAT the public strongly supported the notion of returning the budget to balance, our efforts have received, both at the time and retrospectively, some criticism. Given the wrong-headed nature of these attacks, I would like to set the record straight.

One criticism—an automatic one from the left—is that reducing the deficit crippled public services. The reality is that service to the public was barely touched. The most glaring example at the time was controversy around the closure of some Veterans Affairs offices. We did this because these offices served virtually no one. Visits to them by veterans were as low as single digits in a month. I do admit that the protests against this were effective, but be under no illusion: these protests were led not by veterans but by the bureaucrats who were losing their virtually taskless jobs. The reality was that overall veterans programming expanded enormously during our time in office.

Our successors have repeatedly levelled these kinds of charges against our deficit reduction efforts on many fronts, from vaccine procurement to border security. Fortunately, the public is not so gullible as to believe problems arising some five or ten years later are the fault of somebody's predecessor. The successor government's ability to spend vastly more money with declining service in virtually every area of public administration speaks for itself.

A more intellectually based criticism has come from Keynesian economists. They have alleged that our deficit reduction efforts slowed Canada's economic recovery. More specifically, they claim that we could have avoided the downturn of 2014–2016 with renewed deficit spending.

The first part of the claim is counterfactual. Canada's economy, like Germany's, recovered far better than those that clung to large deficit spending after the global financial crisis. As for the latter part, it is an example of failing to learn from the 1970s. Back then, large-scale deficit spending was engaged in to offset external oil price shocks. This was utterly ineffective in addressing the problem. Deficits went up. Inflation set in. Growth did not recover. It was a similar situation in 2015, and deficit spending then would have been equally ineffective.*

The public should be very skeptical of these Keynesian critiques for a fundamental reason—the underlying assumption that deficit spending somehow creates economic activity that would not otherwise exist. That is only true under the kind of dire, dysfunctional economic conditions that we saw during the global financial crisis. Under most circumstances, deficit spending by government only moves economic activity around—generally from investment to consumption and from the profitable to the subsidized. Any short-term benefit is offset by a hit against long-term economic performance.

There is a third criticism that has cropped up from time to time. It is that our deficit reduction efforts somehow led to the high debt burdens experienced by Canadian households. Once again, this is counterfactual, but it also betrays a lack of understanding of the limits of Canadian monetary policy.

The argument is that, by pushing the deficit down, we lessened demand for government borrowing, which kept interest rates too low. Consequently, households borrowed more than they would have otherwise. The argument

* The difference between 2015 and the 1970s was that oil prices fell rather than rose. Both were effectively "supply shocks." Deficit spending is an aggregate demand tool and therefore not effective in a macro sense in dealing with a supply problem.

goes that if we had let the big deficits go on, the Bank of Canada could have raised interest rates and slowed consumer borrowing.

In fact, the debt burden of Canadian households relative to GDP had been rising since at least the early 1990s. But that trend, completely contrary to the allegation, abated during the period of deficit reduction, when the household debt-burden ratio essentially flatlined. It only resumed its upward trajectory after 2015, when federal deficits returned.

So much for that hypothesis. Yet the truth is that we were concerned that interest rates were too low during this period. Why did we not raise them? Because Canadian monetary policy has limited discretion.

Yes, we have our own currency, but our high level of integration with the U.S. economy severely restricts our ability to diverge on interest rates. What we found was that a gap of over 1 per cent between the Bank of Canada rate and its Federal Reserve equivalent could cause rapid movements in the value of the Canadian dollar.[†] Such fluctuations in the exchange rate, if sustained, will create very serious problems of their own that are best avoided. In short, no big change in the federal budget balance back then would have led to significantly different interest rates.[‡]

APPROACHING THE ELECTION CAMPAIGN

IN THE PERIOD AFTER BUDGET 2015, our minds were increasingly preoccupied by the upcoming election. Our own data mirrored public polling. It indicated that we were going to have trouble getting re-elected. It essentially had the three major parties all polling in the same range (around 30 per cent), but with "time for a change" sentiment running very strongly against us. Of course, we took an optimistic view, as

---

† This was shown again in late 2024.

‡ In fact, the Bank of Canada rate only started moving up in earnest in 2017, not from the Liberals' budget deficit but under pressure from U.S. Federal Reserve rate increases.

lots can happen during campaigns. Still, we never thought our chances were more than fifty-fifty at best.*

As I have said before, time-for-a-change voting tends to become a big motivator for any contemporary electorate after a decade of the same party in office. We saw my Murphy's Law of Politics† first-hand in our focus-group testing. Key swing voters remembered anything we had done that they were against, but they could rarely recall anything that they had liked, unless they were prompted. That is just human nature, but it meant that our campaign would have to lay out measures for the future while also being careful to recall our past achievements.

It came down to this: about 50 per cent of the public thought we were a decent government—which, frankly, is pretty darn good after nearly ten years. We knew that 30 per cent of the electorate were solidly in our camp. But the other 20 per cent, despite giving us passing grades, were inclined to vote for change. Our key challenge would be to convince as many of that 20 per cent as we could that changing the government at this time was an unnecessary risk. It was a steep hill to climb, but we had overcome worse.

On the other side, however, it was unclear exactly whom we had to fight. On the one hand, the NDP had generally been ahead of the Liberals in the polls, and Tom Mulcair had proven to be a very effective Opposition leader. But he also had an unfavourable "likeability" score. Justin Trudeau was viewed much more favourably, if also quite vaguely, by voters. Gaffe-prone when off-script, he rarely said much and came to the House even less. But he did not need to, since his family name gave him instant profile.

---

* How I would have handled the scenario of a minority-government victory was one that I put out of my mind. It would have meant that, although the government might stay in office, I would have had to step down as leader well before a subsequent election. The timing of that, as the Liberals of 2024–2025 discovered, can be challenging.

† I defined it earlier: "friends may come and go, but enemies accumulate."

THE DECISION TO SET THE DATE

ON AUGUST 2, I requested the dissolution of Parliament for the election to be held on October 19. By recent standards this would be a very long campaign, but we had to call it early. We were now up against one of the unintended consequences of the fixed-date election legislation that we had passed back in our first term and were experiencing for the first time.‡

What was happening was an explosion of "third-party," that is, non-political-party, advertising. While this is severely—I believe too severely—restricted during the campaign period, it is not regulated at all before an election call. With the election timing now known, such entities could bombard the airwaves with their messages in the election lead-up.

The challenge was not so much that most of this advertising was overwhelmingly against us and, frankly, quite partisan in character. Media coverage was typically like that, so that was nothing unusual. Much of the time, these campaigns preached to the converted, really speaking only to those who had already made up their minds. There was, however, one advertising campaign that was quite problematic.

The Public Service Alliance of Canada, a public-sector union, had launched a "Vote to Stop the Cuts" campaign. It loudly accused our Government of reducing healthcare spending by a staggering 36 billion dollars. A major advertising buy, we could see that this message was slicing into our potential support. After all, the "cuts" claim seemed to be based on hard numbers.

There would have been nothing wrong with the union or anyone else bringing this to the public's attention—if it were true. But it was a flagrant lie. Its origin was based on the Canada Health Transfer funding formula in place before 2014. Under it, the transfer rose at 6 per cent per year. When that expired, we brought in a new formula that based the escalator

---

‡ I had pre-emptively called the election in 2008 after Mr. Dion had vowed to grind Parliament to a halt. In 2011, Mr. Ignatieff had triggered the election by moving the defeat of the Government in the House. Thus, we had not had previous experience in dealing with the fixed-date scenario.

on nominal GDP, with a 3 per cent minimum. The union took the difference between sets of future increases (6 per cent versus 3 per cent) and claimed that healthcare spending was being cut. In fact, it not only would continue to rise under all circumstances but also had already gone up by over 50 per cent under our Government.*

There is, of course, legal recourse against false advertising, although that would have taken more time than we had. That is why the usual safeguard is with big media companies themselves. They maintain boards that scrutinize advertising, including political advertising, for falsehoods. We would know; they went over anything our party ever ran with a fine-tooth comb, often claiming to find untruths where none existed. Yet this major, black-and-white numerical lie was perfectly acceptable to them in this instance.

The reality was that we faced a media hostility that went beyond the normal antipathy we got from the press gallery in Ottawa. It now also came from the executive ranks in the media. Our Government had been working to open competition in the wireless sector, where costs to Canadians were high due to its excessively concentrated nature. The big telecommunications companies had opposed this, which included running a false advertising campaign claiming that our reforms would allow American industry to take over the sector. Bell Canada, which owned the Liberal-leaning CTV network, was a key part of these efforts.†

Their campaign, being demonstrably untrue, had fallen flat. However, they did something else. In the weeks leading up to the campaign (and after

---

* While the Liberals promised to bring back the old formula, they instead introduced one that was virtually identical to ours.

† I should note that, despite this campaign by the telcos, the incoming Liberal Government, to its credit, did not reverse our efforts to create more competition in the wireless space. Consequently, wireless costs for consumers have fallen by 50 per cent over the past decade. My successive industry ministers Tony Clement, Christian Paradis, and James Moore deserve recognition for having fought the battles over many years to implement these changes.

the closing of the Conservative-leaning Sun News TV), the broadcasters wrote a collective letter to our party indicating that they would not run any of our ads featuring excerpts from their news broadcasts. Again, this was improper, as any clips we used were clearly in the public domain.

This new policy had a purpose. We had demonstrated an ability to effectively use such clips against other party leaders, particularly Stéphane Dion and Michael Ignatieff. We were quite careful in how we did this. I always reviewed the footage to be sure the other leaders were not being taken out of context. That being true, showing such footage of another leader saying something very controversial or very dumb makes the statement undeniable. Merely quoting such a statement is not as impactful, and the public will almost always be skeptical.

However, what should have been evident—it was not our concern at the time—was that this tactic was not merely about hurting us. If you thought about it, it also had another clear political objective. There was not going to be footage like that—at least very little of it—of Tom Mulcair or me. Justin Trudeau was another matter, and the networks knew we had those kinds of clips.

By early August, we had concluded that we had to be able to get our own messages out in our own advertising—at least to the extent that the networks would allow. We could not have blatantly false, third-party commercials defining our record. We needed to end that and have a direct debate with our political rivals. That is why I called the election so early.

FIGHTING AN UPHILL BATTLE

AS IN OUR PREVIOUS CAMPAIGNS, we planned most days around a policy announcement. Almost all the announcements in 2015 built upon existing initiatives. I would then contrast those initiatives with Liberal and/or NDP pronouncements in the same general policy area. There would then be a clear distinction in either substance or financing. All our announcements hinged on a credible commitment to not raise taxes or incur a deficit.

The latter was reinforced by the release of the Public Accounts for 2013–2014 during the campaign, which showed that we had, in fact, reached a balanced budget a year ahead of schedule.

I made literally dozens of such policy announcements over the course of the campaign, but I was particularly proud to visit the great people at Bison Transport in Winnipeg on September 22. There, I detailed our plan to add another 1.3 million new jobs by 2020. This ambitious objective was only achievable due to our plans to further lower taxes and aggressively focus on economic growth. It was our conservative agenda at its best, focused on delivering real results for the average working Canadians and their families and keeping our country on a sound economic path for the future.

If readers do not remember many of these announcements, they should be forgiven. Most of them received scant coverage. However, the media did have time to run fabricated stories, like our Government being somehow responsible for the heartbreaking death of two-year-old Syrian refugee Alan Kurdi in Turkey, the Prime Minister's Office secretly deciding which Syrian refugees could enter the country, and some kind of plan to ban the wearing of the niqab. In any case, the media had a ready-made excuse for ignoring the substance of our campaign: the ongoing coverage of Senator Mike Duffy's (ultimately farcical) corruption trial.*

THE "BARBARIC CULTURAL PRACTICES HOTLINE"

DESPITE THE UNPRECEDENTLY HOSTILE media coverage, our vote was actually holding up pretty well during the campaign. But that was not enough. As the election progressed, the Liberals began to steadily consolidate the opposition vote, pulling ahead of us and the NDP. That was leading

* I say "ultimately farcical" because, while some of Duffy's expense claims were indefensible—that was always my position—there was no evidence that they were criminal.

to increasing tensions in our campaign team, and it led to one regrettable announcement: the "Barbaric Cultural Practices Hotline."

From the start of the campaign, a minor but well-reported issue had been our policy against face-covering during a Canadian citizenship ceremony—the "niqab" controversy. This was not, as sometimes said, about headwear. It was about the concealment of identity during what is supposed to be a public declaration of allegiance.

We were deeply troubled by this practice in Canada, and the public was overwhelmingly on our side on the issue. This was not just true in Quebec, where opinion was virtually unanimous. Some three-quarters of opinion in the rest of Canada was the same. The media (and the other parties) were strongly on the other side of the debate, and they were doing their best to drive it as an issue. They failed to understand that the public (correctly) saw this in the context of women's equality and not of religious practice.

Despite public support on this issue, I did not wish to pursue any new policies along these lines. Early in the campaign, when presented with a range of possible such announcements—I do not recall if the hotline was one of them—I rejected them all. The economy was what our Government was about, and I made it clear that I thought it unwise to introduce a major focus beyond that.

I did not believe the public at large would be comfortable with a cultural focus to our campaign, even if they agreed with us. My opinion was that, for women locked in the kind of cultural space that says they must cover their faces in public, the approach should be to find ways of better integrating them into Canadian society. More conflict along these lines could well be unhelpful for that ultimate objective.

I was thus stunned when, on October 2, it flashed across my screen that Ministers (and Conservative candidates) Kellie Leitch and Chris Alexander had announced the hotline. I was locked away in a Montreal hotel room preparing for the French-language leaders' debate that evening. I had not been consulted.

I was furious, but my options were limited. While I never wanted this policy in the first place, there would be serious questions about our campaign if I disavowed it. It would also strand the ministers who made the announcement, no doubt believing they were acting on my instructions. In the end, I gave a pro forma defence of the policy, simply noting that hotlines are common for various crimes and abuse situations.

An unfortunate side effect was the quick overshadowing of my debate performance. It had been my best French-language one ever. Ironically, I had done particularly well on the niqab issue.

SUPPORT FROM FRIENDS AND "SMALL, TEMPORARY DEFICITS"

OF COURSE, NOT EVERY DAY on the campaign trail was a bad one. I enjoyed the energy our supporters brought to the dozens of rallies and campaign stops across the country, and I valued the moments of conversation with voters, particularly when the cameras were not rolling. Despite the headwinds, at no point was there ever a sentiment of giving up or ceasing to give every effort on every single day. We were proud of our record, confident in our agenda, and kept our heads held high.

On September 18, I was truly humbled to be joined on the campaign trail in Toronto by my friend Wayne Gretzky. We did a fireside chat together onstage and Wayne was very generous, not only in his presence but also in his praise for our Government's record and focus. He went out of his way to give us a boost, and I value his friendship to this day.

Later in the campaign I spoke to a large rally in Etobicoke, Ontario, joined by Doug Ford and his brother, former Toronto mayor Rob Ford. The Fords had built a remarkable political following in their own right, one that crossed traditional political boundaries, bringing together blue-collar voters from a range of backgrounds. We delivered some important projects to Toronto during Rob's time as mayor, and I have valued Doug's friendship since. He has, of course, gone on to win three consecutive majority governments in Ontario, an impressive feat.

August 27 was another day that stands out and still resonates a decade later. That was the day Justin Trudeau announced that a Liberal Government would run "small, temporary deficits" if elected—up to ten billion dollars per year over the next three years, with a pledge to return to balance by 2019. I mocked that statement at the time, joking about "teeny weeny, maybe three years . . . maybe a little bit bigger than teeny." Those clips still play.

Yet the Liberal position was as clever as it was cynical. For the voters they were trying to appeal to, it enabled them to play both sides of the fence. Since the mid-1990s, Canadians had been averse to deficits. However, they had just witnessed our Government run what (at the time) were very large deficits, and, with seemingly little hardship, balance the budget a few years later. So the argument went: you could promise both deficits—at least "small, temporary" ones—and a balanced budget at the same time.

The 30 per cent of Canadians who were Conservative voters were not fooled. But this sleight of hand was key to the Liberals consolidating the opposition vote. Thomas Mulcair's NDP also offered a program of greatly increased spending, along with a balanced budget. That did not seem credible to many centrist voters, making the Liberal approach sound more believable. But for voters on the left, deficits did not matter anyway, so the Trudeau line was appealing to them too. In essence, Mulcair was outflanked on both the centre and the left at the same time.

The important thing to remember, however, is that this promise was rubbish from the beginning. Trudeau was not proposing a deficit because he wanted short-term spending to stimulate the economy. He was proposing a deficit because he wanted to increase spending permanently. He was, in short, proposing a permanent, structural deficit. The history of small structural deficits is clear: they become large structural deficits sooner or later. And that is exactly what happened.

ANNOUNCING A TRADE BREAKTHROUGH: THE TRANS-PACIFIC PARTNERSHIP

ODDLY, OUR MOST EFFECTIVE and widely covered policy pronouncement of the 2015 campaign was one we had no intention of making: the Trans-Pacific Partnership (TPP) Trade Agreement. In fact, it is extremely unusual for an announcement of this nature to occur during an election. And we did not want it. The agreement was large and complex, and it is impossible to predict how such a thing will play out in an election environment.

The truth, however, was that the United States was driving the TPP train at that point. They felt that they had to keep the momentum going and get this done as soon as possible to head off mounting resistance to trade agreements in various countries, including their own. They refused to wait. Accordingly, on October 5, the announcement was done. Making the best of things, I characterized it as "a historic day" and nothing short of "the largest economic partnership in the history of the world."

Because Canada already had trade agreements with four of the eleven other TPP members, this was not, for us, an agreement on the same scale as NAFTA or CETA. However, it was still a very large trade alliance and gave us new access to several important markets, of which Japan was the biggest prize. This was no small thing, as Canadian governments had forever wanted a trade deal with Japan.

It turned out any concerns we had about the announcement were ill-founded. We had done our stakeholder homework, and the agreement received the widespread welcome that our consultations had told us that it would. Opposition came almost exclusively from organizations on the far left that were ideologically opposed to free trade.

Ironically, this was probably our best day of the campaign. It reinforced our record as the government that had concluded the widest range of trade deals in Canada's history. Now, we were opening a whole new set of opportunities, adding the Asia-Pacific to the Americas and Europe in a free-trade network that included two-thirds of global GDP.

The reaction of the opposition was interesting. In fact, it parallelled the way the NDP and Liberals had handled the deficit issue. And, I believe, it again played into Justin Trudeau's rise.

The NDP, with its long history of opposition to virtually every trade deal, came out quickly and strongly against the TPP. Tom Mulcair focused on the negative impact expected on the supply-managed agricultural sectors in dairy and poultry. That was a serious tactical error. Mulcair's reaction put the NDP back into an ideological stance during a campaign in which he had been systematically moving it to the centre.

In fact, the supply-managed sectors were not up in arms. We had made minimal concessions in this area. With wide-ranging global market access secured and supply management intact, we had every reason to believe that the system was safe.*

The Liberals, by comparison, again played this issue cleverly and cynically. They took no position, committed to study the deal, and sent mixed messages to different groups about their eventual position. It was strategic ambiguity all over again, enabled by a compliant broadcast media cartel that had no intention of pressing Justin Trudeau on this (or any other) issue. Mulcair got no such breaks.

Ultimately, the agreement was re-named the Comprehensive and Progressive Trans-Pacific Partnership or CPTTP, and the Liberals ratified it in 2018. That was consistent with their record. The Liberals rarely conclude trade deals, but they always go along with them once they are in office.

GENERAL DYNAMICS

THERE IS ONE OTHER policy controversy from the 2015 election that I wish to address. This is the 2014 General Dynamics Land Systems contract with Saudi Arabia for non-combat military transport vehicles. It was the largest export contract in Canadian history, at fourteen billion dollars, and would employ about three thousand workers, mostly in the London, Ontario, region.

While much of the criticism of this deal was couched in civil rights terms—supplying a country with Saudi Arabia's human rights' record with military hardware of any kind—I do not believe that is what it was really about. The Bloc Québécois led the charge, and the criticism started

* Obviously, this situation changed unexpectedly after Donald Trump's election as president the next year.

in Quebec. Frankly, I strongly doubt that there would have been such criticism if the benefits of the contract were going to Quebec instead of Ontario.

Either way, I offer no apologies whatsoever. We worked hard to get this contract, as did every other Western supplier. In selling this type of equipment, we were doing nothing at all extraordinary or unusual.

I am not going to tell you Saudi Arabia is a Western liberal democracy. What I will say is that, even then, it was a valuable geopolitical partner in that part of the world in both the fight against ISIS and the dangers posed by the Iranian regime. True, this had not always been the case, as there had been tacit support in the past for extremist Sunni elements within the Saudi ruling class (though not the government per se). However, even then that was changing, and since then, Crown Prince Mohammed bin Salman has put a complete end to any such support. In any case, the threat to the Kingdom of Saudi Arabia is not some outbreak of Western liberalism; it is the rise of jihadist extremism.

Besides being good business, the deal was also a statement of our support for the direction Saudi Arabia was taking. From an economic point of view, cancelling the contract would have been just plain stupid. Even the Liberals recognized this reality, eventually ratifying the deal in early 2019. Any Canadian government would have done the same, and had they not, the noise of countries clamouring to take the contract from us would have been deafening.

ELECTION NIGHT

DESPITE THE UPS AND DOWNS of the campaign, our support had barely fluctuated one way or the other. But we were never ahead or even on the verge of being ahead. With the consolidation of the opposition vote, the outcome had become steadily clearer.

Thus, on election night, there was no surprise as to the result. Justin Trudeau's Liberals charged from third place to first, winning 184 seats—a strong majority. We were down 67 seats, from 2011 to 99 seats. The NDP suffered as badly, dropping from 103 to just 44 seats. The Bloc Québécois managed to claw itself back from the brink, gaining 6 seats for a total of 10, but it had not recovered its status as a recognized party in Parliament.*

I was still disappointed with the result. I knew by then that we stood no chance of winning, but the greater disappointment was in the numbers. We felt—certainly I felt—that with the kind of support level we achieved—32 per cent of the vote—we should have won more seats. But if you look at the ridings, we lost in almost every close race. That was not all bad luck; we had virtually no get-out-the-vote campaign in the national war room. There was no excuse for losing some of those close constituencies (almost all of which we got back in 2019).

We did commission Brian Loughnane, the former executive director of the Liberal Party of Australia, to do a deep dive on the campaign. While hoping this would highlight some lessons learned, the big picture of our defeat really went well beyond any campaign deficiencies or errors. We easily retained our core vote, but we simply could not convince many of those time-for-a-change voters of the economic risk of a Justin Trudeau Government.

The data we had on this was interesting. Voters who were dealing with the (brief and regional) economic downturn of 2014–2015 were the ones most inclined to vote for us. But most voters were convinced that the economy would be fine. We were the victims of our success. After years of stable economic leadership, many simply felt the economy was not at risk anymore. And the better a voter felt about the economy, the less likely they seemed inclined to support us.

Regardless of the reason for the loss, the election defeat was my responsibility. Therefore, although I did not say it in my concession speech—it was not the clip we wanted—my office announced immediately afterward that I would step down as leader as soon as possible. I had committed to Laureen in 2001 that the moment I had clearly passed my political peak, I would walk away. And that is what I would now do.

---

* This requires a minimum of 12 seats.

This was also a commitment I had made to myself. I did not want to fight the same battles for the rest of my life. I had watched too many other leaders do that, and it is no way to live. At fifty-six, there would still be more phases to my life. I was not going to expend any energy reliving the old one. My years in office had been a great experience, but that period was over.

A TIME OF FAREWELLS

IN OUR SYSTEM, you remain prime minister until a new government is sworn in. Upon returning to Ottawa, I met immediately with Governor General Johnston to recommend that he ask Justin Trudeau to form a government. The date of transition was set for November 4.

There were a few pieces of official business to take care of in that sixteen-day period. One of them was a preplanned national ceremony on October 22—the one-year anniversary of the attack on Parliament and the murder of Corporal Nathan Cirillo. I also met with Justin Trudeau since a brief transition meeting is standard practice. I asked him to lay the wreath together with me at the National War Memorial. I believed we should do that in tandem as a symbol of the peaceful transition of power and the continuity of our democratic institutions.

Much of the rest of that period was spent packing and moving out of offices and residences. There were many tearful farewells. They began at the Ottawa airport when I was greeted by a couple hundred of my longest-serving employees. They were both cheering and crying. These people had been the backbone of our staff and our national campaign team for up to a decade and a half. They had much reason to be both proud and sad.

These emotional meetings continued in the caucus, in the office, and with my official residence staff. People who had given their hearts and souls to our movement, to my career, and to the welfare of my family and me were saying goodbye. Of course, many we would see again. Just the same, many hearts were breaking.

ENDING ONE PHASE . . .

I USUALLY KEEP my feelings to myself. When I have been in positions of leadership, I especially try to demonstrate control over my emotions if the situation around me is otherwise. Particularly when my people are grieving, I attempt to be comforting.

Thus, as odd as it might sound, I approached that sixteen-day period as dispassionately as I could. There was a lot to do and little time to do it in. And, truthfully, I was mentally moving on quickly. I had always thought of being prime minister as an extraordinary, almost surreal, privilege. I had treated it as my duty, not as my identity. I had long resolved that, the day I left office, I would return with my family to my Calgary neighbourhood and my old friends.

Of course, I took a few last moments, in my Parliament Hill office, in my 24 Sussex residence, and on the last Challenger flight back to Calgary, to reflect on things. Overall, I felt pretty good. I believed that when the dust cleared, it would be recognized that, by any meaningful measure, our Government had left the country better than we had found it.

The country was wealthier and had outperformed others during a unique global crisis. We had left a balanced budget, the lowest federal tax burden in fifty years, a relatively low national debt, and record investments in vital priorities like health, education, and infrastructure. Even the *New York Times* noted Canada had achieved "the richest middle class in the world."* We had also created a global trade network whose potential we had barely scratched. Canada was more united than it had been in decades, with Quebec separatism on an ongoing decline and Western alienation forgotten. And we had been playing a meaningful role in the world, cutting out the finger-wagging and replacing it with hard contributions to shared allied objectives.

---

* See David Leonhardt and Kevin Quealy, "The American Middle Class is No Longer the World's Richest," *New York Times,* April 22, 2014, and Ian Austen and David Leonhardt, "Life in Canada, Home of the World's Most Affluent Middle Class," *New York Times,* April 30, 2014.

Regrets? Every leader will tell you that the biggest regret is that they did not do more. I felt that way as well, but I also believed that we had been an energetic, active, and decisive Government during the time that we had. I had given it my best, and my overall feeling was one of satisfaction.

What about the fact that much of what we had accomplished was later reversed or squandered? I am less upset about that than people might think. When handed the keys of office, your responsibility is to do what you can with the time you have. Democracy is a battle that never ends. There are no permanent winners and no permanent losers. Anything can be built upon. Anything can be undone. And anything can be restored.

AFTERWORD

THE ELECTION DEFEAT OF 2015 had, in effect, moved my plan to leave office up by a year and a half. One way or the other, my time remaining as prime minister had been limited. Yet I had given no thought to the next stage of my life. That was deliberate. I believed that to do so could potentially influence my judgment as PM. It just felt like a conflict of interest.

I expected to experience a huge physical and psychological letdown after fifteen years of unrelenting activity and stress. It was not that bad. In fact, I would say that, in no time at all, it felt liberating.

After Laureen and I were settled back in our family home in Calgary, I flew to Las Vegas for a week. I took in some shows, did some modest gambling, and walked the Strip. I enjoyed the (close to) anonymity and solitude.* I later joined some friends at a condo in Florida for a few weeks.†

I resolved to take three months to relax and put the future out of my head. I also said I would not accept any future commitment for six months. And I resolved that I would not start any new job for a year. Those timelines got moved up somewhat, but I stuck to the framework.

My initial breaks were interrupted by the return of Parliament in early December 2015. After all, I had won my riding of Calgary Heritage in the

---

* Also in Las Vegas at the time were longtime Ottawa friend Murdock MacLeod, staffer Matt McBain, and Devin Dreeshen, son of Alberta MP Earl Dreeshen and a future provincial Cabinet minister.

† These were also friends from Ottawa—Ken Guarisco and Kevin Pidgeon.

election.* I made a point of being in Ottawa during sittings, and I showed up for most votes. However, I did not attend caucus meetings or Question Period. I wanted our interim leader, Rona Ambrose, and the party to be able to do their work without me hovering over them. She and they did a great job. In the meantime, I was in my office and available for those who wanted to visit or to chat.

My reflections in the first months led to a couple of decisions. The most important was that I had no desire to retire. I doubt I ever will, at least for as long as I am able to work. I do not believe that men† should retire, unless there is a good alternative plan. My father, for example, had very demanding pastimes in retirement that kept him busy. If men retire, they must make the effort to remain active and connected—intellectually, socially, emotionally, and physically.

A second big decision was that I wanted one more career. I felt I still had it in me. It had to be disconnected from Canadian politics, as there would be no going back to that. But it still had to build on what I had done for most of my life.

In short, I decided to pursue the business career that I never had, by building my own enterprise. No former Canadian prime minister had really done that. Most, if they had not retired, joined corporate boards or did some personal consulting. However, at least one former prime minister had built his own business, and I borrowed elements of the model from my friend Tony Blair.

On August 26, 2016, I announced my resignation as the member of Parliament for Calgary Heritage. I then launched Harper & Associates (H&A) Consulting, taking my best longtime staff and making them partners. They run the day-to-day operations. They are a generation younger than me, and as I frequently say, they have to make this last a lot longer than I will be around. Ray Novak, Jeremy Hunt, Anna Tomala, and Nick Koolsbergen have been

---

* The local campaign that year had been managed by perennial volunteer Bob Huff.

† I believe that women are different and much less likely to fail in retirement.

the key partners, but many of my former employees and colleagues have been involved at one time or another.‡

In very general terms, we try to further the kind of business we wanted to see done while we were in government. Conversely, I do not maintain any associations that I would not have cultivated when I was in public office.

We now have a few linked businesses in different verticals. In H&A, my focus is largely on the investment world. We have had several investment funds as clients, both as consultants and/or equity holders. As a consequence, we decided that we wanted to establish our own such fund. That led us to partner in the formation of Vision One, a highly differentiated public-equity fund based in Miami.§

My work in the investment world led the Government of Alberta to ask me to accept the role of the board chair at the Alberta Investment Management Corporation (AIMCo). This position at the province's pension and sovereign wealth fund dovetails well with my experiences of the past decade. I took the job (and declined compensation) because I remain open to public service—but not politics!

The only political role I have is as chairman of the International Democracy Union, the global alliance of some eighty-plus conservative parties. We are an international network that shares best practices on campaigning and governing and promotes freedom and democracy in authoritarian states. We also do a modest bit of mentoring of future conservative leaders.

I have joined just two corporate boards—Colliers International of Toronto, led by Jay Hennick, and Alimentation Couche-Tard of Montreal, led by

---

‡ I should mention Carl Vallée. Although he has not been part of any of my enterprises, he has been a constant help on any Quebec-related business.

§ Our Vision One partners are CEO/CIO Courtney Mather, a highly skilled investor with an impressive track record, and Dennis Wallace, whose experience includes years in the Canadian pension fund and family office space. Dennis is also the son of longtime supporter Blake Wallace and brother of my former PMO economics advisor Andrew Wallace.

Alain Bouchard. They are the kind of success stories I wanted to encourage as prime minister—Canadian businesses that have become global in scope. That Hennick and Bouchard and their associates have created world-leading enterprises in their own time is proof that Canadians can do it. We need to do so much more often.

That leads me to reflect on the state of our country today. Only a couple of months before writing this, many of my former colleagues and supporters marked the 20th anniversary of the swearing in of our Government. It was a massive celebration during which even the current Liberal government acknowledged our achievements. However, it was tempered by the ongoing poor performance of the Canadian economy, the renewal of separatist threats in Quebec and Alberta, and the existential hostility of the United States under the second Trump administration.

Despite writing this book, I do not spend a lot of time looking back.* My life is still about looking forward. And, while the current environment makes me very worried, I believe that the best moments in our history can guide us to a better future.

Our country, Canada, is a magnificent achievement. We brought together disparate regions and peoples in a remarkably harmonious and compassionate society that has welcomed virtually every nation on earth. That said, I have often observed that we are underachievers. With our huge natural wealth alone, we should be the wealthiest country on the planet. Instead, after the decisions of the past decade, our living standards are lower, our vital resources unharnessed, our export capacity limited, and our dependence on the United States unresolved.

Our relationship with the United States today is not unlike the situation we faced in the year 1866. That was when the American government cancelled our free trade agreement (and yes, we had one back then). It published

---

* While I had been in no hurry to publish my memoirs, this manuscript emerged from my team's work with Library and Archives Canada. Please see the Acknowledgements section.

maps showing how Canada could be annexed to the United States. And it even covertly sponsored armed attacks on Canada for the next five years—the Fenian Raids—designed to force our capitulation. These were repelled, although many people, including Father of Confederation Thomas D'Arcy McGee, died in the process.

But John A. Macdonald and his colleagues did not just resist; they built. The following year, 1867, witnessed Confederation—the single biggest act of nation-building in our history. Within six years, virtually all the colonies and territories of British North America were under one government—the federal institutions that endure to this day. The transcontinental railway system was constructed, and in the decades that followed, countless other initiatives laid the groundwork for everything we now have.

We are equally capable of building a country less dependent on our southern neighbours. We can be more internally competitive. We can be more globally connected. And we can end the actions that threaten Quebecers and alienate Albertans. It is all within our power.

I hope this book will provide a record of how we tried to create that kind of a Canada. I also hope it may give insight to those who come to have what I call "the best job in the best country in the world."

ACKNOWLEDGEMENTS

I had not intended to do memoirs until much later in life. This project began earlier because of Library and Archives Canada (LAC). After my team submitted my prime ministerial archives, LAC arranged for me to record nearly fifty hours of interviews on my career and time as prime minister. These transcripts then provided the basis on which this book was based.

When these interviews become publicly available, discerning observers may note some discrepancies in events recounted in these pages and on the recordings. Further research corrected some errors in my oral accounts, so this book should be considered authoritative.

I want to use this opportunity to acknowledge LAC for all the work they did over many years on the archive project. Special thanks to manager Élizabeth Mongrain, as well as to project manager Emily Reza, senior archivist Patrick McLean, and senior archivists Kelly Ferguson and Rachel Klassen. There were literal dozens of others who worked with them. LAC is a great institution.

The archive project was completed with help from members of my team. Thanks for many hours of work go to Shauna Wright, Art Milnes, Darrel Reid, and Jill Thompson. Jill, a former PMO photographer, was assisted by her former colleagues in that role, Jason and Deb Ransom. Darrel, a former PMO deputy chief of staff and policy director, conducted the oral interviews, for which Jill acted as videographer, assisted by Caitlyn Madlener.

Several former colleagues reviewed this manuscript and offered both suggestions and corrections. They include Ray Novak, Jeremy Hunt, Anna Tomala, Matt McBain, and, once again, Art Milnes. Many other people provided their thoughts during the time I was working on this manuscript.

Some are already named somewhere in the text. A couple of others that come to mind provided help on some specific issues. They are my former deputy chief of staff Derek Vanstone (from his time in Jim Flaherty's office), fellow Colliers International director Poonam Puri (who provided some background on the asset-backed commercial paper crisis), and my former policy advisor Sean Speer (on any number of matters).

Thanks are due to Canada's great literary agent Michael Levine and the folks at Westwood Creative Artists, for managing the contractual business around this publication.

My publisher is once again Signal/McClelland & Stewart, an imprint of Penguin Random House Canada, and, as always, they assembled a great team. It included Noelle Zitzer as managing editor, Andrew Roberts as designer, Eleanor Gasparik as copyeditor, Tara Tovell as proofreader, Erin Kelly as publicity director, and, of course, as editor and publisher, Doug Pepper, who led them all. Doug dedicated much personal time to this project, despite his many other responsibilities. Any remaining errors and omissions are solely my responsibility.

I reserve the biggest thanks, however, for my family. My late father, my mother, and my brothers, Grant and Robert, gave me the loving start in life that made everything else possible. My wife, Laureen, and children, Ben and Rachel, gave all the support and comfort I needed during what was a rewarding, though often stressful, political career.

As I said at the unveiling of my official portrait on February 3, 2026, I tried to devote the majority of my working life to making this country a better place for hard-working Canadians and their families. But it was my own family that made that possible. Whatever price a person pays for being in public life and, in particular, for being prime minister—and frankly, I always found it far more an honour than a burden—a bigger price is paid by those closest to them. I can never fully appreciate the burden that Laureen, Ben, and Rachel bore, nor adequately express the love I feel for them.